Visual Basic® 6 COM+ Programming Bible

Visual Basic® 6 COM+ Programming Bible

John Paul Mueller

IDG Books Worldwide, Inc.
An International Data Group Company

Foster City, CA ✦ Chicago, IL ✦ Indianapolis, IN ✦ New York, NY

Visual Basic® 6 COM+ Programming Bible

Published by
IDG Books Worldwide, Inc.
An International Data Group Company
919 E. Hillsdale Blvd., Suite 400
Foster City, CA 94404
www.idgbooks.com (IDG Books Worldwide Web site)

ISBN: 0-7645-4731-3

Printed in the United States of America

10 9 8 7 6 5 4 3 2 1

1B/RX/RQ/QQ/FC

Distributed in the United States by IDG Books Worldwide, Inc.

Distributed by CDG Books Canada Inc. for Canada; by Transworld Publishers Limited in the United Kingdom; by IDG Norge Books for Norway; by IDG Sweden Books for Sweden; by IDG Books Australia Publishing Corporation Pty. Ltd. for Australia and New Zealand; by TransQuest Publishers Pte Ltd. for Singapore, Malaysia, Thailand, Indonesia, and Hong Kong; by Gotop Information Inc. for Taiwan; by ICG Muse, Inc. for Japan; by Intersoft for South Africa; by Eyrolles for France; by International Thomson Publishing for Germany, Austria, and Switzerland; by Distribuidora Cuspide for Argentina; by LR International for Brazil; by Galileo Libros for Chile; by Ediciones ZETA S.C.R. Ltda. for Peru; by WS Computer Publishing Corporation, Inc., for the Philippines; by Contemporanea de Ediciones for Venezuela; by Express Computer Distributors for the Caribbean and West Indies; by Micronesia Media Distributor, Inc. for Micronesia; by Chips Computadoras S.A. de C.V. for Mexico; by Editorial Norma de Panama S.A. for Panama; by American Bookshops for Finland.

For general information on IDG Books Worldwide's books in the U.S., please call our Consumer Customer Service department at 800-762-2974. For reseller information, including discounts and premium sales, please call our Reseller Customer Service department at 800-434-3422.

For information on where to purchase IDG Books Worldwide's books outside the U.S., please contact our International Sales department at 317-572-3993 or fax 317-572-4002.

For consumer information on foreign language translations, please contact our Customer Service department at 800-434-3422, fax 317-572-4002, or e-mail rights@idgbooks.com.

For information on licensing foreign or domestic rights, please phone +1-650-653-7098.

For sales inquiries and special prices for bulk quantities, please contact our Order Services department at 800-434-3422 or write to the address above.

For information on using IDG Books Worldwide's books in the classroom or for ordering examination copies, please contact our Educational Sales department at 800-434-2086 or fax 317-572-4005.

For press review copies, author interviews, or other publicity information, please contact our Public Relations department at 650-653-7000 or fax 650-653-7500.

For authorization to photocopy items for corporate, personal, or educational use, please contact Copyright Clearance Center, 222 Rosewood Drive, Danvers, MA 01923, or fax 978-750-4470.

Library of Congress Cataloging-in-Publication Data

Mueller, John, 1958–
    Visual Basic 6 COM+ programming bible / John Paul Mueller.
        p. cm.
    ISBN 0-7645-4731-3 (alk. paper)
    1. Microsoft Visual BASIC. 2. BASIC (Computer program language) 3. COM (Computer architecture) I. Title.
QA76.73.B3 M82   2000
005.2'768--dc21   00-058120

ABOUT IDG BOOKS WORLDWIDE

Welcome to the world of IDG Books Worldwide.

IDG Books Worldwide, Inc., is a subsidiary of International Data Group, the world's largest publisher of computer-related information and the leading global provider of information services on information technology. IDG was founded more than 30 years ago by Patrick J. McGovern and now employs more than 9,000 people worldwide. IDG publishes more than 290 computer publications in over 75 countries. More than 90 million people read one or more IDG publications each month.

Launched in 1990, IDG Books Worldwide is today the #1 publisher of best-selling computer books in the United States. We are proud to have received eight awards from the Computer Press Association in recognition of editorial excellence and three from Computer Currents' First Annual Readers' Choice Awards. Our best-selling ...For Dummies® series has more than 50 million copies in print with translations in 31 languages. IDG Books Worldwide, through a joint venture with IDG's Hi-Tech Beijing, became the first U.S. publisher to publish a computer book in the People's Republic of China. In record time, IDG Books Worldwide has become the first choice for millions of readers around the world who want to learn how to better manage their businesses.

Our mission is simple: Every one of our books is designed to bring extra value and skill-building instructions to the reader. Our books are written by experts who understand and care about our readers. The knowledge base of our editorial staff comes from years of experience in publishing, education, and journalism — experience we use to produce books to carry us into the new millennium. In short, we care about books, so we attract the best people. We devote special attention to details such as audience, interior design, use of icons, and illustrations. And because we use an efficient process of authoring, editing, and desktop publishing our books electronically, we can spend more time ensuring superior content and less time on the technicalities of making books.

You can count on our commitment to deliver high-quality books at competitive prices on topics you want to read about. At IDG Books Worldwide, we continue in the IDG tradition of delivering quality for more than 30 years. You'll find no better book on a subject than one from IDG Books Worldwide.

John Kilcullen
Chairman and CEO
IDG Books Worldwide, Inc.

Eighth Annual Computer Press Awards ≥1992

Ninth Annual Computer Press Awards ≥1993

Tenth Annual Computer Press Awards ≥1994

Eleventh Annual Computer Press Awards ≥1995

IDG is the world's leading IT media, research and exposition company. Founded in 1964, IDG had 1997 revenues of $2.05 billion and has more than 9,000 employees worldwide. IDG offers the widest range of media options that reach IT buyers in 75 countries representing 95% of worldwide IT spending. IDG's diverse product and services portfolio spans six key areas including print publishing, online publishing, expositions and conferences, market research, education and training, and global marketing services. More than 90 million people read one or more of IDG's 290 magazines and newspapers, including IDG's leading global brands — Computerworld, PC World, Network World, Macworld and the Channel World family of publications. IDG Books Worldwide is one of the fastest-growing computer book publishers in the world, with more than 700 titles in 36 languages. The "...For Dummies®" series alone has more than 50 million copies in print. IDG offers online users the largest network of technology-specific Web sites around the world through IDG.net (http://www.idg.net), which comprises more than 225 targeted Web sites in 55 countries worldwide. International Data Corporation (IDC) is the world's largest provider of information technology data, analysis and consulting, with research centers in over 41 countries and more than 400 research analysts worldwide. IDG World Expo is a leading producer of more than 168 globally branded conferences and expositions in 35 countries including E3 (Electronic Entertainment Expo), Macworld Expo, ComNet, Windows World Expo, ICE (Internet Commerce Expo), Agenda, DEMO, and Spotlight. IDG's training subsidiary, ExecuTrain, is the world's largest computer training company, with more than 230 locations worldwide and 785 training courses. IDG Marketing Services helps industry-leading IT companies build international brand recognition by developing global integrated marketing programs via IDG's print, online and exposition products worldwide. Further information about the company can be found at www.idg.com.   1/26/00

Credits

Acquisitions Editor
Greg Croy

Project Editor
Sharon Nash

Technical Editor
Russ Mullen

Copy Editors
S.B. Kleinman
Richard H. Adin

Proof Editor
Neil Romanosky

Project Coordinators
Marcos Vergara
Danette Nurse

Graphics and Production Specialists
Robert Bihlmayer
Jude Levinson
Michael Lewis
Victor Pérez-Varela
Ramses Ramirez

Quality Control Technician
Dina F Quan

Permissions Editor
Carmen Krikorian

Media Development Specialist
Travis Silvers

Media Development Coordinator
Marisa Pearman

Book Designer
Drew R. Moore

Illustrators
Karl Brandt
Brent Savage
Rashell Smith
Gabriele McCann

Proofreading and Indexing
York Production Services

Cover Illustrator
Joann Vuong

About the Author

John Paul Mueller is a freelance author and technical editor. He has writing in his blood, having produced 47 books and almost 200 articles to date. The topics range from networking to artificial intelligence and from database management to heads down programming. Some of his current books include a COM+ programmer's guide and a Windows 2000 performance, tuning, and optimization book. His technical editing skills have helped over 23 authors refine the content of their manuscripts, some of which are certification related. In addition to book projects, John has provided technical editing services to both *Data Based Advisor* and *Coast Compute* magazines. A recognized authority on computer industry certifications, he's also contributed certification-related articles to magazines like *Certified Professional Magazine*, *SQL Server Professional*, *Visual C++ Developer*, and *Visual Basic Developer*.

When John isn't working at the computer, you can find him in his workshop. He's an avid woodworker and candle maker. On any given afternoon, you can find him working at a lathe or putting the finishing touches on a bookcase. One of his newest craft projects is glycerin soap making, which comes in handy for gift baskets. You can reach John on the Internet at `JMueller@mwt.net`. John is also setting up a new Web site at `http://www.mwt.net/~jmueller/`; feel free to take a look and make suggestions on how he can improve it. One of his current projects is creating book FAQ sheets that should help you find the book information you need much faster.

This book is dedicated to my wife Rebecca who has stayed with me through thick and thin during our 20 years of marriage.

Preface

Windows 2000 is the most anticipated and exciting release of the Windows product line in history. There are more new features in this product than many individual companies will even use and definitely enough features to keep programmers busy for quite some time to come. In fact, the Windows 2000 operating system is so large and complex that some people wondered whether it would ever be released. However, the fact that you're reading this means that Microsoft finally got all of the pieces together and we now have an operating system that'll provide the functionality for which programmers and customers alike have clamored.

This book looks at a very specific area of the new Windows 2000 release, COM+. We'll discuss everything from what makes COM+ different from COM and its predecessors to the details of the component parts that make COM+ work. This book contains a wealth of examples that demonstrate everything from using Component Services or Queued Components alone, to using them together to create a complex application. This book also covers some other new Windows 2000 technologies like Active Directory and how these new technologies can interact with COM+. One of the book's examples will help you to understand how to work with both thick and thin clients, something that most developers need to know about today.

So, what can this book offer you that you can't find anywhere else? There are three key features that make this book special. The first is in-depth theory. Unlike many books on the market, this one talks about the various COM/DCOM/COM+ interfaces, discusses the Registry in detail, and allows you to see how the various pieces go together. The second is source code. The accompanying CD-ROM contains at least one fully functional example per chapter (most chapters contain code snippets as well) and several chapters contain more. Finally, this book is about resources, most importantly, those that you can find on the Internet. Throughout the book, you will find references to Web sites and newsgroups that'll help you to learn just about anything that you ever wanted to know about the topics being covered.

If you're looking for a good book about all of the ins and outs of working with COM+, then you've come to the right place. While I don't provide encyclopedic coverage (who could, given the complexity of COM alone, much less COM+), you'll garner enough information to really understand the important new principles that Windows 2000 includes. The whole purpose of this book is to make you a better Windows programmer with an emphasis on both corporate and Windows 2000-specific programming.

Whom This Book Is For

This book was written for the Visual Basic 6 developer who has a good understanding of programming principles and has used Visual Basic sometime in the past. In other words, this isn't the book that you want to buy if you are a complete novice; but if you are someone with a little programming experience, then you will get some information from it almost immediately. All of the examples were written on the assumption that you know something about Visual Basic programming and have worked with COM in the past. You won't find simple ActiveX components in this book, nor will you find a detailed description of terms like interface.

As the book progresses, the topics get harder and the expected level of understanding of the reader increases. By the time you reach the chapters on remote database programming principles, I assume that you're at least an intermediate- to advanced-level reader who has spent some time programming. This doesn't mean that I'm overloading you with arcane information; the various topics are discussed in simple terms that are easy to understand. However, a beginner will still very likely become lost as the book progresses because there's little in the way of introductory information.

The entire book is meant to help a wide variety of readers who want to know about COM+ programming. We won't look at add-on products or other technologies; COM+ is a complex topic that requires focused attention. (There are a few side topics about additional tools that you can download from Microsoft's Web site or that are available on the CD-ROM included with this book, but these tools are designed to make COM+ development easier and therefore fit in with the topic at hand.) With that in mind, you won't find a lot of esoteric information that some books provide. My goal is to give you the information that you need along with resources that you can use to find additional information as needed to complete your projects.

How Things Are Organized

This book is organized in two ways: theoretical to practical and relatively simple to difficult. Everything in this book is about COM, DCOM, MSMQ, MTS, COM+, or an associated technology. You won't find much general information in this book because I assume that you already know it. As a result, this book has a fairly narrow focus, which means looking in the index if something doesn't catch your eye immediately.

I placed the single database example and both Web programming examples for this book at the end. This isn't a database programming book, so reading these chapters won't make you into a database management guru. The database example is fairly complex, which is why I placed it near the end. Web programming is still a somewhat esoteric topic for some developers, which is why I made that topic the last chapter in the book. You may find that your experiences are different from mine, so something that I would consider hard may be child's play for you.

Organization

Now that you have a brief overview of what the book will and won't cover, and why I placed certain topics where I did, let's look at the content in a little more detail. The following sections provide an overview of what you'll find in this book.

Part I: Fundamentals

Many developers will view COM+ as an entirely new technology; its not. The first part of this book will help you understand what COM+ is, the tools you need to work with it, and how you'll administer COM+ applications. COM+ does provide important new capabilities, but it also consolidates many existing tools and allows them to work better together.

Chapter 1, "An Introduction to COM+", begins with a historical view of COM and COM+, which is an important way to discover why some things in COM+ work in the way that they do. It also provides you with a quick overview of COM+ features. Finally, we'll talk about the workstation and server setup that I've used for this book so that you have some idea of what you'll need to set your test system up.

In Chapter 2, "COM+ Administration Issues", we'll discuss all of the administrative issues of working with COM+. We'll talk about everything from creating a COM+ application (the container, not the code) to understanding how applications generate entries in the event logs.

Chapter 3, "Working with COM/COM+ Tools", helps you to understand which tools are at your disposal when working with COM+ and where you can get them. All of the tools are provided with either Visual Basic 6.0 Enterprise Edition or the Windows Platform SDK. Some tools won't be available to Visual Basic 6.0 Professional users.

Part II: COM+ In Theory

Once you know what COM+ is and how it can make your next development project easier, it's time to look at the details. The second part of the book helps you understand how COM+ works internally. We'll look at the various technologies that make COM+ what it is today—the constituent parts. Once we get past the existing technologies, we'll look at what makes COM+ a unique and special technology that you need to consider for your next project.

The first theory chapter is Chapter 4, "Starting with Components". This chapter provides a very quick overview of how components work. We'll also talk about DCOM in some detail because DCOM is currently used as the transport technology for COM+. Finally, we'll discuss two very important COM+ specific topics: contexts and interceptors.

We'll discuss detailed theory about DCOM, and DCOM's benefits and limitations in Chapter 5, "Understanding DCOM". We'll also talk about monikers, a very important topic for any COM programmer because you need a moniker to access most resources. Finally, this chapter tells you about some of the problems of using Visual Basic with DCOM.

So what makes COM+ unique and why should you use it for your next project? Chapter 6, "COM+ Specific Issues", is a COM+ component chapter. We'll begin by discussing both MTS and MSMQ at a detailed level. This chapter also talks about COM+ events and the difference between the COM and COM+ event systems. Finally, we'll discuss the types of applications that you can create with COM+.

The security issues surrounding COM+ are discussed in Chapter 7, "COM+ and Security". Distributed applications are subjected to higher levels of scrutiny by crackers, so you need to provide a better level of security. This chapter discusses the Windows 2000 technologies that are available to ensure that your server, application, and data remain safe.

Microsoft has made COM+ part of a larger enterprise strategy for developing applications. Chapter 8, "COM+ and Distributed interNetwork Architecture", is about n-tier computing. Distributed applications can execute on multiple servers and involve thousands of clients. As a result, it's important to know the latest methods for organizing your application into something more manageable than a massive Web of disassociated components.

Part III: Writing COM+ Applications

Theory is fine, but I know that most of you want to know how to use COM+ in your applications. We're going to look at COM+ from various angles in this part of the book. For example, there are administration issues to consider that you may not need to consider with other application types. We'll look at applications that manage your COM+ application through the use of an MMC snap-in. Of course, we'll also look at using COM+ in large network and Internet environments. We'll even discuss the methods required to make your applications run without a server connection (the disconnected application).

Chapter 9, "Creating Simple Components", is the first programming chapter. I decided to show how to create an MMC snap-in because you need to know how to work with MMC to manage COM+ applications. You'll also learn a lot of the programming techniques to avoid when working with server based components.

Chapter 10, "Creating Distributed Applications", contains the first and last example that you might be able to run on Windows NT. It shows you how to create a DCOM application. We'll discuss how DCOM is used as a transport mechanism for COM+ right now. I also provide some information on how SOAP will replace DCOM as the preferred DCOM transport sometime in the future.

Two complete examples and a lot of code snippets are found in Chapter 11, "A Simple COM+ Example". You'll learn how to create a basic COM+ application in the first application. The second application shows how to work with the COM+ publish/subscribe event model.

Chapter 12, "Working with Disconnected Applications", also contains two complete examples and many code snippets. Queued Components are an important part of COM+, so the first example shows you how to create and test a disconnected application. The second application shows you how to extend disconnected applications to work with Active Directory.

One of the harder examples in the book is found in Chapter 13, "Connecting to Remote Databases". We'll create a database and connect to it with a COM+ component. After the server-side application is complete, we'll look at two types of client application. The first is a standard desktop application, while the second shows a Web-base thin client.

The last chapter is Chapter 14, "Working with Web-based Applications", and it contains a detailed Web-based application. We'll discuss how you can combine existing technology like scripts and ASP with COM+ to create exciting new applications. In this particular case, we'll look at what you need to do to create a help desk application that users can access while on the road.

> **Note**
> This book contains many Internet references that you can use to find updates, to download SDKs and other required development tools, and to locate additional information that will help you in your development efforts. A summary of these URLs is found on my Web site at `http://www.mwt.net/~jmueller`. This is also the place to look for updates to the URLs as they change. The Web site URL summary will contain the Web site name, URL, and location of the Web site information in the book. Every effort was made at the time of writing to ensure that every URL in the book is correct, but URLs tend to change as the Internet itself changes. Please feel free to contact me at `JMueller@mwt.net` if any of the URLs that you see in the book have changed or are incorrect.

System Requirements

There are some assumptions that I've made while writing the application programming examples in this book. First, you need at least two machines running Windows 2000, one of which requires Windows 2000 Server. This two-machine setup is the only way that you'll see some technologies, like DCOM, Queued Components, and Component Services, in action and truly know that they work as expected. Make absolutely certain that you set up your machine so that it'll work properly with Windows 2000 and the various test setups in the book. Chapter 1 has instructions on how to do this. Most of the examples in this book won't work with Windows NT because I'm concentrating on COM+ and new Windows 2000 features like Active Directory. Windows NT won't even work as a client machine, in many cases, unless you download and install support packages that Microsoft provides.

All of the examples in this book were tested with Visual Basic 6.0 Enterprise Edition. They aren't guaranteed to work with any other version of the product and none of them will work with the educational versions of the product. You need, as a minimum, Visual Basic 6.0 Professional Edition to work with the nondatabase examples in this book. In some cases, the tools that I describe are Enterprise Edition specific, so if you're using Visual Basis 6.0 Professional Edition, you may not find them on your hard drive.

You must install Service Pack 3 for Visual Basic 6.0 before any of the examples from Chapter 10 onwards will work. Some examples, like the MTS example, won't even compile without this service pack in place. Other examples, like the DCOM example, may compile, but probably won't work very well without the service pack in place. I've provided information in several places in the book on where to download the service pack. You'll also find it included with an MSDN subscription.

In some cases, you're going to need additional tools because Visual Basic 6.0 was released to the market long before Windows 2000. The most important of these tools is the current release of the Platform SDK. I've provided information in the appropriate places on where you can download the Platform SDK and any other required tools. The CD-ROM provided with this book contains the most current version of many of the tools that I discuss, at least as of the time of writing. You can also get the vast majority of these tools from the CDs provided with an MSDN subscription.

Conventions

There are several conventions used within this book that will help you to get more out of it. The first is the use of special fonts or font styles to emphasize a special kind of text; the second is the use of icons to emphasize special information.

+ There are some situations when I'll ask you to type something. This information always appears in bold type like this: Type **Hello World**.

+ Code normally appears on separate lines from the rest of the text. However, there are some special situations when small amounts of code appear right in the paragraph for explanation purposes. This code will appear in a monospaced font like this: `Some Special Code`. URLs for Web sites are also presented in monospaced font like this: `http://www.microsoft.com`.

+ Underscores are used within the source code as continuation characters. In other words, if you see an underscore, the code on the very next line would normally appear on the same line as the underscore. The only reason that underscores are used in the source code for the book is to make it easier to read. Here's an example of code that would normally appear on one line, but is divided to make it easier to read in the book.

```
MsgBox _
    "Hello World"
```

✦ Definitions are always handy to have. I'll use Italics text to differentiate defini-tions from the rest of the text like this: A *CPU* is the central processing unit for your machine.

✦ In some cases, I won't have an exact value to provide so I'll give you an idea of what you should type by enclosing it in angle brackets like this: Provide a *<Machine Name>* value for the Name field.

✦ You'll always be able to recognize menu selections and command sequences because they're implemented like this: Use the File ⇨ Open command.

The following icons identify useful and important asides from the main text.

Notes help you to understand some principle or provide amplifying information. In many cases, a note is used to emphasize some piece of critical information that you need.

Any time that you see a caution, make sure that you take special care to read it. This information is vital. I always uses the caution to designate information that will help you to avoid damage to your application, data, machine, or self. Never skip the cautions in a chapter and always follow their advice.

All of us like to know special bits of information that will make our job easier, more fun, or faster to perform. Tips help you to get the job done faster and more safely. In many cases, the information found in a tip is drawn from experience, rather than through experimentation or from the documentation.

Finding what you need quickly is more important than ever before. Many people work at a pace that they call Internet time. They no longer have the luxury of per-forming hours of research to find that magic piece of information needed to com-plete an application. With this in mind, I've spent the time that you don't have to find unique information sources on the Internet. This icon will always provide that information so that you can get what you need quickly.

You're going to see a lot of example code in this book. The On the CD-ROM icon will help you to find application source code on the CD-ROM that accompanies the book. It's important to follow along with the book whenever possible so that you can get the most out of the information provided. The demo programs on the CD-ROM help you do just that.

There are times when information in another area of the book will help you to bet-ter understand the current discussion. I always include the Cross-Reference icon to indicate additional material that you might need.

Acknowledgments

Thanks to my wife Rebecca for working with me to get this book completed. I really don't know what I would have done without her help in proofreading my rough draft. She also deserves thanks for helping to research, compile, and edit some of the information that appears in this book.

Russ Mullen deserves thanks for his technical edit of this book. Russ greatly added to the accuracy and depth of the material that you see here. In addition, he spent many hours working with me through e-mail to find solutions to some of the problems that both VB and COM+ presented, and he is responsible for providing many of the Web site addresses sprinkled throughout the book.

Two people deserve a special mention for reading both excerpts and entire chapters from the book. Karen Watterson and Chris Goodale both provided extensive comments about content, ideas for new types of material, Web sites, and even helpful hints to get me back on track. Neither person had anything to gain from this experience and gave of themselves simply because they wanted to see me produce a good book.

Matt Wagner, my agent, deserves credit for helping me get to the contract in the first place and taking care of all the details that most authors don't really think about. His help is always appreciated, but especially so on this book because I was going through some very tough times. It's good to know that there is someone who wants to help.

The technical support staff at Microsoft (especially those on the Internet beta newsgroups) deserve credit for answering the questions that helped fill in the blanks and made the COM+ learning experience go faster. I especially appreciate the information and assistance provided by Mary Kirtland, Jeff DeVos, and Matthew Williamson.

Finally, I would like to thank Greg Croy, Eric Newman, Sharon Nash, S.B. Kleinman, and other members of the IDG Books staff for their assistance in bringing this book to print. I especially appreciate their willingness to work with me on a very demanding schedule.

Contents at a Glance

Contents

Chapter 10: Creating Distributed Applications 417

Chapter 11: A Simple COM+ Example 471

Fundamentals

An Introduction to COM+

Anyone who spends any time at all writing Windows applications will eventually discover a need for some type of component programming. Components make writing applications easier. Of course, the major Windows component technology, the one that's supported by Microsoft, is the Component Object Model (COM). This technology has been around in one form or another since the very earliest days of Windows and forms the basis of many applications today.

Many of you have probably designed applications using COM already and realize that it has many limitations. In fact, a major problem with this technology is that it doesn't scale well to the world of enterprise applications that are commonly distributed across the company local area network (LAN) or wide area network (WAN). Microsoft realized this limitation long ago and made an attempt to fix it with Distributed COM (DCOM). However, DCOM suffers from limitations as well; so now, with Windows 2000, we're looking at another version of COM in COM+.

The first section helps you better understand how we got here from the very beginnings of Windows. It's important to take a look back at where you started because, in many cases, there are certain oddities in the way that COM works that you won't easily understand otherwise. Obviously, it's also good to have a historical view of the technology you're using because you're very likely to run into predecessors of the current technology in your programming adventures.

As previously mentioned, COM+ isn't new; it's an extension of current technologies. The second section of the chapter looks at four very important issues that you'll need to know about when dealing with COM+. The first issue is how this technology will affect application connectivity. Because COM+ is supposed to fix some of the problems that COM users experience with distributed applications, it pays to know how it will actually accomplish the task. The second issue is how COM+ will affect the user personally. COM+ applications will, of necessity, change the user's environment, and you need to know what kind of changes to expect. The third issue is the user interface. COM+ is definitely going to change the way that users interact with the applications you create, but not necessarily the way you think it will or to the extent you might expect. Finally, we'll look at how COM+ will affect you as the programmer. The changes here are significant and will definitely help you develop more robust applications faster than ever before.

It's important to understand how COM and COM+ compare from a nuts-and-bolts perspective, so that's the issue discussed in the third section. This isn't going to be an interface-by-interface comparison—that could take a lot more space than this entire book provides. Instead, I use an overview of the two technologies to give you a general view of how they compare. This section answers this question: What does COM+ offer in addition to what you already get with both COM and DCOM? (In fact, you might be surprised to know that DCOM is still there, lurking under the surface of COM+.)

Major additions to COM+ include two existing technologies, Microsoft Transaction Server (MTS) and Microsoft Message Queue (MSMQ). Both of these technologies appear in the fourth section of this chapter. MTS adds the reliability provided by transactions to COM. It ensures that every COM data transfer takes place at least once, but only once. Obviously, reliability is a major issue for critical enterprise applications. You don't want to bet your business on something that's not going to provide predictable results every time you use it. MSMQ, on the other hand, fixes another COM-related problem, the problem of tightly coupled applications. When you're working with an application on the local machine, it's expected that both the client and server will exist at the same time. A distributed application, however, can't make the same guarantee. The user may be on the road and not even have a connection to the server at the time that the user is creating new orders at the client site. Distributed applications need to provide a robust environment that allows the user to continue working even when the server isn't available, and vice versa.

The fifth and sixth sections are important in that they tell you about the hardware that I'm using to write this book and the minimal hardware that you need in order to develop applications of your own. COM+ is about distributed applications, so the one-machine setup really won't help you anymore. To write COM+ applications, you need two machines coupled together with network cabling. These two sections will help you create a test system to actually do the required work and make things easier for development purposes.

The last section of this chapter addresses a special need of developers. If you try to install SQL Server 6.5 Developer Edition (the version that ships with Visual Studio 6.0 Enterprise Edition), you'll find that your server becomes less functional and that SQL Server doesn't work at all. There's a way around this problem, and this section of the chapter tells you all about it. Not everyone is going to be upgrading to the latest version of SQL Server, so I considered this section essential for your sanity and well being. This section also tells you how to get the Visual Studio 6.0 Plus Pack, which contains SQL Server 7.0 Developer Edition. I highly recommend that you get the Visual Studio 6.0 Plus Pack because it solves many of the problems that you'll encounter in working with Windows 2000. In addition, I'll be using SQL Server 7.0 Developer Edition for all programming examples in the book.

A Historical View of COM+

The history of COM+ doesn't begin where most people think it begins. Microsoft didn't suddenly introduce COM one day, DCOM the next, and finally get around to COM+ on the third — the evolution of COM+ is a long journey that began almost with the beginning of Windows itself. While I'm not going to provide a blow-by-blow account of the progress of COM+ in this section, I do plan to provide you with enough information so that you can understand two important facts. First, COM+ may have some quirks, but those quirks are the result of a long development process. Second, although some developers may feel that COM+ doesn't go far enough, Microsoft has gone a very long way with this technology and there isn't any reason to believe that COM+ won't evolve into something more useful yet.

Starting with DDE

The history of COM+ actually begins with dynamic data exchange (DDE). DDE, also known as linking and embedding, first appeared on the scene in late 1989 to early 1990. DDE allowed two documents to share the same data. DDE-capable programs could trade information while they were running, exchanging text, pictures, and even some simple commands — with no user intervention. Instead of the user's selecting some text, selecting the Edit ➪ Copy command, and then switching to the target application and selecting the Edit ➪ Paste command, all these steps were automated. This automation, although primitive in 1990, had broad implications — in essence, it meant that one program could control the behavior of another. This was Microsoft's first major step toward object-oriented programming.

The whole purpose behind DDE was to create a common macro language for applications. A developer could use DDE to allow communication between applications and to allow one application to control another application's behavior in such a way that the user wouldn't really know where the data came from. Of course, there were lots of problems because each vendor's version of DDE was different and you had to know each application's method of doing things. However, DDE was still better than nothing — at least at the time. DDE is still around, albeit in a very subdued form. You'll find it used with the various file associations in both the Registry and within Windows Explorer. Figure 1-1 is a typical example of what you'll see.

Figure 1-1: DDE, the earliest form of macro control for applications, is still around in Windows Explorer.

Somewhere along the way, someone at Microsoft got the idea that controlling the application using the brute force of DDE just wasn't going to work. It was important to control both the application and the application's data. In addition, many programmers were starting to look at object orientation. Objects are the encapsulation of code and data into a single unit. The outgrowth of this evolutionary spurt was Object Linking and Embedding (OLE)—a technology that took a document-oriented approach to the question of data manipulation.

Introducing OLE

Microsoft introduced OLE 1 as part of Windows 3.*x*. It provided a basic set of linking and embedding features that users soon outgrew. One of the biggest problems was the huge amount of memory that OLE 1 required when creating more than one or two links with other applications. OLE 1 required the client to start every application that it had established an OLE link with—whether that link was actually displayed on screen or not. If the user's document was linked to a spreadsheet, a graphics program, and a charting program, all three had to be in memory when you opened your compound document. Most machines just didn't have the amount of memory that was needed. The lack of speed was also a major concern. Keeping all those applications going at once made a real performance hit; most machines spent their time swapping out one application to disk and swapping in another as you moved from place to place in the compound document. In addition, OLE 1 managed links inefficiently.

Even with the problems with OLE 1, from 1990 to 1993, DDE quickly fell into the shadow of OLE, a technology that included DDE but that expanded its features and added several innovations. OLE 1 was a hit, but not as much of a hit as Microsoft wanted. OLE 1 came closer to making the use of objects the same across all applications, but the performance and usage problems were still too costly for many users. OLE 2 is supposed to remedy some of the OLE 1 problems and provide much more functionality to boot. The following list gives you an idea of all the improvements Microsoft made in OLE 2.

✦ **Visual editing:** One of the problems with OLE 1 was that the user's train of thought got disrupted each time he or she needed to make a change to an object. The reason was simple: OLE 1 loaded a copy of the server and displayed the object in the originating application's window for editing. OLE 2 allows visual (or in-place) editing. Instead of opening a new window, the server merely overlays its toolbar, menu structures, and controls with those of the client. The user simply sees a change in tools, not a change in applications. As a result, the transition between documents is less noticeable. This method of editing has another benefit as well: Because the user doesn't load an entire application, in-place editing is more memory-efficient and reduces the load on the processor.

✦ **Nested objects:** OLE 1 allowed you to place one object at a time in the container document. An object couldn't become a container; all the objects existed as a single layer within the container. OLE 2 treats every potential container as just that — a container. It doesn't matter how many containers you place inside a container or how many ways you stack them.

✦ **Drag and drop:** You used to cut or copy an object in the server application and then place it in the client using the Paste Special command. This option still works, but OLE 2 also provides a new method of creating links to other documents. You can simply grab the object and move it wherever you want. It becomes linked wherever you decide to drop it.

✦ **Storage-independent links:** OLE 2 enables you to create links to other documents, even if they aren't physically located on the local drive, using a Lightweight Remote Procedure Call (LRPC) mechanism. Unfortunately, this linking mechanism has limitations. You'll find that it works fine with some peer-to-peer networks, for example, but that it works only marginally with other network types.

✦ **Adaptable links:** Many users screamed for this feature. If you moved any of the files required to create a compound document under OLE 1, all the links got destroyed, and you had to re-create them. This older version stored the full path, including the drive, to the linked data. OLE 2 stores only enough path information to maintain the link. If you create links between two files in the same directory, you can move these two files anywhere on the drive, and OLE 2 can maintain the link. The only criterion for maintaining a link under OLE 2 is that the relative path must remain the same.

✦ **OLE automation:** OLE automation is part of Visual Basic for Applications (VBA). VBA defines a standard interface for communicating with the server application, which enables the client application to send commands to the server that will change the contents of an object indirectly. OLE automation is the direct descendant of the DDE macro language that many applications still use.

The big difference from the user's perspective is that DDE macros were difficult to write and very prone to error. VBA is the native language of the application and is consistent across platforms. Complex communication between applications became possible with OLE Automation. A Visual Basic application could access and trigger nearly all the features in Word for Windows, for example. This way, an application written in Visual Basic could, for example, "borrow" Word's spelling checker, using it to examine the text in a text box. (This is one example of what's sometimes called OLE Automation.) Beyond that, Visual Basic could make Word do nearly anything; Visual Basic had a relationship to Word that was similar to the relationship between puppeteer and puppet. This was true of any OLE client application — it could put any server through hoops.

✦ **Version management:** Users found that OLE 1 would often try to load a compound document without verifying that the various objects inside had been created with the same version of the application that the user had on his or her machine. This resulted in what appeared to be unreadable or corrupted documents, when in reality only one or two of the objects inside had been created by a newer version of the application. OLE 2 can store the application name and version number as part of the link. If an application developer implements this feature correctly, a server (or client, for that matter) will detect an old version of a file and ask if the user wants to update it.

✦ **Object conversion:** This feature allows an object of one type to be converted to another type. It's normally used to convert an object created by another application into a format that's natively supported by the application. In many cases, this allows the user to view the document without incurring a heavy processor or memory load. However, object conversion can also result in corrupted data, or at least data that loses some of its meaning in translation.

✦ **Optimized object storage:** One of the reasons that OLE 1 failed to garner as much attention as it should have was the large amount of memory that was required if a user built a compound document using several different applications. Optimized object storage is part of the cure. It allows the linked documents to stay on disk until needed. That way, Windows doesn't need to load every application and data file required when reading the compound document. In most cases, Windows uses a buffer-zone technique. A word processor might keep the applications and objects required for the preceding, current, and next page in memory. The rest of the objects stay on disk, greatly reducing the memory footprint of a compound document in some cases.

✦ **Component object model:** That's right, COM began life as part of OLE 2. COM started out as Microsoft's simplified application programming interface (API) for OLE 2. Remember that OLE 2 was supposed to provide a means of data storage and conversion — the combination of data and code in a single object. OLE 1 didn't do this very well, but Microsoft corrected a lot of problems, including the matter of coding, in OLE 2.

ActiveX and COM

Just as DDE was converted into OLE, so, too, in its turn, has OLE evolved into ActiveX, which is just another term for a specific kind of component technology. When originally introduced in December 1995, ActiveX was a broad term for component technology that relied on COM, among other things. *ActiveX* is actually an umbrella term that covers the various concepts and technologies of DDE and OLE. It adds the idea that ActiveX controls (self-contained, usually smaller, specialized programs or libraries of data) can be used by traditional applications or can be embedded into HTML documents for use on the Internet.

The original ActiveX technology introduction confused programmers, so eventually Microsoft defined terms and limited the scope of what ActiveX was supposed to represent. ActiveX is still around today, although the meaning of the term isn't nearly as broad as was originally conceived by Microsoft. In most cases, the name *ActiveX* now refers to a component used to create applications. For example, all of the buttons in an application could be considered ActiveX components. In some cases, the components are hidden but still used to make the application function. For example, there are timers used with many applications that users can't see, but they can see the *effects* of them as they use the application.

Microsoft uses the word *active* to describe many things, not just ActiveX components. The idea is that previously inert, passive, or static objects can come "alive" (and contain their own capabilities — such as methods for self-modification, animation, calculation). Objects are referred to as a combination of data with the capability to act on that data. This capability to act is now being distributed to locations that were previously static. Server HTML pages used to be, for example, simple page-description documents. Now they can contain scripts (behaviors) that execute on the server side. (You're not surprised that they're called Active Server Pages, are you?) The idea of "active" has also been extended to the database used to store user, machine, and operating system information in Windows 2000. Active Directory is another "active" technology that relies on components for dynamic storage and data-manipulation requirements.

But ActiveX did not emerge one day as a full-blown, new technology. It isn't new, nor is it a single technology. ActiveX is simply a logical evolution of what Microsoft has done in the past. It gives the programmer greater flexibility in storing and manipulating data — much like DDE and OLE. In addition, ActiveX makes the distinction between programming and data less rigid.

Microsoft is committed to ActiveX and all that the term *ActiveX* implies. It's a technology, a set of operating system features (DLLs and API functions), a way of programming, and a collection of objects that you can plug into your own programs or Web pages. *ActiveX* is, therefore, a generic term covering a variety of initiatives from Microsoft.

By now, you've probably realized that Microsoft has spent a lot of time and effort making object and component technology work correctly on the desktop. However, enterprise computing isn't about the desktop; it's about corporate data stored in mainframes in some secret room. Enterprise computing is all about distributed applications that can access any data required from any location so long as the user has the rights to access the resource.

The role of DCOM in distributed computing

So, with COM in hand, Microsoft set out to create something like COM, but on an enterprise scale. The first attempt at this process was DCOM, which relies on the Open Software Foundation (OSF) Distributed Computing Environment (DCE) Remote Procedure Call (RPC) network protocol. (The OSF is now part of the Open Group.) DCOM is still a very big success. It allows applications to communicate across the network in ways that users of DDE, OLE, and COM could only dream about. In addition, the links that DCOM creates are both secure and permanent, at least within reason. If you remove the server-side component, the client won't find it no matter how hard it tries. However, excluding the unreasonable, DCOM is very reliable.

Cross-Reference
DCOM is still a very important technology. This chapter provides a simple overview of DCOM from a historical perspective. You learn more about DCOM by reading Chapter 5. In that chapter, we look at detailed DCOM information: how DCOM works and what you need to know from a theoretical perspective. We also work with DCOM using various utilities that Microsoft provides. Finally, Chapter 5 provides a simple DCOM application so that you can see DCOM in action.

However, the problem with DCOM is that it's a tightly coupled protocol. So, what does this mean in terms that the average human can understand? It means that both the client and the server must exist at the same time and have a connection to each other. In short, DCOM is a failure in some situations because it works only in a desktop network environment (or in some close approximation of that environment). Big-iron setups, where everyone had a desk at the company, are gone. Today, the trick isn't providing desktop users access to the data that they need; it's in providing users who are on the road access to the data that they need.

DCOM has other problems. For example, barring any other event, there isn't any guarantee from DCOM that a communication will take place at least once, but only once. To put this problem in perspective, consider what would happen if a salesperson took an order from ABC Corporation. The first time the salesperson visited, the order went in, but it didn't actually arrive at the company. Four weeks later, ABC Corporation is wondering where its widgets are, but there isn't any record of an order for widgets in the company database. Would you want to be the salesperson who visited ABC Corporation a second time?

Let's say that you have plenty of courage and visit ABC Corporation a second time. You give the company president lots of assurances that he'll definitely get his widgets this time. So, you make the order and then verify that the widgets are definitely on order by talking with someone on the phone. Unfortunately, there was a glitch in the line and the server thought that the order was lost, so it asked your machine to repeat the message. Four weeks later, ABC Corporation receives not one, but two orders of widgets.

The COM+ difference viewed historically

DCOM is a great technology, but it isn't up to the demands of today's corporate user. Enter COM+. This is the new technology that we'll spend most of our time discussing in this book. It's also built on DDE, OLE, and COM, just as all of the technologies mentioned so far have been. However, now we also add DCOM to the mix. That's right, moving to COM+ doesn't free you from DCOM.

Cross-Reference

We're taking a very short overview of COM+ in this chapter. Because COM+ is the main topic of the book, you'll find it in most of the chapters that follow. However, if you're looking for the meat of the theory behind COM+, then you need to look at Chapters 6, 7, and 8. Chapter 6 helps you understand the mechanics of how COM+ works — specifically, those areas where COM+ differs from everything that preceded it. Chapter 7 helps you understand the new security issues you'll have to deal with when using COM+. Because COM+ is designed for distributed applications, there are a lot of new security issues to consider. Finally, Chapter 8 tells you how COM+ fits into Microsoft's current vision for enterprise computing, the Distributed interNetwork Architecture (DNA).

So, how is COM+ better? COM+ is actually a combination of three technologies: DCOM, MTS, and MSMQ. Now, it's important to understand how the combination of these three technologies into COM+ makes such a big difference. DCOM has a problem with one, and only one, delivery of information. Adding MTS to the picture solves the problem. Every data transfer can now take place within a transaction, which means that every data transfer will take place only one time, but at least one time. Our salesperson will no longer have to wonder if the order got in at all or if he needs to take a vacation as ABC Corporation tries to sort out an overabundance of widgets. While DCOM is reliable, MTS makes it even more so.

DCOM can't work in a disconnected environment. That's a problem for our salesperson on the road because the salesperson now needs to ask for a telephone line for every transaction. MSMQ solves this problem using a messaging protocol. Every order is stored locally until the salesperson calls into the home office. As soon as a connection to the corporate network is made, the orders are entered into the company database in the background without any user intervention.

COM+ Issues

COM+ is one of the most important new technologies waiting for you in Windows 2000 — new, yet old at the same time. The previous section told you how COM+ relies on technology that has existed since Microsoft introduced Windows. The evolutionary view of COM+ should have helped you understand that this technology is built on a firm foundation — even if it is the new kid on the block.

Note   There's a lot of confusion about the terms *component* and *object,* even among programmers. Part of the confusion is that many technical magazines and trade presses don't use the terms consistently. For our purposes, a *component* is the physical representation of code and data in a DLL or EXE. An *object* is an instantiated form of the component created by a particular application for its use. In short, a component is the template from which objects are created.

I've always viewed components as a sort of programmer's Legos, building blocks for creating something useful out of standardized parts. In this respect, COM+ is no different from any component technology that you've explored in the past. Creating an application still requires talent, even if the talent is in putting building blocks together. COM+ doesn't contain any kind of magic that'll allow applications to appear from nowhere; you still have to put in the time required to create them.

So, if COM+ is still a component technology, what is it offering you? Think of COM+ as a Lego expansion set. Yes, it's still all about building blocks, but now you have new blocks to add to your collection, along with a few motorized parts to make your applications move.

Another way to look at this issue is the ability to do work. OLE was the pathetic 98-pound weakling who appeared in old bodybuilding ads. It was hard to get much done with it and even harder to keep an application going once you did. COM and DCOM are both bodybuilders, but they don't have that really muscular feel. They're like the neighbor who looks impressive but really isn't. Yes, you can get work done with them, but they don't have a good, solid feel. Enter COM+, the Mr. Universe of component technology. This technology has the strength to perform the Herculean feats required by today's computing environment. In short, COM+ is COM on steroids. It represents Microsoft's latest advance in application development for today's complex programming environment.

The following sections explore four very important issues in COM+. First, we explore connectivity, the requirement to create some form of communication between a client and a server. Second, we address the user's needs. In today's work-at-home-and-on-the-road environment, the user's needs can't be fulfilled by standard COM. Third, we look at the user interface and how COM+ will affect it. Finally, we look at the needs of the developer, at least from an overview perspective. This book is for developers, so this overview serves merely as a tour guide of the Microsoft vision for the developer and COM+.

Connectivity

If you have any doubts about the need for better component technology, just look at the kind of environment programmers work in today. When I first started writing code, I had to worry about the local machine, and that was all. That local machine was running DOS, which meant it had limited amounts of memory and very few instructions to worry about. In the days of DOS, programming was quite simple, but also quite limited. I didn't need a large Lego set; in fact, all I really needed were simple tools to create a single Lego.

Even when I moved to Windows 3.x, the programming environment was largely confined to the local machine, with just a few LAN elements thrown in for good measure. Windows 3.x programming focused on the user's desktop, not on a corporation as a whole. Any enterprise applications created during this time ran on mainframes; the PC was still viewed as a toy by most corporations. Very few corporate workers used Windows 3.x machines for serious applications, at least in comparison with the number who use PCs today. In short, from a developer's (and a user's) perspective, Windows 3.x was simply DOS with graphics. (Of course, I'm overlooking the nightmarish task of writing a functional Windows 3.x application.) Even in the days of Windows 3.x, however, Microsoft was already looking toward the future with technologies like DDE and OLE, so you might say that this time period represented the precursor to the Lego days.

There's no local, self-contained machine running DOS or Windows 3.x today in the corporate environment. When you write an application now, you have to worry about how that application will affect the Internet, or a LAN, or some other machine. Computers today are connected in ways that I couldn't even imagine they'd be when I started programming. The Internet is a major part of many application development efforts; you really can't write an application today without at least thinking about how it'll work in a network situation. In addition, users are no longer happy to store their data locally while on the road. They want to be able to connect to the company's intranet using a Virtual Private Network (VPN). The same VPN connection will allow them to update their local data to reflect changes at the office. People today are connected to one another in more ways than one, and applications have to keep pace with the changing needs of these users.

Tip   Although disconnected applications that allow the user to connect using the Remote Access Server (RAS) can easily be written using COM+, using VPN makes a lot more sense financially for most companies, especially if the company already has a Web site in place. The Internet allows easy connectivity anywhere in the world for the price of a local call. Both VPN and COM+ offer data security and encryption features that make this mode of data transfer safe and reliable. RAS can't offer this kind of connectivity either using Public Switched Telephone Network (PSTN) lines or at this price. Imagine the cost of connecting to the corporate network from overseas, if you can get a connection that works. However, if you have just one or two employees on the road in the local area, RAS does make sense as an alternative to using a VPN.

COM+ helps you with connectivity in two ways. First, the inclusion of MTS ensures that communications remain reliable. Every communication is guaranteed to happen one, and only one time, time. Second, disconnected application development means that data entry can occur anywhere, even without a direct connection to the company. When a connection is made, the accumulated data is transferred to the corporate database in the background, without any kind of user participation. Fully automated communications means that there's less of a chance that the user will encounter problems when working with the application and that those communications will actually occur as expected. (You're not relying on the user to remember to transfer the data; the data transfer takes place automatically.)

The user

In addition to connectivity, people expect more assistance out of applications today. A character-mode application like the ones I used to create in DOS just wouldn't work. Those applications were designed with an advanced user in mind. Today, many users have turned on their computer for the first time and have no idea how to run it. In short, the application has to be smart enough to keep users from shooting themselves in the foot. Applications that are designed to prevent users from hurting themselves are very complex and difficult to create. It's not enough to think about the logical considerations; you have to think about the illogical things, too.

COM+ can help you address some user issues that may have required a phone call or other form of communication in the past. For example, it's now possible to maintain help-desk statistics for local desktop computers as well as laptop computers on the road. The same MSMQ facility that allows the user to make data entries in disconnected mode allows your application to maintain statistics on user help requirements. Best of all, these statistics will get uploaded to your network quickly — which is a requirement if you want the data in time to actually use it for application tweaks.

A user who has a question about application use can write a query while on the road. As with all of the other disconnected application data mentioned so far, the question will get uploaded to the help desk during the user's next check-in with the company network. In short, users can now get the help they need while on the road without the inconvenience of having to make a long-distance phone call directly to the company help desk.

Obviously, the main focus of COM+ is the application itself. There are certain connectivity and ease-of-use issues that COM+ is designed to handle for both the user and the programmer. For example, if a user on the road needs to enter a new order in the database, can you really expect the user to remember some arcane procedure that you taught at the office for working on the road? It's very likely that the user isn't going to remember and that you'll have a mess to clean up when the user returns to the office. A COM+ application can act the same no matter where the user is. Because the user uses the same procedure for entering data each time and the programmer doesn't need to do much more in the way of application programming, everyone's a winner in this scenario.

User interface

We're still not done with the issues programmers face today versus the issues of yesterday. There's one additional technological difference that you need to consider. A graphical user interface (GUI) may be wonderful for the user, but I'm not convinced that the programmer gets anything at all out of it other than a major writer's cramp. Getting all of those icons on screen takes time and lots of code. In the days of DOS, I didn't need much in the way of input. Everything was character-driven, so the user interface was often an afterthought after the rest of the application was working.

As soon as Windows 3.x came into the picture, the programmer needed to worry about graphics. The user interface moved from the back burner the front burner and became the very first thing that the programmer had to worry about when creating an application. In short, application programming went from being business-logic-driven to being user-need-driven; today, it is, finally, data-driven. Today, the data you manipulate and the expertise of the user that you're writing for determines what an application will look like. High-end users, the ones who were easy to deal with in the days of DOS, are now the ones who are the most difficult to develop for because they require more control over the data they create.

Component technology has come to the programmer's rescue in a big way when it comes to dealing with a GUI. Instead of writing miles of code to draw every control and handle every event that the user generates, the programmer can now use pre-defined objects to get the job done. All that the programmer really needs to worry about is the appearance of a form and the business logic required to make that form work. COM+ extends the kinds of things that you can do with a GUI. For example, it's possible to set up a COM+ application to download component updates automatically, which means that you change an application once on the server and then rely on the server to update everyone else automatically. Again, we're looking at connected applications that change to reflect current conditions in the company as a whole.

However, the most significant user-interface development in COM+ is what it *doesn't* change. In times past, you had to write all kinds of strange logic to get applications to work in a disconnected environment. The forms and the procedures for using them were different for the user on the road than for the user at the desktop. Even a simple application can become a support nightmare in this environment. Disconnected mode applications mean that you write one interface with a single set of rules that everyone uses, no matter where they're located. So, in COM+, look for the ways in which you can create a consistent, unchanging user interface, rather than new bells and whistles to add to an existing interface.

The programmer

Programmers won't ever have the simple programming environment of DOS again. They'll have to face the consequences of working in a world where the PC has really taken over as a primary business tool, running critical applications that have to be available 24 hours a day, 7 days a week. COM+ allows a programmer to create an application quickly, but with all of the connectivity and ease-of-use issues taken care of. As previously mentioned, COM+ is really an expansion set for the component technology that you already use in your applications, not something entirely new.

We're just getting started with COM+. However, if you want to get right to the action, start looking at Chapter 9. It teaches you to create simple components, providing you with an understanding of the underpinnings of COM+. Chapter 10 addresses a more complex DCOM application that includes more features than the one you find in Chapter 5 (the DCOM theory chapter). Chapters 11 through 14 contain progressively more complex COM+ examples. We start out with simple components in Chapter 11, move on to disconnected applications in Chapter 12, add database management in Chapter 13, and end with Web-based applications in Chapter 14. Obviously, because the Web is where most applications are headed today, the example in Chapter 14 is especially important to your understanding of how COM+ can help you create the kind of applications that users really need.

No one today could create the kinds of complex applications required for Internet use in a GUI environment using straight procedural code — or not without expending a lot of time. In short, using COM (or some other component technology) is no longer a luxury because you need the component technology to create an application of any kind. It won't be long before COM+ will be a requirement as well, because people will have to be connected at all times to their sources of information.

So what does COM+ offer the developer? That question is hard to resolve because COM+ will mean different things to different developers, depending on the kinds of applications they create. However, the following list provides an overview of the things that most developers will get out of COM+.

✦ **Faster development time:** COM+ fills holes in the COM environment as far as developer support goes. In addition, you don't have to worry about adding certain features to an application anymore, like the requirement to check for a network connection.

✦ **Less debugging time:** COM+ does more for the developer, which means that the developer spends more time coding business rules and other unique application elements. Smaller amounts of custom code means less debugging time because more of the code is already debugged for you.

✦ **More automation:** As this book progresses, you'll notice that Microsoft has added a lot of new wizards to the ones that you're already using. More automation means that you spend more time thinking about how the application should work, rather than how to implement your ideas.

✦ **Better reliability:** Let's face it, developers get blamed for all kinds of application issues that they can't control. If an application suffers from line noise, it must be the developer's fault and has nothing to do with the lightning storm currently raging outside. Because COM+ adds reliability features, you're less likely to spend your day trying to explain why acts of nature would affect an application's operation.

How COM+ and COM Compare

From a component creation perspective, COM and COM+ are about the same. Despite all of the hype to the contrary, you can create a component using either form of the technology. In fact, COM+ is merely an augmentation of existing COM technology when it comes to working with components. The important thing to remember is that COM+ is a true superset of COM, so you lose nothing by using COM+ in place of COM in your applications.

Now that you have some idea of how COM and COM+ are the same, it's time to look at how they differ. The following sections provide an overview of these differences. I'll refine this overview as the book progresses. What this overview is designed to do is help you separate the hype of COM+ improvements from changes that'll really make a difference when it comes time to create an application.

COM+ design goals

To better understand what you do gain using COM+, it's important to understand some of the goals that the design team had in mind when putting COM+ together. A main goal was to make developing components for server use as easy as developing components for client use. Before COM+ there were a lot of server-specific issues to take care of (like multiple users' accessing a component at the same time). COM+ removes a lot of the problems that come with a multiuser environment like the one you find on servers. Of course, the result is to promote distributed application development.

A secondary goal was to make it just as easy to develop enterprise applications as to develop workgroup applications. What this means is that COM+ allows you to create components that'll scale to any size. *Load balancing* is a term that you'll hear more and more as companies try to create an environment in which a single programming effort will result in components that continue to work as the company grows.

In short, these two goals define part of what COM+ is all about. Unlike COM, COM+ is designed to allow you to create distributed applications that rely on component technology that scales to any size. This COM+ difference greatly affects how you create future applications. In many cases, you'll now create components that applications on the client will use to access data on yet another server.

Let's talk about the client and server situation a little further. COM+ is also part of Microsoft's DNA. Essentially, this is an *n*-tier architecture where various servers perform specific tasks. Those tasks are just part of a whole application. In other words, a single application on the user's machine may actually require the services provided by more than one server. One server might have the components that include the basic business logic for the request, another server might access in-memory databases containing, for example, a list of the 50 states, and a third server might provide access to the company's main data store. The whole idea is to create an environment where the user doesn't care which server has what the user needs to get the job done, just that the job gets done as efficiently as possible.

Transactions and COM+

Accomplishing the two goals of distributed application development and component scalability that we talked about in the previous section is harder said than done. Anytime you have two machines talking with each other over a cable (be it a telephone wire or coaxial cable), you have to create some type of protocol for the discussion. In addition, there's a much greater chance for lost data, which means that you need some type of transaction technology in place. MTS is part of the COM+ universe. MTS is the mechanism by which COM+ guarantees delivery of data from one machine to another. I discuss exactly how MTS comes into play in the section entitled "The MTS Difference."

Messages and COM+

COM+ also introduces a new concept: disconnected applications. However, it uses an old technology to implement this concept in the form of MSMQ. In the past, an application that required services from the server or wanted to provide input to the server had to maintain a live connection. Obviously, this is impossible for employees on the road, so companies often had to rely on cumbersome, often unreliable technologies that forced employees to use different methods in different situations. In addition to the problem of getting an employee trained to use more than one data entry and management method, there was a problem with getting the employee to use the right method at the right time.

These old technologies also forced the programmer to do more work. Even if the programmer needed to worry about only two data-entry scenarios, that's still twice the amount of code and debugging. In essence, the programmer was actually writing the same application twice because of a lack of disconnected application tools. Of course, the doubling of data-entry features also resulted in larger applications that required more memory to load. A disconnected application takes only slightly more disk space and memory than a single interface application designed for desktop-only use.

MSMQ and COM+ have been teamed up as Queued Components to allow a programmer to build logic into the application that doesn't care about the current connected state of the application. Data that an application wants to send to the server gets stored in a local message queue if the application can't establish a connection with the server. When the user does make a connection, the data in the message queue is automatically uploaded.

Note   You'll see *MSMQ* and *Queued Components* used almost interchangeably throughout this book. MSMQ is the base standalone technology originally introduced for use within Windows NT. It provides both an API and component-based interface for developers. Queued Components are the new COM+ version of MSMQ and offer a true superset of the older technology. All of the older MSMQ interfaces are still in place, but now you also have more automation and integration with COM available in Queued Components. I use *Queued Components* whenever I'm talking about a Queued Component–specific feature like a wizard, while *MSMQ* always refers to the underlying technology or an existing feature like a programming API. It's important to see Queued Components as a slightly augmented version of MSMQ that's designed specifically for use with COM+ and not as a new product.

Resources that the application will require from the server can also be downloaded before the user attempts to break the connection. This will allow the user to request at least a subset of the data from the server, never realizing that there isn't a connection in place for getting the requested information. The only time the user will notice any difference is if the data requested is needed immediately and the need to download it from the server wasn't anticipated. Even so, as soon as the user establishes a connection, the user can download the requested data in the background.

As you can see, coupling COM+ and MSMQ means that the user will need to know only one application's usage procedure. No longer will the administrator have to pull his or her hair out when the wrong procedure is used for data-entry purposes. In addition, the programmer can deliver a working application much faster because there'll be only one set of data access routines to write.

COM+ services

So far, we've seen that COM+ is an amalgam of various existing technologies. In short, nothing I've said so far is all that new. However, the fact that COM+ provides a wrapper for making all of these technologies work together is a new idea. Microsoft has found that it's not enough to provide disparate services that could allow applications to talk with servers using components rather than some of the older technologies we relied on in the past. Creating a single package for all of these technologies is the way to ensure that programmers actually use the technologies that Microsoft has provided.

COM+ isn't merely a wrapper for existing services, however. It also provides some unique services that you won't find in any of Microsoft's older offerings. The following list provides you with an overview of what these offerings are. We'll study these features in greater detail as the book progresses.

Chapters 2 through 4 act as an introduction to this new technology. In Chapter 2, we look at some administration tasks that you'll need to know about in order to work with the examples in the book. You'll also need to know about these procedures in order to show an administrator how to work with the applications you create. Chapter 3 discusses the assortment of utilities that we use in this book. All of these tools come with Visual Studio, but C++ programmers normally use many of them. These tools will greatly enhance your ability to write applications quickly, debug them, and figure out potential sources of error when they do occur. You'll find the theoretical introduction to COM+ in Chapter 4. We'll look at all of the underpinnings of COM+ in Chapter 4, including how interfaces, contexts, and interceptors work. Chapter 4 is the chapter to read if you want to know how things work beneath the surface. It's not an essential chapter if you want to write applications using just the wizards (in which case, however, you'll be extremely limited in the kinds of applications that you can write).

✦ **Events:** Applications can receive events generated on the server as if they occurred on the local machine. This means that the server-side components you create will have a direct connection to the client. COM+ allows you to use *unicast* (event is sent to one event sink), *multicast* (event is sent to multiple event sinks), and *unbound* (event occurs when client makes contact) events. The unbound event is particularly useful because it can inform a client about conditions on the server after the client performs an initial login. In other words, every client who logs into the system will receive the current (dynamic) status of the server that the client is logging into.

✦ **Security:** COM+ actually relies on MTS for the security of its data in many cases. However, there are still security concerns when instantiated objects on the server need to communicate with a client and there isn't any transaction. In addition, COM+ allows the creation of queued components — essentially a component in a message. Security is a requirement if you don't want another company taking a look at your business logic. COM+ checks security at several levels, including the class itself, any interface requests, and all method calls. These security roles are mapped through Active Directory to the Windows 2000 domain accounts.

Component Load Balancing (CLB) wasn't provided as part of the released version of Windows 2000. However, as of this writing, Microsoft has promised to release CLB both as a separate product and as part of the Windows 2000 AppCenter Server product. In other words, if you want the benefits of this particular feature, you'll need to perform a separate download and installation sometime after the release of Windows 2000, or install the Windows 2000 AppCenter Server product in place of the other server products currently available. CLB is a must-have technology for large COM+ applications because it's unlikely that a single server will meet all of your needs. Using CLB automates the process of distributing a component load between several servers (as described in the bulleted item that follows). You can find out more about CLB at http://www.microsoft.com/windows2000/news/fromms/clb.asp. This change in CLB support doesn't affect other forms of multiserver use such as Network Load Balancing (NLB) and Cluster Server. Both of these products are available in Windows 2000 Advanced Server and Windows 2000 DataCenter Server.

✦ **Component Load Balancing:** Large companies very rarely get by with just one server. In the past, the company would divide users into groups, and each group had its own server. This method worked fine as long as none of the servers went down. However, it was very inefficient because one server might have a light load while another struggled to keep up. Load balancing allows everyone to access all of the available servers through a router. The router keeps track of how heavy each server's load is and balances new requests accordingly. In addition, the router can move current requests from a failed server to the good ones in the cluster without the user even realizing that a server failure has occurred.

COM+ was supposed to provide access to another feature called the In-Memory Database (IMDB). Essentially, this feature was to give an application faster access to static data, like ZIP codes or state abbreviations, by keeping that data in memory. Some beta users will probably remember the inclusion of this feature in early Windows 2000 beta releases. Unfortunately, Microsoft pulled this feature from Windows 2000 with the intent of releasing something better later. You can find out more about this feature and its future at http://msdn.microsoft.com/ vstudio/comapps/imdbquestion.asp.

✦ **Queued components:** Clients require updates to the components they hold from time to time and, in some cases, require a new component before they can perform a specific task. In the past, the administrator had to install new components on each machine individually or create cumbersome batch files to do the job. The use of queued components allows each client to update itself automatically, and in the background. The administrator doesn't need to do much more than install the component on the server and send the proper broadcast message.

✦ **Compensating Resource Manager (CRM):** This particular service is used with legacy applications. It actually builds a framework around the old server application so that clients can access the application using all of the new features that COM+ provides. The main goal of this service is to allow you to maintain your investment in established applications yet enable the old application to interact with other resources on the server. Of course, this feature comes at the cost of performance, so upgrading your components to COM+ is something that you should consider.

✦ **Administration:** COM+ uses a Microsoft Management Console (MMC) snap-in to provide administrative services for your server-side components. This snap-in allows you to manage all COM components and to administer all of the new services that COM+ provides. This snap-in also provides a programming interface that allows you to install, configure, and automatically deploy your COM+ components.

It relies on Active Directory's catalog to store the attributes for each of the components installed on the server. The COM+ component attributes include transactions, security roles, and activation properties.

✦ **Publish/subscribe event model:** COM+ provides a new type of event model. The new model enables the developer to create applications that don't need to know quite as much about each other to perform a task. The component publishes events and doesn't care where those events go. An application can subscribe to events without really knowing their source. Between these two applications are Windows 2000 component services, which manage the connection between publisher and subscriber. Contrast this with the request/reply event model used by COM, in which the application and component needed to know specific details about each other, making application development more complex than it needed to be in some cases. We'll look at this particular feature in more detail in Chapter 6.

The MTS Difference

MTS is an important part of COM+. This section provides you with a very brief overview of MTS. We'll discuss the two most important aspects of MTS — the services it provides and the purpose of resource pooling. Chapters 6 and 11 look at MTS in greater detail and define its place in the grand scheme of things a bit better. There's a lot more to know now about MTS from both a management and a programming perspective than you needed to know when working with Windows NT.

MTS service description

As previously mentioned, COM+ relies on MTS to perform specific services which ensure that data gets delivered from one machine to another. These services ensure that the data is delivered and that both the sender and the recipient are sure of the integrity of the data. The following list provides an overview of the services that MTS provides for COM+.

✦ **Transactions:** A transaction is a single group of instructions that have to be carried out in order for a task to be completed. Either a transaction is completed, or it's rolled back so that the application environment is the same as it was before the transaction started. MTS frees the programmer from having to manage transactions. All the programmer needs to do is specify that a given set of instructions constitutes a transaction.

✦ **Resource pooling:** Today's servers have huge quantities of memory and hard-disk space that components can use to complete tasks. However, given the complex environment in which components are often placed, trying to manage resources can be difficult. MTS also features automated resource management. Not only does resource pooling free the programmer from micromanaging system resources, but it also ensures that each component gets the resources it needs.

✦ **Security:** Getting data from one point to another and ensuring that it gets recorded properly won't do much for you if someone breaks into the connection between the client and server and corrupts the data. Consequently, security is an important feature of MTS provides.

✦ **Administration:** Managing your MTS setup so that you can get optimum performance from your server is an important task. Microsoft provides a MMC snap-in that makes MTS management easier. In addition, using a MMC snap-in reduces the administrator's learning curve because all administrative tools in Windows 2000 now use the MMC interface.

As you can see, MTS provides a lot more than just transaction management, although that's its main function. The other services that MTS provides merely augment the main function of making sure that data gets from one point to another without interruption and that all of the operations formed on that data are completed successfully, or not at all. Without these services, COM+ as a whole would fail because data security is a primary requirement when creating distributed applications.

One service that doesn't appear in our list is serialization. This particular feature of MTS ensures that both data and commands arrive at the database in the same order in which they were created on the client, even if the network protocol used to transfer the packets of information doesn't guarantee any order of delivery. This means that you won't need to worry quite as much about the features provided by the underlying network protocol — at least not when it concerns the order that your data will arrive in.

The role of resource pooling in COM+

One MTS service requires special mention. Resource pooling is an important reason to use MTS because resource pooling is a requirement for efficient transactions on a large scale. A smart resource-pooling scheme doesn't just allocate and deallocate system resources. Allocating and deallocating resources takes time that could be used for other purposes. Marking resources that are already allocated for use allows reuse and eliminates some of the inefficiencies of transaction management. MTS does provide four different levels of resource status. It uses the notion of enlisting a resource for use, and then using it. Each of the four levels of resource status is described in the following list.

✦ **Resources in unenlisted inventory:** This is a resource that's available for assignment to any object or transaction. All resources start in this state and remain that way until they're needed by an application for processing purposes.

✦ **Resources in enlisted inventory:** Transactions may involve more than one object. If one object no longer needs a resource, the resource can be set aside for use by another object in the same transaction. This resource status allows a transaction to maintain control over a resource until none of the objects contained within it requires the resource any longer.

✦ **Resources in unenlisted use:** An object that owns a resource that isn't part of a transaction owns that resource in an unenlisted state. This particular resource status also gets used if an object is operating within a transaction, but the resource is marked as not being transactional.

✦ **Resources in enlisted use:** Three conditions must exist before this resource status can be used. The resource must be assigned to an object. The object instance must be part of a transaction. Finally, the resource dispenser must successfully enlist the resource as part of the transaction.

You now have an idea of why resource pooling in MTS is important. It allows MTS to allocate, deallocate, and manage resources efficiently. Resource pooling also promotes resource reuse so that the server doesn't waste time allocating a resource that was just used by another object in the same transaction. Considering that COM+ is all about objects, wise object-resource management is a requirement for successful implementation of the COM+ strategy.

Where does MSMQ fit in?

MSMQ is the messaging arm of the COM+ strategy for Microsoft. It allows applications to do things that were impossible in the past. MSMQ aids in application development, among other things, with communications. COM+ requests and responses are sent and received as messages. This means that all COM+ really needs is a message queue to put the message in. MSMQ places such queues on both the server and the client, and then provides a method for transferring data in these queues between the two machines without the user's assistance. The server and the client don't really need to connect directly as long as they pick up their messages.

A lot of programmers find this particular issue confusing because we're all used to looking at synchronous real-time communication. It helps to look at this messaging arrangement in the same way you that look at e-mail on the Internet. You can have a conversation with an associate using e-mail without contacting that associate in real time on the phone. Using e-mail allows both of you to communicate ideas and learn new ways of doing things. Likewise, disconnected applications can use the MSMQ queues to hold a conversation with the server. Obviously, there has to be some way to exchange the information between the queues. Again, it's easy to look at Internet e-mail as a way to understand how MSMQ works. Although you can answer your e-mail offline, you eventually need to get online to upload the responses you create to the Internet service provider's (ISP) server. The same thing happens with a disconnected application using MSMQ.

Microsoft had to provide four features in MSMQ to make it a useful technology. The following list describes these four features and why they're important.

✦ **Delivery guarantees:** Unless MSMQ guarantees delivery of messages, there's no way to ensure that the server or client will actually receive query responses.

Without a guaranteed communication, your application will be unreliable. In sum, a guarantee of delivery, no matter how long such delivery takes, is a requirement in creating a robust, reliable application that ensures the user will get the same results whether connected to the server or not.

✦ **Routing:** The programmer may not have any idea of exactly how the user will connect to the server. The user might require a dial-up connection over a modem one day and a direct network connection the next. As a result, it's up to MSMQ to ensure that messages get from the client to the server and vice versa. Routing these messages is an important part of MSMQs background processing on behalf of the user.

✦ **Disconnected applications:** The whole reason to use MSMQ is to build disconnected applications. Today's user needs a reliable method of accessing and updating server information without having to learn more than one technique of doing so. Disconnected applications reduce both application development time and user training time. In addition, the application is inherently more reliable because there are fewer points of failure. A single way of doing things means that there's a set procedure in place that the user can always rely on.

✦ **Security:** Like everything else in a distributed application, your data must remain secure. In this case, MSMQ provides the means for ensuring that messages are kept secret. Both the client's and the server's data must remain encrypted so that prying eyes don't gain access to them by looking through the messages that MSMQ stores on the hard drive.

MSMQ actually contains three discrete components: the message queues, a queue manager, and the API used to request data from the queue manager. These components are discussed in detail in Chapters 6 and 12. For the moment, all you really need to know is that the client and server never directly access the messages that MSMQ stores. All access is through the API using the queue manager.

There's a fourth MSMQ component that you also need to be aware of that has little to do with the actual handling of the messages. It's the MSMQ Information Service (MQIS). This database holds the definitions for MSMQ sites, machines, queues, and users. The actual database is implemented using SQL Server, which is why Windows 2000 provides a "limited" version of SQL Server as part of the package. MQIS is not found on every machine, and it is not found on any client. MQIS is a central repository of data and is, therefore, found on just a few servers (possibly only one) on the network.

MSMQ is designed to work locally, on a LAN, or at the enterprise level, without any changes in code on your part. The idea is a simple one: use messages to transfer both data and objects from one place to another. The implementation is equally simple. All you really need is a mailbox on each disconnected machine and a background task to deliver the mail. In short, MSMQ makes application development for COM+ a lot easier than writing enterprise-level applications from scratch.

Creating a Workstation Setup

To get anywhere with this book you need a development workstation on which you install Windows 2000, write your code, and perform any desktop-level testing. Avoid using your regular workstation for development for two reasons. First, there's no guarantee that an application is going to work the first time and you don't want to crash the machine that contains all your data. Second, you want to create the cleanest possible environment so that you know for sure that any bugs are the result of application errors, not compatibility problems.

The version of Windows 2000 you install depends on personal taste and the number of machines that you plan to use. You definitely want to install one of the server versions of Windows 2000 if you plan to use only one machine as both a development workstation and a server. However, all of the programming examples in this book work better and demonstrate more if you use two machines. (I'll always assume that you have two machines: one with Windows 2000 Professional installed for development purposes and one with Windows 2000 Server installed for the server.) If you're using two machines, you can set up the development workstation using Windows 2000 Professional. You may want to use this operating system rather than the server version so that you can get a better idea of how things will actually look from the user's perspective. The server versions include a lot of features that the user won't see, and these features might taint the results of any tests you perform.

Caution   Developing applications for production purposes on a single-machine setup is going to result in applications that are unreliable and not fully tested. There isn't any way to develop COM+ applications and completely test them without a two-machine setup. In addition, you want to ensure that you have some flexibility in the methods used to connect the two machines. At the very least, you want a private network setup where you can disconnect the development workstation from the server without disturbing other people working on the network. A telephone connection (or a simulation) is also valuable for testing disconnected applications fully. Make absolutely certain you set up a good development environment before you begin your first production application or you'll definitely get unreliable results.

For a development workstation that you're going to use exclusively for development and not for testing purposes, make sure you get a fast processor, a lot of RAM, and even more hard-drive space. My test workstation includes 512MB of RAM, a 450MHz Pentium II processor, and a 9GB hard drive. This setup worked very well for my needs in creating code for this book—you'll obviously need to increase your hard drive space as you add more features and create more complex applications. I initially tested every application on my development machine, then on the server, and finally on a test workstation. The test workstation is a 166MHz Pentium machine with 64MB of RAM and a 4GB hard drive. The test workstation you use should reflect the standard-issue machine for the environment in which the application will perform. In all cases, I'm using Windows 2000 as my operating system. The server version of the product is used where appropriate.

You may not think about the font you use to work on your machine very often, but working with monospaced fonts all day can lead to eyestrain, bugs (as when, for example, you confuse an l and a 1), and other problems. Microsoft's choice of Courier New as its monospaced font hasn't been well received by many users. Fortunately, there are alternatives, some of which are free. Paul Neubauer's Web site at: `http://home.bsu.edu/prn/monofont/` discusses how monospaced fonts are used on a typical Windows system and what replacement fonts are available should you decide you really don't like Courier. This Web site even includes reviews of the various fonts so that you can make a good choice the first time around.

I installed the minimum number of user-level features on my machine. However, you'll need to install MSMQ support if you want to work with the MSMQ samples throughout the book. You must install MSMQ as an independent client in order to test disconnected-mode applications. This means installing the server software with MSMQ support first, then testing the connection between the client and server, and finally installing MSMQ on the development workstation. The MSMQ installation routine will check for the existence of an MSMQ server on your test server prior to installing the MSMQ software on the development workstation. Make sure you install browser support as well, or some examples may fail when you execute them.

Install Visual Basic next. I performed a full install of all features. You must install Visual Studio Service Pack 3 to get Visual Basic to work with Windows 2000. Service Pack 3 (or the most current service pack available as you read this) is available at `http://msdn.microsoft.com/vstudio/sp/vs6sp3/default.asp`.

Make sure your Visual Basic installation includes data access support if you plan to work with any of the database examples in the book. The only database provider support you need is SQL Server — there aren't any other database engines required for using this book. There are some significant problems with using SQL Server 6.5 with Windows 2000, so I've included some procedures for installing it in the "Special SQL Server 6.5 Developer Edition Installation Requirements" section of this chapter. I highly recommend that you use SQL Server 7.0 for all development efforts and that's the version that I'll use throughout this book. Make sure you read the "Advantages of the Windows 2000 Developer's Readiness Kit" sidebar for details on getting a low-cost copy of SQL Server 7.0 Development Edition.

You must install the latest version of the Windows 2000 Platform SDK in order to work with any of the COM+ examples in this book. The reason is simple: Many of the examples in the book won't compile without the Platform SDK because Visual Basic shipped without the required header and library files. The examples in this book require the September 1998 version of the Platform SDK or a later version.

Anything earlier won't include the required Windows 2000 support (the September 1998 version is a little flaky, but it does work). You'll find the current version of the Windows 2000 Platform SDK at `http://msdn.microsoft.com/downloads/sdks/platform/platform.asp`.

Creating a Server Setup

You must have a Windows 2000 Server setup to work with all of the examples in this book. I wrote the examples using the standard server product on a dual-processor 450MHz Pentium processor machine with 512MB of RAM, although you could probably get by with a single 450MHz processor machine with 256MB of RAM installed. I recommend a minimum of 9GB of hard drive space, although more is certainly better considering how much space you'll need for the various programming language additions.

The test server will require access to a number of Windows-specific components if you want the examples in the book to work. The following list summarizes the components that I installed while writing this book:

✦ Internet Information Server (IIS) (complete)

✦ Management and Monitoring Tools (all)

✦ Message Queuing Services

✦ Microsoft Indexing Service

✦ Networking Services (all)

✦ Terminal Services (optional, but good to have)

After your test server is up and running, you'll need some additional programs in order to work with some of the examples in the book. The number of features that you install depends on which examples you want to work with. Obviously, you need a database manager to work with the database examples. The following application list is based on the assumption that you want to work with all of the examples.

✦ Microsoft Front Page Server Extensions

✦ Microsoft Posting Acceptor 2.0

✦ Microsoft Visual Studio Enterprise Edition (Server Components)

✦ Microsoft Visual Studio Analyzer Server (part of Visual Studio)

✦ Remote Machine Debugging (only if you want to debug your server from a remote location)

✦ SQL Server Debugging (part of Visual Studio)

✦ Visual InterDev Server (part of Visual Studio)

✦ Visual SourceSafe Server (part of Visual Studio)

✦ VSEE APE Server (Part of Visual Studio)

Special SQL Server 6.5 Developer Edition Installation Requirements

The first stop for any "first database project" you work on is to install SQL Server. It may seem a bit odd that I would add an installation procedure at the end of the chapter, but there are some problems with using SQL Server version 6.5 (all editions) and some older versions of SQL Server 7.0 with Windows 2000 (the problems with using any version of SQL Server 7.0 are definitely of the minor variety compared to what you'll experience with SQL Server 6.5). The biggest problem is that the Distributed Transaction Coordinator (DTC) in Windows 2000 is incompatible with both versions of SQL Server. (The newer SQL Server 7.0 Developer Edition that ships with the Windows 2000 Developer's Readiness Kit doesn't appear to have this problem, so I recommend installing it.) Unfortunately, the installation programs for both products fail to recognize that the DTC for Windows 2000 is newer than the one provided with SQL Server and will install the old DTC over the new Windows 2000 DTC. The result is that your Windows 2000 installation will be damaged until you fix the problem with the DTC. The damaged DTC affects a lot of different services, including all component services and MSMQ, which you'll recognize as two of this book's primary topics.

Although you might be able to work with the examples in this chapter without applying Service Pack 5a to SQL Server, you should apply it anyway to avoid potential problems. Unfortunately, Service Pack 5a is no longer available from Microsoft's main SQL Server Web site; you need to download it from the Microsoft Support Downloads site at `http://support.microsoft.com/support/downloads/LNP220.asp`. There are two patches: one for the Alpha processor and another for the Intel platform.

A second DTC-related problem affects SQL Server 6.5 Developer Edition. You'll find that the Back Office portion of the Visual Studio 6.0 Enterprise Edition installation fails for no apparent reason. The only message that you get is that the SQL Server and associated debugger installations failed. However, running the installation programs manually shows that the problem is that the DTC can't be stopped automatically by the setup program. Once you reach this point, you can start figuring out why the whole SQL Server installation process is flawed in the extreme. With this in mind, the following procedure will help you get around the problems with the current SQL Server installation.

Caution   Microsoft doesn't sanction this procedure. I've provided it as a means to get around problems with the SQL Server 6.5 Developer Edition installation. This procedure has been tested only on a single server and probably won't work with server clusters. Use this procedure only on a test machine, as you may lose data on a production machine. There are no guarantees provided or implied with this procedure — you assume all liability for using it. This procedure assumes that you have a good understanding of how to remove and install software when working with Windows.

1. Open the Services MMC snap-in found in the Administrative Tools folder of the Control Panel.

2. Right click the Distributed Transaction Coordinator service, and then choose Properties from the context menu. Click the Dependencies tab and you'll see a list of dependent services similar to that shown in the bottom list in Figure 1-2.

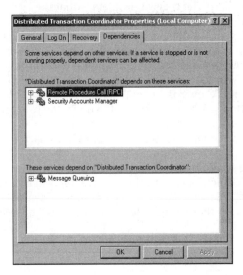

Figure 1-2: You need to determine which services are dependent on the DTC before you stop it.

3. Right-click each service entry listed in the Distributed Transaction Coordinator service dependency list, and then choose Stop from the context menu. This step allows you to manually stop the dependent services so that you can stop the DTC itself. Be sure to record the name of each service that you stop manually because you need to manually restart those services later. In some cases, rebooting Windows 2000 Server won't be enough to restart the service for you; Windows 2000 assumes that you wanted the service to remain stopped for a reason because you stopped it manually.

4. Right-click the Distributed Transaction Coordinator service, and then choose Stop from the context menu. The SQL Server 6.5 installation process will fail unless you manually stop the DTC. This is the problem that caused the installation to fail in the first place.

5. Place Visual Studio 6.0 Enterprise Edition, CD 2 in your CD-ROM drive. Double-click the Setup icon in the \SQL\I386 folder on the Visual Studio 6 CD to manually start the SQL Server 6.5 Developer Edition installation. Follow the installation steps as you normally would. These installation steps don't look like the ones that you'd follow for Visual Studio Back Office installation, but the questions are the same. Make sure that you answer each question just as you would for the standard installation process. When asked for the Product ID number, use the CD Key on the back of your CD holder. Once you have SQL Server installed, you'll want to install the SQL Server Debugger as well — which requires a separate manual installation.

6. Double click the Setup icon in the \SQDBG_SS folder on the Visual Studio 6.0 Enterprise Edition CD to install the SQL Server Debugger. Just follow the installation steps as you normally would. You'll need to provide the CD Key again when asked.

As part of this installation process, you need to install two service packs. The first service pack is part of Visual Studio. You'll find it at `http://msdn.microsoft.com/vstudio/`. The second service pack is SQL Server 6.5-specific. You'll find it at `http://support.microsoft.com/support/downloads/LNP220.asp`. It's very important to install both service packs before you reinstall the DTC. Otherwise, the service-pack updates will damage the DTC again and you'll need to reinstall the DTC.

7. Install Visual Studio Service Pack 3. This is a very important step because not doing it results in your running into Windows 2000-related application development problems. At this point, you need to reboot. After the reboot, the Distributed Transaction Coordinator service no longer appears in the Services MMC snap-in. That's because SQL Server has replaced the Windows 2000 DTC with its own version. Make absolutely certain that SQL Server is working at this point. Open the various utilities and try creating a database. If something doesn't work, repair it now because you won't be able to repair it later.

You can determine the current revision level of your SQL Server installation using the ISQL/w utility (shown as ISQL_w in the Start ⇨ Microsoft SQL Server 6.5 menu). Type **SELECT@@VERSION** on the Query tab, and then click the Execute Query button. The result of the query appears on the Results tab. If the version number is 416 or higher, then you don't need to install SQL Server 6.5 Service Pack 5a.

8. Install SQL Server 6.5 Service Pack 5a, if necessary. A lot of SQL Server bugs are repaired by this service pack, and all application examples in this book assume that you have this service pack in place. Even though the SQL Server 6.5 Service Pack 5a Setup program doesn't ask you to reboot the server, you'll get better results if you do.

9. Use the Start ⇨ Run command to display the Run dialog. Type **DTCSETUP** in the Run field, and then click OK. Running this program should restore Windows 2000 DTC. You'll see a success or failure message box at the end of the installation process. Even though the DTCSETUP program doesn't ask you to reboot the server, you'll get better results if you do.

10. Check the Services MMC snap-in. You should see the Distributed Transaction Coordinator service listed again. If you don't see the Distributed Transaction Coordinator service, perform an upgrade installation of Windows 2000. Performing an upgrade installation may be time-consuming, but doing so ensures that you retain your current operating system settings while restoring any damaged files.

11. Ensure that the Distributed Transaction Coordinator service has started. In most cases, Windows 2000 will automatically start it for you.

12. Open the SQL Service Manager found in Start ⇨ Microsoft SQL Server 6.5. Using the Services drop-down list box, check all three services. All three should be started. If they aren't started, then try starting them manually.

13. Try working with the sample database you created earlier to ensure that SQL Server is actually working. Make sure you test the ability to administrate SQL Server as well by creating phantom users, then deleting them. You may want to try creating a very simple database as part of your test procedure.

14. Restart the services that you manually stopped earlier. It's especially important to restart the Message Queuing service. If Message Queuing won't start, then uninstall Message Queuing and reinstall it. Performing an uninstall followed by a reinstall replaces any missing files. At this point, you should have full SQL Server access and full Windows 2000 Server functionality. Of course, there are always extra steps that you need to take to make this final, and this procedure is no exception. If you stop at this point, you'll find that SQL Server will work but that you won't be able to access it correctly from Visual Basic. You need to do one more thing to complete the setup procedure.

15. Start the ISQL/w utility on the server (you'll find it in the Start ⇨ Microsoft SQL Server 6.5 folder).

16. Use the File ⇨ Open command to display the Open File dialog box.

17. Locate the \MSSQL\INSTALL folder.

18. Open the INSTCAT.SQL script, and then click Execute Query on the toolbar. The script will run for quite some time. The Execute Query button will turn green again after the script finishes. This is your indicator that Visual Basic is now able to access SQL Server normally through the various wizards.

19. Close the ISQL/w utility.

Advantages of the Windows 2000 Developer's Readiness Kit

The Windows 2000 Developer's Readiness Kit is a must-have for all Visual Basic 6.0 developers. You'll find this product at `http://msdn.microsoft.com/vstudio/order`. It's actually a four-CD set that Microsoft has relabeled as the Visual Studio 6.0 Plus Pack. At the time of this writing, the Visual Studio 6.0 Plus Pack was free for the price of shipping and handling (less than $10.00 for U.S. residents in most cases).

CD1 is the Developer's Readiness Kit, which includes some training and white papers, COM+ resources, and the Visual Studio Installer (the new one for Windows 2000).

CD2 contains the Microsoft Data Engine (MSDE) for Visual Studio 6.0. However, the MSDE is the 1.0 version, which means that you should consider it more of a beta than a finished product. This CD also contains a Developer Edition of SQL Server 7.0 that you should use in place of SQL Server 6.5 in new projects.

CD3 contains Microsoft Windows NT4 Service Pack 4, which is kind of a surprise considering that SP5 is already available. Unless you have Windows NT servers to update, this CD won't do you much good. Because we concentrate on Windows 2000 in this book, I won't provide any additional information about this particular CD.

CD4 contains more developer training. However, this training focuses on MSDE and SQL Server 7.0. The main focus of this training appears to be upsizing current SQL Server 6.5 applications to SQL Server 7.0 and using the MSDE.

Summary

COM+ represents a major evolutionary step in Microsoft's plan for component technology. It enables you to perform tasks that you couldn't perform in the past and allows the user greater freedom than ever before in using applications wherever the need arises. In addition, COM+ will represent major cost savings for many companies because it allows its users to use less-expensive communication media and reduces the cost of both development and training. Here are some additional conclusions that you can draw from the contents of this chapter.

✦ COM+ isn't new — it's simply the next step in an existing technology with a very long history. Obviously, this means that you shouldn't think of COM+ as an entirely new product, but that you do need to consider how the new features that COM+ provides will fit within your organization. It's also important to remember that COM+ has many of the quirks of its predecessors. Knowing the history of COM+ means having a better understanding of why some things work the way they do.

✦ The four major areas of COM+ change are connectivity, the user, the user interface, and the programmer. Connectivity is improved because you can now work offline and allow COM+ to take care of server-update features in the background. Users gain new freedom because they can use a single application interface regardless of their location. Using a common user interface means that users don't have to learn new procedures when on the road. Developers gain benefits from using COM+ because it improves application reliability, while reducing development time.

✦ The differences between COM and COM+ can be summed up in three very important words: *transactions*, *messages*, and *services*. Transactions provided by MTS allow COM+ to ensure that data transfers take place only one time, but that they do take place at least one time. Message services provided by MSMQ allow the user to work in disconnected mode, but in a reliable environment. Finally, COM+ provides access to new administrator-oriented services in the form of wizards and MMC snap-ins.

✦ You must provide a two-machine setup to work with COM+ — at least, you must if you really want to get accurate results from machine performance, debugging, and usage testing. A single-machine setup is a thing of the past. It doesn't accurately represent today's computing environment.

✦ There's no doubt that COM+ is a high-powered technology. Get rid of that old 166MHz development machine today and use something with a little computing horsepower to develop your applications. Windows 2000 is a tuned environment, yet it requires far more resources than its predecessors because of all the additional functionality it provides. Unless you want to watch displays draw one line at a time for hours, get a server and workstation that will actually perform well with this new operating system.

✦ SQL Server 6.5 will still work with Windows 2000; it just requires a little additional tender loving care. You'll definitely want to upgrade your DBMS to SQL Server 7.0 for any mission-critical applications. All of the examples in this book rely on SQL Server 7.0 Developer Edition, so you may want to upgrade just to ensure that you can see the examples run as they were meant to. Fortunately, Microsoft has provided a low-cost SQL Server 7.0 Developer Edition update in the form of the Microsoft Visual Studio 6.0 Plus Pack.

✦   ✦   ✦

COM+ Administration Issues

COM+ promises to change completely the way you look at applications. Not only will the applications you create differ from those that you created in the past, but also there will be a lot more automation at your fingertips. In some respects, more automation is good because you can spend more time thinking about how to implement your company's business strategy and less time worrying about the next problem you'll have with a nonbusiness-related coding issue. At the same time, however, more automation means that you're going to have to learn some new methods of doing things. That's what this chapter is all about — I'm going to teach you about the administrative issues that arise when working with COM+. I decided to place some of the more common tasks in this chapter, rather than in the coding section of the book, so that you can find them easily.

On the CD-ROM This chapter uses some pre-made components for demonstration purposes. You'll find these components in the Chapt02\Components folder on the CD-ROM provided with this book. Simply place the components in a convenient place on the server and then work through the example procedures in this chapter. By the time you're finished, you should have a good understanding of what kind of automation COM+ will provide for your application programming needs.

Windows 2000 uses a series of Microsoft Management Console (MMC) snap-ins to allow administrators to perform various kinds of work. MMC itself is a container application, and the various snap-ins are specially designed components. We'll create a snap-in in Chapter 9 so that you can see the inner workings of snap-ins for yourself. For right now, all you really need to know is that the main MMC snap-in for COM+ components is Component Services. This is the snap-in you use to create COM+ applications from standard components. The first section of this chapter looks at the administrative issues you need to know about when installing a component, adding security, and then exporting an application proxy for use on the client.

One feature of COM+ that makes it different from standard COM is the reliability that you can achieve by using transactions. Microsoft Transaction Server (MTS) uses a service known as the DTC. The DTC can track the various transactions that take place on the server for you, as well as log significant transaction events. This means that you need to know how to work with the DTC in order to learn how well your COM+ applications are performing. The second section of this chapter looks at both the type of statistics that the DTC maintains for the server and the purpose of the transaction list.

DCOM still lurks under the surface of COM+. We discussed this issue in Chapter 1. In some cases, you'll want to work with the DCOM configuration of a test machine directly in order to test a component. The third section of the chapter looks at the DCOMCnfg utility. This utility allows you to set the location for remote execution of components, the level of security that these components will use when authenticating users, and the type of impersonation the components can use when requesting services on the user's behalf.

The final section of the chapter looks at services. You'll need to perform a variety of tasks when working directly with the Windows 2000 Services. In many cases, you'll need to perform a special level of configuration or request that the service log in under something other than the default account. You'll also need to know how to perform simple tasks like starting and stopping services, should the need arise.

Working with Component Services

For the COM+ developer, using the Component Service MMC snap-in is an essential part of the development process. This snap-in allows you to install components as part of creating a COM+ application, export a proxy for that application so that the client can access the component, and let the developer or administrator set component security based on the roles users will play in application use. The Component Services snap-in also provides support for the COM+ publish/subscribe event model that we discuss in detail Chapter 6. Finally, given the right application setup, the Component Services snap-in will log significant component events for you; alternately, you can build event logging support directly into the component. In short, this is the one utility that you absolutely must know about in order to make COM+ applications work.

The succeeding sections of this chapter look at four main Component Services areas. For those of you who are new to the MMC snap-in approach to working with administration, we begin by looking at the interface. After you have a basic understanding of the interface, we discuss what you need to do to install COM+ components on the server. This includes everything from creating the COM+ application to exporting a proxy for the client's use. The next section looks at the issue of managing subscriptions. Finally, we discuss the kinds of event logs that you might see as you use COM+.

An overview of the interface

Component Services is found in the Start ➪ Programs ➪ Administrative Tools folder of your server. Starting this MMC snap-in will display a window similar to that shown in Figure 2-1. As with most MMC snap-ins, Component Services uses a hierarchical display similar to that found in Windows Explorer in the left pane and a detailed view of the highlighted item in the right pane. Most of the icons in this view have context menus that you can access with a right click, just as you can with most Windows 2000 applications. The context menus tell you what you can do with that particular icon. In short, there isn't anything too unusual about this interface. If you know how to use Windows Explorer, you also have a good idea of how to use any MMC snap-in.

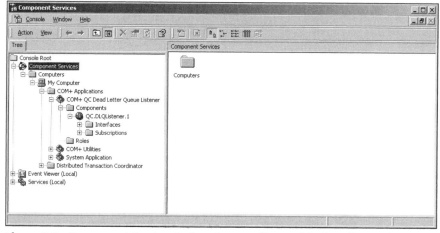

Figure 2-1: Component Services is the primary utility used for installing and managing COM+ components.

Tip   Windows 2000 Professional doesn't install a full set of administrative tools as part of the initial setup. If you want to manage your server from a remote location, find the AdminPak.MSI file in either the \WINNT\System32 folder of the server, or in the main installation directory (\I386 for Intel machines) on the Windows 2000 Server installation CD-ROM. Right-click this file and choose Install from the context menu. Windows 2000 will install a full set of administrative tools for you on your local workstation.

There are three main entries in Figure 2-1. Component Services is where you'll manage the various COM+ applications you create. Event Viewer lets you track any significant COM+ events. In most cases, you use this area to view any errors that the COM+ applications recorded. Finally, Services allows you to work with the various operating system services installed on the target machine.

Both Event Viewer and Services allow you to view a single machine. You can choose the machine to view by right-clicking the appropriate folder and choosing Connect to Another Computer. A Select Computer dialog box similar to the one shown in Figure 2-2 displays. The Browse button allows you to select from any available computer on the network, including servers that you have rights to access. Click OK and Windows 2000 will connect you to the specified computer.

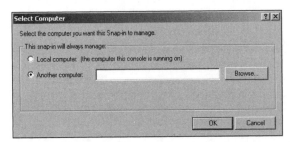

Figure 2-2: The Select Computer dialog box allows you to choose another computer to view.

Component Services lets you view more than one computer at a time. This lets you move COM+ applications from one machine to another in the same way that you'd move files using Windows Explorer. You can add a computer to Component Services by right-clicking the Computers folder and choosing the New ⇨ Computer option from the context menu. An Add Computer dialog box similar to the one shown in Figure 2-3 displays. As with the Select Computer dialog box, you can use the Browse button to find other computers on the network.

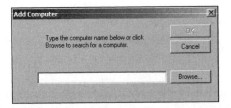

Figure 2-3: The Add Computer dialog box lets you add another computer to Component Services.

Let's take a closer look at Component Services. As Figure 2-1 shows, Component Services contains two folders: COM+ Applications and Distributed Transaction Coordinator. We'll discuss the COM+ Applications folder first. Servers normally have more default applications than workstations do because they have more COM+ roles to fulfill. Figure 2-4 compares the default applications for a workstation

(My Computer) and for a server (WINSERVER). Note that Component Services uses a different icon for a local connection than it does for a remote connection so that you can easily see when you're working with the local machine. In this case, both machines have full COM+ support, along with MSMQ functionality. The server includes additional support for Internet Information Server (IIS) and Visual Studio.

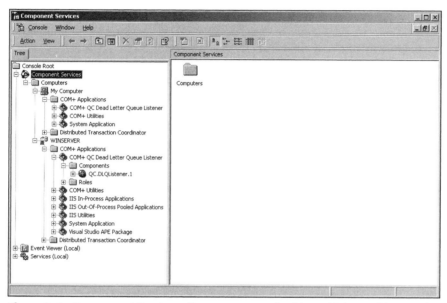

Figure 2-4: Component Services allows you to work with multiple machines at the same time.

Tip   Some books and other documentation refer to COM+ applications as packages. They were originally called packages in MTS, and the term still appears in older documentation. Depending on the document you're looking at, the use of package versus COM+ application can have significant differences because of the way that Microsoft has implemented COM+ in Windows 2000. In short, if you see the term package in the documentation you're using, it's a warning that you may not be getting the COM+ view of this technology but rather an older MTS view for Windows NT4. Not only will you see the term package used in documentation, but you'll also see it used as part of the application name in some cases. For example, the Visual Studio APE Package in Figure 2-4 was originally designed for use with MTS in Windows NT. That this application still works with COM+ shows the effect of backward compatibility. However, that the application name still contains the term package indicates that Visual Studio was originally designed with Windows NT4, not Windows 2000, in mind.

COM+ applications consist of components and roles. A role is a security requirement for a particular component, interface, or method. We'll discuss roles in the "Adding security to a COM+ application" section. For now, let's discuss the construction of COM+ applications from the component perspective.

Components contain one or more interfaces. Each interface contains one or more methods as shown in Figure 2-5. Methods are used to access the functionality that the COM+ application provides. Because servers require more flexibility than workstations do, more components are often found in server applications than in workstation applications. However, each of these components is the same regardless of whether the component is found on a workstation or a server. In short, you won't find one version of a component on a workstation and another version on a server — any extra functionality that the server requires will appear in a separate component.

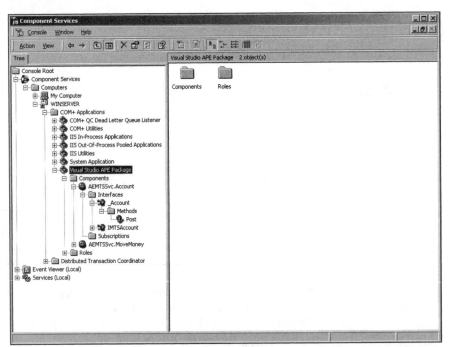

Figure 2-5: Components are made up of interfaces that, in turn, contain methods.

Each application level provides property settings that allow you to modify that level's behavior. For example, you can set role-based security parameters for a COM+ application at the application, component, interface, and method level. This means that you get a very high degree of control over the behavior of an application. Not every level has the same settings because each level performs a different function within the application hierarchy. The folders directly above each application level allow you to organize that level and change the method of presentation. This includes the choices presented by the MMC snap-in, as well as the application itself. In a few cases (where applicable), a New option appears on the context menu for the folder, which allows you to add a new item. You'll see how this works in the "Creating COM+ applications and installing components" section of this chapter.

Creating COM+ applications and installing components

COM+ applications don't appear on your server just because you create all of the required components. Building a COM+ application doesn't require any programming once you create the required components. You do, however, need to use a wizard to create an empty COM+ application. Once the application is in place, you can add components to it by using a different wizard. Each component gets added separately; there isn't any way to add them as a group. Windows 2000 automatically detects component details to make the application complete for you. This section shows you how to perform these two COM+ application-creation steps.

As with any component, you have to register your COM+ components. In the past, you would either allow the integrated development environment (IDE) to do this for you automatically, use RegSvr32 to perform the task manually, or provide the registration feature as part of an installation program or other form of automation. In the world of COM+, you don't use any of these registration methods — Windows 2000 does it for you automatically as part of the process of adding components to a COM+ application. The act of installing a component registers it on a server that it hasn't been registered on before.

Tip
Some Visual Studio products will tell you that you need to register the component on the server using the MTXREREG utility. You'll find that the MTXREREG utility is actually part of the MTS environment provided under Windows NT4. This utility isn't used with Windows 2000 — it isn't even included with the package. The MTXREREG utility was included as part of the Windows NT4 Option Pack, and the instructions in the Visual Studio IDE reflect usage instructions for that older package.

I created a component for demonstration purposes for this chapter. You don't need to create the component or write any code. This example component allows you to see how the two wizards work. Examples later in the book will teach you to create various types of components that you can register using the procedures we discuss here.

We'll use the Component Services MMC snap-in to register and install the OrderAccess component (which includes the COrderModify class). You'll find Component Services in the Administrative Tools folder found in the Control Panel. Figure 2-1 shows what the Component Services MMC snap-in looks like. For those of you who have used MTS Explorer in the past, the snap-in version should look similar except for a few changes in nomenclature.

Tip

Microsoft has provided some tools that you need to know about as part of the Windows 2000 Platform SDK. Some of these tools are installed for you as part of the Windows 2000 Platform SDK installation process. Depending on the options you choose, you'll find a folder containing the tools in your Start⇨Programs menu. Other tools aren't installed automatically. For example, the MTXStop utility is provided in the \Platform SDK\Samples\COM\Tools\MTXStop folder. Make sure you look in the various sample application directories that ship with the Windows 2000 Platform SDK to ensure that you have full access to all of the tools that this product provides. Because MTXStop doesn't ship with Windows 2000, you must install it from the Windows 2000 Platform SDK.

Creating the COM+ application

The first thing we need to do is create a new application for our component. The following procedure shows you how to add a new application to Component Services (this is different from the process that you may have used for other component types).

1. Move the component to a convenient directory on the server. I normally use a central repository for my custom components, but you can use any management scheme that you like, including creating special folders for each project you work with. Now, we need to register the component with the server.

2. Open the Component Service MMC snap-in, if you haven't done so already.

3. Highlight the COM+ Applications entry and select the Action ⇨ New ⇨ Application command from the toolbar. You'll see a Welcome to the COM Application Install Wizard dialog box.

4. Click Next. You'll see an Install or Create a New Application dialog box like the one shown in Figure 2-6. The Install pre-built application(s) option is specifically designed to allow you to install third-party applications. These applications come with an installation file with an MSI extension that contains all of the particulars about the application. We won't talk about pre-built applications for most of the applications in this book. Because we're developing our own application, we need to use the Create an empty application option.

5. Click Create an empty application. You'll see the Create an Empty Application dialog box like the one shown in Figure 2-7. This dialog lets you enter a name for your application. It also asks you to decide between a library and a server application type. Usually, you should choose the Server application option because it allows the components that you create to execute in a separate process. Library applications execute within the creator's process, which means that an errant component can cause the entire application to fail. In addition, library applications don't support load balancing, remote access, or queued components. Library applications do, however, execute faster because there are fewer process boundaries to cross. We discuss the issue of library versus server applications in Chapter 6. Be sure to read about all four types of application that COM+ supports before you begin creating new components that support this technology.

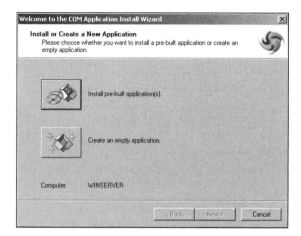

Figure 2-6: The Install or Create a New Application dialog box allows you to choose between pre-built and empty applications.

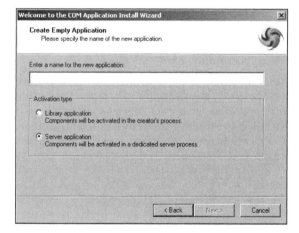

Figure 2-7: You use this dialog box to give your application a name and define the application type.

6. Type a name for the application. The example uses A Test COM+ Application, but you can use any name you like.

7. Choose between the Server application and Library application options. The example application uses the Server application option because it allows more complete testing of the component and better protection during debugging.

8. Click Next. You'll see a Set Application Identity dialog box like the one shown in Figure 2-8. This dialog allows you to choose the identity of the person used to run the component. You'll normally choose the Interactive user option because it allows you to test for role-based security using the identity of the person logged into the server. The second option, This user, allows you to set the component up to run as a specific person. It's handy for those situations when you know another server, rather than a user, will always be the one to call the component. Using this setting is convenient because the component will always allow the same level of access no matter who is logged on to the machine.

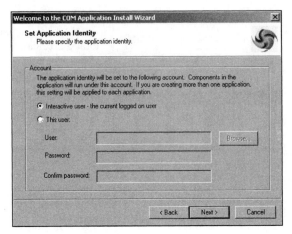

Figure 2-8: The Set Application Identity dialog box is used to determine the identity the application uses while running.

9. Choose the Interactive user option, and then click Next. The example will use the Interactive user option because it provides better application security. This setting will augment the role-based security that we'll talk about later. You'll see a final COM Application Wizard dialog box.

10. Click Finish. The new application will appear in the list of applications in the COM+ Applications folder as shown in Figure 2-9. Notice that Windows 2000 automatically creates a directory structure that you can use for working with the component. We'll use this directory structure in the steps that follow to fully configure the COM+ application for use.

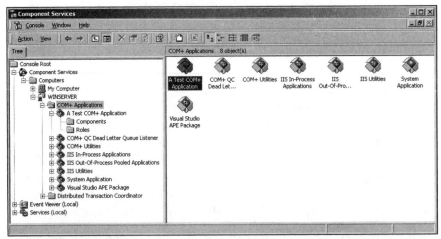

Figure 2-9: Windows 2000 automatically creates the directory structure required to fully configure your COM+ application.

Adding components to a COM+ application

The application that we've just defined acts as a container for our component. In fact, you could place multiple components within this directory structure—the whole idea is to keep the various applications on the server separate, not necessarily to restrict how you add new components to the server. At the moment, we still don't have the example component (found on the CD-ROM provided with this book in the Chapt02 folder as OrderEntry.DLL) installed in Component Services. The following steps will allow you to install the component, even if it isn't registered on the current machine.

1. Open the Order Entry Database application, and you'll see two folders, as shown in Figure 2-9: Components and Roles. (You must highlight the Components folder as shown in Figure 2-10 to add new components to the application.) The Components folder will hold any components that you want to install for the application. The Roles folder allows you to create security roles that you can later assign to the application, an individual component, or a method within the component.

2. Highlight the Components folder, then use the Action ⇨ New ⇨ Component command to display the COM Component Install Wizard dialog box.

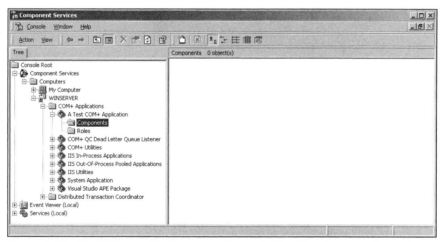

Figure 2-10: All COM+ applications contain two folders like the ones shown here.

Tip

Windows 2000 will keep you informed with status information while using the various COM+ wizards. For example, Figure 2-11 shows that the status information includes the server and application names. By checking this status information as you create applications and install components, you can reduce the chance of errors that may make an application nonfunctional, or change the operational status of an existing application. You can also ensure that you're installing the component on the right machine when you manage more than one machine using a single MMC snap-in setup.

3. Click Next. You'll see the Import or Install a Component dialog box like the one shown in Figure 2-11. The Install new component(s) option allows you to install components that you've placed on the server but haven't yet registered. This is the option that you'll use when your development platform and the server are on two different machines. The Import component(s) that are already registered option allows you to add components that have already been registered on the server. This is the option that you'll choose for updates (when the globally unique identifier or GUID is exactly the same for the new component as it was for the old one) or when the component has been registered for some other reason. For example, you may be using your development machine as the test server. The Install new event class(es) option is used when you want to create event classes for subscription use. This particular component installation requires special programming that we'll discuss in Chapter 6. We'll look at installing a new component first. If you're importing a registered component, then proceed to Step 8.

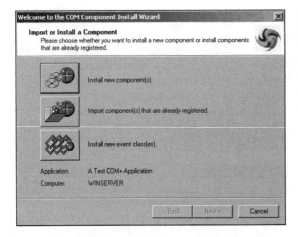

Figure 2-11: The Import or Install a Component dialog box allows you to install new components, import existing components, or create new event classes for subscriptions.

4. Click Install new component(s). You'll see a Select files to install dialog box like the one shown in Figure 2-12. While you can install components that reside on other machines, you'll find that components work more reliably if you place them on a local server hard drive. (You might want to put your custom components in a special place on the server to make them easier to find later.)

Figure 2-12: Windows 2000 will ask for the location of the component that you want to install.

5. Find the component file that you want to install. (The example uses OrderAccess.DLL.) Highlight the file, then click Open to complete the selection process. You'll see an Install new components dialog box similar to the one shown in Figure 2-13. (You may need to check the Details option to get your dialog box to match the one shown in the figure.) Figure 2-13 shows what you should see when working with the example program. The example contains both components and a type library — you need both for COM+ applications. If you create a separate set of component and type library files, then you'll need to add both files to the list to get a complete installation. Clicking Add at this point would allow you to add another file to the list (along with any components that the file contains). Our component is also shown as a COM+ component type, and the wizard has found interfaces within the component (the wizard won't tell you which interfaces have been found at this point — hopefully, it found the ones you wanted to expose). You need to check all of these items as part of the component setup.

Figure 2-13: Make sure you have all of the required parts before you consider the component installation complete.

6. Click Next. You'll see a final COM Component Install Wizard dialog.

7. Click Finish to complete the Install new component(s) installation process. You'll see the new component added to the right pane of the Component Services window as shown in Figure 2-14. This completes the new component installation procedure—don't go on to Step 8.

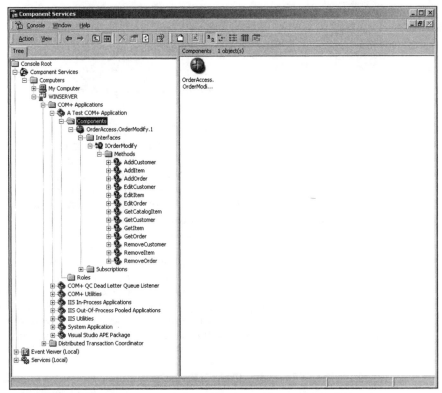

Figure 2-14: The Component Services window will contain the new components you've installed after you complete the COM Component Install Wizard.

8. Click Import component(s) that are already registered. You'll see the Choose Components to Import dialog box shown in Figure 2-15. This dialog contains a list of all of the components that are installed and registered for use on the server. If you don't see your components in this list, then you need to click Back and proceed with Step 4 to install the component and register it (the registration process happens automatically). There's an important feature to note about this dialog box: this list of components comes from the machine that we're working with (the server, in this case), and not necessarily from the local machine.

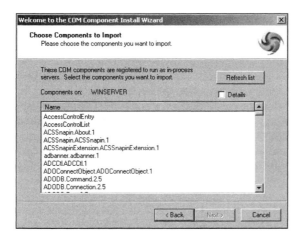

Figure 2-15: The Choose Components to Import dialog box allows you to select a component that is installed on the machine you're working with.

Tip

Clicking the Details check box in the Choose Components to Import dialog box will provide you with additional information about each of the components in the list. The additional information includes the name of the DLL, the DLL path on the machine, and the 128-bit class ID (CLSID) for the component. You can use this information to ensure that the component registered on the machine is the same as the component that you want to use for the COM+ application. There is, however, a performance penalty for using this feature. It takes longer to download a list of components from a remote machine when you request this option, so you should use it only when the identity of a component is in doubt.

9. Locate the OrderAccess.OrderModify.1 component in the list and highlight it (depress the Ctrl key to select a second component).

10. Click Next. You'll see a final COM Component Install Wizard dialog.

11. Click Finish to complete the Install new component(s) installation process. You'll see the new component added to the right pane of the Component Services window as shown in Figure 2-14.

Adding security to a COM+ application

Now we have a COM+ application and an associated component installed within the Component Services snap-in. However, the component isn't yet completely operational because we haven't installed any security for it. Theoretically, we could get by without adding any security, because the application is already protected by the standard Windows 2000 security. However, role-based security is a new feature of COM+ that promises to make life a lot easier for network administrator and developer alike because the security measures used to protect a component, the interfaces it contains, and the methods required to perform the application's work can be refined. Unlike Windows 2000 security, where you have to use a one-size-fits-all approach to security, role-based security allows you to tailor security to the work a user will perform.

To add role-based security to the component, you need to create at least one, preferably two, roles. Let's call the first role Administrator so that someone logged in as
this role can access all of the methods within the OrderAccess component. The
second role can be any other value, but for this example let's use User. Someone
logged in as the User role can access any of the nonconfiguration methods within
the component. In other words, the user can do such things as look up a part in
the catalog, but the user can't modify the contents of the catalog. Obviously, you
don't want to give the user the ability to modify the company's product line. The
following procedure will get you started adding a role to the application.

1. Highlight the Roles folder, and then use the Action ➪ New ➪ Role command to
   display the Role dialog box shown in Figure 2-16.

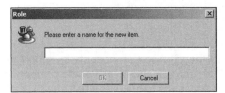

Figure 2-16: The Role dialog box allows
you to give a name to the role you're
designing.

2. Type a name for the role, then click OK. For the example, we'll use
   Administrator for the first role and User for the second.

3. Open the Administrator (or User) folder and highlight the Users folder.
   Use the Action ➪ New ➪ User command to display the Select Users or
   Groups dialog box shown in Figure 2-17. This is where you choose the
   users who can access components using the Administrator role.

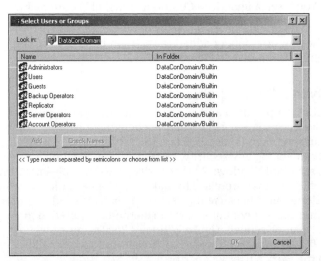

Figure 2-17:
The Select Users or
Groups dialog box
allows you to choose
which users or groups
can perform the task
specified by the role.

4. Highlight the Administrators group entry and click Add. You'll see the Administrators group added to the list of users.

5. Click OK. Administrators are added to the Users folder in the Component Services window.

6. Repeat steps 1 through 5 for the User role. However, in this case, use your own name, a test user name, or the Users group instead of the Administrators group for the Users folder. Figure 2-18 is a typical security setup for this example. Obviously, any production components you create will have a more complex security setup that allows users to access the components you create in specific roles.

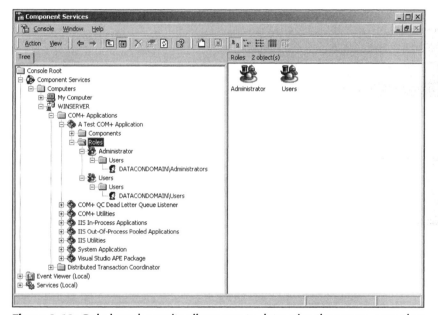

Figure 2-18: Role-based security allows you to determine the access a user has to the methods within a component based on the role that the user performs.

I've chosen not to implement any form of security within the OrderAccess component because that would defeat the purpose of using the highly configurable role-based security option. Had I implemented security within the component, then any change to the company structure might also mean a change to the code within the component. In most cases, you'll no longer want to add security to your component using coding techniques; you'll want to add it using the Component Services snap-in.

With this change in methodology in mind, let's see what you need to do to add security to the OrderAccess component. First, you need to enable role-based security. This means making a change at the application level. Right-click the A Test COM+ Application entry, and then choose Properties from the context menu. You'll see the A Test COM+ Application Properties dialog box. Click the Security tab of this dialog box to see the security options shown in Figure 2-19. This is where you determine what kind of security an application will use.

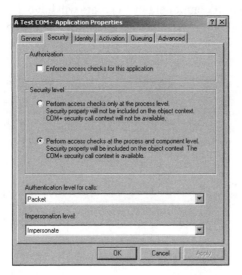

Figure 2-19: You must set security at the application level before you can use role-based security.

Caution   You can't use role-based security with library applications. This feature is designed to work only with server applications. Unfortunately, Windows 2000 won't protect you from adding role-based security to a library application. This means that you could make settings changes that will cause an application to stop working for no apparent reason. In other words, this is one of the settings you should check if a library application malfunctions.

There are actually two settings that you need to look at. First, make sure you check the Enforce access checks for this application option. This will allow you to set security at the component, interface, and method levels. Second, make sure you allow access checks at both the process and component levels. That's the second option in the Security level group shown in Figure 2-19 (the figure shows the Security level properly configured). You also need to select this option if you plan to use role-based security within your components. Otherwise, your components will be limited to whatever security Windows 2000 provides at the application level.

Now that we have role-based security enabled at the application level, right-click the OrderAccess.OrderModify.1 component and choose Properties from the context menu. You'll see an OrderAccess.OrderModify.1 Properties dialog box like the one shown in Figure 2-20.

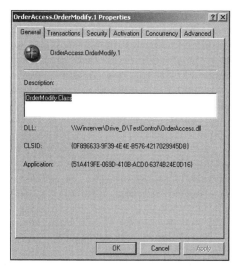

Figure 2-20: The OrderAccess.OrderModify.1 Properties dialog box allows you to configure the application at the component level.

As you can see, the OrderAccess.OrderModify.1 Properties dialog box allows you to configure a relatively wide range of component options, including whether the component supports transactions. There are also options that allow the component to engage in object pooling (normally a good idea with database components) and concurrency. Click the Security tab and you'll see the Security tab of the OrderAccess.OrderModify.1 Properties dialog box; it should look like the one shown in Figure 2-21. Both of the roles we've created are available for use with this component.

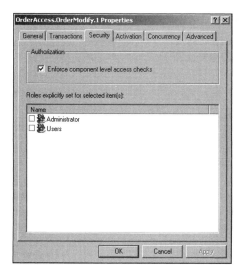

Figure 2-21: Windows 2000 will automatically display any roles that you've created for a COM+ application at all application levels.

Remember that we have role-based security enabled, but as you can see in Figure 2-21, none of the role-based security options are checked. The way that the Security tab of the OrderAccess.OrderModify.1 Properties dialog box is set, no one can access the component right now. What you need to do is check the roles that you want to have access to the component. Let's assume that the administrator will have full access to this component, so check the Administrator entry, and then click OK to make the change permanent.

Now, let's look at the effect of our decision at a lower level of the application. Right-click the IOrderModify interface (located in the Interfaces folder for the application) and then choose Properties from the context menu. Click the Security tab and you'll see an IOrderModify Properties dialog box like the one shown in Figure 2-22. Notice that we still have two options to choose from with regard to role-based security, but that Administrator appears in the Roles inherited by selected item(s) list box. This means that you don't have a choice about the Administrator role—anyone in this role already has access to this interface. You'll find that the same rule holds true for methods. In other words, everyone in the Administrators group can access everything that this component has to offer. On the other hand, the Users role still hasn't been defined.

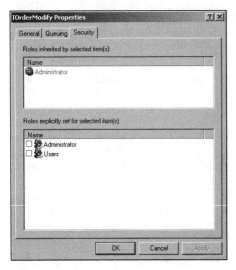

Figure 2-22: Security at the interface and method levels of an application is affected by decisions you make at the component level.

Normally, you'd have a decision to make at this point. You could give the Users role access to the component at the interface level or select individual methods within the interface. However, because our test component only has one interface, you have to set security for the Users role at the component level.

Obviously, this brings a new design issue into the picture when you're working with components designed for use with COM+. No one says that you have to provide specific custom interfaces for your components or lists the methods that the interface has to provide. However, given the method that Windows 2000 uses for assigning roles, it's now a good idea to create custom interfaces based on two criteria (as a minimum): security and function. An interface should always reflect the function that you've designed it for. In this case, we're looking at an interface that's designed to interact with a database manager. However, if I'd wanted to make this component easier for the network administrator to configure, I would have further divided the methods into administrative and user roles. This would have made the job of assigning security easier and less prone to error on the part of the administrator. Of course, just how far you divide an interface based on security requirements depends on the complexity of your application.

Exporting COM+ applications

You're going to find that working with COM+ means thinking about the interaction between the client and server at a functional level. When you work with a desktop application, you can assume that the client and server are easy to locate and running. A COM+ application can't make these assumptions. You must assume that the server is unavailable (especially when working with disconnected applications) and that the server isn't running at the same time as the client. In addition, because the server isn't running on the same machine as the client, your application will require the services of DCOM to make a connection. For all of these reasons (and more that we discuss in the theoretical sections of this book), you need to create a proxy on the test machine that the application can send messages to. This proxy will take the place of the component on the server from the local machine's perspective. Creating a proxy is relatively easy; the following steps show you how.

1. Open Component Services on the server. Locate the A Test COM+ Application application in the COM+ Applications folder.

2. Right-click A Test COM+ Application, and then choose Export from the context menu. You'll see a Welcome to the COM Application Export Wizard dialog box.

3. Click Next. You'll see an Application Export Information dialog box like the one shown in Figure 2-23. This is where you'll choose the name and type of export application created. We need a proxy application in this case, so that the installation routine will direct the A Test COM+ Application requests to the server, not to the local machine.

4. Click Browse. You'll see an Export application to File dialog box like the one shown in Figure 2-24. As you can see, I've chosen a location and name for the exported application file. (The example uses the name A Test COM+ Application Install, but you can use any name that you want.) The COM Application Export Wizard automatically adds an MSI extension to the new application name.

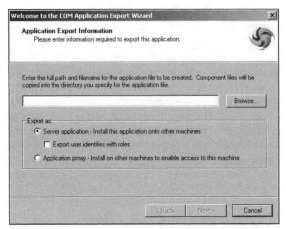

Figure 2-23: Windows 2000 allows you to export your COM+ applications in several different formats, including as a proxy application.

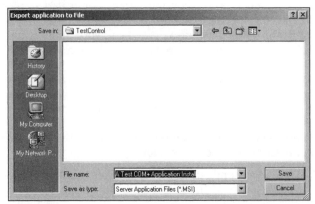

Figure 2-24: You need to choose a name for the application and a place to install it.

5. Click Save. The location is entered in the Application Export Information dialog box.

6. Choose the Application Proxy option.

7. Click Next. A final COM Application Export Wizard dialog box displays.

8. Click Finish. At this point, the application you need is created; all you need to do now is install it.

9. Locate the A Test COM+ Application Install.MSI file from the client machine. In most cases, you'll need to install the proxy application on every machine that will work as a disconnected application. You can use a client-side component as a substitute for a proxy application when working with desktop applications, but the client-side component requires additional development time. Of course, using a custom component instead of the automatically generated proxy application does give you a lot of added flexibility. We discuss this issue in more detail in Chapter 6.

10. Right-click A Test COM+ Application Install, and then choose Install from the context menu. An installation dialog will appear for a few moments, then go away. At this point, you have access to the server-side component through the proxy application. You could create a standard Visual Basic application and use it without ever seeing the DCOM connection between the client and server.

If you open Component Services on the client machine at this point, you'll see that there's a new application named A Test COM+ Application. However, this application isn't the full-fledged application found on the server — it's an application proxy. Open the A Test COM+ Application Properties dialog box and you'll see that you can't change any of the application options. This application is designed to precisely replicate the server application.

Tip Because of the method used to export proxy applications, you usually want to perform a local test of the application and server-side component on a local machine first, if possible. The reason is simple: debugging a local application can be difficult; debugging the same application from a remote location can be impossible. Adding a proxy application, remote communication and security, and all of the other things that COM+ brings into the picture greatly increases the complexity of the debugging process. Always debug your application first, and then export the proxy application and test it from a remote location.

Dealing with events

Clients can interact with servers in two essential ways. First, the client can provide some input data, and then ask the server to massage that data in some way. Second, the client can ask the server to notify it when something happens. The second form of interaction is known as an event. Events are an important part of COM in many ways. For example, stock applications won't work without events. System-monitoring agents won't work without events either. In fact, you can look at events as the action in components — they aren't planned, they just happen at random intervals in response to their environment.

Cross-Reference This section provides a very bare overview of COM events. I discuss COM events in detail in Chapter 6. You should leave this section with an idea of what COM+ brings to the event party.

Originally, COM provided only a single event model. The request/reply model relies on a direct, real-time connection between client and server. The client must know server specifics like the location of the server and what interfaces it supports. When the client wants to be notified about events that the server supports, it makes a request to the server in the form of an interface call. One argument provided to the server as part of the request is a pointer to an interface in the client that the server can use as a callback. The reply part of the picture comes when the server generates an event. Firing the event actually sends a message to the client using an interface method that the client implements.

Naturally, the request/reply event model works fine for desktop applications where there's always a connection between client and server. The model doesn't work at all with remote applications, like those required by users on the road. In fact, this model can even break down on the desktop because a user won't leave his or her machine running 24 hours a day to capture events. In short, this event model works only where the client and server are directly connected and have the same lifetimes. The request/reply event model provides limited, but very important functionality in today's application. However, while we can't get rid of this model because of its importance to applications, we also can't rely on it exclusively for modern enterprise applications.

COM+ provides an entirely new event model — one that's better suited for today's applications. The publish/subscribe model uses several features found only in COM+ like Queued Components (a true superset of MSMQ). When working with the publish/subscribe model, a server will publish a set of interfaces and methods that generate events. These events fire at given times whether anyone is listening or not. All the server cares about is generating events and the information that pertains to those events. The client, on the other hand, subscribes only to the events that it wants to track. It doesn't have to subscribe to all of the events that the server publishes and doesn't particular care if the server is even present. The client will simply listen until a server generates an event. Using this model means that the server and client don't really need to know anything about each other. They don't have to exist within the same timeframe and don't require a direct connection if the event data is stored as MSMQ messages for the client.

This is a very brief overview of what the COM+ publish/subscribe model is all about. Of course, now you need to know how this model is implemented. As you recall from the "Adding components to a COM+ application" section of this chapter, you can add components to a COM+ application that implement event classes rather than act as a service-type component. We'll look at an example of adding an event class later in this book. For now, all you need to know is that the process of adding an event class is about the same as the process of adding a standard component. It's the internal structure of the component that differs. In addition, you'll find that event classes contain additional entries on the Advanced tab as shown in Figure 2-25. These two additional options affect how the component fires events and whether Windows 2000 allows in-process subscribers.

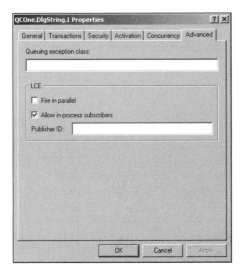

Figure 2-25: Event classes provide additional options that determine how events are fired.

Understanding the event logs

Event logs have been around for quite some time, so they represent one of the better-known methods of providing application information to the administrator in a way that the administrator is already familiar with. There are actually three different event logs (Application, Security, and System) in Windows 2000, and you can create more if needed. These logs are found in the Event Viewer folder of Component Services as shown in Figure 2-26. (There's also a separate Event Viewer MMC snap-in.)

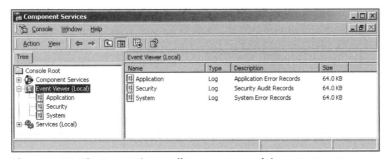

Figure 2-26: The Event Viewer allows you to track important system events.

Normally, a COM+ application uses an Application event log entry. Because this is where the administrator is most likely to look, you'll want to use the Application event log as well if you add event log support to your COM+ application. Each of these log entries provides a quick view of the event, including the event code and source. You can double-click the event entry to see detailed information as shown in Figure 2-27.

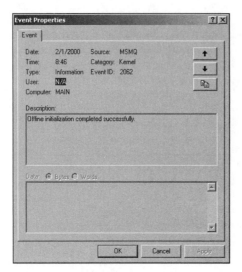

Figure 2-27: Each event log entry provides detailed information about the event that caused its creation.

Tip

There are three buttons shown on the right side of the Event Properties dialog box in Figure 2-27. The first two buttons allow you to move to the previous or next event entry in the log. The third button allows you to copy the contents of the dialog box to the clipboard. You can use this third option to copy the data and send it to another component developer or for logging problems that others have experienced with a component that you developed.

If a COM+ application wanted to provide some additional information to the administrator, it would use the Description field. The Data field (not used for the event shown here) will contain the data associated with the event. For example, the COM+ application could place the data that caused the error here, giving the administrator more clues as to why a transaction or message delivery failed. Obviously, there aren't any limitations as to the content of either the Description or Data fields. The Data field can contain more than text; a COM+ application can include any binary data that might be useful for the network administrator or the developer of the component.

Events are also registered by type. There are five different event types, three of which you can use for components and applications. (The Success Audit and Failure Audit event types are for security use only.) Table 2-1 describes the three event types we discuss in this section.

The event logs are physically stored in the \WINNT\system32\config folder of your hard drive in files with an EVT extension. Because more than one application can write to the event file at the same time, you never want to write to these files directly. What you'll use instead is a series of API functions specifically designed to work with the event logs.

Table 2-1 Standard Event Log Entry Types	
Event Type	**Description**
Information	This is an event that your application can generate to tell the administrator about an application occurrence that didn't result in an error. For example, you could register an event when the component loads or unloads. If the component loads once or twice a day, the administrator might be interested to learn when it does load so that the administrator can anticipate server loads. On the other hand, this isn't the kind of event that you'd want to generate if your component loads every few seconds.
Warning	A Warning event indicates that some type of minor problem has occurred, but nothing that would prevent the application from successfully completing its task. For example, you might include a Warning event if your application detects a low resource condition. The administrator would then be alerted to the fact that the server needs some type of optimization or that the hard drive needs to be cleared.
Error	This is the event that we're most concerned with in this chapter. An error event occurs when the application has encountered a condition that prevents it from successfully completing its current task (if not fully, at least partially). You'll want to use this event as an alternative to displaying dialog boxes on screen.

Working with the Distributed Transaction Coordinator

The DTC is the part of MTS that performs monitoring and directing of component transactions. The direction part of the picture comes into play when a client application initially creates a message that's enveloped within a transaction. Either all of the transaction or none of it is recorded.

However, before an application can even create a transaction for a particular component, the component has to provide the necessarily programming constructs to work with transactions. The network administrator also has to configure the component to work with transactions. Windows 2000 doesn't assume that any component will require transactions, even if the component contains the interfaces required to do so. To set a component up to use transactions, right-click the component icon within the COM+ application and choose Properties from the context menu. Click the Transactions tab and you'll see a display similar to that shown in Figure 2-28.

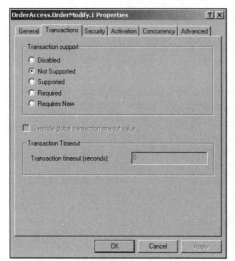

Figure 2-28: The transaction options appear on the Transactions tab of the component's Properties dialog box.

The example component that we used earlier in the chapter is designed to work with transactions. If it hadn't provided the proper interfaces, then one or more of the transaction options in Figure 2-28 would have been disabled. Selecting the Required or Required New options will force the component to use transactions all of the time. If you choose the Supported option, then the client application can request a transaction, but Windows doesn't force the application to do so. If you select either the Required or Required New options, then you can also change the timeout value. This value determines how long MTS will wait before declaring the transaction invalid and rolling back any changes made during the transaction. Normally, you won't have to change this value for desktop applications, but you may find that you need to provide a longer time for remote and disconnected application types.

The monitoring part of the DTC comes in two forms. First, the DTC maintains statistics of the transactions that occur on the local server. You can use this information to determine whether your server is working at full efficiency — at least when it comes to performing transaction-based data transfers. Second, the DTC maintains a list of pending transactions. Depending on the speed of your server, the amount of work that each component has to perform, and a myriad of other factors, you may never see an entry in this list. MTS does slow application performance slightly, but the amount of time spent processing the transaction is so small that many users won't notice the difference on a server with a light to medium load.

Working with the Transaction List

The Transaction List tells you about transactions that are currently awaiting resolution or some other form of processing. Figure 2-29 shows a typical list view. Usually, you won't see any entries in this list unless you server is heavily loaded, there are a lot of remote users with slow connections, or the component in question has a lot of work to do in order to complete the transaction.

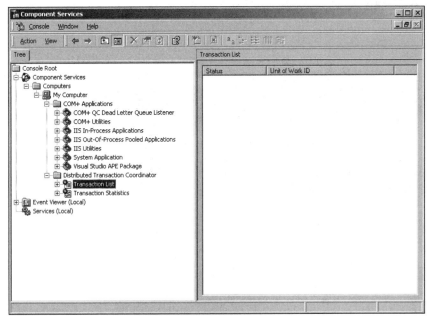

Figure 2-29: The Transaction List should be blank in most cases.

If you do see transactions within the Transaction List, you can right-click the entry and choose Properties from the context menu to see more information about the transaction. You can sort the transactions by their status or by Unit of Work ID (the application instance that the transaction is associated with). We discuss the DTC status indicators in more detail in the "Understanding the Transaction Statistics" section that follows.

You can also manage transactions using the Transaction List. A network administrator can tell MTS to abort, commit, or forget about a transaction. The abort option is handy when a transaction can't complete and the normal method for ending it isn't available for some reason. (A transaction can be affected by outside conditions such as poison messages—a condition that we discuss in Chapter 12 when we create a disconnected application.) The commit option should be used with care because for all intents and purposes you're forcing a commit. The only time this option is handy is when you're developing a component and the component code doesn't vote on the outcome of the transaction. If you know that the transaction is complete and the data is safe, committing the transaction shouldn't cause any harm. Using either the abort or commit option releases locks and makes resources used by the transaction available for reuse.

There are some situations when aborting or committing the transaction won't completely clear it from the DTC. Forgetting the transaction is the same as deleting the transaction without resolving it in any way. As far as the DTC is concerned, the transaction stops. If the transaction is incomplete, the changes that the components make won't be rolled back. If the transaction is complete, but not committed, forgetting it won't allow the transaction to ever commit. What this means is that the transaction's resources and locks will remain in use if you use the forget option by itself. You must either commit or abort the transaction before you tell the DTC to forget it.

Caution   Use the Transaction List management options with the utmost care. If you use these options with a viable transaction, then the transaction will be disrupted and there's no way to determine whether it would have completed normally. In addition, an application is almost guaranteed to suffer some level of data loss when you use these options because the transaction is still in an uncertain state. The only time it's safe to commit manually or abort a transaction is when the transaction status is listed as Cannot Notify Commit or Cannot Notify Abort. These entries mean that the transaction completed successfully, but that the various entities involved with the transaction couldn't be notified of its status. In short, this should be your last-ditch option to resolve transaction problems on the server.

Understanding the transaction statistics

The DTC will also maintain transaction statistics. These statistics can tell you a lot about your system. Naturally, you'll want to know how your server is performing; the transaction statistics give you some idea of how much of a load the server is handling and how fast it is processing that load. However, the transaction statistics are also useful for troubleshooting. For example, a high number of aborted transactions may indicate that machines are disconnecting before the transaction is complete, that users are providing inaccurate input, that there's some sort of network or hardware failure, or that there are some old components on the network. You'll need to confirm your suspicions by checking other performance monitors using System Monitor.

You'll find the statistics in the Transaction Statistics folder shown in Figure 2-30. As you can see, this window provides some straightforward statistics about the current state of transactions on the server. (The statistics on an operational server look different from the ones on the text server shown in Figure 2-30.) The status fields shown in Figure 2-30 are the same as the ones used for the Transaction List, making it easy to coordinate the contents of both folders. Table 2-2 contains a complete list of the status indicators and what they mean.

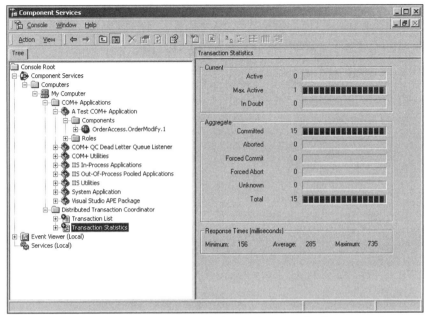

Figure 2-30: Transaction Statistics can help you keep track of server performance, as well as indicate potential setup problems.

Table 2-2
Common DTC Transaction States

State	Statistic Group	Description
Aborted	Aggregate	The number of aborted transactions. When a transaction aborts, the DTC notifies all participants that it has failed (unless the participant is no longer accessible). Windows 2000 will initiate whatever process is required to roll any completed parts of the transaction back. The transaction is removed from the DTC's list, and it's impossible to change the outcome of the transaction.
Active	Current	The number of transactions that have started but aren't resolved. You should never attempt to change the status of an active transaction.

Continued

	Table 2-2 (continued)	
State	**Statistic Group**	**Description**
Average	Response Time	The average amount of time that it takes the server to process a transaction. This number is affected by the server's processing power, the kind of connection the client is using, the amount of work that the component has to perform, and the number of servers involved in the transaction (along with external factors).
Cannot Notify Abort	N/A	The transaction is aborted, but not all of the participants can be notified. This state normally indicates that there's an IBM LU 6.2 transaction manager enlisted in the transaction that the DTC can't contact. You can manually abort the transaction, then tell the DTC to forget about it.
Cannot Notify Commit	N/A	The transaction is committed, but not all of the participants can be notified. This state normally indicates that there's an IBM LU 6.2 transaction manager enlisted in the transaction that the DTC can't contact. You can manually commit the transaction, then tell the DTC to forget about it.
Committed	Aggregate	The number of committed transactions. When a transaction commits, the DTC notifies all participants that it has completed (unless the participant is no longer accessible). The transaction is removed from the DTC's list and it's impossible to change the outcome of the transaction.
Forced Abort	Aggregate	The number of forced aborts. The administrator forced a transaction that was in doubt to abort. (See the In Doubt entry for details about transactions that are in doubt.) The transaction is removed from the DTC's list and it's impossible to change the outcome of the transaction.
Forced Commit	Aggregate	The number of forced commits. The administrator forced a transaction that was in doubt to commit. (See the In Doubt entry for details about transactions that are in doubt.) The transaction is removed from the DTC's list, and it's impossible to change the outcome of the transaction.

State	Statistic Group	Description
In Doubt	Current	The number of transactions where the status is currently unknown due to a lack of connectivity. The transaction has started, but the outcome of the transaction is unknown because the current machine has lost contact with the remote transaction manager that's acting as the commit coordinator. The transaction manager can be the DTC or another type of transaction manager like the one provided with SQL Server. You can manually abort or commit the transaction, then tell the DTC to forget about it. Forcing an abort or commit will update either the Forced Abort or Forced Commit statistic. The local DTC will continue to try to reestablish communication with the remote transaction coordinator as long as you allow it to do so or communication is reestablished.
Max Active	Current	The greatest number of transactions that were active at any given time.
Maximum	Response Time	The maximum amount of time that it takes the server to process a transaction.
Minimum	Response Time	The minimum amount of time that it takes the server to process a transaction.
Prepared	N/A	All of the participants in a transaction have notified the DTC that the transaction is prepared. The transaction is added to the DTC's list, and it's impossible to change the outcome of the transaction at this point.
Preparing	N/A	A client has requested a transaction commit. The DTC has asked all of the resource managers involved with the transaction to prepare for the transaction. It's impossible to change the outcome of the transaction at this point.
Total	Aggregate	The total number of transactions that the DTC has processed. These transactions are no longer in an active state.

Continued

Table 2-2 *(continued)*		
State	*Statistic Group*	*Description*
Unknown	Aggregate	The number of transactions whose status is unknown. The status information for one or more resource managers was lost and the transaction can't be counted as either committed or aborted. This is obviously a serious error condition that you'll want to investigate further.

Using the DCOM Configuration Tool

The DCOM Configuration Tool is a powerful utility that allows you to work with the components registered on a client machine. You can set the component to execute remotely or locally. In addition, this utility allows you to modify the security setup for the component.

This utility also allows you to modify the general DCOM operation on a client machine. For example, even though UDP/IP is the normal protocol used to create a connection between the client and the server, you can set it to any of the protocols that both client and server support. This means that you could create a secure connection between client and server by using an encrypted protocol instead of a plain text protocol like UDP/IP.

This section begins by showing you how the DCOM Configuration Tool works and how you can use it to redirect execution of the component from the local machine to a server. For our example, we'll change the point of execution for the OrderAccess component that we installed earlier. However, the methods we'll use work with any component. We'll also look at some essentials like security and the use of protocols. Getting the right setup is important if you want your DCOM application to work as anticipated.

Setting up the general DCOM environment

Microsoft assumes certain defaults when setting DCOM up on your machine during the Windows installation process. Normally, these defaults work just fine, but you may find that you either need to change the features supported by the DCOM or the protocols used to communicate between client and server.

The first thing you need to do before you can reconfigure anything is start the DCOM Configuration Tool. Use the Run command on the Start menu to display the Run dialog, type **DCOMCnfg** in the Open field, and then click OK. You'll see the initial Distributed COM Configuration Properties dialog shown in Figure 2-31. The Applications tab of this dialog displays all of the out-of-process servers that are installed on the client machine. The out-of-process server must be registered on the client, even if you intend to run it from a remote server. This dialog will only reflect the out-of-process servers that are actually registered locally.

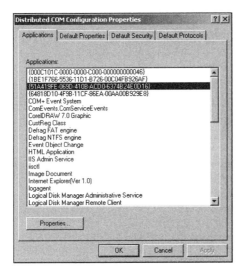

Figure 2-31: The Applications tab of the Distributed COM Configuration Properties dialog shows a list of locally registered out-of-process servers.

Tip The Active Directory support provided by Windows 2000 will obviate the need to register a component locally to use it on a remote server. The client workstation will download global Registry entries from the domain server during login. These entries could include remote component Registry settings that allow a client to access the component on a remote server. The advantage to this method is that the administrator needs to make only a single entry on the domain server for DCOM components.

The Default Properties tab shown in Figure 2-32 allows you to change the general characteristics of DCOM on your machine. By default, Microsoft enables DCOM support on a client. This primary level of support allows you to create trusted connections with servers on a local network. A second check box, Enable COM Internet Services on this computer, lets you enable COM communications over the Internet.

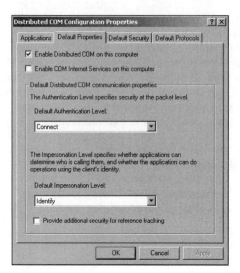

Figure 2-32: The Default Properties tab includes settings for the kinds of communication that can take place and the authentication level used when they do.

The Default Authentication Level list box controls how communication security is handled between the client and server. The default setting is Connect, which means that security is handled only once per connection. We'll talk more about how authentication level is used in the "Setting the Authentication Level" section.

The Default Impersonation Level list box controls what the server can do on the user's behalf when it comes to identification. For example, this setting affects what will happen if the server has to create another component to satisfy a user request. How is that component created? Is the component created in such a way that it looks like the user has created it directly? The matter of impersonation level affects what kinds of things the server can do for the client and how it does them. The default setting for this field is Impersonate. The following list defines the various levels of impersonation that DCOM supports.

✦ **Anonymous:** This is the least secure impersonation level. The server performs processing tasks for the client without knowing the identity of the client application. Unfortunately, this setting limits the server to performing tasks that an anonymous user could perform, which means that many resources will be out of reach.

✦ **Delegate:** The most secure impersonation level. The server is allowed to perform all tasks as if it were the client. This includes requesting services and resources on other servers. Windows 2000 Server authentication service doesn't support this level of impersonation.

✦ **Identity:** Allows the server to identify the client application. What this means is that the client will gain full access to the resources and services available on the server as long as it makes the call directly. The server isn't allowed to impersonate the client, even for local service and resource requests.

✦ **Impersonate:** This is the highest degree of impersonation level that the Windows 2000 Server authentication service supports natively. It allows the server to impersonate the client locally, which means that any services or resources that the server has to request to satisfy a client request will be done in the client's name. The Impersonation level only allows client impersonation on the local server; a server can impersonate the client on other servers.

The Provide additional security for reference tracking check box allows the server to track connected client application requests. This option uses additional server resources, both memory and processor cycles. However, it does enhance server security because a client can't artificially set a server process' reference count to 0, which could kill the process prematurely. The effect of killing a process prematurely is that other clients are likely to crash when they attempt to free reference pointers to objects that no longer exist.

The last set of general settings for DCOM appears on the Default Protocols tab of the Distributed COM Configuration Properties dialog box shown in Figure 2-33. This tab shows the various protocols that DCOM will attempt to use in creating a connection between a client and server. In addition, the protocols are tried in the order in which they appear in the list. Figure 2-33 shows the default list of protocols that DCOM will attempt to use and the default order in which it will try them. Notice that Connection-oriented TCP/IP is at the top of the list because this is normally the first choice for DCOM communications, at least on a LAN.

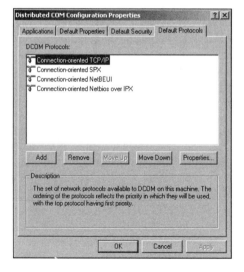

Figure 2-33: The Default Protocols tab allows you to configure the protocols that DCOM will attempt to use to create a connection.

There are various controls on the Default Protocols tab that allow you to modify the protocols that DCOM will use. Clicking Add displays the Select DCOM protocol and endpoint dialog box shown in Figure 2-34. This dialog contains a list of all the potential protocols and endpoints that DCOM will support, not necessarily the ones installed on the client machine. In other words, you have to use some care in choosing a new protocol and endpoint. While nothing terrible will happen if you choose a protocol and endpoint that the client can't support, DCOM will waste time trying to make it work, which will only delay the process of creating a connection.

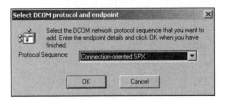

Figure 2-34: The Select DCOM protocol and endpoint dialog box allows you to add a new protocol and endpoint to DCOM's support list.

Some protocol/endpoint combinations also allow you to make some configuration choices. For example, highlighting the Connection-oriented TCP/IP option and then clicking Properties displays a Properties for COM Internet Services dialog like the one shown in Figure 2-35. This dialog allows you to choose port ranges for various types of TCP/IP communication. You can choose one set of port ranges for intranet use only and another set of ranges for Internet use only. Security is the main reason to use this configuration dialog — you need to set specific port ranges when using packet filtering with most firewall products. The firewall product will block access on all but a few ports, making your network more secure by closing open ports that a cracker could use. In other words, you need to synchronize the efforts of DCOM and the firewall software.

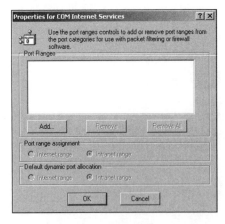

Figure 2-35: Some protocol/ endpoint combinations allow for further configuration using dialogs like this one.

The order in which protocols are tried could make a big difference in some environments. For example, you may not want to use a connectionless protocol if there's a connection-oriented alternative available. To change the order in which a protocol is tried, highlight the protocol, and then click Move Up or Move Down as needed to change its order in the list. DCOM will attempt to use the protocols in turn, starting from the top of the list and going toward the bottom.

Redirecting a component

The whole purpose of using the DCOM Configuration Tool, at least from a programming perspective, is to allow an application on the client machine to access components that you've placed on a server. Distributed processing, coupled with multithreading programming techniques, allows two machines to work in tandem on a single problem. In sum, using DCOM should result in higher system throughput, efficiency, and security, while reducing overall network bandwidth.

This section shows you how to redirect execution of the OrderAccess component that we installed previously on the client machine (most likely your development machine) to a development server. Some of the particulars of my setup will vary from your setup. For example, your development server will have a different name. However, except for the names, this procedure will allow you to redirect the execution of any component from the local machine to a server. The following steps help you redirect the OrderAccess component in particular and most components in general.

1. Start the DCOM Configuration Tool, if you haven't already done so.

2. Highlight the component that you want to redirect on the Applications tab of the Distributed COM Configuration Properties dialog. For the purposes of this example, we'll use the COM+ application that holds the OrderAccess component. The name of this application won't appear in DCOMCnfg because it was added for us automatically. You need to find the application GUID using Component Services. The GUID appears on the General tab of the A Test COM+ Application Properties dialog box shown in Figure 2-36. The GUID used on my test machine was {51A419FE-069D-410B-ACD0-6374B24E0D16}, although it could be different on your machine. (If you don't see the required GUID in the list, make sure that you've registered the component on the test machine.)

3. Click Properties. You'll see a *<Component Name/GUID>* Properties dialog like the one shown for the OrderAccess component in Figure 2-37. The General tab shown in the figure contains an Authentication Level list box. We'll look at this list box later in the "Setting the authentication level" section.

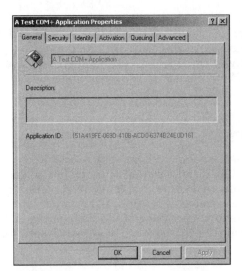

Figure 2-36: You may need to look up a component GUID instead of using the component name in some cases.

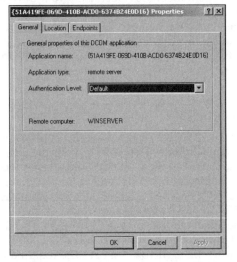

Figure 2-37: The initial {51A419FE-069D-410B-ACD0-6374B24E0D16} Properties dialog shows general component information, including authentication level.

4. Choose the Location tab. You'll see a display similar to the one shown in Figure 2-38. This is where you choose where the component will run. The default setting runs the component on the local machine. However, the COM+ proxy application installation program will always set the application to run on the server where the proxy application was created. There's also an option to run the component wherever the client's data is located. You'll find this option handy for database applications where a single client may need to access the same type of data on several different servers. Using the options

on the Location tab, you could set the proxy application to redirect requests to any server, or even to the local machine if so desired. You can use the Browse button to find the server on the network. At this point, you could click OK to make the changes permanent. However, in many cases, you'll need to configure additional settings to actually gain access to the server.

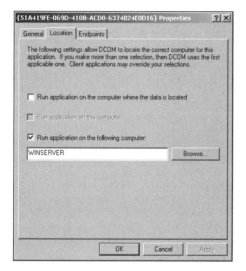

Figure 2-38: The Location tab allows you to choose one or more places to execute the component.

If you choose more than one location to execute a component, DCOM will look for the first viable execution option and execute the component there. The normal search order is to look at the local machine, then a server that you've specified, and finally the location where the client's data is located. If you don't want the client to attempt to execute the component locally, make sure you uncheck this option.

Many components also provide an Identity tab. This is where you define the identity of the user that will execute the component on the server. Using the default option, the launching user works just fine in most cases (this is the identity you used to log on to the server, which is normally the same as your name and password for the rest of the network). The interactive user option uses the name and password of the person that logged on to the workstation and started the client application. This user option allows you to enter the name and password of a user that has the correct level of access to the server for executing the component. Finally, if you want to remotely execute a service, you can choose to use the built-in system account for the server in question.

5. Choose the Endpoints tab. You'll see a dialog similar to the one shown in Figure 2-39. Usually, DCOM simply uses the protocols that were defined on the Default Protocols tab of the Distributed COM Configuration Properties dialog. You can, however, choose to add additional protocols/endpoints, add a specific endpoint, or even disable a protocol/endpoint.

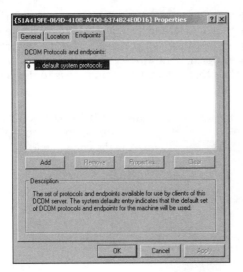

Figure 2-39: The Endpoints tab allows you to change the protocol/endpoint that DCOM uses to create a connection for your component.

6. Click Add and you'll see a Select DCOM protocol and endpoint dialog like that shown in Figure 2-40. The same list of protocols is displayed here that you saw on the Default Protocols tab. Here, however, there are several additional options for configuring those protocols/endpoints. The Disable protocol sequence option allows you to disallow a protocol/endpoint, even if DCOM would normally use it to create a connection. You can also use a static endpoint or the range of port addresses defined for Internet or intranet use. Finally, you can choose the Use default endpoints option, which allows DCOM to use the normal endpoints for the specified protocol. Selecting this last option allows you to change the order in which DCOM chooses protocols for making a connection. DCOM always uses the protocols/endpoints that you define for the component first, and then moves on to the general DCOM choices.

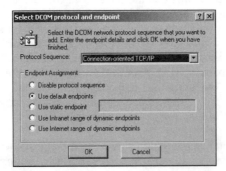

Figure 2-40: You don't have to use the default DCOM protocol/endpoint selections; this dialog allows you to choose custom settings.

7. Choose a Protocol Sequence option, and then add an Endpoint Assignment if necessary to control the protocol/endpoint configuration. Repeat this step for each custom protocol/endpoint required by your application.

8. Click OK to make the component choices permanent.

9. Click OK to close the DCOM Configuration Tool.

This procedure doesn't address security. While COM+ proxy applications won't allow you to set security options, other component types will. The reason you don't need to set security for a COM+ proxy application is that security for this component type is managed at the server, not at the client. We discuss security issues in the next section. For the most part, you won't need to modify the security settings for a component in a development environment. You'll need to check with the network administrator for security settings in a production environment.

Creating a secure environment

Security is a major concern for any distributed application. The reason is simple: making the application available over a network means that more than one person can and will access it. The more open your network environment and the more critical the data being transferred, the greater your need for robust security. You need to be sure that the right person accesses the application, while keeping others out. This is especially important in today's Internet-oriented environment in which a company may want to allow remote access of critical company information using a standard Internet connection.

In previous sections, we discussed some of the basic security measures that you could take when configuring DCOM. For example, you can change the Default Authentication Level to ensure that each communication between client and server is authorized. (This section provides more detailed information on your authentication options.) The default authentication level only ensures authentication when the client connects initially (normally to create the object in the first place or add a reference to an already existing object).

Windows 2000 uses Access Control Lists (ACLs) to control access to most objects on the server. The DCOM Configuration Tool utility can use the security measures provided by Windows 2000 to secure remote component communications as well. You can build an ACL for each component that DCOM will allow users to access remotely. Using an ACL means that only certain people with the right credentials will gain access to the component. In other words, you'll secure the connection to the server itself and the component on the server, making it unlikely that anyone who isn't authorized will gain access to the component itself.

This section shows you how to use the DCOMCnfg utility to secure the components on your server. This utility greatly reduces the external threats to your network.

Caution   Securing the server and the components that reside on it still doesn't secure the data that gets transferred between client and server. Make sure that you always use some type of secure communication protocol to transfer data from one point to another—especially when working on a public network. Check the various options in the "Setting the authentication level" section of this chapter for details on how you can use built-in DCOM settings to make your data more secure (a good encryption product will only enhance the security you can get by default).

Using the general DCOM security options

Making sure that the DCOM environment as a whole is secure is the subject of this section. You'll find the general DCOM security settings on the Default Security tab of the Distributed COM Configuration Properties dialog as shown in Figure 2-41. There are three main security areas that this tab covers: access, launch, and configuration. The access area determines who can connect to your machine for the purpose of using DCOM in the first place. The launch area determines who can remotely run applications on your machine. Finally, the configuration options determine who has permission to configure the DCOM settings on your machine. The following list tells you about these areas in more detail.

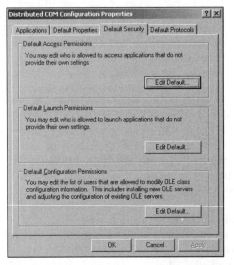

Figure 2-41: Three areas of security are covered by the options on the Default Security tab.

Note   None of the settings in this section override application-specific settings. Windows 2000 uses the application-specific settings first.

✦ **Default Access Permissions:** This option defaults to using the same access-level permissions provided by the system as a whole. In other words, if a person has permission to access your hard drive in some way, that person usually has permission to access the applications found there as well. Of course, access doesn't necessarily mean the ability to execute. All that the Default Access Permissions option does is determine who can access the machine at all.

✦ **Default Launch Permissions:** There are three groups that are normally allowed to launch DCOM applications by default: Interactive Users, Administrators, and System. You must specifically assign a user to the Interactive Users or Administrators groups before they'll have launch permission. Only system-level services are allowed to use the System account. This particular dialog also allows you to add specific groups that aren't allowed to launch an application. However, you need to remember the rules for using an ACL when adding deny entries. The ACL always goes from the top of the list to the bottom and acts on the first entry it sees. So, if a user were part of two groups, one that was allowed to launch DCOM applications and another that wasn't, you would need to put the deny group first. Otherwise, the user would still be allowed to launch DCOM applications based on the group entry that's allowed to launch applications.

✦ **Default Configuration Permissions:** Anyone who can work with the configuration of DCOM on your machine at all is in this list. Normally, the System account and the Administrators group are allowed full control over the configuration. Everyone else is only authorized to read the configuration. You have to allow read permission to anyone who will launch or access applications; otherwise, DCOM won't know how to interact with the test machine. There's also a Special Access setting that allows you to customize settings, but this is a difficult entry to set up and normally you won't need to use it.

All three of these settings work the same way, so I'll discuss them as a single entity, even though each area affects a different area of DCOM communication. Clicking Edit Default will display a Registry Value Permissions dialog for launch permissions like the one shown in Figure 2-42. This dialog allows you to add and remove users from the access list.

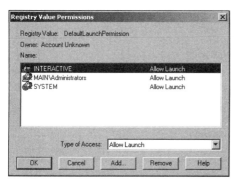

Figure 2-42: The Registry Value Permissions dialog shows access permissions in addition to those normally set for the machine as a whole.

Click Add and you'll see an Add Users and Groups dialog like the one shown in Figure 2-43. This particular dialog shows the list of users and groups for the domain controller; you can also choose from a list for the local machine. There are advantages to using each list. Using the local machine's list allows you to individually control the security settings on a machine-by-machine basis. On the other hand, using the domain list means that you only need to change the settings on one machine to add a new user to a group that will affect all machines that are running DCOM applications.

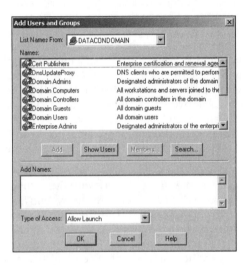

Figure 2-43: DCOM allows you to choose users and groups from the local machine or from the domain controller.

Working with component-level security

Component-level security works much like the general security we discussed in the previous section. Figure 2-44 shows a typical example of a component-level Security tab (in this case, for the Media Player component). Note that you can choose between general security and component-level security for all three areas that we talked about previously. If you choose the default security option, then DCOM will use the options set on the Default Security tab of the Distributed COM Configuration Properties dialog. Otherwise, you need to click the individual Edit button to set the security you want for that area of component level security. Because the actual process of setting component level security is the same as default security, I won't discuss the various options in this section (refer to the section called "Using the general DCOM security options").

Setting the authentication level

There are two ways to set the authentication level for your component: at the DCOM level or the individual component level. Both authentication-level settings determine the minimum security requirements for the client and server to gain access to each other's resources. In other words, this setting determines how the client and server exchange security information during a session.

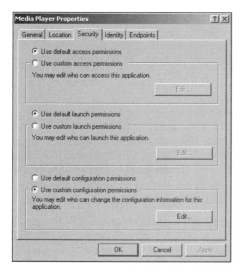

Figure 2-44: The major difference between the component-specific Security tab and the Default Security tab is default/custom option buttons.

The Default Authentication Level setting is found on the Default Properties tab of the main Distributed COM Configuration Properties dialog. The default general setting is Connect. The component-specific setting appears on the General tab of the <*Component name*> Properties dialog. In this case, the default setting is Default. These two settings represent a minimalist approach to DCOM security. There are other settings that may provide you with better security. The following list describes each of the Default Authentication Level settings.

✦ **None:** The client and server don't authenticate each other at all. You must use this setting when creating anonymous connections. However, this setting also comes in handy if you're working in a small workgroup network situation where physical security is high and there aren't any connections to the outside world. This setting reduces overall network traffic to the lowest possible level, but also represents the greatest security risk.

✦ **Call:** Authentication occurs for every call while a connection is maintained. This is a moderately high security level that ensures the client and server verify each other's identity for each method call in the application, which may involve several packets. There will be a slight increase in network traffic when using this level of authentication, and no guarantee of complete security from third-party intrusion.

✦ **Connect:** One-time authentication takes place during object creation. The client and server verify each other's identity during this initial request. There's a good chance a third party could break network security if you use this mode because the client and server don't have any way to verify either packets or requests. The advantage to this method is that initial authentication places limits on what the user can do and network traffic is kept to a minimum.

✦ **Default:** At the individual component level, this setting means that the component will use the general DCOM setting. At the DCOM level, this setting means that DCOM as a whole will use whatever security the authentication method uses in general. For example, the default Windows 2000 Security Services uses Connect-level authentication. The results of using this setting vary according to the authentication method used.

✦ **Packet:** This is the first of three levels of truly secure DCOM communication settings. The sender's identity is encrypted and packaged with the packet. This means that the receiver can verify the authenticity of the sender with every packet and greatly reduce the probability of third-party intrusion. However, this method also bloats the size of the packet and could greatly increase DCOM-related network traffic. This setting represents the most reasonable level of protection for a network that allows outside access.

✦ **Packet Integrity:** The sender's identity and a packet signature are encrypted as part of the packet. Using these two forms of authentication ensures that the sender is authorized and that the packet hasn't been modified in any way. However, this method won't ensure that a third party hasn't read the packet, and it does increase network traffic over Packet authentication. You'd only want to use this setting when the integrity of the data was absolutely essential, but you didn't care who read the packet.

✦ **Packet Privacy:** In most cases, this is the paranoid level of security. Not only does the packet contain the sender's identity and a packet signature, but the packet itself is encrypted to ensure that a third party can't read it. This level of authentication greatly increases network traffic and could actually slow communications to a crawl when used on slower traffic media like a dial-up connection. However, this is the level of authentication that you need to ensure safe financial transactions and the transmission of critical confidential information from one site to another.

Performing service-related tasks

The last management area we need to look at is the services that Windows 2000 uses to perform tasks in the background. Figure 2-45 shows what the Services folder looks like in Component Services. There's also a separate MMC snap-in for managing services if you'd like to use it.

There isn't a lot that you need to know about the services to work with COM+ applications. However, you do need to know how to start, pause, and stop the services. It's also handy to know how some of the service settings will affect the operation of the service.

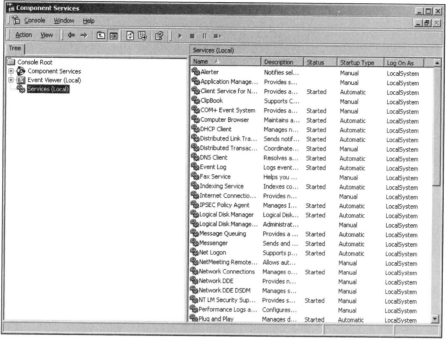

Figure 2-45: The Services MMC snap-in allows you to manage the various Windows 2000 services.

Starting, restarting, stopping, or pausing a service is easy. All you need to do is highlight the service, then click the appropriate button on the Services MMC snap-in toolbar. Starting a service executes the service background so that whatever services it has to offer are available for use by your components. In some cases, you'll need to stop a service to perform system maintenance, as we had to do when installing SQL Server 6.5 in Chapter 1. Pausing a service allows you to temporarily stop it and then restart it without any loss of state information. Finally, restarting a service allows you to place the service in its initial starting state without stopping it first.

There are a few situations where you may want to change some of the service settings to ensure your component will work as anticipated. For example, you may want to start the service automatically each time the server is booted, rather than allow the service to start manually. To make changes to the service's settings, you need to right-click the service entry and then choose Properties from the context menu. Figure 2-46 shows a typical example of the General tab of a service Properties dialog box (in this case, we're looking at the Distributed Transaction Coordinator). This tab also allows you to start, stop, pause, and resume the service.

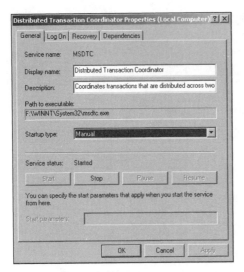

Figure 2-46: The General tab of the service Properties dialog box allows you to set the service's starting state.

The Startup type field allows you to change the startup state of the service. There are three settings: Automatic, Manual, and Disabled. Setting this field to Automatic means that the service will automatically start every time you reboot the server. The Manual setting tells Windows 2000 that you want to start the service only when it's needed. Finally, the Disabled setting means that the service can't start, even if it's fully installed and an application has requested the service.

Note   We looked at the Dependencies tab of the service Properties dialog box as part of the SQL Server 6.5 installation procedure in Chapter 1. For the most part, you won't need to access this tab. However, the SQL Server installation procedure does show one way in which this tab can help you work with services. Refer to Chapter 1 for more information on the Dependencies tab.

The Log On tab shown in Figure 2-47 contains some additional settings that you may need to change. Normally, a service logs in using the system account. This login gives the service complete access to local resources. However, there are times when you need to limit what the service can do or provide it additional access. In this case, you'll want to change the Log On tab settings to use a specific account.

You can also use the Log On tab to enable or disable the service depending on the current hardware setup. This is an option that's designed for use with portable machines, in most cases — not for use with servers. For example, a laptop user may have three different hardware setups: one for use at the office, a second for use at home, and a third for use while on the road.

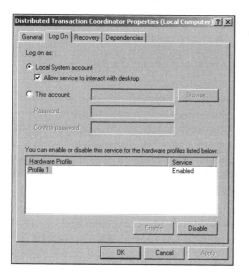

Figure 2-47: The Log On tab allows you to set the account that the service uses to log in to the server.

Summary

As operating systems become more complex, it's more important for the developer to use as many predefined methods for handling administrative tasks as possible. This chapter has shown you the need to learn about the various MMC snap-ins and how to use them. Here are some additional conclusions you can draw from the contents of this chapter:

✦ Component Services is the most important MMC snap-in for the developer to know about. You'll use it for a variety of purposes, including managing your component setup.

✦ COM+ applications require a minimum of three installation steps. You begin by creating a host application that acts as a container for the component. Next, you add one or more components to the COM+ application shell. Finally, you add security and perform any setting changes for both the COM+ application and the components that it contains.

✦ Previous versions of COM allowed you to use the request/reply event model, which required a connection between the client and server. In addition, this older model required the client and server to have overlapping lifetimes. COM+ adds the publish/subscribe event model to the picture, which works much better in a disconnected application environment.

✦ Because a COM+ application can't use most of the error-reporting techniques available to other applications, you need an alternative. Using event log reporting is a perfect alternative that allows you to categorize errors in a number of ways. The two most important reporting elements are the Description and Data fields of the Event Properties dialog box.

✦ The DTC monitors and directs transactions on the server. It provides two methods of monitoring transactions. The Transaction List allows you to view current transactions and manage them as needed. Transaction Statistics allows you to monitor transaction server performance and can help you detect certain types of server problems.

✦ DCOM is still very much a part of COM+. Even the COM+ proxy applications that you create rely on DCOM to transfer data from the client to the server. Because DCOM is still part of the picture, you can use the DCOMCnfg utility to manage the connections between the client and the server. The DCOMCnfg utility is also handy for setting local DCOM security, which is an important part of security for all component communication, not just the communication required for COM+ applications.

✦ Services allow Windows 2000 to perform tasks in the background. These tasks normally provide access to operating system features that applications require. Some back-end applications, like SQL Server, can also install services that allow them to perform certain tasks in the background or to interact with front-end applications. It's important to realize that you can start, stop, resume, and pause services as needed for maintenance or other tasks. You can also change the way services start and how they log on to the server.

✦   ✦   ✦

Working with COM/COM+ Tools

No matter what your trade, there are always tools that you need to perform your job well. In some cases, the tools are so specialized that you need them to perform your job at all. Programmers, like all other people in all other trades, need to know about the tools of their profession. More important, when the need arises they need to know about new uses for those tools. COM+ is an evolutionary technology built on the technology used in the past. It makes sense, then, to use some of the same tools that were used in the past for development. However, because COM+ is a new environment, you may find yourself using those tools in new ways.

The first section provides a summary of the tools that we use throughout the book to create the example applications. You may know how to use these tools, but you probably haven't used them with COM+. This first section provides a quick summary of the tools and their uses and then delves into some of the new ways that you can use them when working with COM+ applications. In addition, we look at some of the ways that you probably shouldn't use the tools, as well as new techniques for performing old tasks in new ways. In short, you may end up looking at Visual Studio differently from the way you have in the past.

This chapter uses some pre-made components and applications for demonstration purposes. It's important to show how the various tools will work with a functional object or running application. You'll find these components and applications in the Chapter 3 folder on the CD-ROM provided with this book. Each component or application appears in a separate directory of the same name. Simply place the components in a convenient place on the development workstation and then work through the example procedures in this chapter. You'll need to register the components using the command line utility RegSvr32 <Component Filename> before you'll be able to see them in many of the utilities. By the time you're finished, you should have a good understanding of how the various tools provided by Visual Studio and the Platform SDK will help your COM+ development efforts.

Visual Studio was developed long before many of the features of Windows 2000. As a result, Visual Studio doesn't include every tool that you need to program effectively. Some tools are missing simply because Microsoft didn't know that a need for the tool would exist. The Windows 2000 Platform SDK provides some new tools that you need when writing COM+ applications or working with new Windows 2000 features in general.

The second section introduces you to some of the features of the Windows 2000 Platform SDK. I'll tell you where to get this product online and include some ideas on what you may want to avoid when setting up the Platform SDK for use. This section of the chapter concentrates on the new tools that you'll find in the Platform SDK. I've divided the tools into two categories: those that are used for normal development and those that are used for databases.

Some people may not view the contents of the third section as a discussion about tools, because it centers on Active Directory. In the strictest sense, Active Directory is a very specialized database, so it really doesn't fall into the tool category. However, programmers do need information. In many cases, the programmer's best tool is the information that the programmer can garner from the operating system. That's why Active Directory is discussed in this chapter. We'll look at two very important information centers that tell a programmer about the configuration of the server, the configuration of the network, and the users who rely on the server and the network to accomplish specific tasks. In short, Active Directory is one of those very specialized tools that were mentioned in this chapter's introduction. In this sense, Active Directory is a tool that you use only occasionally but absolutely need to know about when the need arises.

Microsoft has built up slowly some additional aids to help developers create fully integrated Distributed interNetwork Architecture (DNA) applications. As part of this effort, Microsoft has set up the Microsoft Visual Studio Interoperability Studio, a Web site where you can learn about new products and download add-ons that make the development process easier. For the most part, this site brings together all of the links to other Microsoft Web sites that you'd normally need to collect yourself. It also has case studies (customer examples), tools, and other interoperability resources. You can find this Web site at http://msdn.microsoft.com/vstudio/centers/interop/default.asp.

Visual Studio Tool Summary

Visual Studio provides a wealth of utility-level tools in addition to the main pro-gramming language offerings. The purpose of these tools varies, but for the most part they're designed to make writing and testing code easier. In other words, you need to know what tasks these tools perform to get the most out of Visual Studio as a whole. Look at these as the hand tools that any good craftsperson would have in addition to the latest power tools provided by the main programming-language packages. Just as it takes a combination of tools to build a house or create a meal with eye appeal, it takes a combination of programming tools to craft a really great application.

The following sections will provide you with an overview of the tasks performed by most of the Visual Studio utility programs. This chapter concentrates on the tools that you're most likely to need throughout the book — Visual Studio does provide other tools that you can use for tasks like performance testing. These sections aren't meant as a full-fledged demonstration of every task these utilities can per-form. What you'll get from this chapter is enough information to use these utilities as you build the various applications found in this book.

ActiveX Control Test Container

Component technology has freed many programmers from the need to perform some types of repetitive tasks. For example, the addition of standard dialog box support, like the File Open dialog box, to Windows has reduced the need for each person to create his or her own version of this very standard application feature. Command buttons, labels, and text controls have all contributed as well toward reducing the programmer's workload. Consider what it would take to write a mod-ern application using only the C code that programmers of the past had to use, and you can see why component technology is so important.

Microsoft's latest term for application component technology is ActiveX. Creating an ActiveX control allows you to encapsulate within a single object some of the functionality that you'll need for every program you create (or, at least, a good many of them). ActiveX controls appear everywhere, including Web pages and applications. In fact, every interface element that you'll actually touch in the Windows environment is an ActiveX control.

Tip

ActiveX Control Test Container will work with a variety of objects, not just ActiveX controls. Part of the confusion about the name of this tool stems from the fact that Microsoft originally used the term ActiveX to refer to all COM technology but then decided to use ActiveX to refer to applications components only. The fact remains that you can test most components within the ActiveX Control Test Container to see if they'll work as anticipated. For example, you'll find that many of the Visual J++ design-time controls work just fine with this utility. In addition, most Java classes also work fine.

Because of the faith that many programmers place in the ActiveX controls they use, it's important to test components fully. That's when the ActiveX Control Test Container comes into play. This utility allows you to test the features of your ActiveX control in a special environment designed to help you locate flaws quickly. In addition, the ActiveX Control Test Container utility allows you to test your component outside of the programming language integrated development environment (IDE) or test application, where errors could get introduced outside of the component itself. Figure 3-1 shows what the ActiveX Control Test Container looks like with the MultPB1 component loaded. (You can see how this component works outside the ActiveX Control Test Container utility by using the MPBTest application provided in the source code directory.)

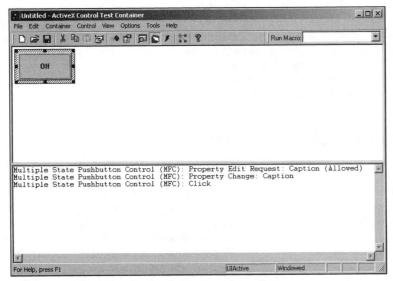

Figure 3-1: The ActiveX Control Test Container allows you to check the operation of components that you create.

Note   To load an ActiveX control in the test container, use the Edit ⇨ Insert New Control command. An Insert Control dialog box that lists all of the components that are currently registered on the local machine will appear. The MultPB1 component used in this section will appear as the Multiple State Pushbutton Control in the Insert Control dialog box. You can also insert an ActiveX control into the current test container from a stream or from storage using the appropriate Edit menu command.

The following sections are going to explore a few of the more important tasks that you can perform with ActiveX Control Test Container. You'll need to perform one or more of these tasks as the book progresses. For example, when using an ActiveX control in a multilanguage environment, you'll normally want to test it using this utility. At the very least, you'll want to check to see that you can access the methods and properties that the component provides.

Checking methods and properties

There have been a number of situations in which I thought I had defined a property or method properly only to have it fail to appear when needed in the final application. In some cases, the failure wasn't anything in my code, but a difference in the way the two programming languages supported ActiveX controls. Unfortunately, unless you can isolate the component and test it in an independent test environment, you'll have trouble determining the precise problem.

ActiveX Control Test Container allows you to check the availability of both methods' properties. In addition, you can change these features of your ActiveX control to see whether they work as intended. Let's look at properties first. The normal method used to change the properties is through a property page (which is one of the reasons I normally include a property page for the most important value). Simply click on the Properties button (or use the Edit ⇨ Properties command) to display the component's Property dialog. Figure 3-2 shows a Property dialog for the Multiple State Pushbutton control (MultPB1.OCX). All of these properties reflect changes that a designer would make during design time (and in many cases, runtime as well).

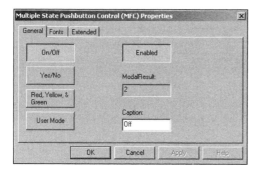

Figure 3-2: All of your components should include a Properties dialog so that you can check their operation with different property settings.

There may be times when you don't want to place a property in the component's Properties dialog box. Perhaps the property affects something that the application designer wouldn't normally change, or something that the designer would change only during runtime instead of at design time. Even if the properties for a component you design aren't listed in their entirety on property pages, you can still access them by looking through the list of methods supported by your component. You'll find that ActiveX Control Test Container creates a get and set method for every property your component supports. However, it's still easier to access properties (at least those created for design-time use) through a property page.

Let's talk about methods for a moment. All you need to do to look at the methods your component supports is use the Control ⇨ Invoke Methods command (you can also click the Invoke Methods button on the toolbar). In addition to the get and set method for various properties, you'll find all of the other methods that your component supports in the Invoke Methods dialog box shown in Figure 3-3. The figure shows the extended Method Name list box so that you can see some of the methods that this component supports.

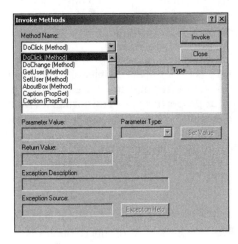

Figure 3-3: You use the Invoke Methods dialog box to test your component's capability to handle method requests.

Two of the methods, `GetUser()` and `SetUser()`, support one of the component's properties. Most components will use get and set methods to allow an external application to change the value of a custom property. An alternative method is to use a `PropGet` and `PropPut` combination, in which case, you'll see the property name first, followed by the action in parenthesis like this: Caption (PropGet). This is the most common method used for inherited properties like Caption.

Tip   You may have a component method that accepts multiple input values using a variant type. The Parameter Type drop-down list box contains a list of the commonly used parameter types. Choosing alternate parameter types allows you to test a method's capability to work with more than one data type as input. You could also use this field to perform various kinds of type checking on your component so that you can see a failure mode before it becomes part of an application and gets hidden. Obviously, you need to use the Parameter Type field with care because setting a parameter to a different type puts you at risk of a component failure that may not be obvious.

Having access to the property change methods means that you can manipulate the properties as an application would during runtime as well as the design-time method of using a Properties dialog box. If you wanted to change the User property, you could select the `SetUser()` method, type a string in the Parameter Value field, and then click Invoke. ActiveX Control Test Container will send this value to the component and then the component will perform the required action.

Tip   Some methods have more than one parameter. You can highlight the parameter that you want to change in the Parameter list, change the value in the Parameter Value field, and then click Set Value. Using Set Value changes the parameter locally. This method allows you to set multiple properties before you try to invoke the method. Clicking Invoke sends all of the parameters that you've changed to the method at one time. In some cases, you must set a group of properties prior to invoking the method to get the desired results.

Tracking events

Events are the basis of a lot of ActiveX control activities. ActiveX Control Test Container has two windows. The upper window displays the components you've loaded for the test, while the bottom window displays any output from the component. Output, in this case, occurs (at least in most cases) because some event has fired. Some events are derived from custom programming, whereas others occur as part of normal component operation. For example, you'll normally see a Click event generated when the user clicks a button as shown in Figure 3-1. In this case, clicking the button also generates Property Edit Request and Property Change events. This second set of events demonstrates the multiple-part nature of some event generations. An application has to ask permission before it makes a change to the Caption property; then the actual change occurs.

ActiveX Control Test Container provides two levels of event logging. The first level is at the container level. To set these logging options, use the Options ⇨ Logging. . . command to display the Logging Options dialog box shown in Figure 3-4.

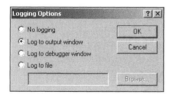

Figure 3-4: The Logging Options dialog box allows you to set the level of logging provided by the ActiveX Control Test Container.

As you can see, the Logging Options dialog box allows you to choose where the logging output appears. As mentioned earlier, the default setting sends any log entries to the Output window. You can also choose to stop logging all events from all components that you currently have loaded or to place the log entries in a file. The Log to debugger window option is supposed to send the log entries to the debug window of your favorite programming language product, but support for this feature is flaky at best. This option works best with the latest versions of Visual C++ and only marginally with Visual Basic.

The second level of logging is at the component level. Normally, ActiveX Control Test Container logs all component events, but logging all events can lead to overload and make the detection of a specific event more difficult. In most cases, to get optimal results it's important to select a specific set of events to monitor. You must select the component that you want to work with before using the Control ⇨ Logging. . . command to display the Control Logging Options dialog box shown in Figure 3-5.

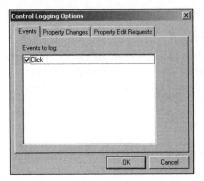

Figure 3-5: The Control Logging Options dialog box allows you to control event logging at the component level.

As Figure 3-5 shows, there are three tabs on the Control Logging Options dialog box. The following list explains how each tab controls a major event logging type.

✦ **Events:** The first tab contains a list of all of the events that your component can fire. When a user clicks the component, it normally fires an event. As Figure 3-5 shows, our test component fires only the Click event.

✦ **Property Changes:** The second tab contains a list of all the standard property changes, but not necessarily all of the properties that the component provides. Figure 3-6 shows what this tab looks like. In the case of the Multiple State Pushbutton control, only the Caption, Enabled, and Font property changes are tracked. These logging events get fired only if an actual change takes place, not if the client requests the current value or the capability to change the property.

Figure 3-6: The Property Changes tab allows you to determine which property changes are tracked.

✦ **Property Edit Requests:** The third tab lists the property edit requests. In this case, only the Caption and Enabled properties listed; the Font property uses a special property page, which handles the request event for a font change. A request event is fired whenever the client requests the capability to edit the property, which in turn generates the logging event. In other words, a request event log entry will appear even if no actual change takes place. Figure 3-7 shows what the Property Edit Requests tab looks like.

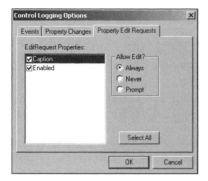

Figure 3-7: The Property Edit Requests tab allows you to track edit requests.

The Property Edit Requests tab allows you to do something that the other logging options don't. The Always, Prompt, and Never options allow you to tell ActiveX Control Test Container what to do with edit requests. In most cases, you want to allow the component to accept changes as normal. However, there are some situations when you may want the component to prompt you before it grants permission or to deny permission so that the property value remains constant during testing. The edit request event will still be logged whichever option you choose, so that you can maintain a record of component activity.

Tip   You can load more than one ActiveX control at a time to see how two or more components interact. For example, you might have a visible component that relies on input from an invisible component like a timer. This feature is especially important when working with data-related components like those used to set the database and table source.

Testing persistence

Persistence is the capability of an ActiveX control to retain its values from one session to the next. In most cases, you want your component to retain any property values that the user sets. Read-only properties, on the other hand, may change from session to session and therefore don't require persistence. It doesn't matter whether a property is persistent or not; you still have to ensure that it reacts as intended.

ActiveX Control Test Container provides three levels of persistence testing: property bag, stream, and storage. Generally, it's a good idea to test your component in all three environments to make sure that the persistence it provides actually works. Two of the testing methods, stream and storage, require that you save the component to disk and then read it back into the test container. The other method, property bag, provides instant feedback.

Let's look at the property bag method first. Set the component properties as needed for the test (verify that they're indeed set). After you've set the properties, use the Control ⇨ Save to Property Bag command to display the Property Bag dialog box shown in Figure 3-8. This dialog box can't tell you about the contents of every property. In this case, it can't represent the contents of the Font property. You can normally count on seeing the values for string, numeric, and Boolean values.

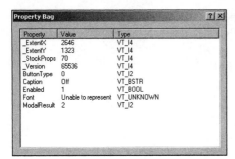

Figure 3-8: The Property Bag dialog box allows you to perform one form of component persistence testing.

So, how do you test the component's capability to persist values in a property bag? All you need to do is make sure that the settings in the property bag match the settings you made to the component. If they don't, then your component has failed the most basic test of persistence. Special properties, like the Font property, will require further testing before you can make a determination.

Tip

The Property Bag dialog box provides the opportunity for you to check more than just the persistence of your component; it also allows you to see how a client views your properties. It's important to note inconsistencies in both the value and type of the properties that your component provides. Some subtle errors, like the size of an integer, are easy to spot this way.

The other two persistence tests rely on saving the component to disk, then reading it back into the ActiveX Control Test Container. This act simulates the actions that an application would perform when working with persistent components. If the component's persistence is working properly, then persistent properties should have the same value as when you set up the component in the first place. Obviously, any non-persistent properties will have a random value, so you don't need to worry if they have the same value or not. The following seven-step procedure works for testing both storage and stream methods of persistence.

1. Set the component's properties.

2. Use the Control ➪ Save to Stream or Control ➪ Save to Storage command to display a Save As dialog box. Notice that test stream files use a file extension of TSM, while test storage files use a file extension of TSG. You can't use a single file for storage purposes — each kind of file uses a different file format. As a result, it's important to make sure you run a separate test for both streams and storage.

3. Type the filename you want to use for storing the component (properties set), and then click Save.

4. Close ActiveX Control Test Container, and then restart it. It's important to restart the ActiveX Control Test Container to avoid contaminating your test with values that exist in memory.

5. Use the Edit ⇨ Insert Control from Stream or Edit ⇨ Insert Control from Storage command to display an Open dialog box.

6. Highlight the test file of the component you want to test, and then click Open to display the component.

7. Check the component's properties to ensure that they're the same (for persistent properties) as when you stored the component on disk. It's equally important to check nonpersistent components for some default value when supplied, or a random value if not.

Depends

Have you ever sent out an application and found out later that the person using it didn't have all the files needed to run it? Most of us have done that at one time or another and, in most cases, it wasn't our fault that a file or two was missing. It seems as if every file in Windows relies on every other file in some way — trying to untie this knot is something even Houdini would have had trouble doing.

 Note   This section discusses the version of Depends that comes with the Platform SDK. This new version includes a lot of features that are different from the version included with Visual Studio 6.0, along with an additional window for logging various types of application checks. As a result, the screen shots in this section may not exactly match what you see on screen if you're using an older version of Depends.

The following sections look at the Depends utility from two perspectives. I've divided the coverage so that you can see clearly what Depends 2.0 adds to an already valuable utility. The old version (included with Visual Studio 6.0) allows you to perform analysis on the structure of your application and the resource files that it depends on. The new version (version 2.0) includes many additional analysis features that will help you move beyond taking the application apart to seeing how it actually works in the runtime environment. Even though the old version is a very capable product that still provides valuable information, the new version is so improved that you really owe it to yourself to test it out.

Standard Depends features

Dependency Walker (or Depends, as it's listed on the Microsoft Visual Studio 6.0 Tools menu) helps you prevent the problem of the missing file. It lists every file that an application, DLL, or other executable files needs to execute. You can use the output of this application to create a list of required files for your application. Loading a file for examination is as easy as using the File ⇨ Open command to open the executable file that you want to examine. Figure 3-9 is an example of the output generated for the SayHello.EXE file. This is a typical example of a minimal Visual Basic application. In fact, you can't get much more minimal than this example program. The point, of course, is that even a very small and simple application may require more support files than you think.

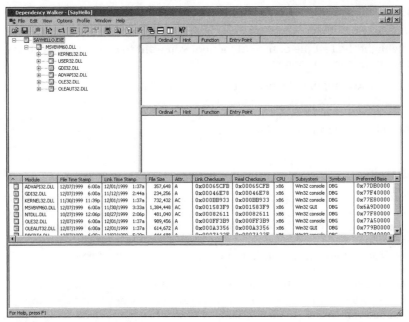

Figure 3-9: Dependency Walker can help you determine which external files your component needs to operate.

 Tip   It's interesting to note that Dependency Walker doesn't include any kind of print functionality. Fortunately, you can highlight a list of the items that you want to print, press Ctrl+C to copy them to the clipboard, and use the Paste function in your favorite word processor to create a document that you can print for future reference.

As you can see, this application provides a lot of information about the dependencies of your file. In the upper left-hand corner is a hierarchical view of dependencies, starting with the executable file that you want to check. The hierarchy shows the files that each preceding file requires to be capable of running. So, while the application itself relies on MSVBVM60.DLL, the support DLL relies on input from a host of other files.

To the right of the hierarchical view are two lists. The upper list tells you which functions the parent executable imports from the current file. The lower list tells you which functions the highlighted executable exports for other executables to use. The sample application doesn't export any functions because it's an end product. You'll typically see a blank export list for applications. Figure 3-10 shows a more typical list of imported and exported functions for a DLL.

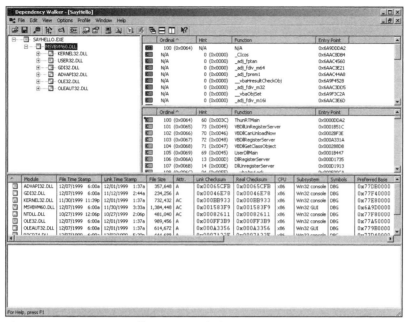

Figure 3-10: DLLs normally import and always export functions that are used by applications and other DLLs.

At the very bottom, you'll see an alphabetical list of all the files along with pertinent information like the executable file's version number and whether you used a debug version of that file while creating and testing your application. This list comes in handy when you're debugging an application. It allows you to check for problems that might come up if you're using an older version of a DLL or detect potential corruption in a support file. You'll also find it handy when you want to check that final release build before you release it for public use. Many applications have tested poorly because they still had "hidden" debug code in them.

New Depends 2.0 features

It's time to look at some of Depends 2.0's new features. An interesting new feature is the capability to profile an application. In this case, profiling doesn't have anything to do with performance; I'm talking about tracing every call that your application makes. To start the profiling process, choose the Profile ➪ Start Profiling command. You'll see a Profile Module dialog box like the one shown in Figure 3-11.

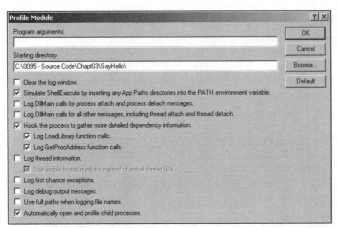

Figure 3-11: The Profile Module dialog box allows you to add a command line argument and adjust the kinds of information that Depends will track.

There are actually two sections in this dialog box. The first section allows you to provide a command line argument for the application and change the application's starting path. In most cases, you won't need to change either entry. You can also choose whether Depends clears the Log window before it begins the profiling process. The Simulate ShellExecute option determines how the application is started. Normally, you'll keep this checked to ensure that the application path information is provided to the application when it starts. The only exception is when you're troubleshooting problems related to the application path. If you uncheck this option, then Depends will start the application using the `CreateProcess()` API call rather than using `ShellExecute()`.

The second section lists the items that you want to monitor. For example, you might only be interested in profiling the libraries that your application loads and when it loads them. In this case, you should select the Log LoadLibrary function calls option. The number of entries in the Log window can build very quickly, so it helps to decide what you really need to monitor at the outset, rather than wading through a lot of useless information that you don't really want. Figure 3-11 shows the default information that Depends will collect about your application. This setup is useful in determining how an application uses the various libraries that it requires to operate. It's interesting to note that you can even use Depends to monitor Debug output messages that you've placed within an application, making it a handy tool for monitoring application activity outside of a programming language's IDE.

Once you've decided how to start the application and what you want to monitor, click OK. Depends will load the application and start displaying profile information. Figure 3-12 shows the Log window entries for the SayHello.EXE application that we looked at earlier. As you can see, there's a lot of activity that occurs even by starting an application.

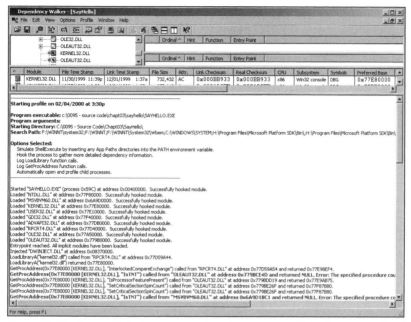

Figure 3-12: Depends helps you monitor the startup activity for any application you create.

Even though you can't see it in Figure 3-12, Depends has noted two problem calls made by the application during startup. These calls are highlighted in red in the Log window. In addition, the affected modules are highlighted in red in both the module list and the hierarchical display. What this means to you, as a developer, is that Depends has gone from being a simple analysis aid to being an application that can help you diagnose application problems. In this case, the two errant calls aren't part of the application code; they're caused by the Visual Basic runtime. Microsoft will probably fix these problems when it updates Visual Studio for Windows 2000.

Depends returns control of the application to you as soon as the application finishes loading. You can work with the application just as you normally would and monitor the results in the Log window. When you finish working with an application, you can stop the logging process using the Depends Profile ➪ Stop Profiling command.

There are quite a few other new features provided with Depends, but the capability to profile your application is the highlight of the list. Another new capability allows you to save a Dependency Walker Image (DWI) file. This option creates a file on disk that allows you to restore your setup as needed. Because Depends 2.0 provides so many new features for configuring the application environment, the capability to save a DWI file is a useful feature that wasn't needed by the previous Depends version.

The View menu contains three options that you really need to know about. The first is a System Information command that displays a dialog similar to the one shown in Figure 3-13. This short summary provides a quick view of your current system configuration, which could be important if you want to stress the application under a set of specific conditions like low memory. There are also options to display the full paths for all files and to undecorate those really weird function names that you'll normally find in C++-generated DLLs.

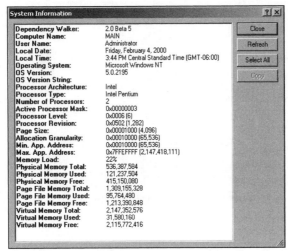

Figure 3-13: The System Information dialog box provides a quick overview of your system.

One final feature that improves the usability of Depends is that it has the capability to search for specific information. For example, you can highlight a module of interest and use View menu options to search for other occurrences of the same module within the hierarchical view. This allows you to see better where specific modules are used and by whom. Another search feature, found on the Edit menu, allows you to search the Log window for words, just as you would with a text editor. You could use this feature to help find errors (the logs do get very long very fast) or to find instances where a specific module is used for tasks like application initialization.

OLE/COM Object Viewer

Every object linking and embedding (OLE) object you create, whether it's an application or an ActiveX control, relies on an interface of some sort. Even language extensions, like ActiveX Scripting, rely on interfaces. An interface is a method for bundling functions independently of programming language. Interfaces are one of the basics of OLE. In addition to the custom interfaces that you create for your object, every object also supports standard interfaces like IUnknown.

Visual Studio provides a handy utility that you can use to see these interfaces in more detail called OLE/COM Object Viewer (Microsoft shortened the name to OLE View in recent versions of Visual Studio). We use this utility several times in the book, so you may want to install it if you haven't already.

Note   The latest version of the OLE/COM Object Viewer as of this writing is 2.10.059, which wasn't shipped as part of Visual Studio 6.0. You can get an updated version from the main COM Web site at http://www.microsoft.com/com/default.asp. This section of the chapter uses the latest version of the OLE/COM Object Viewer, so some screen shots may look slightly different from the ones that you're seeing if you're using an older version of the product. Because the latest version of the OLE/COM Object Viewer fixes several important problems found in previous versions of the product, you'll want to download and install it as quickly as possible. Fortunately, none of the changes affect OLE/COM Object Viewer features, so the version of OLE/COM Object Viewer that comes with Visual Studio 6.0 operates much like the one shipped with the Platform SDK.

A quick overview of the interface

It's important to understand how the OLE/COM Object Viewer can help you during the development process. Say you want to find out about the interfaces provided by a component like the Multiple State Pushbutton Control. The OLE/COM Object Viewer could help you find out about those interfaces and their associated Registry entries. You could use this information to debug problems regarding how a component (or other COM object like a document server) registers itself. This information is also handy when developing a better view of how the component is put together.

Caution   Strange things can happen if you create an instance of an application or component in the OLE/COM Object Viewer and then don't release it. For example, your machine might freeze unexpectedly. Every time you view the interfaces supported by an application or component, you have to create an instance to do it. You can tell whether there's an instance of an object by looking at the application name. The OLE/COM Object Viewer displays any open objects in bold type. To release the instance of the object you created, right-click on the object name (like XYZ Single Document), and then choose Release Instance from the context menu. Fortunately, the OLE/COM Object Viewer is good about closing instances of objects before you leave, but you may need to do this during a viewing session if your machine begins to run out of memory. Remember that every instance you create uses some memory.

Go ahead and open the OLE/COM Object Viewer. You'll see a set of folders that encompass the various types of objects similar to the one shown in Figure 3-14. Notice that these statically defined classes are rather broad. There's a very good chance that a component or other type of COM server could appear within more than one folder, depending on which interfaces it implements.

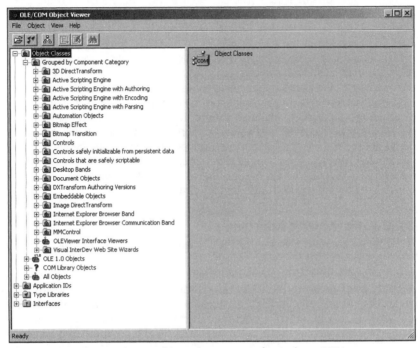

Figure 3-14: The OLE/COM Object Viewer sorts the various COM servers into easily understood categories.

Open the Controls folder, and then open the Multiple State Pushbutton Control folder (or another component folder if you don't have the MultPB1.OCX component registered on your machine). You'll see a list of interfaces that MFC implemented for you as you built the component, as shown in Figure 3-15. The component entry contains information about the Registry, implementation details like the location of files and threading model, activation details like the remote activation site (when required), launch permissions (who can run the application), and access permissions (who can look at the component's settings). All of these settings have default values based on what the developer provided or what Windows 2000 requires.

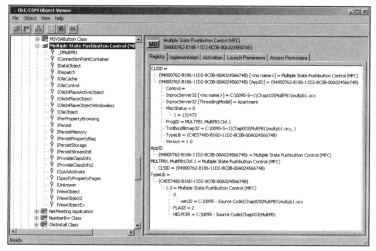

Figure 3-15: The OLE/COM Object Viewer shows a hierarchical view of objects starting with the object type, following with the name, and ending with the interfaces that the object supports.

Performing interface analysis

Highlight the IUnknown interface. You'll see a display similar to the one shown in Figure 3-16. If you look in the right pane, you'll see that this interface has three methods: `QueryInterface()`, `AddRef()`, and `Release`. In addition, you could find the class ID of the proxy stub for this interface. Because IUnknown is a standard interface, you can be certain that it will always contain all three of these methods — this is just part of the interface's standard package.

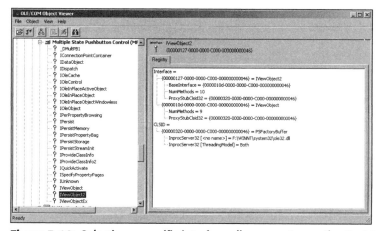

Figure 3-16: Selecting a specific interface allows you to see the Registry entries for that interface, along with details like the number of methods it supports.

In many cases, you can use the information you find in OLE/COM Object viewer to learn more about the way interfaces work together. For example, look at the IView Object2 interface shown in Figure 3-17. This interface depends on the IViewObject interface. So, although the IViewObject2 interface only has 10 unique methods, it can actually provide access to 19 methods by adding the capabilities of the IView Object interface. Notice, also, that this interface includes a CLSID entry. This entry tells Windows where to find the file that contains the interface. Files like OLE32.DLL contain many interfaces, each of which requires a separate entry in the Registry. This is the method that Windows uses for keeping all of the facts about an interface together in one place.

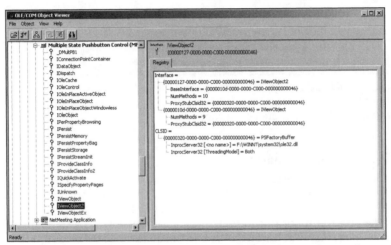

Figure 3-17: Sometimes one interface is actually built out of several interfaces; inheritance plays a role in how you view components.

The OLE/COM Object Viewer can also help you find problems with the interface support in your components. For example, if you look at the contents of the Controls that Are Safely Scriptable folder, you'll find that the Multiple State Pushbutton Control isn't there. Other components that appear in the Controls folder also appear in the Controls that Are Safely Scriptable folder, so it might be helpful to see what they have that the example component doesn't provide. It's important to realize that what you're searching for are clues — you can accept what the OLE/COM Object Viewer tells you as absolute fact; it's certain that this utility will put you on the right track.

Tip If you're confused by all of this talk about interfaces, make sure that you spend plenty of time reading through the various pieces of OLE documentation that Microsoft provides — the most important of which is the OLE 2 SDK. You'll also want to invest in a magazine like *Microsoft Developer Network* (formerly *Microsoft Systems Journal*). This particular magazine painstakingly explains most of the new interfaces that Microsoft designs. I also discuss interface basics in the "Working with Interfaces" section of Chapter 4. A lot of the more common interfaces that you need to implement within components to allow them to work with Windows 2000 will appear in the examples in this book. In short, although interfaces appear confusing at first and there are a lot of them to remember within Windows 2000, you'll find that there's also a lot of documentation available that explains how these interfaces work.

If you take the time to perform the analysis, you'll find that the Multiple State Pushbutton Control doesn't include support for the IOleWindow interface. Further research would tell you that the IOleWindow interface is used to obtain window handles for in-place activation and provide context-sensitive help. Because some scripting environments require components that provide in-place activation capability, a component that doesn't implement IOleWindow isn't safely scriptable.

However, adding the IOleWindow interface would merely make the component safe for scripting — it still wouldn't place the component in the scripting folder. Windows makes no assumptions about a component; Windows only does what you it to do through Registry settings or through the implementation of an interface. This is one of those areas where you need to perform additional research. The component also has to be marked as scriptable before it will appear in the Controls that Are Safely Scriptable folder. This is something that you'd take care of once you knew all of the required interfaces were in place and had tested the component fully. There are two methods that you can use to mark the component as safe. You can either implement the IObjectSafety interface, or make changes in the Registry that show the component is safe. We won't go into the implementation details here; the point is that you could at least get started making your component safe for scripting by using the OLE/COM Object Viewer.

Process Viewer

The Process Viewer utility (shown as PView on the Platform SDK Tools menu) allows you to see what processes are currently running on your machine, what threads they've spawned, and the priority of those threads. You can also use this utility to kill a process that isn't working as intended by using the Kill Process button. Figure 3-18 shows what the Process Viewer utility looks like in action. Notice that I've started a copy of the SayHello test application that we used earlier in the chapter for demonstration purposes.

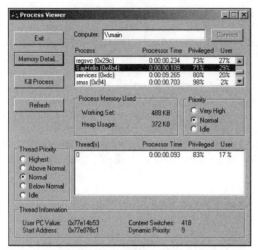

Figure 3-18: The Process Viewer allows you to see what processes are currently executing on your machine.

Tip   The Process Viewer automatically updates its display at a given interval (depending on current processor load). You can force an update of the display by pressing F5 or by using the Process ⇨ Refresh command.

The upper window contains a list of all of the processes currently running on the machine. It includes information about the process like the process ID number, the number of threads that it owns, the base priority of the process (used for multitasking), whether this is a 16-bit or 32-bit process, and the full path to the process.

Highlighting a process displays thread information for it in the lower window. In this case, we see the one thread owned by SayHello.EXE. Thread information includes the thread ID, the ID of the process that owns the thread (useful when you have threads starting other threads), and the priority of the thread (normally the same or lower than the base priority for the process as a whole).

There's one additional Process Viewer feature that you may want to look at. Click Memory Detail to view the Memory Details dialog box shown in Figure 3-19. This dialog box contains very precise and detailed information about how a process is using memory. This dialog will tell you how much memory is used privately, how the memory is mapped into various functional areas, and how much virtual memory the process is using.

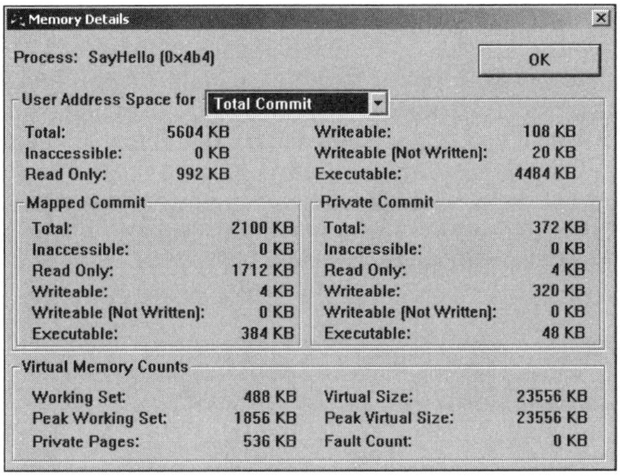

Figure 3-19: The Memory Details dialog box provides extremely detailed information about how a particular process is using memory.

The User Address Space field of the Memory Details dialog box contains the name of the address space that you're viewing. The Total Commit value means that you're looking at the memory used by the entire process. Clicking the arrow next to the combo box displays a list of all of the DLLs and EXEs used by this application. Select one of these entries and you'll see the memory used just by that piece of the application. For example, the executable portion of the file uses a mere 4KB. Because most of these DLLs are shared, the application is most likely using only the 4KB for the executable and the 32KB for the runtime file.

You can use the Memory Details dialog box to troubleshoot applications with subtle memory problems by looking at the values in two of the fields. First, look for a number in the Inaccessible field. Any value other than 0 in this field tells you that the process has some type of memory problem. The second item is the Total memory field. Compare this entry for the Total Commit entry to the Total memory field value for other address spaces. If you see that one DLL is using a substantial amount of memory and the others a small amount of memory, you need to ask why this one DLL is acting in that way. In many cases, you'll find nothing wrong, but there are a few situations when a buggy DLL will keep grabbing memory until it begins to impinge on the resources available to other applications.

ROT Viewer

The IROTView utility (it appears as ROT Viewer in both the Platform SDK and the Visual Studio Tools menus) allows you to view OLE's running object table (ROT). So, what does this buy you? Well, if you're testing the OLE capabilities of your application, you can use this capability to see how well your application interfaces with other objects. For example, what happens if you open a compound document object? Does your application actually make the connection? Figure 3-20 shows what the IROTView utility looks like with several objects loaded.

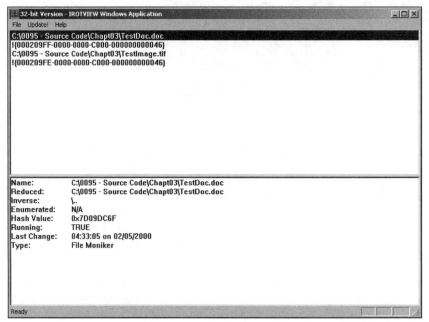

Figure 3-20: The main purpose of the ROTView utility is to track the OLE running object table.

The upper window gives you a complete list of the currently running objects. The GUIDs are running applications that can act as containers for other objects. Figure 3-20 shows two applications: Word and Paintshop Pro. Above each GUID is a list of the documents that the application is running. Each time an application receives focus, this list is updated. You can also perform a manual update using the Update! menu option.

The lower window gives you more information about the highlighted object. The following list describes the contents of each field.

Note

A moniker is a name for some kind of a resource. For example, C:\MyStuff\ MyDoc.Doc is a moniker for a document file that appears in the MyStuff folder on the C drive of your machine. Monikers can include all kinds of resource types. For example: `http://www.microsoft.com` is the moniker for Microsoft's Web site. You can even refer to objects by their moniker by using the class ID (CLSID). For example, the moniker for Microsoft Word is {000209FF-0000-0000-C000-000000000046}, including the curly brackets.

✦ **Name:** The display name of the moniker. For example, in the case of a file, you'd see the complete path for the file. Applications normally use their class ID.

✦ **Reduced:** The reduced name of the moniker. Normally, this is the same value as the Name field.

✦ **Inverse:** The anti-moniker for this object. You add this value to the end of the moniker to destroy it. In most cases, this value is set to: "\..".

✦ **Enumerated:** A list of the items in this moniker. If this isn't a composite moniker (as is the case in most situations), then the field displays N/A.

✦ **Hash Value:** The 32-bit hash value associated with the moniker.

✦ **Running:** Displays TRUE to show that the application is running or FALSE to show that it's halted. The entry for the application will always disappear when the application is terminated, so FALSE always indicates a halted, but active, application.

✦ **Last Change:** This is the last time that the moniker's data was updated.

✦ **Type:** The type of moniker displayed. Standard values include: Generic Composite Moniker, File Moniker, Anti-Moniker, Item Moniker, Pointer Moniker, and Not a System Moniker.

Spy++

Spy++ is a complex utility that can give you more information about your application than you might have thought possible. This section is provides a very brief summary of this utility. I point out some of the more interesting features of Spy++ that will make working with the applications in this book easier. Make sure you take time to work with this utility further after you've learned the basics.

The first thing you'll see when you start Spy++ is a list of windows. A window can be one of any number of object types, but the most familiar is the application window. Figure 3-21 is an example of what you might see when you start Spy++ with the SayHello sample application running.

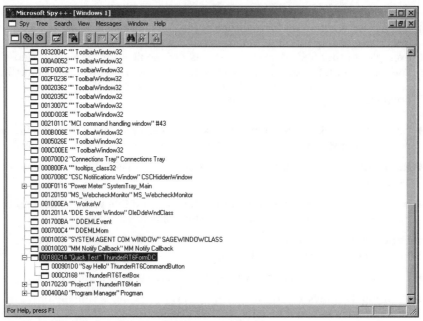

Figure 3-21: Spy++ allows you to take your application apart and see it from Windows' perspective.

There are two windows that belong to the main application window—both of which are components of the dialog box. In this case, the output text and the Say Hello test button are both considered windows. In fact, when you try to change the caption on the button or the text within the text box, you'll find that you're working with an object derived from the CWindow class, which means that Spy++ is right on track displaying the information as it has.

Tip   One of the few places where the Platform SDK doesn't currently provide superior tool support to Visual Studio is the Spy++ utility. The Platform SDK includes only the much-less capable Spy utility. You'll definitely want to use Spy++ because it provides so much more functionality.

Working with window properties

Windows are a central part of working with Spy++. They represent the method you'll normally use to begin deciphering how an application works and how well it runs. It makes sense, then, that you can access every aspect of an application, its child windows, processes, and threads through the Window Properties dialog box shown in Figure 3-22.

Figure 3-22: The Window Properties dialog box allows you to learn the details of the windows in your application.

Accessing this dialog box is easy. All you need to do is right-click the window that you want to view, and then choose Properties from the context menu. You can also access this dialog box using the View ⇨ Properties command.

The General tab of the Window Properties dialog box tells you about the window as a whole. It includes the window's display name, the window handle, the virtual address of the window procedure, the size of the rectangle used to display the window (both present and restored sizes), and various other pieces of general application information.

The Styles tab contains a list of the window style constants used to create the window. For example, you'll commonly find WS_VISIBLE as one of the items in the list unless you're dealing with an invisible window. This same tab contains extended styles for the window like WS_EX_APPWINDOW. These constants should be very familiar to someone with C/C++ programming experience; they may require a little research for the Visual Basic programmer to learn. However, if you're having problems getting an application to display correctly, learning the various constants (or at least knowing where to find out about them) used by your application may help you find the problem.

The Windows tab contains five entries. You can move between windows at the same level by clicking the links in the Next Window and Previous Window fields. The Parent Window field will contain a link if this is a child window or (None) if this is a main window. If the window contains child windows (like the components for the SayHello.EXE program), you'll see an entry in the First Child field. Clicking this link will take you down one level in the hierarchy so that you can examine any child windows that belong to the current window. Finally, the Owner Window field will contain a link if the current window is owned by another window—except for the Desktop, in which case the field displays a value of (None).

The Class tab tells you about the class used to create the window. For example, the main window for the SayHello.EXE program uses the ThunderRT6FormDC class, while the components are all listed as being part of component specific classes like the ThunderRT6CommandButton class used for the Say Hello test button. You'll also find class-specific information like the class style codes, number of data bytes used by this instance of the class, an instance handle for the window, and number of bytes used by the window itself, as well as window details like the name of any associated menus.

The Process tab provides a list of process IDs and thread IDs associated with the current window. Clicking the links associated with each field displays the properties dialog associated with the process or thread ID. We'll look at this properties dialog in more detail in the "Viewing processes and threads" section that follows.

Viewing messages

Windows runs on messages. Every activity that the user engages in generates a message of some sort. It's important to monitor those messages and see how your application reacts. For example, if you expect a certain message to be generated when the user clicks a button, you can monitor the message stream to determine whether it really is generated.

There are a number of ways to display the Messages window for a window that you're debugging. You could right-click on the window and choose Messages from the context menu. However, in this particular case, the best way to start the message monitoring process is to use the Spy ⇨ Messages command. This command will display the Message Options dialog box shown in Figure 3-23 (you don't get this dialog box when you use the context menu method of displaying the Messages window).

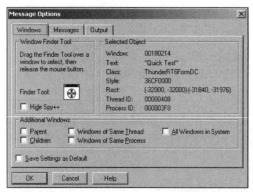

Figure 3-23: The Message Options dialog box allows you to adjust the kinds of messages to monitor.

Notice the Selected Object frame on the right side of the dialog box. This frame provides information about the object that you've selected. This additional information enables you to determine whether this is the window that you want to monitor. The

Finder Tool on the left side of the dialog box is also interesting. Drag this tool to any displayed window and release the mouse button, and the information on the right side changes to match the data for that window. (The windows will be highlighted as you drag the mouse cursor over them so that you can see which window is being selected.) The Windows tab also allows you to choose additional windows. For example, you may want to monitor the child windows as well as the parent window for a specific kind of message.

There are 849 different messages that Spy++ can track for the average window — the Message tab shown in Figure 3-24 gives you some idea of just how extensive the message coverage is. Needless to say, you could end up with a lot of useless tracking information if you don't trim this to a more reasonable number. That's why the Messages tab is so important. This tab allows you to choose which messages are tracked in the Messages window. You can choose messages singularly or by group. A Select All button allows you to choose all of the messages, while a Clear All button allows you to clear the current selections. Make sure you fine-tune these settings before you display the Messages window or your chances of getting the input that you need will be very small.

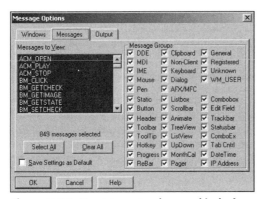

Figure 3-24: Spy++ can track every kind of message traffic that an application can generate.

It's also important to determine how you want information displayed in the Messages window. In most cases, the default options on the Output tab work just fine. Spy++ assumes that you want to display only decoded information and only onscreen. However, there are options for displaying raw message information. You can also send the output to a file as well as to the screen.

After you have set the options for your Messages window, you can click OK and Spy++ will display the window for you. Figure 3-25 is an example of what a Messages window would look like if you chose to monitor a subset of button and mouse events. As you can see, just selecting these two message groups generates a lot of message traffic.

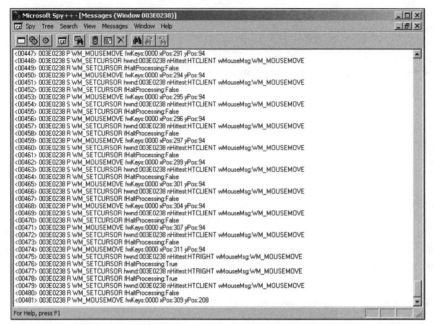

Figure 3-25: The Messages window displays the messages that you choose to monitor for an application.

In this case, I clicked the Say Hello button several times and moved the mouse around on screen. Notice that the log entries contain the handle of the window where the action occurred, the action performed (mouse button up or down, mouse move, or set cursor), and the position where the action occurred. Although this is a simple test case, it's easy to see that monitoring messages can provide you with very important debugging clues for your application.

Viewing processes and threads

Every application that you create has at least one process and one thread. Consider a process as the overall application identifier, while a thread consists of a particular set of actions taking place within that process. In a multithreaded application, each thread of execution is performing a single task that affects the application (the process) as a whole.

Spy++ allows you to monitor both processes and threads. All you need to do is use the Spy ➪ Processes or Spy ➪ Threads command to display the appropriate window. Figure 3-26 shows an example of the Processes window.

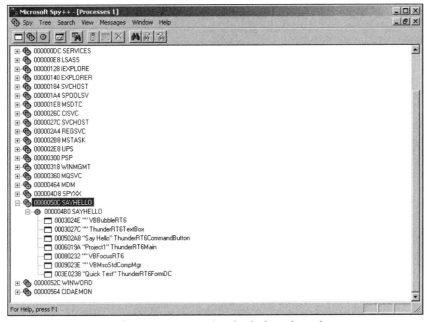

Figure 3-26: Spy++ allows you to monitor both threads and processes.

It's interesting to note that the Processes window also contains a list of any threads owned by the process in a hierarchical format. For this reason, you'll normally want to use the Processes window over the Thread window. You get more information in a more readily understandable format using the Processes window.

Notice also that there's a complete list of windows provided, even those that aren't visible. This listing differs from the one you saw for the Windows window, which lists only visible windows like components. Our application still contains two component windows, but it also includes invisible windows that provide support functions for the rest of the application. Double-clicking any one of these window entries displays a Window Properties dialog box like the one we discussed earlier in the "Working with window properties" section.

Platform SDK Tool Summary

Visual Studio was released long before Microsoft began working on some of the major aspects of Windows 2000. It's no surprise, therefore, that you need the Windows 2000 Platform SDK to write applications that truly make use of all of the features that Windows 2000 has to offer. The simple fact is that you must download the Platform SDK and install it, or the applications that you create that rely on these new features won't run. You'll also find that in many cases you need to provide new redistributable files with your applications. Older Visual Basic runtime files won't have the level of support required by Windows 2000.

Note   At the time of this writing, you could download several different versions of the Platform SDK, the latest of which is the January 2000 Platform SDK (the one I'm using to write the book). However, Microsoft is slowly removing all of the older versions of the Platform SDK from its Web site. I refer to the Windows 2000 version of the Platform SDK as "the Platform SDK" throughout this book. Be sure that you have the newest possible version of the Platform SDK before you begin working with the examples in this book. Some of the Platform SDK features that I talk about in the book are subject to change, so you may not see every feature that I mention and some of the features may have changed since the time of this writing.

Web Resource   There are a number of places to download the Platform SDK. However, one of the easiest places to get it is the Microsoft Platform SDK site at `http://msdn.microsoft.com/downloads/sdks/platform/platform.asp`. This site allows you to download just the Setup program. After you decide which Platform SDK elements you want to install, the Setup program will download them from the Internet for you. If you prefer the Windows Installer (MSI) approach to application installation, use this site: `http://msdn.microsoft.com/downloads/sdks/platform/wininst.asp`. Those of you who want the entire SDK need to go to Microsoft's FTP site, which is currently `ftp://ftp.microsoft.com/developr/PlatformSDK/Jan2000/`. Be prepared for a very long wait if you choose more than just a few Platform SDK elements and you have a dial-up connection. A full download takes approximately 36 hours with a 56Kbps dial-up connection. You can also get the Platform SDK with an MSDN subscription, which is probably the easiest method if you don't have a high-speed Internet connection.

One of the benefits of downloading the Platform SDK is that you get new tools to use and updated versions of old ones. Microsoft's goal is to make Windows 2000 application development as easy as possible. Microsoft wants developers to provide Windows 2000-specific answers to user needs, especially when it comes to the capabilities provided by technologies like COM+ and Active Directory. The following sections explore updates to existing tools and some of the new tools that you'll find in the Platform SDK. The new Platform SDK contains two kinds of tools: general tools and database-specific tools. The general tools are used for all application programs, regardless of type, while the database-specific tools are designed to make enterprise database application development easier.

Same Visual Studio tools, different names

Microsoft has a habit of renaming utilities. Sometimes the utilities have changed, sometimes they haven't. In some cases, even a small change in marketing orientation will prompt a change in the name of a utility. For example, OLE View has gone through several name changes in the past few years. It seems that it has a different name with every release of Visual Studio or the Platform SDK. In short, there are times when you'll be unable to find a tool, only to find it under a different name later. For this reason, it's a good idea to check out every tool in the Platform SDK, just to make sure you know which tools are actually present.

The Platform SDK ships with a fairly full toolbox of utilities that you can use to craft applications. In most cases, you should use the Platform SDK tools instead of the tools provided with Visual Studio because the Platform SDK tools could have features that make development under Windows 2000 easier. Of course, this begs the question: What tools appear in Visual Studio versus the Platform SDK? Table 3-1 provides a complete list of the tools in both packages. Table 3-1 also shows any name changes that you'll encounter when working with Visual Studio tools versus the Platform SDK. Tools that Visual Studio provides that don't appear in the Platform SDK appear with an N/A in the Platform SDK Tool column. Likewise, new Platform SDK tools that don't appear in Visual Studio appear with an N/A in the Visual Studio Tool column.

Note   Table 3-1 doesn't contain a list of the special tools found in Visual Studio Enterprise Edition. You won't find these specialty tools in the Platform SDK for the most part. All that this table compares is the contents of the Tools folders for each product. The Platform SDK also includes additional tools not found in Visual Studio, especially when it comes to database management. I discuss many of these additional Platform SDK tools in the sections that follow.

Table 3-1
Visual Studio versus January 2000 Platform SDK Tool Comparison

Visual Studio Tool	Platform SDK Tool	New in Platform SDK?
ActiveX Control Test Container	N/A	N/A
API Text Viewer	N/A	N/A
DataObject Viewer	DataObject Viewer	No
DDE Spy	DDE Spy	No
Depends	Depends	Yes
DocFile Viewer	DocFile Viewer	Version numbers are equal, file date is newer
Error Lookup	N/A	N/A

Continued

Table 3-1 *(continued)*

Visual Studio Tool	Platform SDK Tool	New in Platform SDK?
Help Workshop	Help Workshop	Version numbers are equal, file date is newer
OLE Client Test	N/A	N/A
OLE Server Test	N/A	N/A
OLEView	OLE-COM Object Viewer	Yes
Package & Deployment Wizard	N/A	N/A
Process Viewer	PView	No
ROT Viewer	ROT Viewer	No
Spy++	N/A	N/A
Tracer	N/A	N/A
Windiff	Windiff	No
Zoomin	Zoomin	No
N/A	ADSI Viewer	N/A
N/A	CPU Stress	N/A
N/A	DBMon	N/A
N/A	Dialog Editor	N/A
N/A	HTML Help Workshop	N/A
N/A	Image Editor	N/A
N/A	Shell Walk	N/A
N/A	Spy	N/A

General tools

General tools are the ones that you use every day to write any application that your company may require. General tools are used to perform a variety of tasks that involve everything from checking application memory usage to verifying that the application will work in memory-starved environments. In short, general tools are the screwdrivers and hammers of the programming world. We've already touched on many of the general tools found in the Platform SDK as part of our Visual Studio discussion. There are a few special tools that you need to know about that are discussed in the paragraphs that follow.

This chapter doesn't cover the HTML Help Workshop application. I discuss that application as part of Chapter 14. You also won't find any coverage of Spy in this chapter because that utility doesn't provide the same level of features as Spy++. Always use Spy++ in lieu of the Spy utility supplied in the Platform SDK. Finally, because the Visual Basic IDE provides everything you'd ever need in a dialog editor, I don't look at the Dialog Editor utility in this chapter.

ADSI Viewer

Active Directory Services is a new Windows 2000 feature that promises to change the way that developers do a lot of things. Essentially, Active Directory is an extremely complex database that gets replicated across the network. It contains a variety of information like user settings, computer configuration data, the operating system setup, and information about security. In short, this is the central configuration database for the entire Windows 2000 network. As such, you'll find good reason to work with Active Directory Services, which means that you have to be at least a little familiar with how this product works.

This section shows you how the ADSI Viewer works. It assumes that you're using Windows 2000. The ADSI Viewer won't run under other versions of Windows until you install the ADSI client service. You can download the ADSI client service at http://www.microsoft.com/ntserver/nts/downloads/other/ADSI25/default.asp.

The Active Directory Services Interface (ADSI) Viewer allows you to see the schema for Active Directory. The schema is what controls the structure of the database. Knowing the schema allows you to work with Active Directory, change its contents, and even add new schema elements. To control the kinds of data stored for the applications you create, you must know the Active Directory schema. Otherwise, you could damage the database (given sufficient rights) or at least prevent your application from working correctly.

When you first start ADSI Viewer, a New dialog box like the one shown in Figure 3-27 displays. This dialog allows you to choose between browsing the current objects in the database or making a specific query. You'll use the browse mode when performing research on Active Directory schema structure or when you're not absolutely certain about what you're looking for. The query approach provides more precise information a lot faster when you already know what you need to find.

Figure 3-27: The ADSI Viewer asks whether you want to ask for specific information or browse through Active Directory.

In most cases, you'll begin your work with Active Directory by browsing through it. This means that you'll select ObjectViewer at the New dialog box shown in Figure 3-27. After you do that, you'll see a New Object dialog box like the one shown in Figure 3-28. This dialog box is already filled out to provide you with some sample entries. You'll need to supply Active Directory path information, which usually means typing **LDAP://** followed by the name of your server (WinServer in my case). If you're using Windows 2000 to access Active Directory, then uncheck the Use OpenObject option.

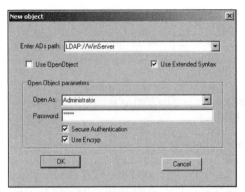

Figure 3-28: The New Object dialog box allows you to make a connection to the server.

After you've filled in the required information in the New Object dialog box, click OK. If you've entered all of the right information and have the proper rights to access Active Directory, then a dialog box like the one shown in Figure 3-29 displays.

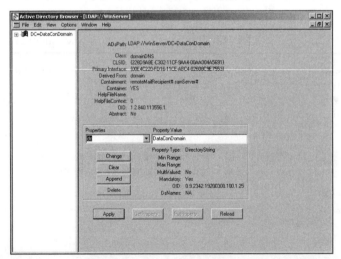

Figure 3-29: Opening a new object browser allows you to see the Active Directory schema for your server.

This is where you'll begin learning about Active Directory. On the left side of the display is a hierarchical list of database structure. Each of these elements is an object within Active Directory. Clicking the plus (+) signs next to any object shows the layers of objects beneath. Highlighting an object calls up detailed information about it in the right pane. For example, Figure 3-29 shows the details of the domain object for the server. The heading for this display includes object class information, help file location, and whether the object is a container used to hold other objects.

Below the header are the properties for the object. You can choose one of the properties from the Properties list box and see its value in the Property Value field. Active Directory is extensible, which means that you can add new properties to an existing object, change an existing property, or delete properties that you no longer need. If you want to add a new property, all you need to do is type its name in the Properties list box, assign it a value in the Property Value field, and click Append. This doesn't make the change final; you still need to click Apply at the bottom of the dialog box. Deleting a property is equally easy. Just select it in the Properties list box and click Delete. Clicking Apply makes the change final.

Leaf properties often have additional features that you can change. For example, the user object shown in Figure 3-30 allows you to change the user password and determine which groups the user belongs to. When working with a computer object, you'll be able to determine the computer's current status and even shut it down if you'd like (although this particular option isn't suggested unless you really do want to shut it down).

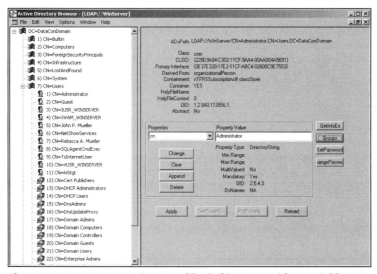

Figure 3-30: Some containers and leaf objects provide special buttons that allow you to perform tasks associated with them.

CPU Stress

The CPU Stress utility does just what its name implies — it places a load on a CPU to see how well it works in a given situation. Figure 3-31 shows the initial CPU Stress display. As you can see, the program is designed to create from one to four threads and specific priority levels. You can also choose how busy that thread should be during the testing process.

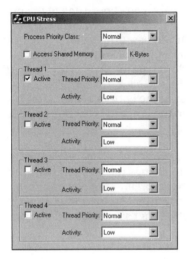

Figure 3-31: The CPU Stress utility tests a workstation's capability to handle a given load.

Other than set the number of threads, the thread and process priority, and the level of activity, you don't have to do anything else with the CPU Stress utility. This program is already doing the work you need it to do as soon as you start it. You can use this utility to measure the ability of your application to work with other applications on a single system. It is also handy for placing a load on your system so that you can simulate the performance characteristics of a less-capable system.

Image Editor

The Image Editor is a typical drawing tool. You could equate it to something like Paint because it has about the same drawing capabilities. However, that's where the similarity to other tools ends. Image Editor allows you to create new icons, cursors, and bitmaps. While Visual Basic allows you a great deal of flexibility in creating new dialog boxes, it doesn't allow you to create new resources, so a utility like Image Editor isn't just helpful, it's a necessity if you want to fully customize your application. Figure 3-32 shows the Image Editor with an icon loaded. While the tools won't vary with the kind of resource you create, the size and the format of the image will. The display you see may vary from the one shown here depending on what type of resource you decide to create.

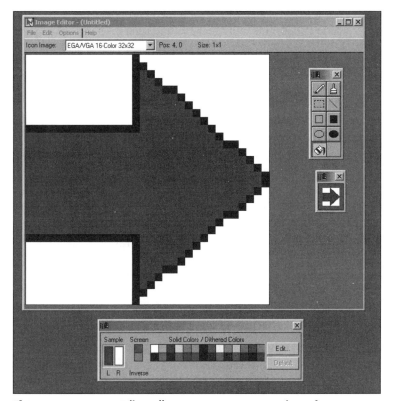

Figure 3-32: Image Editor allows you to create a variety of resources using common drawing tools.

Tip   Some of the other programming languages included with Visual Studio have the same resource-creation limitation as Visual Basic — lots of canned resources, but no tools to create custom resources. Visual C++ is an exception to this rule — you can use it to create custom resources, but it's hardly the right choice for generating them when using Visual Basic. Using Image Editor is the easiest way to create new resources that you can use in any of the programming language environments supported by Visual Studio. In fact, you'll find this limitation in just about any development product. As you can see, Image Editor is one of the utilities that you should always have loaded on your hard drive, no matter what type of application development you're performing.

Image Editor allows you to create three different kinds of resources: cursor, bitmap, and icon. Selecting the File ⇨ New command displays the Resource Type dialog box shown in Figure 3-33 that lets you choose the type of resource to create. After you select a resource type, you may see a second dialog box that allows you to choose the size and (optionally) color depth of the resource you'll create. Choose the settings you want to use for the resource, and then click OK on the second dialog box to create the initial resource.

Figure 3-33: The Resource Type dialog box allows you to choose the kind of resource to create.

ShellWalk

ShellWalk is a handy utility for finding bugs in namespace implementations. You can use it to walk through the namespace hierarchy and look for problems in applications that you create. The testing includes folder, item, PIDL (identifier list pointer), and COM-related checks, which means that ShellWalk will find most namespace-related problems. All data logging occurs through the LOR logging utility.

There are two ways to use ShellWalk. You can use the command-line method or directly interact with the application interface. The command-line parameters include \tp, which makes a single pass through the namespace hierarchy, and \stress, which allows the utility to pass through the namespace hierarchy infinitely. In most cases, you'll want to use the \tp command-line switch to make a single pass through the namespace hierarchy and log problems that the ShellWalk utility finds.

Figure 3-34 shows the ShellWalk utility. The left pane contains a hierarchical view of the namespace. The right pane contains the results for any tests that you run. Unlike the command line, the user interface allows you to select both multithreaded and single-threaded testing. There are also settings for the breadth and depth of testing. The testing depth affects just how deep in the hierarchy ShellWalk will look for errors. There are several test types. The Walk menu options allow you to walk the namespace starting at a specific point in the hierarchy, while the Test Pass menu options test the entire hierarchy. Note that you can't perform a leak test without a checked build of Windows 2000.

Before using ShellWalk for the first time, you need to make some configuration changes. There are two INI files in the ShellWalk directory. The first is MTShellWalk.INI. This file contains the location of the LOR logging DLLs. You need to change the two entries in this file to point to the ShellWalk directory on your hard drive, which, in most cases, is C:\Program Files\Microsoft Platform SDK\Bin\ShellWalk for the Platform SDK. The second is LorLogging.INI, which contains the logging settings. You need to set the log filename and logging path entries as a minimum. The other entries control which logs the LOR logging utility generates.

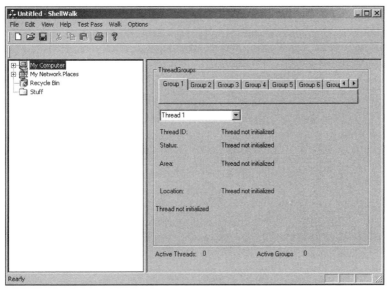

Figure 3-34: ShellWalk provides a method for looking for namespace errors in applications that you create.

Database-specific tools

Writing applications that manipulate the contents of databases can be one of the more complex forms of programming for any developer. The reason is simple. Databases are normally built on complex relationships, the application always has to assume multiple users, and the database management system (DBMS) itself can be akin to working with another operating system. In addition to the problems faced by a developer with the database application and associated DBMS, there's the problem of communication. A database application is one of the few application types where you can always assume a distributed environment. In short, a database application developer needs all the help he or she can get.

Any DBMS-specific tools that you require will be provided by the DBMS vendor, or not at all. However, there are some functions that the operating system will support independent of the DBMS. For example, OLE DB is an independent support option that allows a Visual Basic developer to access the features of a DBMS using common API functions. As a result, the Platform SDK does provide some tools that help the developer test his or her database application using these generic support features. The following paragraphs provide an overview of these generalized tools. Many of these tools reappear in other areas of the book when we perform specific tasks.

Local Test Manager

Local Test Manager allows a developer to perform conformance testing on a database provider using any of a number of languages. A database provider is used to create a buffer between the DBMS and the client application. For example, when you use OLE DB, a database provider translates the calls between your client application and the DBMS on the server. The DBMS sees your generic OLE DB API calls as specific commands to perform various types of work. The Local Test Manager only checks database-provider conformance — it won't perform tests like stress analysis or performance monitoring. Because you usually want to perform these tests, you'll probably want to look into third-party tools or those provided by the DBMS vendor.

Normally, you'd need to create your own test-suite DLL for Local Test Manager. However, the version of Local Test Manager that comes with the Platform SDK also includes a sample test-suite DLL that you can use. You need to load this test suite the first time you start Local Test Manager using the Tests ➪ Tests ➪ Add command. You'll see an Add Test Module dialog box (essentially the same as a File Open dialog box). Find the QuikTest.DLL file in the Platform SDK's Bin directory, and click Open. You'll see QuikTest added to the Default Suite entry as shown in Figure 3-35.

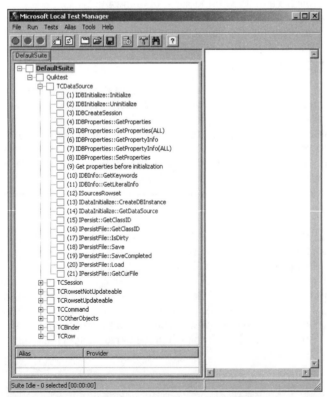

Figure 3-35: You need to select a suite of tests to run against the database provider.

You can expand the QuikTest entry to see which tests it will run. The tests are grouped into categories, then into individual tests. As shown in Figure 3-35, the test entries include an interface name and the method within that interface. What this means is that selecting a test will check the specified method within a given interface. For the purposes of this example, I've chosen to run the TCDataSource group of tests.

Selecting a group of tests is only the first step in the process. You also need to select a data source. Click the Create a New Alias button and you'll see an Alias for MSDASQL dialog box like the one shown in Figure 3-36.

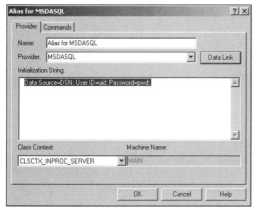

Figure 3-36: The Alias for MSDASQL dialog box is where you configure a provider to use for the test.

To perform a simple test, just choose a provider and create an initialization string. Click Data Link and the Data Link Properties dialog box shown in Figure 3-37 displays. The first step is to select a provider from the list on the Provider tab. Notice that one of the entries allows you to test the provider for Active Directory. I'll be using the Microsoft OLE DB Provider for SQL Server provider for this example.

Click Next and you'll see a list of connection items for the provider. To create a basic SQL Server connection, you need to choose a server, supply some type of username and password (or use Windows 2000 integrated security), and select a database from the list of databases available on the server. I chose to use the Northwind sample database that comes with SQL Server for demonstration purposes, but you can use any database. Click Test Connection to ensure that you actually have a connection to the server, and then click OK. Be sure to select the correct provider in the Alias for MSDASQL dialog box. In this case, I'll use the SQLOLEDB provider. Click OK to close the Alias for MSDASQL dialog box.

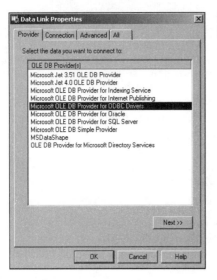

Figure 3-37: You need to select a provider for the database connection.

At this point, you can run a test on the provider of your choice. Make sure that you check both a provider to test and a series of tests to run. Click the Execute Selected Tests button. If the test is successful, all of the checked items will turn green. You'll also see a report similar to the one shown in Figure 3-38.

Figure 3-38: Output from the successful completion of tests on an OLE-DB provider for SQL Server.

ODBC Test

You'll use Open Database Connectivity (ODBC) Test to check the compatibility and functionality of the ODBC drivers and ODBC Driver Manager on a machine. For example, you could check the driver's capability to make a connection to a particular server and obtain data from the DBMS installed on it. This utility checks network connections, DBMS configuration, and other factors as much as it tests the capability of the driver itself. The four different areas of testing or test configuration that you can perform using this utility are:

✦ **Functions:** A single ODBC command. This level of testing is good when you want to check the compatibility of the driver. It allows you to check the availability of individual features.

✦ **Function Tools:** One or more commands work together to complete a given database task. For example, a full connect will test all of the commands required to create a connection to a particular data source. This level of testing allows you to check the capability of all of the database elements to work together to produce a predefined result.

Note ODBC Test allows you to perform tests using ODBC 2.*x* or ODBC 3.0 commands. You can adjust the ODBC Test menus so that they reflect the kind of testing that you want to perform using the options on the ODBC Menu Version tab of the User Options dialog box. Use the Tools ➪ Options command to display the User Options dialog box.

✦ **Tools:** Configuration options within ODBC Test. These options allow you to change application parameters like the level of error reporting to use or whether ODBC Test automatically disables menu options that a particular driver doesn't support.

✦ **Auto Tests:** As with the Local Test Manager utility discussed earlier, you can create a DLL for ODBC Test that will allow automated testing of the ODBC drivers and ODBC Driver Manager on a machine.

Getting started with ODBC Test is relatively easy. All you need to do is click the Full Connect button on the toolbar or use the Conn ➪ Full Connect command to display the Full Connect dialog box shown in Figure 3-39. You can highlight one of the existing data sources, or leave the Data Source field blank, and then click OK. If the Data Source field is blank, you'll be required to create a new Data Source Name (DSN) using the standard ODBC connection techniques (we'll discuss these techniques later in the programming sections of this book). After ODBC Test successfully creates a connection, a display similar to the one shown in Figure 3-40 appears.

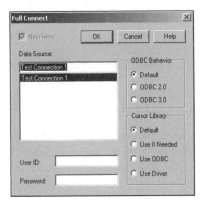

Figure 3-39: The first step in starting a test procedure is to create a connection.

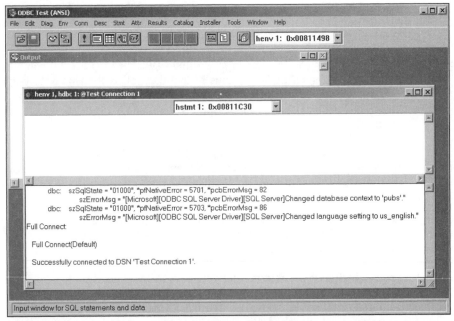

Figure 3-40: ODBC Test generates an output window after it successfully connects to your test database.

After a connection is in place, you can begin working with the database driver. This includes using all of the predefined commands in the various ODBC Test menus, as well as entering SQL statements in the upper half of the result window shown in Figure 3-40.

Tip   The Platform SDK provides both ANSI and Unicode forms for the ODBC Test utility. Make sure you use the right utility for the type of work that you're doing. ANSI and Unicode support usually appear in separate drivers, which means that any testing you do for one won't necessarily reflect the capabilities in the other.

In most cases, you'll combine a set of SQL statements and menu commands. For example, I opened the Northwind database for this example, and then executed a simple SQL statement that selected all of the columns from the Employees table. (Just typing the SQL statement isn't enough; you need to click the Execute button, which appears as a button with an exclamation mark on the toolbar.) After this, I used the Results ⇨ Describe Col All command to display a list of the columns from the Employees table. Figure 3-41 shows the result.

Figure 3-41: Working with ODBC Test often means combining SQL statements with menu commands to achieve a specific result.

As you can see, ODBC Test could double as an SQL statement tester in addition to a utility designed to check driver compatibility. Because Visual Basic has extensive database resources built in, you won't normally need to use this utility while working with Visual Basic directly. However, it can be handy for other purposes.

The last step of every testing session is to clear all of your database connections. The reason is simple. If you don't clear the connections before you exit the program, there's a chance that some resources won't be cleared. As a result, continued testing could result in a large memory leak or other system problems. Just use the Conn ➪ Full Disconnect command to disconnect from a database session. The window shown in Figure 3-40 will disappear, indicating that the connection was cleared.

Rowset Viewer

The Rowset Viewer is yet another utility that allows you to work with a remote database from your local workstation. It's more of a minidesign utility than anything we've looked at so far. In fact, you'll find that this utility provides just about everything that you need to perform any kind of database design work.

To use Rowset Viewer, you begin just as if you were using any of the other utilities that we've discussed. You need to create a connection to the data source. However, there are a multitude of connection types available for Rowset Viewer. For example, you can choose to enumerate the provider root to determine which providers are available. The resulting table will provide you with the GUIDs of the various providers installed on the current machine, along with other information you can use to research the capabilities of a particular setup better. You can also work with the root binder and with service components. However, we're going to look at data links in this section, just as we have in other sections of the chapter.

To create a data link connection, begin with the File ➪ Data Links command. This command displays a Data Link Properties dialog box like that shown in Figure 3-37. As before, you can select the provider that you want, and then fill out the required connection information. I'll use the Microsoft OLE DB Provider for SQL Server in this section of the chapter and the Northwind database as before. If the connection succeeds, then you'll see a command window where you can enter SQL statements and perform other tests on your database. In most cases, a SQL statement will generate a rowset that you can use for working with the data in the selected table. Figure 3-42 is an example of the Employees table in this utility.

At this point, you wonder what makes this utility so important. The Rowset Viewer allows you to add or remove data from the table shown in Figure 3-42, but that's not where the real power of this utility lies. Click the Get Schema Rowset button on the toolbar and you'll generate a list of every table in the database. You can add new tables to the database using this table as a starting point. In fact, you can generate a rowset for any database element and use the resulting rowset to manage that element. Double-click any row in a rowset to see a details table that allows you to change the data in that row. Just click Set Data to make any changes permanent.

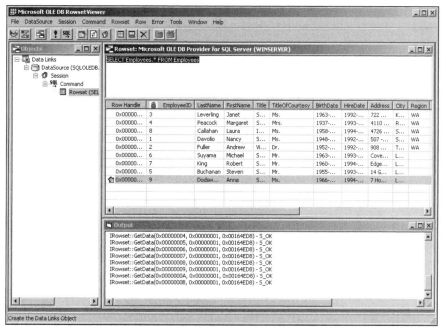

Figure 3-42: Rowset Viewer allows you to manipulate the data in tables or entire databases.

We haven't even begun to look at the menu options. The Data Source, Session, Command, Rowset, and Row menus across the top of the utility contain a list of interfaces associated with that part of the database connection hierarchy. The interfaces are enabled when you highlight an object that they pertain to. Under each interface option is a list of methods associated with that interface. You can use these methods to interact with the database, tables, rows, and associated data. What this means is that you can test coding ideas in real-time using this utility. Because you know the interface and associated method, you can transfer what you learn right to the application code. The result of any command that you issue using the menus will appear in the Output window, along with errors generated by the use of the methods when required.

Table Copy

Have you ever wanted to test a new procedure, but didn't want to do it on an existing table? Table Copy allows you to create a precise copy of a table (or any subset that you might need for testing purposes). Using a copy of the table allows you to test a new procedure using live data, but without the hazards of damaging that data.

As with every other utility in this section, you begin using Table Copy by creating a connection to the data source. After a connection is established, you can create a copy of any of the tables within the selected database. The following procedure shows you how.

1. Highlight a table within the database. The rows for that table will appear in the right pane of the Table Copy utility as shown in Figure 3-43.

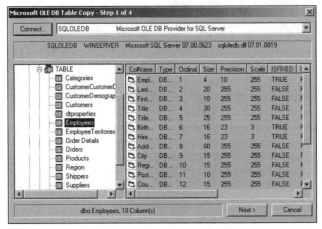

Figure 3-43: Select a table to copy as the first step of the copying process.

2. Highlight the columns that you want to copy to a new table. Table Copy doesn't force you to make a precise replica of the original table, which is handy when you only need to test a procedure on a subset of the data.

3. Click Next. You'll see a list of indexes associated with the current table, as shown in Figure 3-44. Table Copy differentiates between primary keys and foreign keys. It also tells you about any index settings that you need to know about in order to make a decision.

4. Select one or more of the indexes to add to the copy of the table.

5. Click Next. Table Copy will ask you to provide a destination for the new table as shown in Figure 3-45. You'll need to create another connection if you want to copy the table to another database; otherwise, you'll need to supply a new table name for the copy.

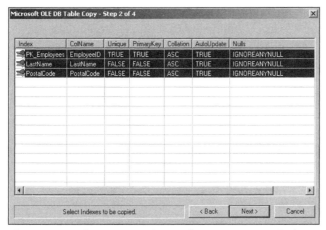

Figure 3-44: The next step is to select one or more indexes to include with the new copy of the table.

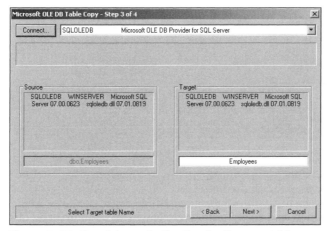

Figure 3-45: Supplying a destination for the new table may mean creating a connection to another database.

Tip

Table Copy doesn't restrict you from making connections to other kinds of databases. In other words, you could theoretically use Table Copy to move tables from one DBMS to another. There are situations when this won't work because the two databases have incompatible data formats and you'll experience some level of data loss during the transfer. It pays to check for incompatibilities before you use this utility, but Table Copy does offer one solution to a problem that plagues many developers.

6. Select another connection. Change the target table name if necessary. Make sure you provide either a unique connection or a unique table name (or both), or the data transfer will fail.

7. Click Next. An Options dialog box like the one shown in Figure 3-46 appears. This is where you choose the options that Table Copy will employ to make the transfer. For example, you can choose to include all data rows, or just some of the rows (enough data to perform the test).

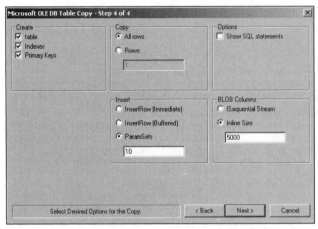

Figure 3-46: The last step in copying a table is to select the options that you want to use during the copying process.

8. Select options as needed to complete the table copying process.

9. Click Next. A final output dialog box that shows how the data from the source table will be mapped to the target table displays. Normally, this table shows an exact copy when you use the same DBMS for both source and target table. However, you'll want to check it carefully when the source and target DBMSs aren't the same. Because DBMSs rarely provide the same level of data-type support, you may find that some data is compromised as a result of data translation.

10. Click Finish if you're happy with the target data and format; otherwise, click Cancel. If you select Finish, then Table Copy will create the new table for you.

Working with Active Directory

For many network administrators, Active Directory is the reason to upgrade to Windows 2000. From a programmer's perspective, Active Directory represents a part of a larger whole in new features. You'll still find that you spend at least some time working with Active Directory, if for no other reason than it provides the means to store application settings on a global network basis.

The following sections aren't designed to tell you about every part of Active Directory, but they do tell you about the most important utilities designed to work with Active Directory at the administrator level. Make sure you couple the information you see here with the information in the ADSI View utility section of the chapter. These two areas go hand-in-hand as the application development project proceeds. Although ADSI View is great for programming issues, you still need the utilities in this section to check the final results from the network administrator perspective.

Sites and Services

The Sites and Services MMC snap-in gives you an overview of your domain. Microsoft uses the term Forest to refer to the collection of domain controllers that make up a network. Think of each domain controller on your network as a tree within the forest, with the oldest and largest tree (or the master tree) being the root domain within the forest. Figure 3-47 is an example of a forest with a single domain controller (or one tree).

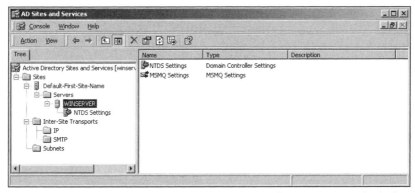

Figure 3-47: The Sites and Services MMC snap-in allows you to see both the forest and the trees.

Each domain controller can provide services to the network as a whole. I'm not talking about DNS or other types of services; I'm talking about services that affect Active Directory in some way. In the case of the sample network, the domain controller provides both MSMQ and Windows NT Directory Services (NTDS) support. (You'll see NTDS used in quite a few places, even though Microsoft has changed the name Windows NT to Windows 2000.) If you want a better (and fuller) view of the services offered by a particular domain, then right-click on the site icon (Default-First-Site-Name in this case) and choose the View ➪ Show Services Node option. Your display will change as shown in Figure 3-48.

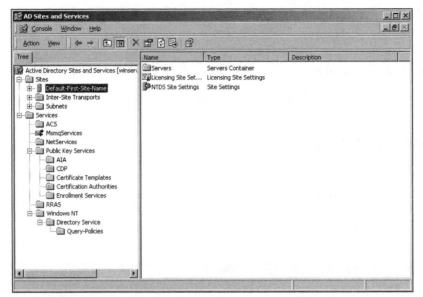

Figure 3-48: You can get a fuller view of the services offered by the currently selected domain by removing some of the filtering.

There aren't many settings that you'll need to worry about at this level of Active Directory. However, there are two things that you do need to be aware of. First, each of the objects shown in Figures 3-47 and 3-48 has some type of security attached to it. If you're running into a security problem with an application that you're developing, this is the front gate. You need to check security starting at this level if there isn't something obviously wrong with your application.

The second consideration is that this is one place where you can start adding policies to a network. For example, you'll find group policy settings associated with the site object on the Group Policy tab of the Default-First-Site-Name Properties dialog box (the name of your site will likely vary from mine — Default-First-Site-Name is the default name of the first site).

Active Directory can introduce some strange problems on large sites. Consider the problem of replication. When your application makes a change to the Active Directory settings on one domain controller, those settings don't automatically appear on every other domain controller on the network—they have to be replicated. Unfortunately, most network administrators are going to be unaware of the replication schedule maintained by the NTDS Site Settings object (this is the one that appears in the right pane when you click on the site icon in the left pane). If you look at the Site Settings tab on the NTDS Sites Settings Properties dialog, you'll see a Change Schedule button. Click this button to see the replication schedule for the site as shown in Figure 3-49.

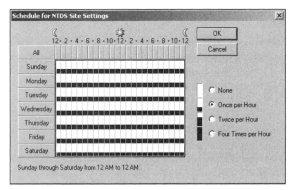

Figure 3-49: The data replication schedule for the domain is hidden in the NTDS Site Settings Properties dialog box.

Notice that the NTDS Site Settings currently replicate Active Directory once an hour, which may be just fine in many situations. However, you may find that some users do experience odd application problems if you make a change to Active Directory during the busiest time of the day. Given the amount of network traffic that occurs when users first log on to the network, a network administrator may make the replication time higher — meaning replication happens less often. While this will reduce network traffic and improve server performance, it's not going to do much for your application. The lesson here is to work with the network administrator to set a replication schedule that will work for your application and ensure that you make major Active Directory changes during the least busy time of the day.

Another odd setting that you'll find using the MMC snap-in is the lifetime of MSMQ messages on the network. You won't find this setting in the service icon that appears beneath the server; you need to show the services node first. You'll find MSMQ Services under the Services node as shown in Figure 3-48. Open the MSMQ Services Properties dialog box to find the message lifetime setting on the General tab. You can choose any lifetime from 1 second to 90 days (or more, if you wish).

There's one other setting that most developers are interested in, and it's in the Services folder. It's possible to get a bad Certificate Server installation or to configure it incorrectly. Unfortunately, there are a lot of application features in Windows 2000 that require certificates because Microsoft has strengthened its security a great deal. If you have any doubt about the viability of the Certificate Server installation, check the Certification Authorities folder. If this folder is blank, then Windows 2000 hasn't recognized any certification authorities on any server on the network — even if the Certificate Server is already installed. You'll need to check the Certificate Server installation and configuration to ensure that applications have access to the required certificates.

Users and Computers

The Users and Computers MMC snap-in is where network administrators spend a lot of their time. It allows the network administrator to manage users, computers, domain controllers, and other system resources. Figure 3-50 shows the Users folder for the Users and Computers MMC snap-in.

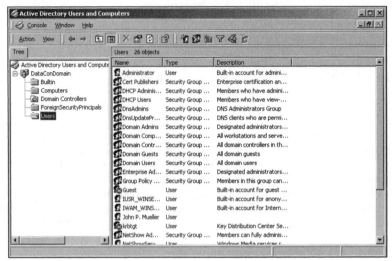

Figure 3-50: The Users folder contains a complete list of users and groups for the network.

Note   There are two MMC snap-ins used for managing users on a network. On a network without a domain controller, you'll use the Local Users and Groups folder found in the Computer Management MMC snap-in. This is the same snap-in that gets used on workstations. As soon as you make a server a domain controller, Windows 2000 automatically installs Active Directory. At this point, the Local Users and Groups folder becomes inactive, and you must use the Active Directory Users and Groups MMC snap-in.

There are some oddities in the way that Active Directory works when it comes to computers and users. For one thing, computers automatically register themselves when they join the domain, but a network administrator has to add users manually. Of course, the reason for this little difference is security—a computer joins the network based on the user's credentials.

Another little problem for the programmer is that Active Directory works fine as long as all the machines on the network are using Windows 2000. When a Windows 2000 machine joins the domain, it registers itself. Users of Windows 9x and Windows NT won't be registered. This means that even though the information in Active Directory is accurate—at least when it comes to the information that's automatically entered— you can't count on Active Directory to track every computer on the network.

Some of the problems that you'll encounter in this area are the result of diligence on the network administrator's part. For example, if everyone is registered properly, you could easily create an address book application that relies on Active Directory as a source of information. The problem is that the network administrator will very likely have other things on his or her mind and won't keep this information current. You could delegate the authority to enter the required data to someone else using the same application that displays the address-book information in the first place, but now you'll need to worry about potential security problems. Therefore, although Active Directory gives you a lot more to work with, you need to find people who are willing to do what it takes to get the information added to Active Directory.

There are two areas of concern, other than gathering information, for the developer in the Users and Computers MMC snap-in. The first is security. As with every other object that we've discussed, every user and computer object on the network has default security attached to it. You need to track changes to user and computer security when an application suddenly stops running because of a security problem.

The second area of concern is related to the Managed By tab of many object Properties dialog boxes in this snap-in. The Managed By tab tells you who's responsible for a particular object. You can use this information when you need to make changes to security or configuration. It also comes in handy for some application-handling requirements. For example, who's responsible for handling a COM-component error? Looking at Active Directory may yield answers that will help your component automatically direct error message information to the right person. Needless to say, this is yet another area in which you have to depend on someone else, likely the network administrator, to enter information to make things work.

Summary

This chapter acquainted you with the tools that you need to work with the examples in the remainder of the book. If you leave this chapter with any new knowledge, it should be that Visual Studio and the Platform SDK provide a wealth of tools that make application development easier. Here are some additional conclusions you can draw from the contents of this chapter:

✦ The ActiveX Control Test Container is designed to help you test your components before you use them in an application. The main reason to use this tool is to isolate the component from outside influences. Testing a component in this environment helps you detect hidden errors.

✦ Depends is a utility that every programmer should have in his or her toolkit. It allows you to trace the dependency between the files in an application or component. Tracing this information allows you to build better installation programs because you can include all of the important files on the installation disk.

✦ Visual Studio provides various OLE test utilities that allow you to check the performance of both applications and components in a lab-type environment. OLE View is very important because it allows you to see your component as Windows sees it, which can help with troubleshooting.

✦ Debugging complex applications means understanding how they appear when they run. Process Viewer can help you take apart any process as it's running to see how it looks to Windows. You can use Process Viewer to kill any errant processes or threads.

✦ Windows 2000 maintains a running object table that tracks the activities of the objects on the local machine. You can use the ROT Viewer to see the objects that your application creates. This information allows you to determine whether the application and the objects created from the components you design are working as anticipated.

✦ Process Viewer provides an overview of the way applications appear to Windows 2000. Spy++ is the utility to use for a detailed view of your applications. You can see both processes and threads, as well as visible elements like windows and components. Spy++ differs from Process Viewer in that you can't use Spy++ to kill errant threads or processes.

✦ It is tempting to think that the Platform SDK and Visual Studio provide the same set of tools. As Table 3-1 shows, they don't. In some cases, the tools in the Platform SDK are newer than the ones in Visual Studio. There are other situations in which either the Platform SDK or Visual Studio has a tool that doesn't appear in the other product.

✦ The ADSI Viewer is the most important add-on tool for the Platform SDK, because it allows you to see and manipulate the Active Directory schema.

✦ ShellWalk is a utility that allows you to test for errors in any namespace extensions you create. There are several levels of testing including the single pass (/tp) and multiple pass (/stress) command-line methods.

✦ The Local Test Manager and ODBC Test utilities share a common goal: enabling you to test the compatibility of your database manager drivers. The Local Test Manager provides the capability to perform very extensive automated testing, while ODBC Test is better suited to manual testing of a subset of driver features.

✦ Rowset Viewer has the potential to be your most-often used utility for performing complex database design tasks when the programming language you're using doesn't provide the right resources to do so. Even with the extensive capabilities that Visual Basic provides when working with database managers, you'll find that Rowset Viewer enables you to experiment at a lower level than does Visual Basic.

✦ There aren't many application designers who can say they don't run into a database conversion problem from time to time. As companies grow, they need larger and more capable DBMSs to manage their data, which means moving the data from one DBMS to another. Table Copy is a partial answer, at least to the problem of moving that data. While it can't perform a perfect data transfer every time, it comes very close.

✦ Active Directory is Microsoft's new strategy for storing system settings in a centralized storage place. You'll use utilities like ADSI View to get the programmer's view of Active Directory. However, you'll also need to look at things from the Network Administrator's perspective, which means using the Sites and Services and Users and Computers MMC snap-ins.

✦   ✦   ✦

COM+ in Theory

Starting with Components

✦ ✦ ✦ ✦

In This Chapter

Learning about the
benefits of using
COM and COM+
for application
development

Understanding the
various classes of
COM and COM+
development

Understanding the
role of interfaces
in component
development

Learning how contexts
allow single-threaded
components to handle
request-specific data

Learning how inter-
ceptors are used

✦ ✦ ✦ ✦

Component Object Model (COM) has caused more confusion since its inception than any other programming technology ever made. Many programmers feel like one of the blind
men trying to describe an elephant, and most of them don't
feel they do any better in figuring out what COM really is. That
Microsoft has made COM a moving object and keeps changing
the definition COM based on marketing needs doesn't help
matters much. For example, Microsoft tried to change all COM
technologies into some form of ActiveX as little as three years
ago, yet ActiveX is now described as simply an application
component technology—a part of a larger whole. Consequently, there's probably less work done with this very useful
technology than could be, and yet the results that programmers do get are nothing less than amazing. In other words,
COM is worth the effort to learn, but you probably won't
learn everything about it in a few days.

If you're just starting out with COM+, it might seem more confusing than COM. The fact of the matter is that Microsoft combined all of the diverse pieces of technology that made up
earlier versions of COM and packaged them as a combined
whole called COM+. Whether developers will find COM+ easier
to learn and use than COM remains to be seen. However, there's
no doubt that this new technology will definitely change how
you view distributed application programming.

This chapter provides an overview of COM and COM+ from
a theoretical perspective. The first section shows you what
COM is and what it can do for you in an application. We also
look at what COM+ can do for you and how it makes programming at least slightly easier than COM.

The second section discusses the various forms of COM and
what they mean to you as a programmer. For example, we'll
look at how DCOM differs from standard COM. It's important
to remember from our historical conversation in Chapter 1

that all of the versions of COM build on one another. In other words, a feature supported by an early form of COM like OLE is also likely to appear in some form in newer versions of COM like COM+ (unless the reason for adding the feature no longer exists).

In the third section, we look at one of the basics of COM, the interface. Briefly, an interface is a way to bundle related or complementary methods. Of course, it's a little more complicated than that. Interfaces are important for a number of reasons, all of which we explore.

One of the new concepts that COM+ introduces into the programming picture is the concept of the context. Context isn't hard to understand—it's a minienvironment that allows your component to know more about the application request that it's servicing. In fact, contexts aren't even new; they were used in Internet Server Application Programming Interface (ISAPI) Filters. However, COM+ contexts go much further than the earlier incarnation of context used in ISAPI. Many developers are very confused about this issue, so we'll look at contexts and what they mean to your application in the fourth section of this chapter.

COM+ also introduces the need for a new programming element known as the interceptor. Essentially, this is a proxy in disguise, but it has added functionality that's required for working in the distributed programming environment. We discuss interceptors and how they're used within COM+ in the fifth section of this chapter.

Note   While this chapter provides the information that you need to work with the examples in the next chapter, it's important to realize that a single chapter can't provide the kind of comprehensive information that has been the subject of entire books. There are many issues that this book doesn't discuss. If you don't have at least a passing familiarity with COM, you need to spend some time learning the basics to make sense of this chapter. We also don't spend any time discussing really advanced topics that are more issues of debate than of practical importance. In other words, this chapter discusses the practical issues that are specifically required for working with this book.

The Benefits of COM and COM+

In the beginning, there was spaghetti code and although the spaghetti code worked, no one could understand it. Then came an age of enlightenment when programmers learned about the usefulness of modular programming techniques. Although coding was still difficult, it was no longer impossible, and people other than the programmer could actually understand the code. Modular programming first gave programmers the opportunity to reuse code. If the programmer could write a function or procedure in a generic manner, then the function or procedure could also appear in another application, thereby easing the programmer's burden.

Next came libraries that allowed the programmer to place compiled and debugged code in a separate file to reduce the complexity of the application, making it even easier to understand. Linking a library to an application to perform generic tasks meant that the programmer didn't need to worry about the details of the function or procedure; only the calling syntax was required. Unfortunately, the programmer had to add the library to the application during the link cycle, which meant that updates to a library file also meant updating a lot of applications.

Finally, the dynamic link library (DLL) arrived on the scene, freeing the programmer from having to incorporate the code into the application. A DLL improves application development in a lot of ways. For one thing, updating a DLL doesn't necessarily mean updating the application because the DLL gets loaded separately from the application. In addition, DLLs use memory more efficiently because more than one application can access the code they contain — you only need one copy of the DLL in memory instead of the multiple copies that libraries required. However, DLLs still have problems because two applications might need two different versions of the same DLL to work properly, and there isn't an easy way to tell which version of the DLL was loaded into memory. Some developers have coined a term for this situation *DLL hell*, which means developers really don't know which version of the DLL to use because they require both applications.

Now we have COM, which incorporates every advance that has come before and makes it even easier to write bulletproof applications. (COM even includes version control, which makes it easier to detect which version of a component you're using and prevents certain errors.) COM provides the programmer with a lot of functionality. It incorporates the notion of code reuse and reduced memory consumption. Updating a COM application doesn't necessarily entail updating the applications that rely on the COM application. However, COM provides more than these simple benefits — features that we now take for granted. Other benefits that COM provides are:

✦ **Language Independence:** Depending on the programming language you use, a string might consist of a null-terminated array of characters or an array of characters where the first array element contains the number of characters that follow. This is just one example of how languages can differ. In the past, you had to use libraries that were developed for your programming language or convert your data and calling methodology to meet the library's expectations. COM allows you to create libraries of routines that don't rely on the language used to develop them.

✦ **Platform Independence:** Theoretically, COM allows you to move your application source code from platform to platform without any major recoding. Because the interface for COM is always the same, an application can use the same calls on every platform. COM automatically takes care of the hardware differences between platforms, effectively isolating the programmer from the hardware and reducing application complexity. Unfortunately, this is one area where much of COM's potential has yet to be realized.

✦ **Extensibility:** COM is an object-oriented programming (OOP) methodology, which means that it allows you to create a new object based on an existing object type. In other words, if there's a generic bit of code that does almost what you want, but not quite, you can create a new version of the code that incorporates all of the features that you need without rewriting everything from scratch. In addition, the original object can appear in a library, while the new object appears in your code.

✦ **Encapsulation:** There are actually two benefits to encapsulation. The first is protection. When using COM, you get access to the properties and methods that the original programmer wants to make public, but no more. This means that the objects that you create are less likely to fail or produce unexpected results — at least not if you use the object with the vendor's guidelines in mind (you'll learn later that nothing is perfect). The second encapsulation benefit deals with the interface. The interface defines how the client (the application using the component) and the server (the component itself) interact. As long as the interface doesn't change, the client and server will interact in the same way. This means that you can change the internals of a component to fix bugs or optimize performance without having to recompile the client (as long as you don't change the interface). The reverse is also true.

✦ **Locality:** Older applications relied on their resources being local to the executing machine. In addition, all of those resources had to reside in the same process as the application itself. COM allows a component to execute within the same process as the application it services, in a different process on the same machine, or even on a remote machine (given certain circumstances that we discuss as the chapter progresses).

Classes of COM and COM+ Applications

COM didn't happen overnight; it evolved over a period of years. Unfortunately, the older versions of COM didn't go away overnight either; they've stayed around in older applications and in new applications that don't require the full capabilities that a newer version of COM provides. What this means to you, as a programmer, is that you'll actually deal with several classes of COM. Each time Microsoft comes up with a new set of features, it adds them to the existing version of COM and comes up with an entirely different name. In essence, each COM class builds on the capabilities of its predecessor.

The following sections help you learn about the different classes of COM that you may run into as you develop applications. What you'll see is a history of how COM developed. You'll also get a better understanding of why some things are the way they are. For example, you might gain a new understanding of how some oddity got introduced into what appears to be an otherwise logical method of promoting code reuse and application modularity.

OLE

There are actually two versions of object linking and embedding (OLE) used within the various versions of Windows. The first version of OLE relies on dynamic data exchange (DDE), while the second version relies on a very early version of COM. You'll see why this distinction is important as the section progresses.

The Windows Registry maintains the entries for the two versions of OLE in completely separate sections. The OLE1 entries appear in the file association section of the HKEY_CLASSES_ROOT hive. One entry in the OLE1 section of the Registry, CLSID, does refer to OLE2 entry, thereby linking them. Figure 4-1 shows a typical OLE1 Registry entry. This entry relies on DDE scripting to accomplish the four tasks listed (New, Open, Print, and Print To). The script and script-specific information (the filename used in place of the %1 in the script) is passed to the application listed in the command key. An application making an OLE1 call to this document type uses the application entry in the server key, along with the other StdFileEditing subkey entries.

Figure 4-1: OLE1 Registry entries rely on DDE.

The OLE2 entries appear under the HKEY_CLASSES_ROOT\CLSID key as part of the class identifier entries. A CLSID is a 128-bit number that uniquely identifies the various components installed on a machine—no two components have the same class identifier. Programmers also know the CLSID keys as globally unique identifiers (GUIDs), and we use them as a method to identify the component instantiating a COM object. (More on this topic appears in the programming areas of this chapter and the chapters that follow.) Figure 4-2 shows a typical OLE2 Registry entry. This is the OLE2 GUID for the Word.Document.8 entry described in the previous paragraph. This entry relies on COM. In other words, OLE2 and COM are intrinsically linked.

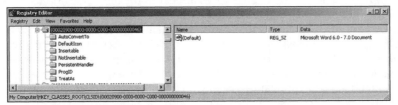

Figure 4-2: OLE2 Registry entries rely on COM.

Tip   There are several places where you might find the same GUID listed for one COM component in HKEY_CLASSES_ROOT. The first is obviously the OLE1 CLSID key shown in Figure 4-1. The second is the OLE2 CLSID entry shown in Figure 4-2. A third is within the AppID section of HKEY_CLASSES_ROOT. The AppID entries are used to identify quickly, in human-readable form, the application responsible for working with a particular file type. The fourth is within the TypeLib section of HKEY_CLASSES_ROOT. COM uses type libraries as a method of describing a component and its interfaces when a programming language (or COM-enabled application) uses this form of data exchange. Finally, you may find the GUID listed within subkeys of other GUIDs. For example, if the COM container supports more than one view (in the document/view architecture used by SDI and MDI applications), you'll see that the ancillary document formats make a reference to the GUID of the primary document. This reference links the various views together.

The following sections discuss the technical differences between OLE1 and OLE2, and why they're important to you as a programmer. Even though most programmers have forgotten that OLE1 and OLE2 ever existed, OLE1 and OLE2 still lurk under the covers of Windows 2000, and it's important to understand the roles they play in the development of COM+ applications. In addition, you'll see how OLE2 evolved naturally from OLE1 as part of Microsoft's learning process. Finally, you'll see why OLE2 was a significant start for Microsoft and how it led to the COM technologies that we use today.

This section of the chapter is an extension of the historical view of COM+ that we discussed in Chapter 1. The following sections of this chapter gloss over historical details in favor of more technical information. For an in-depth historical view, read the section entitled "A Historical View of COM+" in Chapter 1.

OLE1 and DDE

Let's talk about DDE for a moment. DDE used to be the way to transfer data between applications and make them work together (sort of). Then OLE arrived on the scene and made life easier, but COM is the way to go today. There are some significant problems with using DDE, such as that DDE creates a static link, much like the one you get using cut-and-paste. That it provides a stable macro language that you can use to open files and perform other fancy maneuvers from the command line doesn't change much.

DDE is a messaging protocol. It sends a message from one application to another and asks it to do something. Originally, DDE was supposed to provide the means to open another application and copy some data to the Clipboard. You could also get it to do other chores such as printing files.

A DDE macro contains part DDE and part application macro language. This is another problem with using it. Not only do you need to learn the native language of the application you're using and DDE itself, but you also have to learn the macro language for the server application. Needless to say, DDE didn't get the kind of reception that Microsoft originally hoped it would. DDE is simply too hard for the average user. Even programmers find it difficult to use (unless they use it on a regular basis).

Saying that DDE is completely gone might be going too far — it still exists because it does provide some useful services. In the case of Windows 2000, many applications still use DDE as a method for starting the application with the proper settings or for performing automated tasks like printing from the context menu without opening the document. Of course, these are user-related issues and not really a major concern for the application developer unless you plan to provide support for this type of automation within your application.

Like DDE, OLE1 entries still exist in the Registry because there are still some uses for the features that OLE1 provides. Today, no one uses OLE1 to develop applications, but it helps to understand how OLE1 is used in other places in Windows. For our purposes, both OLE1 and DDE support for Windows 2000 can be summarized in part by the Registry entries that you find. The Registry entries in HKEY_CLASSES_ROOT describe the full extent of DDE and OLE1 support that most application developers are concerned about. Table 4-1 talks about all the potential OLE1 entries that you might find. I don't think any application uses them all.

Table 4-1
OLE1 Entries in the Windows Registry

Key	Description
AppRegistry	This key's value points to the location of additional application configuration or installation data in either HKEY_CURRENT_USER or HKEY_LOCAL_MACHINE. You can use this value to find the main application configuration key. Depending on the application, you may find additional subkeys and associated values. This particular entry doesn't appear in older versions of Windows. It will help you to determine how to handle interactions with other applications, so it's an important addition to the OLE1 entry section of the Registry.
CLSID	This is actually part of the OLE2 and COM entry even though it appears in the OLE1 section. It's a pointer to an entry in the CLSID section of the hive. You can use this GUID to find additional information like the in-process server associated with the application and additional Registry entries like type libraries and application identifiers. We'll discuss OLE2 and COM entries in the next section of the chapter; just remember that this particular key is a pointer to other areas of the Registry that contain OLE2 and COM information.
DefaultIcon	A pointer to the location on disk of the default icon used for the application's files. This key's value contains a pointer for the file extension in question. Other file extensions can (and will) use other icons within the application for representation.
DocObject	The OLE DocObject technology allows Windows to perform tasks like in-place editing. This means that a document embedded within a foreign container (like an Excel spreadsheet within a Word document) can start an in-process server that will take over the host's IDE, including menus. Microsoft changed this technology's original name to Active Document, yet the Registry retains the original name.
Insertable	Normally, you won't see any value associated with this key. A blank value means that Windows can place this file association in the Insert Object (or equivalent) dialog provided by many applications, such as Microsoft Word. Some OLE1 objects aren't insertable for a variety of reasons. Many applications have moved this particular key to the OLE2 section of the Registry because other applications are more likely to look there for this information.
Protocol	This is a header key (think of it as a heading in a book, a means to group like information together in one place). Look again at Figure 4-1 and you'll see the hierarchical format of the keys beneath this one. Underneath this key you'll find all the standard actions that this OLE1 application can perform. In most cases, the only supported function is a standard file edit.

Key	Description
StdFileEditing	This key is another header. In this case, it's the heading for all the keys that will define a particular action — standard file editing.
Server	You'll find the name of the application that Windows will call to service any OLE1 calls for this file association. The string always includes the application's name, extension, and path.
Verb	Several verbs are associated with an OLE1 object. Each verb defines a specific action that the server will perform. This key doesn't have a value associated with it; its sole purpose is to organize actual verb entries. A client application can use only the verbs that are defined for a specific server.
-3 = Hide, 0, 1	This verb allows the client application to hide the server window. The first number following the verb is a menu flag. The second number is the verb flag.
-2 = Open, 0, 1	This verb allows the client to open the server in a separate window rather than allow it to take over the client window.
-1 = Show, 0, 1	A client would use this verb to display the server window in its preferred state. The whole idea of a state can get to be quite complex. Think of it as the way the window looks, and you'll have a pretty good idea of what to expect from a user's point of view.
0 = &Edit, 0, 2	Every server provides this verb. It allows the client to call the server to edit the object.
1 = &Play, 0, 3	The only time you'll see this verb is when you're looking at some form of multimedia object.
RequestDataFormats	This entry allows the server to define what data formats it supports for retrieval purposes.
SetDataFormats	This entry allows the server to define what data formats it supports for storage purposes.

OLE2 and COM

As previously stated, OLE2 doesn't rely on DDE with its static links and difficult macro language, it relies on COM. Using COM allows OLE2 to deal with documents as objects and makes it possible for client and server to improve independently of each other by maintaining the same interface. To give you a better idea of how this works, look at the DocFile Viewer display shown in Figure 4-3. This document contains three objects, a sound file, a graphic file, and a Microsoft Word document. As you can see, the effect of COM is real when it comes to working with OLE2.

Figure 4-3: COM is a very real part of OLE2, as shown by the objects in this document file.

Tip

The DocFile Viewer is found in both the Visual Studio and Platform SDK Tools folder. It allows you to analyze the composition of compound documents like those used by Word. It's also a handy way of looking at data stored by components that persist their data. You can combine the capabilities of the ActiveX Control Test Container and the DocFile Viewer to perform low-level analyses of your components. Even though the DocFile Viewer looks very simple, it's a valuable aid in analyzing the contents of compound documents of all types.

Note

We didn't cover the DocFile Viewer in Chapter 3 because you needed the registry information in this chapter to understand how this utility works. There are several test files in the Chapter 4 folder on the CD-ROM provided with this book. SampleComponent.TSG contains the output from the Multiple State Pushbutton Control that we worked with in Chapter 3. This file is viewable because we saved the settings to storage. On the other hand, the SampleComponent.TSM file can't be viewed because it uses a stream format. This example demonstrates that you must use a storage format when testing components using DocFile Viewer. SampleDoc.DOC contains a compound document that contains the other files in the Chapter 4 folder. Use both sample compound document files to test the capabilities of the DocFile Viewer.

It's because of the COM difference that OLE2, and not OLE1, is now used for most application links. (You'll still find both DDE and OLE1 in Windows in some form, but not as a major component.) However, not all of OLE2 is involved with current COM development efforts, but rather an important subset of features that's now referred to as Active Document. It's the DocObject portion of OLE2 that makes all the difference for today's application user, and this is the part of OLE2 that you'll see most often as you develop applications. Active Document is also the portion of OLE2 that you'll use within components that you create to allow them to work with foreign data types, including documents generated by applications. The following list provides an idea of all of the ways that using COM for OLE2 improved the situation.

✦ **Visual editing:** One problem with OLE1 was that the user's train of thought got disrupted each time the user needed to make a change to an object. The reason was simple: OLE1 was forced to use the DDE macro language to load the original application and display the object in the originating application's window for editing. OLE2 allows visual (in-place) editing because it uses COM, which supports both in-process and out-of-process servers. Instead of opening a new window, the server application merely overlays its toolbar, menu structure, and controls with those of the client. The user simply sees a change in tools, not a change in applications. As a result, the transition between documents is less noticeable.

✦ **Nested objects:** OLE1 allowed you to place one object at a time in the container document. An object couldn't become a container; all the objects existed as a single layer within the container. OLE2 treats every potential container as just that — a container. It doesn't matter how many containers you place inside a container or how many ways you stack them. To get a better idea of how nesting will help you, look at the way Windows versions (starting with Windows 2000) implement folders. You can treat OLE2 container objects the same way.

✦ **Drag and drop:** You used to cut or copy an object in the server application and then place it in the client by using the Paste Special command. This option still works. However, OLE2 provides a new method for creating links to other documents — drag and drop. You simply grab the object and move it wherever you want. It becomes linked to wherever you decide to drop it.

✦ **Storage-independent links:** OLE2 allows you to create links to other documents, even if they aren't physically located on the local drive. It implements this using an LRPC (lightweight remote procedure call) mechanism. Unfortunately, this linking mechanism has limitations. For example, you'll find that it works fine with some peer-to-peer networks, but it works only marginally with other network types. It is thought that the next revision of OLE will fix this problem by supporting RPCs (remote procedure calls).

✦ **Adaptable links:** If you moved any of the files required to create a compound document under OLE1, all the links were destroyed, and you had to re-create them. This older version stored the full path, including drive, to the linked data. OLE2 stores only enough path information to maintain the link. If you create links between two files in the same directory, you can move those two files anywhere on the drive without obliterating the link. The only criterion for maintaining a link under OLE2 is that the relative path remains the same.

✦ **OLE automation:** This particular feature is tied into Visual Basic for Applications (VBA), which is a subset of the Visual Basic programming language. VBA defines a standard interface for talking with the server application. This allows the client application to send commands to the server that will change the contents of an object indirectly. OLE automation is the direct descendent of the DDE macro language that many applications still use (with a COM twist, of course). The big difference from the user's perspective is that DDE macros were difficult to write and very prone to error. VBA is the native language of the application and is consistent across platforms.

✦ **Version management:** Have you ever received a document from someone only to find that part of it wouldn't work with your software? OLE2 can store the application name and version number as part of the link (they're stored as object properties). If an application developer implements this feature correctly, a server (or client, for that matter) will detect an old version of a file and ask whether you want to update it. This means that you'll never have an old file sitting around just waiting to make life difficult.

✦ **Object conversion:** Your friend uses Excel and you use Lotus 1-2-3, yet you need to share OLE documents containing spreadsheets. One of you could go through the inconvenience and expense of changing to the other's application and document format, but OLE2 can probably solve this problem without such a change. Object conversion allows Excel to act as a server for a compound document containing a Lotus 1-2-3 object. Just select the Convert option from the object menu. (Obviously, the application must support the data format before the Convert option will become available.)

✦ **Optimized object storage:** This feature allows the linked documents to stay on disk until needed. That way, Windows doesn't need to load every application and data file required to support the compound document. In most cases, Windows uses a buffer-zone technique. A word processor might keep the applications and objects required for the preceding, current, and next page in memory. The rest of the objects stay on disk, which, in some cases, greatly reduces the memory footprint of a compound document.

As with OLE1, the way that OLE2 is used in the system is determined by the Registry entries created by the applications and components that use it. However, unlike with OLE1, the entries contained in HKEY_CLASSES_ROOT are only the beginning for the COM implementation. Component entries, usually identified by GUIDs, appear throughout the Registry. We'll concentrate on the HKEY_CLASSES_ROOT entries for now because these entries are common for most applications and components. Table 4-2 describes these Registry entries in detail. An application doesn't necessarily need to provide every entry that is described in Table 4-2 in the Registry; components are even more selective than applications are. Application-oriented entries depend on what OLE2 features the application vendor decided to support, whereas component entries are dependent on the application types they're designed to work with. You can use these Registry entries to determine the capabilities of your application, just as you can with OLE1.

Table 4-2
OLE2 Entries in the Windows Registry

Key	Description
AuxUserType	This key is a heading for all of the user type keys that follow.
2	The 2 AuxUserType always contains the short name for the application. A client can use this name in a list box to identify the object's owner.
3	This key contains the full name of the application that created the object. Like the 2 key, the 3 key value can be used to provide an English application name for the object.
DataFormats	This key is a heading for all the data format keys that follow.
GetSet	This key is a subheading for all the data formats the server can store and retrieve. For example, an OLE server like Microsoft Word would support a DOC, RTF, and standard text format. Its OLE2 entries would reflect this fact. Each entry below this one defines a specific format type.
n = format, aspect, medium, flag	Each of the sequentially numbered keys contains a different format. Format contains the type of format as a string. You might find some as easy to read here as "Rich Text Format" or as cryptic as "Embed_ Source". In every case, this string tells you the name of the format that the application supports. The client displays this string (for get formats) in the dialog box where you select the format that you want to use when performing a Paste Special command. Aspect tells the client what display orientation the object supports. This usually means portrait and/or landscape. You'll usually find a value of 1 here for portrait. Medium contains the supported format as a computer-readable number. Flag tells the client whether this is a get, set, or both format—a value of 1 is get, a value of 2 is set, and a value of 3 is both.
DefaultFile	This entry works much like GetSet, but it identifies the default file format for this particular object.
DefaultIcon	The value of this key tells the client which application icon to use when displaying the object as an icon.
InProcHandler	This key contains the name of the in-process handler. In most cases, this is OLE2.DLL for applications unless the application provides its own OLE2 handler. (A handler is a special program that helps two programs communicate.) You'll find that components can use any number of in-process handlers, including OLE2.DLL (the in-process handler we'll use for all of the components in this book).

Continued

Table 4-2 *(continued)*

Key	Description
Insertable	Normally, you won't see any value associated with this key. A blank value means that Windows can place this file association in the Insert Object (or equivalent) dialog provided by many applications such as Word for Windows. Some OLE1 objects aren't insertable for a variety of reasons, but most OLE2 objects are insertable by definition.
LocalServer	Every OLE2 object must have a server. This key contains the name of the server on the local machine. Because OLE2 doesn't support RPCs, you'll always need a local server. The same can't be said for components. An application or component can access another component through DCOM using an RPC, which means that the component could appear on another machine. We'll talk about the ramifications of this difference in Chapter 5.
MiscStatus	This key contains the default value for all data format aspects.
ProgID	The program identifier is a pointer back to the file association that this class identifier belongs to. The file association is always a character string of some sort. It's the same string that you look for when you try to find the file association that goes with a file extension in the HKEY_CLASSES_ROOT category.
Verb	Several verbs are associated with an OLE2 object. Each verb defines a specific action that the server will perform. This key doesn't have a value associated with it; its sole purpose is to organize actual verb entries. A client application can use only the verbs that are defined for a specific server. See Table 4-1 for a list of verbs and their meanings.
InProcServer	An in-process server is a component instantiated within the client's process. This has the advantage of enhancing performance (because there aren't any process boundaries to cross) and reducing the memory required to load the component (because there isn't any proxy or stub required). However, it also has the disadvantage of reducing application reliability (because a flawed component can crash the entire application). Some applications will use this approach to handle embedded objects because it makes the handler much faster. All that the host application has to do is call on an in-process server that handles the data processing details. A component can either be an in-process or out-of-process server depending on the way you code it. Normally, in-process servers have a DLL extension, while out-of-process servers have an EXE extension.

Key	Description
TreatAs	When this key is present, it contains the CLSID for another file format. The client can treat the current file format as it would the specified file format. For example, if you looked at the Paintbrush Picture OLE2 entry, you'd find a TreatAs value with the same 128-digit value as a Bitmap Image. This tells you that Windows 2000 uses the same application to service Paintbrush Picture files as it does for Bitmap Image files. A little more research would tell you that the OLE2 server for Paintbrush Pictures is Microsoft Paint.
AutoTreatAs	This key forces the client to treat the current file format the same way it would treat the file format specified by the CLSID. From a user perspective, it works just like the TreatAs entry described previously.
AutoConvert	Some objects' context menus contain a Convert option. This key allows you to convert automatically the current file format to the one identified by CLSID. For example, Microsoft Word allows you to convert many types of data to a format that it specifically supports. This conversion process changes the embedded or linked object into a Word object. In other words, it changes the data into something that Word might have created itself.
Convertible	There are two levels of subkeys below this one. The first level contains two keys, Readable and Writeable. Below them are keys that contain a list of readable or writeable file formats that you can convert this file format to. For example, you'll find that Word supports several formats including Word Document. The number of entries in this area usually varies by the number of file filters you install for the application. For example, if you install WordPerfect file support for Microsoft Word, then you'll likely find an entry for it here. Remember, though, that these are OLE2 entries. Even if an application supports another application's file format as part of a Save As option, it might not support it for OLE purposes.

OLE Support File Requirements

There's a whole group of files in either the \SYSTEM or \SYSTEM32 folder that provide support for OLE2. A programmer seldom needs to know about these files unless there is a corrupt file or a need to check on the version of OLE being used. The following list provides some details of the tasks each file performs. You can use this list if you ever run into a problem with corruption or if you'd simply like to know what level of support you can expect from a certain application. The presence or absence of these files might also indicate problems with your installation.

Continued

Continued

✦ **OLE2.DLL:** This DLL provides some "foundation" functions. It's the first DLL to be called when any type of OLE2 call is made by an application. (This is the 16-bit version of the file — we'll discuss 32-bit version files later in the list.)

✦ **OLECLI.DLL:** This file contains all the basic client code your application needs to implement OLE2 client calls. Your application uses this file as a base for building its own client features.

✦ **OLESRV.DLL:** This file contains all the basic server code your application needs to implement OLE2 server calls. Like the client code, this DLL won't provide everything. Your application uses it as a basis for building its own set of features.

✦ **OLE2CONV.DLL:** This file provides the generic routines a program needs to convert an object to the client program's native format.

✦ **OLE2DISP.DLL:** Every OLE client application uses this program to help it display the objects it contains.

✦ **OLE2NLS.DLL:** Most versions of Windows provide National Language Support (NLS). This program helps OLE keep pace with the rest of Windows in providing support for other languages.

✦ **OLE2.REG:** You can import this Registry file into your Registry to install OLE2 support. In most cases, your application will do this automatically, so you don't need to worry about it. The only time you need to use it is when you can't get OLE2 to work and you discover that the Registry doesn't contain the correct entries.

✦ **MCIOLE.DLL:** Sounds and other multimedia objects require special handling under Windows. Unlike most objects, you don't display a sound, so the normal handling won't work. Other multimedia objects require special supports in addition to displaying an image. This special DLL provides the support that an application needs to handle a sound or other multimedia object.

✦ **OLE32.DLL:** A whole group of OLE files in the \SYSTEM or \SYSTEM32 directory have a 32 somewhere in their names. These files provide the same services to 32-bit applications as their 16-bit counterparts. OLE32.DLL is the main 32-bit OLE2 DLL. You'll also find other 32-bit files that contain 32-bit support for all of the other OLE features in this list.

✦ **MFCOLEUI.DLL:** This file (and any with similar names) provides the Microsoft Foundation Classes (MFC) support interface to OLE. Normally, this file is used only by C++ programmers.

COM

In the previous section, we talked about how OLE2 relies on COM. We looked at how using COM as a basis, rather than DDE, made OLE2 a much better product than OLE1. OLE2 is actually a specific implementation of COM; it's not the whole picture. COM is also used as the basis for controls, compound documents, automation, data transfer, storage, and naming. There isn't one area of Windows computing that isn't tied into COM in some way, which makes this an important technology to know about.

The one thing that you need to understand is that COM is actually a specification — a documented method for dealing with the interaction between clients and servers. COM isn't a language, a set of APIs, or anything of a physical nature; it's simply one of several ways to create connections using a known technology. Some people use the term *programming model* to refer to what COM represents. In other words, COM tells you what needs to happen, not necessarily how to do it. COM represents a programming methodology, not an actual programming implementation. As such, many details are left to the implementers rather than defined as part of the specification itself.

Over the past few years, Microsoft has introduced a plethora of new OLE-related technologies like ActiveX, DCOM, and COM+. Trying to keep up with these technologies could prove daunting for even the best programmer. Not only is Microsoft constantly evolving COM, but there are also new technologies and developments within those technologies to learn about. The general page for all of Microsoft's current COM technologies appears at `http://www.microsoft.com/com/default.asp`.

COM is a Microsoft-specific extension of OOP techniques. As such, the central idea of COM is the object, which is a programming method that attempts to model applications after the real world. Objects have the following components (at least when referred to with respect to COM):

✦ **Methods:** Things you can do with the object. A method allows you to perform a specific task with the object. It may rely on the values of any properties that the object exposes and may require you to provide values as input.

✦ **Properties:** Specifications that determine what the object looks like and how it interacts with the user. A property is a value that affects the internal operation of the object and determines what it will do when that application calls any associated methods.

✦ **Events:** An object-specific occurrence that alerts the application to respond to a user or internal action. Examples of user actions include mouse clicks and key presses. Internal actions cover a lot of territory but are normally associated with some type of status- or error-reporting need.

✦ **Interfaces:** A convenient grouping of methods and properties. Gaining access to an interface allows you to use the methods and properties that it contains.

✦ **Connection Points:** The physical link between the server and the client that allows the object to signal an event.

Overall, the purpose of COM is to hide the underlying complexity of a programming task and allow the user of the object to deal with the task at a higher level of abstraction. For example, a programmer may not care how a string is created or manipulated internally, but will care about how the string appears externally. That a string object allows you to make all of the characters uppercase is important; how the object performs this transition isn't. In other words, COM is a results-oriented programming methodology where the client doesn't care how the server performs a task, and the server doesn't care what the client does with the results.

Objects are also easier to work with than a library because an object is a cohesive whole that includes both code and data in a single package. When you create a COM object, you don't need to specify the internal arrangement of that object, create variables that get used internally within the object, or worry about things like the programming language used by the object designer. All you need to know is that the object has a certain method and that calling the method produces a certain result given certain property values and method arguments as input.

Microsoft set specific goals for COM. These goals allow COM to provide the level of services that Windows requires without exacting such a high performance penalty that the operating system runs too slowly. The following list tells you about these goals.

✦ **Binary compatibility:** Every COM object uses the same calling convention, which means that any client can call any object as long as they both use a standard COM interface. COM relies on double indirection. The client holds a pointer to a virtual table of object functions, which, in turn, point to the actual functions within the component object. Using a virtual table allows the server to interact with multiple clients at the same time. Even components use this methodology. One component will never call another component directly; the interface is used for all communication.

✦ **Strong typing:** If the return value of a function is ambiguous, then the client may not interpret the result correctly. Likewise, if the client provides input values of unknown type, the server may not be able to function properly. Strong typing ensures that clients and servers are both using the same basis to pass information.

✦ **Base interface:** A client may not know what services a server can provide. The use of a base interface allows the client to query the server and ask it what services it provides in the way of properties and methods. In addition, a query can determine the name of the server specific interface used to bundle these methods and properties. All COM components must support the IUnknown interface, and all clients call that interface to learn more about the component. We'll discuss the IUnknown interface in the "Working with Interfaces" section of this chapter.

✦ **Reference counting:** One or more clients could create more than one instance of a particular server. Reference counting allows the server object to keep track of how many instances of itself exist. When there aren't any more active instances, the server object can delete itself.

✦ **Unique identification:** Objects could exist on more than one machine, and object confusion would lead to unpredictable results from client requests. The GUID allows COM to identify every object using a unique 128-bit number. GUIDs actually conform to an Open Software Foundation standard called universally unique identifiers (UUID). This standard ensures that each GUID is unique, no matter its source.

✦ **Component loading:** Every component uses the same loader to load itself into memory. This component loader also tracks interactions with objects on other machines.

As you can see, COM represents a fundamental shift from procedural languages. When COM is combined with the Windows event-driven programming technique, the programmer is left with an environment that's easy to use. The user, in turn, is left with a responsive environment that should be able to react almost immediately to most inputs.

Now that you have a better idea of what COM has to offer, it's time to look at some COM implementation details with regard to application types. One of the easiest ways to categorize COM applications is into functional areas. We've already done that to a certain extent and will continue to define COM applications by function as the book progresses. However, there's another way to divide COM into application types: by sorting the ways in which the application is invoked. COM includes two kinds of component: an in-process server that gets invoked within the client application's process and an out-of-process server that gets invoked within a separate process. The following sections discuss these two application classifications in more detail.

In-process

Of the two component memory models, the one used by in-process servers is the easiest to understand and work with. A good example of an in-process server is an ActiveX component — you add it to your application using the development language's IDE. Most ActiveX components have some type of visual interface, and you set their properties using property pages that get exposed in a variety of ways depending on the development language's IDE.

In-process servers also include the DLLs used to display foreign data within an application. You'll find listings of these types of components within the file association entries in the Windows Registry (HKEY_CLASSES_ROOT is the main key for this type of data). The DLLs used for displaying various types of foreign data, on the other hand, are normally accessed directly from the code in your application. In short, in-process servers, for the most part, are part of the application you create from the very beginning of the design process.

A new category of in-process servers includes the Microsoft Management Console (MMC) snap-ins used in Windows 2000. MMC itself is simply a container used to hold the snap-ins. The snap-ins are DLLs that allow a network administrator to monitor and configure various elements within Windows 2000. In-process servers cover a broad range of application-specific categories, but not nearly the range covered by out-of-process servers (as you'll see in the next section).

Note   In-process servers are normally contained in DLL files — so some developers call them DLL servers. It's important to remember that, in this case, OCX files are essentially renamed DLL files. On the other hand, because out-of-process servers are normally stand-alone applications, they reside in EXE files and are called EXE servers by some developers.

When an application calls upon the services of an in-process server, the object that Windows creates resides within the application memory space. This means that the application has direct access to the object. It's easy to see how an in-process server and a container communicate. After all, they're in the same address space, which makes passing data back and forth relatively easy. All that the container needs is an address for the required interface and a list of methods to work with.

All in-process server calls are local. What this means, to the programmer, is that you don't need to take some potential out-of-process server problems into account. For example, your in-process server will never get disconnected because of a bad network connection. This makes the process of troubleshooting errant components much easier. On the other hand, the inability to use in-process servers from a remote location also reduces their flexibility — you're limited to using the resources on the local machine.

The capability to make local calls and use addresses between server and client makes in-process servers faster and easier to program than out-of-process servers. There are no address or data translations that need to take place. An in-process server represents the most efficient way to work with component technology, despite several limitations that we discuss in the next section of this chapter. The application programmer interacts with the object just like any other part of the program.

While it's important to understand that there are in-process servers from a COM perspective, we don't spend a lot of time working with them in this book. The main event for COM+ is the out-of-process server that we discuss in the following section. With that in mind, this chapter doesn't discuss in-process servers in much more detail except to look at the way they affect the operation of applications in general and their differences with out-of-process servers.

Out-of-process servers

Out-of-process servers come in a very wide variety of shapes and sizes. For example, any COM component that resides on a server, yet provides services to a workstation, is an out-of-process server. So, any component used with DCOM is an out-of-process server, as are those used for Microsoft Message Queue (MSMQ) and Microsoft

Transaction Server (MTS). In short, the most common use of out-of-process servers right now is within the realm of remote execution where an application makes use of resources on another machine.

Don't get the idea, however, that out-of process servers are limited to remote execution scenarios — this just represents the latest in a series of out-of-process server uses. Out-of-process servers are also used in a number of application scenarios in which data integrity and multiple threads of execution are both important considerations. For example, graphics libraries often use the out-of-process server approach. The library starts up in a separate process to ensure that its data remains secure.

Tip Some people find it easy to confuse an out-of-process server with an application that supports OLE. The first is a component, the second is a container. Components can't execute on their own; they need the services of a container. This is equally true whether the component is an in-process server or an out-of-process server.

An out-of-process server relies on a proxy/stub mechanism to accomplish its work. The proxy gets installed in the client's memory space. As far as the client is concerned, it's still talking with a local server. In reality, though, it's talking with the server's proxy. The proxy stands in for the real object, which is executing in a separate process. Likewise, the stub gets installed in the server's memory space. As far as the server is concerned, the container is installed in local memory. The operating system takes care of any communication required to transfer information from the proxy to the server and from the stub to the container. Because the proxy/stub mechanism is fixed, the data transfer can take place safely.

Out-of-process servers don't share the ease of programming or the speed advantages enjoyed by in-process servers. The very fact that an out-of-process server resides outside of the application's memory space means that all addresses must be translated, a time-consuming task to say the least. However, the out-of-process server is protected from direct access by another process of the operating system. In other words, while any address that the container might get from the server would be useless, both enjoy the security and reliability that separate process execution can provide.

There are actually two forms of out-of-process server call: LPC (Local Procedure Call) and RPC. Looked at simply, the difference between the two is that an LPC occurs on a local machine, while an RPC occurs on a remote machine. When a container calls on the services of an out-of-process server that requires the use of RPC, it could run into a myriad of problems including disconnections and delays. We discuss the use of RPC more in the section entitled "DCOM."

Web Resource Microsoft didn't create the RPC specification. It was created by the Open Software Foundation (now the Open Group). You can find out more about the Distributed Computing Environment (DCE) RPC specification at `http://www.opengroup. org/`. There's also a good overview of how RPC works at `http://www.ja.net/ documents/NetworkNews/Issue44/RPC.html`.

ActiveX

ActiveX is a COM derivative. In other words, like OLE2, ActiveX relies on COM as a defining standard. There's been a lot of confusion about ActiveX controls in the past, and part of the problem stems from Microsoft's continuing redefinition of all terms related to COM. The following sections are designed to help you gain a fuller appreciation of precisely what ActiveX is and how it relates to COM as a whole. We'll define what an ActiveX control is, and, more important, what it isn't (at least in terms of ActiveX in this book).

You don't have to learn about ActiveX by yourself. If you'd like some help from fellow programmers, check out the `microsoft.public.activex` newsgroup folder. This folder contains newsgroups that you can join to get various kinds of COM help, although they do specialize in ActiveX support. A great place to learn about the use of ActiveX on the Internet using current browser technology is the `microsoft.public.inetexplorer.ie4.activex_contrl` newsgroup. There are also a lot of component newsgroups spread throughout the Microsoft news server like those in the `microsoft.public.inetsdk.programming.components` newsgroup folder.

Here's the simplest definition of ActiveX that you'll ever find: ActiveX is an advanced form of OLE Control eXtension (OCX). A modern ActiveX component can be 50% to 75% smaller than an OCX of the same functionality when using certain types of programming methodologies like the Active Template Library (ATL) used by Visual C++ programmers. (Visual Basic ActiveX components tend to be marginally smaller than the original OCX version, but usually contain added functionality.) In addition, ActiveX components support incremental rendering and asynchronous connection features required for Internet use. Finally, most ActiveX components are faster than their OCX counterparts because an ActiveX component uses a lower-level interface. As the OLE in OCX indicates, an OCX goes through an extra processing layer by using OLE—ActiveX has direct access to COM.

The OCX was originally designed to create components for Visual Basic and represents a very simple implementation of COM technology (maybe a component form of OLE is a better way to look at it). These components were designed exclusively for desktop application use. The OCX, in turn, was originally designed as a 32-bit replacement for the 16-bit Visual Basic eXtension (VBX). Microsoft's original use for VBX was as a technology for creating controls that a programmer could place on a form to create applications with relative ease. These controls represented a new way to write applications—you just built an application's interface using graphics, much as a graphics artist would use primitives to create a drawing.

It's easy to see that ActiveX is yet another example of the evolution of COM over a period of time as Microsoft learned about programmers' needs. However, this simple definition of ActiveX doesn't even begin to scratch the surface. (We'll look at the process of creating and testing ActiveX components in Chapter 9 as part of learning to create simple components for COM+ implementations.) ActiveX controls include a lot of features that those earlier component forms didn't. For example, you can use ActiveX to create both windowed and nonwindowed components. In addition, an ActiveX component doesn't necessarily have to have a user interface (as we'll see in Chapter 10 when creating a component for server-side use).

So, how does ActiveX affect applications you write? The answer is fairly complex because of the number of ways in which ActiveX gets used, not because the technology itself is so overwhelming. For the most part, ActiveX components are self-contained modules that you can use to create applications. Think of ActiveX in the way that you'd think of building blocks. Both represent basic objects that have no real functionality on their own. For example, a push button component by itself wouldn't make much of an application, even though it's a self-contained, fully-operational module that's commonly created using ActiveX. However, when you combine a group of ActiveX controls and then add some glue code to make them do something as the result of user input, you have a functional application where the individual components work as a single unit.

ActiveX components follow the COM specification fully. When you install an ActiveX control in your programming environment, what have you really accomplished? In most cases, you have a new control that you stick on a form somewhere. You really don't need to know about the control's inner workings. The only important factors are what the control will do for your application and how you interact with it. Again, you're calling a particular module of code installed on your machine using a standard interface—that's what COM is all about.

ActiveX controls are in-process servers. This means that ActiveX relies on the client application for a container in which to store itself and that, from a traditional perspective, it has no application-specific capabilities of its own. ActiveX controls are essentially DLLs with very special capabilities that aren't designed for stand-alone use. That an ActiveX control is an in-process server means that it relies on the client's address space for resources like memory, and that an errant ActiveX control can crash the entire application.

The building block approach to programming has other benefits as well. For example, what happens if you have a defective component that doesn't work as anticipated? ActiveX allows you to fix the component without recompiling the application. All you need to do is correct the error, recompile the component, place it on the affected machines, and then register the new version of the component. That's right, ActiveX controls use the Windows Registry, just like every other form of COM. The Registry entries identify the ActiveX component, specify its location, and define certain component characteristics like whether the component is scriptable.

There's one other significant difference between ActiveX and older technologies. You can use an ActiveX component in a variety of places that aren't in the usual realm of libraries for new types of applications that programmers of yesterday could only imagine. For example, ActiveX is used on the Internet with client-side scripts to develop Web-based applications. In this case, ActiveX components are added to the Web page itself using the <OBJECT> tag. You can also use ActiveX with server-side scripts. The interesting thing is that the same ActiveX component could be used in a variety of environments without any recoding.

There's a wealth of other types of COM component types that use ActiveX technology on a stand-alone, out-of-process server basis like the Active Document (previously know as ActiveX Document) applications that are designed for stand-alone use. Active Scripting also falls under the ActiveX umbrella. This is the scripting technology used by applications like Internet Explorer. The Active Script implementation currently ships with two supported scripting languages: VB Script and JavaScript.

The Hidden Component

Microsoft uses component technology heavily in its own applications and often makes those components available for developer use. The problem for most developers is figuring out whether a component exists and then finding the documentation required for using it. Of course, there's also the problem of whether the component appears on Microsoft's distribution list (should you decide to market an application based on the component) and whether the component will be supported in the future.

In addition to discrete components, there are also times when a technology is embedded as part of a product like Internet Explorer. There could be a wealth of functionality at your fingertips depending on the application, but figuring out where the feature is included, when you can use it, and how to use it can be a daunting task. The interfaces exposed by the product allow you to create ActiveX objects using the same `CoCreateInstance()` method call that you'd use with a discrete component.

To give you an idea of just how severe this problem can get, consider some of the interfaces exposed by Internet Explorer 4. For example, most developers aren't aware that there's an Internet Shortcuts API and that you can use it to manipulate the Internet Explorer Favorites folder for your own needs. Or that a network administrator could use this interface to create a set of links for the company intranet. The administrator could simply add URLs to a Favorites folder using the standard Internet Explorer interface and be certain that those links would appear on the company intranet for everyone to use. This would make updating the link list for the intranet easy. This particular interface not only allows you to get the URL but also allows you to execute a command against the URL as well as set it.

The number of objects you can create using Internet Explorer 4 interfaces alone is pretty astounding. Even smaller parts of the application, like the ratings system, are available for use by other applications. The Internet Ratings API makes resources like the Rating Access Denied dialog available for your use. A network administrator could use this interface for all kinds of purposes, including denying employee access to Web sites that the company considers non-job-related. Instead of placing this Web site list in each employee's browser, you could place it in a SQL database on a main server and provide a utility for changing the database settings. (Interestingly, the Rating Access Denied dialog can be set to allow an employee to enter a special username and password to override the setting when necessary.)

The bottom line for most developers today is that it pays to discover whether there are any existing solutions to problems before reinventing the wheel. If you see a feature that you find beneficial in an operating system, take the time to discover whether there's a documented interface for using that feature. In many cases, finding the hidden component that already exists will save you a lot of time and effort in creating a new component of your own.

DCOM

Microsoft's distributed component object model (DCOM) is the next step in the evolution of COM. It was originally called Network OLE, but, like many things COM, has been given a new name. This version of COM allows components and applications to communicate over a network, no matter how widely separated the participating computers are from each other. DCOM allows components to work together over a LAN, a WAN, or the Internet.

This chapter contains an in-depth overview of DCOM. However, because this communication protocol is so important to COM+, we also take a detailed look at how DCOM works. Chapter 5 moves from an in-depth overview of DCOM to a detailed discussion of how DCOM works internally. We'll build a simple application and use the various tools supplied by both Visual Studio and the Platform SDK to see DCOM in action. Once you complete Chapter 5, you'll have a better understanding of why the new additions to COM+, MTS, and MSMQ are so important.

DCOM is designed to communicate over a broad range of network protocols. This includes both the HTTP and TCP/IP protocols used by the Internet. In other words, a component on a laptop in New York could communicate with a server running in Paris and use that server's resources as if the two were in the same room. In addition, DCOM handles the network protocol details so that you can concentrate on the business logic of the component that you're designing.

DCOM is modeled after the Open Software Foundation (now the Open Group) distributed computing environment remote procedure call DCE-RPC specification. It's supposed to work with both Java applets and ActiveX controls, but with its COM basis, DCOM is definitely oriented toward ActiveX use.

DCOM's benefit for the developer is that it allows a client application to communicate directly with a service running on a server using a standard COM interface. In essence, this means that you could design a control or applet that allows the client application to receive data from the server, and then perform local calculations using that data. In addition, DCOM allows secure communication between client and server regardless of the protocol used.

There are quite a few resources at your disposal when it comes to DCOM on the Internet. The best place to start looking for the latest information about this technology is Microsoft's DCOM Web site at http://www.microsoft.com/com/dcom.asp. This site provides a link to the DCOM specification, books on how to work with DCOM, programming samples, white papers, and links to other Web sites with additional DCOM information. One of the better places to get information about the Open Group DCE-RPC specification (the underlying technology for DCOM) is http://www.dstc.edu.au/AU/research_news/dce/dce.html. This Web site will help you find specifications, frequently asked question (FAQ) sheets for using DCE-RPC in a variety of environments, and a list of vendors who support DCE-RPC in their products.

There are three additions to COM that apply specifically to DCOM. The first is the use of a proxy object. The local client uses the proxy object to work with the component. As far as the client is concerned, the component resides on the local hard drive. However, what the client is really working with is a component substitute. The second is a stub that resides on the server. The stub takes the place of the client on the component machine. As far as the component is concerned, the client is local to its machine. The third addition is the communication that goes on between the proxy object and the stub—that's where the DCE-RPC part of the picture comes into play. DCE-RPC allows the proxy object and stub to stay in sync with their real counterparts.

With the mechanisms that DCOM uses to provide service in place, a client need never know whether a component is local or remote. Part of this seamless interface is incorporated into the Registry. This form of DCOM access requires you to make new Registry entries. The first is an application identifier (AppID) entry in the HKEY_CLASSES_ROOT\CLSID\<class id> entry for the requested GUID. This application identifier uses a 128-bit number, just as the GUID does. A RemoteServerName key in the application identifier entry tells Windows that it needs to use DCOM to access this component on a remote machine. In sum, even the CLSID entry is the same as before—it just points to a remote location instead of a local one.

Note With Windows 2000, many COM Registry entries reside on the domain controller, rather than the local machine when using Active Directory. This reduces the administrator's workload by providing a central location for registering components and applications. It allows an administrator to install or move components without reconfiguring every machine on the network. Any change to the COM entries on the domain controller automatically propagates to all the clients on the network.

In addition to an automated method of creating connections using Registry entries, there's a way to specify the server name during object creation for applications that require it using a COSERVERINFO data structure. This data structure allows you to specify the server name as a domain naming system (DNS) string, universal naming convention (UNC) string, or TCP/IP address. For example, if you wanted to create an administrative tool that allowed access to multiple servers, it would hardly pay to specify the remote server name as part of the Registry entry. When you need to specify the server as part of the object instance creation process use the `CoCreateInstanceEx()`, `CoGetInstanceFromFile()`, `CoGetInstanceFromStorage()`, or `CoGetClassObject()` functions.

The second method of creating a DCOM connection has the added advantage of allowing you to specify the level and type of security access required using a COAUTHINFO data structure. The automated method uses the current user's name and password to log on to the server, which may not be enough to gain the access required to create the object in some cases. The COAUTHINFO data structure allows you to do things like impersonate someone else. If you set the COAUTHINFO data structure to NULL, then Windows will use the current user's security information to gain access to the server as usual.

DCOM is used in a variety of ways in today's computing environment. We'll spend more time looking at DCOM in general in Chapter 5. Chapter 10 will give you a better idea of how you can use DCOM to create remote execution tools; we'll look at what you'd need to do to create a simple remote administration tool for your server.

The best way for a developer to view DCOM is as a transport mechanism for remote out-of-process servers based on the COM specification. Of course, this is a very simplistic view of a more complex process. It's time to look at more specific information about how an out-of-process server works when used to create distributed applications. The DCOM connection is one of the most common uses for the out-of-process server. In addition, DCOM is one of the more all-encompassing connection types because it relies on the use of an RPC connection between the client and the server. With this in mind, we're going to take a detailed look at how DCOM works in the following sections. However, it's important to remember that this information also details how out-of-process server connections work in general.

Note Another reason that this information is so very important is that it forms the basis of what we're going to work with throughout the rest of the book. You must know this information because DCOM forms the basis of the COM+ technologies that we'll study as the book progresses. Both MTS and MSMQ rely on RPC to create new application types like the disconnected application. In short, without the historical context of DCOM to fall back on, learning COM+ will take longer.

Typical out-of-process connections

One thing that you need to worry about when working with a remote access protocol like DCOM is how the connection will occur. After all, without a good connection, many other considerations are rendered moot. Of course, it's important to understand the technical details behind the connection and why connections are made in the way that they are. Because DCOM could encounter problems initiating and maintaining a connection, you also need to consider how error trapping works. A good connection may not remain good long enough to complete a given task, which means that an application that relies on DCOM needs another plan to ensure that the user's data remains safe.

Tip One of the issues that we don't talk about in this section of the chapter is Component Load Balancing (CLB). Load balancing in general allows a cluster of servers to operate more efficiently by spreading the processing load across all servers equally. Normally, a network administrator would need to perform this task manually, which is an error-prone and time-consuming process. Unfortunately, while Windows 2000 does provide Network Load Balancing (NLB), the current release (at least as of this writing) doesn't provide CLB. The beta version of Windows 2000 offered this feature, but Microsoft pulled it. Look for Microsoft to release either a new version of Windows 2000 that includes CLB or an update to existing versions of Windows 2000 that will include this feature. Either way, you need this feature to balance your server cluster's processing load when working with large-scale applications like database management. You can learn more about CLB at http://www.microsoft.com/Windows/server/news/bulletins/clb.asp.

This section of the chapter answers several questions. First, we'll look at how the connection actually works — at least from an overview perspective. As previously mentioned, DCOM relies on an existing technology. However, it's important to understand how this technology works and how DCOM implements it. Second, we'll look at the question of how DCOM keeps the connection from becoming so mired in detail that the user gets tired of waiting for something to happen. Many network administrators worry about performance under Windows 2000. Although the operating system promises to keep data safer, network administrators are worried about the cost in terms of user productivity.

How does the connection work?

In this section, we take a bird's-eye view of how DCOM creates and manages a connection between the client and server. It's important to understand how this connection works so that you can troubleshoot problems in your own applications. Figure 4-4 is a flowchart of the flow of data from the client to the server. The following list describes each of the diagram elements.

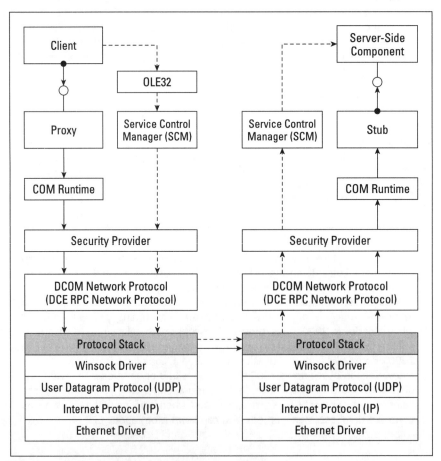

Figure 4-4: The data flow in a DCOM connection.

Note Figure 4-4 assumes a very generic component setup. We aren't doing anything fancy here because the idea is to learn how the connection between client and server works. A real-world component would provide more features and, there-fore, would perform a lot more communication to complete a task. The underlying communication technology will remain the same no matter how complex or sim-ple your component is. The only thing that will change is the amount and type of communication between the client and server.

✦ **Client:** Originates requests to the server for resources and support.

✦ **OLE32:** DLL containing the methods used to create an instance of an object (along with a wealth of other functionality). There are five methods available for remote object creation: `CoCreateInstanceEx()`, `CoGetInstanceFromFile()`, `CoGetInstanceFromStorage()`, `CoGetClassObject()`, and `CoGetClass ObjectFromURL()`.

✦ **Service Control Manager (SCM):** Creates the initial connection between client and server. The SCM is only used during object creation. This feature gets implemented by the `TransportLoad()` method in the RPCLTSCM.DLL file.

✦ **Proxy:** The server's presence within the client's address space. The proxy, which is actually a table of interfaces, is created and managed by the operat-ing system at the request of the COM runtime. It allows the client to think that the server is local, even though the server is actually located on another machine. Windows uses a method like `CreateProxyFromTypeInfo()` found in the RPCRT4.DLL file to create the proxy.

✦ **COM runtime:** Operating system elements that host objects and provide client/server communication. The COM runtime is part of any COM-related scenario — both in-process and out-of-process and local and remote.

✦ **Security provider:** The security provider logs the client machine into the server machine. Windows 2000 provides support for several standard security providers for both Internet and local network use. These providers include NT LAN Manager (NTLM, the standard Windows NT security protocol), Kerberos, Distributed Password Authentication (DPA, which is used by CompuServe and MSN), secure channel security services like Secure Sockets Layer (SSL)/Private Communication Technology (PCT), and third party DCE providers. Some secu-rity providers will also ensure that all data transferred between the client and server is protected in some way — usually through the use of encryption.

✦ **DCOM Network Protocol (DCE-RPC Network Protocol):** Defines a protocol for creating a connection with a remote server for the purpose of using objects. In addition to implementing a component protocol, this block contains all of the elements to implement the Object Remote Procedure Call (ORPC) specifi-cation at an application level. This particular component is known by several different names in the Microsoft documentation — the most popular of which is *DCOM wire protocol*. We'll discuss the DCOM network protocol in detail later in this chapter.

✦ **Protocol stack:** Actual network communication requires more than just one protocol—there are network-related protocols to consider as well. The protocol stack consists of all the protocols required to create a connection between the client and server, including network specific protocols like TCP/IP. Figure 4-4 shows a typical protocol stack consisting of a Winsock driver, UDP, IP, and an Ethernet driver. Not shown is the Ethernet network interface card (NIC) that is actually used to create the physical connection between the client and server.

✦ **Stub:** The client's presence within the server's address space. The stub is created and managed by the operating system at the request of the COM runtime. As far as the server is concerned, it's working with a local client. Windows uses a method like `CreateStubFromTypeInfo()` found in the RPCRT4.DLL file to create the stub.

✦ **Server:** The COM object that the client has requested services and resources from.

The are actually two communication paths shown in Figure 4-4. The first path (the dotted line) is used to create an instance of the object. The second path (solid line) is used for normal communication between the client and the server. Creating a line of communication between a client and server usually follows these steps:

1. Client issues one of the five object-creation method calls that we discussed earlier in the section (the OLE32.DLL bullet). The call must include both a CLSID and a server name (along with any information required to log on to the server). As an alternative, the client can issue a standard call that OLE32.DLL will resolve to a remote location based on a registry entry, or the client can use monikers.

2. OLE32.DLL calls on the client-side SCM to create a connection to the server machine because it can't service the call locally.

3. The DCOM network protocol creates the required packets to send information from the client to the server.

4. The server-side SCM creates an instance of the desired server-side component and returns a pointer to the object instance to the client.

5. The server-side SCM calls on the COM runtime to create a stub for the component to interact with.

6. The client-side SCM calls upon the COM runtime to create a proxy for the client to interact with.

7. The SCM returns a pointer to the proxy to the client.

8. Normal client- and server-side component communications begin.

Connection-oriented data-flow optimization

Sometimes, the development and placement of a component depends on just how much communication occurs. Consider a situation in which a client needs access to the contents of a database. You could place a component directly on the client machine that would access the database manager, gain access to the required data, and then format it for the user. However, this design would require a lot of network communication because the client would need to communicate constantly with the database manager as well as send or receive the data.

Splitting the component in two would allow you to reduce the amount of data traversing the network. One component on the client machine could send data requests and format the incoming data. A second component on the server could make the data requests and deliver only the required information to the client. Using this approach would simultaneously reduce network traffic significantly, enhance both client and server efficiency, and make the user more productive.

DCOM does perform some connection manipulation on its own. An important DCOM connection manipulation feature is connection optimization. If you have a server-side component that's manipulating a database using ODBC, DCOM will more than likely copy the component to the client and then get out of the picture. Because the connection to the database is through ODBC, neither the client nor the database manager notices any difference in the performance of the component. However, because DCOM is out of the picture, the component executes more efficiently. Obviously, this is a very specific kind of connection change and is only implemented when the client will see a significant performance gain.

A detailed look at the DCOM network protocol

The first thing we need to discuss in this section is what the term *DCOM network protocol* means. The DCOM network protocol is a superset of the Open Group DCE-RPC network protocol. Essentially, the DCOM network protocol defines the methodology for enabling COM to work across two machines and making it appear to both client and server that there's only one machine involved. In short, DCOM is simply COM that operates across more than one machine. DCOM uses protocols and a network infrastructure to enable the communication.

Note
After you've done a little reading about DCE, you'll learn that DCE is actually composed of several components, only one of which is RPC. There are also the Cell and Global Directory Services (CDS and GDS), the Security Service, DCE Threads, Distributed Time Service (DTS), and Distributed File Service (DFS) components. In addition, DCE isn't a stand-alone protocol; it's designed to allow an operating system vendor to include its services within an operating system. This is precisely what Microsoft has done with DCOM by basing DCOM on DCE-RPC.

The following sections will help you better understand the DCOM network protocol and where it fits in the scheme of things for you as a programmer. We do not discuss every detail of this protocol because there are entire volumes on the topic. Instead, I cover the highlights of DCOM network protocol as a whole and what makes it different from the protocol it's based on, DCE-RPC.

Many names, same functionality

Trying to nail down what the term DCOM network protocol means can prove frustrating unless you know where to look. Unfortunately, although there are a lot of Microsoft-generated drawings and presentations available with "DCOM network protocol" written on them, searching the various resources that Microsoft provides will shed very little light on this technology. What you really need to look for is the DCOM wire protocol.

The DCOM wire protocol standard defines the kind of packets that get put on the wire between the client and the server. (Other network protocols are required to actually create the connection between client and server, as shown in Figure 4-4.) The DCOM wire protocol standard defines the format of these packets and what the client and server should expect to see in them. In other words, the DCOM wire protocol specifies how the information gets physically transferred from one machine to the other.

DCOM network protocol goes by yet another name, ORPC. The ORPC moniker shows the close relationship between DCOM and DCE-RPC. This particular name for the single technology that we've been talking about throughout this chapter is the most common one you'll see. The "object" part of ORPC points to the fact that Microsoft has extended RPC to support remote handling of objects. In fact, it has added several additional data structures—the most important of which is the interface pointer identifier (IPID). IPID is discussed as the chapter progresses. These additional data structures allow DCOM to request remote instantiation of an object from a server.

The point of this discussion is that you need to perform some research to discover every detail about DCOM. For the remainder of this section, I'll refer to the whole array of DCOM communication names and specifications as DCOM network protocol. However, it's also important to know that you can find this technology listed under other names.

Microsoft has prepared a complete specification for the DCOM wire protocol. Reading this specification will give you a better idea of how DCOM transmissions are supposed to work. You'll find the specification at `http://www.microsoft.com/oledev/olecom/draft-brown-dcom-v1-spec-02.txt`. One of the best places to find out more about DCE-RPC is `http://www.opengroup.org/public/tech/dce/info/`. This site contains an overview of DCE, a copy of the DCE specification, and a wealth of other information that you'll find useful when learning about how DCOM works. If you have questions about DCE that you'd like help with, there's a newsgroup you can go to at `comp.soft-sys.dce`. There's also an interesting presentation of how DCOM works within the DCE environment at `http://www.opengroup.org/dce/proggrp/meetings/july98/FrankHayes/`.

The IRemoteActivation interface

Like many other object technologies, DCOM network protocol relies on an interface to encapsulate the methods required to create, maintain, and eventually sever a connection between client and server. In this case, we're not talking about a COM interface, but an RPC interface called IRemoteActivation. The IRemoteActivation interface is exposed by the SCM on each machine (see Figure 4-4). The SCM is physically located in the RPCSS.EXE file and isn't associated with the SCM that Windows 2000 uses to manage services.

Interestingly, IRemoteActivation contains only one method, RemoteActivation(), which activates the COM object on a remote machine. RemoteActivation() makes up for the lack of a pure DCE-RPC implementation by enabling remote activation of the server by the client. In a pure DCE-RPC implementation, you must run the server first and then allow the client to access it remotely. It's instructional to look at the arguments that the client passes to the server using the RemoteActivation() method and what the server passes back to the client. Table 4-3 lists the input arguments for RemoteActivation() and Table 4-4 lists the output arguments.

Table 4-3	
RemoteActivation() Input Arguments	
Argument	**Description**
hRpc	RPC binding handle used to make the request.
ORPCthis	A data structure that contains the version of DCOM that the client is using, one or more flags that indicate the presence of additional data, the causality ID (CID) of the client, and an array of special extensions. The client's major version number is compared to the server's major version number. If the major version numbers don't match, the server sends back an error message result. A server can have a higher minor version number than the client. The CID is actually a GUID used to link the method calls between two or more machines. For example, if machine A requests that machine B activate a component, and machine B has to request that machine C activate a component first, then the calls are causally related, and DCOM will generate a CID for them. The CID will remain in effect until the original call created by machine A is satisfied by a return call from machine B. Currently there are only two special extensions that you'll find in use in the ORPCthis structure. The first is for error information, while the second is for debugging purposes. We won't discuss these extensions because of their special-purpose nature.
CLSID	Class ID of the object that the client wants to create and activate on the server. This argument is typically used if the application calls CoCreateInstanceEx(), CoGetClassObject(), or CoGetClassObjectFromURL().

Continued

Table 4-3 (continued)

Argument	Description
pwszObjectName	A pointer to a wide character string containing path and executable filename information for the object that the client wants to create. This argument is typically used if the application calls `CoGetInstanceFromFile()`.
pObjectStorage	A client-side interface pointer to an object that supports the IStorage interface. The server will use this interface to determine which object to instantiate. This argument is typically used if the application calls `CoGetInstanceFromStorage()`.
ClientImpLevel	Constant value taken from RPC_C_IMP. This value determines the client's default impersonation level.
Mode	This argument is normally set to MODE_GET_CLASS_OBJECT when instantiating a new object. The Mode argument gets passed to the server's `IPersistFile::Load()` method if either the pwszObjectName or pObjectStorage arguments contains a value.
Interfaces	Contains the number of interfaces that the client is requesting.
pIIDs	A list of interface identifiers (IIDs) that the client wants. One of the more common IIDs is IID_Unknown for the IUnknown interface.
cRequestedProtseqs	Number of protocol sequences specified in the RequestedProtseqs argument.
RequestedProtseqs	An array containing a list of the protocol sequences that the client wants OXID binding handles for.

Note   Not every argument in either Table 4-3 or Table 4-4 is required. A `Remote Activation()` call typically includes only the arguments required to satisfy the object creation request. For example, if you include the CLSID argument, then you usually don't need to include the pwszObjectName argument as well.

Table 4-4
RemoteActivation() Output Arguments

Argument	Description
OPRCthat	This parameter appears at the head of every protocol data unit (PDU) for COM methods. It contains a list of flags that define the presence of other data and an extension array used for special purposes.

Argument	Description
pOxid	The object export identifier (OXID) for the object that the server has just created for the client. This is the binding information that the client will need to connect to the interface specified by the IPID.
ppsaOxidBindings	Contains the endpoint and security bindings required to reach the OXID. In most cases, the SCM is the endpoint, which resides at a well-known port address for each of the major protocols. For example, the SCM port for UPD and TCP is 1066. The endpoint is an UNC-based string instead of a port number when named pipes are used.
pipidRemUnknown	The IPID of the OXID's IRemUnknown (remote unknown) interface. This is the equivalent of the COM IUnknown interface, but for a remote, rather than a local, machine.
pAuthnHint	Constant value taken from the RPC_C_AUTHN list. It provides a hint to the client about the minimal level of authentication that the server will accept.
pServerVersion	The version of DCOM supported by the server. The client and server must support the same major version number of DCOM. In addition, the server's minor revision level must be equal to or greater than that of the client, or an error will occur. If the server's minor version number is greater than that of the client, then the server automatically scales its level of DCOM support to match that of the client.
phr	The HRESULT of the activation operation. This is the COM object's instantiation return value to the client, and shouldn't be confused with the value returned by the server itself for the operation as a whole.
ppInterfaceData	An array of interface pointers. This array contains one entry for each interface requested using the pIIDs argument and in the same order as the interfaces appear in the component. Each interface pointer is actually a data structure consisting of two elements. The first element contains the size of an object reference data structure. The second element is the object reference data structure itself (we'll discuss this data structure in the section that follows). There are three kinds of object reference data structures: standard, handler, and custom. All three of these structure types begin with a signature, flags, and a GUID for the interface pointer. The end of the structure is object-reference-data-structure-type specific.
pResults	An array of HRESULTs for each `<Object>::QueryInterface()` method call performed on the server while gaining access to each of the IIDs requested by the client. This array won't include an object instantiation HRESULT value, because that HRESULT is returned in the phr argument.

As Tables 4-3 and 4-4 show, the interactions between client and server are very straightforward, and there isn't much more information required than what you'd provide for a local object instantiation. The big difference is how the call is handled by the SCM. As a matter of fact, you'll never need to worry about creating a `Remote Activation()` method call unless you begin to work with DCOM directly. If you issue a standard `CoCreateInstance()` call and OLE32 finds that the object doesn't exist on the local machine, it'll create the required DCOM call for you based on the information provided in the `CoCreateInstance()` call and on any Registry entries it finds.

Tip

The DCOM network protocol transmits method arguments using the network data representation (NDR) format. The NDR format determines how the various values get marshaled into data packets for network transmission. Knowing how the DCOM network protocol formats data allows you to do a few things that you couldn't normally do, like use a network sniffer to see how packets get transmitted from one machine to the next. There's one extension to NDR for DCOM so that NDR can support interface pointers. The MInterfacePointer data type (the object reference data structure mentioned in Table 4-3) doesn't contain a pointer to a vtable (virtual table) containing pointers to functions; it's merely an object reference. An interesting thing about the MInterfacePointer structure is that it begins with a signature field that spells MEOW when you look at the data stream in ASCII. Some programmers have speculated that this is actually an acronym for Microsoft Extended Object Wire, but Microsoft hasn't documented it as being so. One thing is certain: You can always tell when you're looking at an object reference in a network sniffer if you see the word MEOW at the beginning.

Object references

From the preceding sections, you now know that the main purpose of all these data transfers between the client and server is to provide the client with access to a specific instance of an object interface using the object reference. Each interface requires a separate object reference that the client uses to access the methods that the interface contains. Object references are passed back to the client using the ppInterfaceData array (MInterfacePointer data type).

There are two main types of object reference data structure (OBJREF_STANDARD and OBJREF_HANDLER) and one ancillary type (OBJREF_CUSTOM). Each data structure includes a signature (MEOW), a flag specifying the kind of object reference, and a GUID containing the interface identifier. Each object reference data structure type also contains specialized data. The data contained in the main object reference types can be broken down as follows:

✦ **Standard object reference:** A data structure containing a reference to the object that was created on the server.

✦ **Dual string array:** A data structure containing two strings. The first string contains the information the client needs to bind to the object on the server. The second string contains security information the client will need to access the object on the server.

✦ **Handler class ID:** This is applicable only to the OBJREF_HANDLER object reference data structure. It contains the GUID for the handler code.

Let's look at the standard object reference in more detail. This is a data structure consisting of five elements: flags, the number of reference counts associated with the object, the OXID for the server that owns the object, the object identifier (OID) of the object that implements the interface, and the IPID. The flags define special settings for the object reference. The only flag that you'll ever need to worry about when working with DCOM directly is SORF_NOPING, which tells DCOM that the object interface doesn't need to be pinged to keep it alive. The cPublicRefs field, which contains the number of reference counts associated with the object, reduces network traffic by allowing a single call to replace multiple IUnknown::AddRef() calls.

The network name difference

It's important to understand all of the theory behind how DCOM works, but, at some point, you have to start working on the practical aspects of implementing DCOM. Obviously, you can create a low-level connection that manipulates DCOM itself, but for the most part, you'll never need to. In fact, creating a DCOM connection can be as easy as creating an alternative type of Registry entry (which requires no changes to your code) or adding the name of a network resource as part of your object instantiation call.

There are a variety of ways to create a DCOM connection. The most common method is to issue a special call from within your application to create the DCOM connection. All five of the following function calls include a method for requesting the name of a network resource where the object will get instantiated. (Notice that CoCreateInstance() isn't included in this list because it lacks the means to define a precise server name.)

✦ CoCreateInstanceEx()

✦ CoGetInstanceFromFile()

✦ CoGetInstanceFromStorage()

✦ CoGetClassObject()

✦ CoGetClassObjectFromURL()

The method argument that you're interested in for the first four calls is pServerInfo, which is a data structure of type COSERVERINFO. This data structure contains several elements that describe the connection to the server as shown in Table 4-5. The CoGetClassObjectFromURL() method relies on the szCodeURL argument to point to the server containing the object that you want to instantiate.

Table 4-5
COSERVERINFO Data Structure Description

Parameter	Description
pwszName	A pointer to a string containing the name of the server in wide-character format.
pAuthInfo	COAUTHINFO data structure pointer containing access information for the server. This data structure has to contain the information required to access the server, like the user's name and password. Setting this argument to NULL will force DCOM to use the default security provided by the user's account.

What happens if you don't want to create special code to create a connection? DCOM also allows you to use a standard CoCreateInstance call by creating a special Registry entry. Using this technique allows you to create a client application that will work on any machine; it won't matter whether the component is local or remote. Creating the required HKEY_CLASSES_ROOT Registry entries for remote activation of a component is a two-step process as shown here.

1. Create an HKEY_CLASSES_ROOT\APPID\<Application Identifier GUID> entry for the remote server like this:

   ```
   "RemoteServerName"="<DNS Name>"
   ```

2. Create an HKEY_CLASSES_ROOT\ClsID\<Class Identifier GUID> entry for the component like this:

   ```
   "AppID"="<AppID GUID>"
   ```

The AppID concept was originally introduced for security reasons. All of the COM objects that share the same AppID will also get the same security levels when accessing the server. However, the AppID also allows you to avoid redundant Registry entries by enabling all of the components that reside on a single server to share one AppID. This makes the administrator's job easier when a group of components moves from one server to another.

Fortunately, you don't have to worry about modifying the Registry entries directly (unless you want to do it as part of the application installation process). Microsoft provides the DCOM Configuration Tool, which makes the required changes for you after you've provided the correct level of information. Unfortunately, using this tool means modifying each user's machine individually and installing the required support on the user's machine. As a result, we won't look at the DCOM Configuration Tool because its usefulness to the programmer of large projects is limited.

At this point, you might think that modifying the user's local Registry entries would cause problems for a large organization even if Microsoft has provided a tool to perform the task. The solution is Active Directory. Windows 2000 provides the capability to create Registry entries in a central location that the user downloads as part of the process of logging into the domain. What this means is that you'll create the required DCOM entries on the server and everything else will happen automatically. Changes will require a single change on the server as well, which should greatly ease the administrator's burden. Obviously, you must run Active Directory to gain this benefit.

COM+

COM+ is yet another extension of the existing COM standard. In this case, COM+ is also an extension of several other technologies, including both DCOM and ActiveX, making COM+ a truly evolutionary product. Of course, COM+ brings some new elements to the party like updated security, reliability through transactions, and the capability to work in disconnected mode. Yet, for some people, these aren't additions that will cause management to invest in Windows 2000 or COM+ immediately.

Cross-Reference

The section about COM+ in this chapter is relatively short. All you need for right now is an overview of COM+. Throughout the chapter, we've already looked at the technologies that make up the basis for COM+ in some detail. COM+ is essentially the combination of COM, DCOM, MTS, and MSMQ. However, we aren't going to stop with the coverage in this chapter. Chapters 6, 7, and 8 will provide the in-depth coverage that you'll need to begin creating the examples in the rest of this book.

So, why develop yet another standard? One problem with existing component technologies is that they're difficult to learn and implement. Most of Microsoft's current component technologies require the skills of an advanced programmer who understands the intricacies of COM to fully implement a programming solution. COM+ makes it easier to develop components in several ways. The following list describes these advantages.

✦ **Language-neutral:** COM+ components are completely language-neutral. No longer do you need to worry about the component that you wrote in Visual C++ while working in Visual Basic. Compatibility between languages was a problem in the past. You might write and test the component using Visual C++ only to find that Visual Basic was expecting something different.

✦ **Ease of use:** COM+ components are completely self-describing. This makes the component accessible to any tool or language that understands COM+. In addition, it eliminates the need to create a type library for the component as is required for COM.

✦ **New features:** This feature allows developers to build advanced controls using special COM+ calls. Some of the more important new features include load balancing, in-memory databases, a publish-and-subscribe-events service, and a queued-components service.

✦ **Fewer requirements:** You'll create a COM+ component using the features of the language you're familiar with. The COM+ tools and runtime will help you turn the resulting classes into COM+ components and applications. This feature eliminates the need for a class factory in your component (at least in most cases) — all you need is the class required to implement the component.

✦ **Ease of programming:** The MTS programming model is a vast improvement over past Microsoft offerings. You'll find that you can develop server-based components faster by using COM+.

✦ **Database support:** An important COM extension that is provided with COM+ is data binding, which enables a component to provide database access. Adding database access means that you can use COM+ to build components for the Internet that can access remote data.

✦ **Common data types:** An ongoing problem with component technology is that different languages use varying data types. In addition, even if two languages do support a common data type, it's very likely that each language will support it differently. COM+ eliminates this problem by supporting one set of common data types that anyone developing components will use. Because the COM+ specification states what these data types look like, they can be duplicated using native language data types or data mapping between COM+ types and native language data types. In addition, COM+ will attempt to coerce any data type that it doesn't recognize into the appropriate COM+ data type. COM+ does allow you to extend the defined data types by defining enums, classes, and structures using native COM+ data types.

COM+ is the basis for DNA architecture, which is Microsoft's latest vision for the Internet. Theoretically, DNA will allow COM components to execute on any platform and the developer to use any language to write the component. As previously stated, however, the language and tools used by the developer must have an understanding of COM+ in order to make the new ease-of-programming features a reality. In addition, much of the new technology is based on Microsoft Transaction Server and related server technologies.

Because COM+ is such a new technology, you might not be able to find much information about it, even on the Internet. You can, however, go to the main COM+ Web site at `http://www.microsoft.com/com/complus.asp` to find the latest Microsoft-supplied information. This Web site has pointers to the latest information about COM+, Web sites that support COM+, white papers, articles in the press, and a variety of Microsoft-supplied materials.

Part of the capability to work with any language and any platform will come from a new COM+ feature called interceptors. Using interceptors will allow a COM+ component to call a variety of services during runtime rather than relying on a specific service. You'll use interceptors to receive and process events related to instance creation, calls and returns, errors, and instance deletion. Interceptors also provide the mechanism to perform transactions and system monitoring.

Microsoft didn't want to make creating COM+ components that much different than anything programmers did in the past. In fact, the goal of COM+ is to keep everything as close to being the same as before while reducing the complexity of creating the code required for a COM+ component. With this in mind, Visual Basic programmers will be happy that you can use COM+ with the relatively minor addition of some new coding procedures and the use of some additional SDKs. (Chapters 9 through 14 show you how to work with various types of COM and COM+ components.)

There are a few COM+ limitations that really make sense when you think about them. The most important limitation is that all properties must use accessor functions (get and set functions). Because Visual Basic uses accessor functions by default, you won't need to worry about this particular requirement. Using accessor functions means that COM+ can always tell when a property has been read or modified by the client. However, you don't have to use properties for every element of your component. Internally you can use fields, which aren't accessible by the client. Fields are maintained by your class for maintaining state information and aren't tracked by COM+ at all.

Working with Interfaces

Working with COM components is all about communication. You want to create some code that's easy to reuse because it can communicate with the client using it and adapt, if necessary. ActiveX control communication consists of a client, a server, and an interpreter between them named COMPOBJ.DLL. Essentially, these three objects are the basis of what we'll discuss throughout the book because they encompass the three objects that most people work with.

Tip

If you're absolutely and totally confused by all of this talk about interfaces, make sure you read through the various pieces of OLE documentation that Microsoft provides—most important of which is the OLE2 SDK. You'll also want to invest in a magazine like *Microsoft Systems Journal*. This particular magazine painstakingly explains most of the new interfaces that Microsoft designs. Finally, although we've already gone through quite a few details about interfaces, we'll discuss a lot of additional details in the sections that follow. The bottom line is that you must understand interfaces and how they work before you can use COM at all. Between the OLE2 SDK, magazines, and the information in this book, you should have everything needed to gain a full understanding of interfaces.

That's not all there is to know about the communication, though. An ActiveX control (for that matter, a COM component of any kind) needs to provide a standard interface in order to be created. When an application instantiates a copy of an ActiveX control (the component object), it receives a pointer to a list of functions. That list of functions is housed in what's called an interface. To make it easier to understand what an interface is (at least in the context of an ActiveX control), think of it as a set of semantically related functions implemented as part of a component object. You'll normally see an interface as an array of functions defined in the OLE2 headers for your programming language.

An interface can perform a variety of tasks. For example, you might add a data operation interface like GetData or SetData. The more complex an ActiveX control, the more interfaces it requires to perform its task.

Understanding IUnknown

There's one interface called IUnknown that every ActiveX control must provide. It's the basis of all other interfaces. This is the interface that gets passed back to your application when you instantiate a copy of the control as a component object. Within this interface (and every other interface supported by an ActiveX control) are the three function calls listed here.

- ✦ `QueryInterface()`: This function allows the application to determine what interfaces the object supports. If the application queries an interface and the ActiveX control supports it, the application receives an array of pointers to the functions supported by the interface. Otherwise, the application receives a null pointer.

- ✦ `AddRef()`: This function creates a new relationship to a component object interface. Using this function creates another pointer to the array of function pointers supported by the interface. A component object maintains a reference count of the number of relationships that it's established. The component object only gets unloaded from memory when the reference count is 0.

- ✦ `Release()`: This function allows you to destroy the relationship between an application and an ActiveX control. It decreases the reference count by 1. If the component object's reference count is 0, then this function call also requests the destruction of the component object.

The presence of IUnknown means that your application can communicate with any component object it encounters. If your application recognizes the interfaces that the component object supports, it can communicate with that object at a fairly high level. For example, an ActiveX control provides very specific interfaces that your programming environment will know about if it supports them. If your application only recognizes a few of the interfaces, it still might be able to communicate with the component object, but at a much lower level.

There are a lot of interfaces that the OLE2 specification already supports for specific kinds of component objects. The Microsoft OLE2 SDK provides a full synopsis of all of these component object types and the interfaces that they're required to support. We'll also cover a few of the ActiveX-specific requirements throughout this book. However, just because Microsoft hasn't defined a particular interface doesn't mean that you can't define it yourself. The specifications we talk about throughout this book, and those that you'll learn from other sources, are the minimum interfaces that you can implement. There isn't any documentation that says that you can't implement more interfaces and then publish an API that tells how to use them. That's the beauty of using COM — you can extend it as needed to meet specific requirements.

Understanding the ActiveX interfaces

Interfaces encompass the idea of standardized access, which is the main goal of using component technology to build applications. Not only do components allow you to reuse code, but they also allow you to do so using standard methods that don't rely on an in-depth knowledge of the inner functioning of the component itself.

Microsoft publishes standards that allow everyone who creates an ActiveX control to create something that everyone can use. These standards enforce the idea that the interface will follow a specific set of rules when providing information about the control that it supports. So, at a higher level, an interface is also a standard.

No matter how you view interfaces, they're a fact of life for anyone who creates ActiveX controls. You must create specific interfaces that do certain things for the control to work properly. For example, you must implement an IPersist interface if you want the property values set by the programmer to remain constant from session to session. If a component doesn't include one of these interfaces, then the client has no idea that the component can actually perform this task. Even the interface name is important because both the client and server must agree on the same name if the client is to find out that the server can persist property values. As you can see, it's important to remember that an interface defines the relationship between the client and the server, so that both the client and the server have something to say about the interface requirements. Because Microsoft publishes standard interfaces that define specific methods, clients and servers that know nothing about each other can communicate using an interface.

Visual Basic supports a variety of ActiveX control types, everything from a standard ActiveX control to one that's optimized for working with Internet Explorer alone. The interfaces that you need to provide for the component to work with a specific environment depends a great deal on the environment itself. In other words, a component designed for Internet Explorer use may have different needs than one designed for use with applications in general. We're going to look at some of these standard interfaces as the book progresses. By knowing which interfaces you need to perform a specific task with a component, you can build components that will talk to any client with a need for the server's resources. (We look at some of the most common interfaces in the next section of the chapter.)

There are many other interfaces that ActiveX controls have to support in order to reach certain levels of functionality. For example, if you want to support events in your ActiveX control, then you'll need to provide an IConnectionPointContainer interface. There are some cases when you need to provide interfaces in addition to the one that you want to support. For example, the IConnectionPointContainer interface also requires that you implement the IEnumConnectionPoints, IConnectionPoint, and IEnumConnections interfaces. Another common supplementary interface is ISpecifyPropertyPages, which tells the container application that your control includes at least one property page. The property page itself will need to support the IPropertyPage or IPropertyPage2 interface.

Using the ActiveX interfaces

Now that you have a better idea of why interfaces, especially standard interfaces, are important, let's talk a little about what those interfaces are for. The following list provides a brief description of each major ActiveX control interface. Of course, these are the interfaces that you'll use most often — there are a lot of special-purpose interfaces that will give your component a specific "flavor" when working with various clients.

✦ **IDataObject:** This interface defines everything needed to transfer information between two objects, including the data format and the method used to transfer the information. If there's more than one format that the data can appear in, this interface will provide an enumerated list of available formats. This is also the interface that provides information about data rendered for a specific device (making it unsuitable for devices that don't conform to a specific standard).

✦ **IDispatch:** There are two methods for accessing the methods and properties provided by an ActiveX control. IDispatch provides an indirect method that relies on a type library for implementation purposes. This interface is always used as part of a dual-interface control. A dual interface isn't necessarily a requirement by Microsoft standards. However, most developers today implement a dual interface to allow their control to work with more than just the language that it was developed in. IDispatch is a late-bound interface.

✦ **IPersistStreamInit:** Making sure that a control's data remains intact between uses is important (otherwise you'd have to reconfigure your applications every time you used them.). You'll use this interface to make sure that any stream data required by your control is persistent or saved between sessions. This is a replacement for the older IPersistStream interface. The main difference between the two interfaces is that IPersistStreamInit also includes initialization code in the form of the `InitNew()` method, which initializes a control to a default state.

✦ **IOleControl:** Communication is key with ActiveX controls. The overall purpose of this interface is control communication between client and server. The normal purpose of this interface is to provide keyboard information. For example, a client could ask about the control's keyboard behavior and whether it provides full or partial support for control-key combinations.

✦ **IOleObject:** This is the most essential of all interfaces for an ActiveX control because it provides both basic control functionality and communication features. Along with this interface, a control must provide support for both IDataObject and IPersistStorage for every embedded object that the control supports. IOleObject contains a wide variety of methods designed to enhance control functionality. There's a minimum of 21 interface-specific methods along with the three standard methods (`QueryInterface()`, `AddRef()`, and `Release()`) for a total of 24 methods in a standard IOleObject interface. Of the 21 interface-specific methods, 6 can be ignored by returning E_NOTIMPL (error not implemented) if you don't require the functionality they provide: `SetExtent()`, `InitFromData()`, `GetClipboardData()`, `SetColorScheme()`, `SetMoniker()`, and `GetMoniker()`. Three of the methods — `DoVerb()`, `Close()`, and `SetHostNames()` — require a full control-specific implementation.

✦ **IOleInPlaceActivateObject:** Some types of ActiveX controls require a method for communicating with the container frame and documents. Normally, you'll find this interface when a control needs to support MDI or other complex application environments. This particular interface allows visual editing of the control in certain application types like a programming language IDE.

✦ **IViewObjectEx, IViewObject2, and IViewObject:** These three interfaces have one thing in common: they allow the ActiveX control a certain measure of autonomy in displaying itself without passing a data object to the container. Not only does this speed up the drawing of the control, but it ensures there's a minimum of drawing problems as well. The caller can request specific types of drawing features. For example, the caller can choose between a full or iconic display of the object. The IViewObject2 improves on IViewObject by returning the size of the drawing required to represent the object when using a specific presentation. You'd normally use this interface when working with compound document containers. The IViewObjectEx interface includes all of the features of IViewObject2. It improves on IViewObject2 by adding flicker-free drawing for nonrectangular objects, hit testing for nonrectangular objects, and control sizing. You'd use this interface to implement irregularly shaped controls.

✦ **IOleInPlaceObjectWindowless:** This interface allows a windowless control to receive window messages and to participate in drag-and-drop operations.

✦ **IPersistStorage:** Storing your data objects from one session to the next is an important part of making the control react the same way each time you use it. This interface provides a structured storage medium where each object has its own storage area within the container's storage medium. You must implement this interface along with IOleObject and IDataObject to make the control work within an embedded environment.

✦ **IQuickActivate:** Performance (control execution speed, loading time, and other performance factors) is often an important consideration when working with ActiveX controls, especially if the user has already spent time waiting for the control to download from the Internet. This interface allows the control and container to combine load-time or initialization-time handshaking into a single call, greatly improving control performance.

✦ **IDataObject:** This interface works with the control's data. It allows the container and the client to exchange information and also provides the means for one object to notify the other of data changes. The data-transfer methods supported by this interface enable objects to specify the format of the data or enumerate the available data formats. The client can also specify that data is rendered for a specific device.

✦ **IProvideClassInfo and IProvideClassInfo2:** Use this interface to access a control's coclass entry in its type library. The IProvideClassInfo2 interface is simply a faster version of the IProvideClassInfo interface. It also provides an ancillary method, GetGUID, which returns the object's outgoing IID for its default event set.

Reference counting

Reference counting is an important part of component technology. You don't want to destroy an object and then release the memory it used before all references to that object are also deleted. On the other hand, you don't want to keep an object around that no one is using. An object requires memory and system resources that you'll only want to maintain while the object is in use. As a result, there has to be some way of keeping track of whether the object is in use or not. That's where the reference-counting mechanism comes into play.

The IUnknown interface includes two methods, `AddRef()` and `Release()`, as does every other interface that you'll ever use. These two methods allow you to increment the reference counter (`AddRef()`) or decrement the reference counter (`Release()`) as needed. When the reference count within the object goes to 0, then Windows knows that no one is referencing the object anymore and the object can be released.

Understanding contexts

Putting things in context is something that's common to every form of communication, including the communication used by COM+. Consider for a moment the effect of context on human language. Depending on the surrounding words, a single word could mean many different things. For example, the word "fancy" could be adjectival (meaning "finely wrought"), a verb (meaning "to be enamored of"), or a noun (meaning "preference"), depending on context. In fact, it's the language recognition programs' lack of capability to interpret words in context that keeps them from being really useful.

COM+ is all about working in a distributed environment. Components reside on a server where one or more clients can access them easily. This means that the components need to provide some method of recognizing which client is making a request so that there aren't problems like security breaches. In addition, in the multithreaded environment required by enterprise-level applications, there are certain thread-synchronization issues that must be taken care of to ensure that only one thread accesses a given resource at a time.

At one time, application developers resorted to API calls to take care of the matter of thread synchronization. For example, a developer would use an `EnterCritical Section()` call to ensure that only one thread at a time could access a critical piece of code. Adding all of these extra calls took a lot of time and not every developer was diligent about adding them. Consequently, some code ended up not providing the right amount of thread safety, and, naturally, crashes occurred.

Microsoft has worked hard to solve the problem of thread safety by moving the thread synchronization code into the operating system. As a result, a COM+ application is always single-threaded. It relies on Windows 2000 to handle the issues of thread safety. That's where the whole idea of context comes in. Both the component and the operating system need to keep track of which threads are currently executing and that means assigning them an identity called a context.

The following sections are a guide to the whole idea of contexts. It's an important idea to consider when creating COM+ applications. In fact, the context is one of those background items that make a COM and COM+ application different.

Note The idea of context raises another issue: the methodology used to move data from one context to another (we're not talking about the process boundary movement that's handled by marshalling here — context is another issue). Interceptors are tied up with the movement of data. We'll discuss them in the section that follows.

An overview of object context

Context in application programming isn't new. Internet Server Application Programming Interface (ISAPI) applications have had the concept of context for quite some time. In most cases, an application context defines the environment of the client for the server in terms that the server can understand. For example, a context could be as simple as identifying the client machine or the thread in which the client application executes. A server normally uses the context to keep various requests separated. The context acts as an identifier that enables the server to determine which answer goes with a particular request.

Using a context means performing a translation of some kind. The most common method of passing object references from one context (normally the client) to another (normally the server) is by using a method argument. COM automatically translates the object reference so that the server can see the object reference within the proper context. This is the method recommended both by Microsoft and by many industry experts. A second method is to use the

CoMarshallInterface() function or the IGlobalInterfaceTable interface. You can use these techniques to gain more control over the translation process, but the programming required can become quite intense.

Tip

It helps to view context as another form of apartment. An apartment keeps objects with similar concurrency requirements together. Apartments also separate objects with different concurrency requirements to prevent them from corrupting each other's environment. Likewise, contexts group objects with the same attributes, while separating objects that differ by even one attribute. (We discuss these attributes as the section progresses.) Every object belongs to just one context; however, a process may contain multiple contexts (up to one for each object that the process contains).

So, how is an object associated with a context? Consider our human-language example again. The words are put into context as you say them. The same holds true for an object. Issuing CoCreateInstance() or another object-creation call also generates a context for that object. However, the context for an object doesn't exist in a vacuum, any more than you'd say a single sentence about your favorite place or food. The contexts of the words in a sentence are mainly determined by the organization of the words in that sentence. However, they also inherit some of the meaning from the surrounding sentences — at least the ones in the same paragraph. Likewise, the application that creates an object can allow that object to inherit some of the context of the application itself. For example, the PID of all threads in an application is the same because there's only one process in any given application.

Object context versus call context

The topic of context, however, goes beyond just the individual object. When a client and server establish some form of communication, there are actually two levels of context to consider. The first is object context, which is the context we've been discussing. An object context remains constant for the lifetime of the object, or perhaps longer, depending on how the object is destroyed. The communication itself involves a context as well. When a client calls on a method within a server, there's a call context. This is a transient context that lasts only for as long as the call is active. As soon as the method returns, the call context is destroyed. In short, just as creating an object attaches a context to the object, making an interface method call attaches a context to the call itself.

While the object context defines the object, the call context is used for entirely different purposes. For example, security settings for an object aren't contained in the object context because the security settings can vary depending on what the object is doing at any given moment. Security information is contained in the call context so that each call can have a separate set of security settings that match the type of call being made. You can determine the current call context using the CoGetCallContext() function. The idea of a context is somewhat new for Windows 2000. So, while Windows NT will support the IServerSecurity interface associated with call context, only Windows 2000 will support the new ISecurityCallContext and ICancelMethodCalls interfaces.

So, what information do you need? The object context contains concurrency, transaction management, thread affinity, just-in-time (JIT) activation, and object-specific (nonchanging) security settings like roles. You can obtain the current object context using the `CoGetObjectContext()` function.

Tip   If you've worked with MTS, then you're familiar with the `GetObjectContext()` function. Microsoft has maintained this function for the current COM+ implementation, but the call is really translated to `CoGetObjectContext()`. All new applications should use the new form of the function call, rather than relying on the continued existence of `GetObjectContext()`. The same holds true for the IObjectContext, IObjectContextActivity, and ISecurityProperty interfaces. These interfaces won't be supported in newer versions of Windows. You should use the IObjectContextInfo, IContextState, and ISecurityCallContext interfaces instead because these are the new interfaces supported by COM+. The IObjectContextInfo and IContextState interfaces are new for Windows 2000 and shouldn't be used with older versions of the product.

Now that you have a better understanding of contexts, you have a better idea of why objects with different attributes need to appear in different contexts. When an object in one context needs to communicate with an object in another context, COM+ sets up a proxy and stub, just as it would for cross-process communication. The difference is that contexts deal with the physical. The translation required by a change of context will transform the attributes of one object into attributes that another object can understand. This is the same process that occurs when you interpret the meaning of a word based on the meaning of the other words around it and the paragraph as a whole.

Understanding Interceptors

There are a number of ways to view interceptors, and how you view them will likely depend on how you use them (if you use them at all). We looked at the task of installing and configuring components in Chapter 2. These administrative tasks should have told you something about COM+ that's different from COM. When you're writing a standard COM component, everything about that component is hard-coded. You add security and methods to change properties at the time you develop the component. An administrator doesn't really have much to say about how the component works — unless that feature is added to the component as a configurable item.

The COM+ component that we configured in Chapter 2 allowed us to set security based on the roles of the user who would use the component. This outside configuration wasn't added to the component — it's a separate feature that we didn't need to worry about as developers. This is just one view of the work of an interceptor. The security interceptor in Windows 2000 validates each method call before the component gets to see it. This extra level of indirection is totally invisible to the user, the client application, the component, and even the component's developer. Only the network administrator is concerned about the changes that role-based security makes to the operation of the component.

So how does this magic take place? In the case of role-based security (but not necessarily with all forms of interception), the component is registered in the Catalog Manager, not within the Registry. The Catalog Manager, in turn, controls the Registry settings for the component. We saw earlier how Registry settings can make a very big difference in the way an application views a component. Change the Registry settings and you'll change the application's view of that component—at least to a certain extent. Because the Catalog Manager controls the Registry, it also affects the capability of Windows 2000 to perform component pre- and postprocessing. This means that the component calls can be redirected to the object that handles role-based security for interrogation before they're sent on to the component itself.

Tip Because interceptors are built right into Windows 2000, you no longer have to worry whether MTS will provide interception services for your object. Any required interceptors are provided automatically. This means that you no longer need to use SafeRef to ensure that your component receives interception services.

Interceptors need one other capability to do their job. They need to be able to cross context boundaries. Consider that any number of components on your server could use role-based security and that each of these components has a different context. Likewise, each application calling on the component for services will have its own context. Because Windows 2000 handles the application context in other ways, the interceptor only requires a reference to its own object context and the object context of the real object. As the interceptor performs its work and passes calls along to the real object, it has to translate the context from the interceptor context to one that the component will understand without changing the original application settings.

Note Interceptors are not limited to role-based security. I only used this example because it's a common interceptor that every component is likely to need. There are, for example, interceptors that track performance statistics for the components on your machine. You could even create custom interceptors to perform pre- or postprocessing of component calls.

Summary

This chapter provided a lot of theoretical information about ActiveX and COM. We discussed a variety of usage and theoretical concerns that you need to be aware of when using these technologies. In addition, we looked at some of the most important tools that you need to be familiar with when working with both ActiveX and COM. Here are some additional conclusions you can draw from the contents of this chapter:

✦ COM offers all of the cumulative effects of the advancements in programming technology like code reuse.

✦ COM offers many new benefits to the programmer like language independence, extensibility, and platform independence.

✦ OLE1 and OLE2 aren't different versions of the same product; the underlying technology is totally different. OLE1 relies on DDE, whereas OLE2 relies on COM.

✦ OLE2 benefits greatly from using COM as a basis, but the more important features rely on the OLE2 capability to view documents as objects.

✦ COM is a specification that defines how clients and servers interact.

✦ COM objects consist of several components, including methods, properties, events, interfaces, and connection points.

✦ Microsoft goals when creating COM, included binary compatibility, strong data typing, a base interface, reference counting so that the object could delete itself when no longer needed, a unique identifier, and a special component loader.

✦ Always look for the hidden component instead of creating one from scratch.

✦ DCOM works with components over a variety of network connections using protocols. It relies on the Open Group DCE-RPC as a method of communication and Registry entries to provide a seamless environment for both the client and the component.

✦ There are two ways to specify the remote server for creating an object when using DCOM. The first is to include two Registry entries that tell Windows which server to use. The second method is to specify the server during the object creation process using a COSERVERINFO data structure.

✦ COM+ is the latest update to Microsoft's component technology. It incorporates a lot of new features, most of which are designed to make COM+ easier to use, faster, and less prone to bugs than its predecessors.

✦ Interfaces are a big part of COM technology. There's one interface that's common to every component: IUnknown, which includes three functions. `QueryInterface()` allows you to determine which interfaces the component supports. `AddRef()` is called when you create a new instance of the component and `Release()` is called when you destroy an instance of the component.

✦ Objects are automatically destroyed when their reference count reaches 0.

✦ A context is a set of attributes that define an object in various ways. The main reason to use a context is for identification and security purposes.

✦ There are two types of contexts: call and object. The call context is transient and lasts only over the time that a method call takes place. The object context remains in place during the entire lifetime of the object.

✦ Interceptors intercept calls to or from a component, perform some extra processing, and then allow the calls to proceed as usual. COM+ applications are registered in the Catalog Manager instead of the Registry. Interceptors rely on the Catalog Manager to make Registry changes that allow the interceptor to gain control as needed over the processing stream. This is the technology that makes new features like role-based security possible.

✦   ✦   ✦

Understanding DCOM

This chapter helps you understand Distributed Component Object Model (DCOM). The first section is devoted to a discussion of the importance of DCOM as an adjunct to both COM and COM+. DCOM is actually a facilitating technology — it's a communication extension for COM and COM+ that makes distributed applications possible. In fact, it's the capability to communicate that makes DCOM an important technology today.

The second section contains a theoretical discussion of what DCOM is all about and what it means to you as a programmer. We'll look at the DCOM architecture as a whole and the various methodologies that you need to know to actually implement DCOM. Of course, while you do have the option of implementing these details directly, COM+ can hide them for you so that all you really need to know about is the needs of the component that you want to access from within the application.

We'll examine the network requirements of DCOM in the third section of the chapter. It's important to understand how network naming works. Other sections look at request forwarding (the act of sending a client request to another machine), the limitations of using a standard component as a distributed component, and the kinds of connections that you can create using DCOM. All of this information is important in learning how DCOM communicates. Remember that it's the communication feature that we're most interested in learning about.

One thing that often occurs when working with server-based components is that there are one or more instances of the component already running when the client makes a request. Sometimes it's necessary to access one of these existing objects in order to allow certain types of application communication to occur. The fourth section looks at the requirements of connecting to a specific object instance. Equipped with your new knowledge of how objects get accessed on a remote host, you'll be able to perform some types of object lifetime management, the next topic of discussion in this section. We'll also talk about one of many utilities that you'll need to use when working with COM, DCOM, and COM+ applications, the Running Object Table (ROT) Viewer.

The final section discusses DCOM and monikers. A moniker is simply a convenient name for a resource on another machine. This section explores monikers in general and then applies them to DCOM. You can discover how using monikers allows you to access resources on other machines without really knowing a lot about the other machines' configuration. In other words, using monikers helps you to avoid the problems of using specific Registry entries to make the connection between a container and server.

Why Use DCOM?

Let's talk for a moment about the real world of application development. You may be tasked to create an order-entry system. This system would definitely need links to your customer, order, and inventory databases. There may be other special requirements as well. For example, if your company handles hazardous materials, the order entry database would have to check for client licenses to handle the materials that the client ordered. If there are design elements in the order, a fax server or other graphics exchange system would need to be in place, and you'd need some way to catalog all of those images so that the customer orders wouldn't get mixed up. There are also credit checks to perform and details to check. In short, getting an order might not be as simple as looking up the client's name and what stock to order.

In the past, people would create a single, large application on a mainframe to handle all of these tasks. The application wouldn't work until all of the application elements were in place. Once the application did work, it would require the services of two or more programmers to keep it up-to-date. Obviously, these programmers would need to know how the entire application worked to service it, so any brain drain within the company could be disastrous. Such a system is large, unwieldy, and definitely too slow to develop in today's competitive market.

Distributed applications allow developers to create codependent applications that form a system. An order-entry system might include several applications, each providing one or more services to the system as a whole. Each application might rely on information supplied by other applications on the system. The applications don't have to exist on the same machine and don't even need to be developed at the same time. A distributed application allows you to get an incremental benefit from an order-entry system (or any other application system for that matter), while the rest of the applications are in development. In addition, the loss of one server may mean only losing one service that the system provides, rather than everything, as would happen in the mainframe environment.

DCOM is Microsoft's answer to the distributed application question—at least it's the first answer they came up with. It allows you to leverage the component technology that you're already familiar with in the form of COM across multiple machines on a network. DCOM offers two things that developers need today: distributed application support and code reusability. The distributed application support part of the picture allows you to develop entities like order-entry systems one component at a time. Even though the entire system isn't in place, the user can still derive some benefit from the components that are accessible. Code reuse means that once you've created and debugged a particular component, you can use it in a number of places within the system as a whole. It pays to look at DCOM as a method for creating service-oriented applications that you can put together like Legos to form a much larger system. The following sections look in more detail at the issue of how DCOM helps you develop better applications.

Uses of distributed applications

There are practical issues to consider when looking at DCOM as an application solution for your company. Distributed applications have become a requirement, rather than a luxury, in today's computing environment. Everywhere you look, someone is talking about better ways of creating a distributed computing environment. The following list provides some of the reasons that distributed applications are a must today.

✦ **Employees on the Road:** You need to provide some means for these employees to communicate with the company or at least work with standard applications like order entry in order to remain competitive.

✦ **The Internet:** You'll find that distributed applications and the Internet go hand-in-hand. Even if you aren't running an e-commerce site, there are business-to-business computing needs to consider. Many businesses can't afford to slow down for the communication lags caused by older technologies. Finally, there are the needs of your own company to consider. Larger companies often occupy more than one building, and using private leased lines to connect satellite offices to corporate headquarters is relatively expensive when compared to using Internet technologies.

✦ **Task Management:** Companies seldom have one type of client. This means that you could have one set of employees working with businesses, another with partners, and another with retail customers. Depending on the time of year, one set of employees could be swamped, while another set is wasting time playing solitaire while waiting for calls. DCOM can help you track the level of activity for the various parts of your order-entry system and adjust employee roles as needed to handle system demands.

✦ **Resource Management:** DCOM can help prioritize the use of scarce company resources like the fax server based on employee need and network load. In the past, most systems were static, which means that one group of employees might always get top priority to a device, even if they didn't need it at the time.

✦ **Centralize Business Processing:** DCOM allows you to place sensitive components on the server where they'll be well protected from prying eyes. You really
don't want other people to know how you bid on projects or perform other
kinds of business calculations. Using server-side components reduces the risk
that you'll inadvertently allow information to leak out of your company.

DCOM allows you to exploit fully the benefits of distributed applications to which
it also adds the features of COM. This means that DCOM applications can react to
a variety of user requests in addition to those normally associated with distributed
application development. A simple example of this is the capability to use file
associations that rely on applications located on other machines. Technically,
a user could double-click a file on the local machine and execute an application
located on the server rather than on the local hard drive.

Code reuse issues

Let's talk some more about code reusability. Although this has been a priority for
quite some time, developers are still looking for new ways to make code reusability
more of a reality and less of a pipe dream. Companies are trying out a variety of
component technologies that promise to provide them with the edge they need in
the marketplace. Normally, moving an application from the desktop to the server
means writing completely new code — or at least creating new applications to hold
the existing business logic. So, even if part of the code is reusable, a move from the
desktop to the server still requires a major expenditure of development time.

COM was yesterday's technology of choice for many Windows developers. In the
past, a developer's main concern was making things work on the desktop. COM
will no longer answer all of the application development needs of a growing company because it doesn't support a distributed environment. In short, what we're
really talking about is moving at least part of the application from the desktop
to the server.

Code reusability is part of the reason that Microsoft has extended COM through
the use of technologies like DCOM. Using DCOM means that you can take a tested
component from the desktop and place it on a server. The resulting application will
probably work with a few very minor changes and perhaps without any changes at
all. With a few additional modifications, you can make the component more secure
and better capable of running in the distributed application environment. This is
code reuse in the truest sense of the word.

DCOM as a COM add-on

DCOM is an add-on technology to COM. In its simplest form, DCOM allows a client to
call on the services of a server located on a remote machine. More than that, DCOM
allows the server to execute on the remote machine, which frees up resources on

the client. In other words, DCOM is a technology that will work in a distributed environment and still provide the component technology that companies require. It's DCOM's capability to work across machines that allows it to provide all of the distributed application benefits that we talked about earlier. The use of server-side components ensures that you maintain control over application functionality and data, yet provide the user with the flexibility needed in today's mobile computing environment.

Unlike COM, where the resource location must be known and registered on the client machine, DCOM allows communication between objects on a LAN, WAN, or the Internet. Yes, you must know the location of the object at some point (otherwise, the application would never find it), but DCOM relaxes some of the requirements for having the object registered locally.

DCOM is also used as the basis for COM+ communication. Whenever communication takes place between two machines, DCOM is the agent that is used to allow that communication to occur. However, when working with COM+, you no longer need worry about many DCOM details, even though these details are still essential to communication. COM+ automates many of the processes that take place beneath the surface of Windows 2000, to the point where you may not realize DCOM is in action until something goes wrong.

The reason to study DCOM when working with COM+ applications, therefore, isn't necessarily to learn about every intricacy of the technology. What you really need to learn is what's going on beneath the surface so that you can fix errant applications faster when something does go wrong. While this chapter does focus on DCOM as a separate technology, the information that you need to take away when working with COM+ applications is an understanding of what happens automatically when your COM+ application executes.

DCOM imperfections

Any generalized technology will fail in some way when given specific application requirements. Most of us are used to compensating for flaws in the overall design of a generalized technology. (Developers tend to view technology omissions as flaws, even when the technology wasn't designed to provide a specific service.) So, what are some of the problems encountered when using DCOM? The following list shows the four main problems that developers need to be aware of, even though COM+ fixes quite a few more problems than that.

✦ **Security:** DCOM provides a modicum of security, but not at the same level as COM+ does using newer technologies like Kerberos.

✦ **Connectivity:** Both the client and server must exist at the same time when using DCOM, something that COM+ users don't need to worry about.

✦ **Lack of Data Delivery Guarantees:** A DCOM connection doesn't provide transactional guarantees of any kind unless those guarantees are provided through the underlying network protocol.

✦ **Protocol Intolerance:** For the most part, you'll find that a DCOM client requires a TCP/IP connection to the server before it'll work. Theoretically, TCP/IP can coexist with other protocols like IPX/SPX and NetBEUI, but in practice, using more than one protocol can create problems. There have been times when I've had to remove the NetBEUI support from a client to force it to use TCP/IP when connecting to the server. Although this isn't a major problem, it's one that you need to be aware of even when using COM+.

There are also a few minor pitfalls to consider when using DCOM, none of which is likely to cause problems for the majority of DCOM users. You can't use DCOM on a Windows 3.x machine. This means that older machines require an upgrade to Windows 9x, Windows NT, or Windows 2000 to use DCOM. You might want to use this as an excuse to simply get rid of your old machines. Some versions of Windows don't come with DCOM support automatically installed. If you have an application that doesn't appear to work on a Windows 95 workstation, for example, you probably need to download DCOM support from Microsoft's Web site and install it. You'll find DCOM support at `http://www.microsoft.com/Com/resources/downloads.asp`. There are also security requirements to consider. In many cases, a DCOM connection won't work simply because the user has insufficient rights to the required component. The reason that many developers don't think of this problem is that they aren't used to thinking about it on the desktop.

An Overview of the DCOM Architecture

In this section, I answer a lot of theoretical questions about DCOM. For example, many of you may not know why DCOM is such a great architectural addition. Before you read this section, however, you may want to familiarize yourself with the architectural details of COM, DCOM, and COM+. We examined many of these architectural details in Chapter 4. The Classes of COM and COM+ Applications section of that chapter explored the progression of technologies beginning with OLE1 and OLE2, progressing through ActiveX, and finally ending with the latest Microsoft technology, COM+.

In the first section that follows, we'll look at the question of why you'd use DCOM as a developer (we've already explored the business reasons for doing so in "Why Use DCOM?" above). As part of the initial discussion, we'll also look at the question of when DCOM is either overkill or inappropriate (when other technologies can take care of the situation better). For example, COM is still the best choice when creating components for pure desktop applications. However, it's important to realize that there are very few pure desktop applications written today for business use, which means that DCOM is probably less overkill than you might think.

The second section will discuss what makes DCOM different from COM (other than the fact that the COM object executes on one machine and the application on another). It's important to have an overall understanding of what makes the technology work. Because DCOM is used as the basis for COM+ communication, you'll also want to understand how it works within that environment. We'll look at this issue in various sections of Chapter 6 as part of the discussion of the COM+ components.

Why DCOM?

There are a lot of reasons to use DCOM. The simple reason is that it's an existing technology that allows you to create distributed applications. However, DCOM provides a lot more than just the capability to run COM objects from a remote location. The following list provides just a few of the reasons why using DCOM is essential in some situations.

✦ **Fault Tolerance:** DCOM can endure both hardware and network failures. What this means is that you gain some level of reliability. Obviously, the size of the gain depends on your current network configuration and what you expect DCOM to do.

✦ **Scalability:** Theoretically, you could write a single DCOM object and use that same object no matter how large your company gets. There are some practical considerations that you need to take into account, such as a multiple server scenario; but for the most part, DCOM is more scalable than COM. DCOM is less scalable than COM+, however, because it only works for client/server connections. DCOM also lacks the reliability features of COM+.

✦ **Load Balancing:** One problem with the desktop computer is that one machine might have an overloaded processor, while another wastes processor cycles waiting for work. DCOM helps you balance the load on your entire network and makes it more efficient by using more of those wasted resources.

✦ **Maintenance Ease:** Placing a single COM object on the server, and then enabling all of the clients on your network to access it is one way to reduce the amount of time required to implement a solution. Initial releases and updates can now be performed by making one change to a single machine instead of the same change to every machine on the network.

✦ **Flexibility:** DCOM hides many implementation details from the client. The client thinks that it always has a local connection to the server, which greatly simplifies the development process. Server hiding allows you to place the server where it's needed without rewriting any application code. Using DCOM also enables you to fine-tune the application for maximum performance by creating the best possible environment for both client and server. For example, you can move the server object from one machine to another when resources on the first machine become strained. All you need to do on the client machine is make a simple configuration change in the Registry.

✦ **Connection Management:** DCOM uses the same reference-counting mechanism as COM does to know when it's safe to release a component. However, DCOM goes beyond reference counting when it comes to the connection itself. Because network connections are uncertain at best, DCOM sends a periodic "ping" to the client (at approximately two-minute intervals). If the client doesn't respond for three consecutive pings, then DCOM considers the connection broken and decrements the component count. This ensures that the component only remains active when there are active clients to service. Of course, the requirement to ping the client constantly wastes processing cycles, which is something that you can get around in COM+. You'll also find that DCOM allows both client/server unidirectional communication and the peer connections required for two-way communication. COM+ solutions lack two-way communication, which is another reason DCOM will hang around for the foreseeable future.

As you can see, there are a lot of good reasons to use DCOM in a distributed application environment. Of course, that begs the question of what a distributed environment is and what kind of applications it can support. A distributed environment occurs whenever two or more machines are physically involved with application execution. In other words, an application that relies on data stored on a second machine doesn't constitute a distributed environment. It's only when part of the processing takes place on the second machine that you can say that the application is distributed. Microsoft has slightly extended the meaning of distributed application to include three machines. A two-machine application is more properly termed a client/server application in Microsoft parlance.

There are actually two kinds of distributed environments, at least in the context of this discussion. The first type involves an application designed from the ground up for a distributed environment that really doesn't work in any other environment. Applications that fall into this category include teleconferencing and many forms of database management. The second type consists of two machines working together toward an end result. The application could just as easily execute on a single machine; however, the primary purpose of distribution is to gain some performance advantage through load balancing.

Obviously, you don't get all of the advantages that DCOM provides for free; there's always some cost involved with implementing any technology. These drawbacks help determine when DCOM is the appropriate choice for a specific application programming need. For example, you may not want to use DCOM in place of COM when all processing can be performed locally. The following list provides an overview of some of the problems that occur when working with DCOM.

✦ **Security:** Any time you send data over a network, you take the risk of enabling someone to see it. COM not only deals with code, it also works with data. Because the component is executing on the server, the only thing that gets transferred over the network connection is the data, which is also the element that you want to protect most. As with any distributed technology, DCOM raises many security issues that you need to consider before implementation. Fortunately, with Windows 2000, your choice of security features has improved, making DCOM a much safer networking choice when only Windows 2000 machines are involved.

✦ **Performance:** Using DCOM involves many performance inhibitors. You can't expect to get desktop performance from DCOM unless the remote machine offers a great amount of resources in terms of memory, hard disk space, and raw processor speed. In short, the remote machine needs to process the information at a much higher rate of speed than the client to get what appears to be desktop performance for that particular user. The first performance problem is the connection itself. Using DCOM means that you go through more layers to create and maintain a connection to the server. Of course, the network connection itself adds further delays. Finally, you have to consider server latency—the time the component waits for the server to allow it to execute.

✦ **Reliability:** DCOM normally relies on the User Datagram Protocol (UDP) subset of TCP/IP to transfer data when this protocol is available. UDP is a connectionless protocol that relies on a combination of an IP address and port number to get data from one point to another. Unfortunately, UDP can present a number of problems, including the inability to guarantee a successful data transfer. The use of acknowledgements reduces the impact of using UDP. In addition, using UDP allows DCOM to perform several data transfer optimizations by merging acknowledge packages with data and pinging (client keep-alive) messages.

Note

Although DCOM prefers to use UDP when it is available, there isn't any rule that says your application must use UDP. DCOM is flexible enough to allow the use of other protocols—even custom protocols. Many of the shortcomings mentioned here can be overcome by using custom protocols. For example, you can overcome the security issues by using a protocol that sends the data in encrypted form. We'll see later that there are many configuration options for DCOM that allow you to determine exactly how a communication should take place. You have the option of encrypting the data in several ways, making it more secure.

✦ **Connection Availability:** Any distributed application needs to deal with the problem of lost or garbled connections. In addition, there's no guarantee that a connection will be available when the user actually needs it. Although solutions like data caching do alleviate part of the problem, you still need to consider connection management when building a COM object for distributed use. COM+ gets around the problem of connection availability by using disconnected application technology. This technology relies on queued components to store a communication on disk if no connection between client and server exists. The problem with this technique is that the connection only works one way. You actually have to create a second connection for two-way communication.

SOAP, the replacement for DCOM

Microsoft recently introduced a new technology (actually a protocol) for Windows 2000 DNA called Simple Object Access Protocol (SOAP). SOAP will eventually replace DCOM for Internet use. Although the initial release of SOAP will be for Windows 2000 DNA, the technology will definitely be used in other places as time passes. SOAP provides the means for exchanging data between COM and foreign component technologies like Common Object Request Broker Architecture (CORBA) using XML (extensible markup language) as an intermediary. Unfortunately, SOAP wasn't included as part of Windows 2000, which means that we'll be spending more time working in a mixed technology environment after SOAP is released. In addition, you'll find that Microsoft has a very poor track record in removing old technologies from its operating systems, especially if that technology serves some purpose. Consider that Windows Explorer still uses DDE for file associations. (You can verify this by looking at the file associations for Microsoft products like the Word DOC file.) SOAP is expected to appear in new Microsoft products sometime soon. You can learn about Microsoft's business plans for SOAP at http://www.internetwk.com/story/INW19991013S0004.

Microsoft plans to release an update to Visual Studio next year that will allow a developer to access SOAP directly. (The actual date of release for any new version of Visual Studio or service packs for existing versions that include SOAP aren't set in concrete — SOAP may be available sooner than anticipated.) However, the smart developer will retain knowledge of DCOM because this technology is unlikely to go away anytime soon. In most cases, new DCOM development will take place with LAN or intranet applications. SOAP is the best technology to use for new Internet applications because it allows for a much higher level of interactivity with other component technologies and is much more flexible. You can find out more about the Microsoft view of SOAP at http://www.msdn.microsoft.com/workshop/xml/general/soaptemplate.asp.

In times past, Microsoft would have created its own proprietary standard for SOAP as it has for technologies like COM. However, some new thinking is occurring at Microsoft, and it is hoped that SOAP will go through some type of public forum for approval. With this in mind, Microsoft has submitted a SOAP draft to the Internet Engineering Task Force (IETF) for approval. If you want to see the publicly available specification for SOAP in request for comment (RFC) format, look at http://search.ietf.org/internet-drafts/draft-box-http-soap-01.txt. The standards document includes such features as language element descriptions, statement of purpose, and examples of how the language would appear when used on a Web page. Because this is an IETF draft, all of the details are up for discussion. However, the document still provides a good idea of how SOAP may eventually affect your Web development. It will also help you to understand how Microsoft plans to support remote procedure calls (RPCs) over the Internet.

The DCOM difference from the Visual Basic perspective

One thing that you need to worry about when working with a remote access protocol such as DCOM is precisely how the connection is to take place. After all, without a good connection, many other considerations are rendered moot. You also need to be aware of the many kinds of connection that an application could establish with the server. Because the big difference between COM and DCOM is the distributed application orientation of DCOM, you can no longer assume certain things when you create a DCOM application. For example, you can't assume that the server will be available. A network connection may not be available at the time of the client request, or the server may be down. So, although a desktop application can always assume that it will find the component it needs as long as the component is installed on the local machine, a DCOM application can't assume anything about the connection.

You also need to consider things like error recovery and what to do if the connection is severed half way through a communication. Unlike COM+, which provides built-in features that ensure data gets transmitted once, and only once, DCOM offers little in the way of error handling. Depending on the network protocol you use, DCOM may not even know whether the data made it safely to the recipient machine. When using DCOM, you have to provide the logic that checks for transmission errors after an unexpected loss of connection. Obviously, reliability concerns are high for any business that relies on technologies like DCOM to conduct business — the connection that DCOM creates is at the center of any discussion about the viability of using the technology for a certain kind of application.

This section answers several questions. First, we'll look at how the connection actually works from the Visual Basic developer's perspective. You've already seen an overview of this information in the DCOM section of Chapter 4, but that section dealt with the API. Microsoft provides much better methods for Visual Basic developers to instantiate an object on another machine.

Second, we'll look at load balancing concerns. We'll answer the question of what you do when an application becomes very large and you need more than one server to run it successfully. An enterprise application can have so many users that there's no way to guarantee fast response times without having multiple servers operating in a cluster environment. Obviously, using multiple servers is also a prerequisite for ensuring application reliability. A single server failure may affect performance, but it won't make the application inaccessible if you use a cluster to run multiple copies of the same application.

Creating a connection with Visual Basic

There are a few circumstances when you may want to create an object using one of the Windows API function calls that we talked about in Chapter 4. For example, there isn't a convenient way to create an object from a stream or file using standard Visual Basic functions. However, most applications don't need to do this—all they really need to do is perform the equivalent of a `CoCreateInstanceEx()` API function call to create the object on a remote machine using the component as a template.

The Visual Basic function that you'll use to create remote objects, in most cases, is `CreateObject()`. You may already be familiar with this function. Some developers use it with the local machine in mind and never consider the fact that this function will also work with a remote machine. The only caveat is that you must know the remote machine's name during design time, or create a Registry entry that will allow you to retrieve the server's name during runtime. Here's a very simple example of the `CreateObject()` function in use.

```
Dim MyObject as Object
Set MyObject = CreateObject("ObjApp.ObjType", "RemMachName")
```

Tip   Another alternative to direct programming of the DCOM connection is to use the same methodology that you use for creating a local connection, then make a special entry in the Registry that redirects the DCOM connection to another machine. We talked about this issue in Chapter 2. The advantage of using the generalized programming approach is that you don't have to worry about the location of the component at design time. In addition, changes in component location won't affect the operation of the application as long as the correct Registry entries are made. Of course, this also means that you must create the requisite Registry entries on every workstation. There are automated methods for doing this, but they're error prone. Depending on the network administrator to make the required changes on a large network would be error prone as well. In short, even though the direct coding approach reduces the flexibility of your application and increases the need for application updates, it's also the most reliable method for making contact with the correct server.

As you can see, the process is relatively simple. All you need to do is create an empty object as usual, then assign it to the output of the `CreateObject()` function. Notice that `CreateObject()` requires two inputs. The first input is a dot format class name. The first part of the class name is the name of the application that contains the object you want to create. This is normally the same as the name of the component's DLL. The second part of the class name is the class type within the component file. This is the name that you assign to the component so that other people can access it. For example, if you had a financial DLL named FINANCE.DLL and it contained a class called AddIt, then the dot format class name would be Finance.AddIt. The second input is the name of the remote machine. There isn't any reason to use the universal naming convention (UNC) format here—just use the actual name of the machine as it appears in My Network Neighborhood. We'll see how this works in a real-world example when we create a DCOM application in Chapter 10.

So, what happens if there's a connection problem, the server is down, or the component isn't installed on the remote machine? Visual Basic creates a runtime error. Because you don't want the application to display a runtime error that the user won't understand, you need to provide error handling of some type. In most cases, adding an On Error statement along with the appropriate error-handling code works well.

Tip

Any client-side application that you create should be capable of handling errors passed back by the server-side component. What this means is that the server will need an On Error statement just like the client-side application needs one. The difference is that the server will pass the Err object back to the client for handling, rather than handle it internally (unless the error is such that the component can perform some level of self-correction). A server-side component should never have any form of user interface. You don't want the component to display an error message on the server screen that no one will ever see. As a result, one of the better ways to handle component failures is to pass the data back to the client for handling by the client. At least this technique allows the user to see what's happening and take steps to fix the problem whenever possible. (We'll look at things like event-log handling later in the book.)

Load balancing concerns

Load balancing is another connection-related problem. Normally, you begin with all of the server-side components required for an application loaded onto a single machine. As people get added to the application user's list, you may have to move some components to other machines to avoid overloading the original machine. Breaking the component into smaller pieces may also relieve some server stress. However, at some point, even a well-designed component may overload a single server. At this point, you need to balance the component load across multiple servers.

DCOM intrinsically supports two types of load balancing—static and dynamic. The first relies on the assignment of users to specific servers, while the second relies on component referral techniques. Windows 2000 adds a third form of load balancing in the form of a COM+ feature called, oddly enough, Network Load Balancing (NLB). This third form of load balancing relies on one or more routers and a cluster of servers.

Web Resource

NLB works by measuring the total load on each server, and then assigning a user to the least busy server without regard to the individual applications running on that server. This means the user won't get the best application performance, simply the best server performance based on specific criteria. Microsoft originally provided a COM+-specific alternative to Network Load Balancing called Component Load Balancing (CLB) during the Windows 2000 beta. This feature was pulled for the reasons found at http://www.microsoft.com/windows2000/news/fromms/clb.asp. As mentioned in the article, CLB will reappear as part of Microsoft's AppCenter Server. Using CLB in addition to NLB and Cluster Services will increase the performance of COM+ components dramatically because CLB will allow the router to account for individual application performance, as well as to server performance as a whole.

Static load balancing

Static load balancing occurs when you assign specific users to specific servers. Older versions of Windows normally rely on Registry entries to enforce the assignment of user machines to a specific server. Fortunately, administrators can use the Win32 remote Registry functions to make any changes.

Another way to statically load balance DCOM connections is to use a database containing usernames and the servers that they're assigned to. While this method does allow the administrator to make reassignments quickly, it also means adding some processing overhead to the connection and some complexity to the application. The overhead comes into play in several ways, the most important of which is the time required for the client to look up the appropriate server prior to requesting component services. In addition, the client has to be rewritten to use the database, which may make the application unnecessarily complex and inflexible.

Yet another method of overcoming problems with static load balancing is to use a referral component. In this case, the client is designed to request the component's services from the referral component at the outset, so no extra programming is required. After the referral component receives a request, it automatically makes the connection for the client, reducing the amount of overhead from using this technique. The obvious downside of this form of static load balancing is that you need to write a special referral component.

Active Directory is the storage medium of choice for Windows 2000 developers. Instead of placing the DCOM entry in the Registry, the DCOM entry appears in the Active Directory centralized storage. The actual storage location is called the COM+ Catalog; it unites the COM and Microsoft Transaction Server (MTS) Registry entry methods. Obviously, this second method allows the administrator to make all required configuration changes from one location to a store that's always online, rather than to multiple Registries, some of which may be offline because the associated machines are turned off. In addition, this second method allows the administrator to assign a specific user to a specific server, rather than assigning a machine to a server.

Both developers and administrators will be able to interact with the COM+ Catalog using the COM+ Explorer. In addition, Microsoft is developing a series of new COM interfaces that will allow the developer to interface with the COM+ Catalog directly.

Two problems with static load balancing are that you need a predictable load and that you need administrator intervention to implement it. In other words, static load balancing works fine for an order-entry system where the same number of users log in each day. It doesn't work well for an Internet site where the number of users may vary by a large amount over a period of a few hours.

Dynamic load balancing

Dynamic load balancing can also rely on the referral component technique described earlier. However, in this case, the referral component considers factors such as current server load, past user request history, and current network topology when assigning a user to a machine, instead of assigning the user based on a static list. Using this technique means that the referral component requires more time to get the job done, but that the network processes requests more efficiently once the connection is made.

There are several problems with this approach. For one thing, the complexity of the referral component is greatly increased. Instead of just directing the user's request to another component, the referral component now has to make some decision as to which server to select. In addition, this technique relies on a database for storing user request history, the availability of server statistics (which must be refreshed for each request), and the availability of network topology data. In other words, dynamic load balancing is much harder to implement because you essentially replace the network administrator with some software.

Balancing a load at connection time doesn't necessarily mean that the load remains balanced either. True dynamic load balancing needs to incorporate some type of reconnect strategy. As the load from a user on one machine increases and the load from a user on another machine decreases, it may be necessary to reconnect them to different servers to keep the load on both servers balanced. Unfortunately, DCOM doesn't provide any built-in functionality for implementing a reconnection strategy, which means that the developer needs to create yet another component that monitors the current situation and makes reconnection recommendations as necessary.

Implementing a reconnection strategy is complicated by the requirement of the component to retain state information for the client. The component and client both need to decide that the current state information is no longer required, then request a reconnection before the next method invocation. As you can see, building a reconnection strategy is extremely complex, making the prospect of adding yet another server to the network quite appealing. The complexity of the problem is most likely one of the reasons that Microsoft didn't implement a reconnection strategy as part of DCOM itself.

Network load balancing

NLB is a new feature that's built into Windows 2000. This method assumes that you have many users to manage and that the application you create adheres to Microsoft's new Distributed interNet Applications (DNA) Architecture.

Implementing the COM+ form of NLB is relatively easy. The first thing you need is an application cluster, which is a set of up to eight machines that are capable of running the requested component. After you have the application cluster machines loaded with the server-side components that you want to use, you need to add a load-balancing router to the picture. The load-balancing router sends client requests to one of the machines in the application cluster.

The client application won't access the application cluster machines directly. What happens instead is that client requests are sent to the load-balancing router. The load-balancing router uses an algorithm to determine which application cluster machine is least busy and then routes the request to that application cluster machine. The load-balancing router needs to ascertain what criteria to use to determine application cluster machine load. The default algorithm uses a response-time algorithm to determine which machine to use. You can, however, write your own load-balancing engine that determines which application cluster machine is least busy. For example, you may conclude that the number of available resources is a better way to determine which application cluster machine has the lightest load if your component requires a lot of resources to execute.

The bottom line from a developer's perspective is that you write your application to direct all server-side component requests to the load-balancing router. If the configuration of the network changes, it doesn't matter because the load-balancing router still accepts all component requests. As you can see, using the COM+ methodology for balancing the component load on several servers is the easiest method to implement, as long as you have all the required hardware running Windows 2000.

Note   The current MTS method for creating components in a load-balanced environment is to create the reference early and hold on to it as long as possible. This approach ensures that the client gets the resources required to complete execution of a given task and that MTS operates as efficiently as possible. The new approach for COM+ is to create components only when necessary and to release them as early as possible to free resources. Obviously, these two approaches are completely opposite to each other, which means that you may have to rewrite some of your older applications to take advantage of the latest COM+ technology. Unless performance isn't a problem on your network, it's usually well worth the effort of rewriting a component to take advantage of this new technology.

Connecting to a Specific Object Instance

There are times when you may want to connect to an existing instance of an object, rather than create a new instance of the object. For example, you may need to access a running component from within a thread of an application or as a connecting link from another application.

This section looks at the problems of connecting to a running object instance. Connecting to an existing object not only entails problems with the object itself, such as managing state information, but also problems with managing the lifetime of that object (you don't want the object to self-destruct if there are references to it). The following sections help you to understand both of these issues.

Object lifetime management

When an application programmer creates a standalone application designed to operate on a single machine, there's no doubt as to the lifetime of the objects that application creates. The objects are no longer needed when the user or the system closes the application. The reason is simple: the application using the objects determines their lifetime because they're part of the application itself. Of course, this scenario assumes that the developer has created everything within the application and that nothing within the application is accessible to the outside world.

Things change a little when an application is composed of components that are created by other programmers and the application isn't certain when the object instances are no longer needed. In this case, COM uses reference counting. Each time an object gains a new connection, its reference count rises. Likewise, when an application no longer needs the object, COM reduces the reference count by one. When the reference count reaches zero, the object is destroyed. This is the typical scenario for an in-process server (normally a DLL of some type).

The problem becomes even more difficult to manage when an application and its associated components execute in more than one process. There are times when this happens on the local machine. For example, if you create a compound document, the embedded document requires the services of a server that exists outside of the current process for display and editing needs. Every out-of-process server (normally an EXE) falls into this category. In this case, reference counts alone won't allow proper object lifetime management because there are connections from outside of the current process.

Note
DCOM applications, which execute on more than one machine, always fall into the out-of-process server category because they're no longer in a single-process environment. While DCOM is actually COM with a longer wire, it treats every component as an out-of-process server even though many of the components appear to the client as an in-process server. In other words, DCOM does add complexity to the object lifetime management problems that occur when using components. COM+ makes the problem worse because it uses DCOM as a basis for communication with two or more machines. As the number of machines involved with an application transaction increase, the complexity of object lifetime increases as well. A COM+ application could theoretically span an infinite number of machines, making object lifetime management critical.

To give you a better idea of why a reference alone can't do the job, consider the following scenario. Begin by thinking about what happens when a user embeds a CorelDraw drawing into a Word document. Every time the user opens the Word document, Word creates an instance of the CorelDraw out-of-process server to handle the display of the CorelDraw drawing embedded in the Word document. When the user closes the document, the reference count for the CorelDraw out-of-process server goes to 0 and the object destroys itself.

What happens when the user clicks on the CorelDraw drawing within the Word document, uses Edit ➪ Select All to grab the entire document, copies it, then embeds it into an Excel document? When the user opens the document in Excel, there are actually two references to the CorelDraw out-of-process server. The first is obvious; Excel needs a reference to the CorelDraw out-of-process server to display the figure. The second comes from Word, which acts as the container for the CorelDraw drawing. When the user closes Excel, the first reference to the CorelDraw out-of-process server is released, but because Excel has no direct link to Word, the second reference remains in place.

This is where the concept of strong and weak references comes into play. A strong reference ensures that an object remains open, while a weak reference doesn't. In other words, Excel has a strong reference in our example, whereas Word has a weak reference. The use of a weak reference allows Word to act as a container for the CorelDraw document, but the weak reference isn't enough to keep the document open after Excel is closed by the user. Both the Word and CorelDraw out-of-process servers are released automatically when the user closes Excel, which is how things are supposed to work from the user's perspective. (All this assumes that every programmer out there observes every COM rule, which doesn't happen. This section looks at a perfect scenario in which all of the components behave exactly as expected.)

What actually happens is that the CorelDraw out-of-process server keeps track of both locks (strong references) and weak references. When the number of locks reaches zero, CorelDraw's out-of-process server issues a `Close()` method call. The `Close()` method does everything needed to "encourage" the reference count to go to zero, including revoking its ROT entry (so that no other clients can attach to the current instantiation of the object), sending an `OnClose()` notification to any attached clients with weak references, closing any internal pseudo-objects, and disconnecting any remote connections. After the reference count reaches zero, the object is destroyed and the memory is freed.

Working with the running object table

So far, we've looked at the requirements for maintaining the lifetime of an object. In the previous section, we talked about an example application that requires two links to a CorelDraw out-of-process server: a weak one from Word and a strong one from Excel. The inclusion of a weak link means that somewhere along the way Word created a reference to the already running CorelDraw object. Obviously, compound documents are just one situation when multiple references to the same object are needed; but this is a very good example because compound documents are often created.

Of course, the question is how Word obtained the information necessary to create a reference to the CorelDraw out-of-process server. Components that allow a client to create a connection to a running instance need to register themselves in a special COM table called the running object table (ROT). In short, the ROT contains a reference to the object so clients can attach to it.

There are two levels of registration: strong and weak. The main difference between strong and weak ROT registration is that a strong registration prevents an object from shutting down until all of the connected clients have also shut down. A weak reference is shut down automatically after all strong references to the object are cleared. In most cases, you want to use the default registration level of weak.

Objects register themselves in the ROT using the `IRunningObjectTable::Register()` method. The object itself determines whether the registration is strong or weak. The default is to create a weak registration. Adding the `ROTFLAGS_REGISTRATIONKEEPSALIVE` flag creates a strong registration. In addition, the object can control which clients get to create a reference to the object. The default allows only clients that are part of the original application window to gain access to the object. However, adding the `ROTFLAGS_ALLOWANYCLIENT` flag allows any client to create a reference to the object. An object removes itself from the ROT using the `Revoke()` method.

You can use the `GetObject()` function to create a strong link with Visual Basic. All you need to do is leave the first argument blank and provide a class name as the second argument. (Remember that the class name consists of the component file name and the internal component name separated by a period. Excel.Application is an example of a class name.) If the object doesn't exist at the time you make the call (Excel isn't running), the `GetObject()` function will return an error. Detecting the error allows you to create a new instance of the object using the `GetObject()` function and the name of the file that you want to open.

Note Microsoft provides a handy utility for viewing the ROT called the ROT Viewer. We'll discuss this utility later in this chapter. Along with the discussion of the utility's operation, we'll look at how you can use it to make development easier. Combining the OLE/COM Object Viewer with this utility also tends to solve problems in working with controls for which you don't have the source code.

DCOM and Monikers

DCOM provides an array of methods for identifying the specific object instances that an application needs to use. While a unique CLSID and (optionally) a server name always identify the object itself, the instantiated object can be identified by a variety of methods, such as a URL for a Web page. The process of naming a specific instance of a COM object is called creating a moniker. The moniker is used to identify the object.

The following sections visit several issues related to DCOM and its use of monikers. Obviously, the first topic we need to cover is how monikers work in the first place. Part of this operational view of monikers requires the use of the ROT Viewer utility supplied with Visual Studio and the Platform SDK. The second section tells you about this utility and how you can use it to better understand the way objects on your machine are accessed. The third section discusses the Remote Automation Connection Manager, a utility that makes creating connections faster and easier. The fourth

section shows you how to use the ROT Viewer, along with other utilities like the
Registry Editor and the OLE/COM Object Viewer, to reduce application coding time.
The techniques in this section also ensure that your applications work correctly the
first time and allow you to debug applications in a relatively short time.

How monikers work

The monikers supported by DCOM can vary a great deal in part because the moniker
itself is an object. The moniker object contains the logic necessary to find the running
instance of the object that it identifies. In fact, like so many other areas of COM,
there's a standard interface designed to perform this work known as IMoniker.

All of the moniker API calls are located in OLE32.DLL, a standard part of every
Windows installation. This means that even though Visual Basic doesn't directly
support functions that access the moniker API, you can add this support with
relative ease. Figure 5-1 shows a Dependency Walker view of OLE32.DLL. This DLL
contains quite a few of the API calls that you need for detailed DCOM work. It's no
surprise that RPCRT.DLL (remote procedure call runtime) is one of the support
modules for OLE32.DLL because of its role in supporting monikers.

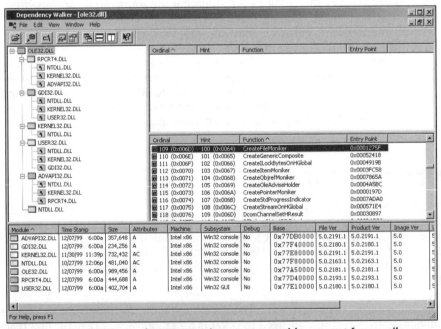

Figure 5-1: OLE32.DLL and RPCRT.DLL interact to provide support for monikers
in DCOM.

Before you get the idea that every component you create will appear in the ROT with a moniker attached, you need to know that the moniker refers to a file or other storage reference of some sort. In fact, there are five different types of monikers supported by Windows, each of which has a special purpose. The following list will help you understand the various moniker types (the two most common of which are file and item monikers).

✦ **File Moniker:** A standard file object. Whether the file appears on the Internet, a WAN, a LAN, or on your local hard drive is immaterial — the moniker binds an object and a file together. The object then registers this combination in the ROT, which allows other applications to interact with that object. You can use the `CreateFileMoniker()`API function to create a file moniker. This method requires you to input parameters: the name and path to a file, and a pointer to the variable used to hold the interface pointer.

✦ **Item Moniker:** Not every object that you need to reference is a file; some objects are contained within files or other objects. An item moniker references an object stored within a container of some type. Item monikers can also be used to refer to pseudo-objects such as a range of cells in a spreadsheet. Use the `CreateItemMoniker()` API function to create an item moniker. This function requires three inputs: a delimiter used to separate the object's name from the container's name in the ROT display, a string containing the name of the object, and the address of a variable used to hold the IMoniker interface pointer.

✦ **Generic Composite Moniker:** The generic composite marker combines several monikers into a single moniker. The monikers don't have to be of the same type, which means that you can use different classes of monikers in tandem. Use the `CreateGenericComposite()` API function to create a generic composite moniker. This method requires three parameters as input: a pointer to the first moniker, a pointer to the second moniker (which can be another generic composite moniker), and the address of a variable that holds the resulting IMoniker interface pointer.

✦ **Anti-Moniker.** This is the inverse of a file, pointer, or item moniker. It's used primarily to create a relative reference to an object. In essence, you create a moniker that provides a relative reference of one moniker when compared to another moniker. (It helps to think of this relationship as a relative file path — the relative file path is a reference to a particular file using the current position in the directory structure as a starting point.) Use the `CreateAntiMoniker()` API function to create an anti-moniker. This method only requires one input parameter: the address of a variable used to hold the resulting IMoniker interface pointer.

✦ **Pointer Moniker:** This is a reference to an object in memory. This is the only moniker type that can't be saved to permanent storage. Use the `CreatePointer Moniker()` API function to create a pointer moniker. This method requires two inputs: a pointer to the interface that you want to create a moniker for, and the address of a variable used to hold the IMoniker interface pointer.

Using the running object table viewer

Now that you have a better idea of how monikers and DCOM work together, it's time to see the ROT in action. Microsoft provides the ROT Viewer utility for the purpose of seeing what objects are registered in the ROT. Not only is this a great diagnostic tool for your own applications, but it also provides a great way to find out more about how other applications work.

You can find the ROT Viewer listed with the other Visual Studio/Platform SDK tools installed on your machine. Figure 5-2 shows a typical example of a ROT Viewer window. In this case, we're looking at the compound document created in Excel used earlier for explanation purposes. (The Excel and Word documents are on the CD-ROM provided with this book, along with the embedded image file.)

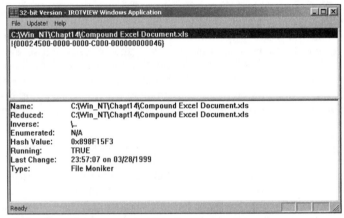

Figure 5-2: This is an example of a file moniker.

The top half of the ROT Viewer window contains a list of 32-bit applications that have registered an object with the ROT. An application can register more than one object. Figure 5-2 shows that Excel has registered two objects: one is a file moniker and the other is an item moniker.

The bottom half of the ROT Viewer window contains information about the object currently selected in the top half. In Figure 5-2, the selected object is a file moniker, and the bottom half of the ROT viewer shows information about that moniker. A file moniker entry includes the path and filename for the file. There's also status information that tells the last time the file was modified and whether the application is running. In addition, the ROT Viewer tells you what kind of object you're seeing.

Select the second object in the top half of this display and you'll see the item moniker display shown in Figure 5-3. This display contains some of the same information as the file moniker. We know that this is an item moniker, when it was last modified, and that the application it belongs to is running. Notice that the item moniker uses a delimiter of an exclamation point (!). On the left side of the item moniker Name field is the embedded object name (blank in this case); on the right side is the container name (a class identifier in this case). If you look up the class identifier in the Registry Editor, you'll find that it refers to a Microsoft Excel 97 Application, as shown in Figure 5-4.

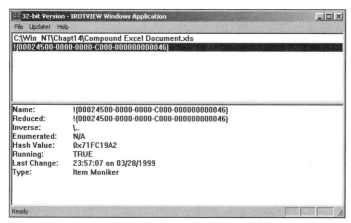

Figure 5-3: Item monikers normally have an object name, a delimiter, and a container name in the moniker Name field.

Figure 5-4: It pays to look up the class identifier for a ROT entry in the Registry to verify the container name.

Using the Remote Automation Connection Manager

The Remote Automation Connection Manager was originally included with Visual Basic to make creating remote connections a lot easier. You can find it distributed with the Enterprise Edition of most Microsoft programming products (the Professional Edition lacks this tool). While we won't use the Remote Automation Connection Manager for that purpose, it does provide another good way to look at your DCOM connections. Figure 5-5 shows a typical example of the Remote Automation Connection Manager display. Notice that I've already selected the AddIt control. (A compiled version of the AddIt control is provided on the CD-ROM provided with this book.)

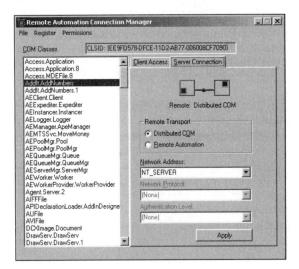

Figure 5-5: The Remote Automation Connection Manager provides another way of looking at your DCOM connections.

Tip   Your display may not show the CLSID field shown in Figure 5-5. You can activate this field by using the Register ⇨ Show CLSID command or by pressing Ctrl+C.

The Remote Automation Connection Manager display is actually a little easier to understand than the DCOM Configuration Tool display that we worked with in Chapter 2. Although it isn't nearly as complete in some ways, it's a little more complete in others. For one thing, you see all the Registry entries, not just applications. This more complete display allows you to see items that the DCOM Configuration Tool hides — making it possible to find errant Registry entries, instead of trying to dig the information out of your code. For example, an errant Registry entry may prevent you from seeing a component that you just created, making it difficult to determine whether the problem lies in your registration code or in the Registry entries themselves. If you see the missing component in the Remote Automation Connection Manager, then you know that your registration code is fine and that it's the Registry entries that are to blame.

Unfortunately, creating the connection is counterintuitive. There isn't a browse button that allows you to find the server that you want to connect to. The Remote Automation Connection Manager won't allow you to change the protocols used for the DCOM connection either — which may actually be a plus for developers who just want to create the connection and don't really care how it gets made.

Fortunately, you can set security at the individual component level, but not for DCOM as a whole. To set individual component security, use the Permissions ⇨ Edit ACL command. You'll see the Remote Class Permissions dialog box shown in Figure 5-6. This is where you can determine the access that each group can have to a particular object.

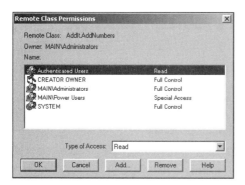

Figure 5-6: The Remote Automation Connection Manager allows you to change the security attached to individual components.

Now, let's say that you want to find out what special access the MAIN\Power Users have in Figure 5-6. All you need to do is double-click the MAIN\Power Users entry in the Remote Class Permission dialog box. You'll see a Special Access dialog box like the one shown in Figure 5-7. This dialog box allows you to control precisely what a particular group can do when accessing or launching a control from a remote computer.

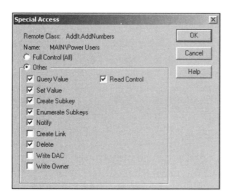

Figure 5-7: The Special Access dialog box allows you to change the type of access a particular group has to a component.

As you can see, the Remote Automation Connection Manager isn't a tool that you use in lieu of the DCOM Configuration Tool — they serve different purposes. It's important to realize that both tools are different. The Remote Automation Connection Manager is actually a better tool for creating quick connections. On the other hand, the DCOM Configuration Tool is better for initial setups and occasional custom setups.

Solving component usage problems with the ROT Viewer

All of the information that I've provided in this chapter is great as long as you know how to use it. Most of these utilities and the other information I've provided are best used for two tasks: developing and troubleshooting. We can actually talk about both tasks using a very simple example. (The source code and compiled version of this example are both located on the CD-ROM provided with this book.) Listing 5-1 shows the code for this example.

Listing 5-1: A Simple ROT Viewer Usage Example

```
Private Sub Command1_Click()
    'Create an out-of-process server object.
    Dim oExcel As Object
    Set oExcel = CreateObject("Excel.Application")

    'Break into the application if necessary
    MsgBox "It's Created"

    'Make the application visible
    oExcel.Application.Visible = True
    MsgBox "It's Visible"

    'Release the object
    Set oExcel = Nothing
End Sub
```

Most of this code should be very easy to understand. The only things that might be a little new are the call to CreateObject()and the method used to make the application visible to the user. Let's talk about CreateObject() first. The CreateObject() function, as previously stated, takes up to two arguments. The first argument is the dot syntax class name that you want to create. The second is the name of a server. In this case, because we're not making a remote machine call, we can eliminate the second argument. The first argument still isn't easy to figure out if you don't have the source code for the server you want to use unless you employ one of two simple techniques.

Open the OLE/COM Object Viewer and find the Microsoft Excel Worksheet entry in the Document Objects folder. You'll see a list of entries like the ones shown in Figure 5-8. Notice that I've highlighted the ProgID entry. Every category of COM object has a ProgID entry with the same information—the dot syntax you'll need for the CreateObject() function.

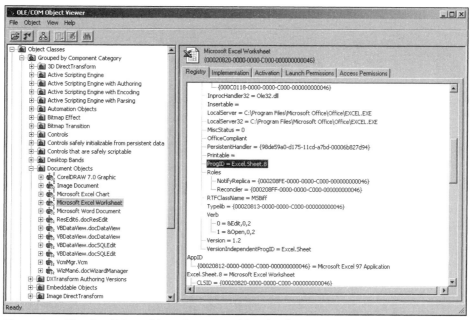

Figure 5-8: The OLE/COM Object Viewer provides the dot syntax you need for most objects.

Unfortunately, there are times when you might not find the information you need in the OLE/COM Object Viewer. For example, although you can find all of the documents supported by Excel, you can't find Excel itself. In some cases, you need to access the application, rather than the data the application manipulates. When this occurs, you need to look in the Registry Editor (RegEdit) utility. You know that the Excel worksheet class is Excel.Sheet.8 from working with the OLE/COM Object Viewer. Use this information to find all of the Excel entries in the Registry. Figure 5-9 shows the kind of information that you'll normally find when working with an application. As you can see, looking in the Registry can help you learn the dot syntax for a variety of objects as long as you do a little detective work first.

Now that you have some idea of where the dot syntax for the `CreateObject()` call comes from, let's look at the second issue—Excel methods. Start the example in the Visual Basic IDE. Click Start Excel. When the application stops at the first MsgBox call, press Ctrl+Break to pause the application. The IDE will highlight the line where the application stopped in yellow. Right-click one of the oExcel entries and choose Add Watch from the context menu. You'll see an Add Watch dialog box with oExcel already entered in the Expression field. Click OK. A Watches window similar to the one shown in Figure 5-10 will appear. Clicking on the plus (+) sign next to the object will show you all of the properties and methods associated with that object. Make sure you finish clicking through the dialogs and stop the application after you're done looking at the properties and methods associated with it.

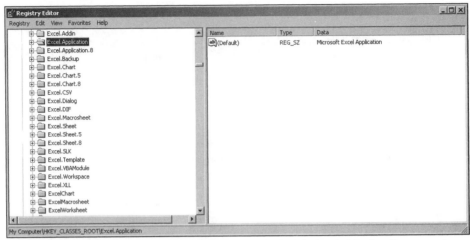

Figure 5-9: Registry Editor allows you to see that Excel.Application is the dot syntax for Excel itself.

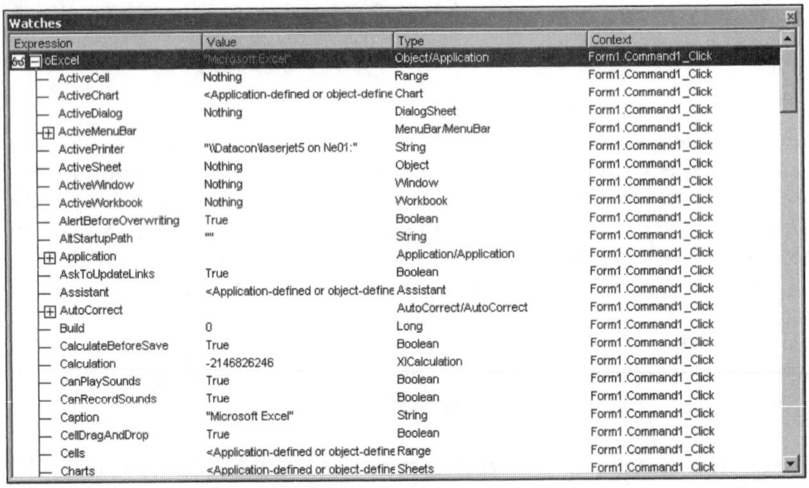

Figure 5-10: The Excel application will reveal its methods and properties for you if you know where to look.

There's one other piece of information that you can learn from this simple example. First, close every application on your desktop except for the ROT Viewer to ensure that you don't get any interference from other applications. Start the compiled version of the example and look in the ROT Viewer. Unlike Figure 5-2, there isn't a file moniker associated with the ROT Viewer entry. As shown in Figure 5-11, all you get is an item moniker until you add a worksheet to Excel using direct programming methods. Creating a server, then seeing how it behaves when you use various method calls, can tell you a lot about that server, even if you don't have the code. For example, we've just learned that Excel creates an item moniker when it starts, so if you want to interact with Excel, you need to access the object associated with the item moniker. On the other hand, if you want to interact with a specific worksheet, then you need to find the associated file moniker.

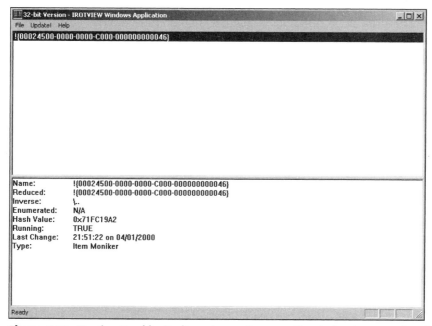

Figure 5-11: Starting Excel by itself creates an item moniker, but not an associated file moniker.

Summary

DCOM provides one way of creating a distributed computing environment. You can use it to allow one machine to borrow resources from another machine on the network, including the components contained on that machine. Here are some additional conclusions that you can draw from the contents of this chapter:

✦ DCOM extends COM so that it can work with remote connections. It's a protocol that manages the remote connection in a manner that's transparent to both client and server. COM still manages all local connections.

✦ DCOM allows you to write applications that service users on the road and meet the requirements of the Internet. It also helps with task and resource management, as well as centralizing business processing.

✦ In many cases, DCOM extends current code reuse and enables the developer to do more in less time.

✦ The main reasons that you should use DCOM are for fault tolerance, scalability, load balancing, ease of maintenance, flexibility, and connection management.

✦ There are some situations when you shouldn't use DCOM because of security, performance, or connection availability concerns.

✦ DCOM relies on DCE RPC to get data packets ready for transmission from one machine to another.

✦ SOAP will eventually replace DCOM as the underlying communication protocol for COM+, especially on the Internet.

✦ Creating a DCOM connection with Visual Basic is easy; simply use the `CreateObject()` function with the name of the server as the second argument.

✦ There are two standard methods of load balancing for DCOM: static (which relies on Registry entries or server references within the client) and dynamic (which relies on a referral component).

✦ COM+ allows you to load balance components using a combination of a load-balancing router and an application of up to eight servers.

✦ There are two main issues when connecting to an existing object: object lifetime and gaining access to the object IUnknown interface pointer. The object lifetime is automatically maintained through the use of strong and weak references. The ROT allows an object to register itself so that clients can create the required connections.

✦ There are five different kinds of monikers that you can bind to an object, and then register in the ROT. They are file moniker, item moniker, generic composite moniker, anti-moniker, and pointer moniker.

✦ The ROT Viewer allows you to see the objects that are registered in the ROT. The two most common object types are file monikers and item monikers.

✦ The Remote Automation Connection Manager provides another method for working with DCOM connections. In this case, the utility provides the means to create quick connections without wading through a cumbersome interface.

✦ You can combine various Platform SDK tools to learn about the components installed on your workstation. Learning more about standard components will reduce the amount of time you spend developing and debugging applications.

✦   ✦   ✦

COM+ Specific Issues

Some developers view COM+ as a new technology with a very long learning curve. In part, this perception is a result of the way that Microsoft's marketing team is presenting COM+ to the public. In reality COM+ is a combination of older product consolidation, product updates, wrappers that make accessing the products easier, and a few new features thrown in for good measure. So, the long learning curve that you might think exists with COM+ is more marketing hype than reality. Nevertheless, COM+ is a very valuable product, and one that's long overdue, but you may know more about it than you think if you've been keeping up with Microsoft's technology releases to date.

Besides COM, COM+ contains two features that are designed to make it work better than COM does now in the enterprise: Microsoft Transaction Server (MTS) and Microsoft Message Queue (MSMQ). Together, these technologies represent Microsoft's latest method for moving components from the desktop machine and local network to the Internet with better reliability than before. The shortest possible way to define MSMQ is as a smart and automated message container (we'll see how this works later in the chapter), while MTS can be defined as the insurance that a transaction will complete as anticipated. As the chapter progresses, you'll see that MTS provides a lot more than this basic functionality; we'll focus, however, on the transactional capability that it provides.

Cross-Reference If you need an overview of the various COM+ technologies, be sure to check Chapter 1. You'll find historical information at the beginning of the chapter that helps you to understand why COM+ works the way it does. The section entitled, "How COM+ and COM Compare" contains the best information on how much of a learning curve you can expect when making the transition to COM+. Finally, check "The MTS Difference" to get the full story on how COM+ combines existing technologies to create a greater whole. This chapter assumes that you've already read Chapter 1 or are familiar with its contents.

Tip   Part of the marketing of COM+ involves renaming an existing technology to make it look new. Microsoft has combined Microsoft Transaction Server (MTS) with the Distributed Transaction Coordinator (DTC) and a wrapper of administrative tools, and renamed it Component Services. Likewise, the combination of Microsoft Message Queue (MSMQ) and associated administrative tools is now called Queued Components. (Interestingly enough, some of Microsoft's documentation also refers to MSMQ 2.0, the version used in Windows 2000 — Windows NT uses MSMQ 1.0.) You can still access all of the underlying technologies, and your old applications will run fine. If you used MTS and MSMQ under Windows NT, then you already know that part of the COM+ story. What you really need to learn is the wrapper that Microsoft has provided to make using MTS and MSMQ easier. Both underlying technologies also contain new connectivity features and provide better integration with the operating system.

Let's look at the MTS and MSMQ portion of the COM+ picture in a little more detail. To make COM+ a reality, you need the COM specification to develop a component that uses common interfaces, MTS to ensure that the results (data output) of using the component are safeguarded, and MSMQ to make the entire application mobile. In short, this chapter looks at the difference between standard COM and the new COM+ technology by examining the methods used to combine the separate technologies that comprise COM+.

As previously mentioned, MTS provides transaction support for COM+. Safeguarding your data is only part of what MTS will do for you. Obviously, there has to be a way to ensure that the transactions that the user creates are recorded on the server, even if the user has no connection when the transaction is created. That's where MTS comes into play; it works in the background to ensure that only whole transactions are recorded and that incomplete transactions are rolled back to a known good state. The combination of MTS and MSMQ makes it possible to create an entire range of application types that you never dreamed possible before.

MSMQ allows the developer to create an application that works — in the same way regardless of whether the user is connected to the LAN. The connected state is what most developers are accustomed to using today — you create a connection to some type of data source, perform some work, and then disconnect from it. Because they're on the road so much, users require a new type of application, one that works even if there isn't a connection. Although some applications now allow you to work in disconnected mode, they normally require you to employ a second set of procedures, which is unsatisfactory because this requires additional training.

Developers will also want to learn about disconnected applications, which act as if there's a connection, even when no connection exists. These applications are the secret to making sure that the application you write today works in a wealth of scenarios, even those that involve users on the road.

However, there are types of message-based applications that you may want to create using MSMQ. For example, network administrators may want to track the status of all of the machines under their control. This is a relatively easy task to perform on the local network. All you need to do is load an agent on the client machine and use some type of server-based product to query the agents for status information. Today's monitoring packages can tell an administrator everything from what applications a user is working with currently to the speed of the cooling fan.

Laptops form a special class of machine because they're used extensively on the road where the network administrator can't get in contact with them. How can a network administrator keep track of these machines while on the road? A message transmitted each time the user makes contact with the corporate network is one answer. Just like the agent on desktop machines, an agent on the laptop can make log entries that get transferred to a queue. When the user is connected to the corporate network, these log entries automatically appear on the server immediately after they're made. On the other hand, when the user is on the road, the log entries appear on the server when the user makes contact. As far as the user and the agent are concerned, everything works in the same way no matter where the user is located physically. MSMQ provides the means for a network administrator to track machine conditions even when that machine is on the road.

Even if MTS and MSMQ functionality stopped there, you may want to know how they work so that you can create the latest trend in n-tier applications. However, these two components can be used for a lot more than just COM+ implementations — you can also use them in standalone mode or in combination. For example, you could use MSMQ to create a new class of smart e-mail applications, while MTS can be used for any type of transaction, not just database work. Combining these two products lets you create a special kind of e-mail application that works with objects, rather than text or other kinds of information. Consequently, a user on the road could receive interim application updates using an e-mail type connection that is automatically activated in the background when the user logs on to the office network.

Tip Any MTS applications that you created for Windows NT in the past, Windows 2000 will treat as COM+ applications. Obviously, these older applications won't automatically use new features that Windows 2000 has to offer, but at least your current development efforts won't be wasted. You'll be able to move your current MTS projects to the new operating system environment without change.

The first section of this chapter looks at MTS transactions. We'll look at questions like what precisely constitutes a transaction and why transactions are useful. Once you know what a transaction is, we'll discuss how the MTS portion of COM+ helps you develop more reliable applications. This section also talks about the various tasks that you need to perform to make MTS available for use. It's important to understand that MTS is used for a lot more in Windows 2000 than it was in Windows NT (when MTS was installed as a separate product). This section of the chapter helps point out those differences.

Tip   A lot of the latest MSMQ features require you to install the most recent version of the Windows Platform SDK. In fact, many of these features are totally undocumented outside of the Windows Platform SDK. What this means is that Microsoft's latest Visual Studio release doesn't handle MSMQ programming tasks very well without this additional SDK support. The coding examples in this book assume that you at least have Visual Studio Service Pack 3 and the latest version of the Windows Platform SDK installed.

Web Resource   You can download Visual Studio Service Pack 3 (or later if available) from the Visual Studio Web site at http://msdn.microsoft.com/vstudio/sp/default.asp. The latest version of the Platform SDK appears at http://msdn.microsoft.com/developer/sdk/platform.asp. I use Visual Studio 6.0 Enterprise Edition for the examples in this book; other versions aren't guaranteed to produce the same results.

MSMQ deals with messages. The wrapper, Queued Components, makes working with these messages much easier for the developer and administrator alike. The second section of this chapter provides a very quick overview of what messages are and why they're useful. The messages that MSMQ provides contain much more than just the data that you need to move from one place to another. Once you understand the basic unit of data transfer in MSMQ, you'll want to know something about how MSMQ works at a low level. We'll also talk about the detailed theory you need in order to use MSMQ fully to create all kinds of message-oriented applications. Building a business case for MSMQ is also important because this is a new technology. The next topic in this section helps you build a business strategy, making it easier for management to see the need for using MSMQ in the applications you create. As with any technology, MSMQ has limitations that you need to know about, so we'll look at problems and some solutions as part of the section. Finally, we'll look at the MSMQ API. You really won't need to know this information in detail for many applications, but it's good information to know when the automation that Microsoft provides doesn't work.

The third section examines MSMQ and the Internet. More likely than not, if you create a disconnected application, you'll also have to deal with the Internet as part of that application. In most cases, users will want to make contact with the company using something more convenient than a long distance telephone connection. This section isn't meant as a detailed discussion of the entire topic of Virtual Private Networks (VPNs), but it does help you understand some of the issues relating to disconnected applications.

Queued Components, the wrapper provided by Microsoft for Windows 2000, is a utility that you'll want to spend some time with. It can save the developer considerable time during the testing process and reduce the lines of code required to create applications. The fourth section discusses the various configuration issues involved with MSMQ and how you can use the snap-ins provided by Windows 2000 to reduce your workload.

COM always assumes that you have a permanent connection between client and server; COM+, however, doesn't make this assumption. The distinction between permanent and nonpermanent connections also means that you need a new event model to handle disconnected application situations. COM+ supports both the request/reply and publish/subscribe event models. We'll discuss both models and their relative merits in the fifth section of the chapter. You may be surprised to learn that the new publish/subscribe model isn't the right solution for every problem — sometimes the old request/reply model works better.

The sixth and final section discusses the new types of applications that COM+ brings into the picture. It's important to understand that COM+ supports a number of application scenarios in addition to those that COM supports by itself. These new application types will help you create solutions to problems that may have plagued your organization for quite some time.

Understanding Transactions

MTS is the underlying technology used to create transactions within COM+. It provides data and object protection, and the services required for managing both data and object protection. It really doesn't do much more than that. However, considering the cost of failed data transmissions and the amount of work they can cause, getting data and objects safely from one point to another is essential. MTS uses secured transactions to accomplish this task.

Management is accomplished using the Component Services console, which contains three *Microsoft Management Console (MMC)* snap-ins by default: Component Services, Event Viewer, and Services. (A console provides the container used to hold the management components, also called MMC snap-ins.) We talked about the Component Services snap-in as part of creating COM+ applications in Chapter 2. Event Viewer allows you to see various events generated by applications, Active Directory, security, the operating system, and other entities like DNS, depending on what features you've installed. The Services MMC snap-in allows you to start, stop, pause, and manage services. You'll find the Component Services console in the Start ➪ Programs ➪ Administrative Tools menu.

According to Microsoft's latest statistics, COM is running on 150 million systems worldwide, some of which have been using COM since it was introduced as OLE in 1991. These systems will benefit greatly from COM+ because this new methodology packages the various COM-related technologies together and makes them easier to work with. You can find out more about COM+ by viewing Microsoft's COM+ Web site at http://www.microsoft.com/com/tech/complus.asp.

One of the more interesting downloads at this site is a presentation that was given at Tech-Ed 99 that contains Microsoft's vision for COM+ now and in the future. You can find out more about the MTS-specific part of the COM+ picture at http://www.microsoft.com/com/tech/MTS.asp. You may want to visit this site to get the latest SDKs and MTS-related white papers.

Finally, if you need help with your MTS project, look at the MTS newsgroups starting with `microsoft.public.microsoft.transaction.server`. In most cases, these newsgroups can help you to solve both the usage and programming problems that you might experience with MTS.

Using transactions is the short definition of MTS; it's time to look at MTS in a little more detail. The following sections describe various theoretical elements behind using MTS as a component deployment strategy. The first section discusses transactions — what they're about and what they mean to you as a programmer. The second section explores the relationship between MTS and COM+. You'll find that these two technologies are inextricably entwined. The next section explains how MTS does its work from a conceptual perspective. After that, you'll look at what applications (a method for grouping together the components required for one transaction type) are all about.

Understanding transactions

The first question to answer is, "What is a transaction?" There are many different definitions for this term floating around in the trade press, many of which are contradictory. Let's begin by looking at the one thing that most people agree on: A transaction is a way of packaging data and commands and ensuring that they reach their destination successfully. In other words, when you submit a form to the database by using a transaction, you can be sure that either all of the data in the form will be added to the database or none of it will. In short, a transaction is insurance that your database (or other application) doesn't get erroneous data placed in it even if it means losing the data for a single transaction (which is normally an entire record for database applications).

MTS is the Windows 2000 component that ensures that the data or objects (MTS can encapsulate anything, not just data within a transaction) you transfer from one machine to another arrive in good shape and that they are fully executed. Execution may include a variety of things, even though most programmers view transactions as being data oriented and used only within a database management context. A good way to remember what MTS transactions are all about is the acronym ACID. The following list provides an overview of ACID.

✦ **Atomicity:** All of the updates required to complete a transaction are grouped together. Either the entire package of updates succeeds and the change becomes durable, or the package fails and all of the updates are removed.

✦ **Consistency:** The transaction is a correct change of the system state. It preserves the state invariants, which means that you don't get unexpected results from the transaction after it is completed.

✦ **Isolation:** Concurrent transactions can't see each other, and the results from one transaction don't affect other transactions running at the same time. Obviously, this is an extension of the principle of encapsulation for objects. Think of a transaction as a form for an object — all of the updates are encapsulated in such a way that the outside world can't see them.

✦ **Durability:** Durability is synonymous with fault tolerance. A transaction should be able to survive some level of failure. These failures may include obvious problems such as server system failures or unexpected problems such as communication failures.

ACID describes MTS in its perfect state, which is what Microsoft would have you believe is always the case. However, there aren't any foolproof technologies for the PC; you have to plan on some level of failure, even if you use transactions. It's at this point that some people differ on exactly what transaction fault tolerance means. For the purposes of this book, a transaction also implies the capability to roll back the addition of data or the execution of commands until the transaction reaches a point of stability — the point at which the last set of operations were successfully completed. A transaction is never complete until the receiver accepts the data or commands. The second that the data or commands are accepted, the transaction is complete and the event is over.

N-tier application failure points

In a client/server setup, the number of failure points is relatively limited. In the modern n-tier application world, a transaction may involve a number of clients and servers, any of which can fail. Transactions can proceed across multiple boundaries, both physical and electronic. In addition, each of these boundaries could represent another transaction triggered by the primary client request. MTS views transaction completion as the point when the primary request completes. If the original request fails, then all intermediate transactions are rolled back. This means that all of the machines involved in the series of transactions required to answer an original request must maintain state information until that original request is completed. Fortunately, in most cases MTS automatically takes care of this requirement for you (unless your application has some unusual or complex requirements).

Internet-induced failures

One environmental factor that complicates matters for today's programmer is the need for Internet support. Consider that this media is both unstable and prone to connection losses. An Internet-enabled application needs to allow for transactional failures that aren't caused by the application or any associated components, but by the Internet itself. The developer needs to consider the situation when data should have transferred properly, but is either missing or corrupted at the receiving end of the application. A connection failure can still cause the transaction to fail even if all of the required application code works as anticipated. MTS helps application programmers handle this kind of failure by maintaining connection information for the programmer. In addition, the use of MSMQ can make the state of the connection a moot point, as we'll see later in the chapter.

Data recovery when failure occurs

Data recovery is an essential part of many applications, especially those that handle large quantities of data. In other words, the receiver notifies the sender that the data or command isn't accepted for whatever reason. While error recovery is a very important thing to have, especially when it comes to database managers, you may find that some transaction methodologies don't allow for any form of recovery. If the data is lost, then it's gone. It's up to the sender to ensure that the data actually gets added to the database or that the commands are executed on the server. Transactions under MTS do have a level of data recovery, although it's uncertain how robust that data recovery is and exactly what it protects. In most cases, you may want include some type of data recovery mechanism within your application in addition to whatever Microsoft provides.

MTS and COM+

As of this writing, Microsoft would have you believe that MTS and COM+ are so closely tied as to make them impossible to understand apart from each other. Actually, it helps to look at the two technologies together, but as separate entities. Here is the clearest possible view of MTS and COM+ in a nutshell: COM+ is a super-set of MTS, MSMQ, and standard COM combined. The following sections describe this view of MTS and COM+ in more detail.

Understanding the MTS design goals

Microsoft has certain goals when it comes to MTS. That MTS provides transaction support is only part of a larger picture. The following list will help you understand Microsoft's four main goals for MTS within the Windows 2000 and COM+ environments.

✦ **Reduced Development Complexity:** Up until now, many programmers have avoided COM because they consider it too complex. Creating components is an error-prone and time-consuming process. So, the first major goal of COM+ is to make components both easier to use and to create. MTS and MSMQ allow developers to use a simplified programming model. These two services do part of the work that the developer would normally need to do. The MTS contribution is to provide security, reliability, and scalability. Even though these are relatively new requirements for the world of n-tier programming, the developer would normally need to add the code manually if MTS didn't provide the required support.

✦ **Improved Scalability:** Critics complained that Windows NT (the predecessor of Windows 2000) didn't scale very well. A lack of scalability means that you can have a server that works fine with a small load, but the capacity to do work diminishes quickly as load is applied in the form of additional tasks. The same criticism is leveled at COM. As soon as you add the capability to service more than one request at a time, the complexity of the component increases almost exponentially. The use of MTS-supported transactions means that the application doesn't need to keep track of all of the actions that occur to complete a request. Consequently, the application can scale better because the inherent operating support scales better.

✦ **Component Modularity:** Component technology as a whole is designed to reduce maintenance problems in several ways. The most important consideration for MTS is that a developer can create components that make applications truly modular. The business logic that's incorporated within a component only gets tested once, instead of within every application. In addition, MTS allows you to enhance the security of the data that's being manipulated by the component, further reducing potential problems.

✦ **Reduced Support Requirements:** A primary reason to use MTS is to ensure that the components you create are always available. Placing the components on the server means that the user doesn't have to have a local copy of the component to get some work done. Loading the component on the server makes it available to everyone at the same time. In addition, bug fixes and updates are no longer a chore because only the server needs to be updated instead of every machine on the network.

Putting components in context

Part of the difference between COM and COM+ is the idea of context. You can create a component that has no context at all (which is how most components are created using COM), but that means that you really don't have a good idea of how the client uses that component. The object exists and is used by a client, but the operating system doesn't know much about the object except that it's using some resources. The inability of the operating system to assist with component management means that the developer must incorporate logic within the component to handle a wide variety of failure conditions, many of which are generic to all components.

Placing the component within a context tells the operating system which services this component requires so that the operating system can balance the needs of all components within the system. In addition, the context adds attributes to the component that you normally need to hard code during the programming process. Obviously, a major context for any component that needs to provide reliable data transfer is a transactional context that defines how transactions are handled given a certain set of default conditions.

At this point, you may think that COM+ components require a lot of additional work to invoke the services they need. However, the opposite is true. The context for the component defines what services the component requires. Interceptors, which are part of the operating system, look at this context and set the required services up for the component when the client calls it. On return, the interceptors again look at the context and determine what kind of cleanup the component requires because it's finished using these services. In sum, COM+ uses an attribute-based programming model, which differs from the API-based programming model that COM used.

The portion of MTS that handles resource management is the *Compensating Resource Manager (CRM)*. The CRM associates an action, abort logic, and complete logic with your component and sets the resources aside that are required to complete these tasks. For example, you might create a component that processes order forms. The action might be to accept the form from the client, look up the status of the requested items, and then return this status information to the client. As you can see, an action consists of one or more objects that execute on one or more servers on behalf of a single client. The abort logic might be to send an error message to the client instead of the order status, while the complete logic might be to place the order in the order database (pending client approval). In short, the component always performs the same task, but you can independently change the result of the outcome of that task to meet changing company needs.

Note　You're currently locked into the context and interceptors that Microsoft provides as part of Windows 2000. The eventual goal is to allow the programmer to define the context and interceptors used. This, in turn, will allow the programmer to define special services in addition to those normally provided by the operating system. Unless you're creating a third-party product, however, you probably don't need this kind of functionality for most applications.

Working with MTS and COM+ services

Obviously, the goals that Microsoft has set for MTS and COM+ are difficult to reach without some type of infrastructure. Windows 2000 includes additional COM+-related services that allow you to create and deploy components quickly. Many of these new services are found within MTS and MSMQ (with MTS providing the lion's share of the new services). The result is that you spend more time working with the business logic for your application and less time worried about mundane tasks associated with developing just about any component.

Even though Microsoft stresses the MTS and COM+ connection, there's actually a lot more to COM+ than simple transactions. In fact, we look at many facets of this technology in this book. The following is a list of the services that are found in COM+ 1.0.

✦ Server Components (MTS)

✦ Transactions (MTS)

✦ Security (MTS)

✦ Administration (MTS)

✦ Queued Components (MSMQ)

✦ Events

As the list illustrates, four of the six services that are associated with COM+ also have something to do with MTS. Microsoft has literally merged the COM and MTS development teams in order to produce COM+. So, what you see in Windows 2000 is the work of both of these teams.

In the past, writing services for Windows NT was a white-knuckled, low-level programming experience that was enjoyed by masochists everywhere. Microsoft has worked hard to make writing services easy. For the most part, writing a service is now like writing any other component. You create the code required to perform the server-side business logic for your application, put it in a wrapper (the COM interface and COM+ application), and place it on the server.

The MTS portion of COM+ does offer transactional services, as mentioned earlier in the chapter. You can set the transactional attributes within the component itself, or as property values after you install it on the server. However, I didn't mention two important features that MTS provides. The first is AutoComplete, which allows an operation to complete (provided there's enough information to do so) even if the connection is prematurely broken. AutoComplete can also be used if your client leaves the component normally and the component simply lacks the code required to complete the transaction itself. Normally, you have to provide a `GetObjectContext.SetComplete()` method within your component to perform this task. The second is AutoAbort, which means that a transaction is automatically rolled back (or whatever other abort logic you provide) the instant that the connection is lost. Again, you normally implement this logic within the component using the `GetObjectContext.SetAbort()` method.

Security is a major problem for just about every area of computing today. It's important to protect your data at all times and at every point of processing. MTS allows you to create a secure environment, yet reduces the complexity of doing so. Microsoft uses a role-based security model. What this means is that you assign users to one or more roles that profile their rights to the component. For example, a typical user role might have one set of rights to the component, while an administrator role might have other rights that include those of the typical user. Component security is also implemented at the method level now. This means that one method within a component can actually have a higher security setting than other methods associated with the same component.

The rights assigned to a component flow with the context for the component. If you give a user a certain level of access to the component as a whole, then that access is provided at the method level as well unless you specifically assign the user a different set of rights at that level. In addition, rights flow from one object to the next. This is an obvious addition because the user requires access to all of the components needed to complete a particular transaction. Fortunately, you can override this default behavior to ensure that access to sensitive components is regulated properly.

The final MTS contribution is administrative handling of components. In the past, the components would have been managed using some special purpose utility. Microsoft has decided to use MMC for all administration in Windows 2000. You actually will manage your components using a COM+ administrative snap-in for MMC named Component Services. This management tool is based on the MTS management tool used previously. We look at this tool later in the chapter after creating a simple component for use in the example purposes.

Using MTS — An Overview

As does any other COM technology, MTS relies on specific component interfaces. In the case of an object that deals with transactions, you need to implement the IObjectContext interface. Visual Basic gives you access to the IObjectContext interface through the GetObjectContext function, so you can use it to gain access to the IObjectContext pointer. The whole purpose of this interface is to tell MTS when a transaction has started, when it's completed, and what the results of the transaction are so that MTS knows what to do next. You can also accomplish these tasks using attributes as mentioned in the previous section; so even though you need to implement the IObjectContext interface, you don't have to call on it within your component's code.

> **Tip**
>
> To gain access to GetObjectContext and other COM+-specific functions, you need to add support for the COM+ Services Type Library to your application. Use the Project ➪ References command to display the References dialog box. Find the COM+ Services Type Library entry and check it. Clicking OK allows support for this library to your application. If you don't see the COM+ Services Type Library entry, check for the COMSVCS.DLL in the Windows\System32 folder. Make sure that this type library is registered using the RegSvr32 COMSVCS.DLL command. It's also important to realize that there are other pieces to the COM+ picture including the COM+ 1.0 Admin Type Library, which we won't discuss in this chapter. All of these libraries are contained in separate files accessible through the References dialog box. Unfortunately, Microsoft also chose some type library names that don't follow normal conventions. For example, the ComPlus 1.0 Catalog Replication Type Library might be difficult to find unless you know where to look (all type libraries are listed alphabetically in the References dialog box). (See the "Using the Object Browser" sidebar below to learn more about the DLLs used by your application.)

The main purpose of many IObjectContext interface (GetObjectContext function) calls is to provide success information to MTS. There are four different IObjectContext methods that you can call to provide MTS with feedback on the level of success of a particular transaction. In addition, there are three methods used to determine the current context status and one method used to create an instance of this interface. Table 6-1 provides you with an overview of these methods.

Table 6-1
IObjectContext Interface and GetObjectContext Method Summary

Method	Description	Result
CreateInstance()	Allows you to create an instance of another COM+ object using the current object context.	Using this method allows you to create new objects that have the same context as the current object. This allows the new object to execute within the same activity as the current object and to participate in transactions started by the current object (as long as the new object is designed and configured to use transactions).
DisableCommit()	The transaction isn't complete. In addition, some or all of the requested updates are still pending, incomplete, or failed.	MTS can't commit the updates in their current form. Because the transaction isn't complete, the IObjectContext object remains active, even if it returns to the method that first entered the transaction context.
EnableCommit()	The transaction isn't complete.	All of the updates in the transaction were successfully made, so MTS can commit them. Because the transaction isn't complete, the IObjectContext object remains active, even if it returns to the method that first entered the transaction context.

Continued

Table 6-1 *(continued)*		
Method	**Description**	**Result**
IsCallerInRole()	Allows you to determine whether the direct caller of your component is in a specified security role.	This method is handy for determining how your component should react in a given situation. For example, you can determine whether the calling component is in a typical user or manager role, then act accordingly when processing information.
IsInTransaction()	Determines whether the calling component is executing within a transaction.	You can use this method to determine how to process a request. In addition, it allows you to look for configuration errors. For example, an administrator may configure a component that really requires a transaction to work without one.
IsSecurityEnabled()	Normally returns true unless the component is running in the client's process.	MTS always uses security to run components. You can use this method to detect client-side component requests that aren't secure (and are therefore potential security breaches).
SetAbort()	All or part of the transaction has failed.	MTS needs to mark the transaction as a failure and roll back any updates that the component may have made. The IObjectContext object is automatically deactivated upon return to the method that first entered the transaction context.

Method	Description	Result
SetComplete()	The transaction completed as originally anticipated.	MTS can mark the transaction as successfully completed. The IObjectContext object is automatically deactivated upon return to the method that first entered the transaction context.

Transactions are usually surrounded by quite a bit of code, so if you look at a completed component it may be difficult to figure out what the component author is doing. In most cases, a transaction consists of five well-defined steps (shown below) that you always need to implement no matter how complex the rest of the component code may be.

1. Create an object context object.

2. Tell MTS that you're beginning the transaction. You do this by obtaining an object context using the GetObjectContext() method.

3. Perform any work required to complete the transaction. Track all of the updates that you make. Even if the component doesn't deal with a database, it has some type of data transformation work to do. For example, even a computational component accepts raw data as input and provides one or more results as output.

4. Compare the results that the component has obtained with the results that the component was supposed to provide.

5. Provide MTS with feedback. The SetComplete()method tells MTS that the transaction was a success. Part of an error-handling routine is to tell MTS that the transaction was a failure using the SetAbort() method.

One of the first things that seasoned COM programmers may note about using MTS and COM+ is that you can't choose a remote platform on which to execute your code by using the traditional COSERVERINFO data structure that's normally supplied to CoCreateInstanceEx(). The GetObjectContext() call doesn't provide an argument for accepting the COSERVERINFO data structure. So, the question becomes this: How does MTS determine which remote host it should use to service the call? The answer is relatively simple and more flexible than what COM provides — MTS uses a catalog manager to determine the remote execution host. You can configure the catalog used by the catalog manager using either a configuration interface or the MTS catalog interfaces within the component itself. In short, the programmer can leave the decision of where to execute a component to the administrator who can configure the component using a standard methodology instead of a custom configuration program. We'll now take a more in-depth look at the various catalog management features that Windows 2000 provides to the administrator as part of working with the example component.

Visual Basic programmers have access to a number of MTS catalog interfaces. The following list provides an overview of the interfaces that you need to know to perform both high- and low-level maintenance tasks with the component.

✦ **ICatalog:** Allows you to connect with specific servers and access the collections they contain. This interface also lets you retrieve version information for the collections. You can access this interface using the MTSAdmin.Catalog object of the MTS 2.0 Admin Type Library.

✦ **ICatalogObject:** Provides access to a specific object and its properties. This interface lets you change values and provides methods for obtaining the object name and key values. You can access this interface using the MTSAdmin.CatalogObject object of the MTS 2.0 Admin Type Library.

✦ **ICatalogCollection:** Provides access to a collection of objects as well as methods for creating, deleting, modifying, and enumerating objects within the collection. You can use the resulting object to access related collections. You can access this interface using the MTSAdmin.CatalogCollection object of the MTS 2.0 Admin Type Library.

✦ **IPackageUtil:** Lets you import, export, or shut down a package within the Packages collection. Microsoft has replaced the term package with the term COM+ Application. If you compare MTS Explorer and the Component Services snap-in, you may notice this change immediately. The next section discusses the exact nature of COM+ applications. You can access this interface using the MTSAdmin.PackageUtil object of the MTS 2.0 Admin Type Library.

✦ **IComponentUtil:** Contains a set of methods for importing or installing a component into a collection. You can work with the component by GUID or by name. You can access this interface using the MTSAdmin.ComponentUtil object of the MTS 2.0 Admin Type Library.

✦ **IRemoteComponentUtil:** Allows you to access components on a remote server by name or GUID. You can access this interface using the MTSAdmin. RemoteComponentUtil object of the MTS 2.0 Admin Type Library.

✦ **IRoleAssociationUtil:** Lets you associate a role with a component. You can access the component by GUID or by name. You can access this interface using the MTSAdmin.RoleAssociationUtil object of the MTS 2.0 Admin Type Library.

While this list of catalog interfaces is very impressive, it still may not answer the question of why you can't choose a specific server to work with your component. Another part of the COM+ equation is load balancing. Load balancing is taken care of through a combination of a cluster of servers that contain the components you need and a router that determines which server is best able to meet the need given the current network demand and server load. Theoretically, all you need to do is request services from a specific server and COM+ can automatically choose the best server out of a cluster to answer the request. Once the server is chosen, the router isn't even part of the picture. The load-balancing mechanism provides a direct connection between the client and the server running the component.

In short, the need to access a specific server based on load is no longer a real need—all you need is the ability to request services from a "generic" server and let COM+ do the rest.

Understanding COM+ applications

MTS components are usually loaded on the server as part of a COM+ application. In other words, everything that both the client and server need in order to perform a specific transaction type is placed in one location for easy access. A user application can access one or more COM+ applications to provide a full range of services to the end user. When you look at the Component Services MMC snap-in, you see four levels of application hierarchy: COM+ application, component, interface, and method. We see how this works in the real world in the examples later in the chapter. However, for now, it's more important to consider a few packaging requirements that help keep your transactions easy to manage and administer. The following sections outline the three most common problems that you may experience when working with COM+ applications: fault tolerance, component activation, and security.

Maintaining fault tolerance

The first problem that you may encounter when working with COM+ applications is how to maintain fault tolerance. By default, MTS places all of the components in a COM+ application in the same server process. The problem with this approach is that a failure by one component affects all of the other components in the COM+ application. In short, a COM+ application may experience multiple transaction failures because one component experiences problems.

The obvious solution to this problem is to place all of the components in separate server processes. That way, the failure of one component won't necessarily affect the operation of any other component. However, the problem with this approach is that the speed of the transactions slows because each transaction has to cross process boundaries and server resources are wasted.

It's important to understand that a COM+ application helps to keep all of the components required for a particular transaction type together. Applications may require more than one type of transaction to get the job done. Consequently, one of the more efficient ways to handle fault tolerance is to group associated components into separate processes along transaction lines. That way, a failed component affects only one of many possible transactions, enabling the application at least to succeed partially. This solution reduces the impact of using multiple processes on execution speed and incurs a minimal penalty on system resources.

Activating a component

The second potential problem is activation. There are three possible places to activate a component: the creator's process, another process on the same computer, and a process on a remote computer.

The safest place to activate the component is another process on the same computer. This approach does incur some performance penalties, but if the component fails, the main application can recover from the failure.

Activating the component within the creator's process is definitely the most efficient way of doing things and ensures the highest possible performance (with an equally high risk). Other problems associated with using the creator's process for component activation is that you can't make use of declarative security — an important MTS feature.

In most cases, you won't want to activate the component on another computer for several reasons. The most important reason is that MTS provides remote activation mechanisms using the Remote Computer and Remote Component folders in the MTS Explorer. Considering the likelihood of serious problems, you should never directly activate the component on another machine.

Maintaining security

The final COM+ application design problem that you need to consider is security isolation. Security is a major problem on any network. Maintaining security means being able to ascertain that the object requesting access to a resource actually has the required credentials to do so. Declarative security allows you to do just that. When you deploy a component in Component Services, you assign it a security role. This security role gets mapped into Windows 2000 group and user security. In short, each component acts as a security checkpoint to ensure that the user has permission to request a specific service.

Note   Fortunately, the user doesn't have to keep entering his or her password as each component gets instantiated — the identity of the user is checked using his or her token. You can find a good description of COM+ security in Chapter 7. We won't discuss Windows security details in this book. However, you can find a detailed description of Windows 2000 security in the *Windows 2000 Programming Bible* (ISBN 0-7645-3312-6). For further updates, you can check my Web site at http://www.mwt.net/~jmueller.

Understanding Messages

In Chapter 5, I spent a lot of time talking about DCOM and how it works. In some ways, MSMQ works like DCOM. What you're doing is creating a connection between a client and server for the purpose of information exchange. However, instead of creating a direct connection using a network protocol like DCOM does, MSMQ uses queues as an intermediary destination for the data that flows between the client and server. These queues are used to hold messages, which is the method that MSMQ uses in place of the packets normally used by networks to transfer data.

The advantage of using the message as a basis for transferring information is that the client-and server connection doesn't need to exist at the same time. In other words, users can open their applications without checking for server availability first and they won't even notice whether the server is available after the application is open. A salesperson can record an order now and then allow MSMQ to upload it automatically to the server later without modifying the methods that he or she normally would use. MSMQ makes the delivery in the background without any interaction on the part of the user. The orders that the salesperson creates while the connection to the server is severed are stored in a local queue as messages. Each message normally represents a single order's data, although there really isn't a limit on how you can format the messages. A message can hold more than one order or only part of a large order.

The disadvantage of using messages as the basis for data transfer is that there's some additional overhead. When messages are used to transfer data, there are more layers of processing, which means that direct connect scenarios actually run a bit slower. In addition, the developer needs a little additional coding and setup time when using MSMQ. However, the advantages far outweigh the disadvantages; you'll see why as the chapter progresses.

So, what does a message contain? All messages are objects that contain the same number of properties, although you won't necessarily use all of the properties all of the time. Table 6-2 contains a description of the various message properties that you'll use most often.

Table 6-2
MSMQ Message Properties

Property	Description
Additional Queue Information	
Ack	Defines the kind of message that MSMQ places in the Acknowledgment queue. The default setting doesn't place any messages at all in the Acknowledgement queue. You can also choose options that place messages in the Acknowledgement queue based on when the message is received by the queue or retrieved by the listener.
AdminQueueInfo	Specifies the name and location of the Acknowledgement queue
DestinationQueueInfo	Tells MSMQ where you want the message sent. This is a read-only property that's set by MSMQ after you specify a destination using a method argument.
Journal	Determines whether MSMQ stores a copy of the message in the system journal

Continued

Table 6-2 *(continued)*

Property	Description
Additional Queue Information	
ResponseQueueInfo	You can set MSMQ to provide a response when it receives your message. This property determines the location of the Response queue on the client machine. We'll discuss this property in more detail in "Understanding MSMQ Limitations" below.
Trace	Determines whether the message is traced as it travels from machine to machine. The tracing messages are placed in the Report queue.
Data	
Body	Contains the message that you want to transfer from one machine to another. This message is stored as a byte array, which means that you can transfer a variety of data types including objects and strings. You definitely want to consider the method used to pack data because you need to unpack it later.
BodyLength	Defines the size of the message body
Miscellaneous	
AppSpecific	Allows you to add application-specific information to the message
Class	This is a read-only property set by MSMQ that specifies the message type. A message can be a standard MSMQ message, a positive or negative acknowledgement, or a report.
CorrelationId	An application-generated number that relates this message to all other messages sent during a given timeframe. It allows the application to sort the messages when they arrive at the receiving queue.
Id	A read-only property that contains the MSMQ-assigned identification number for the message.
Label	An application-specific moniker for the message. This property can be used for a variety of purposes, but is normally used for displaying a message header in human-readable format.
Priority	The priority determines the importance of the message when compared to other messages. MSMQ uses values from 0 to 7, with 0 being the highest. The default priority setting is 3. Transactional messages are automatically given a priority of 0 by MSMQ.

Property	Description
Security	
AuthLevel	Tells MSMQ whether you want the message authenticated when it arrives at the queue.
EncryptAlgorithm	Defines the algorithm used to encrypt the message prior to transmission. A higher level of encryption provides greater security, but also increases the size of the resulting message.
HashAlgorithm	Determines the hash algorithm used to authenticate a message.
IsAuthenticated	A read-only property that tells whether MSMQ authenticated the message.
PrivLevel	This property tells MSMQ whether the message is private or public. There are three levels of privacy available in the United States: 40-bit, 40-bit enhanced, and 128-bit message body encryption. (The levels of privacy available to you are affected by your current location.) The last two levels of encryption are available only when using MSMQ 2.0, which means that you can use them only with Windows 2000.
SenderCertificate	Represents the message sender's security certificate within a byte array. The security certificate is used to authenticate the message.
SenderId	Provides the identity of the person who sent the message. This read-only property is set by MSMQ when the message is sent, unless you specifically declare that the message won't be authenticated.
SenderIdType	Defines the type of sender identification: none or a standard sender ID (SID).
SourceMachineGuid	Contains the globally unique identifier (GUID) for the sending machine. This is a read-only value that MSMQ automatically adds.
Time Tracking	
ArrivedTime	A read-only property that specifies when the message arrives at the queue.
MaxTimeToReachQueue	Defines the amount of time that the message has to reach the queue.
MaxTimeToReceive	Defines the amount of time that the listener has to remove the message from the queue for processing.
SentTime	Contains the time that the message was sent by the client. This is a read-only value that MSMQ automatically adds.

Continued

Table 6-2 *(continued)*	
Property	**Description**
Transactions	
Delivery	Defines how you want the message delivered. See the "Understanding Transactions" section below.

An overview of MSMQ

So, how does a messaging application differ from DCOM? The data is most likely the same, which means that your business logic is the same. However, the delivery method is different. We're now using the idea of messages to transfer data and a queue to hold those messages (a queue is a sort of a mailbox for messages). As a minimum, a queue on the server holds all of the messages that the server components process. Each active component on the server has a separate queue. These components pick messages up from their queue whenever processing on the current message is complete.

In addition to the server queue, some clients also have a queue for local processing. The local queue gets emptied into the server queue anytime there's a connection between the client and the server. In short, messages can be viewed as the packets that normally are carried between the client and server on a network. Obviously, this is a simplification of a more complex process, but it provides a useful starting point.

The obvious advantage of using MSMQ in place of DCOM is MSMQ's capability to perform disconnected application handling. The local client queue allows the client to continue processing information even when there's no direct connection to the server for handling the messages. (Obviously, you need to configure the client for independent use.) Using a local client queue allows the user to continue working as if the connection existed and without performing any special procedures to transfer the resulting messages from the client to the server when a connection is made. MSMQ handles all of the message transfers in the background without the user's knowledge. Figure 6-1 shows the relationship between the client and server, and the kinds of queue setups that you can expect.

Notice that there are actually two client types: dependent and independent. The main difference between the two is that the independent client also provides its own queue, while the dependent client relies on a direct connection to the server. Obviously, you can't use a dependent client setup for a laptop computer that you intend to use on the road because the dependent client lacks a queue. However, a dependent client setup works for a desktop machine that's located in the same building as a server or on a WAN with a reliable connection. Using a dependent client setup reduces the disk requirements for using MSMQ and can result in a slight performance boost because the messages are only placed in one queue rather than two.

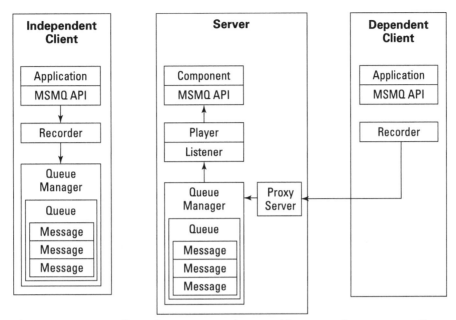

Figure 6-1: MSMQ allows the user to continue working even when no connection between the client and server exists.

There are three elements required for establishing and maintaining a message flow between the client and server: recorder, listener, and player. The *recorder* takes the client output, creates messages, and then either places those messages in the local message or sends them to a proxy server on the server. MSMQ takes the message that the client creates and places it in the server's queue. When the *listener* sees a message in the server's queue, it removes the message and gives it to the player. Finally, the *player* takes the message and turns it into data for the server.

You can look at this process in the same way as the one that goes on with an answering machine in your home. When someone calls and finds that you're not home, they leave a message by talking to the answering machine instead of directly to you. The answering machine stores the message using any number of methods. When you get home, an indicator on the answering machine tells you that you have one or more messages. Pressing a button on the answering machine normally plays the messages back to you, enabling you to determine who has called in your absence. As you can see, the idea of disconnected communication isn't new; MSMQ represents a new implementation of an existing idea.

Earlier in the chapter, we talked about MTS. We also discussed how the use of transactions affects your applications. It turns out that MSMQ applications use a minimum of three transactions for every data transmission, even if it appears that there's only one transaction taking place. The first transaction occurs between the client application and the local queue. MSMQ creates a second transaction when it takes the message from the local queue and places it in the server queue. That's where the third transaction begins. As soon as the server removes a message from the queue, it creates a third transaction that tracks the message's progress on the server. This three-transaction approach makes it a lot less likely that an update will fail because of communication problems, which, in turn, makes the application more reliable. In addition, because there's a special MSMQ transaction for delivering data from the client to the server, you can be sure that each message gets transmitted successfully only one time, but that it does get transmitted at least one time.

Throughout this chapter, I address the topic of queues in several ways. There are two kinds of queues supported by MSMQ: application and system. The application queue is created by the application and is used for messages, administration, reports, and responses. Systems queues are created by MSMQ. There are two types: dead letter and journal. Queues can also be public or private. Public queues are available for anyone to use and are tracked by the *MSMQ Information Service (MQIS)*. Private queues are normally used for one-to-one communications, such as a response from a server on a client machine. I'll talk more about these queues as the chapter progresses.

The business case for MSMQ

Now that you understand what's going on with MSMQ a little better, it's important to understand how MSQM can help you in a practical business way. Sure, being able to complete transactions while the client is disconnected from the server is an important way to make applications reliable, but what are the hidden benefits that you can use to sell your boss on the idea? The following sections provide an overview of some of the business reasons to use MSMQ in place of some of the other technologies that you may have tried in the past.

User training

Right now, you have to train users to perform their tasks in at least two different ways if you want to implement a disconnected application scenario for mobile computers. They have to use one technique when they're directly connected to the server and a second (two-step) technique when disconnected. Of course, this means that you have to invest more time and money training these users, which increases business costs. In addition, because there are two techniques for performing a single task, the probability of user confusion and the resulting user error is much higher.

Reliable database updates

Mobile users are currently required to perform transactions in two phases. First, they take the order at the remote location from a new customer. Second, they have to update all of their orders to the company database in some way. This two-step approach to working with transactions means that the potential for human error greatly increases.

Several problems can occur including the loss of data between the time the order is taken and the time it arrives at the company server: the user simply forgets to upload his or her orders, the order is mangled during transmission, or the order gets transmitted more than once. Because of MSMQ's design, not only is the update process automatic, but the use of transactions also ensures data integrity. In short, you spend a lot less time troubleshooting errant database entries.

Application scaling

One of the MSMQ features that you may not notice immediately is that the disconnected processing scenario also allows the server to scale better. When using a direct connection, the client requests have to be processed immediately or the client will notice a processing delay. Using MSMQ doesn't mean that the requests get processed any faster, but placing the requests in a queue allows the call to return faster, which means that users won't notice a processing delay nearly as fast as before. Users can continue to work as if they have the server all to themselves. When the processing load starts to fall, the server can begin to process the messages contained in the queues at a faster rate. Consequently, the server runs at a higher efficiency and the users are happier.

Noncritical path processing

You can also use MSMQ to prioritize the work that the server needs to perform. For example, the server has to be available to receive customer orders all of the time. Otherwise, you may lose an order to a competitor who's ready. However, once you have the order, you don't need to process it immediately. You can check the customer's credit card validity during off peak times. In addition, order fulfillment can take place during the evening hours when the server is less likely to be busy. All this means that you get better efficiency from your server investment by ensuring that the server is always busy doing some type of work for your company.

Fewer error messages

Consider for a moment the cost of an error message to your business. The user has to call a support technician. If the support technician isn't immediately available, then the user waits instead of processing orders for your business. The more error messages that a server generates, the greater the number of support technicians you require and the more time the user wastes waiting for an answer. Because MSMQ allows your server to scale better, the user receives fewer resource-related error messages, meaning that the capability to scale affects your bottom line in several easy-to-understand ways.

Human processing time removed

When you create a direct connection between the client and the server, the objects created on the server usually exist for the entire time that the application runs on the client machine. This means that the server is allocating resources while the user is thinking about the data needed to commit a transaction. Using MSMQ removes the human part of the equation from server resource allocation. The server-side objects are created only long enough to process the transaction after all of the data is collected. Consequently, the server uses resources more efficiently and usually can handle a larger processing load.

Understanding MSMQ limitations

MSMQ doesn't fix every programming problem that you may have with your applications, and because of the way it's designed, it actually introduces a few new limitations that you need to know about. In short, MSMQ is another tool for your toolbox, but it shouldn't be viewed as the only tool. What Microsoft is attempting to do is create an environment in which more than one tool may meet a particular need; you need to consider the pros and cons of each tool before you use it. Table 6-3 helps you to understand MSMQ limitations.

Table 6-3 An Overview of MSMQ Limitations	
Limitation	**Description**
One Way Message Transport	Previous chapters looked at components that require one or more inputs and produce some type of output. However, when you work with MSMQ you can create components with only inputs and no outputs. The reason for this one-way transfer of information is easy to understand—the client and server may not be available at the same time. As a result, the server may not have a client to which it can send a response.
HRESULT (Return) Value Limited	Because the client may send a message to the server in disconnected mode, you can't expect the same kind of HRESULT or return value that you've gotten in the past. When using MSMQ, a positive return value may indicate that the data was received by the local queue instead of telling you that the transaction succeeded as a whole. This means that you have to limit your assumptions when designing the application.
No Synchronous Result	MSMQ provides asynchronous data transfer through messages. This means that you can't expect instantaneous results from it. For example, the user may query the database for recent customer orders. If you store that information on the user's local hard drive, then you can expect to get a response even in disconnected mode. On the other hand, if the information only appears on the server, then you need to provide users with some type of informational feedback that allows them to retrieve the information that they need.

Limitation	Description
	In short, there are some situations when a connection is required. The best you can do is download a subset of the company's database to the user's machine—those records that you think the user is most likely to need while in disconnected mode. This means that MSMQ applications require some level of intelligent download capability based on the user's schedule.
Complete Messages Only	Because the requestor may be unavailable when the server begins processing a request, the messages that you send to the server's message queue have to contain complete information. For example, if you want to enter a new order into the fulfillment database, then all of the data required for that order has to appear within a single message. Unfortunately (despite assurances to the contrary), this may require some recoding on your part to get an application ready for MSMQ use.
Data by Value, Not by Reference	Visual Basic programmers normally don't worry too much about how data is passed to a component. Large values are normally passed by reference (using a pointer to a location in memory) in order to reduce the load that a data transfer would place on the host machine. That doesn't work with MSMQ. You must send data by value, not by reference. The reason is obvious when you think about it. A lack of direct connectivity means that the reference is worthless. Only discrete values can provide the information that the server requires.

As you can see, most of the limitations of MSMQ are based on the same thing that makes this technology so attractive in the first place. When you create a disconnected application, you have to assume certain things about the client and the server, like the inability of the server and client to talk with each other. This means that you have to think about the kinds of information that the client and server require well in advance of the first trial on the road.

You can partially overcome the problems of disconnected applications by creating two different component message queues: one on the client and another on the server. Because message flow is a one-way process, you need two separate sets of components (or dual-purpose components) to implement this idea. Figure 6-2 shows one way that you can use this methodology to help support a user's need for customer information on the road.

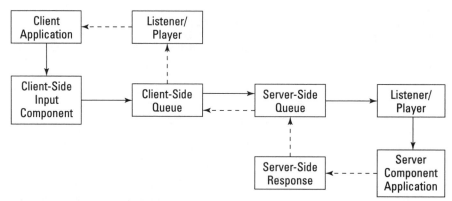

Figure 6-2: MSMQ does provide ways of creating interactive messaging; you just have to be creative in your approach.

As shown in Figure 6-2, this method does require an independent client with its own queue. In addition, the client and the server require a component to manage input to the queue. The client can have a listener component that allows the server to send it messages that respond to client requests. Likewise, the server needs a listener component to respond to client input. (The client-to-server message route appears in solid lines, while the server-to-client route appears in dashed lines.)

Obviously, you still don't get anything close to a real-time response using this method, but it does allow for smarter download of user-requested data. For example, a user can place a list of names for the next day's sales meetings in a client-side queue. When a connection to the server is created, the client-side queue is transferred to the server. The server, in turn, can create a list of local client database entries based on the meeting list and download it to its local queue. The listener on the client receives these new database entries and updates the client's local database in the background as the user completes other tasks. In short, the user always has access to the next day's client records from the company database, even though those records normally require a direct connection. This is an example of smart application downloads. The one-way message connection can be overcome by using multiple components designed to provide a variety of services on both the client and server.

So, at this point, you're probably thinking that you may not be able to use MSMQ because of your application's need to receive a response for every transaction. Actually, there are many situations when the client machine doesn't require a response. For example, when salespeople input orders, they really don't need any response from the server. In most cases, a salesperson simply assumes that the order made it to the server. If an update on order status is required, a salesperson can always issue a status request that is answered during a later connection.

As an alternative, the server can always assume that it needs to download active order status information and provide it during the user's regular connection time. In short, there are many times when you simply don't need an instantaneous response to server input — an update the next day works just as well.

There are going to be times when you absolutely have to have some kind of response to a request. For example, what if an exception occurs during order processing? The salesperson may have forgotten to include the customer ID on an order. In this case, there's another method that MSMQ provides for dealing with the situation. You can pass a reference to a response object on the client machine as part of your request. The messages are still passed one way, and you still need two separate components to achieve two-way data transfer. In this case, however, the response is sent automatically. Obviously, you want to limit this kind of processing so that the connection between the client and server isn't overwhelmed during intermittent user contacts.

Understanding the API

Windows 2000 actually provides two methods for working with MSMQ. You get to choose between the API access method used by previous versions of MSMQ or the newer COM component route. Either route allows you to create, delete, and work with message queues. In most cases, the decision to use either API calls or COM components is a matter of personal taste. However, the big advantage of using COM components is that you can use them with a variety of languages. For the most part, you're limited to using Visual C++ when working with the MSMQ API, which makes the COM component route the best way to go when using Visual Basic. (You could write to the MSMQ API in Visual Basic, but this is time-consuming considering the COM components are already available.) In addition, because the COM components are newer, somewhat easier to work with, and much more flexible than the API calls, you should concentrate on using the COM components in this chapter. Table 6-4 talks about the various COM components and how you use them in an application.

Tip   To gain access to MSMQ COM Components, you need to add support for the Microsoft Message Queue 2.0 Object Library to your application. Make sure you use the 2.0 version, not the 1.0 version that will also be located on your machine. Use the Project ⇨ References command to display the References dialog box. Find the Microsoft Message Queue 2.0 Object Library entry and check it. Clicking OK will add support for this library to your application. If you don't see the Microsoft Message Queue 2.0 Object Library entry, check for the MQOA.DLL file in the Windows\System32 folder. Make sure that this type library is registered using the RegSvr32 MQOA.DLL command. (See the "Using the Object Browser" sidebar below to learn more about the DLLs used by your application.)

Table 6-4
MSMQ COM Component Summary

Component	Description
MSMQApplication	Allows you to perform two machine-related tasks. First, you can obtain the ID of the machine using the `MachineIdOfMachineName()` method. Second, you can register a certification that's used for security purposes using the `RegisterCertificate()` method.
MSMQCoordinated TransactionDispenser	Creates an external transaction that relies on MTS to perform the work. The output from the one method associated with this class, `BeginTransaction()`, is a MSMQTransaction object that you can then use for sending and receiving messages within a transaction. We'll discuss the dynamics of transactions in further detail in "Understanding Transactions" below.
MSMQEvent	Provides an event-handling capability that allows you to monitor various MSMQ events, then react to them within a listener (or other) component. This component allows you to monitor messages arriving at the queue, errors that occur while a message is being delivered to the queue, and messages that don't arrive at the queue before their time-out timer expires. Using the MSMQEvent component allows you to write a single component that can be associated with any number of queues to handle common message-related tasks.
MSMQMessage	Contains all of the methods and properties normally required to work with new messages. You use this component to send messages, as well as gain access, to a security context for the message. The properties associated with this component allow you to define all message characteristics completely including the administration and response queue locations. You can also define encryption and delivery options. We'll look at more message-related features as the chapter progresses.
MSMQQuery	Use this component to ask Active Directory about public queues. The single associated method, `LookupQueue()`, accepts a data structure that allows you to define the parameters of your search. The results of the search are returned in an MSMQQueueInfos object.
MSMQQueue	Allows you to work with queues. This component contains methods for receiving messages, peeking at the contents of the queue, closing the queue, and resetting the queue. A special method, `EnableNotification()`, allows you to set up event-driven message processing for the queue.

Component	Description
MSMQQueueInfo	Use this component to perform queue management tasks. You can create a new queue, open or delete an existing queue, or refresh or update queue properties for the queue. This component also provides access to a wealth of queue-related properties such as privacy and priority levels, creation time, transactional state, time of the last modification, and maximum queue size.
MSMQQueueInfos	An object returned by the MSMQQuery object that allows you to search through a list of public queues meeting certain search criteria. This component relies on two methods, `Next()` and `Reset()`, to manage the position of a cursor within the list of queues. The current queue is returned as a MSMQQueueInfo component that contains properties identifying the selected public queue.
MSMQTransaction	An object returned by a call to the `BeginTransaction()` method of either the MSMQTransactionDispenser or MSMQCoordinatedTransactionDispenser components. The three methods of this component allow you to commit, abort, or initiate a new transaction. You normally use this object as part of a `MSMQMessage.Send()`, `MSMQQueue.Receive()`, or `MSMQReceiveCurrent()` call.
MSMQTransaction Dispenser	Creates an internal transaction that relies on MSMQ to perform the work. The output from the one method associated with this class, `BeginTransaction()`, is a MSMQTransaction object that you can then use for sending and receiving messages within a transaction. We'll discuss the dynamics of transactions in further detail in "Understanding Transactions" below.

Understanding transactions

Let's talk about transactions in more detail. There are two ways to deliver your message: fast or reliable. The fast method sends the message from machine to machine using memory alone, whereas the reliable method flushes each message to disk before sending it on to the next machine. The main difference between fast and reliable transactions is disk access. The disk access time may make the message delivery slower, but it also means that you can retrieve another copy of the message should it get lost between two computers or if a server failure occurs. MSMQ assumes that you want fast over reliable, so it normally uses the MQMSG_DELIVERY_EXPRESS option for your messages. If you want to use the slower, more reliable method, use the MQMSG_DELIVERY_RELIABLE option instead. You'll find both of these options in the MQMSGDELIVERY enumeration.

Whether you use the fast or reliable message delivery methods, the kind of queue you use is also important. Transactions require transactional queues. You can't send a transactional message to a normal queue and vice versa. MSMQ always requires you to determine what kind of queue you want to create during the creation process as shown in Figure 6-3. All you need to do is check the Transactional option in the Queue Name dialog box to make the queue a transactional queue. Obviously, this means that you have to decide whether you want to use transactions during the initial setup of your project or face the possibility of recreating the queues that your application requires later.

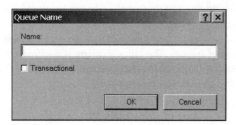

Figure 6-3: MSMQ requires that you determine what kind of queue you need during the creation process—you can't change the settings later.

MSMQ actually supports two transaction types: internal and external. The internal transaction relies on features provided by the MSMQ transport to ensure delivery, while the external transaction relies on MTS. Which transaction type to choose depends on whether you want speed or reliability. An internal transaction runs faster, but provides fewer features than an external transaction.

There are also two kinds of internal transaction types to choose from. You can use the MQ_SINGLE_MESSAGE option to send a single message using a transaction with the `MSMQMessage.Send()` method. If you need to send more than one message using a transaction, then you want to begin by creating a MSMQTransaction object. All of the transactional constants appear within the MQTRANSACTIONAL enumeration.

Besides speed and reliability, there are other differences between internal and external transactions. An important difference from a security standpoint is isolation. MTS transactions run at a serializable isolation level. This means that no one else can see the transaction—it's totally hidden from anyone but the client and server. An MSMQ transaction runs at the read committed isolation level. In other words, there are certain circumstances when a listener or other component can see more than just the current transaction. In short, it's a small breach of security, but still a significant one.

Another potential problem is that other resource managers can't use internal MSMQ transactions. For example, if you want to create a transaction that encompasses both MSMQ and SQL Server, you need to use an external transaction because SQL Server can't participate in an internal transaction. Of course, the lack of resource management coordination also means that internal transactions use less memory than a similar external transaction. Even a small savings can mean a significant difference when your server is processing hundreds (or even thousands) of transactions every hour. In short, the choice is one of resource management versus transaction flexibility. The flexibility that MTS provides comes at the price of system memory and performance.

Handling exceptions

Like anything else, there are situations when the default error handling isn't going to take care of your message queue. For example, a user may inadvertently generate a message with incomplete information, and no amount of rework can fix the message so that it can be processed later. Because the message is handled as part of a transaction and because there's no client to consult with in order to determine how to handle the errant message, an aborted message simply returns to the top of the message queue. In short, your application can find itself in an endless loop trying to process a message that can't be processed.

MSMQ provides a mechanism for dealing with messages that abort in the form of retry queues. What you're really doing is moving the message from the active queue to a background queue for processing later. This means that current messages aren't held up waiting for the errant message to process. Of course, you eventually need to handle the messages in the retry queue. At this point, there are three ways to handle errant messages as shown in the following list.

   ✦ **Fix the Message:** Sometimes the message lacks an important bit of information that you can add to make it process correctly. In this case, all you need to do is fix the erroneous information and move the message back to the normal processing queue from the retry queue. In cases where there's a configuration issue (for example, the user lacks sufficient rights), an administrator can manually fix the problem and then move the message from the retry queue to the normal processing queue.

   ✦ **Gather Diagnostic Information and Delete:** There are situations when no matter what you do to the message it doesn't arrive at the destination in a state that the receiving component can accept. In this case, you need to gather as much information about the message as possible, and then delete it to prevent the message from becoming a problem for the rest of the system. Obviously, you want to generate an event log report using the diagnostic information you've gathered. This will alert the network administrator to potential problems with the MSMQ setup. In addition, you might need to generate an error message for the user so that the user knows that the message failed. In some cases, you may be able to regenerate the message by having the user reenter the information. Finally, you might need to alert the component developer (or an in-house developer) so that the component can be updated and possibly repaired.

✦ **Generate a Compensating Message:** This is a situation in which the message can't complete because of outside influences. For example, you may have an order-entry system that relies on a customer entering a credit card number for payment purposes. The card may be full or out of date, or perhaps the customer has entered the name incorrectly. A compensating message allows you to send a request for additional information to the customer, fix the message, and then place it back into the normal processing queue. As an alternative, you can generate an error message and simply back the transaction out, effectively deleting the entire transaction from the system.

Implementing this error-handling capability requires a number of component configuration changes. The most important configuration item is specifying a queuing exception class for the component. This class has to implement the IPlaybackControl interface, which contains two methods: `FinalClientRetry()` and `FinalServerRetry()`, along with any interface methods that the component normally provides. (You'll find the IPlaybackControl interface in the COM+ Services Type Library, COMSVCS.DLL.) This exception-handing component gives you the opportunity to take care of message problems. If you decide that the message can't be fixed, then call `FinalClientRetry()` or `FinalServerRetry()` to place the message in the dead message queue (just like the dead letter office of the post office—messages enter but in most cases, don't leave).

Using the Object Browser

Sometimes it's hard to know precisely what features a DLL you add to your Visual Basic application contains. I've often found new features that Microsoft added, but didn't document. In some cases, the documentation turned out to be wrong and browsing the DLL turned out to be the only way to get the correct information. In other cases, Microsoft released a new version of a DLL and I wanted to compare the old and new DLL. Whatever your reason for wanting to learn more about the objects used within your application, Visual Basic provides an excellent tool that you need to know about, the Object Browser.

Opening the Object Browser is easy. Just press F2 or use the View ➪ Object Browser command. When you first open the Object Browser, you'll see a dialog box containing all of the objects used by your project—an often dizzying array of objects that you don't want to know about.

Refining your search comes next. Choose a specific library from the top-left drop-down list box (this list box normally contains "<All Libraries>" when you open Object Browser). The following figure shows the display that you'll see when you select the MSMQ library—the one that contains the MSMQ COM objects we discussed earlier in the chapter.

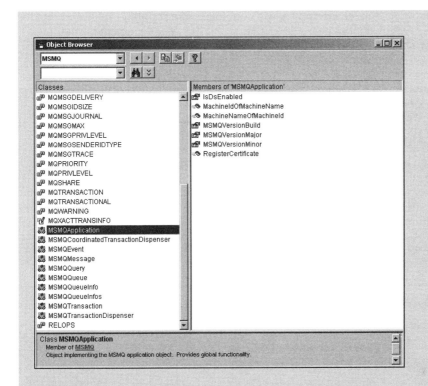

The Object Browser can provide precise information about the contents of a support library.

The figure shows the classes, enumerations, and types for this object in the left pane. Selecting a class, enumeration, or type displays the information for that element in the status bar and the methods, properties, constants, and variables supported by that element. Finally, selecting one of the methods, properties, constants, or variables will display information about that element in the status bar. In short, you can use the Object Browser to better determine what library features are at your disposal.

MSMQ from the Internet

It may be tempting to think that we've discussed everything that you need to know about MSMQ from a theoretical perspective. After all, we've talked about the various components that you need to use, the interfaces that you need to implement, and many of the more important methods. However, the Internet presents some special challenges to the developer when it comes to working with disconnected applications. For example, the client-side interface becomes a concern. You need to ask whether the user will need a full-fledged desktop application (thick client) or a simple browser interface (thin client). It's possible to create a perfectly functional thin client using new technologies like scripting and XML. (See the "Working with XML" sidebar below for details about this new document-formatting technology.) The issue of whether to use a thick or thin client is so important that we'll discuss it in detail in Chapter 13.

Another problem is security. Although MSMQ supports full encryption, it's up to the developer and network administrator to ensure that the data actually is encrypted. The default settings tend to leave your data unprotected, which means that you have to take proactive measures to ensure that your data stays safe. We'll discuss the COM+ portion of security in Chapter 7. On the Internet, however, you'll also want to incorporate a VPN into the security plan. Remember that MSMQ encryption techniques will protect the data, not unwanted intrusions on the server or client. It's also important to use role-based security to your advantage. Make sure that you configure your component carefully to provide full access to those who need it and to deny access to those who don't. The following list summarizes the three levels of security that you need to think about when working on the Internet.

✦ **Data:** Protected by encryption

✦ **Component:** Protected by role-based security

✦ **Client and Server:** Protected through the use of VPN, firewalls, and Windows 2000 security

Assuming that you have the perfect interface and security to protect your data, you still need to consider what level of data access to provide to employees on the road. Obviously, your application has to handle any new information that will affect the employee's ability to get the job done. For example, your application has to consider updates like new pricing information.

Data is relatively straightforward as an update. What happens if you need to update the client software? You may decide on a client software update that will make access from the road impossible unless the employee gets the required update. Using component technology will ease the pain of updates somewhat, but you'll need to provide some type of roll back mechanism if the update doesn't work. In addition, the application should support some type of error reporting mechanism so that the employee doesn't have to endure a barrage of failed updates. Finally, you need to provide some type of contingency planning so that the failed update doesn't become a problem in other ways.

So, how does MSMQ come into play with data downloads and failed application updates? You can use the same techniques that you use to accept orders from the Internet to interact with the employee as well. Using message technology is important for an Internet application in more ways than simple data exchange. It's important to remember that MSMQ can handle everything from a string to an object, and everything in between.

Working with XML

If you work in a large company, then it's quite possible that you're working with several component technologies. COM may be only one of several solutions that you need to deal with on a daily basis. The only problem is that getting the different component technologies to talk to each other has been difficult, if not impossible, until recently. Many companies are looking at eXtensible Markup Language (XML) to solve their compatibility woes. You can find out more about XML in general at the World Wide Web Consortium (W3C) Web site at `http://www.w3.org/XML/`. The draft specification for this new technology appears at `http://www.w3.org/TR/xsl/`. Of course, the best place to get the Microsoft view of things is at `http://msdn.microsoft.com/xml/default.asp`.

It's important to note that XML only provides a standardized method for marking documents up. There still has to be something to define what the content of the document signifies. That's where Microsoft's Simple Object Access Protocol (SOAP) comes into play. We talked about SOAP in the sidebar entitled "SOAP, the replacement for DCOM" in Chapter 5, so I won't talk about it again here. However, look for SOAP and XML to work together to bring a new level of compatibility and flexibility to the component technology used on your Web page.

Don't get the idea that XML is something that exists only on some engineer's blotter. For one thing, you'll find that there are a few XML magazines appearing on the market (a sure sign of interest in a technology). However, the people who are putting effort into making XML a success are the early adopters of this technology. You'll find an outstanding overview of XML, lots of links (including some to those magazines that I mentioned), and the current news about XML at the XML Zone at `http://www.xml-zone.com`. Would you like to see XML in action without spending a lot of time creating a sample yourself? You'll find a list of free XML software at `http://www.garshol.priv.no/download/xmltools/`. Finally, you'll find an XML parser toolkit at `http://www.jclark.com/xml/expat.html`.

Configuring MSMQ

Later chapters will show you how to write applications that use MSMQ, talk about ways in which you can speed the development process, and provide solutions to problems that you might encounter. However, before you can learn all of these tricks of the trade, there are some simple MSMQ configuration techniques that you need to know.

Most of the MSMQ configuration tasks occur in the Computer Management console shown in Figure 6-4. Notice that the Message Queuing snap-in (the friendly wrapper around MSMQ) appears under the Services and Applications snap-in. In addition, the Computer Management console defaults to the local machine. You can always connect to another machine if you have the proper rights by highlighting the Computer Management snap-in, and then using the Action ⇨ Connect to another computer. . . command. The Select Computer dialog box will display a list of computers that you can choose.

Figure 6-4: The Computer Management console is where you configure MSMQ for use.

Message Queuing contains four queue folders that group the queues by use including private, public, outgoing, and system queues. We looked at the uses for these queues earlier, so we won't discuss their use again here. However, you do have to look in the right folder for the queue you want to find. In most cases, you'll need to look at either the Outgoing Queues or Public Queues folder for application data and Private Queues folder for administrative queues. The System Queues folder contains the dead letter queues and other system related queues.

When you first look at a queue folder, you'll see a list of the queues that it contains, the label for each queue, and the number of messages each queue holds, as shown in Figure 6-5. Fortunately, you aren't limited to this list of information. Right-click the queue folder, and then choose View ⇨ Choose Columns from the context menu. You'll see a Modify Columns dialog box like the one shown in Figure 6-6. Notice that this dialog box allows you to add everything from the number of journal messages for the queue to the queue's GUID. The Modify Columns dialog box also allows you to change the order of the various columns using the Move Up and Move Down buttons. In most cases, it pays to display all of the available columns unless desktop space is at a premium. Doing so allows you to better track queue conditions without opening each queue separately. (Some static data, like the Type Guid column, could be eliminated from view if desktop space is at a premium, but you'll definitely want to see dynamic data like the number of queue and journal message entries.)

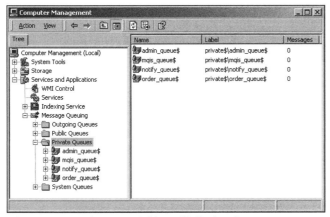

Figure 6-5: Each queue folder will display the queue name, queue label, and number of queue messages as a default.

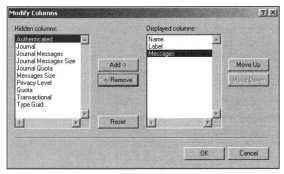

Figure 6-6: You can change the amount of information displayed within the queue folder using the Modify Columns dialog box.

Manually adding new queues to a queue folder is easy; just right-click the queue folder, and then use the New ⇨ <Queue Folder Name> Queue command. You'll see the Queue Name dialog box shown in Figure 6-3. Type a queue name, determine whether you want to make the queue transactional, and then click OK. You'll need to manually configure the queue settings by using the queue Properties dialog box, which is discussed next.

Remember that when you create a queued component and install it using the Component Services snap-in, COM+ will automatically add a queue for you to the correct folder. However, you may want to edit the queue settings later to provide a better label, tweak performance, or update security settings. Right-click any queue, and then choose Properties from the context menu to see the settings for that queue. Figure 6-7 shows the General tab of the queue Properties dialog box. Table 6-5 describes the fields in this tab.

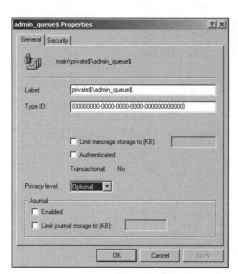

Figure 6-7: The General tab of the queue Properties dialog box contains performance and identification properties.

Table 6-5
Queue Properties Dialog Box Fields

Field	Description
Label	Defines the name of the queue. This is the name that you'll typically use within an application to access the queue.
Type ID	Contains the GUID for the queue. The GUID is used to identify the type of service offered by the queue or the queue's function. A GUID containing all zeros indicates a general-purpose queue. When a queue is assigned a GUID, it's usually associated with a specific application or component.
Limit message storage to (KB)	Determines whether the queue has a size limit. If so, the associated field allows you to define how many KB the queue can hold. When this limit is reached, the queue will no longer accept new messages.
Authenticated	Specifies whether the queue will accept only authenticated messages. This is another queue security feature.
Transactional	Contains the transactional state of the queue. This setting is made when you create the queue.

Field	Description
Privacy level	Determines the amount of encryption that the queue will accept. Queues normally default to Optional, which means that they accept either encrypted or unencrypted messages. The Body option forces the queue to accept only encrypted messages, while the None option forces the queue to accept only unencrypted messages.
(Journal) Enabled	Determines whether the target journal is enabled. The journal holds messages that are removed from the queue by an application. It doesn't store messages that are removed because their timeout value elapsed or as a result of administrative removal using directory services. You must manually remove messages from the journal when they're no longer needed.
Limit journal storage to (KB)	Limits the amount of disk space that can be used to store journal messages. This is an important setting because journal and dead-letter queue messages count against the computer's storage quota.

The Security tab of the queue Properties dialog box appears in Figure 6-8. As you can see, this is a standard security configuration dialog box. It allows you to set the level of access to the queue. Clicking Advanced displays the Access Control Settings dialog box, which allows finer control over the security settings. In addition, you can use the Access Control Settings dialog box to set security auditing for the queue and to change the queue owner.

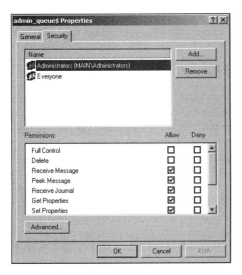

Figure 6-8: The Security tab allows you to configure access to the queue.

Beneath each queue entry are two folders: Queue messages and Journal messages as shown in Figure 6-9. As with other folders we've talked about so far, right clicking on the folder and choosing the View ⇨ Choose Columns command will allow you to specify the amount of information you see for each message. Clearing unneeded messages from the queue message folder is relatively easy. Right-click the queue message folder, and then choose All Tasks ⇨ Purge from the context menu.

Caution   Purging messages from a queue message folder will result in the loss of all messages. The messages won't be placed in a journal queue from a message queue. In addition, you can't select which messages to purge. All of the messages will be removed if you decide to purge the queue. The only way to provide selective message removal is to add removal code to your application.

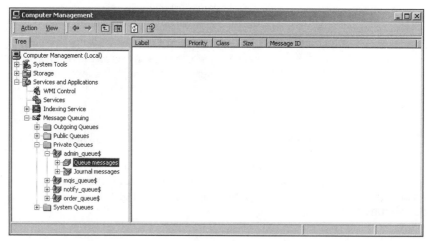

Figure 6-9: Each queue entry has a Queue messages and a Journal messages folder.

Working with COM and COM+ Events

COM and COM+ both support event systems. COM supports the request/reply system in which the client and server are both present to engage in a conversation. COM+ supports both the request/reply event system and the new publish/subscribe event system. The publish/subscribe event system has several advantages over the request/reply event system, most notable of which is the capability to allow events to occur even if the client and server aren't present at the same time. The following paragraphs will look at both event systems, and then help you determine which event system is best for your particular needs.

A short overview of the COM request/reply system

COM was designed during a time when desktop applications ran on one machine. A developer could count on the client and server being present because they were both on the same machine. In addition, the one machine approach meant that communication problems were moot — there just weren't any. Because these two assumptions hold true in a desktop environment, the request/reply event system works as well today as it ever has for a desktop application.

So, how does this event system work? In theory, the request/reply event system is quite simple. The client application requests that the server notify it about events. For example, the client may need to know when the user clicks a button or changes a value. As part of the event request, the client provides a pointer to a callback function. COM marshals this pointer into the server's address space, if necessary.

The request functionality is implemented in the server in a separate interface. When the client wants to request notification about an event, it obtains a pointer to the server's request interfaces and calls the `Advise()`method. Likewise, when the client no longer wants to know about server events, it calls the `UnAdvise()` method. This system allows any number of clients to request notification from the server. Of course, this begs the question of how the server keeps track of each client that it services. The server issues a cookie — essentially a number identifying the client — as part of the return value from the `Advise()` method. The client uses this cookie to identify itself when it calls the `UnAdvise()` method.

When the conditions for the requested event become true, the server fires the event (also known as the reply). In other words, the server calls the client function to notify the client. The client can then act upon the event and perform some work. For example, when the user clicks the OK button on a dialog box, the dialog box destroys itself.

Understanding the COM+ publish/subscribe system

Distributed applications can't rely on a specific connection existing at any given time — the client and server may not even have a connection. Therefore, the request/reply event system that I described in the previous section is unlikely to work with a distributed application. The lack of a connection between the client and server means that we have to create some new method of handling events. COM+ provides this new event-handling methodology, which is known as the publish/subscribe event system.

In the old setup, there was a client and a server with a direct connection. The publish/subscribe event system has three main elements. The server publishes data through an event class that it registers with Component Services. Once the data is published, the server is no longer concerned about where the data goes. In other words, it has no knowledge of which clients receive the data that it publishes.

The client subscribes to an event that the server publishes. However, unlike COM, where the client registers with the server, the COM+ client registers with the COM+ catalog. In reality, the client has no idea of which server provides the data. All it knows is that there's an event that it wants to subscribe to.

So, we have a server publishing the data and a client subscribing to the data, but no connection between the two. That's where the event object comes into play. The event object is created by the server prior to firing an event. When the server fires the event, the event object receives it. At this point, the server can terminate if it wants to — the event has been fired and the event object will handle the details of notifying subscribers. The event object looks through the list of subscribers in the COM+ catalog, and then notifies each subscriber.

At this point, you may wonder what this three-element method buys you in the way of productivity or reliability. Creating the server is certainly easier. The server doesn't need to provide a request interface or handle client function pointers. All it needs to do is fire an event, nothing more. The subscriber, on the other hand, needs to know nothing about the server. All it needs to do is implement an interface. This interface has the same name as the server's interface. In short, you can create two components, change components, or even create entirely new functionality using this method without having the change both the client and server. All that you need to worry about is implementing an interface with the correct name.

The event object is also simple. All it really contains is stub code (empty functions). The COM+ Event System Service handles the actual event object details. It merely uses the event object you create as a template of the interfaces and methods that it needs to handle.

Another advantage of using the publish/subscribe methodology is that you can combine it with MSMQ. A COM server (publisher) could queue up changes that would wait until the host computer has time to service them. Likewise, the fired events could be queued until the client can pick them up. Consequently, neither the client nor the server has to exist during event handling.

Determining which event system to use

We've seen that the request/reply and publish/subscribe event systems are radically different. In some cases, it might appear that the choice of which event system to choose is difficult because of these differences. However, you can ask yourself two questions to make the choice of which event system to use relatively straightforward.

1. Does the application have to work with COM? If the application has to work on both Windows NT and Windows 2000 machines, then it's likely that you'll need to implement a request/reply event system. This isn't a problem when working with desktop applications, but it can be a problem if you need to support users on the road. If you find that you need to support users on the road, then an operating system upgrade may be in order.

2. Does the application need to support more than one client? If you find that you require broadcast capability, disconnected application features, or other COM+-specific elements, then the publish/subscribe model is the event model to use. COM couldn't support these capabilities, which is the main reason Microsoft abandoned the request/reply event system.

There are some potential pitfalls to avoid when using the publish/subscribe event model. A big pitfall to avoid is overwhelming the system with too many messages. The publish/subscribe event model isn't designed to replace modern e-mail systems. If you find that you're sending a lot of messages to hundreds of clients, then an event system is the wrong choice—you need e-mail. The publish/subscribe event model is designed to support a few clients—more than 1, but probably less than 50. Of course, the number of clients your application can support depends on many factors including the amount of available network bandwidth and the capabilities of your server.

Another problem with the publish/subscribe event model is the need to use Windows 2000 to the exclusion of everything else. Theoretically, given the right circumstances, you might be able to get a Windows NT client to work in this environment, but the odds don't favor a workable solution. For the most part, COM+ is a Windows 2000 product that you can't use with older versions of Windows. You'll give up too much development time trying to make the square peg of COM+ fit into the round hole of COM.

COM+ Application Types

Unlike previous renditions of COM, COM+ supports the idea of a true application type. An application type, in this case, isn't the same as the application types that you think about on a client machine. For example, there are no database or spreadsheet application types when talking about COM+. The four COM+ application types are:

- ✦ Library
- ✦ Server
- ✦ Proxy
- ✦ Preinstalled

Microsoft has slowly built up some additional aids to help developers create fully integrated Distributed interNetwork Architecture (DNA) applications. As part of this effort, they've set up the Microsoft Visual Studio Interoperability Studio where you can learn about new products and download add-ons that will make the development process easier. For the most part, this site brings together all of the links to other Microsoft Web sites that you'd normally need to collect yourself. It also offers case studies (customer examples), tools, and other interoperability resources. You can find this Web site at `http://msdn.microsoft.com/vstudio/centers/interop/default.asp`.

Part of the reason for this new direction is that COM+ handles each kind of application differently. For example, the security for a library application is handled differently than the security for a server application. When working with a library application, the object executes in the client process and the client's security context is used for the object. On the other hand, a server application executes out-of-process. The security context is derived using a combination of the component attributes and the client information supplied as part of the component request.

The following sections will help you to better understand how the four types differ. It's important to know about the various COM+ application types because you'll need to know what type of application you want to develop.

Server applications

The server application is an out-of-process server. It executes in its own process and creates its own context. You can access all of the COM+ services using a server application, and the full resources of the host machine are at your disposal (at least within the scope of the security settings).

You'll create the server application more often than any other COM+ application type because this is the most versatile form of application. Obviously, this is the kind of application that will execute on the server and produce the least amount of network traffic (if you optimize it that way).

Library applications

A library application represents one of the newest ways to integrate components in an application. The library application executes in the client process. What this means is that while the library application file physically resides on the server and must be requested from the server, it actually executes on the client machine. The client downloads a library application from the server and uses it locally.

Because of the way that a library application is executed, there are some restrictions on the way that you can work with it and the COM+ services that you can access. These restrictions make sense when you think about the client orientation of the library application. Here's a list of the restrictions.

- ✦ No remote access support
- ✦ Can't use CLB
- ✦ Can't use Queued Components

Library applications can use role-based security. However, the level of access for a library application is limited by the client application's access. In other words, you can't create a component that will provide the client application with more access than it would normally get with its standard security settings. This limitation makes it impossible for a rogue component to damage the system or for users to pry in areas of the server that they have no right to see.

So, what are some of the advantages of library applications compared to standard client-side components? You get most of the same advantages that you would for a COM+ application, but from a client-side perspective. For example, you'll still make component updates at the server, not at the client machine. Access to the component is still secured by the server, not by the client. In fact, the client won't actually see a copy of the component on disk—the component resides at the server and gets loaded into the client's memory. In short, using library applications allows you to get the best benefits of client-side components without many of the problems that client-side components pose.

Proxy applications

When working with DCOM, you had to either use the DCOMCnfg utility to configure the client machine to access the remote application, or find some method to add the required Registry entries through a remote application. Not only was this a difficult and error-prone process, but it required some amount of administrator time for each new client and each new version of the component. In short, the old methodology was time-consuming and almost unsafe from an application perspective.

COM+ provides the proxy application type. This isn't a component, but a proxy for a component that's registered on the server. The proxy application runs on the client machine and automatically adds information into the Registry about the real component that resides on the server. This component information includes class identification (CLSID), program identification (ProgID), the remote server name (RemoteServerName), and marshalling information. This combination of entries allows the client to access the component on the server without any additional intervention on the part of the administrator or developer. In short, Microsoft has automated what could otherwise be a time-consuming and error-prone task in COM+.

Preinstalled applications

COM+ comes with a group of preinstalled applications. Some developers may think that these applications are for COM+ use only—many Windows services in the past have worked exactly this way. The opposite is true with COM+; you're now encouraged to use these preinstalled components to make your own programming job easier.

You'll find all of the COM+ applications in the COM+ Applications folder of the Component Services MMC snap-in. The number of applications you see depends partly on which optional services you install. For example, there are components related to Queued Components within this folder. Here's a list of the potential COM+ Applications folder entries.

✦ COM+ QC Dead Letter Queue Listener

✦ COM+ Utilities

✦ IIS In-Process Applications

✦ IIS Out-Of-Process Packed Application

✦ IIS System Applications

✦ IIS Utilities

✦ System Application

✦ Visual Studio APE Package

Notice that I've added one entry that isn't Windows 2000 specific. The Visual Studio APE (application performance explorer) Package is only installed if you have Visual Studio installed on the host computer. (Obviously, you'll also need to install this component as part of the Visual Studio installation.) You'll find that the COM+ Applications folder of the Component Service MMC snap-in can contain a wide variety of components that you may not have dealt with in the past. The whole purpose of placing components in this location is to make them more accessible to you. You'll find that using the Component Service MMC snap-in will give you a new appreciation of how COM as a whole works and provides flexibility that you've never had before.

Working With Visual Studio Installer

A lot of the new tools in this chapter will use the Microsoft Installer (MSI) file, which is also known as a package. In fact, use of the Microsoft Installer is one of the logo requirements for Windows 2000. Sometimes the way that you install a product plays a role in the way that the product operates later. Certainly, the installation options that you use will control what the user sees during the product's installation. Finally, when installing a product on the server from a remote location, you don't want dialogs to pop up on the display. For all of these reasons and more, it pays to know the MSI file command line options. A complete list of all of the command line switches is found at http://support.microsoft.com/support/kb/articles/q227/0/91.asp?LNG=ENG&SA=TECH. If you're also a developer and need additional information about MSI, look at the SDK site at http://msdn.microsoft.com/downloads/sdks/platform/wininst.asp. There are also some helpful hints about creating installation programs at http://www.installsite.org/. Even though this last site concentrates on information about past Windows installation techniques, it includes an entirely new section on Windows 2000 that you'll want to view.

Summary

This chapter shows you the theory behind COM+. Here are some additional conclusions that you can draw from the contents of this chapter.

✦ COM+ is a combination of standard COM (including DCOM), MSMQ, and MTS.

✦ A transaction is a method of packaging data or commands in such a way that either the whole package is accepted by the receiver or none of the package is accepted.

✦ The best way to remember what features MTS transactions provide is through the use of the acronym ACID (atomicity, consistency, isolation, and durability).

✦ COM+ provides eight essential services for creators of components. Of these eight services, four services are provided by MTS. These services include server components, transactions, security, and administration.

✦ Like all COM technologies, MTS relies on interfaces for communication during a transaction. The interface used with MTS is IObjectContext.

✦ The IObjectContext interface provides four important methods that a component can use to report the success or failure of a transaction: `SetComplete()`, `SetAbort()`, `EnableCommit()`, and `DisableCommit()`.

✦ The easiest way to look at MSMQ is as a form of DCOM that uses queues as an intermediary destination for data flowing between the client and server.

✦ MSMQ provides some important business benefits including reduced user training costs, improved data integrity, enhanced server scaling, noncritical path processing, and reduced support costs.

✦ There are some limits to using MSMQ, most of which have to do with the disconnected nature of this technology.

✦ MQIS is the central database of MSMQ information.

✦ There are certain limitations that you may experience when using MSMQ. The most important limitations include one-way message transport, limited return value, and no synchronous result.

✦ MSMQ provides two methods of access by outside applications: API and COM component. Of the two, the COM component is more flexible, easier to understand, and usable by more programming languages.

✦ The two common methods that a listener uses to detect new messages in a queue are event processing and polling. The polling method is self-contained and requires no additional coding. The event-processing method requires creation of a separate event handler (MSMQEvent) component.

✦ There are two methods of transferring messages in MSMQ: express or reliable. An express message is transmitted using memory only. A reliable delivery is flushed to disk at every computer — making the transfer slower, but easier to recover.

✦ MSMQ also supports internal and external transactions. An internal transaction relies on the MSMQ transport. An external transaction relies on MTS — so it's more reliable, but also slower.

✦ Exception handling is an important part of every programming effort. When using MSMQ, you can handle exceptions in one of three ways: fix the message, gather diagnostic information and delete the message, or generate a compensating message.

✦ Queued Components, the wrapper that Microsoft provides for MSMQ, allows you to easily manage and configure queues.

✦ There are four queue types: public, private, system, and outgoing.

✦ The request/reply event system is the method used by COM to fire events. It requires the client and server to exist at the same time.

✦ The publish/subscribe event system is the new COM+ way of handling events. It uses a three-element system of publisher (server), subscriber (client), and event object.

✦ COM+ defines four specific types of application: server, library, proxy, and preinstalled.

✦   ✦   ✦

COM+ and Security

Windows 2000 provides a wealth of new security features that will make your job as an application developer easier. In fact, security has become so broad and all encompassing under Windows 2000 that a large book on the subject might not be enough to plumb the depths of security features. Suffice it to say then, that this chapter concentrates on developer issues. More precisely, we look at new developer issues — those that you may not have dealt with in the past. Of course, there will be a little overview material to help fill in the gaps.

Security, at least for this chapter, involves four different areas. The first is Windows 2000 security — this is the operating system-level security that you're most familiar with and that we discuss least in the chapter. The second is COM+ specific — component developers no longer have to rely on the operating system features alone to ensure their data and code remain safe. The third is large-environment security. This is security at the domain level and could include connections to the Internet. The fourth is security monitoring. This is an important facet that some developers fail to consider, but ongoing security is the only way to ensure that the application that you write today will be safe tomorrow.

All the security elements that we discuss in this chapter are essential for the COM+ developer. You'll use all of them on an ongoing basis as your project develops and enters maintenance mode. Any kind of practical security is an ongoing process. You don't just set up security one day and then never worry about it again. Even the best application programming methods won't replace maintenance like performing security audits and monitoring unusual user-access patterns. To give you a good example of how important a complete security effort is, consider a recent Caterpillar, Inc. break-in by relatively novice crackers. It seems that the system administrator had left a default password in place, which allowed the crackers to bypass security with ease. In other words, the system administrator left the door wide open for the crackers.

The developer also works with the network administrator and the company staff in general when it comes to security. It's up to the developer to help the network administrator with the human side of the security picture. You can include application code that checks each user's security measures and ensures that those measures comply with the settings provided by the system administrator. In addition, you can keep the system administrators from shooting themselves in the foot. For example, you can include code that automatically asks the system administrator if he or she wants to delete an account that hasn't been used for a given amount of time. In addition, your application can force the user to develop good security habits by doing such things as requiring difficult-to-guess passwords of sufficient length to make it hard for a cracker to use computing power to overcome security.

Note This chapter provides an overview of the theory behind Windows 2000 security. We'll look at potential solutions for generic problems. What you shouldn't be looking for in this chapter are concrete answers that are going to work in your specific situation. It would be silly to try to cover all of the various technologies available today, or even every security issue you'll ever run into, in one chapter. What we'll concentrate on, instead, is the programmer's perspective on security matters. We'll talk about the technologies available to you as a programmer, but we won't get into specific solutions to specific problems. The solutions you finally decide to use will have to be based on your company's needs and the tools you have at your disposal.

The first section looks at Windows 2000 security as a whole. We'll begin with a simple overview of the security provided by the operating system. Because this chapter is devoted to looking at new elements, however, we'll quickly move on to new Windows 2000 security features. We'll look at the new Kerberos and public-key infrastructure (PKI) additions to Windows 2000. These new technologies not only make your network more secure, but they also do it with less stress on the part of both the administrator and the developer. This section also discusses data-encryption concerns. It's not enough to make sure that your system is secure if the data being transmitted from site to site is open to scrutiny. Today's computing environment requires security on many levels including both system-level and data-level security. Finally, we'll talk about a fairly recent addition to Microsoft's arsenal of utilities — the Security Configuration Editor. As a programmer, you need to know how to set up various security scenarios while testing your application. What this means is that you should be familiar with every administrator-level tool, as well as the special programming tools at your disposal. The Security Configuration Editor is an important new addition to the war on computer crime.

Note For the purposes of this chapter, the term cracker always refers to an individual that's breaking into a system unauthorized. This includes any form of illegal activity on the system. On the other hand, a hacker refers to someone who performs low-level system activities, including testing system security. Sometimes you need to employ the services of a good hacker to test the security measures that you have in place, or suffer the consequences of a break-in. This chapter uses the term hacker to refer to someone who performs these legal forms of service. By the way, this is the way that hacker and cracker are commonly defined in security books and by most security professionals. The trade press usually uses the terms incorrectly.

The second section of the chapter addresses COM+ security concerns. As with any development scenario, there are special considerations in the area of security when you use advanced operating system features. The ability of COM+ developers to create new application types like disconnected applications means that some of the old security rules won't work. We'll talk about the main area of COM+ security, the component. This section will also address role-based security — the new way to ensure that your applications are completely secure.

The third section of the chapter shows you how to use role-based security to make your applications more secure. We'll add security to an example component. You may be surprised at just how easy and flexible role-based security really is.

An Overview of Windows 2000 Security

Windows 2000 offers a lot in the way of operating system-level security. You'll find all of the features found in Windows NT, plus new features designed to make security more robust. Microsoft has also spent a lot of time fixing holes in the security system. Of course, security holes will very likely always exist with any operating system as complex as Windows 2000. In most cases, you can count on the operating system to delay breaches, not prevent them. However, even this negative view of Windows 2000 basic security still doesn't negate the usefulness of the security system. You'll find that a properly implemented application design will deter all but the most determined cracker, which is why any good security implementation includes monitoring.

Note This chapter contains an overview of Windows 2000 Security, not a detailed blow-by-blow description. This chapter's purpose is to provide you with the knowledge you need to work with Windows 2000 security effectively. For a detailed security description, you may want to look at my book, the *Windows 2000 Programming Bible* (ISBN 0-7645-3312-6). For further updates, you can check my Web site at `http://www.mwt.net/~jmueller`.

The following sections look at Windows 2000 operating system security. The first section, "Windows 2000 Security Internals," is a very short overview of the basic security that Windows has provided since Windows NT. In most cases, you're already familiar with this information, so I've provided just enough of an overview to clarify technical points that we'll discuss later in the chapter.

The next section, "Kerberos, Public-Key Infrastructure, and Distributed Password Authentication Support," will aid your understanding of some of the exciting new security features of Windows 2000. We'll look at these new technologies in depth because it's unlikely that you've worked with them in the past. For the most part, these new technologies make it much harder for a cracker to decipher your security measures, making a security breach much harder to achieve.

The third section, "Windows 2000 Data-Encryption Support," tells you how Windows 2000 can protect your data from prying eyes. For the most part, a network exists to manage data. In other words, the data is the most important network element. Yet, data is the one element that most application developers fail to protect. As a result, the network itself might be secure, but crackers can gain access to data as it moves from one place to another. Data encryption is a very important feature for keeping your data safe.

The final section, "Using the Security Configuration Editor," helps you understand how to use this new utility. The Security Configuration Editor is actually an MMC snap-in, and it provides detailed access to just about every area of the operating system. As a result, this very powerful tool can greatly reduce the amount of time that you spend configuring security, which means that you spend more time doing what you know best — programming.

Windows 2000 security internals

A famous cracker once said that it's not a matter of if, but when, someone will break into your system. This statement can easily be extended to any computer scenario. It's important to realize that a determined individual can always break your security, so constant hardware/software upgrades and scrutiny on the part of both developer and network administrator are essential. For example, the simple act of tracking security events will allow you to detect security failures before they become a problem.

The amount of security support that you get from an operating system can be crucial, especially on the Internet. Crackers are no longer content to work with one computer at a time; they'll often attack computers in groups or enlist the aid of other computers. For example, the distributed denial of service (DDoS) attacks that caused Yahoo!, Buy.com, ZDNet, eBay, CNN, Amazon.com, and E-Trade.com to lose packets is an example of a mixed OS environment in which crackers used one set of computers to attack another set. The use of zombie computers (essentially computers that are slaves to the will of a master computer run by the cracker) is a new tactic, and one that you need to protect against online. However, you have to consider the legal ramifications of DDoS attacks as well. A lack of due diligence in maintaining the security of your server could affect other systems, and those other owners might decide to sue you (or your company) over the issue in order to recoup part of their losses. Fortunately, software that will scan for DDoS additions to your server is available, but it's still up to you to install and use that software to ensure that your system remains clean of other people's code. The DDoS attack on these Web sites also shows that many network administrators are lax in their use of security software.

Windows 2000 provides a level of security for an operating system that almost verges on paranoia. It allows you to set security in a variety of ways, including both the familiar user and file levels. You can also create groups and assign security by using groups instead of individuals. In addition, you can monitor every aspect of the security system by using various alarms and log files. Windows 2000 excels in the way that it actually monitors system activity. Not one event goes without some kind of scrutiny. In fact, the simple act of passing information from one process to another undergoes some level of scrutiny by Windows 2000.

Web Resource Smaller companies can now take advantage of an alternative to Microsoft's offerings. RSA recently introduced the Keon Software Suite of products. This suite includes a security server, desktop-component, agents, SDK, and a certificate server (most likely tied in with VeriSign in some way). Keon is designed to help companies get past some of the interoperability problems that they've experienced in the past by offering them a complete security solution. The SDK will allow programmers to develop add-on products for the suite, making it possible to tie the suite into custom applications. You can find out more about Keon at `http://www.rsasecurity.com/`.

Developers need to address two main levels of security: local and remote. A user logging onto a company terminal is an example of local security. This is the kind of security that developers have had to deal with for quite some time, and the procedures for doing so are fairly well known. Local access also implies fewer potential security problems because you can secure the lines of communication between the client and server. Less well-known are the procedures for remote security. For example, how does a server-side component deal with a user who's attempting access from an Internet connection rather than a local connection? The data flow between the component and client is now a source of concern — something that the developer will need to address as part of the component.

Fortunately, the Windows 2000 Security API can help you create a more secure local, intranet, and Internet environment. Adding API calls to your application, especially for new features, can make local access much more secure. Obviously, many of these new features were designed with the Internet in mind. Fortunately, you can mix these new solutions with older technologies. You can use ActiveX controls to access Windows 2000 security features from both the server and the client site, ISAPI extensions to access them from the server side, and ISAPI filters to perform behind-the-scenes monitoring of security events.

Security Issues Across Mixed OS Environments

A lot of developers will find themselves creating applications for mixed operating system environments that include both Windows 95 and Windows 98 (and by the time you read this, Windows Millennium). Unfortunately, Windows 95/98/Millennium doesn't provide the same level of security that Windows 2000 does, so you'll find yourself doing without added security under Windows 95/98/Millennium at times. However, when Windows 95/98/Millennium does provide a security feature, it uses the same setup as Windows 2000, so one security module will work with all of them. Of course, sometimes you'll definitely want to detect the operating system and then use a separate DLL module for Windows 2000 to make better use of its enhanced security capabilities.

For those of you that are developing in a mixed operating system environment, remember that the following discussion applies equally well to Windows 2000 and Windows 95/98/Millennium. The main difference is that Windows 95/98/Millennium won't support some of the features that Windows 2000 does.

Whether you're creating an application for Internet, intranet, local, WAN, or LAN use, you'll find that a good understanding of the underlying network security architecture is essential. In this section, the term application is used to refer to any number of executable formats including standard applications like word processors, ActiveX controls, and standard DLLs. As previously stated, Windows 2000 provides a wealth of security features that you can use to make your information more secure. However, we can break the low-level implementation details of those technologies down to make them more generic and easier to understand. That's the purpose of this section—to help you understand the low-level methods that Microsoft uses to make security work in Windows 2000.

Windows 2000 and Windows 95/98/Millennium both use the term object rather loosely. It's true that a lot of objects are lurking beneath the surface, but you may find that they don't fit precisely within the programmer usage of the term. In fact, in many cases, these Windows objects don't necessarily fit within the COM definition of an object either. Nomenclature aside, each security object is a self-contained unit designed to fulfill a specific role.

Note

In many places in Windows 95/98/Millennium and Windows 2000, Microsoft chose to use the full C++ definition of an object mainly because it implemented the required functionality using the MFC libraries. (The Visual Basic and Visual C++ definition of an object are essentially the same, but there are implementation differences, so I chose to use C++ as the standard in some places in the chapter in order to avoid confusion.) In other words, you may find that the full COM implementation of the object is missing, at least with regard to the definition of COM as Microsoft has spelled it out in the specification. However, when reading either the Microsoft documentation or this chapter, you shouldn't depend on the definition of an object to mean a strict C++ object—think of an object more in the generic sense of the word. (Theoretically, all parts of the operating system, including security, will eventually use COM exclusively, but that isn't the case right now.)

Knowing that everything is an object makes security a bit easier to understand—at least it's a starting point. However, objects themselves are just one part of the security equation; users are the other part. A user accesses an object, so security in Windows is a matter of comparing the object's protection against the user's rights. If the user has sufficient rights (rights that meet or exceed those of the object), then the user can use the object. The Windows documentation refers to an object's level of protection as a security descriptor. This is the structure that tells the security system what rights a user needs to access the object. Likewise, the user has an access token, which is another structure that tells the security system what rights a user has in a given situation. "Token" is a good word here because the user will give Windows 2000 the token in exchange for access to the object. (Think of the object as a bus, with Windows 2000 as the driver and the user presenting the required token to board.) Figure 7-1 shows both of these structures.

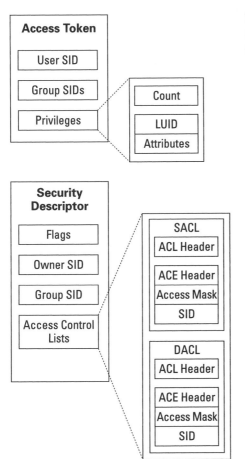

Figure 7-1: Access tokens define the user's rights, while security descriptors define the protection level for a process.

You'll find that there are two of ways of looking at a user's rights under Windows, and both are related to objects in one form or another. The user's access token has a security identifier (SID) to identify the user throughout the network — it's like having an account number. The user token that the SID identifies tells which groups the user belongs to and what privileges the user has. Each group also has an SID, so the user's SID contains references to the various group SIDs that the user belongs to, not to a complete set of group-access rights. You'd normally use the Local Users and Groups snap-in (an add-in module) for Microsoft Management Console (MMC) under Windows 2000 to change the contents of this access token. (This same snap-in can be used to manage remote machines that support remote management.) The access token also includes a list of privileges; a counter keeps track of the number of privileges that the user has. Each privilege is defined by a locally unique identifier (LUID) and associated attributes.

Security descriptors are attached to objects — resources that a user will need. The security descriptor defines what rights the user needs in order to access the object. There are five elements within a security descriptor as shown in Figure 7-1 (the Access Control Lists block contains two elements). The flags tell you the descriptor revision number, format, and ACL status. The figure shows two SIDs, but only one of them is normally used. The Owner SID allows a single person to own the object, which is normally the case under Windows 2000. The Group SID allows a group of people to own the object, which can be the case for the Macintosh and POSIX. The final two elements are the access control lists (ACLs). The security access control list (SACL) controls Windows' auditing feature. Each time a user or a group accesses an object and the auditing feature for that object is turned on, Windows makes an entry in the audit log. The discretionary access control list (DACL) controls who can actually use the object. You can assign both groups and individual users to a specific object.

Addressing Security Interoperability Concerns

Most of the security software that you can use today is vendor-specific and proprietary, which means that you're stuck looking at security through one vendor's eyes. The problem with this approach is that you may not find a single vendor who can address all of your security concerns. Sure, Windows 2000 itself is protected by the security built in by Microsoft, but today's computing environment doesn't limit itself to just one isolated company.

In a world-based Internet economy, you need the ability to secure a wide range of computer equipment from a large number of security threats. The ability to make security solutions from more than one vendor work together is no longer a luxury — it's a necessity.

Security vendors see this problem as well and are working to make their software interoperable through a number of initiatives and APIs. The latest initiative to hit the market is Common Content Inspection (CCI) API, a project started by Aventail, Corp, Finjan Software, Ltd., and Check Point Software Technologies. This group joins others like Adaptive Network Security Alliance (ANSA) and Open Platform for Secure Enterprise Connectivity (OPSEC) Alliance. The goals of these three groups vary slightly, but the main goal is to make it possible for more than one vendor's products to work together. The largest of these groups is OPSEC Alliance with 260 members (as of this writing).

The CCI API seeks to promote interoperability through the use of common interfaces for inspecting content. In other words, each vendor's software might provide completely different features and capabilities, but they would be able to work with the same data because the means for inspecting it are the same. The resulting specification is supposed to work with data at whatever level it appears, including firewalls, antivirus checks, and mobile code. You can find out more about CCI API at http://www.stardust.com/cciapi/ and http://www.finjan.com/cciapi.cfm.

OPSEC Alliance is providing a similar set of APIs through Convent Vectoring Protocol (CVP). The difference, in this case, is that they're concentrating on a single firewall product, Check Point's Firewall-1. In addition to content, OPSEC is working on APIs that allow various vendor products to work together at the application level. At the time of this writing, the OPSEC Alliance offering is pretty much in place and even includes a certification program. You can find out more about OPSEC at http://www.opsec.com/index.html.

Like the OPSEC Alliance, ANSA caters to a specific vendor product. In this case, the target software is Internet Security System (ISS) Group's intrusion detection software. ANSA currently has 40 companies participating in the standardization effort. Unlike the other two security interoperability efforts discussed in this section, ANSA offers a software development kit (SDK) that contains Adaptive Network Security (ANS) modules designed to make interoperability easier. The ANS modules allow ISS Group intrusion-detection software to issue alerts to firewalls, extranet management applications, and other software as soon as an intrusion is detected. These other applications would then deny system access to the intruder. You can find out more about ANSA at http://ansa.iss.net/ or http://www.iss.net/.

Kerberos, Public-Key Infrastructure, and Distributed Password Authentication Support

Windows 2000 supports three relatively new additions to the tools available to administrators for securing a network: Kerberos, Public-Key Infrastructure (PKI), and Distributed Password Authentication Support (DPA). Each of these new technologies is designed to circumvent a particular type of security threat, whether on the Internet or on a local network. Obviously, the developer usually implements anything used by the network administrator. The following list provides an overview of how each of these technologies can help you to develop more secure applications.

✦ **Kerberos:** This is Microsoft's primary replacement for the Windows NT LAN Manager (NTLM) security, which is currently used to ensure that your data remains safe when using older versions of Windows. Kerberos Version 5 is a relatively new industry-standard security protocol devised at MIT that offers superior security support through the use of a private-key architecture. This protocol supports mutual authentication of both client and server, reduces server load when establishing a connection, and allows the client to delegate authentication to the server through the use of proxy mechanisms. Kerberos connects to an online Key Distribution Center (KDC) and the Directory Service (DS) account to obtain session tickets used for authentication purposes.

Note

Windows 2000 will continue to support NTLM when accessing Windows NT 4.0 or earlier. An application can use NTLM for a wide variety of access needs including remote procedure calls (RPCs), pass-through network authentication, and remote file access.

✦ **Public Key Infrastructure (PKI):** This protocol allows two sites to exchange data in an encrypted format without any prior arrangement. The default method for initiating the exchange is to create a secure sockets layer (SSL) connection. The main difference between this technology and others on the market is that it relies on a public-key system of certificates to ensure secure data transfer. The latest specification for SSL is SSL3, which the Internet Engineering Task Force (IETF) is calling transport layer security (TLS) protocol. A newer addition to the mix is Private Communication Technology (PCT). PCT still uses public-key encryption, but there are some distinct advantages to using it that we'll discuss later in this section. One benefit of using PKI is that there's no online authentication server required because the certificate is issued by a well-known certification authority (normally a company like VeriSign when the technology is used publicly).

✦ **Distributed Password Authentication (DPA):** This is a shared-secret authentication method originally started by some of the larger online services like CompuServe and MSN. It lets you use the same membership password to access a number of Internet sites when those sites are linked together as a membership organization. In essence, this methodology replicates some of the same features that you can get when using the same password to access multiple servers on a local network. DPA relies on the Microsoft Membership Service for membership authentication and server-specific access information.

All of these new security methods, along with NTLM, are grouped under the Windows 2000 Security Support Provider Interface (SSPI). Essentially, SSPI allows any application to use any of the security methods to ensure secure transmission of data from one point to another. In fact, SSPI is actually a new Windows 2000 API that you'll be able to use to create more robust applications in the future. SSPI is based on the same architectural concepts as the IETF Generic Security Services Application Programming Interface (GSS-API). You can find out more about this standard at `http://www.ietf.org/rfc/rfc1964.txt`.

The main purpose of SSPI is to keep the application protocols like DCE RPC separate from the security protocols. Doing so provides an application developer with more flexibility in choosing the kind of transmission and security technology to use in a specific situation.

Hardware-Based Security Makes Break-ins Harder

While software security has gone a long way toward making your PC more secure, some hardware-based solutions are on the horizon that will make the PC more secure than ever before. Some of these hardware changes are relatively obvious. For example, Cisco and other router vendors are adding IPSec security as a standard feature to their products. This means that each segment of your network gains some level of protection from prying eyes. Your direct involvement with a router is going to be limited, but these types of hardware solutions may offer more opportunities to reduce application complexity and make security more automatic.

There are some developer-oriented kinds of hardware security to consider as well. Intel is making changes to the design of the Pentium III that will allow administrators to sleep better at night knowing that the machines they administer are at least less susceptible to break-ins than before. Intel's solutions reside inside the processor itself.

The first processor-specific addition is a unique identification number. This particular feature will make it possible to positively identify the machine being using for a particular purpose. Obviously, this feature could be used to infringe on someone's privacy; so Intel is including the capability to turn this unique number feature off when a machine is used privately. (On corporate machines, only the administrator would have the power to turn this feature off, making it impossible for a user to bypass this security feature.)

The second processor-specific addition is a random number generator that's based on the thermal noise produced by the processor. Software-based random number generators aren't truly random because they rely on complex algorithms and a seed value to produce the number. In other words, the numbers produced by the software pseudo-random number generator will eventually repeat. Because thermal noise is a nonrepeating natural occurrence, the numeric sequence produced by a processor-based random number generator is truly random, meaning that no one can predict what number will be produced in advance.

These two features will allow programmers of the future to create nearly unbreakable security for PCs that will definitely keep crackers at bay for quite some time to come. The reliance on hardware to help create these security offerings will keep security monitoring fast. For example, the use of a hardware-based random number generator alone will greatly enhance application speed. That you're getting better output as well only makes these new hardware features more desirable.

By this time, you should have a very good understanding of the various forms of software protection that Windows 2000 provides. However, Windows 2000 goes beyond the offerings made by previous versions of Windows. It also offers support for hardware protection in the form of smart cards. A smart card is a new credit card-sized device that allows for offline storage of various types of sensitive data. A complete discussion of this new technology is outside the scope of this book, but it does pay to know that there are other secure technologies available for making your data completely secure.

Caution   A lot of people still think it'll take weeks to break the 40-bit DES (data encryption standard) security and months to break the 56-bit DES security. Nothing could be further from the truth. A recent trade press article noted that a hacking group was able to break the 56-bit security within one day during an RSA yearly DES Challenge contest. The contest was held in San Jose, CA, and the hackers involved (Electronic Frontier Foundation and Distributed.Net) were able to break the previously difficult-to-break DES security within 22 hours and 15 minutes. What this means to you, as a programmer, is that you can't rely on a security scheme to remain secure forever. It's absolutely essential to keep yourself apprised of new security schemes as they become available. You can find out more information about DES Challenge III at http://www.rsasecurity.com/.

Now that you have some idea of what these new security technologies are all about, it's time to discuss them in a little more detail. The following sections will provide a better look at these three new Windows 2000 security technologies and how they can help you create better applications.

Understanding Kerberos

As previously mentioned, Kerberos is a private-key protocol. This means that Kerberos is limited to use between sites that know each other because the keys have to be agreed upon in advance. In other words, you'll normally restrict your use of Kerberos to the local network, a virtual private network (VPN), or intranet communications.

 Note   Microsoft is always looking for ways to enhance the security that Windows provides. One of the new features of Windows 2000 is an authentication requirement. A user must be authenticated before the user gains any access to an NTFS partition. In addition, NTFS uses the Kerberos 5 Protocol to secure data on the drive. These upgrades in protection will reduce the probability of someone stealing data from your drive, but they won't eliminate all risk. It's always important to combine security monitoring with new security features.

The concept behind Kerberos operation is fairly simple. Kerberos uses the concept of tickets to enforce security. The user must have a ticket for each service that the user wants to access. The following sequence of events occurs every time a user requires access to a local server that is using Kerberos.

1. The user requests access to a server or other resource.

2. The server, in turn, asks for the user's identification.

3. After the server receives the user's identification, it sends the information to the KDC.

4. The KDC checks the user's identity.

5. If the user has the required permissions, the KDC provides tickets for each of the required services or resources.

6. The user provides a ticket for each service or resource needed. This ticket identifies the user; it also includes an option to carry the user's access-level information so that the service or resource doesn't provide the user with too much access.

Kerberos represents the primary authentication method for Windows 2000, which is a departure from the NTLM authentication used in the past. The version of Kerberos used in Windows 2000 is fully compatible with the Version 5 Kerberos used for authentication on other platforms. In addition, Microsoft has made it possible to extend Kerberos to allow nonstandard methods of user identification. For example, you could use a smart card in place of a username and password for identification purposes.

As previously mentioned, Kerberos is actually an internationally approved authentication standard that's currently being worked on by the Internet Engineering Task Force (IETF). You can find out more about Kerberos at `http://www.ietf.org/rfc/rfc1510.txt`. However, it's also important to mention that Microsoft's version of Kerberos includes some permitted extensions; so, while it does provide the full standard's based compatibility, it also provides some additional features that are not found in the standard. The most notable extension is support for smart card authentication. Another good place to look for non-Microsoft Kerberos information is the MIT site at `http://web.mit.edu/kerberos/www/`. The information on this second Web site isn't as technically intense as the IETF information, but it's a lot more readable.

The KDC will normally run on a domain controller (DC) as a privileged process. Every DC replica will have access to its own KDC to reduce the time required for user authentication. The actual user identification information is contained within the Active Directory, which also runs on the DC as a privileged process. It takes the combination of these two processes to perform user authentication.

The Active Directory also performs other Kerberos-related tasks. For example, it performs multiple master update and replication so that new users can be added at any DC. This same feature allows the administrator to make changes to the user's group membership or change the user's password.

Understanding public-key infrastructure

We'll discuss two components with regard to PKI. The first is SSL. SSL relies on encryption and digital certificates to do its work. If you're really paranoid about security, you can even combine these two security methods — they're not mutually exclusive.

The second component is PCT. Microsoft and the IETF have worked together to create this new low-level protocol. Like SSL, PCT is designed to prevent crackers from eavesdropping on communications between a client and server through the use of encryption, authentication, and digital signatures. As with SSL, client authentication is optional.

Working with SSL

SSL is a protocol that's fairly easy to understand. Windows NT/2000 can (and definitely will) request a digital certificate from the client machine. The client can likewise request a digital certificate from Windows NT/2000. These digital certificates are obtained from a third-party vendor like VeriSign that can vouch for the identity of both parties. However, the certificate exchange procedure is a little more complicated than simply sending a digital certificate from one machine to another. There is a six-step process for SSL authentication:

1. The client sends Windows NT an unencrypted random message along with its VeriSign-issued certificate (which contains the client's public key). The VeriSign-issued certificate was encrypted using VeriSign's private key. Because everyone has VeriSign's public key, Windows NT can decrypt the certificate and check it for accuracy. Also, because the certificate was encrypted using VeriSign's private key, no one can forge a public key of their own — they have to get it from VeriSign.

2. Once Windows NT confirms that it has received a valid certificate and public key from the client, it tells the client to send an encrypted version of its original message.

3. The client computes a digest of its original random message and then encrypts it using its private key.

4. Windows NT uses the client's public key to decrypt the digest.

5. Windows NT compares the decrypted digest to a digest it generates from the random message originally sent in unencrypted form by the client.

6. If the two digests match, the client is authenticated.

At this point, you might ask how a programmer would get involved with what appears to be an administrator issue. Even though Windows 2000 comes with a wealth of built-in methods for controlling access to the server, nothing is stopping you from creating an ActiveX component or an ISAPI filter either to augment or to replace the standard security. All you really need to do is monitor the security-related events generated by the server. The most important of these events are the client-authentication requests. Monitoring client-authentication requests allows you to add any requests needed to make sure that the party on the other end is actually someone you want wandering around your Web site.

Working with PCT

PCT assumes that you have a reliable transport protocol such as TCP in place. Some people look at TCP/IP as a single protocol, but it isn't. TCP is the transport part of the protocol, while IP is the data-transfer portion of the protocol. IP doesn't provide any form of data encryption. So, when you use TCP/IP, your data is open to anyone who wants to see it. Using a protocol such as TCP/PCT or TCP/SSL makes your communications secure. The first version of PCT corrects several problems with SSL, as described in the following list.

✦ **Simplified message and record structures:** Reconnected sessions require a single message in each direction if you don't enable client authentication. Even with client authentication, a reconnection requires only two messages in each direction.

✦ **Extended cryptographic negotiation:** PCT supports a greater variety of algorithms than SSL. This means that it can support a broader range of protocol characteristics and that those characteristics get negotiated individually. For example, the common characteristics include cipher type, server-certificate type, a hash-function type, and a key-exchange type.

✦ **Improved message authentication keys:** The message authentication keys are separate from the encryption keys under PCT. This means that messages can use a very long key, ensuring secure transmission even if the encryption key is short or nonexistent. The main reason for this feature is to circumvent the 40-bit key limitation imposed on secure transmissions by the U.S. government.

✦ **Patched security hole:** PCT uses a client authentication based on the cipher negotiated during a session. This prevents someone from capturing the client authentication key, disconnecting the original client, and then reconnecting to the server using the stolen key. The client must know both the cipher and the key to gain access to the server.

✦ **Addition of Verify Prelude field:** During the original handshaking process, communication between the client and server is carried out in the clear. The addition of this field makes it possible for the client and server to detect any tampering with these "in-the-clear" communications.

Note
Even though SSL version 3 also provides a Verify Prelude field-type capability, a cracker can get around it by changing the protocol version number to 2, which didn't include this feature. Because SSL version 3 is fully version 2 compliant, neither client nor server will notice the change.

Microsoft is currently working on the second version of PCT. It's fully compatible with the first version, but offers several important features that the first version didn't. The following list provides an overview of these features.

✦ **New datagram record type:** Individual records are sent independently as "datagrams." In essence, this means that the protocol doesn't guarantee an order of delivery or that the record will even get to its destination. It's up to the client to put the records that it receives in order and then verify that they're all present. The main advantage of this approach is speed.

✦ **Recognizable record types:** The record header contains information that tells the receiver what kind of record to expect.

✦ **Continuation records:** PCT version 1 allowed data to span more than one record even though the record header didn't indicate any form of continuation. Version 2 adds a continuation field to the record header, which also allows protocol messages to span more than one record.

✦ **Intermediate processing of data records:** Data records are encapsulated now, which allows the sender to perform some form of intermediate processing, such as compression.

✦ **Independent decryption of datagram records:** Because datagram records could be sent across an unreliable transport, this particular feature is essential to secure communication. Each record is encrypted individually, making it possible for the receiver to decrypt them one at a time even if they're received out of order.

✦ **New key management record type:** This record type allows the sender to temporarily change either the encryption or message authentication keys during a session. In essence, this allows PCT to transmit pre-encrypted data.

✦ **New closing connection key management message:** This is a special message that tells the other party to close a connection. Because this is an encrypted message, it's harder for a cracker to send a simulated message and close the connection prematurely.

✦ **Enhanced message authentication:** Message authentication now includes record headers.

✦ **Improved handshaking:** Both the client and server authentication phase include a greater variety of options, including key exchange, signature, public-key, and certificate.

✦ **New private authentication feature:** This feature allows a client and server to authenticate each other using a previously shared identity-associated private key, rather than a certified public key.

Now that we have a few of the basics down, let's look at how PCT works. PCT uses variable-length records as a means of communication. Every record contains a header that defines the kind of message it contains. There are two kinds of messages: application and protocol. Application messages always contain data and can use either the standard PCT or datagram formats. A protocol message can key management, error, or handshake information. PCT uses two additional layers. Records are always transmitted using a connection. Normally, there's one connection between a client and server, but there isn't any reason why there can't be more. Every connection is part of a session. Usually you'll only have one session between a client and server, but you could have more. (Multiple sessions would require more than one physical connection between the client and server.)

Web Resource If you want to find out about the current status of PCT, look at `http://www.1ne.com/ericm/pct.html`. This document contains the current draft of the second version of PCT. In addition, you'll want to reference the W3C Web site at `http://www.w3.org/Security/` for details on current Internet security technologies including PCT and SSL.

A PCT protocol connection begins with a handshake phase. This is where the handshake-management message type comes into play. The client and server exchange several pieces of information, beginning with the negotiation of a session key for the connection. In other words, the client and server decide on a secret password to use for talking to each other. The client and server also authenticate each other during this phase. It doesn't pay for them to talk if the client or server doesn't know who the other party is and whether the other party can be trusted. Once the client and server determine that they can trust each other, they decide on a master key that's used for encrypting all other messages.

Understanding Distributed Password Authentication

DPA is a challenge/response password-based security methodology that relies on a trusted third-party authentication server. It's part of the Microsoft Commercial Internet System (MCIS). MCIS is used as a back-end Internet service that multiple sites can link to, enabling a user to move from one membership site to another without reentering any authentication information (unless required for higher-level access).

When using this protocol, the user provides a username, which isn't necessarily unique to that user, along with a valid password, when requested to do so by a server. The server then requests validation from the authentication server prior to granting access to the user.

Three different levels of username are supported by DPA: single user, group name, and generic name. The generic name option is the most interesting because it allows the server to access usernames like WORD_USERS in place of specific usernames like Tom. In addition, generic names don't have to appear on the server as a specific group like Administrators would.

Windows 2000 data-encryption support

Preventing someone from reading your data has been the topic of discussion in just about every part of this chapter so far. We've studied protocols and a variety of security techniques that are going to help you make the work of a cracker nearly impossible. However, there isn't a lock that can't be picked given enough time. In fact, that's the whole purpose behind using a 128-bit key instead of a 40-bit key. Picking the 128-bit lock is too time-consuming (at least at the moment) to make the data contained in a record attractive to a cracker. It's not that the cracker can't pick the lock; it simply isn't efficient to do so.

Caution   A recent trade press article talked about how one vendor's claim of having an unbreakable encryption scheme was causing problems with the cryptographic community. Anyone who constantly deals with security would just love to have a truly unbreakable method of encrypting data. Unfortunately, no matter what the vendor tells you, there aren't any security schemes for the PC that can protect your data with absolute certainty. The main reason that you can't create absolutely reliable security on a PC is that the average PC can't generate a truly random number. (This will change once the Pentium III gains enough of a stronghold in the market for developers to write code that uses its onboard random-number generator.) The best you can hope to achieve currently is a pseudo-random number — one that's generated based on a solid mathematical principle. The difference between a truly random number and a pseudo-random number is that somewhere along the way the random-number sequence will repeat and someone will be able to predict the next encryption number in a series.

As a result, even given the best math in the world, a dedicated cracker with enough processing power can find ways to get into your system. Even the DES, which has withstood more than two decades of scrutiny, was recently broken because of the amount of processing power available on the market today (it did take a whole bank of computers to do the job). In sum, always greet any claim of unbreakable security with a healthy dose of skepticism. One of the more interesting Web sites to look at for additional information about data encryption and cryptographic technology is the Counterpane Systems Web site at `http://www.counterpane.com/`.

Adding layers of protection is another way to guard against crackers. Encrypting the data at several different levels adds "doors" that the cracker must pass through to get to the data. Put enough doors between your data and the cracker, and the cracker will find something easier to break into.

Microsoft's CryptoAPI (Cryptography Application Programming Interface) falls into the layer category of protection. It's a means of adding yet another layer of protection to your sensitive data. Are the encryption techniques that you'll find supplied here unbreakable? No, but they do extend the time required for someone to unlock your data and read it. Using the routines in the CryptoAPI will help you to better protect the data transferred between a client and server on the Web.

Web Resource   As with just about everything else dealing with the Internet, the CryptoAPI is new and evolving. At the time of this writing, the CryptoAPI is part of several Microsoft SDKs including the ActiveX SDK and the Windows Platform SDK — you'll need to download a copy of the specification from the Internet. Even though this section provides the best overview possible at the time of writing, you'll want to visit the CryptoAPI site at `http://www.microsoft.com/security/tech/cryptoapi/default.asp` for the latest information. The Platform SDK documentation also has a lot to say about the CryptoAPI. You can find it on your MSDN subscription or at `http://msdn.microsoft.com/library/psdk/crypto/portaltool_3u3p.htm`.

The CryptoAPI has another objective: It's a general-purpose tool designed to allow encryption of data in any environment, not just the Web. For example, you could build an application that stores data using the same encrypted format whether the information was stored locally, transferred through a modem, uploaded to a Web site, or sent through the mail on a disk. That's a big advantage to your company. Using encryption all the time for sensitive data means that a cracker breaking into your system will find that the job has suddenly gotten a lot harder, yet a common encryption technique means that your users won't be inconvenienced by the added security. You can bet that a user is more likely to use encryption when it's convenient (and for the most part automatic). Making things difficult, hard-to-understand, or simply too time-consuming is the best way to convince the user that it's too much trouble to protect the data on your system.

Note   Windows NT 4.0 comes with CryptoAPI 1.0 support built in. When you install Service Pack 3 (or higher), the level of support gets upgraded to CryptoAPI 2.0. This is the same level of support provided by Windows 2000. A major difference between the two versions is that CryptoAPI 2.0 provides core cryptographic support, which allows a developer to incorporate cryptography within an application. CryptoAPI 2.0 supports X.509 certificates, ASN.1 encoding, and both PKCS #7 and #10 encapsulation. You'll find the Windows 2000 support required to implement CryptoAPI 2.0 support in the CRYPT32.DLL file. However, this file can't be accessed directly by Visual Basic—it's intended for Visual C++ users. In fact, CryptoAPI support is very sparse for Visual Basic users as a whole; your best bet is to create a component in Visual C++, and then use that component to build your application. If you do decide to implement cryptographic functions directly with Visual Basic, then you'll need to add the CryptExt.DLL file to your project. You can add support for this file using the CryptExt 1.0 Type Library entry in the References dialog box (accessed using the Project ⇨ References command in Visual Basic).

Microsoft has also moved to a modular approach in its operating system design in the past few years, so it's no surprise that the CryptoAPI is modular as well. The CryptoAPI could be compared to the GDI (Graphics Device Interface) API under Windows. Any vendor can add a new device driver that tells the GDI how to work with a particular display adapter. The same holds true for the CryptoAPI. It uses the idea of a Cryptographic Service Provider (CSP) just as you would a display adapter device driver. Windows will come with one CSP—the one provided by Microsoft. However, if Microsoft's encryption feature set doesn't meet your needs, you can either design a new CSP yourself or buy one from a third party. The installation procedure will work much like the one you currently use to add a device driver. In fact, this device-driver approach makes it easy for you to mix encryption hardware and software on your machine—a real plus in a world where you normally install hardware and software as separate entities.

Web Resource   Microsoft has developed a DDK (Device driver Development Kit) for the CryptoAPI called the Cryptographic Service Provider Developer's Kit (CSPDK). You can get more information about it at http://msdn.microsoft.com/workshop/security/capi/cryptapi.asp.

Using the Security Configuration Editor

The Microsoft Security Configuration Editor is a new MMC snap-in designed to make life a lot easier for the network administrator by reducing both security management and security analysis time. Initially, you'll use this tool to configure the various operating system security parameters. After these parameters are in place, you can use the Security Configuration Editor to schedule periodic tests. These automatically executed tests help ensure that your operating system maintains the level of security that you initially set up for it.

Note   You can use the System Configuration Manager MMC snap-in to work with the security database (SDB) and security configuration (INF) files that you create using the Security Configuration Editor.

The overall goal of the Security Configuration Editor is to provide a single place to manage all of the security concerns for a network. However, it doesn't actually replace all of the tools that you used in the past; the Security Configuration Editor augments tools like the User Manager, Server Manager, and the Access Control List (ACL) Editor. The Security Configuration Editor also provides auditing tools that Windows has lacked in the past. When working with Windows NT 4, the developer had only the Event Viewer to use, which obviously doesn't provide much in the way of information.

One of the unique ideas behind the Security Configuration Editor is that it's a macro-based tool. You'll create a set of instructions for the Security Configuration Editor to perform, and then allow it to perform those instructions in the background. Obviously, this saves a lot of developer time because the developer doesn't have to wait for one set of instructions to complete before going to the next set. Tasks can also be grouped, which further saves input time because all of the instructions required to implement a given setup can be configured at one time.

At this point, you may wonder why a developer should care about this tool at all. After all, configuring network security is a network administrator's task. That idea used to be true—a network administrator was responsible for all security on the network. However, as computer networks have become more complex and the technologies used with them more flexible, part of the responsibility for network security has shifted from the network administrator to the developer responsible for creating the various components that make the network operational. As a developer, you need to know how this tool works so that you can test the applications you create.

Creating a security setup begins when you either choose an existing template or create a new one. If you want to use an existing template as a basis for creating a new one, you can right-click the desired template and use the Save As command found on the context menu. Microsoft supplies a variety of templates designed to get you started in creating this security database, as shown in Figure 7-2.

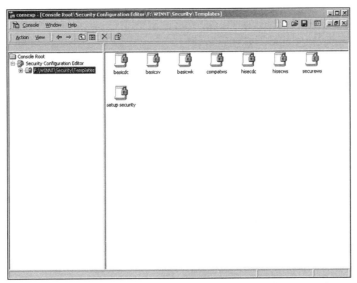

Figure 7-2: The Security Configuration Editor provides a number of standard templates that you can use to create your security setup.

Each security template is designed for a different purpose (which is indicated by its name). The one that I'll be using throughout this section is the basic workstation template (basicwk), but all of the other templates will work about the same as this one. All of the templates contain the same basic elements shown in Figure 7-3. The following list describes each of these elements for you.

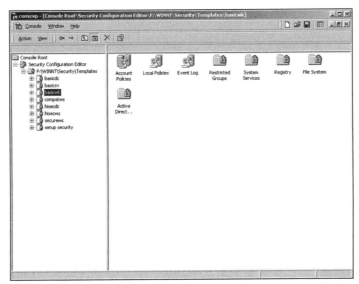

Figure 7-3: Each security template contains the same security elements.

✦ **Account Policies:** Defines the password, account lockout, and Kerberos policies for the machine. Password policies include items like the minimum password length and the maximum time that the user is allowed to use a single password. The account lockout policy includes policies like the number of times a user can enter the wrong password without getting locked out of the system. Kerberos policies feature elements like the maximum user ticket lifetime.

✦ **Local Policies:** Defines the audit policy, user-rights assignment, and security options. Audit policies determine the types of data that you want to collect. For example, you could choose to audit each failed user logon attempt. User-rights assignments should be of special interest because this policy affects the kinds of rights that you can assign to a user (the access token). The security options policy contains all of the elements that determine how the security system will react given a specific set of circumstances. For example, there's a policy that will forcibly log a user off when his or her usage hours expire.

✦ **Event Log:** Defines how the event log stores data and for how long. This set of policies also determines maximum event log size, which can view various event logs, and what to do if the event log gets full.

✦ **Restricted Groups:** Defines groups that aren't allowed to access the workstation or server at all, or restricts the amount of access that they can obtain.

✦ **System Services:** Displays a complete list of all of the system services on the target machine. Double-clicking a service will display a dialog box that allows you to set the security policy for that specific service. This same dialog box will allow you to adjust the startup mode for the service. Normally, you'll want to leave the standard icons in this policy alone. However, you can safely change any system-service DLLs that you create.

✦ **Registry:** Contains all of the major branches of the registry. Double-clicking a branch displays a dialog box that allows you to set the security level for that branch. In addition, you can choose the method of security inheritance by children of this branch.

✦ **File System:** Contains a variety of protected-file system entries. You can add new files to the list or modify exiting entries. Double-clicking a file system entry displays a dialog box that allows you to set the security level for that file system member (which could be a folder or a specific file). In addition, you can choose the method of security inheritance by children of this file system entity (applies only to folders).

✦ **Active Directory Objects:** This entry is only available if you have Active Directory enabled (which means that you must have a domain controller set up). It allows you to edit the security settings for any Active Directory objects, including users and groups.

After you define a security template, you simply right-click the template and choose the appropriate option to apply the template's policies to the system.

Optionally, Microsoft plans to provide a command-line utility that you can use to apply the template or you can use the Security Configuration Manager snap-in to apply the template. Of all the options for applying a template, the Security Configuration Manager snap-in for MMC is probably the best. The following steps will get you started in applying a template to a specific machine.

1. Right-click the Security Configuration Manager icon and choose Open Database from the context menu. You'll see an Open Database dialog box like the one shown in Figure 7-4.

Figure 7-4: The Open Database dialog box allows you to open an existing security database or create a new one.

2. Type the name of the new database that you want to create, and then click Open. You'll see a Select Configuration to Import dialog box like the one shown in Figure 7-5. This is where you need to enter the name of the template that you've created using the Security Configuration Editor.

Figure 7-5: Make sure you know the location of the security template that you want to apply to the current system.

3. Find the template file on your drive, highlight it, and then click Open. At this point, the Security Configuration Manager will start analyzing the template. You should see a Perform Analysis dialog box like the one shown in Figure 7-6. This dialog box allows you to choose a location for the error log that the analysis process will create. It's important to view the contents of this log later, so that you can fix any problems with your template before retrying a failed application.

Figure 7-6: The Perform Analysis dialog box allows you to choose a location for the error log.

4. Choose a location for the error log, and then click OK. Security Configuration Manager will display the Analyzing System Security dialog box shown in Figure 7-7 as it performs the analysis of the security template file.

Figure 7-7: The Analyzing System Security dialog box shows you the progress of the analysis process.

5. After the Security Configuration Manager is finished, you'll see the standard Security Configuration Editor display shown in Figure 7-3. In this case, however, you won't see any of the template names. These entries are the security settings that you've just added to a security database.

6. Right-click the Security Configuration Manager icon, and then choose Configure System Now. You'll see the warning dialog box shown in Figure 7-8. Click OK and the System Configuration Manager will apply the new policy to your machine.

Figure 7-8: The System Configuration Manager will display this warning before it applies the new security policy to your machine.

At this point, you have enough information to work with the Security Configuration Manager. As you add new components to the system, it's important that you test various security options for them, and then work with the network administrator to create a policy for the component.

COM+ Component-Level Security Considerations

So far, we've looked at the traditional object-based security provided by Windows 2000. If you were creating a standard application, object-based security would be the end of the story. In fact, if you're developing components that will be used on Windows NT and Windows 2000, it's still the end of the story. Only when you're working with COM+ under Windows 2000 exclusively do you get the enhanced benefits of role-based security.

Let's take a more detailed look at this new Windows 2000 feature. The following sections will help you understand how role-based security fits into the COM+ component programming scenario. It's important to understand how role-based security will benefit you, so that's the first thing we'll talk about. Role-based security can be used in addition to or in lieu of authentication, which is the topic of the next section. After you have some idea of what the requirements are for using role-based security, we'll take a look at the main interface that you need to know about, ISecurityCallContext.

Tip

To gain access to the ISecurityCallContext interface, you need to add support for the COM+ Services Type Library to your application. Use the Project ⇨ References command to display the References dialog box. Find the COM+ Services Type Library entry and check it. Clicking OK allows support for this library to your application. If you don't see the COM+ Services Type Library entry, check for the COMSVCS.DLL in the Windows\System32 folder. Make sure that this type library is registered by using the RegSvr32 COMSVCS.DLL command.

Role-based security advantages

While object-based security works fine, in many cases, it also has some severe limitations that force a developer to either ignore security issues or perform a lot of hand coding. The most important limitation of object-based security is granularity. You set the security of the entire object, and a user's access to that object is based on an individual or group access token. Role-based security gets around the granularity problem to a certain extent by allowing you to set security at the method level. In addition to allowing you greater flexibility in setting how much access a user gets to a component, role-based security provides benefits, which the following list describes.

✦ **Configuration:** Usually, you'll use the Component Services administrative tools or scripts to configure the component to use role-based security. However, you can also set certain types of security as part of your component's initialization process. (Normally, you won't add any code to the component so as to give the administrator full flexibility in creating a security configuration that meets company needs.)

✦ **No Extra Coding:** COM+ automatically takes care of all of the security details for you if you can get by with method-level security. There are some other restrictions that you need to know about, which we'll talk about in the "Role-Based Security Requirements" section below. In addition, you'll need to add the ISecurityCallContext interface to your component. Obviously, the reduced coding requirement also translates into a smaller design specification — there aren't any security requirements at either the interface or component design levels.

Tip

COM+ doesn't prevent you from adding code to your component to control role-based security; it only makes it possible to create the component without adding the code. If you add code to your component to enforce role-based security, the component is using programmatic security control. On the other hand, if you allow the administrator full control over security and don't add any code, then the component is using declarative security.

✦ **Easier to Understand:** Basing security on roles allows administrators to do a better job of configuring component security. You can still add groups or individual users to a role; the difference is one of perception. It's easier to assign a user or group access to individual methods within a component based on the tasks that the user or group is expected to perform.

✦ **More Flexible:** Unlike hard-coded security features, role-based security is configured outside of the component. This means that there are no coding changes required when the needs of the company change. Instead of changing component code (with the requisite debugging and testing), an administrator can make a change that will take just a few seconds to complete.

✦ **Detailed Auditing:** We've already looked at the issue of auditing several times in this section of the chapter. The main reason that you want good auditing capability is to ensure that you can track the activities of anyone who breaks into your system. Role-based security allows you to audit security at the method, rather than the object, level. This means that you get a better picture of exactly what a cracker was trying to do with a component and allows you to better assess what remedial action to take.

Role-based security can also provide some protection that object level security doesn't really cover. Normally, a user's credentials are checked at the application level. What this means is that the user is granted access one time. The resulting access token is used for all other resource access. In the world of monolithic applications where a single server provides everything that the user will need, this kind of security check is fine. However, what happens if the original application calls a component on one server, and then the component on that server needs the services of a second component on a second server. The user's access to the first server is verified as part of the application startup, but what about access to the second server? As you can see, there's a chance for a security breach between the two servers — another one of those security holes mentioned earlier in the chapter.

Windows 2000 offers something called a security boundary—you can force the security checks at either the process (application) or the component level. What this means is that you can reassess the user's credentials each time another component request is made. This ensures that no security breach between servers occurs. In addition to finer control of security, component-level access means that the current security information is included as part of the context information sent to your component during a call. In sum, when you enforce component-level security, the component can use security as one of the methods for determining how to answer a user request, making the component more flexible and better able to respond to changing network conditions. Like everything else, however, there's no free lunch. The use of a component-level security check comes at the cost of reduced application efficiency and means that the user will spend more time waiting for the application. In addition, there's a small increase in network traffic, which may become a problem in networks that are already hard pressed for enough bandwidth to perform company-required tasks.

Note   COM+ library applications always use component-level security. You can't enable process-level security for library applications because they always rely on roles, which means checking security at the component level.

Dealing with authentication and roles

Authentication and role-based security aren't mutually exclusive. You can create components and install them in such a way that one or both methodologies are used to verify the user of a component and the level of access that the user has. However, it's important to understand that the verification process happens differently depending on how you configure the component. The following list will help you understand how authentication and role-based security can work hand-in-hand.

✦ **Authentication enabled and role-based security used:** Authentication occurs at the process level. A user who can't be authenticated, doesn't make it to the component level. Once at the component level, role-based security allows the user to access zero or more methods within the component, based on the role that the user was assigned. If a user is authenticated to use the component, yet doesn't have a role assigned, then the entire process still fails and the user request is rejected. This is the default COM+ security setup.

✦ **Authentication enabled and role-based security not used:** A user is only authenticated at the process level, not at the component level. If the authentication succeeds, then the user gains access to everything that the component has to offer. This is the default setting for Windows NT 4.0. It's also the settings that any COM component that you migrate to Windows 2000 will use unless the administrator specifically sets role-based security or the developer adds role-based security to the component.

✦ **Authentication disabled and role-based security used:** Even though Windows 2000 still goes through the motions of authenticating the user, the authentication process is essentially short-circuited. The only user access-verification occurring is through role-based security. This methodology is used when standard Windows 2000 authentication isn't flexible enough to account for the various roles that a user may fulfill, or when most of the component's resources are in the public domain. For example, you may want to allow everyone to perform lookups within your parts catalog database, but you may also want to restrict access to edit and delete features.

✦ **Authentication disabled and role-based security not used:** This is the "I don't care" security setting. By disabling both security check levels, you're enabling everyone access to all resources that the component has to offer. In most cases, you'll only use this setting for components that are completely in the public domain. For example, you might use this setting for components that handle mundane tasks for your public Internet site. Obviously, such a component has to be rigorously tested for any security holes and you need to limit component access to network resources.

Understanding the ISecurityCallContext interface

The ISecurityCallContext interface provides access to the security data for a particular component in a particular context. What this means to you as a developer is that you determine what role the current user is in and what the user's rights are. That this interface is for a particular context means that you can only work with the request associated with this particular instance of the component. In addition, you won't be able to gain information about the component as a whole.

This interface is normally accessible to your COM+ component if the administrator enables role-based security, but you won't always need to use it. The only time that you'll need to use it is when you decide to handle security within the component, rather than allow the administrator to handle security as part of the component's configuration. You'll get an E_NOINTERFACE error message if you attempt to obtain a pointer to the interface when role-based security is disabled, so it's pretty easy to figure out when you can use this interface within the component.

You'll normally use the ISecurityCallContext interface to discover specific kinds of information about the current component context. All of this information is contained in the security call context collection — essentially an array of information about the currently executing instance of your component. The information obtainable from the security call context collection is:

✦ Number of Callers

✦ Minimum Authentication Level

✦ Callers

✦ Direct Caller

✦ Original Caller

In addition to the security call context collection information, the ISecurityCallContext interface allows you to determine whether a caller or user is in a specific role. This is the kind of information that you'd use to either grant or reject a request for access to specific methods within the component. You can also determine if role-based security is enabled for this component (versus being available on the server).

Now that you have a little better idea of what the ISecurityCallContext interface can do for you, let's look at the available methods. Table 7-1 provides a list of the methods that you'll use most often.

Table 7-1
ISecurityCallContext Method Summary

Method	Description
get_Count	Returns the number of properties available in the security call context collection.
Get_Item	Retrieves the value for a specific item within the security call context collection. Obviously, the item that you specify must be within the range of available properties, so you should use get_Count first to determine how many properties are available.
Get__NewEnum	Obtains an iterator for the security call context collection.
IsCallerInRole	Determines whether the direct caller is in a specified role. This method won't list all of the roles that the caller is in, it merely allows you to determine whether the caller is a member of the role that you specify. You can use this method to determine whether a caller should have access to a specific method or resource within the component.
IsSecurityEnabled	Determines whether role-based security is enabled for this instance of the component. This method won't determine whether role-based security is enabled for other instances of the component. You already know that role-based security is available on the server because any effort to obtain a pointer to the ISecurityCallContext interface will fail if the server doesn't support role-based security.
IsUserInRole	Performs essentially the same task as IsCallerInRole, but for a specific user. The difference between the caller and the user is that the caller is the one currently using the component. The user call can refer to any user who has access to the server — not necessarily the user making the current call.

Adding Security to Individual Components

Now we have a COM+ application and an associated component installed within the Component Services snap-in. However, the component isn't completely operational yet because we haven't installed any security for it. Theoretically, we could get by without adding any security, but role-based security is one of the new features of COM+ that promises to make life a lot easier for network administrator and developer alike.

To add role-based security to the component, you'll need to create at least one, preferably two, roles. We'll call the first role Administrator so that someone logged in as this role will be able to access all of the methods within the OrderAccess component. The second role can have any other value, but for this example, we'll use User. The User role will be capable of accessing any of the nonconfiguration methods within the component. In other words, the user will be able to do things like look up a part in the catalog, but the user won't be able to modify the contents of the catalog. Obviously, you don't want to give the user the ability to modify the company's product line. The following procedure will get you started in adding a role to the application.

1. Highlight the Roles folder, then use the Action ➪ New ➪ Role command to display the Role dialog box shown in Figure 7-9.

Figure 7-9: The Role dialog box allows you to define the name of a new role.

2. Type a name for the role, then click OK. For this example, we'll use Administrator for one role and User for the second.

3. Open the Administrator (or User) folder, and then highlight the Users folder. Use the Action ➪ New ➪ User command to display the Select Users or Groups dialog box shown in Figure 7-10. This is where you'll choose the users that can access components by using the Administrator role.

4. Highlight the Administrator entry, and then click Add. You'll see the Administrator added to the list of users.

5. Click OK. Administrator will be added to the Users folder in the Component Services window.

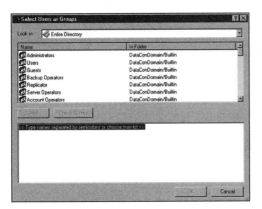

Figure 7-10: The Select Users or Groups dialog box allows you to give users and groups access to a component.

6. Repeat steps 1 through 5 for the User role. However, in this case, use either your own name or a test username instead of Administrator for the Users folder. Figure 7-11 shows a typical security setup for this example. Obviously, any production components that you create will have a more complex security setup that allows users to access the components that you create in specific roles.

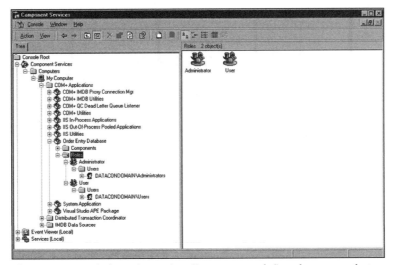

Figure 7-11: Role-based security allows you to define the access that a user has to the methods within a component based on the role that the user performs.

I've chosen not to implement any form of security within the OrderAccess component because that would defeat the purpose of using the highly configurable role-based security option. If I had implemented security within the component, then any change to the company structure might also mean a change to the code within the component. In most cases, you don't want to add security to your component anymore; instead, you'll want to add security using the Component Services snap-in.

With this change in methodology in mind, let's see what you'd need to do to add security to the OrderAccess component. Right-click the OrderAccess.OrderModify.1 component and choose Properties from the context menu. You'll see an OrderAccess.OrderModify.1 Properties dialog box like the one shown in Figure 7-12.

Figure 7-12: The General Tab of the OrderAccess.OrderModify.1 Properties dialog box contains the component name, component GUID, and application GUID.

As you can see, the OrderAccess.OrderModify.1 Properties dialog box allows you to configure a relatively wide range of component options, including whether the component supports transactions. There are also options for enabling the component to engage in object pooling (normally a good idea with database components) and concurrency. Click the Security tab and you'll see the Security tab of the OrderAccess.OrderModify.1 Properties dialog box, which is similar to the one shown in Figure 7-13. Notice that both of the roles that we've created are available for use with this component.

As soon as we added roles to the application, Component Services assumed that we wanted to use security and enabled it for us. The way that the Security tab of the OrderAccess.OrderModify.1 Properties dialog box is set, no one currently has access to the component; you need to check the roles that you want to access the component. For the purposes of this example, check both Administrator and User so that anyone can access the OrderAccess component. You can also adjust security at the application and method levels by opening the Security tab for either object level.

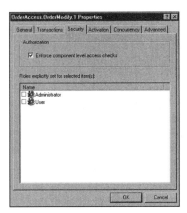

Figure 7-13: Once you've set up role-based security, you can use the roles to allow or deny access to a component at various levels.

Summary

Understanding how security works is an important part of learning what you can expect from your security system. Each form of security available today has some potential flaw, some place where a cracker can get in and damage your data. However, the form of security that you choose can at least deter novice crackers who don't have the experience to handle complex systems and delay entry by others. In addition, a good security system will tell you when it's been breached so that you can take the appropriate countermeasures. Here are some additional conclusions that you can draw from the contents of this chapter:

✦ Ensuring the interoperability of the various security solutions that you implement is an important part of application planning.

✦ Hardware-based security features that you'll find in tomorrow's processors will definitely ease the problem of ensuring that your data remains safe. For example, Intel's Pentium III processor will include both a unique identification feature and true random-number generator, both of which will give programmers the tools that they need to make software safer.

✦ Never assume that any software solution will enable you to provide complete and totally reliable security for your network; always assume that a cracker can break into your system given enough time and computing power.

✦ Security descriptors determine what level of security is attached to an object and what a user needs to access the object, while access tokens determine what rights that user has. If the user's access token has a level of security equal to or greater than the requirements defined by the security descriptor, then the user can use the object.

✦ The SACL works with Windows' auditing feature, while the DACL controls who can actually use an object.

✦ Windows 2000 supports four main types of security: NTLM, Kerberos, PKI, and DPA. Kerberos is the main security provider, while NTLM is supplied for backward compatibility with older versions of Windows.

✦ Microsoft's CryptoAPI enables you to protect the data sent from one site to another by using data encryption.

✦ Physical security is often a required add-on for systems that are exposed to possible threats from within an organization. For example, if you can't lock a server away from public view, the next best thing is to physically secure the server so that no one can access it without a key.

✦ You'll use the System Configuration Editor to create security templates for a machine and the System Configuration Manager actually to deploy those security polices.

✦ Role-based security is an extremely flexible COM+-specific strategy that only works with Windows 2000. It works in addition to any other security that you provide for the system.

✦ Role-based security allows you to protect a component at the component, interface, and method levels.

✦ The ISecurityCallInterface allows you to access directly role-based security from within an application. However, keeping security out of your code and enabling the administrator to configure security as needed ensures that your component won't require additional coding as security requirements change.

✦ Using the Component Services snap-in will add security to your components.

✦   ✦   ✦

COM+ and Distributed interNetwork Architecture

Some developers have been around long enough to see application development move from the desktop, to a client/server network, and finally to the n-tier environment of today. Unfortunately, for some developers, the move from one environment to the next has been fraught with disaster. The desktop is the last place that many of them can remember reliable applications executing in a relatively secure environment. Fortunately, things don't have to continue this way. While it's too soon to say just how good the n-tier approach to development will be, it's definitely better than many of the technologies that preceded it.

This chapter tells you about the n-tier approach to computing. More than that, we'll see how n-tier development can give you the flexibility that you need in a distributed environment, while maintaining or even improving upon both the reliability and the security of days gone by. In some cases, you'll even see an improvement in performance, although much of this improvement comes as a result of things other than the direct effect of n-tier programming. Of course, all of this discussion takes place in the context of Microsoft's new plan for computing, the Distributed interNetwork Architecture (DNA).

The first section focuses on n-tier computing. We look at what n-tier computing is and how it affects the way that you develop applications. The short version is that n-tier computing allows you to create applications that can span multiple servers across both physical and electrical boundaries. The n-tier computing model is a necessary change for a world that's moved from local area networks (LANs), to wide area networks (WANs), to metro area networks (MANs), and beyond.

One problem with all of these great new technologies is that everyone has existing applications. The boss doesn't want to hear that the company needs a new application simply because Microsoft has come out with a new strategy. The second section shows that moving from client/server applications to n-tier applications doesn't have to be a painful process; you can move slowly toward distributed, n-tier applications by carefully evaluating the applications' component requirements.

N-tier applications would use up a lot of network bandwidth if you created them with precisely the same techniques used by desktop and client/server applications. The problem is that there are multiple machines involved in every transaction, so communication between machines needs to occur in an efficient manner. However, there are techniques that you can use to reduce network traffic and free bandwidth for all of the users that you need to support. An n-tier application requires careful planning if you want to get the maximum benefit from the technology. The third section teaches you to plan the modules within your application in such a way that they'll reduce network traffic and work in special circumstances like disconnected mode. This section also deals with some of the problems that you might see as a developer who needs to update existing components to fit within the n-tier model.

The last section examines Microsoft's database technologies. There are three technologies in use today: Open Database Connectivity (ODBC), Object Linking and Embedding for Databases (OLE-DB), and ActiveX Data Objects (ADO). It's very likely that you'll run across all three of these technologies while updating applications on your current system, so it's important to know the relative advantages and disadvantages of each technology. We look at these three technologies and how they affect you as a developer. Of course, part of the learning process includes learning to configure applications to use these technologies.

Understanding the N-Tier Approach to Computing

Everyone is talking about distributed application environments, the n-tier computing model, and the role of the Internet in future business computing. The trade press is especially interested in n-tier computing and spends a lot of time telling you about it in the pages of magazines and newspapers. For many developers, however, there are questions that none of these sources answer. One of those questions is the hype factor. How much of what you read is hype versus real world? Are desktop applications going away in favor of n-tier solutions?

Another potential problem is the ambiguity brought about by a lack of definition for new technologies. Some developers may feel that n-tier computing is simply client/server in disguise or may feel that they have the wrong answers to questions about using n-tier computing. In some cases, developers may even wonder what n-tier computing brings to the computing environment. When a new technology appears on the scene, it's easy to lose track of why that technology is important and what issues it solves.

Finally, n-tier computing isn't just a Microsoft invention—a lot of vendors are introducing similar concepts with their own products. To understand fully the n-tier computing model as it applies to Windows 2000, you have to understand how COM+ fits into the picture. The whole concept of n-tier computing covers a broad range of technologies—COM+ is a specific implementation of the n-tier computing concept.

This section looks at the three questions that we just asked. In the first section, you'll find out what's hype, and what's not. The second section tells you what n-tier computing is and how it affects the way that you develop applications. Finally, we'll look at the COM+ contribution to n-tier computing.

Overcoming the hype factor

There are many misconceptions about n-tier computing. Some developers think that n-tier actually means three tier: client, business logic, and back-end processing because that's the way n-tier computing is often presented. Of course, this limits n-tier computing to database applications in the minds of some developers, which is entirely wrong. N-tier computing involves as many tiers as you need to complete a task. The three tiers shown in many diagrams are simply there to provide you with some idea of the types of jobs that each tier can perform. In other words, the three-level diagram shows one way to organize components into useful categories.

Another misconception is that n-tier computing involves rewriting all of your code from scratch. Components that you wrote in the past will work just fine with COM+. The n-tier concept and the Windows 2000 supporting architecture simply allow you to reorganize your application in a modular fashion. Obviously, you'll have to add some new code to make complete use of the features that COM+ provides, but you can make the transition slowly, COM+ isn't an all or nothing prospect. In fact, with the use of interceptors, you can already take advantage of many COM+ features by packaging existing components. (We looked at component packaging in Chapter 2.)

The COM+ learning curve has also been greatly exaggerated. If anything, COM+ makes development easier, increases reliability, and enhances flexibility. It's true that you'll need to learn some new concepts, especially if you haven't worked with MTS and MSMQ in the past. To get the greatest benefits of this new technology, you'll need to build support for MTS and MSMQ into your components. You'll also need to learn how Component Services and Queued Components work. (See Chapter 6 for more details about how MTS, MSMQ, Component Services, and Queued Components relate to COM+.)

Microsoft would have you believe that using COM+ will automatically make your applications execute faster. It's true that Windows 2000 itself offers a small speed boost if you provide the resources that it requires to run efficiently (the minimum requirements for doing so are much higher than in Windows NT). So, if you use the same components that you have now and provide Windows 2000 with the resources that it needs, then the operating system, not COM+, will give your applications a noticeable speed boost. In many cases, you'll see a 30 to 50 percent speed increase by moving from Windows NT to Windows 2000 because of operating system enhancements.

Visual Basic Limitations for COM+

Visual Basic 6 was introduced long before COM+ became a reality. It's no surprise then that there are some COM+ programming tasks that require a little more effort to do. For example, creating an MMC snap-in is very doable, but it requires a little added effort, as we'll see in Chapter 9. Previous chapters told you about the references that you'll need to add in order to gain access to specific COM+ features like MTS. We'll discuss more of these reference requirements as the book progresses, so that you won't have to spend much time figuring out which module to add. Fortunately, unlike Visual C++, the only reason that you need the Platform SDK when working with Visual Basic is to access the advanced tools and documentation that it provides. In short, Visual Basic is ready to go once you install Service Pack 3.

Unfortunately, there are some new Windows 2000 and COM+ features that you can't access with Visual Basic 6. These features won't become available until the release of Visual Basic 7 because Microsoft (as of this writing) has no plans to provide a service pack to cover this need for Visual Basic 6. For those of you who absolutely must make use of these new features, the best choice is to write a wrapper component with Visual C++, and then access that component through your Visual Basic application. (You must install the latest Windows Platform SDK to gain access to Windows 2000- or COM+-specific features that use Visual C++.) Let's look at the two most important features that aren't accessible through Visual Basic.

Microsoft has introduced a new apartment type for Windows 2000 that's specifically designed to meet the needs of COM+ developers. Like the multithreaded apartment (MTA), there's at most one thread-neutral apartment (TNA) within a process. One thing that differentiates TNA from the other two apartment types is that it contains objects only — no threads are allowed within this apartment. Instead of executing within the TNA, when a thread requests access to a TNA object, it receives a lightweight proxy that switches to the object's context without the penalty of a thread switch. MTA threads can request this access directly, while single-threaded apartment (STA) threads will need to create a new thread-neutral object. The point is that without TNA support, Visual Basic loses out on some of the potential performance enhancements offered by Windows 2000.

Visual Basic also doesn't provide support for the free-threaded model. This means that object pooling won't work. Object pooling is part of the resource pooling feature that we discussed in Chapter 1. When an object is marked for object pooling, COM+ will retain any instances of that object in memory for reuse by other applications (at least as long as there's memory to do so). What this means is that applications will gain access to objects faster if an instance of the object is already available in the pool. This feature alone can greatly speed application execution, but you can't access it from Visual Basic 6.

Even though you can't use all of the features that COM+ provides within your Visual Basic application, you can still use the vast majority of them. For the most part, all that you'll loose is a little speed until Visual Basic 7 arrives on the scene and you can recompile your components to make use of these new features.

To get the speed enhancements that COM+ provides, you have to rewrite your components to take advantage of COM+ features. For example, while the use of interceptors will allow you to configure the component to use MTS, you still have to add code that will allow the component to vote on the outcome of a transaction, or provide logic that will allow COM+ to automatically detect error conditions. You also need to configure your application to use these special features (see the "Visual Basic Limitations for COM+" sidebar below for additional details about configuration and programming requirements). In short, there's no free ride — every time Microsoft changes the operating system, it is likely to mean at least some small change in your application's code or configuration — Windows 2000 is no exception.

Even though Microsoft refers to COM+ as a fully integrated technology, the seams of sewing the various elements together are nevertheless evident. For example, consider the case where you create a transactional application that requires absolute assurance that the transaction has completed properly. MSMQ is no longer an option in this environment because MSMQ supports one-way messaging and can't guarantee a server connection for receiving the receipt. As a result, even though you can create COM+ applications that take the paranoid approach to transactions, the use of receipts prevents you from using all of the COM+ features. The solution to this particular problem is to rely on MTS to ensure that the transaction completes and not to request a receipt within your application. Obviously, it's not a perfect solution, but it's the best one that COM+ can provide.

Not every COM+ feature provides a speed enhancement. Using MSMQ automatically delays the delivery of data, but it also means that you can write disconnected applications. Some speed bumps aren't quite so evident. Consider the use of context with all COM+ components. Context is a requirement if you want to use interceptors and gain the flexibility that COM+ provides. Unfortunately, creating a context also requires processor time — not a lot, but enough that you might notice a small performance loss with some applications. The bottom line is that Windows 2000 and COM+ both run applications faster, but within limits determined by the number and type of features that you use within the application.

What is n-tier computing?

There's a lot of misunderstanding about the role of n-tier development today and its effect on the developer. In the past, a client would send data requests to a server. The server would answer back. This is known as the client/server model. It's not limited to two machines — there can be as many servers as required to get the job done. The limitation is in the number of levels of communication. When using the client/server model, the client requests data directly from the server, which implies that the client knows the identity of the server. In addition, the server can't request data from another server on the client's behalf — the client and the server always have a direct relationship.

Unfortunately, the client/server model won't work very well in the distributed computing environment. As server farms become more prevalent on large networks, it's not always possible for the application to know which server will fulfill a request. Load balancing and other concerns make it possible that a client will be serviced by one server during one request and another server when making a second request. In fact, it's possible that a server will go offline and hand the request to another server midway through the transaction. In other words, direct contact is no longer feasible.

Another problem with the client/server model is that the client has to directly request every piece of data it needs, which means that the client has to have a lot of intelligence. Adding intelligence to the client, rather than the server, means writing a lot of redundant code. In a distributed environment, the client should only need to worry about making an initial request for data. It's up to the server to figure out how to get that data for the client. If the server has to call on several other servers to fulfill the request, then the client shouldn't be aware of the background transactions taking place. Building applications this way means that the server can handle a wider range of clients, all of which use a similar request format.

N-tier computing is an answer to distributed application development. It doesn't assume that a particular server will handle a client request. In addition, one server can call upon another server to handle part of a client request on the client's behalf. This means that the client receives data without worrying about the details and the developer spends less time hard coding specific locations in an application.

It's important to understand that n-tier applications can work across many kinds of boundaries because the request format is always the same. A thin client that uses a browser as a container will request data by using the same request format as a thick client operating on the desktop. The server no longer needs to know what kind of client is making the request, only that the client needs data and resources that the server can provide. In short, n-tier computing and the distributed environment both require self-contained servers and clients, each of which only knows about the data and objects that are being exchanged.

As you can see, n-tier computing isn't about specific roles — it's about modularity and flexibility across vast distances. Unlike client/server, which is designed for use in a LAN environment, n-tier applications are designed to work in the WAN or MAN environment, where you can't assume anything about the connection between the client and server.

Understanding the COM+ role in n-tier computing

Because COM+ allows an application to work across multiple machines and even networks, you need to create a detailed picture of what you expect to provide as application input and to get as output. Unlike many applications, a COM+ application specification should also include the servers on which various parts of the application will execute so that you can take the purpose of a specific server into account when designing the components that will handle the requirements of that server.

Unlike many application specifications, the server need not refer to a specific physical device—a server could refer to a cluster of Windows 2000 machines just as easily as it could refer to a single machine running a single component. A server is therefore a component, or group of components, that execute(s) a specific set of functions based on the input from a given client. This principle holds true whether you use two machines, or hundreds of machines, which is what happens in large corporate applications. Of course, the number of physical machines required to handle a particular server is based on the client load, which is something that we don't discuss in detail in this book.

In Microsoft's n-tier approach to application design specified by the Distributed interNetwork Architecture (DNA), there are multiple server types involved in servicing the needs of a particular application as shown in Figure 8-1. Each of these servers has a distinct purpose. For example, one server might be responsible for ensuring that user input is correctly formatted before adding it to the database.

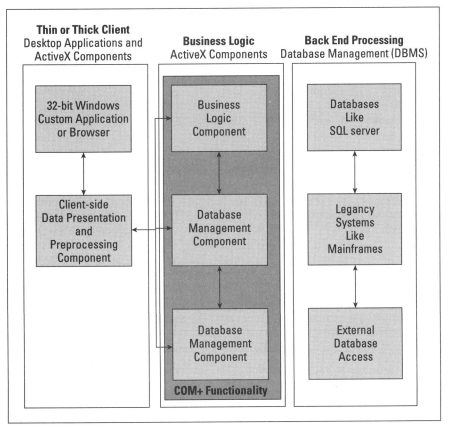

Figure 8-1: Microsoft's DNA allows you to separate the elements of an application into easily managed modules.

Note The blocks shown in Figure 8-1 are meant as aids for component and server categorization. As previously mentioned, n-tier computing is not limited to database applications — you can create n-tier applications that monitor the state of the physical machines on the network. The idea behind n-tier is a complete client request that's handled by one or more servers. You'll also notice that Figure 8-1 is a little more detailed than some of the drawings out there — it's important to realize when creating a real-world application, that the middle tier, for example, consists of more than just business logic. Obviously, you can add custom blocks to this generalized drawing to meet specific needs.

Even if your application is made up of multiple components that reside on multiple servers, you can still ease the complexity of defining the application specification by first taking a DNA view of the application. For practical purposes, what you're really looking at in Figure 8-1 is an extension of the common three-level approach listed here.

✦ **Client:** Contains all of the user and client-side processing. This is the level that formats data for output to the user and checks user input for errors (as much as is possible). You can also use this level for data preprocessing and to anticipate user data requests in an effort to reduce network traffic. Components used for client-side processing can be in-process or out-of-process servers — depending on the kind of client that you need to service. The client level contains all of the thick or thin clients and components required to provide the server with a formatted request and to accept the data requested from the server. The components required for a thin client may physically reside on the machine reserved for server activities, but these components are still performing client-side tasks like formatting data for viewing by user (in the case of a browser and Web page).

✦ **Business logic:** Allows the client application to interact with the server in a way that is defined by the rules of your business. For example, this is the level that determines whether the user has sufficient rights to access the requested data and what elements of the data record the user is allowed to see. This is also the level that requests data from any back end processors and sends formatted data from the user to the database. Business logic can also include a number of other things. For example, a single record may require input from multiple users, so this level could alert users to the presence of new records that require their attention. I call this type of component a state management component because it helps keep the various parts of your application in sync. In short, the business logic level incorporates all nondatabase processing. It could be the end of the line for some applications, so calling it the middle tier or middle level isn't precisely accurate in many situations.

✦ **Back-end processing:** Provides database access and the input/output of complete data. This is the level that manages the data for you, but doesn't format it for use. Every business runs on data that is normally stored in the form of data records on a high-speed server. However, the contents of a single data record may actually come from several sources. In short, the efficient storage of data isn't always matched by the efficient use of the data by the end user. As Figure 8-1 shows, Microsoft has built technologies that will allow you to access data from a variety of sources, including PC-based databases like SQL Server, legacy systems like mainframes, or even data that resides in unconventional locations.

The fact that you can no longer depend on seeing the application as a single entity makes it imperative that you understand how the application works from a design perspective. Even using just two machines makes it much more difficult to see the application in action than in the days when everything resided on one desktop. As a result, monolithic applications no longer work. Modularity has taken on a new level of importance, which will become apparent as the chapter progresses. The main reason that you'd use any component programming approach like COM+ is to ensure that you can move pieces of an application around without making any change to the application code. COM+ is all about application flexibility and writing applications that don't depend on seeing each application as a whole.

Determining Where Your Application Modules Fit

Even in the best of circumstances, your company will have applications that you'll need to move from either a monolithic or a client/server environment to Microsoft's new DNA model. The problem is that most of these older applications weren't designed for a distributed environment. They aren't organized to use such an environment and may not be coded in such a way that the move will be an easy one. The fact remains, however, that your company is moving to the Internet (or may already be there) and you have to support users on the road for the least possible investment.

Some applications contain so much spaghetti code that attempting to make any sense at all out of them is a task better suited to the talents of a cryptographer than a programmer. In some cases, you either have to live with the application or design it from scratch. Revising the application to work in a new environment may be too time-consuming or too costly to attempt. Obviously, there's only one remedy for this situation, which we won't discuss here. Once you get rid of the spaghetti code and uncommented applications, most other applications can be moved from their current environment to COM+ in five steps.

1. Create an application diagram.
2. Decide where you want to place various application functions.

3. Create the components required to service the application.

4. Move your current business logic from the existing application to the new components.

5. Test the new application on a single machine first, then move to a distributed environment, and finally perform live testing.

For applications whose code you can make some sense of and whose organization isn't too bad, you usually begin by creating an application diagram. We're not talking about a blow-by-blow description of the application code or a simple overview for the company CEO; you need a diagram that breaks the application down by function and by task. Creating this diagram will force you to think about things like repetitive functions, where the same code is used by more than one application. You'll also need to look for superceded functionality. It could be that your old application contains functions that are performed for you by Windows 2000 or modern application languages.

After you have an application diagram, it's time to decide where to place the various functions. A monolithic application may have all of the required code on one machine, but that's decidedly not the best way to do things in a distributed environment. You'll want to place the various functions on machines where the client load can be balanced and the application run at top efficiency. Figure 8-1 provides some generic application function classifications that you can use. However, because every application is unique, you'll also want to make your classifications unique. Make sure that anyone working with you can understand how the various application pieces will go together. Consider how the organization that you use will affect reliability, scalability, disconnected applications, and other modern application needs.

Creating the component shells comes next. The shell that you create will be nonfunctional, but it should provide the structure required by the application. If you need to move a function from the old application, make sure that there's a method to hold it in the new application. It's also important to consider application interfaces and other COM+ requirements that your old application may not have required.

At this point, you know where the various components will be located, how you'll implement the flow of data, and you've created component shells. It's time to move the business logic from the existing application to your new application. Of course, this brings up other problems. For one thing, you may find that the existing code won't port directly to the new environment. You may have to make some coding changes to allow the code to run (or run efficiently) on the new system.

The testing phase is where you'll begin to see just how much better the application works in its new form. The first few tests may be a disappointment unless you've really done your homework. Testing the application on a single machine first will help you eliminate problems related to remote machine connections. Next, you'll want to test the application in a simulation of the environment in which it'll eventually run. The final test will start integrating users — begin with a small number of users, perform stress tests, and then (if successful) move larger numbers to the new application.

So far, we've moved an application from an existing environment to a new one, but we haven't done anything else. Now that the application is completely modular, scalable, and reliable, you can add new features as needed to support the company on the Internet. For example, you may want to add MSMQ support so that the users on the road can access the application in disconnected mode.

Creating Components that Reduce Network Traffic

Distributed applications create a new problem that you may not have had to deal with in the past — excessive network traffic. In a client/server environment, there's one path of communication between the client and server. A distributed application may generate several paths of communication, which increases network traffic. Fortunately, there are several ways to reduce network traffic, or at least make the load consistent. The following list will give you some ideas on how you can write new components to accomplish this task.

✦ **Use complete requests:** Every time the server has to ask the client for additional information, the request generates network traffic. Making a complete request reduces the probability that the server will have to ask for additional information. Not only do you have to check the component for completeness, but you need to check user input as well. Make sure that the user enters the required information before sending the request to the server.

✦ **Reduce server feedback:** The more information you request from the server, the larger the network packets. Obviously, you have to request enough information to satisfy the client request. Reducing unnecessary information, however, will conserve network bandwidth. If possible, make data communication between the client and server one way so that you can completely cut one data communication path. For example, when entering a new record, the client can simply send the data to the server without requesting any return value.

Tip

The first two points in this list are especially important for Queued Components. Because the client and server may not exist at the same time, you must create components that will use MSMQ in such a way that they provide only input values and make a complete request. The server may not be able to ask the client for additional information, so the request has to be formatted correctly the first time.

✦ **Use queued components:** Requests that require no server feedback should use a queue, even if you know that the client and server will exist at the same time. The reason is simple: after the client sends the data to the server, it no longer cares about the data. Using a queue will allow the server to operate more efficiently because it can handle the request during off-peak processing times. In addition, if the server requires input from other servers on the network to complete the request, it can do so during off-peak network times. In short, using Queued Components won't reduce network traffic, but they'll make the network traffic more consistent so that you get full efficiency from available network bandwidth.

✦ **Use numbers in place of strings:** I've been guilty of this one myself. A string normally requires more bits to represent a number than using a numeric representation will. You can gain further efficiency by reducing the size of the numeric representation, within reason. For example, using an integer in place of a double reduces the size of that field within the data packet. Of course, you have to consider future data needs. Don't use an integer today if the data might need decimal representation tomorrow.

✦ **Increase client-side error detection:** Many of the problems with components today can be summed up as a lack of error detection. You need to check user input for range, type, and other kinds of error. Prevent errors from happening in the first place by using drop-down list boxes as often as possible. UpDown controls also make it easier for users to select correct values, as do data pickers.

Tip

The distributed computing environment can make it easier for the network or data administrator to automatically update application values. Every time the application starts, it should check for the availability of a server. If the server is available, the application should request the most current data ranges and values, and store them locally. Use these values to check user input prior to sending data to the server; doing so will reduce the number of user errors. Adding this feature to your application means that an administrator can change application behavior without changing every application on the network. Yet, storing the data locally will mean that the user can access the application even when on the road.

✦ **Include administrator and user error feedback:** Applications will often display a simple error message dialog on screen—end of question (there is no additional error processing). The user will often click OK without even reading the message. Frustration mounts as the user clicks OK repeatedly without understanding the application's request for additional input. As a fix, many users will input the first value that comes to mind that also satisfies the pesky dialog box that's getting in their way. The result is that your database receives corrupted data input because the user doesn't understand the requirements. It's possible to add event messages to any application that will inform the administrator about problem areas. When users are having trouble with a certain area of an application, event messages can tell the administrator about the problem. The administrator can then schedule training sessions to help users understand what the application requires as input. User training not only makes the application more pleasurable to use, but also reduces unnecessary network traffic and makes the application run faster.

This foregoing list provides many good tips on creating a new class of component — the intelligent component. As networks get larger and the number of users per administrator increase, intelligent components become a viable solution for many problems. The use of intelligent components will reduce network traffic, make applications run faster, reduce user confusion, and help administrators learn about application problem areas. COM+ makes it possible to increase network efficiency and even out the workload on many servers. Using technologies like Queued Components can help a company use its current network setup for a little longer by extending the time a server works into the nonpeak hours.

Working with Data Sources

A data source can take many forms. Most developers automatically think about databases as data sources. It's true that databases are the most common data sources used in applications and will remain so for the foreseeable future. However, data sources can take other forms as well. For example, you might need to monitor scientific or manufacturing equipment (the constant output of this equipment is a data source). Some Web site software now allows administrators to monitor the areas where users click, making it possible to tailor a Web site to user usage patterns. No matter what data source you need to access, it's important to know how to build support for that data source into an application.

Microsoft currently provides three technologies for accessing data sources: ODBC, OLE-DB, and ADO. Each technology has different uses. For example, ODBC is the oldest, most familiar, and most widely used of the three technologies. OLE-DB allows low-level access to data, yet reduces the amount of programming required to do so. ADO is the highest-level access technology available today. It allows you to access a data source with very little programming. ADO is also the preferred method for Visual Basic developers because it's easier to develop applications by using graphical tools than by using hand coding.

The following sections will provide you with an overview of all three data access technologies. We don't take an in-depth view of these technologies — there are entire books devoted to that topic. Instead, we concentrate on the techniques that you need while working with the examples in this book. We'll continue this discussion within the example setup sections of the chapters that follow.

Creating an ODBC data source

ODBC is one of the older database interface technologies that Microsoft has introduced. It's actually the predecessor of ADO, which we'll discuss in the "Understanding How ADO Differs from OLE-DB" section below. One of Microsoft's principal reasons for introducing this technology was to give programmers an easy way to access the contents of databases in a very nonlanguage-specific manner. In other words, you don't need to know the xBase programming language (like FoxPro's native language) to access a DBF file, or Access Basic to grab data in an MDB file. In fact, Visual Basic and Visual C++ are two of the programming platforms that Microsoft originally targeted with ODBC.

You'll find that ODBC works much the same as the rest of Windows — it uses drivers contained in DLLs to get the job done. In essence, ODBC provides a set of two drivers — one that speaks the language of the database manager and another that provides a common interface for the programming language. It's the meeting of these two drivers through a common interface that allows Visual Basic to access the contents of the database by using a standard set of function calls.

Of course, there are also other utility-type DLLs associated with ODBCll. For example, one DLL allows you to administer ODBC data sources. The actual administration interface for ODBC is in a CPL (control panel) file, like ODBCCP32.CPL, which is found in the SYSTEM32 folder (we'll talk more about it later). The CPL file will call upon an executable like ODBCAD32.EXE that displays a dialog box for managing the database sources. Finally, when you create a database source, ODBCAD32.EXE will load a DLL, like SQLSRV32.DLL for SQL Server, to help with the particulars of a data source configuration.

ODBC does fulfill its promise to provide access to the contents of a database without too many problems. There are situations in which it doesn't provide the best data conversion possible between the database manager and Visual Basic, but for the most part it works as advertised. The only thing that mars an otherwise great future for ODBC is that it's exceedingly slow — at least the older versions of the product are. When ODBC originally came out, some developers said that it would never make much of an impact in the database community because of the speed issues. However, given Microsoft's marketing clout, ODBC has become a qualified success. Just about every database manager worth its salt ships with an ODBC driver of one sort or another.

Working with ODBC

Before you can do anything with ODBC, you have to have a database (at least in mind). It's usually easier to create the database shell within an application like Access, which provides the tools needed to create the shell with the least amount of effort. However, you can create the shell in C++ if you have the required ODBC drivers installed. After you have a database designed, you need to create an ODBC data source for it. That's what we look at in this section. The following procedure isn't meant as a rigid course of action; rather, it shows one technique for getting a data source configured.

Note

This is a general setup procedure for ODBC databases. This procedure focuses on Windows 2000, because that's the main target for this book, but the procedure includes notes as appropriate for other versions of Windows. The SAMPLE.MDB database used for this procedure appears in the Chapt08 folder of the CD-ROM provided with this book. The procedures for the database-specific portion of the procedure will vary by database vendor, so you may not see the same exact screenshots when working with other database products. This example uses an Access database for ease of demonstration.

1. Double-click the Data Sources (ODBC) applet found in the Administrative Tools folder of the Control Panel. (Some versions of Windows use a simple ODBC applet if there are no 16-bit drivers installed on the current system or 32-bit ODBC if there are only 32-bit drivers installed in the main Control Panel.) You'll see the ODBC Data Source Administrator dialog box similar to the one shown in Figure 8-2. Figure 8-2 shows the User DSN (Data Source Name) tab, which is used for general database entries. Other options include a System DSN tab for system-level databases and a File DSN tab for file-level data sources (which may or may not be a database in the truest sense of the word).

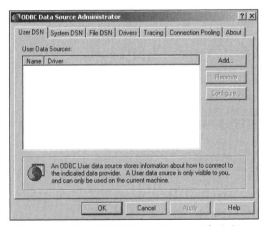

Figure 8-2: The ODBC Data Source Administrator dialog box allows you to configure ODBC connections on the local machine.

 Note

The ODBC Data Source Administrator dialog box shown in Figure 8-2 contains several additional tabs that you'll need to know about. The Drivers tab contains a list of ODBC drivers installed on the local machine. The Tracing tab contains options for troubleshooting your database connections. You may not see the Connection Pooling tab on all versions of Windows — it's used to make ODBC more efficient by allowing the operating system to cache database connections, rather than create new ones for each request. This tab also contains an option for adding the ODBC driver to the Performance Monitor for database tuning. (See Chapter 1 for details.) The About tab contains a list of ODBC core component files and tells you about their function.

Caution   You'll normally need to create an entry on the User DSN tab for local databases and on the System DSN tab for remote databases. Under no circumstance should you create an entry with the same name on both the User DSN and System DSN tabs. Using the same name on both tabs will likely result in really strange and inconsistent error messages from your server when you attempt to access the database remotely. In fact, the 32-bit ODBC applet is one of the first places that you should look if you get strange error messages during remote database access.

2. Click the Add. . . button. You'll see a Create New Data Source dialog box like the one shown in Figure 8-3.

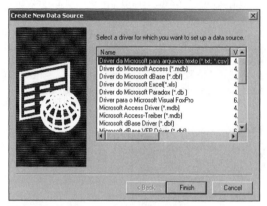

Figure 8-3: The New Data Source dialog box allows you to choose from among all the ODBC data-source DLLs installed on the local machine.

Tip   You can ensure that you're using the most current ODBC drivers available by checking both the Drivers and About tab of the ODBC Data Source Administrator dialog box. These two tabs contain the version numbers of the various ODBC DLLs, the name of the vendor who created them, and the name of the file as it appears in the SYSTEM folder. In most cases, you'll be able to use the version number as a method for verifying that your ODBC driver is up-to-date.

3. Choose one of the data sources (I'll be using the Microsoft Access Driver (*.mdb) option), and then click Finish. You'll see a configuration dialog box similar to the ODBC Microsoft Access Setup dialog shown in Figure 8-4. Note that some ODBC drivers will provide a specific version number as part of the dialog box name. In addition, you'll want to use the correct driver for the language that you're working with. Figure 8-4 shows a generic English language driver dialog box.

Note   The steps that follow use the SAMPLE.MDB Access database that appears on the CD-ROM provided with this book. If you select a different data source, the steps required to configure it will differ from the ones shown here—each ODBC driver requires a different type of configuration.

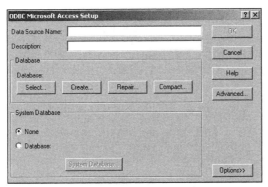

Figure 8-4: After you select a data source, you'll see a data source-specific setup dialog box similar to the one shown here.

4. Type a data source name in the Data Source Name field. Make sure that you choose something descriptive, but not overly long. I chose Food Database because I'll eventually create a link to a food inventory-related database.

5. Type a description in the Description field. You'll want to make this entry a bit longer than the previous one because it describes the purpose of your database. On the other hand, you don't want to write a novel the size of *War and Peace*. I typed, "This database contains inventory information for a food store." for this example.

6. Click the Select. . . button. You'll see a Select Database dialog box similar to the one shown in Figure 8-5, where you can choose an existing database. The ODBC driver will automatically choose the correct file extension for you. You can choose to open the database for exclusive or read-only access by using options in the Select Database dialog box. Once you've selected a database, click OK in the Select Database dialog box.

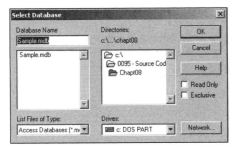

Figure 8-5: The Select Database dialog box allows you to choose any database that you can access through a local or network connection.

Tip

You don't absolutely have to design your database in advance. The Access ODBC driver also includes a button to create a new database. Most, but not all, ODBC drivers provide this feature. Clicking this button will start the database manager application and allow you to design the database. It's interesting to note that the Access ODBC driver will also allow you to compress or repair your database from this dialog.

7. Choose a system database option. In most cases, you'll choose None unless you specifically created a system database for your application. If you do add a system database, it'll appear on the System DSN tab of the ODBC Data Source Administrator dialog box.

8. Click the Advanced. . . button and you'll see a Set Advanced Options dialog similar to the one shown in Figure 8-6. You won't need to modify many of the entries. However, it almost always pays to add the guest username to the Login Name field and the guest password to the Password field. This allows a guest to access your database without really knowing anything about how the access was obtained — not even the name that they were logged in under.

Figure 8-6: The Set Advanced Options dialog box allows you to choose a default login name and password, along with other settings like those that affect performance.

Tip

You may want to look through the list of advanced options provided by your ODBC driver for access and other usage settings. Most ODBC drivers also provide performance settings along with the advanced options. For example, the Access ODBC driver provides a MaxBufferSize entry that lets you fine-tune the size of the buffer used to hold data. Selecting a size that corresponds to an even record size will enhance system performance without wasting memory. As another example, the Access ODBC driver allows you to change the number of threads that the DBMS uses. The default setting of 3 usually provides good performance, but you may find that using more threads in a complex application will speed foreground tasks. However, using too many threads will slow your application because Windows uses some processor cycles to manage the thread overhead.

9. Click OK once you've set any advanced options that you need.

10. Click OK again to close the ODBC Microsoft Access Setup dialog. You should see a new entry added to the ODBC Data Source Administrator dialog similar to the one shown in Figure 8-7. If you need to change the settings for the Food Database later, simply highlight it and click Configure. Getting rid of the database is equally easy. Just highlight it and click Remove.

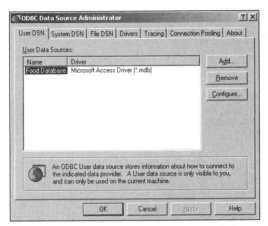

Figure 8-7: Any data sources that you configure will appear on the appropriate tab of the ODBC Data Source Administrator dialog box.

Creating a system DSN is about the same as creating a user DSN. The big difference between the two is what they're used for. A system DSN tells your application how to connect with the database and, in some cases, how to interact with it. A system DSN doesn't contain any of the data for the database — it contains the connection criteria. This could include everything from a user list to the location of important files. While user DSNs are specific to the current user, system DSNs can be used by any user logged into the local machine.

File DSNs

You may have noticed a problem with the example in the previous section. It works fine as long as you want to configure every machine on your network individually, which probably isn't your idea of a good time. There's another way to store the information needed to create a data source — the file DSN. That's what we'll look at in this section. The following procedure provides a general idea of how to set up a file DSN.

1. Double-click the Data Sources (ODBC) applet found in the Administrative Tools folder of the Control Panel. (Some versions of Windows use a simple ODBC applet if there are no 16-bit drivers installed on the current system or 32-bit ODBC if there are only 32-bit drivers installed in the main Control Panel.) You'll see the ODBC Data Source Administrator dialog box. Select the File DSN tab and you'll see a dialog box similar to the one shown in Figure 8-8. The first thing that you'll need to do is choose a place to store the DSN information.

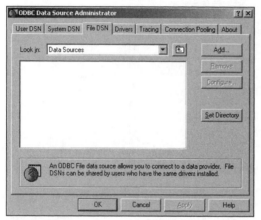

Figure 8-8: File DSNs store configuration data in a portable file format that you can move to other machines.

2. Click on the Look in drop-down list box. You'll see a list of directories and drives for the current machine. You can use any storage location for the DSN. I normally choose the database storage directory on the network. Using UNC (universal naming convention) directory paths means that everyone will access the DSN file using the same path.

The Up One Level button next to the Look in drop-down list box works just the way it does in Explorer. You can use this button to go up one directory at a time. Eventually you'll end up at My Computer and see a list of all the drives on your machine.

3. Click Add. You'll see a Create New Data Source dialog box similar to the one shown in Figure 8-3.

Clicking the Advanced button on the Create New Data Source dialog box allows you to configure some additional file DSN parameters. The dialog will already contain the default DRIVER= entry that determines the name of the driver that you want to use. The most common additional entry is the SERVER= parameter that provides the name of a specific server to use for this DSN.

4. Choose one of the ODBC drivers in the list, and then click Next. You'll see the next page of the Create New Data Source dialog as shown in Figure 8-9. This is where you'll choose a name and storage location for your data source. Click Browse. . . and you'll see a Save As dialog box in which you can choose a storage location. Type a filename and the ODBC wizard will automatically add DSN as the extension. I chose SAMPLE.DSN as the name for the DSN file in this example. Click Save to close the dialog box.

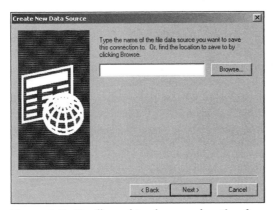

Figure 8-9: You'll need to choose a location for the file DSN. Windows uses a default location of the Data Sources directory on the local drive.

5. Click Next and you'll see a summary dialog similar to the one shown in Figure 8-10. It tells you the parameters for the DSN that you're going to create.

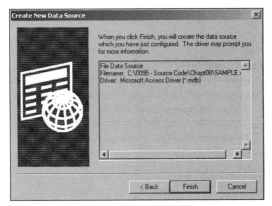

Figure 8-10: This summary dialog box allows you to check the settings for your file DSN before you create it.

6. Click Finish. At this point, you'll see a modified version of the ODBC Microsoft Access Setup dialog box as shown in Figure 8-11. You won't be able to add a Data Source Name or Description like we did in the previous section. However, everything else will work in the same way.

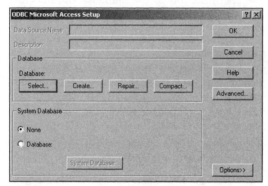

Figure 8-11: This modified form of the ODBC Microsoft Access Setup dialog box allows you only to select a database and access options.

7. Make sure that you enter the name of a database by clicking the Select. . . button and then choosing the database that you want to use. (You can also click Create. . . if you want to create a new database.)

8. Click OK when you complete the configuration process. You'll see a new DSN file entry similar to the one shown in Figure 8-12 in the ODBC Data Source Administrator dialog box.

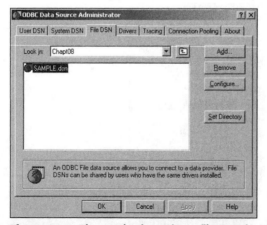

Figure 8-12: The result of creating a file DSN is a new entry in the ODBC Data Source Administrator dialog box.

Unlike the previous DSN that we created, this one actually creates a file that you can view and edit with a text editor. Figure 8-13 shows what this file looks like. Notice that it follows a standard INI file format. You can see the [ODBC] heading at the top, followed by all of the settings that you chose. This file will allow you to choose a data source from Visual Basic, yet it's very easy to transfer from machine to machine. You could even change the locations as required during the installation process — a real plus when you don't know what kind of setup the user will have.

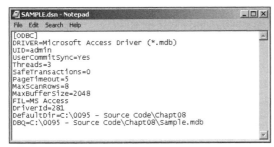

Figure 8-13: The SAMPLE.dsn file contains all of the settings that are required in order to use your database from within Visual Basic.

Logging your ODBC transactions

It's always nice to have a log of whatever you're doing when it comes time to debug an application. The ODBC Data Source Administrator dialog box offers this capability. You can choose to track the various transactions that you make to a database through ODBC. Of course, these logs can get rather large, but you won't be using them all the time.

All you need to do to start logging your transactions is open the ODBC Data Source Administrator dialog box and choose the Tracing tab. You'll see a dialog similar to the one shown in Figure 8-14.

The trace won't start automatically. You'll need to click on the Start Tracing Now button on the left side of the dialog. The push-button caption will change to Stop Tracing Now as soon as tracing starts. Click on the button again to turn tracing off.

The Log file Path's Browse button allows you to change the location of the log file. ODBC normally places the transaction information in the SQL.LOG file in your root directory. However, you may want to place that information on a network drive or in a location hidden from the user. The default location normally works fine during the debugging process.

Note   Unless you want to create your own logging DLL, don't change the setting in the Custom Trace DLL field. The DLL listed in this field, ODBCTRAC.DLL, is responsible for maintaining the transaction log.

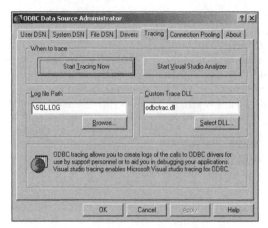

Figure 8-14: The Tracing tab of the ODBC Data Source Administrator dialog box allows you to troubleshoot ODBC data-source connections.

If you have Visual Studio Enterprise Edition installed on your machine, you'll also see a Start Visual Studio Analyzer button. This button allows you to perform detailed analysis of your database connection. When you click the button, the caption will change to Stop Visual Studio Analyzer. Clicking the button a second time will change the caption back and stop the Visual Studio Analyzer.

Understanding how OLE-DB works

So, what is OLE-DB? As the name implies, it uses OLE (or more specifically, the component object model — COM) to provide a set of interfaces for data access. Just like any other COM object, you can query, create, and destroy an OLE-DB object. The source of an OLE-DB object is called a provider. You'll get a variety of OLE-DB providers as part of the Visual Basic package and more will likely arrive as vendors upgrade their database products. The nice thing about OLE-DB is that the same provider works with any Visual Studio product: Visual C++, Visual Basic, Visual InterDev, and Visual J++.

OLE-DB also relies on events, just as any COM object would. These events tell you when an update of a table is required to show new entries made by other users or when the table you've requested is ready for viewing. You'll also see events used to signal various database errors and other activities that right now require polling.

Microsoft defines four major categories of OLE-DB users. It's important to understand how you fit into the grand scheme of things. The following list breaks the various groups down and tells you how they contribute toward the use of OLE-DB as a whole.

✦ **Data provider:** Someone who uses the OLE-DB SDK (software development kit) to create an OLE-DB provider. The provider uses interfaces to interact with the database and events to signal special occurrences.

✦ **Data consumer:** An application, system driver, or user who requires access to the information contained in a database.

✦ **Data service provider:** A developer who creates standalone utilities (services) that enhance the user's or administrator's ability to use or manage the contents of a database. For example, a developer could create a query engine that allows the user to make natural language requests for information in the database. A service works with the OLE-DB provider and becomes an integral part of it.

✦ **Business component developer:** A developer who creates application modules or components that reduce the amount of coding required to create a database application. A component could be something as generic as a grid control that allows you to display a subset of the records in the database at a glance, or something specific to the type of database being accessed.

So, how does OLE-DB differ from ODBC? Table 8-1 shows the major differences between the two products. We'll discuss how these differences affect your usage decisions in "When Should You Use OLE-DB, ADO, or ODBC?" below.

Table 8-1
OLE-DB to ODBC Technology Comparison

Element	OLE-DB	ODBC	Description
Access type	Component	Direct	OLE-DB provides interfaces that interact with the data. User access to the data is through components designed to interact with OLE-DB.
Data access specialization	Any tabular data	SQL	ODBC has always been designed to use SQL as the basis for data transactions. In some cases, that means that the programmer has to make concessions to force the data to fit into the SQL standard.
Driver access method	Component	Native	As mentioned earlier, all access to an OLE-DB provider is through COM interfaces using components of various types. ODBC normally requires direct programming of some type and relies heavily on the level of SQL compatibility enforced by the database vendor.

Continued

Table 8-1 *(continued)*			
Element	**OLE-DB**	**ODBC**	**Description**
Programming model	COM	C	OLE-DB relies on COM to provide the programmer with access to the provider. This means that OLE-DB is language independent, while ODBC is language specific.
Technology standard	COM	SQL	OLE-DB adheres to Microsoft's COM standard, which means that it's much more vendor and platform specific than the SQL technology standard used by ODBC.

Don't get the idea that OLE-DB and ODBC are two completely diverse technologies meant to replace each other. There's an ODBC OLE-DB provider that allows you to access all of the functionality that ODBC provides through OLE-DB or ADO. In other words, the two technologies compliment each other; they're not meant as complete replacements for each other. Can you replace ODBC with ADO or OLE-DB? Yes, but you won't get the very best performance from your applications if you do. The whole idea of OLE-DB is to broaden the range of database types that you can access with your Visual Basic applications. Obviously, if you do need to access both ODBC and tabular data with a single application, then OLE-DB provides one of the better solutions for doing so.

Understanding how ADO differs from OLE-DB

ADO is the preferred (and easiest) method for creating data source connections in new Visual Basic applications because all of the design tools are designed to work with it. The following sections will tell you about the differences between OLE-DB and ADO (and associated component features), and provide you with an overview of ADO. A third section will help you to understand how each of the connection types that we've talked about so far fits into the grand scheme of database access.

ADO features

Microsoft is constantly trying to improve data access for its programming language products. ADO represents a new way to provide database access through the combination of data-bound ActiveX controls and an ADODC (ADO Data Control). The ADODC acts as a data source that defines where the information you want to display is stored and the requirements for accessing that data. You'll need to provide the ADODC with six pieces of information: OLE-DB provider name (like SQL Server); DSN (the data source name as specified in the ODBC applet of the Control Panel);

username; password; record source (usually a SQL query); and connection string. The ActiveX controls are used to display the contents of the data source.

ADO provides several advantages over previous database access methods. The following list will describe them for you.

✦ **Independently created objects:** You no longer have to thread your way through a hierarchy of objects. This feature allows you to create only the objects that you need, reducing memory requirements and enhancing application speed as a result.

✦ **Batch updating:** Instead of sending one change to the server, you can collect them in local memory and send all of them to the server at once. This results in improved application performance (because the update can be performed in the background) and reduced network load.

✦ **Stored procedures:** These procedures reside on the server as part of the database manager and are used to perform specific tasks on the dataset. ADO allows you to use stored procedures with in/out parameters and return value.

✦ **Multiple cursor types:** Essentially, cursors point to the data that you're currently working with. Theoretically, you can even use back-end-specific cursors.

✦ **Returned row limits:** You only get the amount of data that you actually need to meet a user request.

✦ **Multiple Recordset objects:** Allows you to work with multiple recordsets returned by stored procedures or batch processing.

✦ **Free threaded objects:** Enhances Web server performance.

There are two data-binding models used for ActiveX controls. The first, simple data binding, allows an ActiveX control like a text box to display a single field of a single record. The second, complex data binding, allows an ActiveX control like a grid to display multiple fields and records at the same time. Complex data binding also requires the ActiveX control to manage which records and fields are displayed, something that the ADODC normally takes care of for simple data binding. Visual Basic comes with several ActiveX controls that support ADO, including:

✦ DataGrid

✦ DataCombo

✦ DataList

✦ Hierarchical Flex Grid

✦ Date and Time Picker

An overview of ADO

Now that you have a slightly better understanding of OLE-DB, where does ADO fit in? As previously mentioned, ADO provides an easy method for accessing the functionality of an OLE-DB provider. In other words, ADO allows you to create applications quickly and Visual Basic to take care of some of the details that you'd normally have to consider when using OLE-DB directly.

Like OLE-DB, ADO is based on COM. It provides a dual interface: a program ID of ADODB for local operations and a program ID of ADOR for remote operations. The ADO library itself is free-threaded, even though the Registry shows it as using the apartment-threaded model. The thread safety of ADO depends on the OLE-DB provider that you use. In other words, if you're using Microsoft's ODBC OLE-DB provider, you won't have any problems. If you're using a third-party OLE-DB provider, check the vendor's documentation before assuming that ADO is thread safe (a requirement for using ADO over an Internet or intranet connection).

There are seven different objects that you'll use to work with ADO. Table 8-2 provides a list of these objects and describes how you'll use them. Most of these object types are replicated in the other technologies that Microsoft has introduced, although the level of ADO object functionality is much greater than that offered by previous technologies.

Note   Some ADO objects are represented by interfaces rather than actual classes. Table 8-2 also tells you about object associations, which will help you understand how to derive the objects that are not directly represented by Visual Basic classes.

Table 8-2 ADO Object Overview		
Object	**Class**	**Description**
Command	ADOCommand	A command object performs a task using a connection or recordset object. Even though you can execute commands as part of the connection or recordset objects, the command object is much more flexible and allows you to define output parameters.
Connection	ADOConnection	Defines the connection with the OLE-DB provider. You can use this object to perform tasks like beginning, committing and rolling back transactions. There are also methods for opening or closing the connection, and for executing commands.
Error		An error object is created as part of the connection object. It provides additional information about errors raised by the OLE-DB provider. A single error object can contain information about more than one error. Each object is associated with a specific event like committing a transaction.

Object	Class	Description
Field		A field object is composed of a single column of data contained in a recordset object. In other words, a field could be looked at as a single column in a table and contains one type of data for all of the records associated with a recordset.
Parameter	ADOParameter	Defines a single parameter for a command object. A parameter modifies the result of a stored procedure or query. Parameter objects can provide input, output, or both.
Property		Some OLE-DB providers will need to extend the standard ADO object. Property objects represent one way to perform this task. A property object contains attribute, name, type, and value information.
Recordset	ADORecordset	Contains the result of a query and a cursor for choosing individual elements within the returned table. Visual Basic gives you the option of creating both a connection and a recordset by using a single recordset object, or by using an existing connection object to support multiple recordset objects.

When should you use OLE-DB, ADO, or ODBC?

Trying to figure out which technology to use when accessing your data is never an easy job. You may need a common utility to handle more than one database type; part of your data may appear on a local hard drive, part on a network, and still other parts on a mainframe. Even the products that a client normally installs on a local machine may make the choice more difficult. For example, the level of ODBC support that you can expect might rely on which version of Microsoft Office is installed, because this product does provide ODBC support. You'll also find that ADO classes offer more objects and methods than do ODBC classes. ADO may offer some features that you absolutely have to have in your program, but you'll pay a penalty in speed to get them. For example, you'll find that both OLE-DB and ADO support DFX_Currency, which has no counterpart in ODBC.

There are a few general rules of thumb that you can use for making the choice between OLE-DB and ODBC. Because ADO is actually a wrapper for OLE-DB, the same rules that apply to OLE-DB apply to ADO. The following list provides some guidelines that will help you choose between OLE-DB and ODBC.

✦ **Non-OLE environment:** If you're trying to access a database that already supports ODBC and that database is on a server that doesn't support OLE, then ODBC is your best choice.

✦ **Non-SQL environment:** ODBC is designed to excel at working with SQL. OLE-DB provides some very definite advantages when working with a non-SQL database.

✦ **OLE environment:** The choice between OLE-DB and ODBC may be a toss-up when looking at a server that supports OLE. Normally it's a good idea to use ODBC if you have an ODBC driver available; otherwise, OLE-DB may be your only choice.

✦ **Interoperability required:** If you need interoperable database components, then OLE-DB is your only choice.

Other issues tend to compound the problem, or at least remove a handy rule that you can use to differentiate between the two technologies. For example, there are a few features that both ADO and ODBC have in common. One feature is that Visual Basic allows you to access either technology directly. This means that you'll always have full access to every feature that both ADO and ODBC can provide. (Yes, this really is a plus, but it's also a minus because one can't be called definitely superior to the other when it comes to access.)

Some of these technological similarities actually help you move your application from ODBC to ADO or vice versa if you make a wrong decision. Both technologies rely on database objects to manage the underlying DBMS, while recordset objects contain the results of queries made against the DBMS. In addition, both ODBC and ADO use database and recordset objects with similar members. Even though you'll need to make some changes to class and member names, you'll find that the code for both ODBC and ADO programming is remarkably similar.

Both ODBC and ADO rely on external drivers to get the job done. However, with ADO you also get additional help from the Microsoft Jet engine. How can this extra support make programming easier? Consider the case in which you need to perform an outer join on two databases that rely on different engines. Under ODBC, you have to perform all of the required setups manually. Using ADO means that the Microsoft Jet engine will perform these setups for you. Unfortunately, having ADO do the work means that you'll lose a level of control and part of the flexibility that you wanted to use Visual Basic to get in the first place.

There's one situation in which you absolutely can't use ADO. If you need 16-bit data access, ADO is out. You'll have to use ODBC whether you want to or not. However, very few people are working with 16-bit databases anymore. Most of your new projects will use 32-bit interfaces, which means that you'll have a choice. Because old projects already have a data-access method embedded in the code, you really won't need to make a decision there either.

One thing in which ODBC falls short is that you can't follow transactions as precisely as you can with ADO. When using ADO with the Microsoft Jet engine, you get workspace-level support for transactions. ODBC only offers transaction support at the database level, which means that you could be tracking transactions from several different workspaces at once. (This makes debugging very difficult and could cause other kinds of problems as well.)

Note   ADO provides database-level support when used with an ODBC database, the same level of support that ODBC provides. You don't gain the workspace-level-of-transaction-support benefit unless you use the Microsoft Jet engine.

Summary

This chapter has provided you with insights about COM+, n-tier computing, and the Microsoft DNA model. Here are some additional conclusions that you can draw from the contents of this chapter.

✦ There's a lot of hype in the media about COM+. Separate the hype from real-world expectations before you begin application development or you'll find that your application doesn't meet anticipated flexibility or performance requirements.

✦ The two major Visual Basic COM+ limitations are the lack of support for TNA and an inability to use object pooling with Visual Basic components.

✦ N-tier computing doesn't equate to the three level diagrams that you see at seminars and conferences. An n-tier environment means that the client makes a single request that requires a response from one or more servers acting as a unit.

✦ The three levels of DNA model application support are client, business logic, and back-end processing.

✦ There's little you can do to save spaghetti code that's lurking around in your company. In most cases, you'll want to redesign the application from scratch prior to moving it to Windows 2000.

✦ Moving old applications to Windows 2000 includes five steps: creating an application diagram, deciding what type of components you need to replicate the application's functionality, creating the components, moving your business logic to its new location, and testing your new application.

✦ Reducing network traffic is essential in the distributed application environment. A poorly formatted or incomplete data request will often affect more than one server and will have an impact on the network bandwidth available for other requests.

✦ Distributed application development allows developers to create a new class of intelligent component that can better handle user input errors and to provide users with enhanced feedback on the source of a problem.

✦ Use smaller or one way packets to reduce network traffic. Adding Queued Components allows you to even out the remaining workload so that network servers can handle a larger load by working during off-peak processing times.

✦ There are three main access technologies used for databases in the Windows 2000 environment: ODBC, OLE-DB, and ADO.

✦ ODBC provides three main connection types: user, system, and file data source names (DSNs).

✦ The Tracing tab of the ODBC Data Source Administrator dialog box contains troubleshooting and diagnostic options for your ODBC connections.

✦ OLE-DB provides some of the same services as ODBC, but in a completely different way. While ODBC uses direct programming methodologies, OLE-DB relies on components, interfaces, methods, and properties to do its work.

✦ ADO is actually a component wrapper for OLE-DB. It's the level up from the low level access that OLE-DB provides.

✦ Choosing between ODBC, OLE-DB, and ADO can be tough in some situations. It's important to choose the best technology for your project that also maintains the correct level of interoperability.

✦   ✦   ✦

Writing COM+ Applications

Creating Simple Components

Component technology has been around for a very long time now. We've all used simple components to make our applications more modular and work better. Whenever you have code that you use in more than one application, that code is a good candidate for inclusion within a component. In fact, a number of the common components in use today exist because someone used a bit of code often enough to create a component that could standardize access and eliminate the need to write the code yet again. Using components allows a developer to work faster and create applications with fewer bugs. Suffice it to say, there's little doubt about the usefulness of components.

This chapter looks at simple component technology. You've probably visited this issue many times in your development efforts. However, the kind of component technology that we'll look at is different. Instead of looking at standard components that you could use to build an application, we'll look at components that are applications by themselves. That type of component is essentially what a Microsoft Management Console (MMC) snap-in is; it's a component that exists as a separate entity to perform some kind of configuration task for a much larger application. MMC itself is a container application used to hold components of a very specific type.

Of course, MMC snap-ins are just a subset of a new type of component for Windows 2000. As the book progresses, we'll look at a wealth of other component types that are now part of large-scale application development. The two major reasons to work with the example in this chapter, therefore, is to learn how to build your own configuration components that rely on MMC and to see one of the new component types for Windows 2000.

The first section of this chapter introduces you to the various component types. Most of the information in this section is a repeat of what you've read in the past. Of course, we'll also look at the new component types for both COM+ and

Windows 2000, so even those of you who are experienced programmers will want to read this section. However, we'll go through the new component types more thoroughly as the book progresses (this is the overview), so those of you who are experienced COM/COM+ developers may want to skip this section.

MMC snap-ins are useful for a variety of tasks, not just application configuration. The second section of the chapter looks at some of these uses. Although the majority of your programming efforts with MMC will revolve around application configuration, it pays to know these alternative uses as well.

The third section is where the main event takes place. I'll show you how to create an MMC snap-in. We don't create anything too exotic, but the sample shows you some of the basics that you need for any type of snap-in. Of course, part of any component creation is knowing what interfaces you need — we'll look at some of the ways that you can view the interfaces of existing and new components. There are several important features in this section. For example, we spend time discussing some of the things that you can do to speed the development process. We also look at what you need in the way of server setup, as well as how to install the component after you create it.

After you've created a component, you need to test it. That's what we do in the fourth section of the chapter. We'll discuss two testing strategies, one of which is quick, and the other of which is more thorough. Both testing strategies are important because you need to know that a component will work as anticipated on any system. Of course, we all create absolutely perfect code, but sometimes, even after our best efforts, bugs show up in the components that we create. Part of the testing process is to find these bugs and wipe them out quickly. This section shows you how to do that. Finally, after testing is complete, you'll want to install the component on a production system. The last topic in this section discusses the various pitfalls of production system installation.

You can create a perfect component, thoroughly test it, avoid every pitfall, and still run into problems. The fifth section of the chapter will look at some of the component problems that you can run into and methods for fixing them. Obviously, there are phase-of-the-moon problems that won't appear in this section, but the problem descriptions that you do find will help with those that aren't discussed.

Understanding the Various Component Types

Visual Basic allows you to create an assortment of components limited only by imagination and coding ability. We've already looked at the issue of what constitutes a component in Chapter 4, so we won't discuss it again here. Visual Basic comes with five component project types that are designed to make component creation easier. Table 9-1 provides a list of these projects and describes how you'll use them. (You'll find all five projects in the New Project dialog box.)

Tip The five component project types shown in Table 9-1 are only the beginning. Consider these as the base project types from which you can derive specific projects. Microsoft and third parties also make other projects available, as we'll see later in this section.

Table 9-1 **Visual Basic Component Project Types**	
Project	*Description*
ActiveX Control	Creates an in-process server specifically designed for application development. For example, use this to create a new type of pushbutton.
ActiveX DLL	Creates a standard in-process server. Remember that an in-process server always executes in the same memory space as the client, which means that it can't execute on another machine. This type of component is often used for windowless (no user interface) components or container components like the MMC snap-in that we create later.
ActiveX Document DLL	Creates a form-based in-process server designed to manipulate data in some way and present it to the user. The DLL version is normally used to display data exclusively within a browser. It provides better performance and a smaller memory footprint than the EXE version.
ActiveX Document EXE	Creates a form-based out-of-process server designed to manipulate data in some way and present it to the user. The EXE version is normally used when the server will also act as a stand-alone application. It features better reliability and security.
ActiveX EXE	Creates a standard out-of-process server. Use this type of component to execute code on a remote machine by using DCOM. This is also the correct choice when (for reliability or security reasons) you want to use a separate memory space for the component.

As you can see from Table 9-1, the ActiveX DLL is the most appropriate project type for the MMC snap-in example in this chapter. It's also the project type to choose for COM+ components. However, choosing the right project isn't the only requirement for getting a successful component; you also need to add the correct interfaces. The first section that follows tells you about the interfaces required for various MMC snap-in functions.

Because we're talking about tools in this chapter, it's handy to classify administrative tools by type. The second section will help you to understand that various type of administrative level tools that you can create by using component technology. It will also discuss the times when a component isn't the right choice, is one of several available choices, or is only part of the solution. Of course, you can also make these tools by using desktop applications, but doing so isn't as flexible as using components. That flexibility is one of the major advantages of using a container like MMC. All you have to do is write the essential code to display data, allow the administrator to manipulate data and component settings, and output event information. You can leave the user interface management elements up to the container.

The final section will help you to decide which tool is appropriate to use in a given circumstance. Choosing a tool type is an important first step. Some situations appear to require a manual tool, when, in reality, automated monitoring of a condition will work better. For example, you can easily monitor the status of a network by using polling, but this technique wastes such system resources as bandwidth. A better choice is to place a service on each server that sends a message to the network administrator only when an error event takes place. Having to make decisions like this makes it difficult to develop the right administrative tools, especially if you don't do a lot of planning prior to creating your code.

MMC snap-in interface description

As previously mentioned, the basic component projects allow you to create just about any type of component for Windows 2000. This isn't always the most efficient way to do things, as we'll see in the "Creating a Simple MMC Snap-In" section of the chapter. If you decide to go this route, however, you need to create a type library for your project by using the interfaces found in Table 9-2. These interfaces are those that are specific to MMC snap-ins. In other words, they aren't used for other purposes.

Table 9-2 Overview of Required MMC-Specific Snap-In Interfaces	
Interface	**Description**
IConsole2	This is the main interface that allows your component to communicate with the console. It allows you to do things such as set the Result View Pane column heading text. You'll get a pointer to this interface through the `IComponent::Initialize()` and `IComponentData::Initialize()` methods.

Interface	Description
IConsoleNameSpace2	This interface allows you to enumerate subcontainers within the Scope Pane. For example, you might create a main node for all of the employees in your company and a series of subcontainers that contain the employee name and other pertinent information.
IConsoleVerb	Think of action words when you think about this interface. It allows you to request actions from the console such as cut, paste, copy, delete, properties, rename, refresh, and print.
IContextMenuCallback	This interface allows you to add menu items to a context menu. Within MMC, there's one default context menu that's associated with the Scope Pane and the Result View Pane for your snap-in. In most cases, the default context menu for a snap-in contains a single entry, Help. You need to implement any additional context menu items separately.
IContextMenuProvider	Allows you to create custom context menus for your snap-in. You'd use this when the default context menu would require too many changes to implement property for a particular item in either MMC pane. For example, you might write a wrapper for an ActiveX control that requires a different context menu than the main snap-in does.
IControlbar	Use this interface to create control bars for your snap-in. The control bars work just like any application control bar — the main difference is that you're implementing them within MMC instead of within a standard application frame.
IDisplayHelp	Not every snap-in requires extensive help, but you should at least provide instructions on how to use the snap-in and what the various elements are used for. This interface allows you to add the custom help for your snap-in to the main MMC help. As far as the user is concerned, the help that you add was part of the main MMC help file all the time.
IHeaderCtrl	This interface allows you to modify and manipulate the Result View Pane column headings. You can add or remove columns, change the text that they contain, and change their width by using the methods in this interface.
IToolbar	Use this interface to create toolbars for your snap-in. These toolbars work just like any application toolbar — the main difference is that you're implementing them within MMC instead of a standard application frame.

Continued

Table 9-2 (continued)

Interface	Description
IImageList	This is one of the more common interfaces that you'll implement because it contains the list of images that you'll use to display items in both the Scope Pane and Result View Pane. Normally, you need a minimum of two icons: a 16 × 16-pixel image for small icon item displays and a 32 × 32-pixel image for large icon item displays. In addition, you may want to add an icon for each of the node types that you add to the MMC display. The image list uses virtual index numbers because it gets shared by all of the snap-ins currently loaded by MMC. The index number that you provide for an image gets mapped automatically to the real number within the image list.
IMenuButton	This interface allows you to add, delete, or modify custom buttons on the menu bar. These buttons are associated with your snap-in and allow the user to perform special tasks within your snap-in without having to rely on actual menu entries.
IPropertySheetCallback	Use this interface to add or remove a property page to the property sheet for your snap-in.
IPropertySheetProvider	This is the interface that you use to create, find, or show a property sheet for your snap-in. Extension snap-ins can also use this interface to add extension property sheets to the property sheet created by the main snap-in.
IResultData	You always need to use this interface because it contains the methods required to add items to the Result View Pane. This interface also contains all of the required item management methods, allows you to define the total number of items displayed in the Result View Pane, and performs visual modifications like sorting the items currently displayed in the Result View Pane.
IRequiredExtensions	Use this interface to add and enable any extension snap-ins required by your snap-in.

COM communication is definitely a two-way street. You have to implement certain interfaces within your MMC snap-in to make it work at all. In addition, there are optional interfaces that you can implement to extend the functionality of your MMC snap-in. In fact, as we've seen in other chapters, the interfaces that you implement often determine the functionality of your component and give it a unique personality when compared to other components of nearly the same type. Table 9-3 provides an overview of the required and optional interfaces for an MMC snap-in. Other types of components also use these interfaces, so you'll definitely see them used in other places. This table isn't all-inclusive — it doesn't cover common interfaces that generic components might implement.

Table 9-3
Overview of Required and Optional MMC Snap-In-Related Interfaces

Interface	Description
IComponent	This is one of several required interfaces that allow MMC to communicate with your component. You override the methods in this interface to provide a unique implementation of the Result View Pane. The two most commonly overridden methods are `Initialize()` and `GetDisplayInfo()`. Most MMC snap-ins use this interface to work with the Result View Pane of MMC.
IComponentData	This is the second of several required interfaces that allow MMC to communicate with your component. In this case, you override the default methods in order to allow MMC to work with the data provided by your component. Most MMC snap-ins use this interface to work with MMC's Scope Pane.
IExtendContextMenu	This interface allows an MMC snap-in extension to add new entries to a context menu.
IExtendControlbar	This interface allows an MMC snap-in extension to add a custom control bar to MMC.
IExtendPropertySheet2	This interface allows an MMC snap-in extension to add property pages to the property sheet for an item. You can also use the methods in this interface to query existing pages and to obtain the watermark and header information for existing property pages.
IEnumTASK	Use this interface with the IExtendTaskPad interface. It allows you to enumerate the tasks that will be added to a taskpad.
IResultDataCompare	This interface allows your MMC snap-in to compare items in the Result View Pane against one another when they're in sorted order.

Continued

	Table 9-3 *(continued)*
Interface	**Description**
ISnapinAbout	Although from a strict functionality perspective this interface isn't required, most MMC snap-ins implement it. The methods in this interface allow the MMC snap-in to display information about itself so that the user can learn more about the MMC snap-in without too much difficulty. Most of the information obtained by using this interface is simple. For example, MMC can call on the `GetProvider()` method to learn who created the MMC snap-in.
IResultOwnerData	This is an optional interface that allows you to create virtual lists. While it does take some time to implement this interface, you'll notice a performance increase in some types of data-intensive snap-ins by doing so.
ISnapinHelp	This interface allows MMC to determine the location of the MMC snap-ins help file. The file is then added to the main MMC help file so that the user can more easily locate information about the MMC snap-in while looking through the standard help file.
IToolbar	Use this interface to create, delete, and manipulate toolbars associated with your MMC snap-in. Each toolbar is created in its own band on the control bar.

There's an easier way to create an MMC snap-in than implementing a type library. It's the one that we'll use in this chapter. I'll describe the full process for creating an MMC snap-in the easy way in the "Creating the Component Shell" section of this chapter. What you need to do right now is install the Windows Platform SDK. When you install the Windows Platform SDK, you'll see a new project type in your Visual Basic New dialog box similar to that shown in Figure 9-1.

Figure 9-1: Installing the Windows Platform SDK will give you a new project type called SnapIn.

Note   You must install the January 2000 (or later version) of the Windows Platform SDK because older versions don't provide the required MMC snap-in support. There is a Web Resource in the "Creating a Simple MMC Snap-In" section of the chapter that will help you locate a copy of the current Platform SDK.

An overview of tool types

There are many ways to classify the tools that administrators commonly use on a network. In days gone by, these tools would have been created as individual applications that the administrator would have learned about one at a time. Component containers like MMC allow tools to use a common interface, so that they're easier for the administrator to find and master. In addition, using component technology reduces development time.

No matter what type of tool creation technology you use, certain design factors remain the same. Deciding what kind of tool is required to complete a given task is an important part of the tool specification. The job that the tool is required to perform affects the capabilities that it possesses. The following sections discuss the various types of tools that you can create and help you to understand their design requirements.

Classifying by general use

An obvious method of classifying a tool is to determine what you'll use it for in a general way. For example, do you want a tool to monitor the network and alert you to possible problems, or do you need a proactive tool that performs maintenance on a regular basis so that there won't be a need to monitor in the first place? The following list discusses some of the ways to define tool type by general usage.

✦ **Monitor:** This is the type of software that administrators use on a daily basis. It helps them track the status of the network. For example, monitor software can tell an administrator how much memory the server has left or the status of the hard drives. The monitor administrative tool is a perfect example of an MMC snap-in candidate. Administrators normally want to monitor the network from the workstation at their desk. MMC allows this kind of flexibility without any special programming. You won't get this kind of support with desktop applications unless you add special code to make it happen.

✦ **Analysis:** There are times when simply knowing the network's statistics isn't enough. Analysis software takes raw input from monitoring software, studies it, and then returns the result. For example, an analysis tool might try to predict hardware failures based on certain network trends such as the number of errors found while doing normal hard disk maintenance. This is another category of administrative tool that works well with MMC because the administrator will want to track this information from the local workstation.

✦ **Event:** Tools don't always provide a proactive feature; they may be reactive instead. A hard drive failure is something that you can prepare for and even anticipate, but it's not something that you can predict with absolute accuracy. Some developers create desktop applications that periodically poll the servers for failure conditions. You could provide the same (or better) functionality by using an MMC snap-in. However, this is one of those situations when an MMC snap-in may not be the best choice. The best way to monitor failure conditions is to create a service and then allow that service to send e-mail to the administrator when a failure occurs.

✦ **Automated Maintenance:** Some types of maintenance that you need to perform daily don't require any form of administrator input. For example, tape backup software has been automated for quite some time. The administrator needs to set up the parameters only once, and then the software can automatically perform the maintenance from that point on. Any time that you can automate a maintenance task it increases network administrator efficiency and reduces the chance of error. This is one type of administrative software that requires two levels of application support. An MMC snap-in will allow the administrator to configure and monitor the background task, while a service actually performs the task in the background. It's usually not safe to assume that you can answer every administrative software need with a single application.

✦ **Manual Maintenance:** Testing software was probably one of the first administrator tools created. It's important to test the network and verify that it actually works as intended — that there isn't some hidden flaw waiting to cause data corruption or other problems. Some of these testing tasks require constant monitoring, input, or even analysis on the part of the network administrator. These kinds of tasks are perfect candidates for manual maintenance utilities. This is another task that you could perform by using an MMC snap-in. In fact, you'll notice that Microsoft has already moved this functionality to MMC snap-ins for standard Windows 2000 utilities and that this new format has been well received. Any task that requires direct administrative input is a good candidate for an MMC snap-in.

✦ **Configuration:** Software today is more flexible than ever before, which means that there are more configuration options than ever before. Sometimes an operating system vendor hides some of the more powerful configuration options because the vendor fears that the end-user will use the options incorrectly. This particular problem happens all of the time with Windows. Power Toys, a set of utilities designed by some Microsoft engineers, is a perfect example of a tool designed to overcome the limitations of the built-in configuration options of the operating system. Because you can assign individual security restrictions to your MMC snap-ins, they make the perfect configuration utilities. You can hide dangerous utilities from prying eyes by setting the correct security and making it a manual addition to a console, rather than a default console setting stored in the Administrative Tools folder.

✦ **Installation:** Administrators continually perform installations of all kinds — everything from word processors to new operating systems. Consequently, this is one area where even a small amount of automation can produce a large increase in administrator productivity. While you might be able to configure an automated installation setup by using an MMC snap-in, normally you'll want to use the Windows 2000 Installer to perform the actual installation process.

✦ **User Assistance:** All of the large software companies have come to the same conclusion about user support — it's less expensive to write software to do the job than it is to hire support personnel. Witness all of the automated methods that these vendors employ to direct your attention to some other source of help. Telephone lines usually have menuing systems that offer everything from fax-back support to recorded-message help. Online sites provide complex search systems that allow users to find information themselves, rather than depend on human support.

Once you look at these large vendor offerings and analyze why the vendor is going to all the trouble of setting up nonhuman user assistance, it becomes obvious why you might also need to do the same thing to make administrators at your company more efficient. User-assistance software requires constant configuration, monitoring, and updates. You can use MMC snap-ins to perform all of these required tasks. It might be a good idea to place these three functions in separate components, however, so that you can set security for each task individually.

✦ **Tracking:** Records are the mainstays of many administrators. Unfortunately, few administrators have the time to keep records that are both complete and up-to-date. Automating the task of tracking various maintenance and error events on a server makes it easier for an administrator to locate problems based on the history of the system. Of course, all default Windows 2000 monitoring is accessed by using an MMC snap-in. You'll find this MMC snap-in in the Performance console by using the System Monitor MMC snap-in. Figure 9-2 is an example of the System Monitor utility.

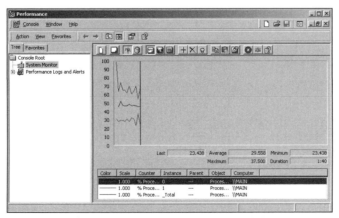

Figure 9-2: The System Monitor MMC snap-in is just one example of an administrator tool used to track system performance.

Note It's not hard to see that there are a lot of different tool functions. There are probably a few tool types that the foregoing list doesn't consider. In short, you need to figure out exactly how you plan to use a tool before you begin to design it. You also need to consider elements like security and the number of tools required to perform the task. The way that you use a tool will decide such things as the user interface and the form factor of the tool itself. It pays to consider using MMC in place of desktop applications, services, or agents whenever possible because of the level of automation that MMC provides.

Classifying by location, user, and data sensitivity

Another way to look at tools is to determine where they'll be used and who will use them. For example, you need a tool with an extensive help system and limited potential for harming the network if the person using it is a novice administrator or trainee. On the other hand, an expert administrator who wants total server control from a remote location will want a tool with robust features and a minimum of chatter (overly helpful messages and help system). This advanced administrator tool also requires a small footprint so that it's portable and easily downloadable.

You can get both of these features by using an MMC snap-in. Many MMC snap-ins will allow you to configure their appearance. Figure 9-3 is just one example of customization. This example is of the Customize View dialog box used with System Monitor. It's also possible to automate the view configuration process by using Registry entries. Using the name of the currently logged in user will allow you to set the view according to that person's access rights. The following list looks at the ways that you could classify tool type by location and user level.

Figure 9-3: Many MMC snap-ins allow you to customize their appearance, a task that could be performed automatically based on the rights of the logged in user.

✦ **Distance:** The distance between your workstation and the server makes a great deal of difference in the type of tool you create. A tool that's used on a LAN doesn't necessarily have to be as small or as network bandwidth efficient as a tool that is created for use on the Internet. In some cases, this means that a tool designed for LAN use can combine more functions into a single large tool, rather than force the administrator to rely on smaller single-use tools that are easy to download.

✦ **Level of Expertise:** A tool designed for a new administrator will normally require more in the way of assistance features. For example, the tool may include more dialog boxes that alert the administrator to potential risks and help screens that fully describe tool features. Unfortunately, adding a lot of these types of features can significantly increase the size of the tool and make the job of managing the network a frustrating experience in button pushing for experienced users. Consequently, you normally want to create tools that consider the needs of the administrator that they're designed to help.

✦ **Communication Media:** LANs normally have high-speed connections, so creating a tool that communicates a lot with the server isn't a big problem. On the other hand, a dial-up connection is almost ridiculously slow. Obviously, you want to optimize communications for the remote administrator who's using a dial-up connection. In some cases, this may even mean cutting features in exchange for speed.

✦ **Data Sensitivity:** Adding security to an application slows it down. It doesn't matter whether that application is an administrator tool or not. Some of the tools that you design will handle extremely sensitive data such as user passwords, while other tools will handle nonsensitive data such as server processing speeds. In short, the sensitivity of the information that the tool is designed to handle determines whether that data needs to be encrypted (as well as the level of encryption), which, in turn, determines things such as tool-processing speed.

✦ **Management Requirements:** A tool that simply monitors network statistics is less complex to build than one that uses those statistics to predict things such as hardware failures. The complexity of the management task that the tool is designed to handle determines its characteristics.

Determining which tool type to use

In some cases, the choice of tool type is relatively easy to make. For example, a sole administrator who works with a small-sized company with three shifts will definitely want a set of tools that work well over a dial-up connection. (Unless, of course, the administrator actually enjoys going to work in the middle of the night only to discover that there's absolutely nothing wrong with the server.) For example, the administrator may want a tool that checks the current level of processor usage or that can determine whether a hardware failure really has occurred. MMC snap-ins work extremely well in a remote access situation because you can dial up another server and have its statistics appear in place of the local machine statistics. Obviously, you need to exercise some care because an MMC snap-in can be just as data intensive as any other application—proper design is critical in this case.

However, some choices aren't quite so easy because you don't know what an administrator will require in the future. For example, just because the administrator performs all network maintenance on the job site today doesn't necessarily mean that this will be true in the future. The company could expand to another building or the company may decide to outsource some of the administrative tasks to an off-site consultant who will need the tools that you build to perform the job correctly. Again, MMC snap-ins are a good choice because they'll work on any Windows 2000 machine that they're registered on and they have the flexibility required to perform the same operation from a local or remote location.

Unless the use, location, and expertise level for a tool is well known, it pays to spend some time looking at both current and future needs. Custom tools take time to build — longer, in many cases, than custom applications — so assessing the requirements for the tool up front is critical. Part of the tool type determination process, therefore, is to figure out how the administrator will use the tool in the present and in the future.

Obviously, part of the longevity consideration hinges on how long you expect to need the tool. A tool designed to answer a shortcoming of one version of an operating system may not be needed for very long. MMC snap-ins are relatively easy to develop, but may not be the best answer for a short-term solution. In this case, you may decide to use a desktop dialog-based application. On the other hand, a special monitoring tool may be useful through several server software updates. Using an MMC snap-in is a great choice when longevity is a consideration because component technology is less likely to change and is modular. This means that change in the user interface is less likely to impact the usability of your tool.

A basic question that you need to answer about using an MMC snap-in versus some other form of tool is what operating system support you'll receive. MMC snap-ins aren't a good choice if most of the workstations on your network use Windows 9*x* or older versions of Windows NT. However, they're one of the best possible choices when a network depends on Windows 2000, because this is the tool of choice for Windows 2000 machines. If all of the administrators are using Windows 2000, but the average user isn't, it might be possible to combine an agent with an MMC snap-in to perform a required level of system monitoring. Remember to combine tools when a single tool won't do the job for you.

Another problem is determining how much and what type of information the administrator actually requires. For example, you may build a monitoring tool that uses existing server data only to learn that the administrator ends up calculating the value that they really needed. In some cases, an analysis tool that does some or all of the calculation work for the administrator is actually a much better choice than the easy-to-build monitoring tool.

There's also a question of how much automation a tool really needs. Too much automation may give the administrator a false sense of security, making it possible that the tool won't actually prevent the catastrophe that it's designed to prevent. Automation should relieve an administrator of needless tedium, not the responsibility of making decisions based on all of the available facts.

Defining level of expertise is something that can also be difficult. Even an expert administrator may have educational or experiential gaps that prevent him or her from getting full use from a custom tool. If portability is a concern, but the administrator's true level of expertise is in question, you might consider making help an optional part of the tool. The administrator could always download just the amount of help he or she needs to do the required work.

As you can see, it's important not only to determine exactly what kind of tool you need to create, but also to specify the range of its operation. In many cases, a custom-built tool starts out as a handy gizmo on the programmer's desktop and ends up in the hands of a user who may not have any idea of what it does. Designing a tool properly from the outset reduces the risk that a tool will be used improperly, even if it does fall into the hands of someone who was never supposed to see, much less use it. In short, always choose the type of tool based on who will most likely end up using it, rather than the person who originally designed it.

Tip   Password protection is a wonderful thing when it comes to administrative tools. Adding password protection doesn't require much code and can take dangerous tools out of the hands of novice users who could use them to damage the network. Obviously, the kind of security that you add depends on just how dangerous the tool is. However, it always pays to err on the side of security rather than to learn later that your tool increased the network administrator's workload after a server failure.

Ranish Partition Manager

The partition manager that comes with Windows 2000 normally does a good job of ensuring that you can set up your hard drive correctly. If you can't get things to work quite right, however, there are tools in both the Windows 2000 Support Tools and the Windows 2000 Resource Kit that can make things easier. Even with these tools, however, you may have to use special software to get the most out of your system or to provide additional boot flexibility. This is especially true for developers who need to test every application with more than one version of an operating system at a time. For example, you may have to test the same component with Windows 9x, Windows Millenium, Windows NT, and Windows 2000. Normally, this means using several machines because you can't place this many versions of Windows on one machine. The Ranish Partition Manager is just one of many tools that can provide the additional flexibility required to perform the required level of operating system testing on one machine.

The Ranish Partition Manager comes in several languages in addition to English, including Czech, Dutch, French, German, Italian, Russian, Spanish, and Swedish. This is a major benefit if you also need to support more than one application language. It also means that you don't always have to do things in English.

Continued

Continued

Another major benefit of the Ranish Partition Manager is that it's shareware and you can download it for a try before you buy. The main Web site for this product is at `http://www.ml.brooklyn.cuny.edu/~mranish/part/`. However, you may want to tag the specific Web site for your language instead of this main page. Because the vendor is constantly upgrading the product and making the product betas available to the public, you'll want to check the Web site for upgrades to any product that you purchase. The author's home page is at `http://come.to/ranish`.

This is an interesting product for several reasons. For one thing, this is a grass roots kind of product that provides a lot of features. The author is genuinely interested in receiving product feedback and even had a survey on his Web site at the time of this writing asking users which features they'd like to see in the product. While the Web site lacks some of the pizzazz normally associated with commercial Web sites, you'll instantly see that this product has a lot to offer where it counts. Here are just a few features that you'll want to know about—the product does support others.

✦ Save and restore the master boot record (MBR)

✦ Create and delete partitions

✦ View integrated device electronics (IDE) hard drive information

✦ Format and resize file allocation table (FAT) 16 and FAT 32 file systems

✦ Comes with Advanced Boot Manager

Note that this product won't format an NTFS partition for you. Therefore, you'd still need to use this product in conjunction with the Windows 2000 boot manager if you need to boot more than just DOS FAT16 partitions. The point is that you can begin with a DOS FAT16 partition, and then convert it as necessary to other partition types by using native operating system features. In addition, even though DOS FAT 16 partition isn't the most efficient partition type for running Windows NT or Windows 2000, you can use the DOS FAT16 partition type as a starting point for Windows NT or Windows 2000 installation. If the ability to boot a variety of operating systems is more important than absolute efficiency, you may still find that the Ranish Partition Manager is the product that you need for development.

The last feature, the Advanced Boot Manager, is interesting because it allows you to reconfigure your system to boot in a variety of ways. This normally isn't a problem with servers, but it may be a plus in some cases. For example, your company may have a development server that you need to boot in several different ways to reproduce certain development environments. You may have a short-term need to boot the server in two different ways while the company goes through a transition. There are also situations when you may need to have multiple boot partitions to meet the needs of the scientific community. The following list tells you about some of the features of the Advanced Boot Manager.

✦ Boot menu with password protection

✦ Automatic partition hide and unhide

✦ Boot any OS from the second hard drive

✦ Create up to 31 primary partitions on a single hard drive

✦ Detect presence of the boot viruses in memory

The first feature in this list is the one that attracted my attention. I normally maintain a DOS partition on my servers so that I can run diagnostics when the server is offline. Even though the DOS partition is small and the server is locked in a closet, someone could use that little breach in security to do something with the server. The ability to password protect the boot manager is a real plus.

The author of the Ranish Partition Manager is currently working on an upgrade of the product. This product is in beta at the time of this writing, but should be in released form as you read this. Some of the expected new product features are:

✦ Handle disks over 8G

✦ Copy disks and partitions

✦ Format and resize FAT partitions

✦ Boot MS-, PC-, DR-DOS and Windows NT from partitions above 2G

✦ Boot Partition Manager from a floppy without any OS

✦ A SIMULATION program that lets you play with Partition Manager without permanently affecting the real disk

Uses for MMC Snap-Ins

Windows 2000 is the first version of Windows to come with MMC support right out of the package. This is an important new feature because it allows you to create consoles (displays of server information) that use a single user interface instead of the myriad of administrative tools used in the past. In addition, the use of MMC snap-in components makes it easy to extend the administrator tool set while keeping the learning curve for the administrator very low.

We've already looked at some of the ways that you can use MMC snap-ins in the, "An Overview of Tool Types" section of this chapter. Saying that MMC snap-ins are limited to administrative functions, however, is like saying that COM is limited to desktop application controls. There are four standard uses for MMC snap-ins as defined in the following list.

✦ **Monitoring:** There are many ways to monitor your system. The most common way is to check system performance or usage statistics by using the System Monitor MMC snap-in. Figure 9-2 shows a typical example of the System Monitor that you can use to check system performance.

However, there are other ways to monitor your system, depending on the features that you install. For example, if you look into the Component Services console, you'll notice that the Distributed Transaction Coordinator snap-in includes a Transaction Statistics folder. This folder will tell you how well MTS is performing and about the current transaction error count. Monitoring could even include something as simple as the activity indicators in the COM+ Applications snap-in (found in the Component Services console). A rotating ball indicates that the COM+ application is active. Otherwise, you see a ball with a plus sign that doesn't move.

✦ **Configuration:** There are so many MMC snap-ins used for configuration purposes, that it's hard to know where to start. Every MMC snap-in includes a Properties dialog box that you'll use to configure the MMC snap-in, but configuring both hardware and software is where you'll use them most often. Look in the Computer Management console and you'll see a wealth of configuration features. Of course, the configuration tools that everyone knows about appear in the System Tools MMC snap-in. It contains MMC snap-ins, like the Device Manager shown in Figure 9-4, that allow you to manage system hardware. Less known, but equally important, are the configuration options found in the Services and Applications MMC snap-in. We'll use some of these configuration options later in the book when working with MSMQ and MTS applications.

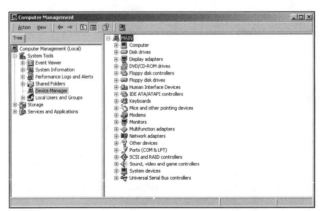

Figure 9-4: The Device Manager is accessible through an MMC snap-in; it allows you to add, update, and remove devices.

✦ **Installation:** For the most part, you'll want to install new applications by using the Windows Installer. Desktop and other application types can be installed automatically by using the Windows Installer with a little help from the user. However, there's one class of application that gets installed by using an MMC snap-in — COM+ applications. You'll install these applications by using the COM+ Applications MMC snap-in found in the Component Services console.

(See Chapter 2 for details.) It's important to realize that nothing limits you from using an MMC snap-in for installation purposes, but it's also important to look at all of the alternatives before you go this route. Consider an MMC snap-in for configuration installs — that is, those types of installs that add features to an existing product.

✦ **Security:** You'll see MMC snap-ins used for a variety of security needs. For example, the Local Security Settings console (Security Settings MMC snap-in) allows you to change the local security policies. Figure 9-5 shows what this MMC snap-in looks like. The Certification Authority console allows you to manage security certificates for your company. Of course, security appears in other forms, too. For example, the only place where you'll find role-based security is in the Component Services console as part of the COM+ Applications MMC snap-in. In short, a security-related MMC snap-in can also perform other tasks.

Figure 9-5: The Local Security Settings console allows you to change the security settings for the local machine.

Tip   One of the best places to look for new uses of MMC snap-ins is in the Administrative Tools folder and within any new applications that you purchase. In general, you'll find that these uses fall within the four categories that we've talked about in this chapter. However, the way that the MMC snap-in is used can help you to define new uses for your own tools.

The standard methods of using MMC snap-ins are fine. You'll find that the MMC snap-ins that Microsoft provides with Windows 2000 are a lot easier to use than all of the individual tools required to manage Windows NT. In addition, creating an MMC snap-in is a lot easier for the developer than attempting to create a new utility every time an administrator has a new management requirement. Unfortunately, these standard uses don't address all of the needs for both users and administrators. There are ways to use MMC snap-ins that aren't immediately apparent. The following list provides some ideas on how you can use MMC snap-ins within your organization to extend the ability of both users and administrators to manage their individual systems and the network. These nonstandard uses open an entirely new realm of MMC snap-in types. Obviously, you'll want to spend time figuring out how to best use the capability that MMC provides and finding the easiest way to allow the user to access this capability.

✦ **Informational:** Many times help desk personnel need to know information about the user's machine. Getting the information out of the user, however, can try anyone's patience. It's not that the user is being evasive; the problem is that the information is spread out into places that the user normally doesn't look at. Informational MMC snap-ins would allow the user to view all of the required information in one place. For that matter, the administrator or help desk personnel could look at the information from their MMC console without even asking the user for input. One example of this alternative use for an MMC snap-in is the contents of the System Summary folder of the System Information MMC snap-in shown in Figure 9-6.

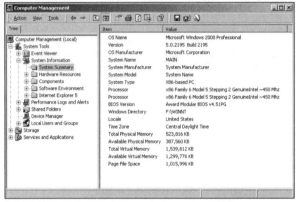

Figure 9-6: The System Summary folder contains one of the only examples of an information-only display for Windows 2000.

Tip

A problem with some Microsoft-supplied MMC snap-ins is that the snap-ins don't provide enough granularity. For example, the System Summary information shown in Figure 9-6 is fairly complete and there isn't any way that a user could damage the system by seeing it. Unfortunately, this same MMC snap-in allows the user to view other information that may not be helpful and definitely adds to the confusion factor. So, even though the System Information MMC snap-in is a good idea, it covers too much territory. Creating a user-specific version of this MMC snap-in isn't difficult and would definitely add to the user's ability to manage his or her own environment.

✦ **Diagnostic:** Windows 2000 still hides much of the system from view. This is a good feature from a security standpoint because the less that a cracker knows about your hardware, the better. It's also good from an application perspective—only the operating system should be allowed to access the one device that's used by many applications. However, the lack of diagnostics often leaves both the user and the network administrator in the dark as to the current system status. Hardware and software problems become apparent only after the device in question stops working entirely. In many cases, diagnostic software can predict a failure long enough before it occurs to ensure that there isn't any loss of service at an inconvenient time. The component nature of MMC snap-ins makes it possible for you to provide a specific level of diagnostic aid to users and a more in-depth level to administrators.

✦ **Analysis:** The ability to make decisions quickly and easily becomes ever more important as systems become more complex. Early PCs were relatively easy to tune because they contained very few parts and the technology used by those parts was easily understood. Today's PC contains many complex parts where the technology is understood by very few people. As a result, it's very hard to tune a system efficiently, much less implement the required changes. MMC snap-ins could perform various types of "what if" analysis and make tuning suggestions as the system configuration, usage, and load change. Obviously, this is only one way to use analysis. You could also use it to determine application performance, check for user interface problems, and even monitor usage habits.

Tip

There's a significant difference between monitoring and analysis MMC snap-ins. A monitoring MMC snap-in will report statistics about the system and allow the administrator to make a decision about which changes to make. While this works fine in theory, the administrator is often at a loss to explain certain system statistics because of the complexity of the system. An analysis MMC snap-in would use the raw statistics to investigate alternatives to the current system setup. While the administrator would still need to make the final decision, the analysis software would help the administrator to better understand the implications of a certain course of action. In short, an analysis MMC snap-in goes one step further in helping the administrator keep system performance at peak.

✦ **Comparative:** At present, it's hard to compare two systems by using the default MMC snap-ins provided with Windows 2000. While you can view the statistics for two machines by using the same console, you can't view them side-by-side, nor can you infer anything from the statistics provided from a system overview perspective. A comparative MMC snap-in would allow you to view two systems as equals. This type of display would be handy in a variety of ways. For example, you could use it if you wanted to judge the overall effect of making a user interface change. The first machine could contain the original version of the application; the second could contain the modified version. Comparing the usage statistics for both machines would allow you to see how the user interface change affects the user's perception of the application.

Creating a Simple MMC Snap-In

This section shows you how to create an MMC snap-in by using the MMC Snap-In Designer for Visual Basic. The snap-in will use two new Windows 2000 functions to display and change the names of the various network servers that you've installed. The GetComputerNameEx() function will allow you to display the computer's NetBIOS and DNS names in various formats (we'll explore them all). Likewise, the SetComputerNameEx() function will allow you to change these names. The example shows how to use most of the features of an MMC snap-in and provide tips on using these features efficiently. Although we won't explore every possibility, you'll walk away with enough information to build just about any MMC snap-in needed for your current projects.

We're going to look at all of the things that you can do with new SnapIn project type, rather than develop a component from scratch with the required interfaces. You'll find that using the MMC Snap-In Designer for Visual Basic is much easier than working with a type library, and that you don't give anything up by using it. If you do want to develop an MMC snap-in from scratch, the MMC Snap-In Interface Description section of the chapter will provide details on which interfaces you need to implement.

You may have heard rumors that there's no reason to install the Windows Platform SDK when using Visual Basic to develop Windows 2000 applications. While this is true for the most part, the application that we'll develop in this section requires that you install the Windows Platform SDK. The MMC Snap-In Designer for Visual Basic is only available after you install the Windows Platform SDK (the January 2000 or newer version). You can read more about this requirement at http://support.microsoft.com/support/kb/articles/q251/0/09.asp. The current version of the Windows Platform SDK is available with an MSDN subscription. You can also download it at http://msdn.microsoft.com/downloads/sdks/platform/platform.asp. In addition to getting a new project type, the Windows Platform SDK will provide you with the latest Windows 2000 programming documentation, administrative and development tools, and example code, which you can use to create better applications.

The following sections examine three important issues in creating COM+ components and administrative components like the MMC snap-in. The first section looks at creating the component shell. We'll discuss a variety of configuration issues that will ease the development process. The second section is more generic. We'll discuss ways to increase your productivity and reduce the time required to develop a new component at any time. The third section will look at the code that you need to add to make the MMC snap-in functional. While this example is somewhat generic, it does show some of the issues that you'll need to consider when creating specific MMC snap-ins of your own.

Creating the component shell

This section shows you how to create a component shell for your MMC snap-in. There are three major steps in this process. First, you create the application and add any required classes to it. Second, you modify the component properties so that the component will work better with the MMC. Third, you configure the MMC snap-in by using the designer. The following paragraphs assume that you've installed the Windows Platform SDK and have access to the SnapIn project type shown in Figure 9-1.

You can skip the configuration procedure by using the contents of the Chapt09/ Start MMC Project folder on the CD-ROM provided with this book. This folder contains the configured MMC snap-in without any of the code added. The project name is Simple MMC Snap-In.

Creating the application

Begin a new project. Select the SnapIn project from the New tab of the New Project dialog box shown in Figure 9-1. You'll see a Project dialog containing a designer and a snap-in control similar to the one shown in Figure 9-7. The designer is the element that you'll work with to configure the component. It defines MMC snap-in elements like the number of nodes and the types of views that the user will see. The control that you see after project creation is used to hold any property pages that you define. We'll look at adding component functionality in the "Adding the code" section of this chapter. I saved this project as Simple MMC Snap-In, but you can use any name that you like. The project name is changed to MySampleSnapIn. The control name is DataView, and the designer name is DataViewDesign.

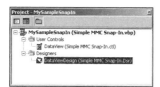

Figure 9-7: The starting SnapIn project consists of a component and a designer.

Defining the project properties

There are several project properties that you have to change to ensure that the MMC snap-in works as anticipated. Open the General tab of the Project Properties dialog box shown in Figure 9-8 by using the Project ⇨ MySampleSnapIn Properties command. You'll need to select the Apartment Threaded option in the Threading Model list box. This dialog box will also allow you to change the project name and add a description for the component. If you plan to add a help file to your project (normally a good idea), you'll want to add the help file information here.

Figure 9-8: The choice of threading model is important when creating component applications.

The Make tab also contains settings that you'll want to change, but they affect the information provided with the component, rather than component operation. For example, this is where you'll set the company name. This information appears when someone views the component's properties. We won't change this information now because it doesn't affect the operation of the component.

The Component tab shown in Figure 9-9 is the next stop. You need to set the Version Compatibility option to Binary Compatibility to ensure that the globally unique identifier (GUID) remains the same for every version of the MMC snap-in. The GUID is used by Windows to identify a particular component, so keeping the same GUID is very important. Microsoft also recommends that you change the component's file extension from OCX to DLL because most MMC snap-ins use this file extension. This change isn't very important — your component will work just fine using the OCX extension. Once you complete all required component changes, close the MySampleSnapIn Project Properties dialog box.

Figure 9-9: Setting the MMC snap-in to use binary compatibility is very important.

Using the MMC snap-in designer for Visual Basic

Configuring the MMC snap-in that you want to create comes next. Figure 9-10 shows what the designer looks like. Notice that the designer uses a hierarchical set of folders to define the various elements that you can add to any MMC snap-in that you create. Table 9-4 describes the design elements. It also defines how they're used to create various effects within an MMC snap-in.

Figure 9-10: The designer uses a hierarchical set of folders to help you design an MMC snap-in project.

Table 9-4
MMC Snap-In Designer Elements

Element	Folder	Description
Auto-Create	Node	Defines the nodes that the MMC snap-in will create automatically. There's only one automatic root node, the Static Node. This node can have any number of child nodes that can be used to create a hierarchical display. Any views that you create for a node automatically appear under the appropriate Result Views folder.
Extensions	Component (DataViewDesign)	Determines how the component extends the MMC environment. You can change the name-space, New menu, property pages, Task menu, toolbar, top menu, and View menu. All of these changes affect how the user will interact with your MMC snap-in. For example, a change to the New menu will allow the user to create new objects of specific types.
Image Lists	Tools	Contains a list of images used within your MMC snap-in. These images can be added manually or through actions on other MMC snap-in elements like a node. Images can be used for a variety of purposes, including node icons.

Continued

Table 9-4 (continued)

Element	Folder	Description
ListViews	Result Views	Lists the list views provided for viewing information that a node provides. This is the default view. However, to make this option as flexible as possible, you need to create a custom ListView. This view works just the same as the ListView common control. It allows you to display information in columns and rows by using several different display formats (large icon, small icon, list, and detail being the most common). Any views that you create for a node automatically appear under the appropriate Result Views folder.
Menus	Tools	Contains any custom menus that you want to add to the MMC snap-in. Normally, you add a menu as an MMC snap-in extension.
OCXViews	Result Views	List the views created using ActiveX controls. This result view requires that you know the GUID of the ActiveX control that you want to display. You also have a few configuration options to consider. For example, you can cache the ActiveX control to make the MMC snap-in perform better or create a new copy every time the user requests it to reduce resource usage. Any views that you create for a node automatically appear under the appropriate Result Views folder.
Other	Node	Defines the nodes that the MMC snap-in will create under specific conditions or by user request. You'll activate these nodes through application code — they don't appear automatically when the user adds the snap-in to MMC. Any views that you create for a node automatically appear under the appropriate Result Views folder.
Taskpad	Result Views	Lists special Taskpad views that you create. This is essentially a custom HTML file that contains bitmaps and other display elements, along with any information that you want to present. A single Taskpad view can contain multiple Taskpads that are accessed through an index. Any views that you create for a node automatically appear under the appropriate Result Views folder.

Element	Folder	Description
Toolbars	Tools	Contains any custom toolbars that you want to add to the MMC snap-in. Normally, you add a toolbar as an MMC snap-in extension.
URLViews	Result Views	Lists the views that contain only an URL in the scope pane. The URL may use any of the protocols available in Internet Explorer, including the file:// protocol. Any views that you create for a node automatically appear under the appropriate Result Views folder.

Note Visual Basic supports four predefined views: list, OCX, URL, and Taskpad. In addition to these predefined views that are defined at design time, you can create message views that are defined at runtime. Message views are helpful for displaying small amounts of volatile information. Usually, you'll want to use one of the other views for formatted or complex data displays. All of these views can be defined during runtime. You can also change predefined views during runtime to include additional information or features.

Now that you have a better idea of what the various views are for, it's time to look at the process for defining an MMC snap-in. The following sections will help you to develop an MMC snap-in. Some of the steps like defining the MMC snap-in name and providing a company name may seem overly simple, but I've provided them here for the sake of completeness. All of these configuration steps are required to create a complete MMC snap-in, but you don't necessary have to complete them all to make the MMC snap-in compile and be visible within MMC. In fact, you could simply compile the MMC snap-in code now, but then you wouldn't see what an MMC snap-in is capable of doing.

Identifying the MMC snap-in

The SnapIn project starts by defining every element in your project with the name SnapIn1. This is hardly useful for identification purposes. The information that we added to the Project Properties dialog box earlier will identify the file, but not the MMC snap-in within MMC. The first task, then, is to highlight the root node (DataViewDesign, in this case) and define some of the identification properties.

This is one instance when the Properties window won't have everything that you need. You'll want to open the custom properties dialog box shown in Figure 9-11. The General tab has everything we need for right now.

Figure 9-11: The General tab of the Property Pages dialog box allows you to configure your MMC snap-in.

A major decision that you have to make in this dialog is what type of MMC snap-in you want to create. The Stand Alone option (the default) allows you to create an MMC snap-in that's used by itself. It can't be called on to extend the services provided by another MMC snap-in. Selecting the Extension option means that the MMC snap-in has to be used as an extension to another snap-in; you can't display it separately in a console. Finally, the Dual Mode option gives you the freedom to use the MMC snap-in by itself or with another MMC snap-in. For the purposes of this example, we'll select the Stand Alone option because it allows you to create a small MMC snap-in that won't interfere with other MMC snap-ins already installed on your machine.

The other fields on this dialog box may seem self-explanatory, but it's important to fill them in. The Display Name field is used in several places, including the MMC tree, to identify the MMC snap-in. The Provider, Version, and Description fields are used in places like the MMC snap-in's About dialog box. Finally, the Static Node Type Name field is used to identify the static node. This data is never displayed, but it's important for making your code readable. If you have more than one result view defined, the Default Result View field will allow you to determine which result view is displayed by default. You can add other result views to the View menu, making them equally accessible to the user.

The Image Lists tab shown in Figure 9-12 becomes active only after you create an image list. MMC provides three default images for large icons, small icons, and open icons. You can, however, change these images to meet specific needs. For example, you might want to use the image of a disk drive for an MMC snap-in that works with the hard drives on a machine. We'll see in the "Designing Image Lists" section of this chapter how image lists work and the methods required to used them within an MMC snap-in.

Figure 9-12: Image Lists allows you to change the appearance of your MMC snap-in display.

Creating nodes

Every MMC project that you create will begin with the static node already included. This is the node that's displayed when you first start the MMC snap-in. However, very few MMC snap-ins use just one node. Consequently, you'll need to add one or more nodes to a project during the design process.

There are two kinds of nodes that you can add: those that get displayed automatically when the MMC snap-in starts and those that don't. If you want a node to appear immediately, you'll normally add it to the Static Node entry under Auto Create. On the other hand, if you want the node to appear later, add it under Other. This example will add two nodes — one that is displayed automatically and another that is displayed after the user selects an Advanced Display option on a menu. (We'll talk about menus in the "Adding menu and toolbar entries" section of this chapter.)

Adding a new node is easy. Just right-click the node that you want to add the node under, then choose Add child node from the context menu. The two nodes that we'll add are called Basic and Advanced. Figure 9-13 shows what they look like.

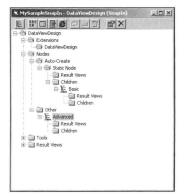

Figure 9-13: The DataViewDesign tree now contains two additional nodes.

You'll want to change the DisplayName properties for both nodes. Give the first node a DisplayName value of Basic Information and the second a DisplayName value of Advanced Information. Notice that the second node's AutoCreate property is set to False. Even if you set this property to True, the node won't appear within MMC until you provide code to display it.

Defining the views

Nodes without a view won't do much for you. You can select the node and see any child nodes that it might have, but that's about it. As previously mentioned, MMC supports five different views, four of which you can create during the design phase and one that you need to create by using code during runtime. We'll create all five of the views for our example MMC snap-in. Normally, you'd use just the views that you actually need to display data.

Adding a view is easy. Right click the Result Views folder that you want to use to hold the view, then choose Add New Result View, and select a view type. For starters, let's add a list view to the Basic node and call it BasicList. It's time to define the properties for our list view. Right-click BasicList and choose Properties from the context menu. You'll see a ListView Properties dialog box similar to the one shown in Figure 9-14.

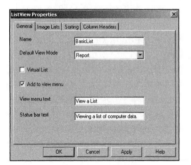

Figure 9-14: The ListView Properties dialog box allows you to configure the BasicList results view.

One of the first choices you have to make is what type of display you want the user to see when he or she first opens the view. The default setting of Large Icons won't work for the example because we're going to display several columns of data. There are five choices: Large Icons, Small Icons, List, Report, and Filtered. The Report and Filtered options refer to special instances of the detail display, which is perfect for the example. Choose the Report option because it displays the data raw form.

The list view offers the powerful feature of using virtual lists. A virtual list allows you to display many items with a single list view. However, instead of populating the entire list during initialization, you simply tell the list view how many items you intend to display. When a user activates the view, the list view will ask you to provide a list of items to display. Each time the user makes a change on the list view (like moving the thumb on the scrollbar) the list view will ask for an update. This feature requires additional code, so you normally won't use it unless you need to conserve resources and still display a larger than average list.

Use the Add to view menu option when you want to allow the user to change views to this particular view. Because we'll be adding more than one view to this node, you'll want to check out this option. Type **View a List** in the View menu text field. This is what the user will see when they look at the View menu with your MMC snap-in loaded. Type **Viewing a list of computer data** in the Status bar text field. This is what the user will see while the BasicList view is active.

As with every other object we've talked about so far, you can use an image list to define the bitmaps used for display purposes with the view. All you need to do is select the Image Lists tab and select values for both the Small Icons and Large Icons fields. Make sure you use a 16-pixel × 16-pixel bitmap for the Small Icons field and a 32-pixel × 32-pixel bitmap for the Large Icons field.

The Sorting tab will let you choose how the data you present to the user is sorted. If you're presenting the output from a database manager, this is a very handy feature. We'll be placing the data in the order in which we want to display it for this example, so you don't need to worry about the sort order for right now.

The final tab, Column Headers, appears in Figure 9-15. This is where you'll define the columns used to display data on screen. All you need to do to add a column to the view is click Insert Column. The Index field will automatically increment to the next available number. Type the text that you want to see at the top of the column in Detail view in the Text field. You have a choice of allowing the column to automatically size itself or setting the size of the column manually. Check the Auto Width option if you want to size the field automatically. Otherwise, type a number in the Width field. Finally, you'll need to choose a key for the column. This key is used within your application to access the column. It's also used by MMC to sort columns when requested.

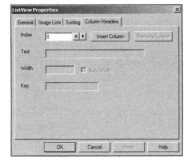

Figure 9-15: The Column Headers tab allows you to define the columns used to display data on the list view.

Because this example is designed to show how to use the `GetComputerNameEx()` and `SetComputerNameEx()` functions, we'll need three columns for the BasicList view. The first column is Computer Name Entry, with a Key field value of Name. This column contains a short name for the value that the user will see. We'll allow this column to size itself automatically. This compensates for font and information size differences on each user's machine. The second column is Description, with a Key field value of Description. You'll want to set the Width field for this column to 100. Because this column could contain more information than the user's display can handle adequately, we need to set the size to a specific value. The third column is Value and it holds the current value of the computer name entry. Give this column a Key field entry of Value and allow it to automatically size itself.

Now that you have a general idea of what the various tabs on the views do, let's add three other views to the example. Table 9-5 contains the information that you'll need to add a URL View to the Basic node and both a List View and a Taskpad to the Advanced node.

Table 9-5
View Configuration Information

Node	View Name	Tab	Field	Value

Basic	BasicURL	General	URL	`http:\\www.`
				`microsoft.`
				`com`

		General	Add to view menu	Checked
		General	View menu text	See Microsoft
		General	Status bar text	Go to the Microsoft Web Site
Advanced	AdvList	General	Default View Mode	List
		General	Add to view menu	Checked
		General	View menu text	View or Change a List
		General	Status bar text	Viewing or Changing a list of computer data.
		Column Headers (Index 1)	Text	Computer Name Entry

Node	View Name	Tab	Field	Value
Advanced (continued)		Column Headers (Index 1)	Auto Width	Checked
		Column Headers (Index 1)	Key	Name
		Column Headers (Index 2)	Text	Description
		Column Headers (Index 2)	Width	100
		Column Headers (Index 2)	Key	Description
		Column Headers (Index 3)	Text	Value
		Column Headers (Index 3)	Auto Width	Checked
		Column Headers (Index 3)	Key	Value
Advanced	AdvTask	General	Title	Computer Names View
		General	Description	A formatted view of the computer name data.
		General	Add to view menu	Checked
		General	View Menu Text	Formatted List
		General	Status Bar Text	View the formatted computer name data.

Note   We didn't add any tasks to the AdvTask (taskpad) view. The "Adding the code" section of this chapter contains more information about this view and adding tasks to it. This section has made the view available and provided some basic configuration entries for it.

Designing image lists

Image lists allow you to provide custom icons for your MMC snap-in. In this case, an image list is essentially a container for the icons that you need for the MMC snap-in display. You'll normally create bitmaps in two standard sizes (16×16 pixels and 32 × 32 pixels). There are several uses for these icon containers. For example, you can use an image list to store icons for each toolbar that you create. Custom icons are also used for the nodes and scope items within the MMC display.

When creating icons for the node and scope items, you'll actually need three sets of icons: two small 16 × 16 pixels icons and one large 32 × 32 pixels icon. Each set of icons is stored in a separate image list. The first small icon is used for closed folders, and the second small icon is used for open folders. Because all of the elements for this example will require at least three icons, we'll simply create three image lists. This first image list is named SmallIcons. It contains the standard and folder closed 16 × 16-pixel icons. The second is named LargeIcons. It contains all of the 32 × 32-pixel icons. The third is SmallOpenIcons, which is used to hold the folder open 16 × 16-pixel icons. Adding a new image list is easy. Just right-click the Image Lists folder and select Add Image List from the context menu.

On the CD-ROM

Visual Basic doesn't allow you to create icons within the IDE; you'll need a separate utility to perform this task. In addition, image lists work with BMP files, which means that you won't be able to use icons that you create in other applications without converting them first. There are icons for the sample application supplied on the CD-ROM provided with this book. Each icon filename includes a number and an icon size to make it easy to work with. For example, the first BMP file for the SmallIcons image list has a filename of 1-16X16.BMP. I added an O to the open file icons.

Once you have the image lists created, you need to add icons. Right-click the image list object, and choose Properties from the context menu. You'll see an ImageList Properties dialog box similar to the one shown in Figure 9-16. (Note that this ImageList Properties dialog box is shown with images loaded.) You can assign a key to each image list item to make it easier to work with in your code. If you do this, however, make sure that you use the same key for each version of the image; otherwise, you may get unanticipated results within the snap-in (MMC won't be able to find the required icon). Normally, using an index number is easier and less error prone when working with an MMC snap-in, even though using a key is suggested for other image list applications. On the other hand, a key value is more legible and easier for developers who follow after you to understand. In addition, a key value is the only way to ensure that you have the right icon if the image list gets reordered.

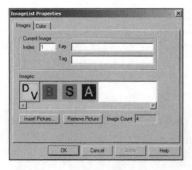

Figure 9-16: The ImageList Properties dialog box allows you to see which images are currently available within the image list, along with their properties.

Tip

The Tag field shown in Figure 9-16 isn't used by Visual Basic. You can use it, however, to provide additional information about the image to your application. For example, you could use it to identify the location of the image on disk or to store flags to queue specific application behaviors.

To add an image, click Insert Picture. You'll see a Choose an image dialog box similar to the one in Figure 9-17 that allows you to browse the hard drive for the image that you want to add. Highlight the desired image and click OK. The image will appear in a slot next to the currently selected icon. It's important to select the correct placement for the icon because MMC relies on icons that are in specific places to present objects as opened or closed, or to select the correct icon by size.

Figure 9-17: The Choose an image dialog box allows you to add icons to the image list.

Now that we have image lists to use, you need to add them to the appropriate places. The image lists are selected by every designer object that includes an Image Lists tab, like the Static Node, and by every result view that we created for this example (an example appears in Figure 9-18). All you need to do is select the image list that you want to use for a particular purpose from the list in the drop-down list box. Make sure that you choose the appropriate image list for the type of folder that you want to display (hence, the method of naming the image lists in this section).

Figure 9-18: Once you've created image lists, you can add them to the various MMC snap-in objects.

You also need to choose a folder for the various Node objects. There are two in this example, Basic and Advanced. Figure 9-19 shows that you need to change the Folder Image value to match the index number of the image in the image list that you want to use. Because there are three image lists, you can see why accurate placement of the images within the image list is important. The Basic node uses image index 2, while the Advanced node uses image index 4.

Figure 9-19: Choosing an image is important for proper display of the MMC snap-in nodes.

Understanding the image list gotchas

At this point, you may feel that everything required to make your MMC snap-in work from a graphical standpoint is in place. All you really need are some menus and toolbars to allow a user to select various snap-in options (we'll discuss menus and toolbars in the next section). Unfortunately, the way that the views work, you'll need to add a little more to the design of this project to make it work correctly.

The first concern is providing an icon for the MMC snap-in. For example, one of the fit-and-finish items that you need to consider is adding an icon to the About dialog box. Adding an icon to your MMC snap-in won't occur on the Make tab of the Project Properties dialog box. Instead, yo need to highlight the root node in the designer (DataViewDesign in this case) and change the Icon property. All you need to do is browse for the icon that you want to use in the normal way.

The various folder icons we've chosen for the Basic and Advanced nodes will also appear as they should, but only in the hierarchical folder list. The scope pane will be devoid of the appropriate result view to the Static Node. To do this, simply add a new list view as you have for the other views that we've added so far. The example uses the name of NoDisplay, but you could use any appropriate name. Choose Large Icons in the Default View Mode field on the General tab, SmallIcons in the Small Icons and LargeIcons in the Large Icons fields of the Image List tab, and add a single column to the Columns tab with a name and key of Name. Select Auto Width for the width of this single column. Adding this phantom view will allow the appropriate folder icons to appear in the scope pane.

Of course, creating the phantom result view doesn't make it the default view. Select the root node (DataViewDesign) and change the DefaultView property to NoDisplay. At this point, if you compiled the application and tested it, you'd be able to see the Basic node with the proper images displayed in the various panes.

There are some places where Microsoft has implemented the property pages for the MMC Snap-In Designer for Visual Basic in an inconsistent manner. While most nodes will allow you to select a folder through the property pages (as shown in Figure 9-19), Static node won't. You have to select the root node entry (DataViewDesign in this example) and alter the StaticFolder entry on the Properties window as shown in Figure 9-20. Inconsistent developer implementations will make it harder than it should be for you to create an application. You'll find yourself constantly looking at both property pages and the Properties window to find what you need to modify the design of your MMC snap-in.

Figure 9-20: Some MMC snap-in properties are implemented in an inconsistent manner, forcing you to look in more than one place for design modifications.

Adding menu and toolbar entries

The last two elements that we need to add to the MMC snap-in design are a menu and a toolbar. Adding both elements is easy. Just right-click the appropriate folder and choose Add Menu or Add Toolbar from the context menu. You can add submenus to a main menu by highlighting the required menu entry instead of the Menus folder.

Tip   Menus and toolbars won't automatically display after you create them with the designer. You must add code to display the menu or toolbar at the appropriate time. We'll discuss the code required to display and change both menus and toolbars in the "Adding the code" section of this chapter.

When working with menus for an MMC snap-in, you always have to include two levels — a main menu and a submenu. Toolbars only require a single entry. A toolbar, however, requires the addition of an image list in order to provide a complete display. Table 9-6 provides details on how to configure the two menus, the toolbar, and the image list for this example.

Table 9-6
Toolbar, Toolbar Image List, and Menu Object Configuration

Object	Tab	Field/Property	Value
Toolbar	Images	Images	Insert the TB1 icon found on the CD-ROM provided with this book.
mnuAdvanced	N/A	Caption	Advanced
	N/A	Key	mnuAdvanced
	N/A	StatusBarText	Allows you to choose Advanced node options.
mnuAdvancedSelect	N/A	Caption	Advanced Options Select
	N/A	Key	mnuAdvancedSelect
	N/A	StatusBarText	Choose this option to display the Advanced node.
tlbAdvanced	General	Image List	Toolbar
	Buttons (Index 1)	Key	tlbAdvanced
	Buttons (Index 1)	ToolTip Text	Select the Advanced view.
	Buttons (Index 1)	Image	1

The Toolbar image list is used to provide one or more button presentations. There are a number of ways to work with buttons. You can even change the button image as needed to show a change of state. Toolbars can also include button menus, and you can choose to keep the button pressed to indicate a two-state button. Figure 9-21 shows what the Buttons tab of the Toolbar Properties dialog box looks like. As you can see, you can choose several of these options during design time or change them as the application runs.

 Tip   Any shadowing required to make the button look three-dimensional is added for you automatically. All the button image needs to include is the icon art and a gray button (so that it blends well with the rest of the buttons on the toolbar).

Now that we've gotten the MMC snap-in configured, let's take one more look at the designer. Figure 9-22 shows what your designer should look like at this point. You can also look at the example supplied in the Start MMC Project folder of the CD-ROM provided with this book to compare your settings to those used to complete the project.

Figure 9-21: The Buttons tab of the Toolbar Properties dialog box provides ideas on how you can change the state of a toolbar within an MMC snap-in.

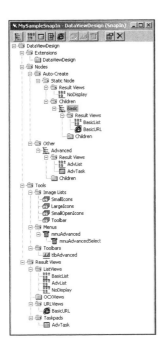

Figure 9-22: The final appearance of the designer used for the example application.

Shortcuts that make development faster

No one wants to spend more time than necessary developing a simple component. After all, project schedules hardly have enough time in them to develop the main application, let alone the components that will be used with the application. This section provides you with very fast shortcuts that you can use to reduce development time.

Make sure that you engage in the number one productivity-enhancing activity—keeping your information up-to-date. Microsoft constantly releases new information about their products, much of which affects bugs that you see or makes development easier in some way. The main MMC Web site is at `http://support.microsoft.com/support/default.asp?SD=SO&PR=MMC`. You can also participate in the MMC development process by sending feedback to mmcnews@microsoft.com. Finally, you'll want to check out the three newsgroups available for MMC users and developers: `microsoft.beta.iis4.mmc`, `microsoft.public.iis4.beta.mmc`, and `microsoft.public.management.mmc`.

Create templates for common projects

Wizards and project templates aren't just the stuff of the Visual Basic CD-ROM. You can create your own templates by using the AddIn project type. These new projects can be based on an existing project, or can be made totally free form. The point is that you can greatly reduce the development time for common projects by setting certain parameters automatically on a project template.

Once you select the AddIn project type, you'll want to select the correct kind of project by using the Project Properties dialog box shown in Figure 9-23. Notice that I've highlighted the Project Type dialog box—this is where you'll choose the kind of project template that you want to create. The Project Properties dialog box also allows you to select various project settings. For example, the Make tab contains settings that allow you to enter default information like your company name, copyright, and trademark information.

Figure 9-23: The Project Properties dialog box contains the essentials for configuring the project type.

The Connect Designer is the second part of the puzzle. Figure 9-24 shows what this dialog box looks like. It allows you to provide a name for your template, along with settings like the development language.

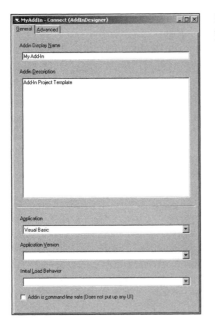

Figure 9-24: The Connect Designer allows you to define project template settings.

Develop only the features you need

It's easy to forget that unlike the developer tools that you created in the past, MMC snap-ins use component technology. This means that you can create only the features that you need right now, and add other MMC snap-ins later to address other needs. Creating the MMC snap-in that you need today allows you to test its utility earlier in the development process and work out any bugs. It also allows you to determine whether other features are actually required.

You'll find that this technique also works to your advantage because it makes the various tools required for your application more modular. Sometimes, both the user and administrator need a general-purpose tool. If you develop that tool as a separate entity, it's easier to add the appropriate security so that everyone who needs it can access it. Modular development means that you can secure dangerous tools and keep them available for administrator use only.

Working with image lists

Decide which MMC snap-in elements will require images during the initial design process. Instead of creating a large number of image lists, which can become a headache to manage, create three. Let the first image list contain the small icons (16 × 16 pixels), let the second contain the large icons (32 × 32 pixels), and let the third contain the folder open icons.

The reason for including three icons, even if you need only one at the time, is to make it easy to reuse icons for other purposes. Keep the number of icons in your MMC snap-in small to conserve server resources. Always including three sizes of each icon makes reuse a lot easier for situations that demand both sizes.

Always design the graphical elements first

If you're used to designing application programs using Visual Basic, it might be tempting to design groups of graphical elements, then code them right away. This usually isn't a very productive method of working with designers like the one used for the MMC snap-in example in this chapter. The reason is simple, all of the graphical elements are intimately connected. As you can see from Figure 9-21, you really don't get a full view of the MMC snap-in until all of the elements that you need are in place (even if those elements won't appear immediately, you need to design your MMC snap-in to accommodate them).

Obviously, part of the design process is configuring all of the graphical elements. Not only do subs and functions derive their names from graphical elements (when they're associated with a graphical element), but the configuration options often determine what optional elements are available during coding. In short, trying to write code before you completely design the graphical elements is akin to walking around blindfolded. A designer setup requires a thorough design before you begin developing the application code.

Adding the code

It's finally time to add some code to the MMC snap-in that we've designed. Unlike most components, the MMC snap-in is actually a hybrid application and component. The user will see an MMC snap-in as an application, not as a component, even though the underlying technology is based on COM. Consequently, we may be working with some coding elements that you may not have worked with for other components.

Note   Any MMC snap-in that you create can be used on other machines. The other machine will require the MMC snap-in DLL file that you create, along with the MMC snap-in runtime file (MSSnapR.DLL) and the Visual Basic runtime module to use the MMC snap-in. When creating a distribution package for your MMC snap-in, make sure that you include all three of these files as a minimum. Of course, it's also helpful to include a saved console file (MSC extension) so that the person using your MMC snap-in can access it immediately. In addition to the files required to run the MMC snap-in, you must register the MMC snap-in runtime file before you register the MMC snap-in DLL that you created; otherwise, the MMC snap-in DLL registration will fail.

The following sections explore various MMC snap-in coding tasks. We'll look at some of the fit-and-finish items that you need to consider, along with standard coding required to make the MMC snap-in functional.

Making menus and toolbars visible

Adding menus and toolbars to your application won't make them visible. You need to determine when, where, and how the menu or toolbar becomes visible. The most appropriate time to make a toolbar visible is when the user selects the root or children nodes of your MMC snap-in. Toolbars always appear on the MMC snap-in window. As a result, you'll normally add the code required to make the Toolbar visible to the View's SetControlBar event as shown in Listing 9-1 for this example.

Listing 9-1: **Making a Taskbar Appear**

```
Private Sub Views_SetControlbar(ByVal View As SnapInLib.View, _
ByVal Controlbar As SnapInLib.MMCControlbar)

    'Add the Advanced toolbar.
    Controlbar.Attach tlbAdvanced
End Sub
```

This code answers the question of when the toolbar becomes visible. However, the way this code is presented, the toolbar will stay visible no matter what view is selected. If you wanted to make the toolbar a little more selective, you could use the View object as a means for determining which view is making the request. (The Key property is the means that you'll use most often to determine which view is making the request.) This technique allows you to provide different toolbars for each view, if desired.

Menus require a little more effort and thought. You can make a menu visible as part of the top menu, the view menu, the new menu, or as a context menu. So, the first decision is determining where you want the menu to appear on screen. The choice of where won't affect the operation of the menu as much as it affects the user's perception of when to use the menu. Each menu location has a different event associated with it as shown in the following list.

✦ **AddNewMenuItems:** Allows you to add a new menu to the New submenu of the console's context menu and the MMC Action menu.

✦ **AddTaskMenuItems:** Allows you to add a new menu to the Task submenu of the console's context menu and the MMC Action menu.

✦ **AddTopMenuItems:** Allows you to add a new menu to the console's context menu and the MMC Action menu.

✦ **AddViewMenuItems:** Allows you to add a new menu to the View submenu of the console's context menu and the MMC View menu.

Notice that there isn't any way to add an entirely new menu. Any menus that you add will always appear as part of another menu. The choice of event does determine where the new menu will appear, however, so it's important to determine where you want to add the menu in advance. Because our menu addition will affect the user's view of the data, the best position of it is as part of the top menu. The code in Listing 9-2 shows you how to make the menu visible.

Listing 9-2: **Making a Menu Appear**

```
Private Sub Views_AddTopMenuItems(ByVal View As SnapInLib.View, _
ByVal Selection As SnapInLib.MMCClipboard, _
ByVal ContextMenu As SnapInLib.ContextMenu, _
InsertionAllowed As Boolean)

    'Add the Advanced node selection menu.
    ContextMenu.AddMenu mnuAdvanced
End Sub
```

Displaying the basic data

This example creates a display that tells you the local computer's NetBIOS and DNS name in various forms. There are separate outputs for the local computer and for the cluster to which the local computer belongs (if any). When the local computer isn't part of a cluster, you'll see two sets of the same information because the cluster name is the same as the local name. We'll see in the "Presenting the Advanced View to the User" section that you can also modify these names to other values. While this isn't a common task, it's something that the administrator might need to do on rare occasions.

All of this functionality relies on two new Windows API functions: `GetComputer NameEx()` and `SetComputerNameEx()`. You can only access these functions when working with Windows 2000, so this example won't work on a Windows NT or Windows 9x machine. Because these are Windows API functions, rather than internal Visual Basic functions, you'll need to create a Visual Basic module and add the required function declarations to it. I've used the default name of Module1 for this example, but you could use any name that you wanted. The reason we have to place these functions in a separate module is that you can't perform certain tasks within an object module, like the DataView control. Listing 9-3 contains the code that you'll need to use these two functions.

Listing 9-3: Using the GetComputerNameEx() and SetComputerNameEx() API Functions

```
'A list of the types of data retrieved using
'GetComputerNameEx() or modify using
'SetComputerNameEx().
Enum Computer_Name_Format
    ComputerNameNetBIOS
    ComputerNameDnsHostname
    ComputerNameDnsDomain
    ComputerNameDnsFullyQualified
    ComputerNamePhysicalNetBIOS
    ComputerNamePhysicalDnsHostname
    ComputerNamePhysicalDnsDomain
    ComputerNamePhysicalDnsFullyQualified
    ComputerNameMax
End Enum

'The GetComputerNameEx() and SetComputerNameEx()
'API function declarations.  These are available
'in Windows 2000 only!
Declare Function GetComputerNameEx _
    Lib "Kernel32" _
    Alias "GetComputerNameExA" _
    (ByVal NameType As Computer_Name_Format, _
    ByVal NameBuffer As String, _
    ByRef BufferSize As Long) _
    As Boolean

Declare Function SetComputerNameEx _
    Lib "Kernel32" _
    Alias "SetComputerNameExA" _
    (ByVal NameType As Computer_Name_Format, _
    ByVal NameBuffer As String) _
    As Boolean
```

There isn't anything special about the function declarations. The only concern is making sure that you use ByVal and ByRef in the appropriate places. Notice that I've included an enumeration. This enumeration includes all of the possible types of data that you can work with. The ComputerNameMax enumeration, although available and usable from within the functions, isn't implemented, as of this writing, so you'll want to avoid using it.

Once you have access to the required API functions, it's time to build the code required to create a results view. Listing 9-4 shows the two steps that are required to create most list result views. These steps include creating the list items that will appear no matter which view is displayed, then adding the list subitems, which are displayed when working with a detail view.

Listing 9-4: Filling the BasicList and AdvList Result Views with Data

```
Private Sub ResultViews_Initialize( _
ByVal ResultView As SnapInLib.ResultView)

    'Create a buffer variable to hold the data.
    Dim ReturnValue As String
    Dim BufferSize As Long
    ReturnValue = String(31, Chr(0))
    Buffer = Len(ReturnValue)

    'Determine if this is the right view.
    If ResultView.DisplayString = "BasicList" _
        Or ResultView.DisplayString = "AdvList" Then

        'Create all of the list items.
        ResultView.ListView.ListItems.Add _
            1, , _
            "NetBIOS Name", _
            3
        ResultView.ListView.ListItems.Add _
            2, , _
            "DNS Host Name", _
            3
        ResultView.ListView.ListItems.Add _
            3, , _
            "DNS Domain", _
            3
        ResultView.ListView.ListItems.Add _
            4, , _
            "DNS Host Name (Fully Qualified)", _
            3
        ResultView.ListView.ListItems.Add _
            5, , _
            "NetBIOS Name (Physical)", _
            3
        ResultView.ListView.ListItems.Add _
            6, , _
            "DNS Host Name (Physical)", _
            3
        ResultView.ListView.ListItems.Add _
            7, , _
```

```
        "DNS Domain (Physical)", _
        3
ResultView.ListView.ListItems.Add _
    8, , _
        "DNS Host Name (Fully Qualified & Physical)", _
        3

'Fill in the information for NetBIOS Name.
ResultView.ListView.ListItems(1).ListSubItems.Add _
    1, Name, _
        "NetBIOS Name"
ResultView.ListView.ListItems(1).ListSubItems.Add _
    2, Description, _
        "The local computer or cluster NetBIOS name."
If GetComputerNameEx(ComputerNameNetBIOS, _
    ReturnValue, Buffer) Then

    ResultView.ListView.ListItems(1).ListSubItems.Add _
        3, Value, _
        ReturnValue
Else
    ResultView.ListView.ListItems(1).ListSubItems.Add _
        3, Value, _
        "Value Not Available"
End If

'Fill in the information for DNS Host Name.
ResultView.ListView.ListItems(2).ListSubItems.Add _
    1, Name, _
        "DNS Host Name"
ResultView.ListView.ListItems(2).ListSubItems.Add _
    2, Description, _
        "The local computer or cluster DNS Host Name."
ReturnValue = String(31, Chr(0))
Buffer = Len(ReturnValue)
If GetComputerNameEx(ComputerNameDnsHostname, _
    ReturnValue, Buffer) Then

    ResultView.ListView.ListItems(2).ListSubItems.Add _
        3, Value, _
        ReturnValue
Else
    ResultView.ListView.ListItems(2).ListSubItems.Add _
        3, Value, _
        "Value Not Available"
End If

'Fill in the information for DNS Domain.
ResultView.ListView.ListItems(3).ListSubItems.Add _
    1, Name, _
        "DNS Domain"
```

Continued

Listing 9-4 *(continued)*

```
ResultView.ListView.ListItems(3).ListSubItems.Add _
    2, Description, _
    "The DNS Domain assigned to the local computer or cluster."
ReturnValue = String(31, Chr(0))
Buffer = Len(ReturnValue)
If GetComputerNameEx(ComputerNameDnsDomain, _
    ReturnValue, Buffer) Then

    ResultView.ListView.ListItems(3).ListSubItems.Add _
        3, Value, _
        ReturnValue
Else
    ResultView.ListView.ListItems(3).ListSubItems.Add _
        3, Value, _
        "Value Not Available"
End If

'Fill in the information for DNS Host Name (FQ).
ResultView.ListView.ListItems(4).ListSubItems.Add _
    1, Name, _
    "DNS Host Name (Fully Qualified)"
ResultView.ListView.ListItems(4).ListSubItems.Add _
    2, Description, _
    "A combination of the DNS host name and DNS domain name."
ReturnValue = String(31, Chr(0))
Buffer = Len(ReturnValue)
If GetComputerNameEx(ComputerNameDnsFullyQualified, _
    ReturnValue, Buffer) Then

    ResultView.ListView.ListItems(4).ListSubItems.Add _
        3, Value, _
        ReturnValue
Else
    ResultView.ListView.ListItems(4).ListSubItems.Add _
        3, Value, _
        "Value Not Available"
End If

'Fill in the information for NetBIOS Name (P).
ResultView.ListView.ListItems(5).ListSubItems.Add _
    1, Name, _
    "NetBIOS Name (Physical)"
ResultView.ListView.ListItems(5).ListSubItems.Add _
    2, Description, _
    "The physical NetBIOS Name of the local computer."
ReturnValue = String(31, Chr(0))
Buffer = Len(ReturnValue)
```

```
If GetComputerNameEx(ComputerNamePhysicalNetBIOS, _
    ReturnValue, Buffer) Then

    ResultView.ListView.ListItems(5).ListSubItems.Add _
        3, Value, _
        ReturnValue
Else
    ResultView.ListView.ListItems(5).ListSubItems.Add _
        3, Value, _
        "Value Not Available"
End If

'Fill in the information for DNS Host Name (P).
ResultView.ListView.ListItems(6).ListSubItems.Add _
    1, Name, _
    "DNS Host Name (Physical)"
ResultView.ListView.ListItems(6).ListSubItems.Add _
    2, Description, _
    "The physical DNS Host Name of the local computer."
ReturnValue = String(31, Chr(0))
Buffer = Len(ReturnValue)
If GetComputerNameEx(ComputerNamePhysicalDnsHostname, _
    ReturnValue, Buffer) Then

    ResultView.ListView.ListItems(6).ListSubItems.Add _
        3, Value, _
        ReturnValue
Else
    ResultView.ListView.ListItems(6).ListSubItems.Add _
        3, Value, _
        "Value Not Available"
End If

'Fill in the information for DNS Domain (P).
ResultView.ListView.ListItems(7).ListSubItems.Add _
    1, Name, _
    "DNS Domain (Physical)"
ResultView.ListView.ListItems(7).ListSubItems.Add _
    2, Description, _
    "The physical DNS Domain Name of this computer."
ReturnValue = String(31, Chr(0))
Buffer = Len(ReturnValue)
If GetComputerNameEx(ComputerNamePhysicalDnsDomain, _
    ReturnValue, Buffer) Then

    ResultView.ListView.ListItems(7).ListSubItems.Add _
        3, Value, _
        ReturnValue
Else
```

Continued

Listing 9-4 *(continued)*

```
            ResultView.ListView.ListItems(7).ListSubItems.Add _
                3, Value, _
                "Value Not Available"
        End If

        'Fill in the information for DNS Host Name (FQP).
        ResultView.ListView.ListItems(8).ListSubItems.Add _
            1, Name, _
            "DNS Host Name (Fully Qualified & Physical)"
        ResultView.ListView.ListItems(8).ListSubItems.Add _
            2, Description, _
            "The physical and fully qualified DNS Host Name for this computer."
        ReturnValue = String(31, Chr(0))
        Buffer = Len(ReturnValue)
        If GetComputerNameEx(ComputerNamePhysicalDnsFullyQualified, _
        ReturnValue, Buffer) Then

            ResultView.ListView.ListItems(8).ListSubItems.Add _
                3, Value, _
                ReturnValue
        Else
            ResultView.ListView.ListItems(8).ListSubItems.Add _
                3, Value, _
                "Value Not Available"
        End If
    End If

End Sub
```

As you can see, the code is relatively straightforward, but there are a few things that you need to consider. Even though it's not really documented, the maximum buffer length required for the computer name data (at least as of this writing) is 30 characters, with an additional character required as a terminating null. As a result, the ResultValue buffer is initialized with 31 zeros.

There are a number of ways to detect which view is being used. I chose to use the DisplayString property of the ResultView object in this case. You could also use keys to find out which view is in place or flags.

The next step in the result view building process is to create a list of items. These items form the icons seen in the Large Icons, Small Icons, and List views. They also provide an object to host the detail information created later. The ListItems.Add method allows you to specify an index number, key, list item text, and the number of the folder icon used to display the object.

Creating the detail view information comes next. There are three detail view columns. You might expect that the first column would get filled in automatically with the information from the list item, but this wouldn't work in every case, so you need to provide the information for all three columns. The first two columns are relatively easy, all you need to do is provide some text. The `ListSubItems.Add` method allows you to provide an index number, key, and detail view text. Notice that, in this case, the keys are the ones that we specified during the design phase.

The Value column requires a little more work. The `GetComputerNameEx()` function returns False if the requested value isn't available. So, we need to test the return value of this function, then provide the actual value or a default text string as output. Notice that the `GetComputerNameEx()` function requires a computer name type, a pointer to a sting, and the size of the string as input. You also have to reinitialize the string after each call or the function won't work.

Presenting the advanced view to the user

The basic view that we created earlier allows someone to view the data on screen, but not to change it in any way. This is a view that would allow a user to participate in a troubleshooting session with help desk staff without any potential for damaging the system as the result of an input error. A network administrator would require more flexibility, however, so we also need an advanced view. The display logistics for the advanced view are the same as the basic view, so I won't discuss them again.

Tip   When creating a ListView that has scope items, make sure that the indexes for the small and large bitmaps are precisely the same. Otherwise, the scope items will display different bitmaps depending on which view the user chooses. Although this won't cause your MMC snap-in to fail, it will reduce the usability of your MMC snap-in and negate the usefulness of the icons that your MMC snap-in uses.

The MMC snap-in does need to provide a means for switching between the basic and advanced views. That's where the menu and toolbar that we created during the design phase comes into play. A user can use either the menu or toolbar to switch between views. Listing 9-5 shows the code that you'll need to make the view switch.

Note   Listing 9-5 only shows the code for the `mnuAdvancedSelect_Click()` method. You also need to provide code for the `tblAdvanced_ButtonClick()` method. Because there's only one button on the toolbar, you can use the same code for both methods, or create a new function and call it from both methods. In either case, the code shown in Listing 9-5 is the same for both the menu and the toolbar.

Listing 9-5: **Switching Between Results Views**

```
Private Sub mnuAdvancedSelect_Click( _
ByVal Index As Long, _
ByVal Selection As SnapInLib.MMCClipboard)

    'Get the root node.
    Dim oSN As ScopeNode
    Set oSN = ScopeItems.Item(1).ScopeNode

    'See which node is displayed.
    If mnuAdvancedSelect.Checked = False Then

        'Make the Advanced node appear.
        ScopeItems.AddPreDefined "Advanced", _
            "Advanced", oSN, siFirst

        'Check the menu item and depress the toolbar button.
        mnuAdvancedSelect.Checked = True
        tlbAdvanced.Buttons(1).Value = siPressed

        'Make the Basic node disappear.
        ScopeItems.Remove "Basic"

    Else

        'Make the Basic node appear.
        ScopeItems.AddPreDefined "Basic", "Basic", oSN, siFirst

        'Check the menu item and depress the toolbar button.
        mnuAdvancedSelect.Checked = False
        tlbAdvanced.Buttons(1).Value = siUnpressed

        'Make the Advanced node disappear.
        ScopeItems.Remove "Advanced"

    End If

End Sub
```

Because the mnuAdvancedSelect object acts as a toggle, I decided to check it when the user has activated the advanced view. This allowd me to verify the current application state simply by inspecting the checked state of the mnuAdvancedSelect object.

You'll use the `ScopeItems.AddPredefined` method to add the new view. Notice that this method requires the name of the view, a key value that will be used to interact with the view later, the node that we want to attach the new view to, and the position of the new node in the hierarchy. While it's possible to place the new node anywhere in the hierarchy, placing it as the first or last item appears to work best.

Changing the menu and toolbar status to match the current view comes next. All you need to do is set the menu's Checked property to true. MMC snap-in buttons allow you to maintain a depressed stated. Change the Value property to siPressed in order to make the required status change.

Finally, you'll need to remove the old view. The `ScopeItems.Remove` method requires a single input, the key value of the view that you want to remove. Make sure that you supply the key value and not the display text value.

Testing the MMC Snap-In

Testing the MMC snap-in is relatively easy. There's a way to run the snap-in from the Visual Basic IDE for debugging, so that's what we'll look at first. The following steps will get you started.

1. Set any breakpoints that you want within the component.

2. Press F5 to start the component. In most cases, a copy of Internet Explorer will launch. You can close the copy of Internet Explorer because it isn't needed for debugging.

3. Start MMC by using the Start ➪ Run command. Be sure to specify MMC /a to ensure that you can enter debugging mode.

4. Use the Console ➪ Add/Remove Snap-in command to display the Add/Remove Snap-in dialog box shown in Figure 9-25.

Figure 9-25: The Add/Remove Snap-in dialog box shows currently installed snap-ins and allows you to add or remove snap-ins as needed.

5. Click Add. You'll see an Add Standalone Snap-in dialog box similar to the one shown in Figure 9-26. This dialog box shows all dual-mode and stand-alone MMC snap-ins. It won't display extensions because they appear on the Extensions tab of the Add/Remove Snap-in dialog box.

Figure 9-26: The Add Standalone Snap-in dialog box presents a list of stand-alone and dual-mode MMC snap-in components.

6. Highlight the MMC snap-in that you want to add to the console (DataView in this case).

7. Click Add, and then Close. At this point, it's usually a good idea to verify the information that you've provided with the MMC snap-in.

8. Highlight the MMC snap-in, and then click About. You'll see an About dialog box similar to the one shown in Figure 9-27.

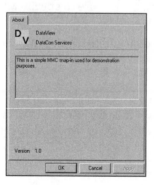

Figure 9-27: It's a good idea to check the About dialog box as part of your initial testing to ensure that the user has everything that the user needs.

9. Click OK twice. You'll return to MMC and see the new MMC snap-in installed.

Start working with the MMC snap-in. Every time you come to a breakpoint in the code, the console will become nonresponsive. It appears to take a few seconds for the Visual Basic IDE to respond as well, so don't be surprised if you need to wait a few moments before you begin debugging the MMC snap-in. Once Visual Basic does respond, you'll be able to see the MMC snap-in in action.

After the code is debugged, you'll want to spend some time working with the IDE to ensure that the component works as intended. Make sure that you test for problem areas like menus that don't work where they need to, but do seem to work everywhere else. It's also important to check the display for ease of use. You may want to change some of the column-width settings to make it easier to see the data without a lot of extra fiddling. Figure 9-28 shows the output for this example.

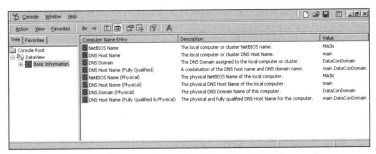

Figure 9-28: Typical output from the DataView MMC snap-in.

A final step in this process is saving the console settings so that the user can access them quickly. All you need to do is use the Console ⇨ Save command. Windows 2000 will normally select the user's Administrative Tools folder automatically. This means that your console will be available from the Administrative Tools folder whenever someone logs in with the required permissions. You may want to save the console settings for powerful tools in another place to prevent them from falling into the wrong hands. The console settings for this example are saved on the CD-ROM provided with this book in the MMC Project Console folder. You can place the Data View console in your Administrative Tools folder, if desired, to gain better access to the compiled application while you work with the code.

Solutions for Component Problems

No matter how well your component is designed and coded, a potential for problems exists. Miscommunication and a lack of standards in some areas of Windows application development both conspire to make your job harder. In addition, under the best circumstances it's difficult to predict how loads and user interaction will affect your original design. The unpredictability of external influences, like new techniques developed by crackers to encroach on your system's security, also create problems. In short, even the best developer will experience a range of problems with the components that he or she designs.

The following sections look at some of the problems that you'll encounter while creating COM+ components using Visual Basic. The goal of this section is to expose some of the weaknesses within Microsoft's component technology. Knowing how these weaknesses will affect your application makes it possible for you to avoid some problems, or at least recognize them so that you can fix them quickly. This isn't an exhaustive reference, but will help you find solutions to other problems.

MMC snap-in fails to work

There are several problems that could keep your MMC snap-in from working as it should. First, you need to make sure that the MMC snap-in DLL is registered. You can do this by using the RegSvr32 <MMC Snap-In Name>.DLL command at the command prompt. Make sure that you register the MMC snap-in runtime file (MSSnapR.DLL) before you attempt to register your own DLL file. If you've used the default file extension of OCX, be sure to use that in place of the more standard DLL extension.

In some cases, the MMC snap-in still won't work. The next thing to check is the location of the MSSnapR.DLL file. It should be in the \Program Files\Common Files\Microsoft Shared\SnapInDesigner directory. If you don't find it there, locate the MSSnapR.DLL file, move it to the new location, and be sure to register it again using the RegSvr32 command.

Another potential source of problems is inaccurate or missing Registry information. You'll find all of the MMC snap-ins registered under HKEY_LOCAL_MACHINE\SOFTWARE\Microsoft\MMC\SnapIns key of the Registry as shown in Figure 9-29. The number of values that you see listed here will depend on the complexity of the MMC snap-in. In many cases, all you'll see is the GUID for the About dialog box and a MMC snap-in name in human readable form. If this information is missing completely and you know that you successfully registered the component, you may have chosen the wrong Visual Basic project as a starting point. Use the OLE View utility to see if the component appears on the machine at all before you begin troubleshooting your code.

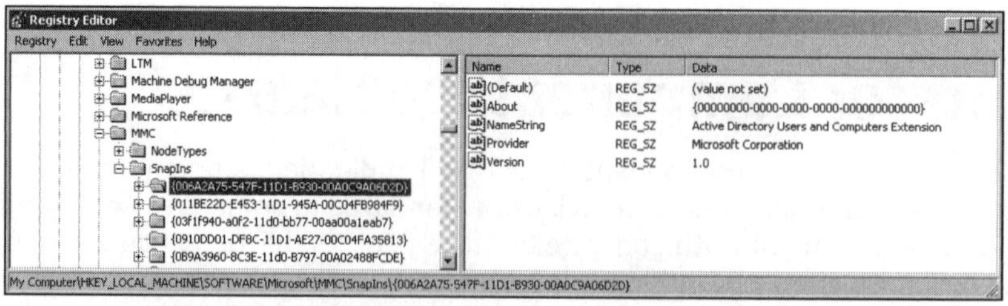

Figure 9-29: Ensure that a MMC snap-in is properly registered before you attempt to troubleshoot other problems.

It's also important to check the viability of your saved console file. Corruption could make it appear that the MMC snap-in is missing, when the problem is that the console can't find the MMC snap-in. This same problem could occur if you failed to select the Binary Compatibility option on the Component tab of the Project Properties dialog box. A changing GUID will make it nearly impossible to create console settings that you can save and distribute as part of the MMC snap-in.

Check for display errors in your MMC snap-in. Visual Basic will compile an MMC snap-in with display errors and never tell you about them. Likewise, RegSvr32 will register the MMC snap-in for you. The only time that you'll become aware of a problem is when you try to use the MMC snap-in and find that it won't display. There are many strange display errors that can occur. For example, make sure all bitmaps are either 16 pixels × 16 pixels (small) or 32 pixels × 32 pixels (large). Image lists can only contain bitmaps of one size — they can't be mixed. In addition, toolbars only use small bitmaps (16 × 16). You'll also want to check for errors of configuration when it comes to displaying information. For example, make sure that the Small Icons field on the Image Lists tab of the ListView Properties dialog points to an image list containing 16 × 16 icons.

COM+ performance problems for Visual Basic

Performance is always a problem for developers. Creating applications that are fast, easy to use, and that minimize resource usage within the time limits allowed by most project schedules is an exercise in frustration. Windows 2000 and COM+ offer many new configuration options, but they also make it easier to introduce performance-inhibiting settings.

Part of the problem is that components can be created with a variety of attributes, some of which contribute to the performance problems that developers experience. For example, if you use one threading model in a component and the client calling your component uses another threading model, then COM will have to create a proxy and marshal the method calls to the component. In addition, the use of two different threading models will mean that a context switch occurs each time that the client makes a component method call. If the first component calls on a second one with yet another threading model, more marshaling and context switches may have to occur in order to ensure that the application will execute as intended.

In a perfect world, every component uses the same threading model and executes in the same process as the client. This ensures that no proxies are required and that there are no context changes when moving data from one component to the next. When a client makes a method call without the use of a proxy, the call requires very few machine instructions to execute, making the method invocations extremely efficient. A client method call that acts this way is more like a wrapper around a `LoadLibrary()` call, rather than an invocation of a method in a foreign object. The client receives a raw reference, rather than a proxy. Creating a context requires both time and resources, so minimizing context changes is always a good goal to achieve. Security, the use of proxy and stub, and context changes, are the three elements that affect component performance the most once programming technique is considered.

Effects of COM+ application-type choices

Of course, components that use the same threading model and execute in-process with the client are very limited. The second that you want to execute a client on a remote machine you give up the efficiencies of in-process execution. Consequently, you may think that COM+ applications are limited to the performance-robbing out-of-process server-invocation scenario. There are actually two types of COM+ applications and choosing the correct one is important from a performance perspective. Figure 9-30 shows the Activation tab of the COM+ application Properties dialog box. (In this case, we're looking at an application named Threading Test, which is available on the CD-ROM that accompanies this book.)

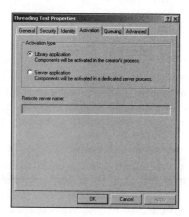

Figure 9-30: Choosing the right application type is important if you want maximum performance from your COM+ application.

Notice that you can choose between a server and a library application. A server application always incurs a performance penalty because it executes on the server — there's both a proxy and a context change. Nothing comes free. Although a library application will execute faster because it shares the creator's process, you won't be able to use some COM+ features like role-based security. These features require the use of an interceptor, which means that they have to execute in a separate process.

Unfortunately, the issue of which COM+ application type to choose isn't as straightforward as choosing between performance and features. Consider the case in which a client application creates an object that we'll call Object A, which in turn creates two more objects (Objects B and C). If Object A executes in the client context, there are two proxies and two context changes to access Objects B and C. On the other hand, if Objects A, B, and C can all reside in a single apartment on the server, there will only be a single proxy and context change between the client and Object A. In short, you can reduce the number of proxy and context change related performance inhibitors in half by using a server application in some cases.

There are also situations when you'll want to use a combination of server and library applications. Use the same situation where a client calls Object A, which, in turn, calls on Objects B and C. What would happen if Objects B and C resided on a second server? In that case, you'd want to create the COM+ application for Object A as a server application and the COM+ application for Objects B and C as library applications. Doing so would allow you to keep performance high by reducing the number of context switches required for the application as a whole.

Tip   Performance-related problems for Visual Basic components can't be completely counteracted at the time of this writing because Visual Basic doesn't offer support for either the free-threaded model or the new thread-neutral apartment. While Visual Basic does offer superior development speed and lower cost of component maintenance, Visual C++ will maintain a speed superiority for the foreseeable future because it does support these alternative threading models. Of course, the only time that using the free-threaded model (ThreadingModel=Both) in Visual C++ helps is when you also refrain from installing the application in the COM+ catalog. So, the whole issue of performance enhancement under COM+ boils down to support for the thread-neutral apartment. This support should appear in Visual Basic 7.

Choosing the right component threading model

Always choose the Apartment Threaded option in the Threading Model field on the General tab of the Project Properties dialog box (shown in Figure 9-8) when creating a COM+ application. While either threading model will work, using single threading incurs a penalty on both resources and time.

Single threading implies that a single object can only be accessed by one thread. Every time an object is needed, Windows must create a new one. Besides wasting resources by creating a new object each time one is needed, the time required to create the object also reduces performance. An apartment-threaded object can be accessed by multiple threads (in an orderly manner), a much more practical arrangement with a COM+ application.

On the CD-ROM   There's an example application on the CD-ROM provided with this book that you can use to demonstrate the difference between single threading and apartment threading. All you need to do is install the COM+ application found in the Threading Test Application folder on your machine, then use the applications found in the Apartment Threaded Test and Single Threaded Test folders to test this principle. Use more than one invocation of each application to see how the threading works. While both applications will perform the same task of adding two numbers together, the apartment-threaded component will perform its task more efficiently.

The question of choosing the single-threaded apartment model when a component contains user interface elements should be moot. You should never include user interface elements of any kind in components that will execute on the server because there's unlikely to be anyone using the server machine as a workstation who can interact with the component. All that will happen is that the component will block (stop executing while waiting for input), leaving the application in limbo. There are two methods for communicating errors when working with a COM+ component as shown below.

✦ Send an error number as part of the HRESULT (return) value.

✦ Use the App.LogEvent "Event Message", `vbLogEventTypeError` method to log the event.

Colocation Problems

As previously mentioned, keeping the number of context switches and proxies low in an application is one of the more significant ways to improve application performance. This means that you need to avoid configurations where colocation of components isn't possible. Table 9-7 provides a list of COM+ application and component attributes (dialog box settings) that affect colocation.

Table 9-7
COM+ Settings that Affect Colocation

Setting	Dialog	Tab	Description
Server application	Application Properties	Activation	Always prevents colocation unless the component is called from the same surrogate process.
Enforce access checks for this application	Application Properties	Security	Always prevents colocation when checked.
Component supports events and statistics	Component Properties	Activation	Always prevents colocation when checked.
Enable Just-In-Time Activation	Component Properties	Activation	Always prevents colocation when checked.
Must be activated in caller's context	Component Properties	Activation	Forces colocation when possible, or instantiation fails if colocation isn't possible.

Setting	Dialog	Tab	Description
Synchronization support	Component Properties	Concurrency	Always prevents colocation when the Required or Required New options are selected. Colocation is never prevented when the Disabled or Not Supported options are selected. Colocation could be prevented if the Supported option is selected.
Enforce component level access checks	Component Properties	Security	Always prevents colocation when checked. This option is check by default, so you must uncheck it if you want to improve performance.
Transaction support	Component Properties	Transaction	Always prevents colocation when the Required or Required New options are selected. Colocation is never prevented when the Disabled or Not Supported options are selected. Colocation could be prevented if the Supported option is checked and the caller has transaction support enabled.

As you can see from Table 9-7, the one setting that most affects colocation is, "Must be activated in caller's context" found on the Activation tab of the Component Properties dialog box. Figure 9-31 shows what this dialog box looks like for the ApartmentThread component used as one of the test applications for this chapter (you'll find the complete application on the CD-ROM provided with this book). Checking this option forces one of two conditions. Either the application will run with the component in the same context as the client application, or the call will fail and the application will display an error message similar to the one shown in Figure 9-32.

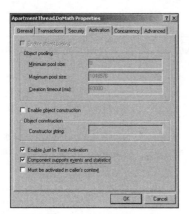

Figure 9-31: The Activation tab contains several settings that affect the ability of objects to colocate.

Figure 9-32: Setting the "Must be activated in caller's context" option when colocation isn't possible results in this error message.

There are also degrees of context switching. If you can't colocate the components for an application, you can at least reduce the context-switching penalty. Each of the settings in Table 9-7 that require a colocation adds to the context-switching penalty of your application. In other words, the fewer of these settings that you use, the faster your application will execute. Obviously, there are times when you have to choose the lesser of two evils, poor performance or lack of application flexibility. If you need maximum application security, for example, then role-based security is the option to choose, even if it will slow performance.

Message boxes or other graphical element errors

It's very easy to develop certain habits when writing code. For example, most people use the MsgBox function without much thought. In most cases, the MsgBox function displays a message box that provides the user with useful information. Some people have used this particular function for so long that they write it without really thinking about the ramifications of doing so.

However, when you're working in some environments, you need to consider the special requirements for that environment. For example, when working with an MMC snap-in, you'll want to use the ConsoleMsgBox function in place of the standard MsgBox function. While this function is completely documented, it doesn't stand out in the Microsoft documentation, so you could easily miss it.

The reason for the change in function is easy to understand. An MMC snap-in is actually a COM object that's being hosted by the MMC.EXE program container. There are several application layers in place, rather than the single layer normally found in a desktop application. If you use the `MsgBox` function, the parent of the MMC snap-in won't properly host the message box. The `ConsoleMsgBox` function allows MMC to keep track of the dialog box and return the proper results to the MMC snap-in.

This particular problem is subtle. It won't look like anything is wrong at first. Using `MsgBox` will always display the message box that you want with the appropriate text and buttons. It's the feedback part of the process that doesn't work. So, if you find that you're not getting the feedback that you thought you would from a message box, one of the first places to look is in your code. Make sure that you used the correct function (`ConsoleMsgBox`) to display the message box.

The `ConsoleMsgBox` function problem isn't an isolated event. Working with components often means following rules that don't make sense until you trace through the code and see what's happening under the surface. In many cases, the graphical element will display and appear to work as anticipated. Only when you try to use the element within your code will you notice that it isn't working as anticipated.

Security

Microsoft keeps enhancing Windows security, but crackers are adept at finding holes in each enhancement. Every advance in security functionality appears to be matched by an equally aggressive cracker who just won't quit. The result is akin to the childproof containers that adults find difficult to open and children continue to circumvent. Needless to say, the never-ending spiral of security measures in Windows 2000 makes security a major source of problems for component designers. A great source of COM+ application failure is a lack of rights for the client on the host system. In many cases, the system won't tell you that there's a security problem — in most cases, the problem won't even appear in the Security Event Log. (We'll see how all of this works later in the section.)

Let's consider, for a moment, the sources of security problems. There are a considerable number of potential security problems that you need to consider when installing a component on a production system, including:

✦ **Client-Side Security:** Interestingly enough, it's possible to install an application in such a way that the user's request never leaves the client, much less gets to the server. For example, an application requires the right Registry entries to access a component located on a server. In addition, you need to configure the application to use the correct username, password, and other identification information.

✦ **DCOM or Other Protocols:** Creating the correct network connection is essential to proper transmission of security data. Ensure that settings like encryption and impersonation level are correct. Although almost all of the transmission details are taken care of for you, most protocols require some level of configuration before they can transmit data securely and reliably.

✦ **Encryption:** There are several encryption levels used with components and the data that they transfer. In Chapter 2, we saw how changing the default DCOM settings affects the way that messages get encrypted. Components can rely on internal security to encrypt data, but it's more likely that they'll use whatever encryption technology the operating system and network protocol offer. Too much encryption can make an application run slow, yet not enough encryption opens your application's data to attack.

✦ **Firewalls:** There are times when an incorrectly configured firewall will prevent security requests from reaching the server. The required data gets dumped in the bit bucket, ensuring that the user will never gain access to the server resources required to use the application. This is one of the issues that Simple Object Access Protocol (SOAP) will eventually fix and one of the reasons that Microsoft is looking to SOAP as the replacement for DCOM. (You can find out more about SOAP in Chapter 6.)

✦ **Server-Side Security:** Remember that a client must have access to the component through Windows 2000 security, even if you plan on using COM+ role-based security. Server-side security ensures that no one gains access to server resources unless they have the proper permissions. One of the problems that users will encounter with applications is a lack of permission to use the server resources required to complete a task. In many cases, a lack of permission is disguised as some other problem. For example, an application may report a missing file, when in reality, the file is present. The user simply doesn't have access to it.

✦ **Role-Based Security:** COM+ provides a great new security feature that allows you to control precisely who gets access to what component resources based on the task that they perform. Using role-based security means that you can give one person read-only access, and another person write access based on the role that they perform within the company. A manager may require read/write access to the data that an employee can only read. Unfortunately, the complexity of using both server-side security and role-based security can turn what would otherwise be a flexible feature into a programmer's troubleshooting nightmare.

Most components that you build today will be used across server boundaries (or at least across machine boundaries from client to server), which means that security is paramount. Face it, the days of building a new pushbutton are all but gone. The components that you'll build today work in the background, manipulating data, or allow access to advanced configuration features (as in the case of the MMC snap-in component for this chapter). Of course, components very seldom transfer code from one location to another, so the most likely element that you'll need to secure for transfer is the data that your company relies on to operate.

Because security is such a big issue, it's important to understand how security works on the system that you design a component to work with. Today COM+ uses DCOM as a transport mechanism, but tomorrow it will use SOAP, which means that there will be a difference in the way that the network transport element of COM+ works. Fortunately, many of the problems that we discussed in this section have a common root and therefore a common fix or source of prevention. The following list tells you about the solutions for component security problems.

✦ **Configuration:** Ensure there are sufficient instructions for configuring the components that you create. COM+ takes security configuration out of the hands of the developer, which is good for many reasons, but also means that you no longer directly control security setups. You can set a default configuration, but the administrator can choose to override those options if the network setup requires something different from the default.

✦ **Programming Control:** COM+ controls should be designed with flexibility in mind. For this reason, you should set security defaults with the assumption that the administrator will change them under certain conditions. However, you shouldn't depend on the administrator to set security — a component should include default settings that are consistent with its intended use.

✦ **Standardized Access:** To some extent, COM+ security access is standardized because of the way that Windows 2000 enforces security checks. In addition, use of MMC snap-ins ensures that every component will appear to work in the same way to the administrator who configures it. However, the inner workings of a component can vary a lot, which means that the interpretation of security settings can also vary somewhat. If you decide to implement role-based security, make sure that every component in the application implements role-based security in the same way. For example, if one component uses the `GetSecurityCallContext.IsCallerInRole()` method to check the caller's role, all of the components within the application should do so.

Tip   The IGetSecurityCallContext interface is found in the COM+ Services Type Library (COMSVCS.DLL). You'll need to add this reference to your application in order to gain access to methods like `IsCallerInRole()` and `IsSecurityEnabled()`.

The Importance of the High Encryption Pack

Some developers feel that security configuration is an administrator-only task, but that isn't always true. Consider the problem of keeping data secure through encryption. The default Windows 2000 setup will allow you to configure data encryption to use Triple-DES (Data Encryption Standard) security. Triple-DES is part of the Internet Protocol Security (IPSec) standard that many vendors are developing. (You can learn more about both of these standards at `http://www.ietf.org/html.charters/ipsec-charter.html`.) This secure data encryption method is more than enough to protect your data — at least for today. So, the assumption is that if you set the server to use Triple-DES, the server will always keep your data secure.

The problem is that there are some situations when Windows 2000 switches to standard (single) DES encryption without letting anyone know about the change in protection level. If two machines both have standard DES installed, the communication between them will take place at this level even if the administrator has configured the system to use Triple-DES. The only notification of this problem is one that appears in an audit log that the administrator may not view on a regular basis. As a result, both the company and the users of an application may have a false sense of security when it comes to data encryption.

Because of export and import restrictions, Microsoft decided to place full Triple-DES support in the High Encryption Pack that the user must download separately and install on the local system. Their reasoning is that some companies wanted to have this security feature as a separate option — a dangerous assumption when it comes to data security. If you plan to write applications that could use the Internet as a transmission media, then you also need to ensure that the right security is in place. You can find out more about the High Encryption Pack at `http://www.microsoft.com/windows2000/downloads/recommended/encryption/default.asp`.

Developers have a responsibility to ensure that their applications provide the level of security that users expect, even if the level of security that should be provided isn't provided by default. The solution to this problem is to check for the presence of the High Encryption Pack when starting your application on a Windows 2000 machine. As an alternative, you could also check the level of data encryption used by individual components.

COM subsystem

It's always important to consider outside sources in your search for application errors, especially after a thorough search of your code doesn't yield answers to your application's COM problem. Bugs exist in other areas of Windows, so it's not a good idea to assume that the COM libraries provided with Windows are perfect. In fact, there are some rather odd bugs in the COM subsystem, depending on which version of Windows you're using at the moment and the conditions under which the application will run.

A look through the various Knowledge Bases that Microsoft provides will usually give you an idea of whether a problem is in your code or within Windows. For example, consider the problem talked about in Knowledge Base article Q167133. In this case, developers found that COM objects mysteriously disappeared after six minutes. It turns out that local COM objects are pinged every two minutes, just like those in remote locations. If the client doesn't respond after three tries to contact it, Windows terminates the client, even if the client is still active and functional. Failing to install network support with Windows NT initiates the problem. Microsoft fixed this particular problem with Service Pack 2.

The Microsoft Developer Network (MSDN) subscription contains a wealth of information that you need to work efficiently. For example, it contains a complete list of all of the Knowledge Base articles that Microsoft has at the time, making it easy to look for problems like the ones we discuss in this section. However, not everyone has access to MSDN and even if you do, there are times when your subscription might not be available to you. That's where Microsoft's online MSDN site comes into play. You can find much of the same information that your MSDN subscription provides online at `http://msdn.microsoft.com`. If you want to search for a Knowledge Base article, simply click Search MSDN on any MSDN Web site page. Be aware that some MSDN services online will require your MSDN ID number, so it's a good idea to record this number on your laptop.

Of course, Knowledge Base article Q167133 wouldn't answer your question if you needed to deal with this problem on a remote server. It turns out that you can have the very same problem of disappearing objects when working with remote objects, but for a different reason. Knowledge Base article 175020 provides a complete description of this problem, which was fixed in Service Pack 4 of Windows NT. The short story is that objects created without authorized users were getting pinged as if they were secure. Of course, the component couldn't respond to the secure query and was terminated after six minutes.

Knowing which service packs are installed on each client and server is very important. Otherwise, you won't know whether a Knowledge Base article applies to you. It's also good to have an idea of what problems those service packs will fix. In some cases, knowing which service packs must be installed to run an application will save your product support staff a lot of time looking for a problem that doesn't exist in your software.

The point is that you could search for hours to find a problem like this without ever discovering the source. Your application would work fine on a machine with network support, but fail on machines without network support. In the long run, knowing how to ask Microsoft about potential problems in the COM subsystem can save you many hours of fruitless debugging time.

Summary

This chapter has shown you how to create a simple component. Because most of you have already created ActiveX controls and other simple component types in the past, I chose to concentrate on one of the new types of components in the Windows 2000 arsenal, the MMC snap-in. For the most part, the MMC snap-in takes the place of all of those separate administrative tools that you used in the past. You can use the snap-ns to configure, monitor, test, and secure an individual server or an entire network. Here are some additional conclusions that you can draw from the contents of this chapter.

✦ While you can create an MMC snap-in by using a basic component and the required interfaces, using the MMC Snap-In Designer for Visual Basic is much easier.

✦ An MMC snap-in consists of both mandatory and optional interfaces. The mandatory interfaces determine basic component features and operation. The optional interfaces normally extend component functionality in some way.

✦ There are two ways to classify administrative tools. The first way is to look at how the tools will be used by the administrator to perform work. The second way is to look at the component usage characteristics like location, user expertise, and the sensitivity of the data being manipulated.

✦ There are many considerations when choosing the type of tool to use. An important consideration is whether the user will have adequate access to Windows 2000 to make use of an MMC snap-in. If not, then some other form of administrative utility might be better.

✦ Most developers work with multiple versions of Windows; some even need to boot other operating systems. The partition manager that comes with Windows 2000 works fine in many situations, but it's not the most complete product on the market. One alternative is the Ranish Partition Manager — a shareware product that boasts support for many languages, in addition to a full set of partition-management features.

✦ There are a number of ways to use MMC snap-ins within Windows 2000. The four general uses are monitoring, configuration, installation, and security. In addition to these general uses, some special uses are information, diagnostics, analysis, and comparison. No matter what type of MMC snap-in you create, you can count on one thing — the user interface will remain the same and the component technology will let you develop the tool in less time.

✦ Make sure that you consider the performance implications of any component that you create. Choosing the right threading model is crucial.

✦ Always verify that you've used the correct graphical elements and that they're in the correct order. It's easy to get the images within an image list out of order, which could result in some very strange results when the user clicks the wrong button. You'll also want to look for other obvious configuration and coding errors before you begin troubleshooting a component at a low level.

✦   ✦   ✦

Creating Distributed Applications

Distributed application development implies an understanding of not only the client side of the application or the server side of the application, but also of the transport mechanism that connects the two. A distributed application implies some level of connectivity between application components executing on more than one machine. The Distributed Component Object Model (DCOM) is the technology that is currently used to provide a connection between COM+ applications. Even though the Simple Object Access Protocol (SOAP) is looming on the horizon, DCOM will likely remain the protocol of choice for some time to come because both the client and server need to support SOAP before it becomes a reality. In short, for now at least, you need to know about DCOM in order to build the very best applications.

This chapter concentrates on what you need to know to work with DCOM. If you want to know more about DCOM in theory, you'll want to read both Chapters 4 and 5. Chapter 4 helps you to understand where DCOM fits into the grand scheme of COM technologies. It also includes a brief overview of why DCOM is so different from the other COM technologies that it tends to support. Chapter 5 provides detailed theoretical information on how DCOM works and how you'll use it within applications. This chapter also talks about some of the challenges of using DCOM, which is part of the reason Microsoft is developing SOAP as an alternative to DCOM. Finally, all of the tools used to work with the application in this chapter are discussed in Chapter 5.

SOAP is still a work in progress as of this writing. However, Microsoft is making every effort to keep developers informed about its progress on the SOAP standard and incorporating SOAP within Windows. You can find the latest specification and discussion at `http://msdn.microsoft.com/workshop/xml/general/soapspec.asp`. SOAP relies on the eXtensible Markup Language (XML) to perform its work, so you need to know about this specification, too. The Microsoft view of XML appears at `http://msdn.microsoft.com/xml/default.asp`. Microsoft isn't the only company working with SOAP, which is why this is such an exciting new technology. If you want to read about how IBM and Lotus are currently working with this product, read `http://www.devx.com/free/press/2000/042800.asp`. Using SOAP will very likely require changes to the programming language that you use today. To find out about Microsoft's current plans for the next generation of Visual Basic, check out `http://msdn.microsoft.com/vstudio/nextgen/`. You can also find an excellent introductory discussion of the capabilities of SOAP at `http://msdn.microsoft.com/msdnmag/issues/0300/soap/soap.asp`. If you want to discuss SOAP with someone, try the SOAP mailing list at `http://discuss.develop.com/`. Some of you may want to try using SOAP right away. If so, you'll want to download the SOAP toolkit for Visual Studio at `http://msdn.microsoft.com/xml/general/soaptemplate.asp` and `http://msdn.microsoft.com/xml/general/toolkit_intro.asp`. Of course, because the specification is still a work in progress, anything you do with SOAP today isn't guaranteed to work tomorrow.

DCOM was used as a mechanism for building applications long before it became the transport protocol for COM+. In fact, you'll find that DCOM has been used for quite some time as an application development protocol. We'll talk about the kinds of applications that you can create by using DCOM alone in the first section of this chapter. It's important to understand how DCOM can make life easier (or at least applications more flexible) before we delve into its use with COM+ in the next chapter. There are still many applications that can be built by using DCOM alone and, in many cases, COM+ isn't even the right choice for these applications today. Sometimes newer isn't always better. For the most part, small networks and applications that will never execute on the Internet still benefit from the capabilities provided by DCOM.

Once you have a better understanding of what DCOM is all about, we'll create a very simple COM component and activate it by using DCOM. Remember that DCOM is a protocol, not a component technology as such. DCOM is Microsoft's expression of DCE RPC. This example shows how a network protocol is implemented. In other words, the component will reside on one machine and the client on another machine. The component will execute on the server and the test application will execute on the client machine. We'll look at the implications of this distributed form of processing and some of the problems that you may encounter by using it in the example.

Part of working with DCOM is understanding the tricks of the trade. Yes, you can use standard components on the server, but you need to ask whether those components will operate efficiently. In many cases, components created for desktop application use won't work properly on a server. Even if they do work properly, they'll waste a lot of resources, slow the network, and generally cause problems. As part of the task of creating a server-side component, we'll discuss the effects of networks and server resources on component design. In other words, we'll look at what you need to consider before building a server-side component. It's important to ensure that the component will make the best possible use of resources.

Writing the DCOM application is only part of the process. Once the client and server parts of the picture are in place, you have to conduct tests to ensure that they'll work as anticipated. I normally use a two-phase testing model. The first phase tests the client and component locally to ensure that the component works as anticipated and to remove the network as a potential source of error. The second phase tests the component on a remote machine to see how it performs over the network and resolves any network induced errors like loss of connection.

The final section of this chapter will look at problems and fixes. DCOM introduces a wealth of potential problems that are beyond your control during the design phase of the application. For example, if the network administrator assigns the wrong security settings to the component, it's unlikely to work even if the code that you write is absolutely perfect. In some cases, there isn't anything that you can to do to prevent the problem; all you can do is detect it and provide code to help the application recover from the problem. For example, a fault in the network cabling or an act of nature like lightning can cause data loss. If the component is halfway through a calculation or a data entry scenario, you need to provide some means of recovery. The component needs to know that the client is no longer present and then do something to reverse any incomplete transactions so that your database doesn't suffer from data loss.

Because this chapter talks about remote COM communication, you must have a minimum of two Windows machines (one client and one server) set up in a network configuration to work with the following exercises. Although the example will work on a single machine setup, you won't see DCOM at work when using just one machine, which is the purpose of creating the example in the first place. Make certain that both machines support DCOM, which leaves out older versions of Windows. All versions of Windows NT 4.0 and Windows 2000 ship with DCOM installed. You can download a copy of DCOM for the first version of Windows 95 from Microsoft's Web site; later versions of the product include DCOM as a default. You'll find a variety of DCOM resources, including DCOM support and updates for both Windows 95 and Windows 98, at `http://www.microsoft.com/Com/resources/downloads.asp`. This Web site also has a link to an interesting Windows Distributed interNetwork Architecture (DNA) Performance Kit that will make it possible for you to check the performance of any COM+ applications that you create.

Uses for DCOM Applications

DCOM can't be used in place of COM+. Even if you discount all of the new security features that COM+ provides, DCOM is essentially a client/server protocol. One client requests services from one server. However, this perceived lack of functionality doesn't prevent you from using DCOM for a number of application types, especially those that are used locally rather than across the entire enterprise.

DCOM has a number of things in its favor. For one, it's a very stable technology and has gone through several years of testing. COM+ is a relatively new and untested technology that builds upon older technology. It's important to consider the stability that DCOM has to offer when designing a new application.

Obviously, I could go on for quite some time discussing the relative merits of DCOM versus COM+. In the long-run, COM+ will be the technology of choice for enterprise applications, especially those that require new COM+ features like transactions and the capability to work in disconnected mode. DCOM is a more suitable choice for workgroups and other situations in which client/server is still a good and reliable technology to use for application development.

Now that we've gotten past some of the preliminaries, let's look at the ways that you can use DCOM to create applications in today's computing environment. The following sections aren't meant to be all-inclusive, but they do provide you with some good ideas of how to use DCOM for development. More importantly, we'll look at some of the caveats of using DCOM, especially in light of the new features that COM+ has to offer the developer.

Utility

Utility applications normally provide some small but necessary task at the server for either an application or user. For example, a utility application might query the server about the status of a print job or obtain equipment status information. You still need to provide some method for obtaining this information, but COM+ is definitely overkill in this situation. Unless your application needs to obtain this information over an Internet connection, a small DCOM utility application is all you really need to get the job done.

Note   DCOM Applications can work over the Internet if you enable COM Internet Services (CIS). There are some relatively difficult problems to overcome if you go this route, so it's not the best option. The "Security Settings" section of the chapter will help you to understand the implications of using CIS with your DCOM application. Although using this particular feature is tricky, you can configure it to provide a maximum of functionality with a minimum of security risks.

DCOM has several advantages when it comes to the utility application. It's smaller and lighter than COM+, so it actually makes better use of critical server resources. You also won't need to retrain the network administrator to use it; a utility application is almost self-supporting in most situations. Utility applications also have to provide consistent results, something the longevity of DCOM would tend to support. Finally, there aren't any disadvantages to consider, like multiple machine queries, because a utility application would need to query each server separately.

Of course, this begs the question of how many utility applications are left to write, especially when you consider the level of support that Windows 2000 provides. Even at this early stage of release, there are a number of Windows 2000-specific utility applications on the market. The third-party development market is definitely alive and well. It's almost certain that third party products alone won't answer every need that a company will have, so the utility application is definitely one category of DCOM application to consider.

Utility applications targeted at Windows 2000 will probably exploit gaps in Microsoft's support for new technologies like Active Directory. In fact, Active Directory is one very large area to look at for DCOM development. This particular part of Windows 2000 carries a great deal of information, much of it inaccessible to the end user. In addition, it's extensible. You can use Active Directory to store any type of system status information desired. In short, Windows 2000 provides more opportunities to create utility-type applications, not less.

Library

Library applications tend to work with logic, rather than physical devices. For example, a set of math routines would fall into the library category. In many cases, libraries reside on the client machine, rather than on the server, so that the user has direct access to them and can gain the advantage of speed that local access provides.

Local client access works only with routines that don't change. If you're working with data that changes from time-to-time, the best place to put the library routine is on the server. For example, you might have a library routine that computes the amount of postage to place on a package based on weight. In this case, the postage rate would change from time-to-time, so the best place to put the calculation program is on a server where the network administrator could make changes as needed.

Library routines are perfect candidates for DCOM for the very same reason that utility programs are. Because library routines are usually designed for everyone to use, security isn't even a problem. As with many small applications, DCOM is still the right choice because it works well in the client-server environment.

Database management

A database management system (DBMS) is a borderline use for DCOM. In fact, there are very few database applications where DCOM is still the right choice because COM+ provides so many useful features that make a DBMS easier to use and more secure as well. There are, however, some cases where the use of DCOM is still warranted, even in the database application arena. The following list provides you with some criteria that you can use when making a decision.

✦ **Size:** DCOM is a good choice for small databases. If the database application was originally designed for client/server, then DCOM will likely work well. Utility databases, like the one used to hold the numbers required for calculating totals in a library application are a perfect candidate for DCOM from a size perspective.

✦ **Security:** DCOM isn't as secure as COM+. If everyone has (or should have) access to the data, and the application security requirements are low, then DCOM will work just fine. If the database contains supersecret data, you'll want to use COM+ instead.

✦ **Mission Critical:** DCOM is a very poor choice for mission-critical database applications. If you think that you might need to use any form of transaction support within the application, then look to COM+, not DCOM. COM+ has the transaction support required to build mission-critical database applications. It ensures that any data that you send to the server will actually arrive intact.

✦ **Multiple Server or Server Cluster:** DCOM isn't even a candidate when it comes to multiple server or server cluster applications. Remember that DCOM is client/server; it simply doesn't provide the support required to build a true distributed application.

✦ **Multiple Components:** DCOM is a relatively poor choice when working with multiple components. Most developers today will divide their application into relatively small modules. This tends to promote code reuse if a module is generic enough. Creating multiple components with a DCOM setup, however, invites disaster when the network administrator reorganizes the network and places some components on another machine. An application that was working yesterday might suddenly break.

 Tip

Always include extra error-trapping code when working with more than one component in a DCOM application. The server-side component that the client initially calls should check for the existence of all components locally before it begins processing the request. If one or more of the components is missing, then the server-side component should report an error indicating the absence of the affected components. The server-side component should also check for accessibility (security) because the network administrator could set security differently for each component.

✦ **Internet Support:** DCOM doesn't provide any form of Internet support, which isn't surprising considering when this technology made its debut. You can probably work around this limitation by providing dual support for your application (desktop and Internet), but this could turn out to be more hassle than it's worth. In most cases, you'll want to use COM+ for Internet applications.

✦ **Older Client Support:** DCOM is a relatively good choice for older clients that may not support COM+. For example, if you have to support a combination of Windows 2000, Windows NT, and Windows 9x machines, then consider using DCOM. There isn't any guarantee that you'll be able to use a COM+ application with all of these clients. One thing is sure: You must have a Windows 2000 client to use some of the best new features of COM+ like disconnected mode operation and some of the security features.

User or application control

User and application control applications aren't necessarily restricted to security applications. An example of a user control application that falls into this category is one that tracks when the user initially logs in during the day and the amount of resources that the user requires before logging back out. Although Windows 2000 does provide a lot of auditing features that help you to perform this task, your company may have requirements that Windows 2000 doesn't handle natively. The ability to extend Active Directory to handle a variety of new object types means that you can log anything, even if Windows wasn't designed to handle the information that you want to store.

There are other forms of user control as well. For example, you may want to create a set of rules that define what resources a user can access depending on environmental factors like the day of week or current server load. The more complex the set of conditions that you need to set up, the better it is to use an external application. However, no matter how complex the setup, control of this type still requires a single level of communication between a client and server. Because the communication doesn't occur on more than one server, DCOM is still the best solution.

Application control can fall into the resource category as well. For example, you may need to monitor an application's use of network bandwidth. Simple communication between the client and server using DCOM will allow you to keep certain types of application activity at acceptable levels, ensuring that all network users get their fair share of resources.

Business logic

There are a lot of forms of business logic. For example, an application needs to have some form of business logic in order to process customer orders. The application may need to check the customer's current account balance and credit rating before completing the order. In most cases, this type of business logic is integrated into a larger application, and therefore might not be a candidate for a DCOM application.

Other forms of business logic do fit within the small application category that DCOM is still very adept at handling. For example, although you couldn't use DCOM for a client-entry application for a large corporation, DCOM will still work fine in the shipping room where orders are simply read. The same holds true for finding standard bits of information like the company's preferred shipping routes for products in different states. In short, if the database is small and the distribution limited, you can use DCOM as a means for allowing access to your business logic across a network. While these applications are small, any resource savings that you get by using DCOM in place of COM+ will help the network to run more efficiently.

Help desk

One application that many people are writing and constantly updating is the corporate help desk. A help desk application reduces the need for a user to directly contact a network administrator. In many cases, the user can fix a problem without ever talking to someone else. This kind of self-help saves company resources and makes the user better able to handle small emergencies that normally wouldn't require a network administrator's help.

Help desk applications are perfect for DCOM because they normally reside on a single server and use a relatively small database that isn't changed by the user. There is no need for transactions and little need for security. All the user really needs is a conduit to the information required to answer his or her question.

Of course, all of this discussion assumes that you're using a thick client. What happens if you need thin-client support via an Internet connection or wireless network? At this point, you're using Web pages and perhaps need to set communication up between more than one server. DCOM is the right solution for small networks that don't require Internet support and rely on thick clients. The moment that you bring a thin client or the Internet into the picture, DCOM becomes a much poorer choice.

At this point, it may sound like I've contradicted myself and that DCOM really is no longer part of the picture. However, you need to consider company policy regarding users fixing equipment on the road. Will the help desk application that you design really see use from users on the road or is this simply wishful thinking on the part of those road warriors who are tired of returning their machine to the company for every small glitch. Obviously, this is a question that you'll need to answer, but it's important to do so before you begin the design and coding process.

Data collection

It's surprising to think that many developers forget that a computer is essentially a data-collection device. The fact that you can write tomes like this one or play games on a computer has nothing to do with its original function. The computer was originally designed to collect data and perform computations from the resulting input, a job that it still performs admirably.

Data collection is still one of those back burner projects in many companies, but that doesn't mean that you can ignore some very real programming issues when working with a data-collection application. For example, one company recently created a data-collection application that allowed a client to upload current hardware configuration and usage information to a central server. This information allowed the network administrator to detect missing equipment and determine how long that equipment had been in use. The sole purpose of this application is to predict when a piece of equipment is likely to fail, something that's becoming more useful as computer part reliability becomes more predictable.

Besides data collection of this type, there are thousands (or even millions) of scientific applications that require many data-collection features. Every type of assembly line application also relies on data collection, as do hospitals and a host of other specialty environments. Data collection is actually more prevalent than many developers realize because monitoring the environment in which we work is an important task.

DCOM is the best solution for data-collection applications even if multiple computers are involved. There's a simple difference between this application type and the others that we've discussed so far. The client is collecting data; it doesn't care what the server does with that data and doesn't need any feedback about the data. Consequently, if the server collecting the data does need to interact with other machines, it doesn't have to impersonate the client to ensure that security is maintained. In addition, because the client doesn't require feedback, there's no need for transactions or any of the other trappings of an order entry system.

Creating a DCOM-Enabled Component

Before you can create an application that will use a component, you have to create that component. We're going to build a simple library component that adds two numbers together. The component doesn't provide any form of user interface. All it does is accept two numbers as input and output the sum as a result. The purpose of this example is to show that components used in a remote application don't require much in the way of special programming. Obviously, you need to avoid providing a user interface because there isn't anyone at the server to interact with it.

This component is unique in another way; it's not designed to be included directly within the application. (This is an out-of-process server, versus the in-process servers that you may be used to working with.) As a result, there's no need to worry about creating a property page or the other paraphernalia that normally goes with working with a component in an IDE. The AddIt component is designed to interact with the client during runtime, not during design time. There are actually a lot of applications for a component like this. Any time that you want the client to request information from the server without having to ask the user for input, you can use this method. In fact, there are several advantages to using this method. For example:

✦ **Reduced Complexity:** Any time that you can reduce the complexity of a component, you can also reduce the number of things that can go wrong with it, enhancing reliability as result.

✦ **Reduced Code Size:** A component that doesn't include user interface elements or IDE elements will be much smaller than a component that relies on these features. Obviously, a component of this nature won't be nearly as friendly to use. You have to weigh the benefits of reduced memory requirements and enhanced execution speed against programmer concerns.

✦ **Reduced Development Time:** Graphic elements take time to develop. Because this type of component doesn't include any graphics or associated code, you may find that development time of the core logic is greatly reduced.

Creating the component shell

Remember that DCOM relies on an out-of-process server, whereas COM+ uses in-process servers for the most part. This means you'll begin a DCOM project differently than you'll begin the COM+ examples in the chapters that follow. Creating an out-of-process server like the one used in this example is easy. All we'll need to do is create a standard ActiveX component project and change a few properties to get started. The following steps will get you started.

1. Select the ActiveX EXE option from the New Project dialog box, and then click Open. The ActiveX EXE project always creates an out-of-process server, while the ActiveX DLL project creates an in-process server. (Remember that in-process servers execute in the same process as the client.)

2. Change the Project Name property to AddIt and the Class Name property to AddNumbers. The name that you choose for the project and class is important because you'll need this information to access the component later. The component Registry entry will use the project name separated from the class name by a dot. We'll see how this works later in this chapter in the "Designing the Coding Method Example" section.

3. Use the Project ⇨ AddIt Properties command to display the AddIt Project Properties dialog box shown in Figure 10-1. You'll need to set the Unattended Execution option to ensure that the component won't display any dialog boxes on the server. If the component does try to display a message box, Windows will send the message to the event log instead. You'll also want to select the Thread per Object option to ensure that each new object instance is created in a separate thread. This reduces interference between threads.

4. Click OK to close the AddIt Project Properties dialog box.

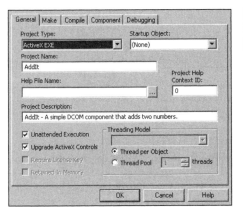

Figure 10-1: Setting the Unattended Execution option is essential.

5. Select the AddNumbers class module and set the Instancing property to 3 – SingleUse. This forces the component into single-threaded mode, which is a safer way to create components for access by more than one application.

6. Use the Tools ⇨ Add Procedure command to display the Add Procedure dialog box shown in Figure 10-2.

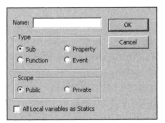

Figure 10-2: You'll use the Add Procedure dialog box to add methods to the component.

7. Type DoAdd in the Name field. This is the name of the method that we'll work with later. Select Function as the Type and Public as the Scope. Click OK to complete the process. At this point, you're ready to add code.

There are two other class module properties that we haven't talked about. The first is DataBindingBehavior. This property affects the way that the component interacts with a data source. If you set it to vbSimpleBound, then the object will bind to a single field of the data source. On the other hand, setting it to vbComplexBound will allow the object to bind to an entire row of the data source. The easiest way to look at this property is that simple components like a text box are simple bound, while components with more flexibility like a grid control are complex bound. Because we don't access a database with this component, the default setting of vbNone works just fine.

The Persistable property is only important if you want to save the settings for a component. For example, if a user places your component within an application and makes settings change to it, then the component should be persistable. On the other hand, the simple component that we're creating in this chapter doesn't have any properties to save, so setting this property to NotPersistable is the best choice. Setting a component to NotPersistable does save some system resources and makes the component operate slightly faster because Windows doesn't have to constantly monitor the component for changes.

Design tricks for distributed applications

It's never a good idea to rush development of an application, especially if the short-cut you're taking will result in a security breach or loss of data later. Of course, at the top of the user's list of things to dislike about any new application are bugs, and careful design can help you to avoid them. However, there are many development shortcuts that you can take that will maintain the current quality of the resulting application, yet reduce overall development time. While the following sections don't provide every shortcut ever conceived, they do provide you with food for thought. These shortcuts will help to reduce your development time without any loss of application quality.

Write individual component test routines

DCOM applications often rely on more than one server-side component to perform a given task. That's because DCOM sets security at the component level; you don't get the granularity of security control with DCOM that you do with COM+. In addition, there are times when you can't create a one-stop shop component; sometimes it makes sense to create a general-purpose component that you could use with other applications as part of the current development effort. Consequently, it's likely that you'll spend a lot of time debugging individual components, the interactions between components and the client application, and interactions between the components.

Writing individual component test routines allows you to check the component's operation with fewer interaction problems. You can use a small application to test the capabilities of a single component or you can create a larger test application that tests several of the components individually (using separate test buttons, for example). In most cases, this separate-component test methodology also allows you to see how efficiently the individual component works.

After you've tested the components separately, you can begin combing their output to create a cohesive application. Again, it pays to add one component to the application at a time, rather that trying to add all of the components at once. Designing and testing an application this way may take more time at the outset, but this technique will save you a considerable amount of time during debugging. If your application breaks during integration, you have the advantage of knowing precisely which component broke the application and a better idea of where to look for the cause.

Variable interference

It's possible that you'll see strange results from your component if it suffers some type of global variable interference. DCOM applications execute as out-of-process servers and on a server, rather than a desktop machine, so it's very likely that the component will have to handle more than one client request at a time. You can create a multithreaded component, but that requires a lot of added coding. Because more than one thread can execute in the same address space, they all have access to the same set of global variables. Generally, you'll want to create a single-threaded component where each instantiated object executes in a single thread.

To ensure that your component is single-threaded and that there's no chance of global variable interference, make sure that you set the component's Instancing property to 3 – Single Use. You'll also need to select the Thread per Object setting on the General tab of the Project Properties dialog box. These two settings will ensure that your object's variables remain safe and that you won't see global variable corruption.

What do you lose by going this route? Using these two settings means that every client request creates an entirely new object, rather than creating a thread on an existing object. This means that your application won't run as fast because it takes some amount of time to create the object. In addition, it won't use resources as efficiently because there are some resources devoted to the object itself. In short, you're paying in resources and execution speed for a gain in component reliability and a reduction in development time.

Always provide a return value

It's easy to forget that a DCOM component has no user interface while you're writing the code. However, once you begin using the component as part of an application, the lack of a user interface quickly becomes evident. With this in mind, you should always write DCOM component methods as functions and provide a return value that indicates the result of the method call. Even if the method call succeeds, you should provide a return value of vbOK so that the client knows that the method call was successful, rather than not knowing how the call turned out.

When the method call does fail, try to use standard error messages first, and if they won't work, create custom error messages that tell the user the precise cause of failure. The reason that you want to use standard error messages first is so that the user can easily convert them to human-readable form. Custom messages tend to be a lot more difficult to decipher, so it's important to use them with constraint.

Because you'll be using the return value as a success or failure indicator, you need to pass both input and output values as method arguments. Most developers will place the inputs to a method call first, then the outputs. Of course, this methodology isn't set in stone, so you can pass the arguments in any order that you like. Consistency does have the benefit of making your component easy to use, however, so it's a good idea to at least consider passing arguments in some specific order.

Diagram data flows

It's easy to get mired in detail and miss the big picture when creating distributed applications, so the first thing that you should do is create the big picture. Start with the idea that data exists on a server somewhere and that you have to present it to the client by using the most secure and efficient method possible. Every distributed application development scenario begins this way, yet many developers begin by looking at the details before they look at what the application needs to do as a whole.

Use realistic data when you diagram your application. Include the amount of data that you need to transfer and see if there's some way to minimize the size of each transfer. It's also important to consider the number of transfers. A data transfer of 1 byte still consumes network resources. Try to combine data transfers into one request whenever possible.

Tip   As important as diagramming your application is to DCOM, it's even more important when working with COM+. Instead of working with one client and server, you may find yourself working with one client and several servers, each of which can also communicate with other servers. An application can quickly get so complex that no one really understands what's going on. Diagramming data flows, knowing what data is flowing where and how much, is absolutely essential when designing distributed applications.

After you have a data flow designed, you can begin to figure the inputs and outputs of the components that you'll need to create the server side of an application. DCOM requires quite a few components, in many cases, because you set security at the component level. So, as part of the diagramming process, you need to set up security zones to ensure that the data that you access is accessed in the safest possible manner. The combination of security zones and data flow determines the number of components that you require for the application and how they'll interact with both the client and each other.

Test on more than one client

When you're writing desktop applications, you at least know that the application will execute on a single machine, which has certain advantages. For example, you can check for specific versions of DLLs as part of the installation process, so that you know the machine meets minimum requirements. Unfortunately, distributed applications don't afford the same comfort level as desktop applications do; you can't always check which version of a DLL will be used to access your component.

DCOM support is built into Windows 2000 and Windows 98 SE. However, it's an add-on for Windows 95 and the original version of Windows 98. Even if DCOM is supplied as part of the operating system, you still can't be absolutely certain which version of DCOM you're using. As a result, you need to test your DCOM application with several different clients before you can be certain that it'll work with a wide variety of machines. If you need to support all versions of Windows 9x, Windows NT, and Windows 2000, you need to test your application within all those environments to ensure that you get the results that you anticipated.

So, how do you determine which version of DCOM you're using? There isn't any method for determining the version with absolute certainty, unless you want to compare every DLL individually. However, the rpcrt.dll file will normally give you an indicator of which version you're using as shown in Figure 10-3. (A number showing the general version number will normally follow RPCRT.) You'll find the rpcrt.dll file in either the SYSTEM or SYSTEM32 folder. If this file isn't present, then you need to install DCOM support.

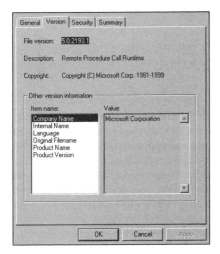

Figure 10-3: Check the rpcrt.dll file for an indication of which version of DCOM you're using.

Adding some code

Now that we have a simple component shell put together and you have some ideas for creating a better component design, let's add some code to the AddIt component. Listing 10-1 shows the code that we're going to use for this example.

Listing 10-1: **AddIt DoAdd() Method**

```
Public Function DoAdd(Input1 As Long, _
    Input2 As Long, _
    Answer As Long)

    'Determine if we received good inputs.
    If (Input1 >= 0) And (Input2 >= 0) Then
```

Continued

Listing 10-1 *(continued)*

```
            'Add the two numbers.
            Answer = Input1 + Input2

            'Return a result code.
            DoAdd = vbOK

        Else

            'Return an error code.
            DoAdd = vbError

        End If

    End Function
```

As you can see, this example is ridiculously simple and for good reason — we're only looking at how DCOM works for now, we're not trying to create a complex library routine application. There's one item in this example that you should always add to your applications. Notice that we use a value of vbOK as the function's return value. You should always return status information as part of your DCOM component. We'll see in Chapter 12 that this isn't always so. When working with a COM+ application that allows the user access in disconnected mode, you'll want to report errors to the event log instead of returning an error to the client.

Notice that there's also an opportunity for failure, even with this component. You should always range check any input variable. In this case, range checking is very easy. For one thing, txtInput1 and txtInput2 are set to accept only numeric input. In addition, using a Long means that DoAdd( ) will accept only integer input. In this case, the range checking is provided for example purposes only, but it should be an important element of every component that you build. Knowing that the component is receiving good data is essential because there isn't any way that the component can ask the user for additional or different input.

Normally, you'll also want to use a specific error constant for feedback. Because this is a very generic example, I've also used a generic error code. As applications get more complex, it's important to provide a specific error code so that the user has a better idea of precisely what went wrong with the application. For example, you should have a different error code for a variable range problem than for an incorrect variable value. In some cases, this means that you'll have to create custom return values, but try to use standard Visual Basic error codes whenever possible.

Creating Two DCOM Client Applications

Let's create two very simple applications for this example. Because the component we've built will only add two numbers together, we'll create two different applications that accept two numbers as input, then display a result based on the component's output. The point of these applications is to illustrate for you the remote connection between a component on one machine and a client on another machine.

The first client in this example uses the Registry method of accessing the remote component, while the second client has this information directly programmed into the application itself. DCOM doesn't limit you to one method of access. In fact, you could easily create a hybrid of these two applications and store the coding information required for the second client in the Registry. In general, you'll find that the Registry method offers more flexibility, while the coding method is less prone to configuration error and could offer more security because the user doesn't need to know where the data is stored.

Note   This application is set up to work on my server. You need to substitute some of the information in the source code for your setup. Make absolutely certain that you change any server arguments to match the name of your server, along with any required security information. In addition, make certain that you configure the test server to work with the component. We'll look at the process of installation and configuration later in the chapter.

Web Resource   Writing COM and DCOM applications involves creating components and applications to use them. No matter how careful you are, there's a good chance that you'll leave small pieces of these applications in the Registry. In many cases, the extra Registry information will simply bloat the size of the Registry on your hard drive. However, there are situations when old Registry information could cause other kinds of problems. Microsoft provides a special utility for cleaning up old Registry entries from a development workstation called RegMaid. Information about this utility is found at `http://support.microsoft.com/support/kb/articles/q156/0/78.asp`.

Creating the program shell and designing the dialog

We'll be using a standard dialog application for this example. All you need to do is start Visual Basic, select the Standard EXE option from the New tab of the New Project dialog box, and then click Open. You'll see an empty form. Figure 10-4 shows the positions of the components that we'll use for this example. Table 10-1 contains the property changes that you'll need to make to each object in the example. As you can see, this is a relatively simple test application.

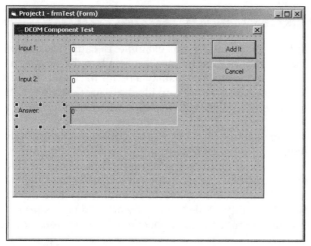

Figure 10-4: A simple test application dialog box.

Table 10-1
Component Properties for the DCOM Test Client

Object	Property	Value
frmTest	BorderStyle	3 – Fixed Dialog
	Caption	DCOM Component Test
	Height	4700
	Icon	DCT.ICO file found on the CD-ROM provided with the book
	Width	7000
cmdAddIt	Caption	Add It
	Default	True
	TabIndex	0
	ToolTipText	Add Two Numbers
cmdCancel	Cancel	True
	Caption	Cancel
	TabIndex	4
	ToolTipText	Exit the Application

Object	Property	Value
txtInput1	DataFormat	Number (0 decimal places)
	TabIndex	1
	Text	0
	ToolTipText	First Input to AddIt Component
txtInput2	DataFormat	Number (0 decimal places)
	TabIndex	2
	Text	0
	ToolTipText	Second Input to AddIt Component
lblAnswer	BorderStyle	1 – Fixed Single
	Caption	0
	DataFormat	Number (0 decimal places)
	ToolTipText	Answer from AddIt

Adding the Registry method code

There's one additional configuration step when working with a DCOM application that uses the Registry method to find the component. You also need to add a reference to the AddIt component. Use the Project ➪ References command to display the References DCOMTest1.vbp dialog box shown in Figure 10-5. Check the AddIt – A simple DCOM component that adds two numbers entry, and then click OK. You'll need this reference in order to access the component when using the Registry method. We'll see that the coding method (discussed in the "Designing the Coding Method Example" section) doesn't require a reference because you're using a different coding technique to access it.

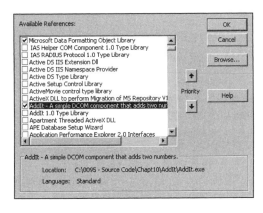

Figure 10-5: Make sure you add the AddIt component to your project.

As mentioned previously, this example is very simple, but it demonstrates how a DCOM application works. Listing 10-2 contains the two subroutines that you need to implement for this example.

Listing 10-2: **Registry Method**

```
Private Sub cmdAddIt_Click()

    'Create a temporary variable.
    Dim liAnswer As Long

    'Create a result variable.
    Dim liResult As Long

    'Create the AddIt object.
    Dim oAddIt As New AddIt.AddNumbers

    'Add the new numbers.
    liResult = oAddIt.DoAdd( _
        CInt(txtInput1.Text), _
        CInt(txtInput2.Text), _
        liAnswer)

    'Check the results.
    If liResult = vbOK Then

        'Display an unnecessary success message.
        MsgBox "Success!"

        'Place the results in the answer.
        lblAnswer.Caption = CStr(liAnswer)

    Else

        'Check for a range error.
        If liResult = vbError Then

            'Display a specific error message.
            MsgBox "Please use positive numbers only!"

        'Otherwise, it's a generic error.
        Else

            'Never displayed with our code.
            MsgBox "Failure"

        End If

    End If

    'Release the object.
```

```
        Set oAddIt = Nothing

    End Sub

    Private Sub Command2_Click()

        'End the application
        End

    End Sub
```

There are a few things to notice in this code. First, we're using the New keyword to create the object. This saves one line of code because you don't have to set the object's value, it's set as part of the creation process.

Notice that we provide direct input in the form of the two textbox Text properties. When it comes to the return value, however, we need an intermediate variable. No matter what you do, you can't pass an object to a remote server with DCOM. You can, however, pass an object when working with COM+, even a disconnected COM+ application. The capability to pass objects is a big advantage when using COM+.

I've used the return value from the DoAdd() method call to determine which course of action to take. You'll normally do this in your code as well. Because the DCOM component can't provide any form of feedback, you need to check the return value for errors. If the call is successful, you can take the normal course of action. Failure messages might mean simply displaying an error message or trying the call again, but you might need to ask the user for additional input or to take some other course of action depending on the type and severity of the failure.

You know from Listing 10-1 that the only possible error-return code for this example is vbError. The application code specifically checks for vbError and provides a meaningful message to the user. Because we want the user to enter only positive numbers, the vbError return code indicates that the user entered a negative number. The Else clause in the error-checking section might seem unnecessary, but you'll never know when the component developer will add a result code that your application doesn't handle. If this happens, you need to have some code in place to at least acknowledge the error, which is what MsgBox "Failure" does in this case.

I placed an unnecessary MsgBox() call in the code as well. The reason for this message box is to show you the DCOM application in action. If the code was written as normal, lbliAnswer would receive the return value from the DoAdd() method call so quickly that you wouldn't get to see the AddIt object created on the server. This MsgBox() call simply delays freeing of the oAddIt object long enough for you to see the results on the server.

The final piece of code might seem inconsequential, but it's very important. By setting the oAddIt variable to Nothing you free the object created earlier. This frees resources on the server immediately and allows other applications to use them.

It also means that your application will leave a clean environment behind on the desktop. While DCOM will eventually release the objects that you create (through pinging to test whether the client is still alive), it may take up to eight minutes for it to do so. In server time, this is a lifetime and you'll definitely see the result in reduced application performance.

Designing the coding method example

There's a second major method of accessing a component on a server by using DCOM: the coding technique. We'll need a second application to test this second methodology. You can use the steps in the "Creating the Program Shell and Designing the Dialog" section to create the application shell. After you've completed the application shell, you can add the code shown in Listing 10-3.

Listing 10-3: **Code Method**

```
Private Sub cmdAddIt_Click()

    'Create a temporary variable
    Dim liAnswer As Long

    'Create a result variable.
    Dim liResult As Long

    'Create the AddIt object.
    Dim oAddIt As Object
    Set oAddIt = CreateObject( _
        "AddIt.AddNumbers", _
        "WinServer")

    'Add the two numbers.
    liResult = oAddIt.DoAdd( _
        CInt(txtInput1), _
        CInt(txtInput2), _
        liAnswer)

    'Check the results.
    If liResult = vbOK Then

        'Display an unnecessary success message.
        MsgBox "Success!"

        'Place the results in the answer.
        lblAnswer.Caption = CStr(liAnswer)

    Else

        'Check for a range error.
        If liResult = vbError Then
```

```
                'Display a specific error message.
                MsgBox "Please use positive numbers only!"

            'Otherwise, it's a generic error.
            Else

                'Never displayed with our code.
                MsgBox "Failure"

            End If

        End If

        'Release the object.
        Set oAddIt = Nothing

    End Sub

    Private Sub Command2_Click()

        'End the application.
        End

    End Sub
```

At first glance, this code doesn't look much different than the code in Listing 10-2. We're still creating an object, calling the DoAdd() method, testing the result, and releasing the object when we're done. The major difference is in how the object is created. You'll remember from discussions in Chapter 5, that you can add a remote server to the CreateObject() function call. However, to use this capability, we need to create the object first, then use a separate set to create and initialize the object. In short, this method is slightly less efficient than the Registry method.

 Note   Notice that I've hard coded the remote location of WinServer in this example. You could easily extend this example to look in the Registry for the required information. In fact, if you'll look on the CD-ROM provided with the book, you'll find another version of this example called DCOM Test Application (Hybrid Method) that allows you to store the location of the server in the Registry, rather than hard coding it in the application.

Testing the DCOM Application

At this point, we have two (actually three) versions of the same DCOM application to test. Both applications create the AddIt object and use the DoAdd() method that it contains to add two numbers together. The client applications receive the results from the components, then display them on screen for the user to see. There really isn't anything too complex about the example or associated code.

Testing and debugging applications have to be the least favorite part of any developer's day and DCOM doesn't do anything to make life simpler. DCOM applications normally require three main phases of testing as listed below.

1. Build and test the components individually. If you don't test the functionality of each component, you'll find yourself chasing interaction errors down during integration testing. A component should be able to stand on its own while adding the whole application. If you have trouble testing individual components, you may want to take another look at the application design before you move forward.

2. Build and test the application locally. A DCOM application should be able to run on a single machine. You may need to jury rig a data source, in some cases, but it's important to do so. Local testing allows you to keep network and server issues out of the initial testing phase. What you end up with is an application that you know works — at least locally.

3. Distribute the applications components on test servers, and then check for network and server interaction problems. Never test your application on a production system; always use a test server setup that replicates the production system for testing purposes. By the time you reach this level of testing, you should have eliminated the majority of the bugs from the application. The only elements that this level of testing should check for are server and network compatibility problems.

Our test application isn't complex enough to require individual component testing — there's only one component to work with. However, we do need to perform both the local and remote tests of the application. For the Registry method example, you won't have to make any changes to the component between phases. You will, however, need to change the source of the component in the coding method example. After you've tested the example locally, you'll need to change the application code to start the component on the server. This is one additional complication of using the coding method that you won't have to deal with when working with the Registry method.

Testing the result locally

At this point, you can compile the DCOMTest1 and DCOMTest2 applications, and the AddIt component for a local test. While you can perform the initial component and application tests within the Visual Basic IDE, you'll need to compile both to ensure that they work, because they may act differently in the IDE than they will in a standard runtime environment. When you start the application, you see a simple dialog box similar to the one shown in Figure 10-6 asking for two numbers as input. Entering the two numbers and clicking Add It displays the result in the Answer field of the dialog box. Both of the test applications should work in precisely the same way (and, in fact, look precisely the same).

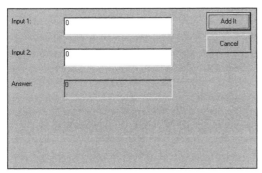

Figure 10-6: The DCOMTest application allows you to test the component locally before running it on another machine.

Configuring for a remote test

When you finish testing the component's local operation, copy the component to the machine that you want to use as a server and register it there. Normally, you use RegSvr32 to register either an OCX or DLL version of a component. Out-of-process servers are EXE files and come with their own built-in registration feature. All you need to do is type AddIt/RegServer at the command line to register the AddIt component. Likewise, typing AddIt/UnregServer at the command line unregisters the component on the server (or the client). Unfortunately, Visual Basic hides the implementation details of the registration process from you, so it's difficult at best to modify it in any way. Fortunately, there probably isn't any reason for you to do so.

You'll also need to modify the `CreateObject()` call in DCOMTest2. Make sure that the call uses the remote server in place of the local machine. Otherwise, DCOMTest2 won't be able to find the remote component when you execute it. Unlike DCOMTest1, DCOMTest2 doesn't rely on any configuration Registry entries (as we'll see later in this section of the chapter.) DCOMTest2 does, however, rely on one Registry entry that allows it to determine the GUID of the component. You'll have to recompile the application once you make the change so that you can test it outside of the Visual Basic IDE.

DCOMTest1 won't automatically know that you've placed a copy of AddIt on the server. You need to tell DCOMTest1 where to find a copy of AddIt. Let's begin this part of the configuration by looking in the Registry. Open RegEdit and find the AddIt.AddNumbers key under My Computer\HKEY_CLASSES_ROOT. Expand the hierarchy and you'll see two keys as shown in Figure 10-7. The Clsid key is the one you're interested in because it contains the globally unique identifier (GUID) for this class.

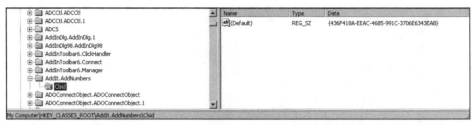

Figure 10-7: Finding the first entry for your component class in the Registry is easy, just look for the class name.

Use the GUID to find the next entry in the Registry. The first entry that you should find will be under the AppID key. This key doesn't contain any subkeys right now, but as we'll see later, this will change. The second entry that you'll find will appear under the CLSID key as shown in Figure 10-8. This is where the name and location of the server are stored, along with any required configuration variables. When you select the local execution checkbox in the Distributed COM Configuration Properties dialog box, what you're really doing is adding this key to the Registry.

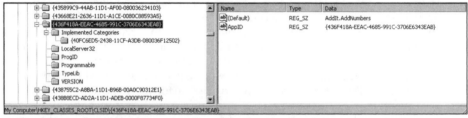

Figure 10-8: Local machine data for a component is stored under the CLSID key.

Tip   You'll also find this set of three keys under HKEY_LOCAL MACHINE. However, the two sets of keys are normally synced, so making a change in one location with a utility will usually make it in the other. It's important to realize that there are two sets of keys, though, when making manual changes to the Registry. If you make a mistake changing a value under HKEY_CLASSES_ROOT (the active set of entries), you'll find a duplicate set under HKEY_LOCAL_MACHINE.

Now that you have some idea of the implications of the changes that we're going to make, let's set AddIt up for remote operation. Start DCOMCnfg using the Run dialog box (you can display this dialog box using the Windows Start ➪ Run command). Once you start the Distributed COM Configuration Properties dialog box, highlight the AddIt.AddNumbers application and click Properties. Click the Location tab and you'll see an AddIt.AddNumbers Properties dialog box similar to the one shown in Figure 10-9. This is where you'll choose a new location for the component to run. Uncheck Run application on this computer and check Run application on the following computer. You'll need to supply a remote computer name as well.

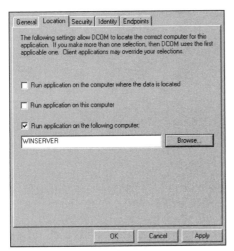

Figure 10-9: It's important to reconfigure your application for remote execution.

Making a change to the Registry by using the Distributed COM Configuration Properties dialog box doesn't really show what happens. If you still have the Registry Editor open, press F5 to refresh the view. Move to the top of the Registry and locate the GUID for our component again. The first entry that you find will be the original AddIt.AddNumbers entry under HKEY_CLASSES_ROOT. This entry hasn't changed because even remote execution requires a GUID entry. The second entry under the AppID key has changed as shown in Figure 10-10. There's a RemoteServerName value now that tells Windows where to find the required component. The third entry has changed as well as shown in Figure 10-11. Notice that the LocalServer32 key now begins with an underscore. So, even though the local entry remains in place, Windows won't find it and try to execute the component locally.

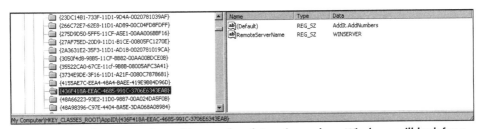

Figure 10-10: The RemoteServerName value determines where Windows will look for a remote component.

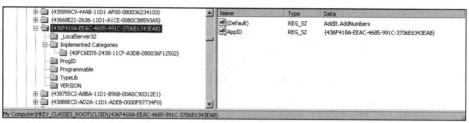

Figure 10-11: The local entry remains in place, but the key changes, making it inaccessible to Windows.

Here's something interesting to try. Save the key under CLSID to disk, and then delete it from the Registry. Now, try the two test applications. What you'll find is that the application that depends on the Registry method of execution (DCOMTest1) fails with an error message, while DCOMTest2, which relies on the coding method, executes correctly. In short, this demonstrates that the coding method does rely less on the Registry. The only Registry entry that the coding method requires is the initial AddIt.AddNumbers entry under HKEY_CLASSES_ROOT that contains the GUID for the component.

On the CD-ROM There's a copy of the three Registry entries on the CD-ROM provided with this book that will work with the AddIt component (also on the CD-ROM). If you inadvertently delete your Registry entries without saving them first, you can restore them by using AddIt/RegServer or by adding the supplied Registry entries. (Don't use the supplied Registry files if you created your copy of AddIt from scratch because your GUID will be different than mine.)

Performing a remote test

The test application is ready for remote testing. There's an easy way to verify that the component is executing on the remote server. Right-click the Task Bar on the remote server (the bar normally found at the bottom of the Windows display) and choose Task Manager from the context menu. A Windows Task Manager dialog box will display. Click the Processes tab to see a list of processes executing on the machine. Click the Image Name column header to view the process names in alphabetical order (this helps you to find a process faster). Look through the list of processes; you shouldn't see AddIt.EXE anywhere in the list. Now, run the DCOMTest1 application, type two numbers in the input fields, and then click Add It. You'll see the AddIt.EXE component added to the process list in the Windows Task Manager dialog box as shown in Figure 10-12. Click OK at the Success message dialog box. After a few seconds, the component disappears from the list. This is your assurance that the component has executed on the machine that you indicated.

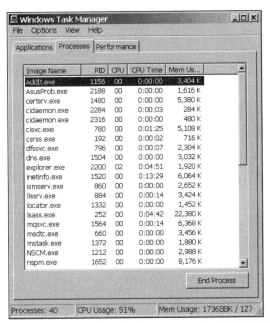

Figure 10-12: Using the Processes tab of the Windows Task Manager dialog box allows you to monitor the execution of components.

Check out the same display on the client machine. What you see is that DCOMTest.EXE appears on the list, but that AddIt.EXE doesn't. This may seem like an overly simplified way to see DCOM in action, but it does show you how even complex setups work in the real world. Repeat these two steps for DCOMTest2 and you'll see the same results, even though the two applications use different component-creation techniques.

Quick Fixes for DCOM Communication Problems

DCOM is COM with connectivity added. We've discussed the COM part of the picture in Chapter 9. There are a number of component problems that affect COM and they affect DCOM as well. For example, a DCOM application can experience the same performance issues as a COM application. However, in many cases, those problems are more pronounced under DCOM. A small performance problem under COM is likely to become a big performance problem under DCOM because you're also dealing with a network connection. In short, where you have to be careful creating COM applications, you need to be decidedly paranoid when creating DCOM applications.

DCOM does introduce a new set of problems. Your application is no longer tied to the desktop, it's located on two machines with a network connection in between. This means that besides dealing with component problems, you also have connectivity problems to worry about. Some communication problems are programmer controlled. For example, you'll experience a performance loss by transferring too much data to the server, but the amount of performance loss is under your control. A lost connection, on the other hand, isn't under your control. You can't even predict when one will happen. The best that you can hope to do is detect the connection error and provide some code that will help the application to recover from it.

The following sections will look at DCOM communication problems. We'll see how various networking issues can affect your application and what you need to do to prevent errors, at least most of the time. The important idea to take away from this section, however, is that you can't prevent all of the problems from occurring. Sometimes a problem occurs and there's nothing that you could add to your code to prevent it. So, DCOM applications need to incorporate error detection and recovery code, in addition to following good programming techniques.

Component specific

DCOM components execute on the server, while the requesting application resides on the client machine. Consequently, when you design a DCOM component, you have to remember to consider the additional requirements of server-side processing. Of course, a major requirement is security, something we'll talk about in the "Security Settings" section of this chapter. The following sections look at some component-specific issues that you need to consider when building DCOM applications.

Resource management

One big source of problems for component developers is that a server may appear to have limitless resources, but the amount of resources available for any given task are actually smaller than on the client. Servers are responsible for handling requests from multiple clients simultaneously, so the resources need to be shared between multiple copies of the component. Therefore, when writing a component for server use, the component should gain access to resources as soon as possible (to ensure that processing can complete) and release them only when they're no longer needed (to ensure that the client call doesn't block).

Note COM+ introduces new technologies that make some of the advice I'm giving you here irrelevant or outdated. For example, COM+ provides much better resource handling than does DCOM, so you'll find that you use different resource management techniques for a COM+ application than you do with a DCOM application. While a DCOM application gains access to resources early and releases late, a COM+ application gains access to resources only when needed and releases them as early as possible. The difference in resource management does mean that you should create new components (or at least update the existing ones) when creating a COM+ application.

This resource management strategy could also have an effect on communications between the client and server. What should happen is that the client makes a request and the server does everything it can to service that request. If it can't service the request for any reason, including a lack of resources, the request should fail. In short, there should be at most two trips across the network. If you find that your component is making more than two trips, you'll need to figure out why those additional trips are required. In most cases, you should handle resource management problems on the server and keep the client in a request-only mode.

User interfaces

Server-side components, unlike desktop components, can't have any user interface like dialog boxes. The reason is simple: There's no one at the server to click OK in response to a message or to provide input that the component may need. Normally, you'll need to communicate errors through return values or by using the event log. Even with the event log, however, there's little chance of an instant response. You should always use return values when you need instant feedback on a problem or require additional user input. Event log entries allow a network administrator to monitor network problems, but you'll normally find that event logs are more for historical use than immediate response. (There are ways to create alerts from event log entries, so using an event log entry isn't always a bad idea — it's just not the optimal way to create the application.)

It turns out that the capability to always use return values for a DCOM application is one area where this technology is actually ahead of COM+. While there isn't any rule saying a COM+ application can't use return values, the truth is that you give up that capability to create disconnection applications. The knowledge that your component will always have a client to communicate with is one of the perks of using DCOM. It allows you to design components in such a way that they always provide solid feedback to the client. We'll see in Chapter 12 that there are kludges that you can use to get around this feedback problem, but for the most part, COM+ applications are limited to using the event log to report problems that the client isn't aware of.

Effects of pinging

One of the stranger DCOM problems that you'll run into is the timeout value. A client must send keep-alive messages to the DCOM server to indicate that it's still available and that the connection is in good shape. When the DCOM server fails to get a keep-alive message from a client for two minutes, it sends out a ping (another form of message) to the client to see if it's still available. If the client misses three ping intervals, then DCOM assumes that the client is no longer available.

As soon as DCOM considers the client dead, it frees any components in use by the client, which allows the server to recapture valuable resources. Because the ping interval is two minutes, keeping the component alive usually isn't a problem. However, you could run into a situation where the two-minute interval isn't long enough, which might mean that you can't use DCOM for the application in question or that you need to code the application in such a way that it can ping the server faster.

Pinging also has an effect on system performance. Normally, you won't see this effect, but it's present. What happens, however, if you have thousands of clients all pinging to keep themselves alive? At some point, system performance will degrade noticeably and you'll need to consider some method of reducing the number of machines on a network segment to a more manageable level.

Fortunately, DCOM requires pinging on a per-machine basis. Therefore, whether a single machine makes 1 or 100 requests, the ping requirements are the same. A single ping will keep all of the components for a single client machine alive on the server. In addition, instead of sending a keep-alive message with all of the references that a client has included, DCOM allows the client to send a meta reference, which keeps all of the components alive with a single reference.

Network-related problems

Many of the network-related problems that you'll experience with DCOM fall into the unavoidable category. For example, a lightning strike and a careless user crimping a cable are two situations in which you could lose the connection between client and server. Both situations require the server-side component and client-side application alike to detect the error, and then take steps to recover from it, or fail gracefully.

As mentioned in the "Effects of Pinging" section, DCOM will automatically detect a loss of client communication and either lower the component's reference count, or, if the reference count is zero, free the component. However, this still leaves you with data at the server end and an application running at the client end.

Using a timer at the client end usually works well. If a server-side component doesn't respond within a given interval, your application can query the server to ensure the connection is intact. If the connection isn't intact, you could either recreate the connection or tell the user about the problem. On the other hand, if the connection is intact, you should reset the timer and wait for a longer time or ask the user about terminating the current component and creating a new one. Make absolutely certain that you can modify the timeout interval to account for various network scenarios.

The server-side data is a lot more difficult to deal with. When working with COM+ you have the option of using transactions, which will automatically perform rollbacks if the transaction doesn't complete as anticipated. You can get the same support with DCOM by using Microsoft Transaction Server (MTS) directly. Otherwise, the data may very well be lost or the database corrupted.

Security settings

Security is always a problem when working with servers. You need to protect the data and resources that the server provides, but you also need to provide access to the data and resources in such a way as to make the access transparent to the user.

There are actually two levels of security that you need to consider when working with a server-side component. First, you must get the data from the client to the server securely. If the server wants to send a response back to the client, the data needs to be secured again. Second, the component must remain secure on the server. Only those people with the proper rights should be able to gain access to the server side component.

Securing data transfers

The problem of securing data transfers is relatively easy to take care of. We saw in Chapter 2 that you can set various levels of DCOM security by using the DCOM Configuration Tool. If you're working with sensitive data and don't mind the performance penalty, you can always encrypt both the data and the encryption key before it moves over the network.

Unfortunately, all of this automation can be a trap. A network administrator not only has to set security for every component used in an application, but the administrator needs to set that security consistently to ensure that the application works as anticipated. It's very easy to set components in a way that prevents that application from working at all (or at least exchanging data). Yes, the DCOM Configuration Tool makes configuration easy, but if the network administrator doesn't use it properly, there isn't any sense in having the tool available in the first place.

Component security settings

A common problem that developers face when working with server-side components is that of security settings. In most cases, it's not possible to test access to an application by using every potential setting, so it's important to use groups in place of individual users. Using a group makes it possible to test access to an application for an entire group of people.

However, there are still security-setting problems to consider. When Component A calls upon services provided by Component B on the same server, how do you set security for Component A to ensure that Component B will react properly? For example, you could use impersonation to ensure that the user's security plays a role in determining what level of access Component A should get to services provided by Component B. In a perfect world this would probably be the optimal answer, but it isn't always the right solution. What if Component C also requires access to Component B, but you still need to provide some level of security for Component B's services? In this case, you'll probably want to set access for both Component A and Component B to a special security account to ensure that both gain access to Component B, but that no one else will. Unfortunately, a security-minded network administrator could easily break your application, in this case, by setting security differently than anticipated. In short, security settings are always a prime target for investigation if an application works fine when you test it, but won't work when another user tries to access the application.

Tip   Always test security settings by using different accounts but the same machine. Unless the machine has some type of failure during the test (an unlikely event, but possible), you've eliminated a wealth of potential causes of application failure. If the administrator can access and use the application, but a user can't access that application, or the application fails for some reason using the same machine, then you know that it's not a network connection, installation, server, or local machine problem. The only three possible causes are local machine configuration, server configuration, or some type of security problem.

DCOM has a lot of problems when it comes to security. We'll see in Chapter 11 that COM+ overcomes many of these security deficiencies by providing the component with a context. The context allows the developer to check security settings with relative ease and act upon any problems in those settings. We'll also see that there isn't any need for certain types of security problems to occur at all. For example, instead of the three components I used in my example in the previous paragraph, you could build a single component containing all three objects. Role-based security allows you to perform these types of tasks without incurring any loss of security. Security is one of the reasons why you should use COM+, not DCOM, for large-enterprise applications where security enforcement is a prime consideration.

Overcoming problems with COM Internet Services (CIS)

In most cases, you won't want to use DCOM over an Internet connection, even though this feature is available through CIS. The problem is that DCOM doesn't provide the same level of security that a COM+ application will; additionally, you have to leave a port exposed on your machine. To make matters worse, an incorrect configuration could leave more than just one port open to the prying eyes of a cracker.

Let's look at what you need to do to use CIS first. Run the DCOMCnfg utility and select the Default Properties tab. You'll see a Distributed COM Configuration Properties dialog box similar to the one shown in Figure 10-13. Notice that the Enable COM Internet Services on this computer option isn't checked. To use DCOM over the Internet, you must check this box on both the client and the server (it's not checked by default). Simply checking this box won't make the feature completely available, but it's the first step.

After you have checked this option, you'll need to add an endpoint that will use the Internet connection. There are two places that you can do this. Adding it to the Default Protocols tab of the Distributed COM Configuration Properties dialog box will enable this feature for every component on the machine. The problem with this approach is that it leaves the entire machine open. A more conservative approach (and the one we'll use here) is to add the endpoint only to the application that needs it.

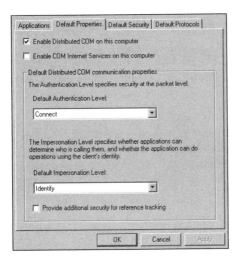

Figure 10-13: The first step to using DCOM over the Internet is to check the Enable COM Internet Services on this computer option.

Adding the endpoint to an application is easy. Select the Applications tab of the Distributed COM Configuration Properties dialog box, highlight the application that you want to work with, and then click Properties. Select the Endpoints tab and you'll see an application Properties dialog box similar to the one shown in Figure 10-14. Notice that this application is currently set to use only the default protocols.

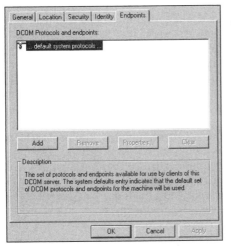

Figure 10-14: The Endpoints tab is where you add new protocols for an application.

Click Add and you'll see the Select DCOM Protocol and Endpoint dialog box shown in Figure 10-15. This dialog box allows you to choose a protocol. If you're working with the Internet, you'll want TCP/IP. You'll also want to select the Use Internet range of dynamic endpoints if the application will work with the Internet or Use Intranet range of dynamic endpoints if the application will work with a company intranet.

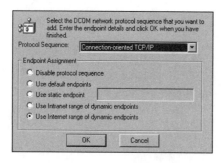

Figure 10-15: Selecting a protocol and endpoint type for this specific application is an important part of the configuration process.

At this point, you might be tempted to close the application dialog box and say that setup is complete. The second that you added a new protocol to the list, however, you told DCOM that this application would use a custom set of protocols and endpoints. This means that you have to add any protocols and endpoints that the application will use on your network or the application will fail to work.

We have one more configuration step to perform. Now that we've configured a specific application to use a particular protocol and endpoint type, it's time to reduce the potential for crackers to gain access to the system. Not only do you need to set more stringent security for the application in question (using options found on the Security tab that we discussed in Chapter 2), but you also need to restrict port access to the machine. You'll perform this task on the Default Protocols tab of the Distributed COM Configuration Properties dialog box. (Click OK to close the application Properties dialog box after you've completed the application configuration.)

To configure the ports used for a particular protocol, highlight the protocol on the Default Protocols tab and click Properties. You'll see a Properties for COM Internet Services dialog box similar to the one shown in Figure 10-16. This is where you'll choose the ports that an application can use to communicate with the server and vice versa. It's important to choose ports that won't be in use by your Web server. Choosing a unique port number will also deter some inexperienced crackers, but most crackers will find open ports on your system anyway.

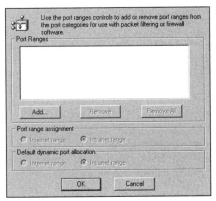

Figure 10-16: The COM Internet Services dialog box shows you which ports your application can use for communication.

As you can see from Figure 10-16, we don't yet have any ports configured for this protocol. To add a port, click Add. You'll see the Add Port Range dialog box shown in Figure 10-17. Type in a single port number above 4000. Selecting a port range provides a cracker with even more access to your system. Click OK to close this dialog box, and OK to close the Distributed COM Configuration Properties dialog box. At this point, your system is configured to use CIS. Obviously, you'll want to document this change to ensure that it doesn't stay in place after its useful lifetime.

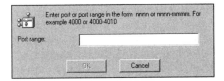

Figure 10-17: To maintain security at a higher level, always enter a single port number rather than a range of ports.

Application security is essential in today's computing environment. DCOM has never provided the best security available and CIS is an open door. The configuration suggestions provided in this section will reduce the risk of a cracker gaining access to your system, but you'll still need to watch for unwarranted attacks. Because you're using just one port for DCOM, the task of monitoring for problems is greatly reduced in complexity.

Compatibility and version issues

There are more compatibility and version issues popping up daily with regard to Windows in general and applications in specific. A common source of grief for the developer is the well-known problem of DLL hell. An application may expect one version of a DLL, when there's actually another version installed on the system. This problem doesn't just occur when you're working with applications from multiple sources, it can occur with the custom-built applications on your network as well. A poorly designed component can cause a variety of DLL hell problems by failing to observe some simple rules for component building.

Anyone who's used Microsoft's components knows that they have a habit of providing several methods with almost the same name. The only difference is a number or the addition of "Ex" to the end of the method name. There's a reason for this practice. Any time that you change the interface for a method within the component, you need to change the name of the method. Older applications will look for the old method name by using the original interface. New applications, those designed to use the new features that you added to the method, will also know to use the new name that you've provided. In short, never change the interface for a method or you'll experience some of the problems of DLL hell within your custom application.

Compatibility issues can affect component development in other ways. For example, there are well-known issues in using components built with Visual C++ under Visual Basic. Unless the component designer is careful to test the component with both languages, you may find that your application can't access the component correctly.

There are version issues with data as well. Consider what happens when you change the design of a database table. The obvious problem is that you'll also need to change all of the client applications and components that work with that table. Otherwise, the client and components will expect data in a format that the database isn't prepared to provide. The moment that the database rejects input from the client, the application will generate a wealth of network traffic in the form of error messages, retries, and other data. All it takes is one old application to generate enough traffic to jam your network.

An alternative to the database problem is to ensure that all of the original columns remain in their original form and position within the table. A version upgrade can usually get around problems with data format by ensuring any change makes the field bigger, rather than smaller. Old applications will simply ignore the additional space. If you add new fields, ensure that the fields are at the end of the table and that you provide new scripts within the database to handle these new fields. New applications will use the new queries, while old applications will use the old queries and simply ignore the new fields. No, it's not a perfect solution, but it's one that will keep you application working.

Data-specific problems

Many developers get used to the idea that they can create components that transport just about anything over the desktop. The problem with DCOM is that you're using a network connection. Every piece of data that you transport requires resources from the client, the server, and the network itself. Because bandwidth is a relatively scarce commodity on some networks, it pays to conserve as much of this resource as you can through careful programming. Using too many client, server, or network resources will cause your application to slow and could cause problems like lockups and data loss. One of the hardest and yet most devastating communication problems to fix when working with DCOM is too much data.

It may seem that finding this problem would be too difficult for the average programmer to do, much less predicting that the problem will occur. Fortunately, there are things that you can do to reduce network traffic and to make your application work faster. The following list provides some ideas on how to fix an application before it breaks the network.

✦ **Send Complete Requests:** Every communication between the client and server uses network bandwidth. In some cases, a developer may feel that the server should request the data it needs from the client, rather than send all of the potential data in one request. In some very rare requests, this would be true, but if you have that much data to send to the server, you should be using COM+, not DCOM. Make sure that every request sent from the client to the server contains complete information to ensure that the server can process that request without additional requests for data.

✦ **Minimize Data Transfers:** There was a time in computing when programmers would count every byte and ensure that they really needed to use it. The Y2K problem was an example of overzealous programmers saving the last bit without fully considering the ramifications of their decision. Still, the fact remains that developers today will often err on the side of too much data rather than figuring out what they really need. For example, if an integer will do, then don't use a real number in its place. The big savings come from other sources, however. For example, it's not always necessary to send a complete graphic over the wire when a partial graphic showing a change will do.

✦ **Decide Between Finished and Raw Data:** In some situations, there may be a question of sending raw or finished data to the server. Sending raw data means that the server will have to spend time processing it before it can send a response. In addition, the raw data could be larger than the finished product. When dealing with this problem, you need to consider whether there will be a need now or in the future for the server to use the raw data for additional processing. If there is, then sending raw data is your only option. You also need to compare the size of the finished product to the raw data. In some cases, the raw data is actually smaller than the finished product that it produces. Always choose the smaller data transfer when you can in order to save network bandwidth.

✦ **Avoid Disruptive Data:** This may seem like one of those bullets that a book should never have, but this particular problem occurs more frequently than most of us want to admit. It's possible today to have security set up on a network in such a way that some data actually disrupts the flow of traffic between a client and a server. For example, you may have set your server to reject data containing certain words no matter what the source of that data is. While this may be a good way to avoid getting hit by the "love" virus, it's not a particularly good way to configure a network. You have to configure the client application to avoid using disruptive data, verify the source of a data entry before you accept it, or perform a more discrete level of filtering at the server.

Even if you follow all of these tips, you may still run into a problem where client-processing demands exceed server capacity or network bandwidth. Unfortunately, there isn't any quick fix for this problem because you need to consider all of the factors that affect the processing load of the server and the use of both server and network resources. For example, you need to determine what the precise source of the problem is. It may be nothing more than an errant piece of hardware making it look as if your application is having problems. (A router, for example, could be producing an excess of messages or resending messages that failed to reach the server the first time.)

The first solution that many network administrators will reach for when it appears that the network has slowed to a crawl is more hardware. Adding another server and dividing your processing load in two will make the application run faster for some amount of time, but it usually doesn't fix the underlying problem. If a piece of network hardware or software has failed, throwing more hardware at the problem only makes the problem's cause harder to find later.

Monitoring will allow you to spot the vast majority of the network hardware and software problems that you'll encounter. The Performance console shown in Figure 10-18 contains two MMC snap-ins: System Monitor and Performance Logs and Alerts. The System Monitor MMC snap-in allows you to see current performance statistics for the network and applications running on the server. The Performance Logs and Alerts MMC snap-in allows you to set thresholds for applications and other system objects. As soon as an object exceeds the threshold that you set, you'll see a message warning you of impending doom.

After you've monitored the data flow of your application and ruled out potential sources of problems, like failed hardware and misconfigured software, you need to look at other potential sources of application slowdowns. The way a user interacts with an application often determines its performance characteristics. Every time the user needs to send another request to the server, there are network bandwidth and resource usage problems to consider. An interface design problem can cause a variety of user interaction problems, so ensuring that you spend time looking at user interface issues and training the user to work with the application will solve many data-related communication problems.

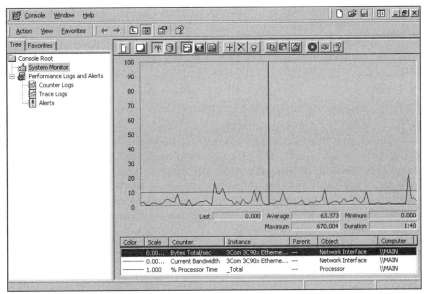

Figure 10-18: The Performance console is the programmer's best friend when it's time to find the source of a network slowdown.

Obviously, there comes a point when you need to throw some additional hardware at a problem. Even if you fully optimize your application, train users to interact with the application properly, remove every interface problem, and have hardware that works at the peak of performance all the time, you still have to move data from one point to another. The point is that you shouldn't add hardware until you've solved the underlying causes of data related communication problems.

Network hardware performance problems

Some of you may be wondering why I've included a network topology section in a book on programming. I've found that many developers have no idea of how the hardware they're working with affects the application they're trying to develop. As a result, they're often surprised when the application that they developed on a high-speed test system crashes and burns on the real network. Often, the application was doomed from the start because the developer failed to consider the implications of the hardware that they were working with on the production system.

DCOM is COM with a network connection; I've probably repeated that phrase to the point of boring some of you, but it bears repeating. The network part of the picture will cause you as many performance problems as any other aspect of your application design, which means that you have to consider the implications of the network topology when assessing the performance of your application. If you only have

10MB/sec of bandwidth, then you're not going to get 100MB/sec of performance—it just won't happen and there's no reason to anticipate getting performance that you haven't designed into the system as a whole. With this in mind, the following sections tell you about the most common network topology problems that you'll run into.

Network topology performance overview

A network's topology defines the combination of hardware and software required when making connections between the various nodes of the network. In a very real sense, the network topology is the network; the nodes merely serve as endpoints that give the network a purpose. It's important to understand how the network topology affects network performance because the network topology allows very little in the way of tuning potential. In short, the network topology reflects the upper limits of the performance curve that you can hope to achieve. Any further increase in performance will require you to change the network topology at a basic level.

The configuration of a network determines certain physical characteristics that you can't alter with any ease. A 10MB/sec Ethernet network won't suddenly provide 11MB/sec worth of bandwidth after tuning—there's a physical limitation to the topology that would prevent any performance in excess of the topology limit. In fact, you'll find that the specified topology limits rarely reflect real-world performance. You'd be very lucky to get the full 10MB/sec out of the Ethernet network because there are other factors that you have to consider. We'll discuss these limitations in the "Theoretical Versus Real-World Performance" section of this chapter.

The important thing to remember is that your DCOM application is transferring a specific amount of data over the network. That data consumes a certain amount of the available bandwidth. If you write an application that transfers 10Mb (or 1.25MB) every second, then it's unlikely to perform well on a low-end Ethernet network because such a network rarely transfers more than 6Mb/sex (0.75MB/sec) of data.

Many of you are probably wondering why I've wasted precious book space talking about old 10MB/sec Ethernet technology. It's because many companies continue to use this older technology because it provides acceptable performance given the task that the company needs to perform on the network. Consequently, when you're designing a DCOM application for commercial distribution, you have to consider the type of client that will use the application. If you envision a small business user with limited funds for equipment upgrades and little reason to do so, expect to work with a 10MB/sec Ethernet network for the most part.

Of course, not every company is using older technology. A lot of larger companies are moving to fiber optic technology, which transfers data at much higher rates, has fewer losses, and is upgradeable. We'll discuss this technology in more detail in the "Understanding Fiber Optic Performance Characteristics" section of this chapter. The reason that we're looking at this technology in a special section is that fiber optics impose special restraints on network topology — these restraints are seldom mentioned outside of the circles of electronics specialists, so you may not even be aware that they exist. The point is that your application's capability to transfer data over a fiber optic network is much greater than its capability to transfer data over a network that is using copper.

Programmers rarely have to consider hardware failure problems such as old cabling, but it's a mistake to forget this potential source of problems. No, I'm not suggesting that you turn into a hardware guru and fix your company's network when the need arises; but leaving hardware out of your application planning is a mistake. Here's why. A new network has new cables, connectors, and electronics. These new components will provide the very best performance that you can hope to achieve once they're tuned for your company's needs. So, if you design an application and test it on new equipment, you're seeing your application perform at the highest performance it will ever perform (all other elements remaining constant).

However, as the equipment ages, you'll notice a drop in performance. It's not because the equipment is broken, the loss of performance simply reflects the vagaries of aging. You have to consider this particular network bottleneck during your design and setup phase because it's unavoidable unless you want to continually change your equipment. Because no one realistically replaces network components until they're either broken or so out of date as to be unusable, you have to plan for some drop in performance due to aging as part of your design. In short, if your company needs a certain level of performance today and tomorrow, you need to consider the performance that you'll get out of the hardware tomorrow, not the performance that you're getting today. We'll talk more about the problems of aging equipment in the "Performance and Aging" section of this chapter.

Theoretical versus real-world performance

When you look at the specifications for a network, you need to remember that these are the theoretical performance parameters of the network topology. Let's discuss a real-world example. When you read on the NIC package that the device is capable of transferring data at a rate of 10MB/sec, that's the theoretical delivery speed. In the real world, collisions, noise, and other performance inhibitors lower the amount of data that actually gets transferred across the wire. In fact, you may be surprised to learn that in a normal network setup, the 10MB/sec that you're supposed to get actually translates into 6MB/sec real-world rates.

Note The example in this section is just that — an example. Any network topology will be affected by enough outside influences that a precise calculation of network bandwidth will require on-site measurements. In addition, any change to the network will change the performance characteristics of that network. For example, if you add a node to a network, the performance characteristics of that network will change due to insertion losses, increased collisions, and various media losses like the increased resistance of a copper network.

The point of this example is that there are certain realities in the world of networks, one of which is that there are factors outside of the realm of the operating system that affect perceived operating system performance. A user who experiences slow network performance will more than likely blame a slow server because it's the easiest part of the network to see and understand. The reality is that you may need 10MB/sec of network bandwidth when only 6MB/sec worth of network bandwidth is available. The user sees a slow network not because of a faulty server, but because of the physical limitations of the network topology.

Of course, the network bandwidth is just one source of theoretical versus real-world performance problems. Consider for a moment the length limitations of most network topologies. Many network administrators would take the specifications at face value and extend their network within the limitations of the topology-specified length criteria. However, these specifications assume a network in perfect environmental conditions. For example, as the noise around the network increases, the length that you can make the network cabling decreases in proportion to the noise level. Obviously, many network administrators don't account for this problem and pay with decreased network bandwidth.

The situation becomes even worse when a network administrator tries to extend the network the extra five feet needed to connect one more workstation. In this case, you not only have signal strength and noise problems to deal with, you also have timing problems to contend with. In short, even the specifications for a network topology have to be read with a grain of salt. These specifications always assume that your network is operating under perfect conditions because the engineers who create the specification can't anticipate every network problem. They assume that the on-site network administrator will take noise and other environmental hazards into consideration during the network design process and act accordingly.

Real-world performance is also based on the load that the unique combinations of your company's applications provide. Theoretical performance values are usually created by using test suites of applications that your company may not use. Someone writing a specification will very likely try to achieve a generic application load — one that could reflect the load that a majority of companies will place on the network. Unfortunately, there isn't any such thing as the generic company or the generic load. As a result, the performance that you actually see when you design a network will vary from the theoretical norm.

Let's consider the problem of application load for a moment on the theoretical versus real-world network throughput. If your company uses applications that place large continuous loads on the network, like a graphics application, then you can expect that the network will provide maximum throughput, but that the applications could appear to run slowly because of their ravenous appetites for network bandwidth. On the other hand, a database application creates small, record-sized packets that may require padding. The use of padding characters wastes network bandwidth, so the efficiency of the network will decrease. However, because of the kind of load that the database places on the network, you might see very little in the way of performance drop on a fully loaded network. There are other applications that place other kinds of load on the network—depending on how they create a load, you may see a loss of either performance or efficiency, or, in some cases, both.

There's one final real-world consideration to make. When the theoretical limits of a network topology are created, the engineers use lab-type equipment in a lab setting. This equipment is specially designed to help the engineers make the required measurements. In short, even if everything else is equal, the hardware that you'll use to create a network isn't equal to the hardware used for testing. There just isn't any way that you'll achieve the highest performance that's possible with a network because no one will purchase lab equipment for general office use.

Understanding fiber optic performance characteristics

The emergence of fiber optic cabling as the media of choice for networks is easy to understand. Companies need to move more data, faster than ever before. It doesn't matter what application you work with, there isn't a single environment today that couldn't benefit from some sort of performance boost. Of course, there are copper solutions that get almost the same level of performance as a modern fiber optic network will achieve, and with a lot less hassle. Recent technology advances in the production of fiber optic cable and the components required to make it work have made fiber optic cable a viable choice for most companies. Not only does fiber optic cable lack some of the potential security risks of copper, but it's also achieved cost parity with copper, making fiber optic networks a very attractive choice. In short, fiber optic networks have earned a place in many companies because of their performance, cost, and security characteristics.

As we've discussed throughout this section, tuning in the general sense can go only so far in making a network run faster. At some point, you will run up against the wall of the network topology. No matter what you do, at some point, no amount of tuning will change the performance characteristics of your network. So, the alternative is to change the network topology, and that's precisely what many companies are doing today. The move from copper to fiber optic alternatives means that network administrators have to learn new skills when it comes to diagnosing and fixing network performance problems. Don't make the mistake of thinking that all network cabling is the same—fiber optics are completely different from copper when it comes to performance characteristics and problem areas.

Note This section covers some of the more technical performance details of fiber optic cabling. The reason that this information is important to a developer is that you need to know what types of losses to account for when calculating the amount of load that you can place on a server given the current network configuration. Large-enterprise applications move huge quantities of data, so any chance that you have of being successful at planning the network capacity required for adequate application performance depends on knowing the specifics of the topology that you're working with. In addition, knowing these performance factors can help you locate and fix hardware-induced problems with your applications such as those induced by poorly maintained connectors.

Fiber optic cabling started out as a single-wavelength, single-mode telephony system. Unfortunately, it wasn't long before the market reached the limits of this technology. Today, fiber optic cabling normally means using dense-wavelength, division-multiplexed (DWDM) broadband systems. These systems include high-quality components like splitters, couplers, and optical amplifiers.

Unfortunately, as you increase the complexity of a network topology, you also increase the number of things that can inhibit performance. Because of the added complexity of today's systems, fiber optic networks require more advanced testing and performance-monitoring equipment. You can't use the simple equipment found in early fiber optic networks simply because they can't handle the multiple wavelengths of data that these new configurations can work with. The following list provides some ideas about the performance inhibitors that affect fiber optic networks as a whole.

✦ **Connectors:** Unlike copper, fiber optic cabling is affected by a number of problems at the connector. For example, the way that the end is cut can make or break the connection. Fiber optic networks require perfectly straight cuts that can only be achieved by special equipment. In addition, there are reflection losses from the end of the cable and insertion losses.

✦ **Fiber Optic Cabling:** Like copper, fiber optic cabling suffers from span losses — a degradation of signal strength as the length of the cable increases. Fiber optic cabling also suffers from chromatic loss (the refraction of some light into other wavelengths), polarization-dependent loss (PDL), and polarization modal dispersion (PMD). Polarization is the effect you get from sunglasses. It reduces glare by changing the characteristics of the light in one direction. Unfortunately, because you're trying to maintain a consistent light condition on a fiber optic network, polarization is an undesired side effect of using glass for the cable.

✦ **Dispersion-Compensating Devices:** These devices recollimate the laser light that moves through the fiber optic cable. You have to perform this step to keep the light from dispersing so much that the signal becomes gibberish at the receiving node. However, even these devices suffer from various losses that include insertion loss, PDL, and delay ripple (moving the signal through the dispersion-compensating device incurs a delay that degrades the signal). Insertion loss occurs every time you add another device to the cable. The insertion of the device causes some of the light to reflect back toward the source, reducing signal strength in the process.

✦ **Transmitter:** Every fiber optic transmission begins at the transmitter. The accuracy with which the transmitter creates the laser light at a given wavelength determines the starting signal strength. Obviously, some transmitters will do a better job than others at creating the required light at the proper frequency. In addition, the transmitter quality can affect the output power, spectral width (the width of the light in terms of frequency), long-term output stability, and side-mode suppression.

✦ **Receiver:** The biggest factor here is how sensitive the receiver is. A sensitive receiver will pick up a smaller signal. In addition to sensitivity, the power range, signal degradation, and loss-of-signal threshold experienced by the receiver will affect the overall throughput that you'll get from the network.

✦ **Dense Multiplexers and Demultiplexers:** DWDM requires multiplexing prior to transmission, then demultiplexing once the signal is received. Remember that we're actually sending more than one signal across the fiber at the same time. The process of multiplexing and demultiplexing incurs loss in the form of bandwidth, insertion loss, delay ripple of each passband, and the differential loss between channels.

✦ **Optical Amplifiers:** Increasing the signal strength of the transmitted data incurs a loss of wavelength, in most cases, which means that the signal is louder, but distorted. There are also various types of noise that an amplifier adds to the signal, which means that the quality of the signal is degraded. Finally, there's only so much amplification that can occur before the amplifier produces a flat response and begins to add signal harmonics. As with any other fiber optic device, there's also a certain amount of insertion loss.

✦ **Overall Link:** When viewed as a whole, the fiber optic network will experience end-to-end losses in the form of signal dispersion and other light refraction problems. A certain amount of the light will return to the source because the devices inserted in the line and the walls of the fiber optic cable itself will reflect it. This is called the optical return loss (ORL). Finally, the fiber optic link as a whole will experience a PMD loss.

This section of the chapter has provided a very brief overview of the kinds of losses that you'll incur by using fiber optic cabling. Obviously, this is a very complex and a very new technology. The Rifocs Web site at http://www.rifocs.com/ provides press releases, white papers, a glossary, demos, and other resources that will make understanding this topic a little less difficult. In addition, this site contains descriptions of the test equipment that you'll need to work with fiber optic networks, along with some of the components that these networks require to run efficiently.

Performance and aging

Everything on your network ages. Cables get older, as do connectors, and the electronics that support the network. Unfortunately, this is a part of the network picture that few people plan for and most people wouldn't know how to anticipate even if they did intend on accounting for it. Calculating the amount of performance loss due to aging when you begin a project will help reduce the amount of reconfiguration that you have to do later to maintain a specific level of application performance. In short, the application that you create today has to exceed the anticipated performance specifications if you want to maintain minimal acceptable performance as the equipment ages. This is especially true of DCOM applications where you have a slow network connection to begin with; a network connection that will only get slower as it ages.

Consider the lowly cable. Your network can't operate without some type of cabling unless you're using a wireless technology. If you look at the end of a coaxial cable connector, you'll notice that part of the cable sticks out — the center conductor — and makes contact with the NIC. This conductor can corrode over time and the corrosion will affect the electrical characteristics of the cable. Not only will you see reduced signal strength, but also corrosion can cause problems like intermittent contact with the NIC (corrupting packets as a result) as well. Other cable-aging problems include brittleness — a cable breaks more easily as it gets older. You'll find that there are other vagaries of aging as well, all of which affect the performance of your network in a way that you can't compensate for.

Connectors and plugs rely on metal with a certain amount of spring. Just look at any RJ plug and you'll see four or more connection fingers that are configured as springs. The act of pushing the connector into the plug creates a connection due in part to the spring action of these fingers. Each time the plug is removed from the connector, the little fingers move back out — flexing the metal again. Eventually, the metal fatigues and you don't get the same level of connectivity you once got. The connector doesn't fail; it simply doesn't perform as well as it could.

To give you an idea of just how this problem can affect a system, one building that I worked at shook because of a nearby railroad. The shaking was so slight that no one in the building really noticed — it was a very minor problem. However, this network used older coaxial cabling and the connectors hadn't been replaced in quite some time. The combination of loose connectors and corroded cable greatly reduced network throughput. The simple act of replacing the connectors and exposing new cable as the result of connector replacement garnered a 25 percent performance increase. Needless to say, this act of miracle work was relatively inexpensive and it certainly wasn't rocket science. Aging is a real-world problem that you need to take seriously as you design and maintain a network.

Aging definitely affects any mechanical component within your network. For example, some devices on the network may use relays. A relay is a physical device that has springs, contacts, and other mechanical features that can wear out. Likewise, some devices use hard drives for internal storage purposes. Like any spinning device with bearings, the bearings eventually wear out and you have to replace the device. Of course, it's not too difficult to figure out that the physical devices will fail. What happens, however, during the time that the device hasn't failed, but it's too worn out to perform its job completely? That's the point at which you'll see certain types of performance degradation on your network. Because these devices often appear within hubs or other nonuser-related peripherals, finding the source of the degradation can be very difficult.

The effects of aging certainly aren't limited to the parts of your network that encounter physical stress. You'll find that aging affects every part of the network to some extent, even electronic components. For example, it's not at all uncommon for the characteristics of an amplifier to change over time. Most amplifiers today contain some type of compensating circuitry that helps with the aging process, but the fact remains that even compensating circuitry won't keep the amplifier performing at peak performance forever. At some point, the amplification capability of the circuit will fall below desirable levels, even if the device itself hasn't failed.

Understanding network component interactions

A network is a system of devices that work together toward the same end goal of promoting communication between nodes. Each device is individual and to a certain extent, you can treat the device as an individual device. However, there are limits to what you can assume about any device on the network because all of these devices are connected. All of the devices form a cohesive whole. As a result, a change on an individual device affects the performance of the network in some way.

The following scenario will give you a better idea of how network component interactions affect application performance. You create a DCOM application and test it with one workstation and one server. The application runs great; response time is nearly instantaneous. A second test has ten workstations and one server; again, performance is well beyond anticipated levels. So, you deploy the application on the production system and performance falls through the floor; users, management, and even your own development staff are angry over an application that flies about as high as a lead balloon.

Every workstation, server, and piece of cable on a network affects a distributed application like those created with DCOM in ways that you can't imagine if you're dealing with desktop applications right now. In this case, the problem could be too little network bandwidth, a faulty workstation sending out too many packets, a server that's ill-equipped to handle the load that you are placing on it, or an application that simply isn't tuned properly. Until you understand how the components interact, you won't know which element is at fault. For example, if you only calculate the size of the packets that the network will handle, you're not factoring in the effect of collisions, which, in some cases, can create more of a performance bottleneck. Simple monitoring can save in you many cases. All you need to do is monitor the network, server, and individual workstations to see if their loads are within limits. If they are, you know that you have some tuning to do on the application.

Some problems aren't nearly so obvious as the one we just talked about. For example, it might seem like a good idea to change the setting for Application response on the Performance Options dialog shown in Figure 10-19 from Applications to Background services. (You can access the Performance Options dialog by clicking Performance Options on the Advanced tab of the System Properties dialog box.) However, this change can have the unwanted side effect of reducing overall server performance, especially if the server is used more to run components than to act as a file server.

Figure 10-19: Some changes to a server's configuration can make a big difference in network performance.

Interactions between network components can become even more entangled when you start adding more than one server to the picture. The servers need to communicate to keep each other up to date. Trying to time the updates so that each server gets what it needs without interrupting the other servers at a busy time could quickly turn into a logistical nightmare. Consider the simple matter of replicating Active Directory information. You may find that some times of the day are better than others for performing this task. In short, developing a large-scale application means accounting for the interactions of the components that you're developing the application to work with.

Application testing and users

Users represent the most frustrating part of testing the performance of your DCOM application so that you can ensure that it will work as anticipated on a production system. First, let's look at the question of performance monitoring. A developer can take several approaches to monitoring the network's performance, one of which is to tell everyone that the performance monitoring will take place. This has the advantage of warning users in advance that there may be small glitches on the network and that they shouldn't worry about them. However, it also seems to have the effect of changing everyone's behavior. Unless you schedule enough time to perform the monitoring, what you'll get is a skewed view of the network's performance (and therefore your application's performance) because most users will subconsciously change their behavior. They feel as if they're being watched and won't do some of the performance-inhibiting things that they would normally do.

Another approach to the performance-monitoring problem is telling the network administrator and management about the event, but keeping silent around users who aren't testing your application. Unfortunately, even a single glitch could end up costing the company money because the users will be unprepared for the event. In addition, you'll find that the user cooperation level greatly decreases because they'll associate you with "big brother"—a definite problem when it comes time to making changes to a new application that will keep the user's needs in mind. Finally, given that most applications are tested by groups of users, keeping the test a secret will be difficult to say the least.

Monitoring problems aside, once you do come up with a picture of the application's performance, you'll have to decide what action to take. You may find that application performance could be improved by changing the order in which users complete tasks and by asking them to use certain features (such as using the File ⇨ Save command) less often in order to reduce nonessential use of network bandwidth. Retraining the users to do something different is problematic to say the least. People tend to reject change, especially if they perceive the change as threatening or inconvenient.

Of course, tuning the way that people interact with the network is only part of the process. You'll have to optimize any new procedures later. This leads to the confusion syndrome. Some users will end up using the old method, some will use one of the failed methods, and still others will use the optimized method that you created.

By now, you may be thinking that any change in a user's behavior, no matter how attractive from a performance perspective, just isn't worth the work. Unfortunately, that kind of an attitude will backfire as well. Now the users will perceive that you don't think they're worth the effort of training to do the job better. In short, you're going to have to face the fact that getting great application performance from the user perspective will be an error prone, time-consuming process that few will enjoy (especially the developer doing the work).

Now that you're perfectly terrified about the prospects of doing anything with the users of a network, it's important to understand that a network is designed to serve the needs of the user. As a result, the user has the greatest impact on any application's performance — especially on a DCOM application that relies on workstation, server, and network resources that all interact with each other. Users who aren't completely sure how to use the network will waste precious network bandwidth trying to figure out the best way to get their work done. In addition, poorly trained users won't know that the network can perform certain tasks for them automatically, which means that they'll waste time doing things in some convoluted manual fashion. So, the first user-oriented network bottleneck solution is to ensure that that everyone is actually trained to use the network.

No matter what you do, some users will insist on at least attempting to abuse network resources. Considering the type of application we're talking about in this chapter, network abuse is exceptionally easy. With this in mind, part of your user-oriented application performance solution should be to check network security. Ensure that that users can only reach the applications that they actually need to use. In some cases, you may need to perform the additional work required to secure high bandwidth applications like NetMeeting until the user actually needs them to perform work. However, a good network usage policy (and requisite enforcement) should keep this kind of micromanagement to a minimum.

At some point, your users will be trained to use the network, and will be aware of all of the security and application usage policies for the company. Even with these two goals met, you may still find that network performance lags. That's where certain types of monitoring come into play. You don't want to become "big brother" because that will kill user productivity and could cause your company to lose valuable employees. What you do want to do is look for application usage problems with your custom DCOM applications. In some situations, you may find that a change in the design of the application interface will net improved performance; in other situations, you may find that more user training on specific procedures is mandated. Whichever route you go, it's important to understand what kind of problem the user is facing before you assume that a performance inhibiting usage habit is all the user's fault.

Summary

DCOM provides one way of creating a distributed computing environment. You can use it to allow one machine to borrow resources from another machine on the network, including the components contained on that machine. This chapter discussed the theory and implementation of DCOM. We saw how DCOM gives the programmer additional flexibility in creating remote connections in a world that's ever more Internet and intranet bound. Here are some additional conclusions that you can draw from the contents of this chapter:

✦ DCOM extends COM so that it can work with remote connections. In short, DCOM is a protocol that manages the remote connection in a manner that's transparent to both the client and the server. All local connections are still managed by COM and its associated technologies.

✦ DCOM still has many uses in the corporate environment, despite what Microsoft would have you believe. It's still the best choice for any application that requires one-to-one communication with the server and where the security and transactional requirements are small. COM+ only becomes an alternative when the application that you're creating uses the advanced capabilities that it provides.

✦ Design and test your DCOM applications with care. Diagram the data flow between various components and set up security zones as needed as part of the design process. You'll want to add components to the application one at a time and use a separate test application to check the functionality of each component before you integrate it.

✦ There are two major ways to create components in a DCOM application. You can use the Registry method, which relies on the standard New keyword to create the component, or you can use the code method, which relies on `CreateObject()` to get the job done. While the Registry method is more reliable and perhaps a little faster, the code method is less error prone and, in many instances, more secure.

✦ There are three levels of DCOM application testing that you need to perform. First, test each application individually to ensure that the components work as anticipated by themselves. Second, integrate the components one at a time until the application is complete. Make sure that you perform a complete local test to locate any component or application interaction problems. Third, test the application remotely. Ensure that you use the same test server setup as you will for the production system.

✦ Many DCOM application errors are preventable with good coding techniques. There are, however, some unavoidable errors. In these cases, you need to detect the error as soon as possible, and provide recovery code that will help the application to continue working or fail gracefully. Unlike COM applications, which execute on the desktop, not every aspect of a DCOM application is completely under your control.

✦ Security is a problem when working with DCOM, especially if you want to work with DCOM over an Internet connection. COM+ is a better solution because it offers better built-in security and more robust Internet connection handling. If you must use DCOM for an Internet solution, ensure that you minimize the risk of doing so by configuring the application and associated components correctly.

✦ One of the most devastating DCOM communication problems is that of data transfer. There are two simple rules to remember for maximum application throughput. First, always make sure that you send a complete request to the server, rather than allow the client and server to communicate several times for one request. Second, make sure that you only transmit enough data to complete the request, rather than transferring more information than the server can use.

✦ ✦ ✦

A Simple COM+ Example

CHAPTER

11

There's a lot of confusion about what constitutes a COM+ application because Microsoft has been marketing COM+ as an all-inclusive package. The problem is that it's not an all-inclusive package; COM+ is more like a menu where you get to choose one from Column A and another from Column B. In fact, COM+ is probably the most flexible system that Microsoft has ever conceived. That's why I've decided to present some technologies as separate topics, so that you can see the Column A-Column B effect. The big thing to remember is that COM+ builds on predecessors and is essentially a combination of COM, DCOM, MTS, and MSMQ, all of which are known quantities.

This chapter will look at the first of the COM+ features that you can choose to add to an application, Microsoft Transaction Server (MTS). You'll see references to MTS all over Windows 2000. It appears in several of the MMC snap-ins and always seems to be at the periphery, but not a discrete entity. MTS is, in fact, built into COM+ and you won't install it as a separate entity as you might under Windows NT. For this reason, it's difficult to put a handle on MTS and say precisely what it is. As far as I'm concerned, MTS has always been a programming interface that you can use to add transactions to an application.

Cross-Reference

This chapter doesn't provide a full description of MTS. If you want to learn the theory behind MTS and what it means to the developer, look in Chapter 6. You'll want to look at Chapter 7 for the security issues of using COM+. Chapters 3 and 4 are good places to look for the tools that you'll need to work with MTS and some of the information that you'll need to learn about MTS from a historical perspective.

The first topic that we need to discuss is how you can use MTS to create applications. There are some applications for which MTS is a big help and others for which it's a drain on resources. MTS does reduce application performance, but it also makes your data a lot safer. The first section of this chapter will help you to understand the circumstance in which MTS can make a big difference and those circumstances when it will be a nuisance rather than a help.

Microsoft has steadily improved its products because of customer input and after combating errors in early version releases. As a result, the version of MTS that you used with Windows NT isn't the same version that you'll use with Windows 2000. The second section of this chapter will help you to understand the differences between the two versions, which should make it a lot easier to move applications that rely on MTS from Windows NT to Windows 2000. This section will also help those of you who are already familiar with MTS and simply want an update on its capabilities.

The third and fourth sections of the chapter contain the first example. In this case, we're creating a simple application that demonstrates the basics of MTS development and shows how it works. These sections will also provide you with some helpful advice that will reduce application development time. As part of the development process, we'll also discuss some requirements for MTS applications that you don't need to worry about when working with other application types.

The fifth section of the chapter will show you a more complex MTS example. In this case, we'll also be working with the COM+ publish/subscribe event model. This new event model is more practical than what you may have used in the past because it allows a publisher to communicate with a subscriber without either party knowing anything about the other. In addition, unlike previous event models, the publisher and subscriber don't have to be available at the same time for the event to work.

The sixth and seventh sections of the chapter will help you to debug your MTS applications. We'll look at two separate issues. First, we'll look at ways to fix problems with basic MTS applications, those without any special functionality. Second, we'll look at higher-end MTS applications, especially those that use the publish/subscribe model to communicate with clients.

Uses for MTS Applications

One of the very first applications that everyone thinks about when you mention MTS is the database. The idea of a secure environment for data that traverses the link between client and server is an old one and has been an unobtainable goal for quite some time. A guaranteed method of getting data from the user's machine to the server and then into the database has been a pipe dream for many developers. MTS does greatly improve the security of data for database applications, but there are still times when MTS might not provide the full protection that you'd like. In some cases, the choice of rolling back a transaction is the right one, but doing so still incurs lost time and perhaps lost data.

Custom e-mail setups are another application that can benefit from MTS. This may not be an application type that you've thought about for MTS, but consider the importance of getting a message from one person to the next. If a message contains sensitive data, then the contents of that message are every bit as important as a database record. In fact, you may find that some messages are more important because people often use them as a means for talking about new ideas. An idea may float around in e-mail for weeks before it's well enough defined to appear on paper and get presented to someone in charge.

MTS should be used in any situation in which the data is critical or of a sensitive nature. One choice that makes a lot of sense is any type of custom uploads from a user on the road. Not only is the data open to more potential sources of compromise than normal data is, but the data is critical in itself. Trying to retrieve lost data from someone working at a desktop in the company is hard; it may be impossible for someone on the road unless the machine is sent back to the office (a costly proposition to say the least).

The term, "users on the road" has been used to describe the most common reason for implementing remote application technology. However, this might not be the most precise terminology that you can use for all remote applications. Consider the current rash of e-commerce applications being built. While a business-to-customer application usually requires a secure environment, but not much in the way of transactions (there should be some support), a business-to-business application does require transaction support because of the amount and the sensitivity of the data. Using MTS to ensure that every order from a business partner gets entered in your system is critical if you want to keep the big customers who make the large purchases.

Sometimes you'll use MTS for something other than transactions; you may just want to track the data and determine if it arrives at its destination. For example, someone who works with documentation may keep a copy on the local server, but send a copy to a colleague in another part of the company. Because there's a local copy of the document, you won't lose any data if the message containing the document doesn't arrive at its destination for some reason. However, knowing that the document arrived (and sometimes when it arrived) is very important. So, in this case, even though MTS is protecting the data, the main reason to use MTS is to track the eventual reception of the data by another party.

There are many other uses for MTS; the following list provides some of the more common uses for the technology. In fact, if this list says anything, it says that MTS is underused for some types of applications. You can generalize the uses for MTS within applications from the following list.

✦ **Critical:** Any data that's critical to the operation of your company should be protected within a transaction during transfer. You want to ensure that the data will arrive at its destination the first time because time is usually an element in critical data transfers.

✦ **Sensitive:** Company secrets only remain secret as long as you protect your data. It may not matter how long it takes the data to move from one point to another, but the security of the data does matter. Encryption provides a method of keeping the data from prying eyes. Adding transactions allows you to follow the data and determine where security breaches, if any, occur.

✦ **Fragile:** A user on the road may not make contact with the company every day. If a user sends data to the company, then erases it from their hard drive, the data had better arrive at its destination or it'll be lost forever. Fragile data is the type that can get damaged or lost easily. For many of us, just about every piece of data is fragile to some extent.

✦ **Data Tracking:** There are times when data protection is a secondary reason to use MTS. The primary reason to use it is to track where the data goes and when it arrives at its destination. Think of this type of application as one where you're sending the packet by general mail, but you want to request a receipt to prove that the data arrived.

Don't get the idea that MTS is a solution for every problem. As previously mentioned, new technology attracts those who want to use it for any and every purpose. MTS does have limitations and you need to understand that it's not an appropriate solution for every occasion. The following list presents just a few of the places where you won't want to use MTS within an application.

✦ **Low Resources:** MTS consumes resources, just like any other technology. Not only does it require CPU time to implement, but it makes the data packets larger as well. This means that the data packets consume more memory, more disk space, and more network bandwidth. If you're already struggling to make an application work because of low resources, adding MTS to the picture will only make things worse.

✦ **Non-Windows 2000 Recipient:** If you're sending data to a Windows 95 machine, forget about using MTS. You'll find that MTS is a Windows 2000 solution to problems that companies are just now identifying. So, if you want to use this new technology, you'll need a new operating system.

✦ **Utility or Nonpermanent Data:** There are few, if any, utility applications out there that require the services of MTS. In most cases, the data that they're working with is read from system or hardware registers. In many cases, the data is logged locally so that you can retrieve it again when lost. Wasting processor and other resources to work with data that isn't going to be around for very long anyway is normally a less than optimal use of MTS.

✦ **Time Sensitive:** MTS does require processing and transmission time. The larger packets that it creates can take longer to move from one machine to another. In addition, all of the tracking that takes place for MTS packets requires time at each node that the data passes. If the data you're working with has to be transferred within certain time constraints and isn't critical in nature, then MTS may not be a good solution because it will make the transfer slower.

How MTS Differs Between Windows NT and Windows 2000

We've already talked about how MTS affects COM+ in previous chapters. Essentially, COM+ is a combination of COM, MTS, MSMQ, DCOM, and some new features. It's the new features that we need to talk about in this section. You already know that MTS is built into COM+, but what you may not know is that there are definite differences between the version of MTS for Windows NT and the version for Windows 2000.

Understanding the effects of MTS integration with COM+

Let's begin with the simplest part of the picture. The integration between COM and MTS means that you can use transactions with components that aren't specifically designed to work with MTS. Component Services is a wrapper around MTS that allows access to the base services through an MMC snap-in as shown in Figure 11-1. Even if a component isn't designed to work with MTS, the integration between MTS and COM in COM+ allows you to use MTS, at least to an extent. Contrast this with Windows NT, where an application must be designed to use MTS from the ground up before it will actually do so.

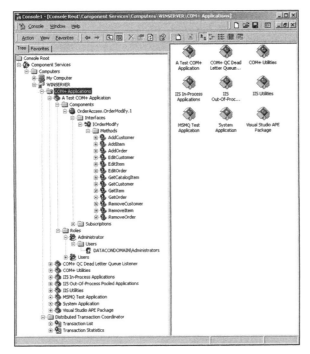

Figure 11-1:
The Component Services MMC snap-in is a key element in managing MTS applications under COM+.

The Component Services MMC snap-in is interesting for several reasons. For one thing, it allows you to manage several components from one location. Notice that in Figure 11-1 there are two computer systems shown and you could easily add more. The Component Services MMC snap-in also organizes COM+ applications hierarchically. It displays components, then interfaces, methods for each interface, subscriptions to the component, and finally, role-based security for the COM+ application as a whole. In short, this MMC snap-in gives you a worldview of your COM+ applications, including those that are MTS enabled, that you can't get when working with Windows NT. The level of integration makes working with MTS much easier because you can easily see the various components of an application at a glance.

Cross-Reference   We talked about the procedures for creating COM+ application in Chapter 2. Chapter 2 also tells you about some of the implications of creating a COM+ application and how that process differs from what you may have done in the past. Be sure that you understand how to work with COM+ applications before you start the application in this chapter. We'll be creating MTS applications that you'll need to install by using the Component Services MMC snap-in to ensure proper operation.

MTS under Windows 2000 also has an advantage that the Windows NT version doesn't have: the capability to make use of interceptors. Figure 11-2 shows the Transactions tab of a typical component Properties dialog box. This dialog gives you full control over the amount of MTS support that a component will get regardless of whether the component is specifically developed for use with MTS. Obviously, although a non-MTS component's data will be protected when you use this configuration dialog to implement MTS, the component's level of participation in the outcome of the transaction is extremely limited.

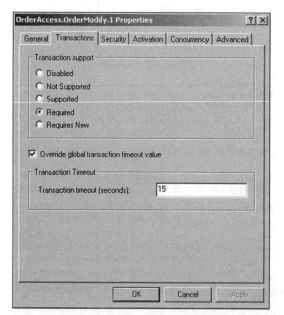

Figure 11-2: The use of interceptors allows non-MTS components to enjoy some of the benefits of MTS.

Contrast the support shown in Figure 11-2 with the MTS Explorer view provided by Windows NT shown in Figure 11-3. Notice that there are two major differences. First, because there's no interceptor support, you can't disable transactions. You can set the level of support for components designed for MTS use only. It's also important to note that you can't control the global transaction timeout value. This setting is important if you plan to create distributed applications over the Internet by using a virtual private network (VPN), or if the wide area network (WAN) technology that you're using wouldn't allow a transaction to take place within the default timeframe.

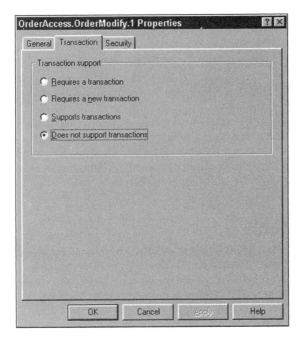

Figure 11-3: MTS Explorer doesn't allow the same level of component configuration flexibility that Component Services does.

Cross-Reference   We discussed interceptors in detail in Chapter 4. Interceptors are an extremely important COM+ feature that affects the operation of MTS. The combination of interceptors and MTS makes it possible to do things with transactions that developers could only dream about when working with Windows NT. Even though the developer doesn't have to worry about the implementation details of interceptors, understanding that they exist and how they affect MTS is important when developing new applications that make maximum use of new COM+ features.

If you compare Figures 11-2 and 11-3, you'll also notice other configuration differences that are all due to the lack of interceptors and tight COM integration with MTS under Windows NT. There are three additional tabs that contain settings for concurrency, activation, and advanced features. In fact, you'll find that you can't perform any of the configuration tasks listed below under Windows NT, even though they're available under COM+ and Windows 2000.

✦ Object pooling

✦ Object construction

✦ Just In Time activation

✦ Event and statistic support

✦ Caller context activation support

✦ Synchronization support

✦ MSMQ exception class configuration

Finally, there's the matter of security. You'll notice that Figure 11-4 shows an equivalent of the Roles folder found in Figure 11-1. However, this screen shot is deceptive in some ways. You can only authenticate user access to an MTS component under Windows NT at the component level. COM+ adds the capability to check security at both the interface and method levels. In short, interface and method property dialog boxes are missing the security tab in MTS Explorer (Windows NT). COM+ is definitely a safer environment, and you can implement this safety feature as a configuration item, rather than adding code to the component.

Usability enhancements

MTS 2.0 is the first version of MTS to make use of an MMC snap-in for management purposes. The MMC snap-in for MTS 2.0 allows the developer to create packages that encapsulate an application and makes the application package easier to work with. Figure 11-4 shows the Windows NT version of the Microsoft Transaction Server Explorer, which has been replaced by Component Services in Windows 2000. A package may look the same as a COM+ application from a purely visual perspective, but it isn't even close to the COM+ application in functionality; we already talked about many of these differences in the previous section of the chapter. We'll discuss additional differences as this section of the chapter progresses. The Component Services MMC snap-in also allows the developer to create installation programs that will add the MTS application to client machines.

The MTS 2.0 features shown in Figure 11-4 are also familiar to COM+ developers. Component Services is merely an extension of an existing technology, so many of the display elements look and act the same. One element that you can't see in Figure 11-4 is the method used to export an application. The installation package concept is the same, but the implementation is different. Instead of using older setup applications for installation, Component Services creates Microsoft Windows Installer (MSI) applications that provide many features that the older installation programs don't provide. A major difference is that you don't have to open Component Services to install an MSI package. On the other hand, you do need to open MTS Explorer or Component Service to install an older MTS 2.0 package (PAK) file.

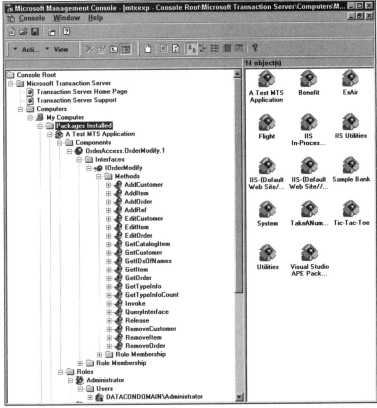

Figure 11-4: MTS 2.0 relies on Transaction Server Explorer to create application packages.

On the CD-ROM

You'll find an example of an MTS 2.0 package file in the Chapt11\MTS Application Package folder on the CD-ROM provided with this book. This package will install under either Windows NT or Windows 2000, which means that this format is less machine dependent. However, you'll also find that the MSI format used by Windows 2000 installs faster and with fewer problems. While the PAK file used by MTS Explorer will work, it doesn't provide the same functionality as an MSI file.

When working with Component Services, you also have the option of exporting a COM+ application in two formats: server application and application proxy as shown in Figure 11-5. MTX Explorer only offers one format, that of the server as shown in Figure 11-6. Remember that an application proxy allows you to install access to the server on a client machine with minimal effort. Using a simple MSI package allows the developer to place a pointer to the server application on a client machine, which makes access of the server application quite easy. Normally, you'd need to perform the required configuration by using other techniques, most of which require Registry manipulation and some additional coding.

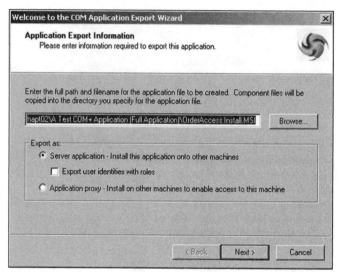

Figure 11-5: Component Services allows you to export an application in both server and application proxy formats.

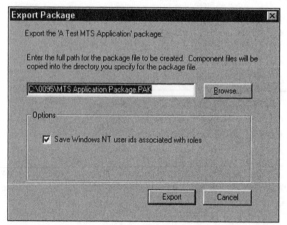

Figure 11-6: MTX Explorer limits export options to the server-only format.

Tip

The MSI file created by Component Services uses new features that didn't appear in the Microsoft Windows Installer versions provided for Windows NT and Windows 9x. If you need to install an application proxy on either of these two operating systems, then you'll need to install the updated version of Microsoft Windows Installer first. You'll find this updated product on any Windows Platform SDK CD that's dated January 2000 or later. If you don't remember to perform the update, nothing terrible will happen; the installation process will start as normal and then fail due to perceived errors in the MSI file. This is your cue to install the update.

You'll find two Component Services versions of the test application used in this section of the chapter (shown in Figures 11-1 and 11-4) in the Chapt02\A Test COM+ Application (Full Application) and Chapt02\A Test COM+ Application (Proxy Installation) folders on the CD-ROM provided with this book. These two versions demonstrate the additional flexibility that Component Services provides over MTS Explorer. Right-click either of the MSI files and you'll see that you can install them on another machine by using Windows Explorer. The MTS Explorer version requires you to open MTS Explorer and install the package manually.

The use of MMC might create another problem for some developers because Microsoft isn't very clear about management issues. Simply because MTS 2.0 and Component Services both use MMC doesn't mean that you can access the MTS applications on a Windows NT server from within Component Services console on a Windows 2000 machine. Likewise, Windows 2000 access isn't permitted from within the Windows NT version of the MMC snap-in. Even though you can install the computer within the snap-in, the applications managed by the computer won't be accessible. The second that you try to click on COM+ applications you'll see the error message shown in Figure 11-7. The moral of the story is that you're going to run into compatibility problems, both large and small, in a mixed environment. There are many ways in which the current version of MTS on Windows NT isn't compatible with the new version on Windows 2000.

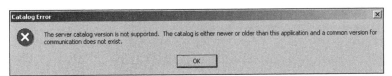

Figure 11-7: Managing a mixed environment means using separate tools for Windows NT and Windows 2000.

MTS Version 2.0 Improvements for Windows NT Developers

Windows NT developers have a choice of two different versions of MTS to choose from. MTS version 1.0 originally appeared as a separate product that you could download and install. It was also distributed with SQL Server. There were a lot of problems with MTS 1.0 that substantially limited its suitability for general application use. For example, it didn't support a wide range of database management systems (DBMS) at a time when many companies had more than one DBMS to work with. This lack of functionality reduced MTS acceptance at first, even if it did provide some of the reliability features that companies were looking for. When Microsoft introduced the Windows NT 4.0 Option Pack, MTS 2.0 was part of the package.

Continued

Continued

One feature that distinguishes MTS 2.0 from MTS 1.0 is its integration with Internet Information Server (IIS) and Microsoft Management Queue (MSMQ). This version also includes connectivity support for both Oracle and DB2 DBMS. Another connectivity feature is support for mainframe access through Microsoft SNA Server 4.0 and the COM Transaction Integrator. Finally, MTS 2.0 features both better performance and manageability (although it's not nearly as manageable as Component Services). Performance enhancements come through support for a multithreaded class factory and a reduction in the number of steps required to perform certain operations.

MTS 2.0 is also extensible. For example, it allows you to work with server clusters—a requirement when you consider how many companies rely on server farms because of the large number of users that they need to support. The addition of clustering support also played a very big part in making MTS 2.0 more acceptable than its predecessor. It's the extensibility factor that makes this product usable for large enterprise development.

Because MTS 2.0 adds so many new features, it pays to use this version of the product on any servers that you can't upgrade from Windows NT to Windows 2000. Of course, the best scenario is to perform the Windows NT to Windows 2000 upgrade whenever possible to gain all of the benefits of COM+. You'll also need to modify any applications that you want to run on both Windows 2000 and Windows NT. It's possible to create such applications, but you also need to realize that MTS 2.0 places restrictions on component development that you wouldn't encounter when working with COM+ alone.

Interface differences

COM and all of its progeny are based on interfaces. An interface bundles all of the methods that you need to perform a given task within in your application. Adding a new feature to a component technology requires the addition of a new interface, in many cases, or at least the addition of methods to an existing interface. It's little wonder, then, that COM+ supports interfaces that weren't available with MTS.

To fully understand the differences between MTS support under Windows NT and MTS support under Windows 2000, you have to look at the interfaces supported by each environment. You'll find the main MTS interfaces in the Microsoft Transaction Server Type Library (mtxas.dll) in Windows NT. The COM+ Services Type Library (comsvcs.dll) contains the main interfaces under Windows 2000 (and any other operating system that supports COM+ by the time you read this).

You can see the differences between MTS under Windows NT and under Windows 2000 at a glance by looking at the Object Browser outputs for the libraries in question. Figure 11-8 shows the Windows NT version and Figure 11-9 shows the Windows 2000 version. As you can see, the Windows 2000 version contains a lot more interfaces as well as functionality. Even though Windows 2000 provides support for the older interfaces, in many cases using the new interfaces will make developing MTS application faster, less error prone, and easier. (Obviously, using a new interface also means that you can't use the component on a Windows NT machine.) Table 11-1 looks at the commonly used interfaces supported by these two versions of MTS and what features you can expect each version of the interface to support.

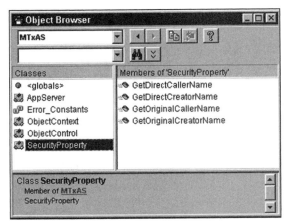

Figure 11-8: The Windows NT version of the MTS runtime library contains just a few interfaces.

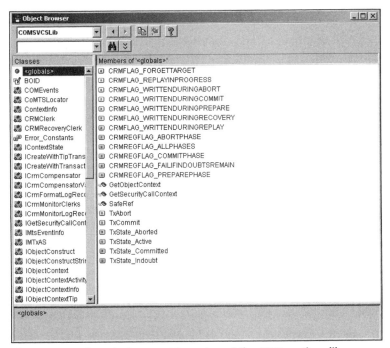

Figure 11-9: The Windows 2000 version of the MTS runtime library contains a wealth of interfaces that provide increased functionality.

Note   We won't look at every interface that MTS supports in Table 11-1. I chose to focus attention on the interfaces that developers are most likely to use in every application that they create rather than to provide encyclopedic coverage of every interface. This information still points out the vast number of new features that COM+ provides when compared to MTS alone. I'm using MTS 2.0 for comparison purposes.

Table 11-1
MTS and COM+ Interface Comparison

Interface	Implementation	Description
AppServer or IMTxAS	COM+ or MTS Runtime	Interestingly enough, Microsoft changed the class name between MTS (AppServer) and COM+ (IMTxAS). Both of these interfaces provide the same functions, including the all-important GetObjectContext() method call.
ContextInfo	COM+ Runtime	Provides information about the current context including activity, context, and transaction. I'll talk more about this new interface later in this section of the chapter. This interface isn't implemented by MTS under Windows NT.
IContextState	COM+ Runtime	You'll use this interface to control transaction state, which includes determining and setting the transaction vote and the completion state. I'll talk more about this new interface later in this section of the chapter. This interface isn't implemented by MTS under Windows NT.
IObjectConstruct	Developer	This interface allows you to create a component by using an initialization string. Using a construction string allows you to set special component features in the same way that a command line will allow you to control the behavior of an application. I'll talk more about this new interface later in this section of the chapter. This interface isn't implemented by MTS under Windows NT.
ObjectContext	COM+ or MTS Runtime	This interface allows the component to vote on the outcome of a transaction, determine whether security is enabled, and determine whether a caller is in a specific role. The COM+ version of this interface also includes a property that allows the component to obtain the current object context.

Interface	Implementation	Description
ObjectControl	Developer	There's an implementation of this interface for both COM+ and MTS that you can extend. The purpose of this interface is to notify the component of activation and deactivation events. In addition, you'll use it to tell the operating system when the component can be pooled.
SecurityCallContext	COM+ Runtime	This interface allows you to implement programmatic security. It parallels some of the methods in the ObjectContext interface, but offers a few additional features as well, like the ability to determine the current user context. I'll talk more about this new interface later in this section of the chapter. This interface isn't implemented by MTS under Windows NT.
SecurityProperty	COM+ or MTS Runtime	This interface allows you to determine specific security information including the direct caller, direct creator, original caller, and original creator names.

As Table 11-1 shows, there are several new interfaces provided by COM+ that allow you to extend the functionality of your components. There are, in fact, many other interfaces that I chose not to cover in the table because they're of limited use for most developers, so you may want to spend some time checking out those other new interfaces. Of course, knowing that an interface exists doesn't make it immediately useful. The problem is determining how to use these new interfaces. The following sections will tell you more about each of the new interfaces and how to use them within your applications.

ContextInfo

A component's context is one of the most important pieces of information that you can obtain from the operating system because it helps you to determine who's calling the component, for what purpose, and at what time. Even if a single user calls your component twice, each component will have a separate context. You can think of the context as providing an identity for a particular instance of your component. A context also allows Windows to keep each instance separate so that a vote from one component instance won't affect the outcome of a transaction performance by another instance.

Sometimes you want to know more about the context than the current vote or whether the happy bit is set. That's where the ContextInfo interface comes into play. It provides you with access to five important methods.

Note   The happy bit determines whether the transaction was accomplished successfully. Setting the happy bit means that the transaction completed successfully and that you're voting to complete the transaction. Some of Microsoft's documentation might refer to the happy bit as the consistency bit. The done bit determines if the component has completed its work. Setting the done bit tells Windows that it's OK to deactivate your component and return it to the pool (or destroy it).

✦ `GetActivityId()`

✦ `GetContextId()`

✦ `GetTranaction()`

✦ `GetTransactionId()`

✦ `IsInTransaction()`

Let's talk about the simplest method first. The `IsInTransaction()` method allows you to determine whether the component is currently involved in a transaction. You can use this information to determine certain courses of action. For example, if your component is in a transaction, you'll want to vote on the outcome in addition to setting the happy bit. On the other hand, if your component isn't involved in a transaction, you may not want to vote on the outcome—you may want to leave the transaction bit alone. You still need to set the happy bit, however, so it may be time to use the `SetDeactivateOnReturn()` method of the IContextState interface instead of using the normal `SetComplete()` method, which sets both the happy bit and the transaction bit.

The `GetTransaction()` method is one of the more difficult methods to understand. Using this method will return a pointer to the IUnknown interface for the current ITransaction interface. You can use this pointer to manually enlist a resource manager that doesn't support automatic transactions. The ITransaction interface supports method for obtaining transaction information, committing a transaction, or aborting it. You'll want to combine this method with the `IsInTransaction()` method, as shown in the following example, to avoid errors induced by attempting to get an interface pointer when there isn't any transaction in progress.

```
Dim oCI As COMSVCSLib.ContextInfo
Dim oTransact As ITransaction
Set oCI = GetObjectContext.ContextInfo
If oCI.IsInTransaction Then
    oTransact = oCI.GetTransaction
End If
```

In some cases, you'll want to know the identifier of a particular activity, context, or transaction. The last three methods `GetActivityId()`,`GetContextId()`, and `GetTransactionId()`allow you to do just that. You can use this information in conjunction with other Visual Studio tools to troubleshoot your application. What you get from these three functions is a globally unique identifier (GUID). Here's an example of how you can place the GUID for the current context within a string and display it onscreen.

```
Dim oCI As COMSVCSLib.ContextInfo
Dim strGUID As String
Set oCI = GetObjectContext.ContextInfo
strGUID = oCI.GetContextId
MsgBox "The current context GUID is: " + strGUID
```

IContextState

Microsoft provided the IContextState interface as part of COM+ for several reasons. The first reason has to do with the ability of the network administrator to disable transactions, yet retain just-in-time activation for a component. So, in some cases, you'll need to set the done and happy bits separately. There isn't any reason to set the happy bit if the component isn't involved in a transaction.

The second reason is to allow you to read the current state of the done and happy bits. This feature wasn't available with Windows NT. Allowing a component to read the state of the done and happy bits allows you to write code more efficiently and reduce the possibility for errors because you no longer have to maintain a state-tracking variable within the component.

The third reason is to provide better error handling. The IContextState methods will return error codes if you attempt to read or set the happy or done bits when it's inappropriate to do so. So, if you try to read or set the done bit when a component doesn't support just-in-time activation, then Windows can return an error code and allow you to change application execution to match the current component configuration.

This interface includes four methods; two for setting each bit individually and two for getting the current bit value. You pass the variable used to hold the new or existing happy bit or done bit values as an argument. Remember that the return value from these methods is used to determine the success of the call, so you can't make a result variable equal to the output of the method. While the GetDeactivateOnReturn() and SetDeactivateOnReturn() methods will accept a Boolean as input, you'll need to use a tagTransactionVote variable with the GetMyTransactionVote() and SetMyTransactionVote() methods as shown in the following example.

```
Dim MyVote As tagTransactionVote
Dim oState As COMSVCSLib.IContextState

Set oState = GetObjectContext

Result = oState.GetMyTransactionVote(MyVote)

If Not Result = vbOK Then
    Exit Sub
End If

If MyVote = TxCommit Then
    Result = oState.SetMyTransactionVote(TxAbort)
End If
```

This is a bare bones implementation, but it provides an idea of how you might handle the result values. The whole point of using the IContextState interface and its associated methods is to improve the reliability of your applications and still gain a measure of control over application execution. Most importantly, however, this new interface allows you to interact more fully with the new features that COM+ provides. In addition, these new methods allow you to interact with the network administrator settings programmatically.

IObjectConstruct

A major problem with using MTS under Windows NT is that everything is completely static. There are a few configuration items, but as we've already seen, COM+ under Windows 2000 has many more configuration features. However, even with all of the configuration options that we've looked at, the component is still essentially static. When a user creates the component, it's the same component that they've always created. Nothing changes and there's no way to make the component react to changing server conditions.

The IObjectConstruct interface contains a single method, Construct(), that allows the developer to create a component that can modify itself to meet specific needs. In other words, the developer can add some flexibility to the design of the application so that as network conditions change, the components that the application relies on can change as well. For example, you might build a component to expect a maximum 15-second propagation delay. What if the size of the network increases so that 15 seconds is no longer sufficient to support the application? In times past, you'd have changed the code to meet the changing condition. Other examples of constructor strings would include adding a Data Source Name (DSN) for components that work with databases or performance parameters for components that require tuning to ensure top performance in real time applications.

The network administrator can now add an initialization string to the component's construction string as shown on the Activation tab of the object Properties dialog box in Figure 11-10. Notice that the administrator will need to check the Enable object construction option in order to tell Windows to call the IObjectConstruct interface implemented by the developer prior to constructing the requested object. (If the developer hasn't implemented the IObjectConstruct interface, checking the Enable object construction option won't accomplish anything — it'll be ignored.) The constructor string is passed as part of this call, making it possible for the component to change internal configuration and other behaviors. Obviously, you need to design the component to accept these construction string parameters much as you would design an application to accept command line parameters.

The constructor string isn't passed directly to the Construct() method of the component. What you get instead is an IObjectConstructString interface pointer. This pointer allows you to access a single unique method, ConstructString(), which lets you retrieve the string entered by the administrator in the dialog box shown in Figure 11-10. The string will still need to be parsed, just like any other command-line string. What this interface allows you to do is provide a means for the network administrator to communicate additional configuration information to the component. Here's a very simple implementation of this method.

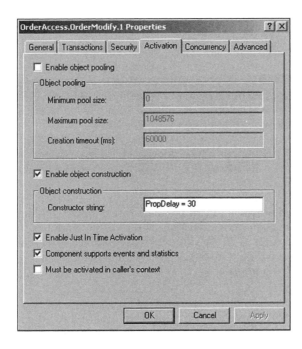

Figure 11-10: Using construction strings makes it possible to create components that change their behavior to meet changing network conditions.

```
Implements COMSVCSLib.IObjectConstruct

Private Sub IObjectConstruct_Construct _
    (ByVal pCtorObj As Object)

    Dim strConnection As String
    Dim oCS As IObjectConstructString

    Set oCS = pCtorObj

    strConnection = oCS.ConstructString

    If strConnection = "LogOn" Then
        SetLoggingOn
    Else
        SetLoggingOff
    End If

End Sub
```

As you can see, if the network administrator adds LogOn as the constructor string, the component will be created with the logging option on. Otherwise, the logging option is disabled and the component won't record any of the actions that it takes.

SecurityCallContext

The SecurityCallContext interface allows you to perform an additional level of security processing not found under Windows NT. For example, in a client/server environment, you can assume that the current caller is also the application that originated the call because there's only one level of processing involved. The same can't be said for Windows 2000 and COM+ applications. When you work with a COM+ application, a client could call on a component that would in turn call upon the services of another component. The chain of calls could get so long such as to make identification of the call originator impossible.

Under Windows NT, you could use the ISecurityProperty interface to obtain the name of the original caller and the direct caller. This would give you the beginning and end of the call chain, but nothing in the middle. The original caller is the one that made the very first call that initiated the current sequence of events. The direct caller is the one that made the call to this particular component. It's the client that called this particular component, perhaps as the result of another call made by another client. In the world of client/server, these two levels of call verification are all that you need, but it definitely won't work within a distributed environment in which many levels of calls could be the normal method of getting work accomplished.

There are two properties that make the SecurityCallContext interface work. The first is the Count property, which tells you how many levels of callers are involved in the current call. The second is the Item property, which contains the security call collection. You use an index to retrieve specific security call context within the collection. Once you have an individual member, you can examine it for specific types of information like the minimum authentication level that it supports.

This interface also supports two methods. Neither method works with the collection, so you can't use them to work with a specific caller's context. The IsSecurity Enabled() method allows you to determine whether security is currently set to on. If security isn't set to on, then there won't be any useful information in the security call context collection. The second method, IsCallerInRole(), determines what role the direct caller is in. You can use this method to determine whether additional processing is required. If the direct caller can't meet the required security requirements for the component, then access is denied and no further processing is required. Here's a typical example of this interface is action.

```
Dim oSecurity As COMSVCSLib.SecurityCallContext
Dim oDirectCaller As COMSVCSLib.SecurityIdentity
Dim strUser As String
Set oSecurity = GetSecurityCallContext
```

```
If oSecurity.IsSecurityEnabled Then
    If oSecurity.IsCallerInRole("Administrator") Then
        Set oDirectCaller = oSecurity.Item("DirectCaller")
        strUser = oDirectCaller.Item("AccountName")
        If strUser = "Administrator" Then
            DoSomeWork
        End If
    End If
End If
```

As you can see from the example code, the SecurityCallContext object allows you to detect the current security settings and look for potential showstoppers before you do any other work. Once you've determined that security is enabled and the direct caller is in the proper role, you can use the Item property to check for specifics on the direct, original, and other callers of this object. The name of the caller is a handy piece of information. You can check both the direct and the original caller's name with relative ease using special Item index values. The account names of other call chain participants are also available with the Callers index.

Information received from this interface is often stored in other objects. In this case, we need a SecurityIdentity object to work with the direct caller data. The original caller data is stored in a SecurityIdentity object as well. If you need to work with the call chain, then you can retrieve it by using a SecurityCallers object. This object uses a numeric index that allows you to scan through the list of all callers. A value of 0 in the index will allow you to determine information about the original caller. Setting the index value to –1 or 1 less than the number in the Count property, will allow you to see information about the direct caller.

Using CreateObject() is safe

Anyone who has worked with MTS under Windows NT knows that you need to use the CreateInstance() method to create new objects safely. The CreateInstance() method provides both a ProgID and a context to MTS in order to ensure that the new object is instantiated with the base client's current activity. You want each client to participate in one, but only one, activity. Otherwise, COM needs to create a proxy between the various activities, reducing application speed. Unfortunately, assigning more than one activity to a single client also uses up an additional thread from the pool. Finally, using more than one activity means that the various objects can't participate in the same transaction, which means that errors in subcomponents won't "bubble up" to root components where they would be reported to MTS. That's why you couldn't use CreateObject() under Windows NT — it doesn't provide context information as part of the call, so Windows NT has no way of knowing precisely which context to associate the new object with.

The problem with Windows NT is that you aren't assured of having all of the objects for a particular base client created in a single activity. That's because the Service Control Manager (SCM) provided with Windows NT isn't context aware. The SCM under Windows 2000 is context aware, which means that you don't have to provide the base client's context as a separate input. The Windows 2000 SCM knows how to flow context information correctly and ensure that every client has only one activity to participate in. Because Windows 2000 can take care of context handling automatically, you now have a choice between `CreateInstance()` and `CreateObject()`.

While the `CreateInstance()` function is still supported under Windows 2000, new applications should use `CreateObject()` instead. The main reason to use `CreateObject()` instead of `CreateInstance()` is that `CreateObject()` requires less code and uses fewer resources. These two differences can make your application run faster, even if nothing else within the component changes. Here's an example of the difference between the two methods of creating an object.

```
'Using CreateInstance() requires more code and resources.
Dim oCtx As ObjectContext
Dim oAddIt As AddNumbers

Set oCtx = GetObjectContext()
Set oAddIt = oCtx.CreateInstance("AddIt.AddNumbers")

'Using CreateObject is more efficient.
Dim oAddIt As AddNumbers
Set oAddIt = CreateObject("AddIt.AddNumbers")
```

Tip Never use the Visual Basic New operator to create objects within MTS components. The New operator will cause problems when the MTS interception scheme isn't handled correctly. Without proper interceptor support, you'll lose access to features like role-based security. Most of the new COM+ and existing MTS features rely on the use of interceptors to perform both pre- and postprocessing. Even though using `CreateObject()` or `CreateInstance()` means that you'll encounter both a slight performance hit and a loss of compile time-type checks, both methods are a safer bet when working with COM+. (New provides a performance boost because Visual Basic doesn't have to resolve a ProgID to a CLSID. In addition, Visual Basic can't check the validity of a ProgID, but can check the validity of a CLSID at compile time, making the New operator easier to debug.) As with every rule, there are exceptions with regard to using the New operator. You can use the New operator when working with components that don't require a context because they're not part of an MTS package. For example, when you create an ADO object, you can use the New operator because ADO objects aren't registered with MTS. The best choice under Windows 2000 however, is to always use `CreateObject()`.

Using SafeRef() is no longer required

Another problem that you'll encounter when working with MTS under Windows NT is that Windows NT isn't always sure when it's time to create a proxy for a component. The purpose of the `SafeRef()` function is to allow an object to create a reference to itself that's safe to pass to another context. An object should never pass the this pointer to another object because that pointer won't be set up for the other object's context.

Unlike MTS under Windows NT, COM+ is context relative. This means that as long as you observe a few simple precautions, COM+ will automatically take care of creating an appropriate proxy as needed. Consider the situation in which Object A calls upon Object B to create Object C and then pass a reference to Object C back to Object A. The following code won't work under Windows NT, but will work fine when using Windows 2000.

```
Function CreateObjectC() As ObjectCClass
    Dim newobj As ObjectCClass
    Set newobj = CreateObject("ADLL.ObjectCClass")
    Set CreateObjectC = newobj
End Function
```

When Object A calls upon the `CreateObjectC()` method in Object B, Object B creates Object C. At this point, there's a proxy between Object B and Object C. Windows will automatically handle any required conversions between the two objects. As soon as Object B passes the reference to Object C back to Object A, Windows also creates a proxy between Objects A and C. This new functionality in COM+ allows you to create references to objects without using the `SafeRef()` function.

Registry entry differences

We've talked about a lot of differences in the way that MTS and COM+ implement object technologies like references and the SCM. All of these differences mean that you get more features from COM+ for a lower cost in development time and system resource. It also means that MTS under Windows NT is configured differently than COM+. We've looked at the same application throughout the chapter configured for both a Windows 2000 and a Windows NT machine. In this section, we'll look at how all of the differences in configuration affect the Registry.

Let's begin by looking at how the OrderAccess.OrderModify.1 component is registered under Windows NT. Normally, the LocalServer32 key for a component points to that component's location on the hard drive. Notice that in Figure 11-11 the LocalServer32 key value points to mtx.exe instead of the component DLL.

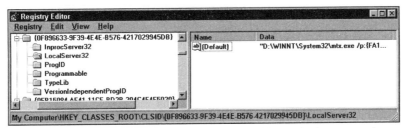

Figure 11-11: MTS components are configured differently than normal components.

There's a simple reason for this change in tactics. The Windows NT SCM doesn't know how to create a component context. As a result, if the LocalServer32 key had a value that pointed directly to the component, the component would get created without a context. Of course, this means that the component wouldn't work properly under MTS for all of the reasons that we discussed in the "Using CreateObject() is Safe" section of the chapter. By calling mtx.exe instead of the component, MTS gets a chance to create an object context before it creates the object. After the context is created, mtx.exe takes care of creating the component.

Things can get stranger still under Windows NT. If you install an MTS component on the machine by using RegSvr32, then the Registry entry will appear under the InprocServer32 key. Instead of using mtx.exe, the component will use mtxex.dll. In short, there are two different ways of creating an MTS component under Windows 2000, neither of which calls the component directly.

Windows 2000 has gotten rid of much of the Registry confusion for MTS developers. As shown in Figure 11-12, COM+ uses the same type of entry for MTS components as it does for standard components. The Windows 2000 SCM has been rewritten to take the type of component into consideration and instantiate the component within a context when required. In fact, the SCM is even able to detect the difference between component setup types. It performs a different kind of instantiation for library applications than it performs for server applications. However, no matter which kind of application you use, the Registry entries never change.

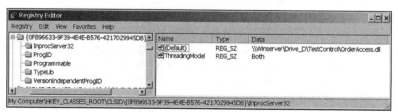

Figure 11-12: COM+ Registry entries for MTS components look the same as standard component entries.

Creating a Simple MTS Component

In Chapter 10, we created a simple DCOM application that consisted of a client-side application and a server-side component. The main difference between this application and any other application that you may have created in the past is that the server-side component has no user interface. This is also a characteristic of MTS components. You can take just about everything that you've learned for building a DCOM component and apply it to what you need to do when creating an MTS component. So, you won't be starting at the very beginning when developing the component in this chapter. The process described in the first section that follows, "Creating the Component Shell," is similar to the process used to create a shell for a DCOM component because the two start at essentially the same point.

There are, however, a few things that you need to consider when creating an MTS component that you didn't need to consider when creating a DCOM component. All components developed specifically for MTS use need to contain code that monitors the state of code processing within the current component, and then vote on the outcome of the transaction based on events within the component. Obviously, you also need to consider how much MTS code you'll implement when developing a COM+ application. We'll discuss these and other requirements in the second section that follows.

The third and fourth sections that follow, "Shortcuts for MTS component development" and "Shortcuts for the DBMS," provide tips that will make the development process faster, easier, or less error prone. We all need tips of this type to get applications out the door in the short time frames that application development is given today. While you may not be able to use all of these tips, you should be able to use many of them in any MTS development scenario.

The final section that follows is the main event; we'll add some code to the component shell and get it ready for use. This section will explore some common MTS coding techniques. We'll talk about both generic MTS coding and coding that's specific to the COM+ environment. Applications typically require both types of coding right now because some companies haven't made a complete switch to Windows 2000.

Creating the Component Shell

There isn't a special project type for MTS applications. However, remember that an MTS component, unlike a DCOM component, is an in-process server. There's an important reason for this difference. Remember that a DCOM component resides by itself on the server. You create a direct connection to it over the network. An MTS application, on the other hand, is placed within a container. This container holds the application and allows COM+ to create interceptors for it, which, in turn, allows advanced configuration, and both pre- and postprocessing. This is an important difference between DCOM application construction and MTS application construction (there are more differences that will be discussed as the chapter progresses).

The sample application will provide an overview of some typical MTS tasks like determining the current security status of the component and the security of the client requesting access to the component. The example will detect various component settings and report back to the client application about them. You'll be able to change component settings by using the Component Services console, and see the effects of those changes on the output of the application. So, while this application won't do anything fancy, it will help you to understand how an MTS component interacts with the system when using COM+ under Windows 2000.

Let's begin by creating a new project for our component (I'm assuming that you've already started Visual Basic). All you need to do is select the ActiveX DLL project from the New Project dialog box, and then click Open. After you've created the application shell, you'll need to configure it before you can do any coding. Table 11-2 contains a complete list of settings for this component.

Table 11-2 Simple MTS Component Settings			
Window or Dialog	**Tab**	**Property**	**Value**
Properties	Project	Name	SimpleMTS
Properties	Class Module	Name	Transact
		MTSTransactionMode	2 — RequiresTransaction
		Persistable	0 — NotPersistable
Project Properties	Component	Version Compatibility	Binary Compatibility

You'll also need to make some changes to the properties for this project. Just use the Project ➪ SimpleMTS Properties command to display the SimpleMTS – Project Properties dialog box shown in Figure 11-13. You'll need to set the Unattended Execution option to ensure that the component won't display any dialog boxes on the server. If the component does try to display a message box, Windows will send the message to the event log instead. Select the Single Threaded option in the Threading Model field. Using a single-threaded component reduces programming complexity.

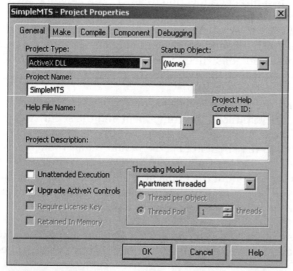

Figure 11-13: The SimpleMTS – Project Properties dialog box is where you choose a threading model.

We'll also need to add support for the various MTS features for this component. Use the Project ⇨ References command to display the References –SimpleMTS.vbp dialog box shown in Figure 11-14. Every MTS component that you create requires a reference to the COM+ Services Type Library (highlighted in the figure) as a minimum. There are other COM+- and MTS-specific libraries that you may need to add depending on the requirements for the component.

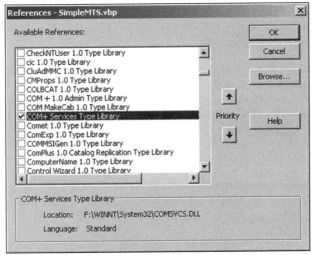

Figure 11-14: The COM+ Services Type Library is the minimal reference required by any MTS component.

Requirements for MTS components

There are few requirements for MTS components that execute under COM+. The ability to configure the COM+ application obviates the need for some types of coding that were absolutely essential under Windows NT. For example, you can set an application to automatically terminate and vote on the outcome of a transaction even if it lacks the required COM+ code.

Of course, taking advantage of every potential configuration option and not implementing any configuration items within the component itself could be an invitation to disaster because you're depending on the network administrator to perform the required work. In many cases, the work won't be done at all or will be done improperly, leaving your application in an unworkable state. As a result, there are a few items that you should consider requirements for any MTS component, regardless of the platform that it executes under.

One of the first requirements is to ensure that the component does mark the done and happy bits as required. These housekeeping chores ensure that your component will participate in the transaction and won't continue using resource long after its work is done. You can allow the network administrator to configure the component for automatic termination, but there should still be some type of default action.

If your MTS component will always be used on a LAN, you should consider providing a return value in addition to any output arguments associated with any methods that you expose. The reason for including a return value is so that the client application can determine the results of any call. If an error occurs, the use of a return value also gives you an option for providing feedback to the client component. Your only other recourse is to place entries in the event log and hope that the network administrator reads them. MTS components should never use any type of user interface elements because it's unlikely that anyone will see them.

The data handled by most MTS components is fairly sensitive. This means that you need to handle security issues by using the resources that MTS makes available. The first step is to ensure that the network administrator configures role-based security for the component. You can check the security status of a component by using the `IsSecurityEnabled()` method. A small piece of additional code like this is well worth the slight performance hit that the component will encounter and the small amount of additional development time required to implement the security check. Make sure that you also check for the client's role. Role-based security makes it less likely that someone will intrude on your application, but it's still not impossible. Make sure that your application is designed to detect a variety of security infractions so that your application will continue to run safely.

Also, ensure that your component is flexible enough. The Component Services MMC snap-in does make a wealth of configuration options available to the network administrator. It's up to you, however, to ensure that your component is designed to work with those configuration settings. This means detecting the configuration setting and performing configuration changes as required. Especially important in your arsenal of configuration features is the ability to send a constructor string to the component by making configuration changes to the Activation tab of the component Properties dialog box.

Shortcuts for MTS component development

Creating any component can be a time-consuming process because there are so many factors to consider and because components present special debugging and implementation challenges. Fortunately, there are a few things that you can do to make the development process faster. We looked at many of these productivity enhancements in Chapters 9 and 10. Make sure that you look at those two chapters to learn about the productivity enhancements for components in general and for components that need to work in a distributed environment. The following sections will look at productivity considerations for MTS components in particular.

Working with the AutoComplete attribute

MTS applications normally require some special coding to handle the transactional requirements of the application. You must tell Windows that the component is done performing its task and that you need to vote on the outcome of the transaction. If these two criteria aren't met, then the application could literally wait forever for your decision. Even if it doesn't wait forever, Windows assumes that a transaction has failed if any party fails to provide an affirmative vote.

COM+ provides a special configuration option for each method as shown in Figure 11-15. Checking the Automatically deactivate this object when this method returns option allows a component to participate in the transaction voting process and to tell Windows when it's completed its processing without any special code. In other words, by using this techniques, you can take any component and turn it into an MTS application component without any worry about the component failing to do its job.

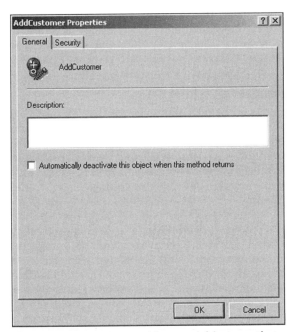

Figure 11-15: COM+ provides special features that allow a component to automatically complete its processing.

So, how does COM+ perform this magic? When you check this option, you're telling Windows to assume certain things about your component — at least about this method within the component. Windows will always assume that exiting a function or subroutine means that the component has finished performing the requested processing, even if the done bit isn't set. Likewise, if the component exits without error, then the transaction is assumed to complete properly and Windows will treat the component's response as a `SetComplete()` call.

The productivity enhancement behind this feature should be fairly obvious by now. If you have a component that can already do the work that you need, but doesn't have the required MTS code in place, you can use this technique to create applications faster. The component will work as anticipated and will participate in transactions, even though it doesn't have a single line of MTS code.

There are potential problems with this method as well. The biggest problem is the network administrator. You have to depend on the network administrator to set the proper options or the component won't engage in the transaction and any data transferred is at risk. In addition, because the component isn't looking for problems that are unique to MTS, there are errors that could pass unnoticed. In short, you might be getting a false sense of security from a component that can't see specific types of errors.

Use constructor strings whenever possible

Application development often ends up being a nightmare for the developer because of changes in system configuration. If you normally develop custom applications, you may be used to including hard coded location information like a DSN within your application. If this information changes later, you'll find yourself rewriting code that shouldn't have to change. Unfortunately, in the early days of MTS, you didn't have much of a choice unless you wanted to use Registry settings or some other less than convenient configuration method.

Using a constructor string allows the network administrator to change configuration details as needed. If the server containing a database required for a particular application changes, a simple component configuration change will make the application work correctly again without any coding change on your part. In addition, because the constructor string is included as part of the application, is always available, and uses the same configuration technique every time, you don't have to worry about creating a special set of administrator instructions. There are no training costs when using this method; at least not if the network administrator is already familiar with MMC and MTS.

As mentioned earlier, constructor strings also allow you to create applications that are flexible enough to handle conditions that you didn't anticipate when designing the original component. Something as simple as a propagation delay can cause major heartache for the network administrator whose application suddenly stops working for no apparent reason. Constructor strings allow you to overcome these potential problems and allow support staff to fix errors with a simple phone call, instead of sending out a technical representative.

There are times, however, when you should not use a constructor string. The most important fact to remember is that a constructor string won't fix sloppy programming. If you think a constructor string will make an application run better, faster, or more error free, think again. The constructor string is just as likely to cause problems as any other part of the application if it isn't coded properly.

You should also avoid using constructor strings when there's a potential security or data integrity risk. Because the constructor string isn't encrypted in any way, it's open to prying eyes. Someone could potentially use the information from a constructor string to help break down application security. Data integrity could also be at risk if you're counting on a network administrator entry that doesn't get made for some reason. A constructor string should be an optional element of your application. There should be a default course of action in case the network administrator fails to configure the component for some reason. If nothing else, you can always use the lack of a constructor string as an excuse to leave a component not configured error message in the event log to remind the network administrator to complete component installation.

Use COM+-specific methodologies

We saw in the "Interface Differences" section of the chapter that COM+ has a lot to offer in expanded functionality when it comes to transactions. It pays to mention, though, that COM+ offer more flexibility and also offers security and performance features that you can't get with MTS 2.0.

All of these differences mean that you'll spend less time coding, because you'll have access to more special-purpose methods and won't need to build your own in as many situations. You'll also spend less time debugging the application because it does offer higher reliability. COM+ applications require less tuning, and you'll find yourself spending fewer Saturdays ensuring that no one has invaded your company.

The downside of using COM+-specific methodologies is obvious. COM is already considered a platform-specific solution to any programming problem. COM+ isn't even found on every version of Windows, so you may find that you lose a lot in the way of portability and cross-platform compatibility by using COM+.

There's also the problem of what to do with existing code. There are few companies out there that can afford to perform wholesale modifications of their code each time Microsoft comes out with a new and improved product. As a result, you may find yourself in the dubious position of having to justify the expense for a component upgrade before you can use COM+. The important thing to remember is that

COM+ need not be an all-or-nothing technology. You can mix and match new technology components with those that rely on older technologies. The disadvantage of doing so is that your entire application won't benefit from using COM+ and that you may have to make a few concessions as the application develops.

Watch out for Visual Basic limitations

Nothing could be more frustrating than trying to get object pooling working, only to discover that Visual Basic doesn't support it. We talked about the majority of these limitations in Chapter 8. In many cases, these errors won't show up as error messages. What you'll see is a loss of functionality during testing. Finding the problem may take days and even then you won't be sure until you fully research the problem. In short, Visual Basic has limits compared to Visual C++ and you need to be aware of them to keep your development efforts on track. We'll see later in this chapter how some types of Visual Basic limitations show up when you install a component and try to configure it.

Shortcuts for the DBMS

MTS applications, unlike many component classes, tend to work with databases and the information that they contain. What this means to you as a developer is that you not only need to find ways to speed development of the component, but you also need to find ways to speed development of the database that the component will work with. It's important to create a good database design at the outset because a poor design will cost you a lot in terms of productivity, data security, and ease of development. The following sections will help you to create a good database design in a minimum of time. Remember that this section does deal with MTS, so I've limited the database productivity considerations to those that would directly affect MTS component development.

Avoid using stored procedures

Many database applications rely on stored procedures to perform at least part of the required work. Using stored procedures allows an application to perform some of the required work within the DBMS itself, providing a small, but noticeable performance gain as well as a small gain in security.

Unfortunately, there are a few problems in using stored procedures within the COM+ or even the MTS environment. When the database manager takes control of application execution, it means that MTS is no longer in control. Any data integrity or security gains that you've made by using MTS could be lost at the database level; depending, of course, on how well the database is designed. The point is that if you're relying on MTS to provide security, reliability, and performance benefits, you should rely on it all the way and leave only the management of data to the DBMS.

Rely on the server component

The more time that you can spend on one machine rather than transferring data across the network, the more efficient your application will be. MTS makes the problems that you get when working across a network with large data sets worse because it bloats the data to a certain extent. Part of this bloat happens as part of encrypting the data for security purposes; part is the housekeeping overhead of using MTS to ensure that data integrity remains high. If you write an MTS application in such a way that the client is requesting data directly, the application is almost guaranteed to run slowly (unless it's using small data sets).

However, you don't have to write applications where the client is working with the database directly — you can create a server-side component to do most of the work. A server-side component can perform all of the work required to create an answer set with only the records that a user will need. Using this approach reduces the bandwidth needed for your application and makes it possible to use MTS and still realize a performance gain.

Adding some code

The test MTS component will provide a series of methods that will allow a test application to determine the current state of the component. For example, there will be a separate method that demonstrates the IObjectConstruct interface. Each section that follows explores one of these method implementations. By the time that we're finished, you'll have a component that can at least demonstrate the basic functionality that MTS offers.

Note   The MTS example in this section isn't designed to run on Windows NT and MTS 2.0. It relies on new COM+ features that aren't available on that platform. As a result, you may be able to install this component on a Windows NT machine, but it won't work as anticipated. To get full use out of this component, you need a two-machine setup consisting of one Windows 2000 Professional/Server workstation and a second Windows 2000 Server.

Implementing IObjectContext

The capability to provide a string as input to a component is more important than you might initially think. We've already talked about the various ways that you can use construct strings to ensure that a component provides all of the functionality that the network administrator requires as the network configuration changes. Listing 11-1 shows one way to implement the IObjectContext interface.

Listing 11-1: **A Simple IObjectContext Implementation**

```
'Enable the component to process a constructor string.
Implements COMSVCSLib.IObjectConstruct
Dim strConstructor As String

'The sub required to support the constructor string.
Private Sub IObjectConstruct_Construct _
    (ByVal pCtorObj As Object)

    'Create a variable to hold the constructor
    'string object.
    Dim oCS As COMSVCSLib.IObjectConstructString
    Set oCS = pCtorObj

    'See if there is a constructor string to
    'process.
    strConstructor = oCS.ConstructString

    'If not, then place a default value in the
    'global constructor string value.
    If Len(strConstructor) <= 0 Then
        strConstructor = "No Constructor String"
    End If
End Sub

Public Function ReadConstructor _
    (pstrConstructor As String)

    'See if the constructor was initialized.
    If Len(strConstructor) <= 0 Then
        strConstructor = "No Constructor Support"
    End If

    'Place the constructor string value in the
    'supplied variable.
    pstrConstructor = strConstructor

    'Return a success code to the application.
    ReadConstructor = vbOK
End Function
```

Before we talk about the code, there's one issue that you need to consider when working with this interface. There are three potential outcomes depending on how the network administrator configures the component. The network administrator could disable the Enable object construction option. In this case, the IObjectConstruct_Construct() method won't get called at all. So, the global string, strConstructor, will remain empty and you'll need to check it before using it. A second option is that the network administrator could check the Enable object construction option, but fail to provide a Constructor string field value. In this case, the `IObjectConstruct_Construct()` method will get called, but won't have any data to process. You'll also need to check for this condition. Finally, if the network administrator checks the Enable object construction option and provides a Constructor string field value, you'll need to parse the string to find out what data it contains and configure the component appropriately.

The operation of this example code is relatively simple. Windows 2000 calls the `IObjectConstruct_Construct()` method when necessary and passes it the constructor string (if any) provided by the network administrator. The component tells Windows 2000 that it implements the IObjectConstruct interface by using the Implements keyword and by adding the `IObjectConstruct_Construct()` method. The first thing that the method does is to create an IObjectConstructString object to receive the value supplied by Windows. It then converts this object to a string that can be examined for a value. If the administrator doesn't provide a value, the method automatically provides a default value. Your code should always provide a default value of some kind, rather than leave the string blank. Doing so will reduce the number of problems that you experience later while debugging the application.

The global string value either has a value now or it doesn't, depending on the Enable object construction option setting. The component is ready to go, however. As soon as the client calls `ReadConstructor()`, the method checks for a value in strConstructor. If this string is empty, it's safe to assume that the Enable object construction option isn't checked and we can provide a default string value saying so. No matter what the strConstructor value is, we place it in the return value for the `ReadConstructor()` method call.

Notice that this method doesn't provide the string as a return value — the string is returned as one of the arguments. The function return value is actually a result value that indicates the success of the method. Because this method is relatively simple and because there's little that can go wrong, the component always returns a value of vbOK. Even if your methods are this simple, you need to use a return value for components that won't be used in disconnected applications. The return value ensures that the component is set up to provide return values later when you need to add more functionality and error codes.

Tip   The reason that you can't provide return values for components used for disconnected applications is that you can't be sure that the client will be available to receive the return values. Disconnected applications rely on one-way data transfers that don't lend themselves to using return values for error reporting. When working with components for disconnected application use, you'll normally need to provide error reporting by using the server's event log.

Implementing ContextInfo

The ContextInfo interface allows a component to determine the current transaction state and then retrieve identifiers for the activity, context, and transaction in the form of GUIDs. This information can be useful, especially while debugging a COM+ application, because there are few tools that allow you to get all of the information that you need in a distributed environment. Listing 11-2 shows the code required to implement a basic ContextInfo interface handler.

Listing 11-2: **A Simple ContextInfo Implementation**

```
Public Function ReadContextInfo _
    (strActivityID As String, _
    strContextID As String, _
    strTransactionID As String, _
    bIsInTransaction As Boolean)

    'Provide error trapping.
    On Error GoTo NoTransaction

    'Create a variable to hold the context information.
    Dim oCI As COMSVCSLib.ContextInfo
    Set oCI = GetObjectContext.ContextInfo

    'Fill in the variables.
    strActivityID = oCI.GetActivityId
    strContextID = oCI.GetContextId
    strTransactionID = oCI.GetTransactionId
    bIsInTransaction = oCI.IsInTransaction

    'Provide a positive return value.
    ReadContextInfo = vbOK
    Exit Function

NoTransaction:
    'An error happened, so use default values.
    bIsInTransaction = False
    strActivityID = "N/A"
    strContextID = "N/A"
    strTransactionID = "N/A"

    'Provide a negative return value.
    ReadContextInfo = mtsErrCtxTMNotAvailable

End Function
```

There's one feature of this code that you must implement whenever you work with the ContextInfo interface: error trapping. If you request transaction information of any kind and there's no transaction taking place, Windows will generate an error that won't tell the user about the true cause of the problem. It's absolutely essential that you trap the error within the component and provide alternative values for each of the output arguments. In addition, you should return an error code that the client can trap. I chose a predefined error code. While this error code may not precisely fit the circumstance, the fact that it's predefined makes things a bit easier on the developer who's using your component. Obviously, the decision of whether to use a preexisting error code or create a new one is based as much on personal taste as on the availability of an existing error code that fits your needs. Finally, if this component is working with sensitive data, you should consider adding an event log entry so that the network administrator knows that an error occurred and can reconfigure the component as needed.

For the most part, there aren't any other surprises with this code. You create a pointer to the required interface, call methods within that interface, and then provide a result to the client. The only part that might be tricky is using the GUID to find out additional information about each of the objects that this series of calls identifies.

Implementing SecurityCallContext

Security is undoubtedly one of the biggest issues facing any developer of COM+ applications today. Knowing how to configure a COM+ application to use security features like role-base security is important because security conditions tend to change as networks face new threads. Equally important is knowing how to detect security settings from within the application. An application should know that security is implemented and that the user has presented a set of valid credentials as a minimum. Role-based security makes it easier for a network administrator to change the access requirements to a component, so hard coding access requirements is something that you shouldn't do with a COM+ application.

There are several security interfaces used with both MTS 2.0 under Windows NT and COM+ under Windows 2000. If you need to build a component that will work under both platforms, then look at the SecurityProperty object. On the other hand, if you need to provide the best security under COM+, then you'll want to look at the SecurityCallContext object because it provides more features for the developer to use in securing an application. This is also Microsoft's preferred method of providing access under Windows 2000. With this in mind, let's look at the simple SecurityCallContext implementation in Listing 11-3.

Listing 11-3: **A Simple SecurityCallContext Implementation**

```
Public Function ReadSecurityCallContext _
    (oDirectCaller As SecurityIdentity, _
    oOriginalCaller As SecurityIdentity, _
    liMinimumAuthLevel As Long, _
    liNumberOfCallers As Long, _
    oCallers As SecurityCallers)

    'Obtain the current security call context.
    Dim oSCC As SecurityCallContext
    Set oSCC = GetSecurityCallContext

    'Fill the variables with values from the
    'security call context collection.
    Set oDirectCaller = oSCC.Item("DirectCaller")
    Set oOriginalCaller = oSCC.Item("OriginalCaller")
    liMinimumAuthLevel = _
        oSCC.Item("MinAuthenticationLevel")
    liNumberOfCallers = oSCC.Item("NumCallers")
    Set oCallers = oSCC.Item("Callers")

    'Provide a positive return value.
    ReadSecurityCallContext = vbOK

End Function
```

The SecurityCallContext object isn't the end of the line for COM+ developers; it only provides access to the security information in the form of collections. (There are two methods for checking whether security is enabled and whether the user is in a specific role at the time.) There are five collection items returned by this call and you access them by using a text index. Table 11-3 lists the five collection items, describes them, and tells you what data type they return.

The source code for this method is relatively simple once you understand the SecurityCallContext collection. The first thing that the code does is to create a SecurityCallContext object, and then set it equal to the current security call context by using the GetSecurityCallContext() method. Note that this call always succeeds, so the only way to trap an error is to check the "OriginalCaller" index for blank data field. A blank field here indicates that security isn't enabled or that some other error happened. You can check this value either at the server or client.

After the current security call context is obtained, the code fills in values in the variables passed by the client application. The call returns vbOK as the last step. Suggestions for other call values include an error value if role-based security isn't enabled, the client application fails to pass the required variables, or if the client application (or a member of the call chain) lacks the proper authorization to make this call.

Table 11-3
SecurityCallContext Collection Items

Item	Index String	Return Type	Description
Direct Caller	"DirectCaller"	SecurityIdentity Object	Contains the security information for the direct caller of the object. This caller may not be the application that originated the calling sequence; it may be a server that's requesting the information on a caller's behalf.
Original Caller	"OriginalCaller"	SecurityIdentity Object	Contains the security information for the originator of a calling sequence.
Minimum Authentication Level	"MinAuthenticationLevel"	Long	Contains the lowest level of authentication used in a sequence of calls. This value indicated the lowest level of security that you can expect a particular call to receive, even if the current level is higher.
Number of Callers	"NumCallers"	Long	Contains the number of callers in the current call chain. If this number is 0, then there are no additional callers and this is a direct client to server call.

Continued

	Table 11-3 *(continued)*		
Item	**Index String**	**Return Type**	**Description**
Callers	"Callers"	SecurityCallers Object	Contains a collection of callers of this object. Each item in this collection is a SecurityIdentity object, which is the same as the Direct Caller and Original Caller entries. You can use this object to trace the call chain and verify the identity of every caller in the chain. This object is useful when you need to verify that everyone involved in a particular call has the required access (no one is trying to spoof access to data that they're not entitled to).

Creating an MTS Client Application

Now that we have a component to use, it's time to create a client application to go with it. This application allows you to see MTS in action. We'll create an application that can test both good and bad transactions. You can see the results of these transactions by using several tools, most notably the Component Services console. This application will also let you test performance, at least a little, when you run several copies at the same time. The following sections will help you to build the client application.

Creating the program shell and designing the dialog

This example will use a simple dialog-based application to test the component that we created in the previous section of the chapter. The first thing that you'll need to do is create a new application. Once you do, use the values in Table 11-4 to configure the application for use.

		Table 11-4 Simple MTS Test Application Settings	
Window or Dialog	**Object or Tab**	**Property**	**Value**
Properties	Project	Name	SimpleMTSTest
Properties	Forms	Name	Main
		BorderStyle	3 — Fixed Dialog
		Caption	Simple MTS Component Tes
		Height	3000
		Width	3500
References	N/A	Available References	Check SimpleMTS — A simple MTS component.

Now that the application is ready to go, let's add some components to it. Figure 11-16 shows the design for this application. Notice that the only interface elements are pushbuttons used to test the various component methods. Table 11-5 contains the setting changes that you need to make for each of the pushbuttons.

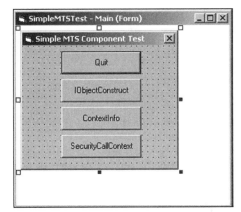

Figure 11-16: The test application will use a separate pushbutton to test each component method.

<table>
<tr><td colspan="3" align="center">Table 11-5
Simple MTS Test Application Component Settings</td></tr>
</table>

Object	Property	Value
cmdQuit	Name	cmdQuit
	Caption	Quit
	Default	True
	ToolTipText	Exit the Application
	Width	1750
cmdIObjectConstruct	Name	cmdIObjectConstruct
	Caption	IObjectConstruct
	ToolTipText	Allows testing of the IObjectConstruct interface
	Width	1750
cmdContextInfo	Name	cmdContextInfo
	Caption	ContextInfo
	ToolTipText	Allows testing of the ContextInfo interface
	Width	1750
cmdSecurityCall	Name	cmdSecurityCall
	Caption	SecurityCallContext
	ToolTipText	Allows testing of the SecuirtyCallContext interface
	Width	1750

We'll need a second dialog box to display the SecurityCallContext data. This object provides more information than a simple message box can hold. Begin by adding a plain Dialog form to your application by right-clicking Forms in the Project window and choosing the Add ⇨ Form option. You'll see an Add Form dialog box similar to the one shown in Figure 11-17. Choose the Dialog option and click Open.

The new form will require some components to display the SecurityCallContext object information. Figure 11-18 shows what the form should look like when you're finished. Table 11-6 contains all of the values that you'll need to create the form. The only addition to the table is that I used a 10-point Bold MS Sans Serif font for all of the major labels on the form to make them easier to read. We'll work more with this form in the cmdSecurityCall Pushbutton section of the chapter.

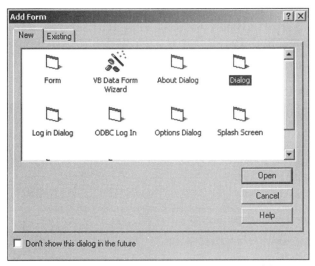

Figure 11-17: Use the Add Form dialog box to add new forms to a project.

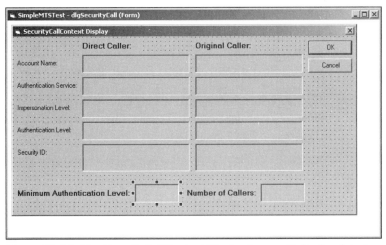

Figure 11-18: The SecurityCallContext Display form will display data from this object.

Table 11-6
SecurityCallContext Display Form Component Settings

Object	Property	Value
Dialog	Name	dlgSecurityCall
	Caption	SecurityCallContext Display
	Height	5145
	Width	9555
OKButton	Default	True
CancelButton	Cancel	True
lblDirectAN	Name	lblDirectAN
	BorderStyle	1 – Fixed Single
	Caption	""
	Font	Bold (everything else is the same)
	Width	2955
lblDirectAS	Name	lblDirectAS
	BorderStyle	1 – Fixed Single
	Caption	""
	Font	Bold (everything else is the same)
	Width	2955
lblDirectIL	Name	lblDirectIL
	BorderStyle	1 – Fixed Single
	Caption	""
	Font	Bold (everything else is the same)
	Width	2955
lblDirectAL	Name	lblDirectAL
	BorderStyle	1 – Fixed Single
	Caption	""
	Font	Bold (everything else is the same)
	Width	2955

Object	Property	Value
lblDirectSID	Name	lblDirectSID
	BorderStyle	1 — Fixed Single
	Caption	""
	Font	Bold (everything else is the same)
	Height	735
	Width	2955
	WordWrap	True
lblOriginalAN	Name	lblOriginalAN
	BorderStyle	1 — Fixed Single
	Caption	""
	Font	Bold (everything else is the same)
	Width	2955
lblOriginalAS	Name	lblOriginalAS
	BorderStyle	1 — Fixed Single
	Caption	""
	Font	Bold (everything else is the same)
	Width	2955
lblOriginalIL	Name	lblOriginalIL
	BorderStyle	1 — Fixed Single
	Caption	""
	Font	Bold (everything else is the same)
	Width	2955
lblOriginalAL	Name	lblOriginalAL
	BorderStyle	1 — Fixed Single
	Caption	""
	Font	Bold (everything else is the same)
	Width	2955

Continued

Table 11-6 *(continued)*		
Object	**Property**	**Value**
lblOriginalSID	Name	lblOriginalSID
	BorderStyle	1 – Fixed Single
	Caption	""
	Font	Bold (everything else is the same)
	Height	735
	Width	2955
	WordWrap	True
lblMinAuthLevel	Name	lblMinAuthLevel
	Caption	""
	Font	Bold (everything else is the same)
lblNumCallers	Name	lblNumCallers
	Caption	""
	Font	Bold (everything else is the same)

Adding Some Code

It's time to add some code to the test application. As with the component, I'll talk about each of the buttons separately. The only exception is the code for the cmdQuit pushbutton, which will appear with the code for the cmdIObjectConstruct pushbutton. The following sections show you the code that you'll need to add to the test application and explain how these buttons interact with the SimpleMTS component.

cmdIObjectConstruct Pushbutton

The IObjectConstruct interface allows a component to receive a configuration string from the network administrator. We've already talked about how this interface works and what you need to do to implement it. However, it's also important to see how this interface could affect a client application. Listing 11-4 shows you how to call upon the services of the IObjectConstruct interface as implemented by the `ReadConstructor()` method. This listing also contains the code for the cmdQuit pushbutton. The sole purpose of this pushbutton is to allow you to exit the application.

> ### Listing 11-4: **cmdIObjectConstruct Pushbutton Source Code**
>
> ```
> Private Sub cmdIObjectContext_Click()
>     'Create the required variables.
>     Dim oMTS As SimpleMTS.Transact
>     Dim strResult As String
>
>     'Instantiate the object.
>     Set oMTS = CreateObject("SimpleMTS.Transact")
>
>     'Get the construct string.
>     oMTS.ReadConstructor strResult
>
>     'Display the result.
>     MsgBox strResult
>
>     'Get rid of the object.
>     Set oMTS = Nothing
> End Sub
>
> Private Sub cmdQuit_Click()
>     'Exit the application
>     End
> End Sub
> ```

There aren't any major secrets in this code. All we do is create a reference to the SimpleMTS.Transact interface and instantiate it. After we have an object to work with, the code uses the `ReadContructor()` method to access the constructor string value (or a descriptive message if there isn't any value). After we have a value, the application displays it onscreen then releases the SimpleMTS.Transact object.

The only surprise in this application is that you don't need to provide a server name when instantiating the object. If you'll remember from the DCOM example in Chapter 10, a DCOM application requires either a Registry entry or direct coding to find the server where the object is located. This requirement is taken care of by the proxy application for a COM+ application. We've already talked about creating and installing COM+ applications (including the proxy application) in Chapter 2, so I won't cover that process again.

cmdContextInfo Pushbutton

This is the pushbutton used to obtain the current transaction status information about a component. We need to identify each type of information (because they're GUIDs you wouldn't know what they identified otherwise) and provide some form of simple formatting from the output of the `ReadContextInfo()` method. Listing 11-5 shows the source code that you'll need to implement this simple output function.

Listing 11-5: **cmdContextInfo Pushbutton Source Code**

```
Private Sub cmdContextInfo_Click()
    'Create the required variables.
    Dim oMTS As SimpleMTS.Transact
    Dim strActivityID As String
    Dim strContextID As String
    Dim strTransactionID As String
    Dim bIsInTransaction As Boolean
    Dim strIsInTransaction As String

    'Instantiate the object.
    Set oMTS = CreateObject("SimpleMTS.Transact")

    'Get the context information.
    oMTS.ReadContextInfo strActivityID, _
                         strContextID, _
                         strTransactionID, _
                         bIsInTransaction

    'Test for a transaction.
    If bIsInTransaction Then
        strIsInTransaction = "Active Transaction"
    Else
        strIsInTransaction = "No Transaction"
    End If

    'Display the result.
    MsgBox "The context information includes: " + _
        vbCrLf + strIsInTransaction + _
        vbCrLf + "Activity ID: " + vbTab + strActivityID + _
        vbCrLf + "Context ID: " + vbTab + strContextID + _
        vbCrLf + "Transaction ID: " + vbTab + strTransactionID

    'Get rid of the object.
    Set oMTS = Nothing
End Sub
```

As you can see, this code is relatively straightforward. The code begins by creating an instance of the remote component, the calling on the ReadContextInfo() method to gain access to the values that the ContextInfo object can provide. The bIsInTransaction variable allows you to determine if the component is currently in a transaction. If so, you'll see GUIDs output as the various ID values. If not, all of the ID values will have N/A after them.

cmdSecurityCall Pushbutton

The SecurityContextCall object provides a wealth of data by using collections. These collections are indexed by using text strings. You can see the discussion of these strings in Table 11-3. Because the data is in a collection, we'll need to do a little more work than with the previous pushbutton code. In this case, we'll need to retrieve the data from the collection, and, in some cases, format it for viewing. Listing 11-6 shows the code that you'll need to implement the cmdSecurityCall pushbutton.

Listing 11-6: cmdSecurityCall Pushbutton Source Code

```
Private Sub cmdSecurityCall_Click()
    'Create the required variables.
    Dim oDirectCaller As SecurityIdentity
    Dim oOriginalCaller As SecurityIdentity
    Dim liMinimumAuthLevel As Long
    Dim liNumberOfCallers As Long
    Dim oCallers As SecurityCallers
    Dim oMTS As SimpleMTS.Transact
    Dim aSID() As Byte
    Dim strSID As String
    Dim iCount As Integer

    'Instantiate the object.
    Set oMTS = CreateObject("SimpleMTS.Transact")

    'Call the security call context.
    oMTS.ReadSecurityCallContext _
        oDirectCaller, _
        oOriginalCaller, _
        (liMinimumAuthenticationLevel), _
        (liNumberOfCallers), _
        oCallers

    With dlgSecurityCall
        'Determine the Direct Caller SID.
        strSID = ""
        ReDim aSID(UBound(oDirectCaller.Item("SID")))
        aSID = oDirectCaller.Item("SID")
        For iCount = 0 To UBound(aSID)
            strSID = strSID + CStr(Hex(aSID(iCount))) + " "
        Next

        'Fill in the Direct Caller data.
        .lblDirectAN.Caption = _
            oDirectCaller.Item("AccountName")
        .lblDirectAS.Caption = _
```

Continued

Listing 11-6 *(continued)*

```
            oDirectCaller.Item("AuthenticationService")
        .lblDirectIL.Caption = _
            oDirectCaller.Item("ImpersonationLevel")
        .lblDirectAL.Caption = _
            oDirectCaller.Item("AuthenticationLevel")
        .lblDirectSID.Caption = strSID

        'Determine the Orignal Caller SID.
        strSID = ""
        ReDim aSID(UBound(oOriginalCaller.Item("SID")))
        aSID = oOriginalCaller.Item("SID")
        For iCount = 0 To UBound(aSID)
            strSID = strSID + CStr(Hex(aSID(iCount))) + " "
        Next

        'Fill in the Original Caller data.
        .lblOriginalAN.Caption = _
            oOriginalCaller.Item("AccountName")
        .lblOriginalAS.Caption = _
            oOriginalCaller.Item("AuthenticationService")
        .lblOriginalIL.Caption = _
            oOriginalCaller.Item("ImpersonationLevel")
        .lblOriginalAL.Caption = _
            oOriginalCaller.Item("AuthenticationLevel")
        .lblOriginalSID.Caption = strSID

        'Fill in the minimum authentication level and
        'number of callers
        .lblMinAuthLevel.Caption = CStr(liMinimumAuthLevel)
        .lblNumCallers.Caption = CStr(liNumberOfCallers)

        'Display the SecurityCallContext dialog.
        .Show Modal
    End With

    'Get rid of the objects.
    Set oDirectCaller = Nothing
    Set oOriginalCaller = Nothing
    Set oCallers = Nothing
    Set oMTS = Nothing
End Sub
```

As with all of the other pushbuttons so far, the first thing we need to do is create an instance of the SimpleMTS component and gain access to the Transact interface. Next, we need to call the ReadSecurityCallContext() method. Notice that the variables used in this case are MTS-specific objects for the most part, rather than generic Visual Basic variables.

After the objects are retrieved, we need to begin retrieving the data from the collection. Both the direct caller and the original caller collection items work in the same way, so I'll discuss just the direct caller code.

The first piece of data that we'll look at is the security identifier (SID) of the direct caller. This data isn't only in a collection — it's stored as a byte array. The dynamic array, aSID, is resized to the upper bound of the "SID" array, and the data from that array is then placed in aSID. A for. . .next loop converts the array of bytes to a hexadecimal string. Placing a space between each element makes the string easier to read onscreen and allows you to display it in a shorter space.

Filling in the direct caller elements of the SecurityCallContext Display dialog box comes next. All of the other collection members are easily placed in the dialog box as is, so we don't need to convert them. After the dialog box elements are filled in, we can display the SecurityCallContext Display dialog box so that the user can see the information.

There's one final note when viewing this code. Notice that I didn't instantiate the SecurityIdentity or SecurityCallers variables before calling the `ReadSecurity CallContext()` method. Because these variables are passed by reference, the `ReadSecurityCallContext()` method will instantiate them for you. What you'll get back is an object that's ready to use. You will, however, have to free these variables before you exit the Sub. Otherwise, the memory they use will remain in limbo because Windows won't know who owns the object afterward.

dlgSecurityCall Dialog

Most of the needs of the secondary dialog box, dlgSecurityCall, are taken care of in the main routine shown in Listing 11-6. However, you may still want to hide the dialog box after you're finished viewing it to test other buttons in the example application. Listing 11-7 shows the simple code that you'll need to hide the dialog box.

Listing 11-7: **dlgSecurityCall Dialog Component Source Code**

```
Option Explicit

Private Sub CancelButton_Click()
    'Exit the dialog
    Hide
End Sub

Private Sub OKButton_Click()
    'Exit the dialog
    Hide
End Sub
```

Testing the Simple MTS Component

Like DCOM, MTS applications consist of a client application and one or more servers. In many cases, the component will provide access to a database. All MTS applications handle critical, sensitive, or fragile data, so complete application testing is essential. We talked about the need to test components individually and as separate additions during integration testing in Chapter 10, so I won't repeat that information here.

The following sections will help you to install and test the simple MTS application that we've just created. The important thing to remember is that this application represents an overview of what you'd normally do with a full-fledged application. It's not designed to represent a real-world example; it acts as a training tool for what will become real-world applications in the future. Likewise, this testing procedure will show you the steps needed to fully test an MTS application, but won't provide as much detail testing as required for a production application. For example, when testing a production application, you'll want to set up a test suite with test users and verify that the application works fully on a test network before moving to the production network for additional testing.

Installing the MTS component

The procedure for installing the MTS component is found in Chapter 2. We'll call this application Simple MTS Example. The component will install within Simple MTS Example as SimpleMTS.Transact. Make sure that you can see two Interfaces and associated methods as shown in Figure 11-19.

Chapter 2 also provides a procedure for adding role-based security to your application. You must add security or the SecurityCallContext part of the application won't work property. The example provides two roles: Administrators and Users as shown in Figure 11-19. Make sure that you assign security to the component, interface, or method levels so that you can access the component by using the test application.

There's one special configuration item in this example. Right click the SimpleMTS. Transact component entry and choose Properties from the context menu. Click the Activation tab. You'll see a dialog similar to the one shown in Figure 11-10. Make sure that you check the Enable object construction option and enter a value in the Constructor string field. The example uses a value of "Hello World" but any value will do because we're displaying it as a simple string in the example application.

After you get the application configured, you'll need to export a proxy and install it on the client machine. We talked about this procedure in Chapter 2.

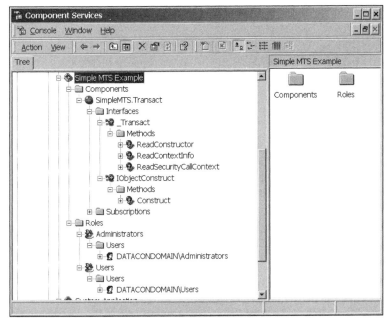

Figure 11-19: The Simple MTS Example

Testing the MTS component

When you run the SimpleMTSTest you'll see a simple dialog box with four buttons. Click IObjectConstruct and you'll see a message box that says Hello World. Open the Activation tab of the SimpleMTS.Transact Properties dialog box and remove the string that you typed in the Constructor string field. Click OK. Press the IObject Construct button again and you'll see a dialog box that says No Constructor String. As you can see, the example is able to detect when the Enable object construction option is checked, but no Constructor string field value supplied. Finally, open the Activation tab of the SimpleMTS.Transact Properties dialog box again and uncheck the Enable object construction option. Click the IObjectConstruct button on the sample application again. This time you'll see a dialog box that says No Constructor Support, which indicates that there's no IObjectConstruct support available.

Let's try the ContextInfo button now. If you click this button you'll see a dialog box that contains GUIDs similar to the one shown in Figure 11-20. These three GUIDs represent the three elements required for a transaction: the activity, the context, and the transaction itself. Open the Transactions tab of the SimpleMTS.Transact Properties dialog box. Select the Disabled option and click OK. Click the ContextInfo button of the example application again and you'll see that there aren't any GUIDs provided. In this case, there isn't any transaction, so there are no GUIDs available.

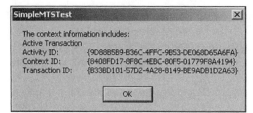

Figure 11-20: A message box showing the three GUIDs associated with a transaction.

It's time to try the final button, SecurityCallContext. Click the button and you'll see the SecurityCallContext Display dialog shown in Figure 11-21. This dialog displays the various security values that are available when using the SecurityCallContext display. Obviously, these values will change by person, so your values won't match mine, even if you install the application right from the CD-ROM provided with this book.

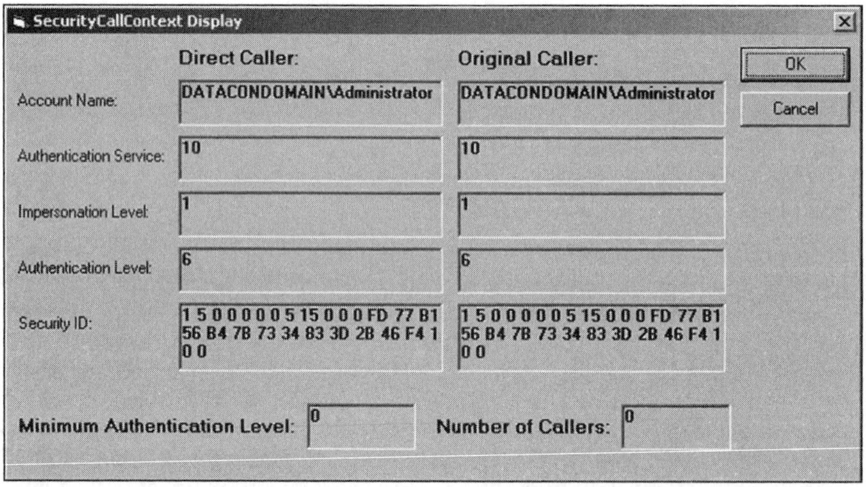

Figure 11-21: A display showing the security information available when you use the SecurityCallContext object.

Creating a Publish/Subscribe Event Model Application

The publish/subscribe event model is one of the more interesting features of COM+ because it allows a server to send event messages to a client without knowing much about the client or even knowing if the client exists at the time that the message is sent. Likewise, the client knows nothing about the server except that it wants the event message that the server can provide. Between these two elements is an event class that handles the details of getting event messages from the server to the client. We talked about the theory behind the publish/subscribe event model in Chapter 6, so I won't discuss the details again here. You do, however, want to be familiar with this information before you begin the example in this section.

The example in this section will show how you can combine COM+ technologies to create interesting applications. A client application will subscribe to events published by a component. Every time that the application receives an event message, it will display a simple message based on the event message contents.

You could combine this example with database management in a real-world situation for several application types. For example, the client application may store production line data locally. The server could be set up to poll the production line every so often for new data. It would send out an event that the production line application would respond to with statistics. There isn't any direct communication required for this type of application. Using this technique would allow a company to add as many production lines as needed to meet current demand, collect data from all of them, and still not require any form of code change. In fact, the only change required to make this work is adding a new subscriber for each production line on the system.

A primary reason to use a transaction with this type of application is to ensure that there are no interruptions in collecting the data. You want to be sure that the data arrives intact. Otherwise, errant data could change production line statistics and create problems for administrators planning upgraded systems or deciding whether another line is needed to meet current demand. In short, because the data collected from the individual production lines will affect the operation of the company as a whole, getting accurate data is essential. The transaction ensures that the data collected from an individual production line is either collected as a whole or not at all.

The sections that follow will show you how to construct all of the elements required for a publish/subscribe event model application. We'll begin by creating a publisher application that you can use to generate events for this application. Next, we'll create an event component. The main purpose of this component is to generate events based on input from a publish application—you could just as easily generate these events by using another component or a timing mechanism. These events will be sent to the client through the event object. After the client receives the event, it will generate a message that tells you what the publisher broadcast contains.

This section will also show you how to create a component, rather than a desktop application client. In some cases, you'll want to create a component client because any data handling can occur in the background without user intervention. You'll learn about transient and permanent subscriptions as part of the component client discussion. We'll also look at configured versus programmed subscriptions.

This chapter discusses other elements of the publish/subscribe model as well. We'll look at shortcuts that you can use to reduce both publisher and client development time. Because the event object is so simple, there really isn't anything that you can do to make development faster in this area. We'll also discuss a very important topic when it comes to any type of COM+ component: the COM+ Catalog. Finally, this section will help you to understand some of the problems of working with transient subscriptions.

Creating the event object

The very first piece of code that you should create when creating a publish/subscribe model application is the event object. You need to use this object when creating both the publisher and the client. Remember that the event object is the middleman—the go-between for the publisher and the subscriber. Although the publisher doesn't need to know about the subscriber, nor the subscriber about the publisher, they both need to know about the event object.

Creating the event object is more a matter of configuration than coding. You'll begin by creating an ActiveX DLL project. Make sure that you give your project and the default class a name. The example uses a project name of SimpleEvent and a class name of SendMsg.

It's absolutely essential that you set certain properties for this project or strange things will happen when you attempt to work with the event object. You'll get error messages that have nothing to do with your application and the usual Windows glitches. I even had Windows restart the machine once while writing this example because of a setting change that I failed to make.

The two most important settings changes appear on the General tab of the SimpleEvent – Project Properties dialog box. Make certain that you check Unattended Execution and set the Threading Model field to Single Threaded. Under no circumstance should you check the Retained In Memory option for this type of object because it interferes with the normal performance enhancing features of COM+. Checking the Retained In Memory option caused my test setup to slow to a crawl (your experience with this setting could definitely vary from mine. Make sure that you select Compile to Native Code on the Compile tab. Finally, make sure that you select the Binary Compatibility option on the Component tab (you'll have to compile the event object to a file for the first time before you can select this option).

At this point, we're ready to write code, which is almost too easy in this example. Because we're only supporting one event for this application, you only have to write one Sub to support it. Here's the code that you'll need to add.

```
Public Sub FireBroadcastMsg(ByVal strMsg As String)

End Sub
```

If you're thinking that there's an error in the book, you're wrong. All you need to provide for an event object is the prototype of each event that you plan to support. COM+ will take care of the implementation of each event, so coding is extremely simple. Make sure that you compile the event object component to a file before you leave this section because you'll need to reference it in other areas of this example.

Creating the publisher

We'll begin this example by creating a simple publisher application. This application could represent anything that generates events. You could use anything from automated monitoring sensors to manually entered data to create the event. The source of the event doesn't matter nearly as much as the linkage between the publisher and the subscriber.

Begin by creating a standard Visual Basic EXE project. Figure 11-22 shows the form that we'll use for this application. Table 11-7 shows the changes that you'll need to make to the various form objects.

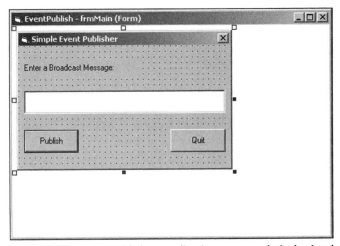

Figure 11-22: The publisher application uses a relatively simple form to generate events.

	Table 11-7	
Simple Event Test Application Component Settings		
Object	**Property**	**Value**
Project	Name	EventPublish
frmMain	Name	frmMain
	BorderStyle	3 – Fixed Dialog
	Caption	Simple Event Publisher
	Height	3000
	MinButton	True
	ShowInTaskbar	True
cmdQuit	Name	cmdQuit
	Cancel	True
	Caption	Quit
	TabIndex	2
	ToolTipText	Exit the Application
cmdPublish	Name	cmdPublish
	Caption	Publish
	Default	True
	TabIndex	1
	ToolTipText	Send an Event Message
txtMessage	Name	txtMessage
	TabIndex	0
	Text	(Blank)
	ToolTipText	Enter a Message to Send as an Event
	Width	4455

Besides the changes shown in Table 11-5, you'll need to add a reference to the component that we created in the previous section. You'll also want to make any required changes to the project's properties.

Now that we have an event publishing application designed, let's add some code to it. All this example needs is a small amount of code to fire an event that sends a message out to a list of subscribers. Listing 11-8 shows the code that you'll need to add to this example to make it functional.

Listing 11-8: **Event Publisher Source Code**

```
Private Sub cmdPublish_Click()
    'Create a message object
    Dim oMessage As SendMsg

    'If an error occurs, display a nice message.
    On Error GoTo PublishingError

    'Create the message object.
    Set oMessage = CreateObject("new:SimpleEvent.SendMsg")

    'Fire the event
    oMessage.FireBroadcastMsg (txtMessage.Text)

    'Perform some cleanup
    Set oMessage = Nothing
    Exit Sub

'There isn't much we can do for error handling except
'display a nicely formatted message
PublishingError:
    MsgBox Hex$(Err.Number) + ": " + Err.Description + _
        vbCrLf + Err.Source, vbCritical + vbOKOnly, _
        "Publishing Error"
End Sub

Private Sub cmdQuit_Click()
    'End the application.
    End
End Sub
```

As you can see, the code is very straightforward. All you need to do is instantiate the oMessage object, which offers access to the event object component that we created earlier. After you have an event object, all you need to do is fire the event. As you can see, the publisher knows nothing at all about the subscribers that it'll serve because of the way that this application is designed.

Complete error trapping is important for this type of application. There are a number of errors that can occur — everything from lost component references to components that didn't get installed properly. The very nature of this application makes it hard to troubleshoot, so error trapping really isn't an option. Displaying the error number, description, and source should be considered the minimum level of error trapping and you'll normally want to check for common errors like missing components.

Shortcuts for publisher development

The publish/subscribe event model provides an entirely new way of looking at application development because this technology allows for maximum expandability and flexibility. You can add as many publishers and subscribers as you want to an application. All without changing anything that you've already written and debugged. This makes it possible to create a publish/subscribe event model application in an ad hoc fashion as your company grows.

The following sections will provide you with some tips on making the whole process of creating a publisher faster, simpler, more efficient, and less error prone. It's important to understand, though, that this technology is in its infancy as I write this, so there are bound to be a lot more new ways to shortcut the development process as you read this. Consider these tips as a starting point for learning more about this exciting new technology.

Think small

Event publishers tend to be very small applications that are designed to make the dissemination or gathering of data simple. Processing the data normally occurs at the subscriber's end of the application. There are several good reasons to keep the publisher simple. The most important reason is speed. An event publisher is often asked to run in real time, which means that any extra processing will be a hindrance to getting the publisher running efficiently.

Publishers also need to provide accurate raw data. You can't guess as to how your company will use data when you first create an application. Performing even a little too much processing may make the data obtained by a publisher of no use for other applications that your company needs later, after the initial application has been online for a while.

The publisher is also more likely to run on a machine with limited resources. For example, events generated by an inventory control system will very likely begin their journey on an embedded system or as output from a small handheld device. These machines aren't known for the vast number of resources that they provide; you may find yourself fighting for every byte of memory with the operating system and other applications.

Use event layering

Most publish/subscribe event model applications assume little processing on the part of the publisher and lots of processing on the part of the subscriber. However, if you're sending events to a palm-sized computer, you can't assume very much about the capabilities of that machine. In fact, the subscriber machine may have fewer capabilities than the publisher machine does. So, there are some situations when you may have to design an application to use minimal resources on both the client and the server end.

There are three ways to handle this problem. The first is also the least attractive for a number of reasons (see the "Think small" section for details). You can always perform more processing on the publisher end, enabling the subscriber to receive the data in usable form. All the subscriber might need to do is perform a little filtering and perhaps change the data's format for display purposes.

A second method of handling this problem is to use a server-side component as the subscriber. The subscriber might generate output in the form of new Web pages or other lightweight content that any client machine could accept. There are several problems with this approach, however, The first is that the client may not want all of the data that the subscriber component has to offer. Unfortunately, using this technique means that you have to provide data that the majority of the users will require, rather than customizing output for each user.

A third method, which is the method that I recommend, is to use two or more levels of event layering. A publisher can send data to a server-side subscriber component through the event object. The server-side component can perform most of the required processing, and then generate events itself. These events will be in nearly final format, which means that client-side processing will be minimal. A second subscriber on the client will receive the event messages and allow for additional custom manipulation of the data with a minimal use of resources. The advantage of this method is maximum flexibility and the ability to use the application even on thin clients. The disadvantage is application complexity. You now have to create multiple components with the requisite configuration and linkage problems. In short, there are no perfect solutions, but this third solution does have a lot more to offer than other solutions that you may have tried.

Enhance efficiency with subscriber monitoring

It's possible to monitor the subscribers assigned to a particular publisher. All you need to do is monitor the COM+ Catalog for specific data strings (see the "Understanding the COM+ Catalog" section of this chapter for details). If the publisher doesn't have any transient or permanent subscribers, a server-side component could tell the publisher to turn itself off until a subscriber is available. The publisher machine can use the freed resources and processing cycles to perform other work.

This is one programming solution that you'll want to use with care because you're trading a loss of efficiency on the server for a gain of efficiency on the publisher machine. Running a component that monitors the subscribers for a particular publisher will cost the server some processing cycles and resources. However, this is the method to use if the publisher machine is already overwhelmed with other tasks.

Creating the subscriber object

Most developers will think about the publish/subscribe model as a means of getting data from the server to a client. A proliferation of stock-ticker applications in just about every magazine makes this view one that a lot of developers will have difficulty shaking. Yet the publish/subscribe event model, like any event model, can be used for other purposes. Nothing says that you have to start at the server and end at the client—you could start at the client and end at the server, or even use this programming methodology to allow communication between two clients or two servers. In short, don't limit your vision to sample applications that you may see in other places.

If you're going to work with publish/subscribe events on a server, the easiest way to do it is with a subscriber object. The object sits in the background and waits for events to occur. When the events do occur, it receives the data and processes it in the background without any interaction from users or the network administrator.

Like any other publish/subscribe application, the subscriber has to subscribe and enable the event object before it receives any data from the publisher. There are three ways to subscribe with a server-side component:

✦ **Self-Register:** A subscriber object can include an initialization routine that allows it to subscribe to an event object. However, there are severe limitations when using this technique and you should avoid it whenever possible. The main limitation is all of the hard coding that you'll need to do. Moving or changing the event object will necessitate coding changes in the subscriber object as well, which is something to avoid whenever possible.

✦ **Manual Register:** This is the most time-consuming method of creating a subscription, but also the most flexible in some ways, and it requires no coding at all. You'll want to rely on this method for a smaller network where maximum flexibility is essential. We'll talk more about this method in the "Creating a Subscription Manually" section of this chapter.

✦ **Installation Program Register:** The COM+ Catalog is, essentially, a large hierarchical database. There are several methods for traversing this database, as we discussed in Chapter 6. Creating an installation program is one of the better ways of configuring subscriptions on a large system. We'll talk about this technique in the Working with Permanent Subscriptions section of the chapter.

Creating a subscriber object isn't any more difficult than creating a subscriber client application for the desktop. In some respects, it may actually be easier because you don't have to add any code for the user interface. Of course, both subscriber types have their uses.

To create a subscriber, you start with an ActiveX DLL application. Unlike a subscriber client, you don't have to add a reference to the event object or implement it within the code. We'll see why there's this difference later after we create a client and begin to configure the application. You do, however, have to implement all of the method calls that the event object contains, even if you include only Subs without any code in them. The example has a project name of EventSubscribe and contains a single class called SendMsg.

If this will be a standalone component — one that operates in the background processing events and not being accessed by a client — you can use the default Visual Basic settings. It's usually a good idea to check the Unattended Execution option on the General Tab of the EventSubscribe–Project Properties dialog box. If clients will access this component, then you'll also want to change the Threading Model to Single Threaded and the Version Compatibility option on the Component tab to Binary Compatibility.

After the component is configured, you can add some code. We'll use a simple message box, in this case, just to show the component in action. Normally, you'd want to perform some type of background task that requires no user interaction. For example, you might want to update a database that contains performance statistics for the various servers in your organization. Here's the code we'll use for this component.

```
Public Sub FireBroadcastMsg(ByVal strMsg As String)
    MsgBox strMsg
End Sub
```

Creating the client

The client application for this example will be a lot more complex than the other elements you've seen so far. The client will need to react to events that the publisher generates. For the sake of simplicity, we'll generate a simple dialog box again with the understanding that you could do a lot more. Client applications normally provide a user interface and the means to interact with the user to filter and otherwise manage the data.

The application will also have two different subscribe buttons. The first will create a subscription for the subscriber object we discussed in the previous section. You can also create this subscription manually (which we'll do in the "Creating a subscription manually" section of the chapter). This first subscription is a permanent subscription because it survives a reboot of the server. It also shows up in Component Services, so you can manage it as you would any other subscription. Component subscriptions usually use permanent subscriptions because you want them to be capable of returning to work immediately after a server reboot. In addition, because the component is local to the server, there isn't any need to worry about a sudden disconnection.

The second subscribe button will create a transient subscription for the client. A client application will normally use a transient subscription because it isn't connected to the server 24 hours a day. In addition, if the server is down for any reason, you don't want to load it up with client requests immediately after a reboot. Finally, clients do disconnect without removing their subscriptions. Transient subscriptions are easier to remove and therefore a lot less work for the network administrator.

To begin this example, you'll need to create a standard Visual Basic EXE application. Figure 11-23 shows what the form for this application should look like. Table 11-8 shows you how to configure the various application elements.

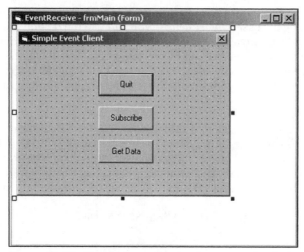

Figure 11-23: The client application has two subscription buttons that are used to subscribe to the event object.

	Table 11-8 Simple Event Test Client Application Settings	
Object	**Property**	**Value**
Project	Name	EventReceive
frmMain	Name	frmMain
	BorderStyle	3 – Fixed Dialog
	Caption	Simple Event Client
	ShowInTaskbar	True
cmdQuit	Name	cmdQuit
	Cancel	True
	Caption	Quit
	Default	True
	TabIndex	2
	ToolTipText	Exit the Application
cmdSubscribe	Name	cmdSubscribe
	Caption	Subscribe
	TabIndex	0
	ToolTipText	Create a Permanent Subscription

Object	Property	Value
cmdGetData	Name	cmdGetData
	Caption	Get Data
	TabIndex	1
	ToolTipText	Create a Transient Subscription

Now that we've gotten application configuration out of the way, let's look at what you'll need to do to code the application. We'll begin with a very short discussion of some of the COM+ Catalog mechanics. Chapter 6 provides an in-depth theoretical discussion of this topic. After a brief overview of the COM+ Catalog, we'll look at the code required to create both transient and permanent subscriptions.

Understanding the COM+ Catalog

As previously mentioned, the COM+ Catalog is really a special-purpose database that Windows 2000 uses to store information about the various COM+ applications that you create. Each element of that database can be changed by using standard interfaces and search techniques, as we'll see when working with both the transient and permanent subscription code in this chapter.

It often helps to look at Component Services when you need to envision what you'll do next with the COM+ Catalog. For example, if you need to find out information about a specific component, you'll need to find the associated application first, then the component. You'll always use an ICatalogCollection object to access a node within the COM+ Catalog like a component or an interface. After you find the object that you want to work with, you'll use an ICatalogObject object to access individual properties. These two interfaces and a few methods within them are all you'll need to find any piece of information within the COM+ Catalog.

Every property can be accessed within the COM+ Catalog by using the `Value()` method ICatalogObject interface. You'll access the properties by providing an index value in the form of a keyword. Unfortunately, Visual Basic won't list these keywords for you, so it takes some research at times to find precisely what you need. The examples in the transient and permanent subscription code sections will provide you with enough keywords for many uses.

Tip

Those of you lucky enough to have an MSDN subscription will find at least some of the keywords that you need there. Searching for topics like IEventSubscription Properties and TransientSubscriptions Collection will often yield information that you need when a direct look at ICatalogCollection or ICatalogObject doesn't help. Much of the MSDN subscription material is also available online and is often updated from what you get in the subscription. While some of this information is available publicly, most of it requires you to log in by using your MSDN member information. You can find out more about MSDN at `http://msdn.microsoft.com`.

There's also the idea of a collection within the COM+ Catalog. When you create an object, you have the equivalent of an empty vessel. Before you can do anything with the object, you need to fill it up. COM+ uses a special method for this purpose called Populate(). As soon as you've identified a unique resource within the COM+ catalog, you can use the Populate() method to retrieve the entire collection of those types of objects.

The Populate() method creates a local copy of the object information that you need to work with the COM+ Catalog. Any changes that you make are on the local copy and the changes won't affect what anyone is seeing until you save them. In addition, the changes are all validated. Any changes that don't fit within the validation specifications are denied. You'll always use the SaveChanges() method of the ICatalogCollection interface to make any changes permanent. Make sure that you save changes before you move to another area of the COM+ Catalog or, in many cases, they'll be lost.

Working with transient subscriptions

Transient applications allow you to make a quick subscription to an event object without spending a lot of time traversing the COM+ Catalog. In addition, transient subscriptions won't survive a reboot, which means that applications that fail in the middle of a session won't leave permanent bits of themselves behind. The client application for this example uses a transient subscription to receive broadcast messages from the publisher. Listing 11-9 show the code that you'll need for this example. This listing also shows a few global variables that we need to make the example work and the cmdQuit_Click() method that allows the application to exit.

Listing 11-9: **Creating a Transient Subscription**

```
'You must implement the event object class in
'a client application.
Implements SimpleEvent.SendMsg
Option Explicit

'Two variables used to store global event information. The
'gTransID variable holds the identifier for the subscripton,
'while oAdmin holds the current administration object.
Dim gTransID
Dim oAdmin As Object

Private Sub cmdGetData_Click()
    'Two variables that hold the COM+ Catalog information
    'for the current subscription.
    Dim oSubColl As ICatalogCollection
    Dim oCatObj As ICatalogObject
```

```
Dim iCount As Integer

'Get the current administration object, then find the
'transient subscription collection.
Set oAdmin = CreateObject("COMAdmin.COMAdminCatalog.1")
Set oSubColl = oAdmin.GetCollection _
    ("TransientSubscriptions")

'Depending on the current button setting, we'll either get
'a new subscription or free an existing one.
If cmdGetData.Caption = "Get Data" Then
    'Add a new subscription to the transient subscription
    'collection. You need to provide the EventCLSID,
    'subscription name, and the suscriber interface as a
    'minimum. You also to enable the transaction if
    'necessary.
    Set oCatObj = oSubColl.Add
    oCatObj.Value("EventCLSID") = _
        "{291CE3B1-E329-475B-AD4E-2B57E971FFA5}"
    oCatObj.Value("Name") = "Transient Subscription"
    oCatObj.Value("SubscriberInterface") = Me
    oCatObj.Value("Enabled") = True

    'Save the changes we've made to the transient
    'subscription collection.
    oSubColl.SaveChanges

    'Make the button an unsubscribe button.
    cmdGetData.Caption = "Don't Get Data"

    'Store the subscription ID for later.
    gTransID = oCatObj.Value("ID")
Else

    'Obtain a list of all the current subscriptions.
    oSubColl.Populate

    'Look for the subscription we created earlier.
    For iCount = 0 To oSubColl.Count - 1

        'When we find the subscription, remove it, then
        'update the transient subscription collection.
        If oSubColl.Item(iCount).Value("ID") = gTransID _
            Then
            oSubColl.Remove (iCount)
            oSubColl.SaveChanges
```

Continued

Listing 11-9 *(continued)*

```
                GoTo EndSubscription:
            End If
        Next

EndSubscription:
            'Change the button caption to allow subscriptions.
            cmdGetData.Caption = "Get Data"
        End If

    End Sub

    Private Sub cmdQuit_Click()
        'Exit the application
        End
    End Sub
```

The application begins by instantiating the oAdmin object and using it to find the "TransientSubscriptions" collection in the COM+ catalog. You don't need to know anything more about this collection other than that it's the area of the COM+ Catalog that is used to store transient subscriptions. At this point, oSubColl has the location used to store the transient subscription.

The next task that the code performs is to detect whether the application is making a subscription or releasing one. If the application is releasing a subscription, then the code will use the Add() method of oSubColl to add a new subscription to the COM+ Catalog. After the subscription is added, the code fills out various values for the entry including the event CLSID, the name of the subscription, and the subscriber interface (the application responsible for handling events). Make sure that you also enable the subscription as part of the configuration process. Once the changes are made, the code saves them and changes the caption of the pushbutton to Don't Get Data. You'll also need to save the subscription ID for later in order to remove it from the COM+ Catalog.

The event CLSID may give you a few problems because it's not really available in the application code. There are two very convenient places to find this information. First, you can use the OLE/COM Object Viewer to find the event object. Second, you can create the event application on the server, register the event object, and then get the event CLSID from the event class Properties dialog box. Figure 11-24 shows the event CLSID for our example. You can copy the event CLSID directly from this property page by pressing Ctrl+C.

Figure 11-24: The event CLSID is available from at least two easy-to-access locations.

Removing the subscription from the COM+ catalog requires a little more work because you have the find the subscription's location first. The first thing that the code does is to populate oSubColl with the contents of the Transient collection of the COM+ catalog. After that, a simple For. . .Next loop allows us to compare the ID of each subscription to the one located in gTransID. After the subscription is found, the Remove() method will request it's removal. To make this change permanent, you must use the SaveChanges() method. The last step in removing the subscription is to change the pushbutton's caption.

Working with permanent subscriptions

Permanent subscriptions are located in another part of the COM+ catalog and require a lot more work because you have to locate the right application first. The advantage of a permanent subscription is that it survives reboots and tends to be more efficient for long-term applications like server-based components to use. Listing 11-10 shows the code that you'll need to implement a permanent subscription.

Listing 11-10: **Creating a Permanent Subscription**

```
Private Sub cmdSubscribe_Click()
    'There are three catalog collection levels manipulated
    'in this Sub. The first is at the COM+ application level,
```

Continued

Listing 11-10 *(continued)*

```
'the second is at the component level, and the third is
'at the subscription level.
Dim oAppColl, oCompColl, oSubColl As ICatalogCollection
Dim oCatObj As ICatalogObject

Dim iCount As Integer

'Obtain the curent application collection and then populate
'the oAppColl variable with the members of that collection.
Set oAdmin = CreateObject("COMAdmin.COMAdminCatalog.1")
Set oAppColl = oAdmin.GetCollection("Applications")
oAppColl.Populate

'Locate the application we're interested in subscribing to.
For iCount = 0 To oAppColl.Count - 1

    'When we find the application, obtain the current
    'component collection for that application. Populate
    'oCompColl with the contents of the component
    'collection.
    If oAppColl.Item(iCount).Name = _
        "Simple Event Subscribe" Then
        Set oCompColl = oAppColl.GetCollection _
            ("Components", oAppColl.Item(iCount).Key)
        oCompColl.Populate
        GoTo GetComponent:
    End If
Next

'Locate the event object component. We need to subscribe to
'that particular component in order to receive events.
GetComponent:
For iCount = 0 To oCompColl.Count - 1

    'When we find the event object, obtain the current list
    'of interfaces that it supports. We need the SendMsg
    'interface for this example. Once you find the correct
    'interface, you can create a subscription for it.
    If oCompColl.Item(iCount).Name = _
        "EventSubscribe.SendMsg" Then
        Set oSubColl = oCompColl.GetCollection _
            ("SubscriptionsForComponent", _
            oCompColl.Item(iCount).Key)
        oSubColl.Populate
        GoTo MakeSubscription:
    End If
Next

'Depending on the current button setting, we'll either get
'a new subscription or free an existing one.
```

```
MakeSubscription:
    If cmdSubscribe.Caption = "Subscribe" Then

        'Add a new subscription to the application subscription
        'collection. You need to provide the EventCLSID,
        'and subscription name. You don't need the suscriber
        'interface in this case because it's supplied by the
        'application collection for you. You also to enable
        'the transaction if necessary.
        Set oCatObj = oSubColl.Add
        oCatObj.Value("EventCLSID") = _
            "{291CE3B1-E329-475B-AD4E-2B57E971FFA5}"
        oCatObj.Value("Name") = "Permanent Subscription"
        oCatObj.Value("Enabled") = True

        'Save the changes we've made to the application
        'subscription collection.
        oSubColl.SaveChanges

        'Make the button an unsubscribe button.
        cmdSubscribe.Caption = "Unsubscribe"

        'Store the subscription ID for later.
        gTransID = oCatObj.Value("ID")

        'When working with an application subscription, you
        'should start the application to reduce request delays.
        oAdmin.StartApplication ("Simple Event Subscribe")
    Else
        'Obtain a list of all the current subscriptions.
        oSubColl.Populate

        'Look for the subscription we created earlier.
        For iCount = 0 To oSubColl.Count - 1

            'When we find the subscription, remove it, then
            'update the application subscription collection.
            If oSubColl.Item(iCount).Value("ID") = _
                gTransID Then
                oSubColl.Remove (iCount)
                oSubColl.SaveChanges
                GoTo EndSubscription:
            End If
        Next

EndSubscription:
        'Change the button caption to allow subscriptions.
        cmdSubscribe.Caption = "Subscribe"
    End If

End Sub
```

Like the transient subscription, this method begins by instantiating the oAdmin object and using it to find the starting point in the COM+ Catalog. Unlike the transient subscription, a permanent subscription appears in the applications collection instead of the transient subscriptions collection. After we have the applications collection starting point, it's time to populate oAppColl with a list of all of the current COM+ applications.

As you can see, the code uses a series of For. . .Next loops to traverse the COM+ Catalog. The next step is to find the application that we want and place a collection of the components that it supports in oCompColl. After that, we find a particular component and locate the interface that we need. Finally, knowing the interface that we want to subscribe to, the code makes a decision about whether the user wants to subscribe or unsubscribe.

The subscription and unsubscription process is the same as for the transient subscription. The only difference is that we don't need to provide a subscriber interface. That value is already known because it's supplied by the component that we're registering through the subscription process. It's important to start the application right away by using the `oAdmin.StartApplication()` method to ensure that the component handles any events promptly.

Receiving events

There's one last task that any subscriber will need to handle. There has to be a method to receiving any events that the publisher creates. This method has to provide exactly the same interface as the publisher, or the event won't get handled. Listing 11-11 shows the event handler for this application. As you can see, there isn't anything spectacular about this code; all it does is display a dialog box in response to publisher events.

Listing 11-11: **Receiving Events from a Publisher**

```
Private Sub SendMsg_FireBroadcastMsg(ByVal strMsg As String)
    'Every time we receive an event, display this message box.
    MsgBox "The Get Data Message Is: " + strMsg, _
        vbInformation + vbOKOnly, _
        "Broadcast Message"
End Sub
```

Component configuration

Creating an application for the EventSubscribe.DLL is the same as for any other COM+ application. You'll find the procedure for doing so in Chapter 2. I gave this application the name of Simple Event Subscribe, but you can use any name that you want. We're not testing security or any special component features in this example, so you won't need to perform any configuration after the application is created and the component is installed.

You can also use the same process as normal to create the event object application. I named the example Simple Event Example. Installing the component, however, is different from the process that we covered in Chapter 2. The following steps will show you how to install an event component.

1. Right-click the Simple Event Object\Components folder and choose New ⇨ Component from the context menu. You'll see a Welcome to the COM Component Install Wizard dialog box.

2. Click Next. You'll see the Import or Install a Component dialog box as shown in Figure 11-25. Notice the Install new event class(es) pushbutton near the bottom of this dialog box.

3. Click Install new event class(es). You'll see a Select Files to Install dialog box.

4. Locate the event object DLL that you want to install (Simple Event Class.DLL for this example), highlight it, and then click Open. You'll see an Install new event class dialog box similar to the one shown in Figure 11-26.

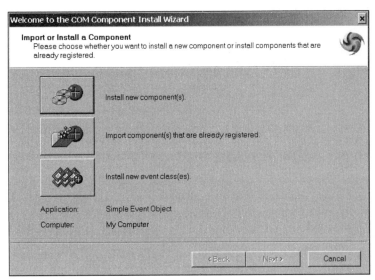

Figure 11-25: The Import or Install a Component dialog box allows you to install several component types.

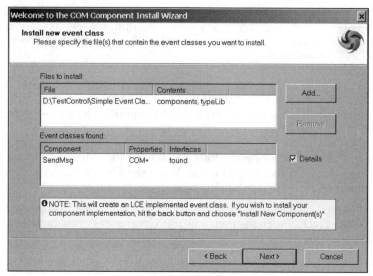

Figure 11-26: The Install new event class dialog box allows you to check the event object that you want to install.

5. Verify the DLL that you want to install, and then click Next. You'll see a success dialog box.

6. Click Finish.

The two applications that we need are ready. Export both applications as proxies, and then install them on the client application. We talked about the method for creating a proxy application in Chapter 2. Chapter 2 also tells you how to install them on a client.

Creating a subscription manually

There are two ways to check the operation of the subscriber component. The first is to create a subscription manually, which we'll do in this section, while the second is to make the subscription by using application code, which we'll do in the next section of the chapter. In both cases, publishing an event with the publisher application will cause the component to display a message. Remember that there are two recipients of events in this example, an application and a component. The following steps will help you to create a subscription manually.

1. Right-click the Simple Event Subscribe\ComponentsEventSubscribe\ SndMessage\Subscriptions folder and choose New ⇨ Subscription from the context menu. You'll see a Welcome to the COM New Subscription Wizard dialog box.

2. Click Next. You'll see a Select Subscription Method(s) dialog box similar
   to the one shown in Figure 11-27. This is where you choose the methods
   that you want to use to accept events from a publisher.

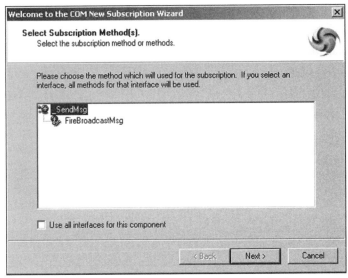

Figure 11-27: The first step is to select the methods that you want
to receive events.

3. Choose the Use all interfaces for this component option, and then click Next.
   Windows will search the COM+ Catalog for components that publish events
   that might fulfill your component's needs. After this search process is complete, you'll see a Select Event Class dialog box similar to the one shown in
   Figure 11-28. Notice that the event object that we created appears in this dialog box. If you don't see the event object, then you need to stop the procedure
   now and check the Simple Event Example application. Make sure that you see
   the right event object listed here; otherwise, the example won't work (and neither will your application in real life).

4. Select the SimpleEvent.SendMsg class, and then click Next. You'll see the
   Subscription Options dialog box as shown in Figure 11-29. This is where you'll
   provide a name for your subscription and enable it. Always enable the subscription unless you don't want to receive events right away.

5. Type a subscription name (the example uses MySubscription), select the
   Enable this subscription immediately option, and then click Next. You'll see
   a success message.

6. Click Finish.

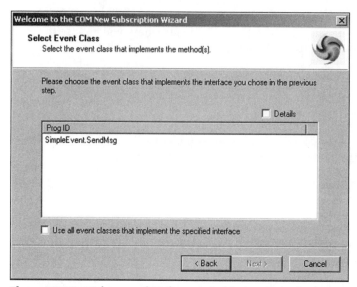

Figure 11-28: Make sure that the event object appears in the Select Event Class dialog box.

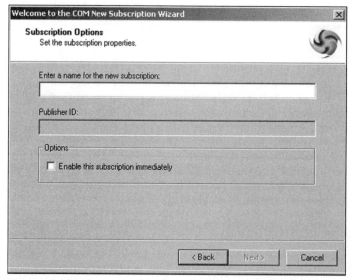

Figure 11-29: Always enable the subscription as part of the configuration process.

At this point, you're ready to test the manual subscription. Start the Event Publish application, type a message in the Enter a Broadcast Message field, and then click Publish. You'll see an EventSubscribe dialog box that contains the message that you typed. After you've tried this application several times, remove the subscription and proceed to the next section.

Testing the publish/subscribe event model application

Testing the Event Receive application is fairly easy. We'll begin by testing the component again. Click Subscribe. Wait a second or two and look in the Simple Event Subscribe\ComponentsEventSubscribe\SndMessage\Subscriptions folder. You should see a new subscription titled Permanent Subscription. (You may have to right-click the Subscriptions folder and choose Refresh from the context menu to see the new subscription if you already have the folder open.) Use the Event Publish application to publish a message, and the message will appear onscreen, just as it did in the previous section.

Click the Unsubscribe button on the Event Receive application. Look in the Subscriptions folder again and the subscription should be gone. (You may have to right-click the Subscriptions folder again to update the display.)

Creating a transient application is as easy as clicking Get Data on the Event Receive application. When you click Publish on the Event Publish application you'll see another dialog box, but this time it will be from the application, rather than the component. Look in the Subscriptions folder and you'll notice that there aren't any subscriptions because this is a transient subscription. Make sure that you click Don't Get Data before you exit the Event Receive application or you'll have an extra entry in the COM+ Catalog until the next time that your machine boots.

Quick Fixes for MTS Problems

MTS applications begin to show the complexity of COM+ applications as a whole by combining the capabilities of COM, MTS, and DCOM. Consequently, any problem that can occur when working with a desktop COM application, or with a distributed application that relies on DCOM, can happen to a DCOM application. You'll definitely want to review the problem solutions in Chapters 9 and 10. These two chapters address concerns about the client application, the component's internal functionality, and the network protocol that connects them both.

MTS applications, however, add features that neither a desktop COM application nor a DCOM application addresses. The most noticeable of these features is the capability to use transactions; essentially error handling that ensures that each transaction happens once, and only once. New problems come with this capability; you'll need to solve them as you debug and usability test that application. While the following sections don't address every potential problem, they do address common problems that you should know about.

Role-based security

There are a lot of potential problems that you can run into that are role-based security related. For example, one strength of role-based security is the enabling of security settings for each component, interface, and method. However, that strength can quickly become a problem if you grant access to one method that a user needs and but no access to another needed method. In many cases, the problem will bubble up from the server-side component level to the client application as a true security error. There are other cases, however, when no error is indicated or something other than a security error will appear (the inability to create an ActiveX control error message set is common). When this occurs, the network administrator will have few clues as to what methods to use to fix the problem. Always double-check your role-based security settings if you think that there might be a configuration problem.

Certain COM+ interfaces and objects, like SecurityCallContext, also require role-based security. You can enable standard security to protect the application, but the call will still fail because role-based security is a separate item. You must select the correct application-level security options as shown in Figure 11-30 before these interfaces have any chance at all of working. Some calls will require further configuration. You'll have to define roles and assign them at the component, interface, or method levels before the COM+ objects or interfaces become active. The odd problem that you'll face is that the methods within these interfaces and objects will succeed in many cases, but the call will come back with an empty set. What this means is that the application won't indicate an error, it will simply lack the information needed to complete the current task. In short, using certain role-based security calls within your application requires additional error trapping code.

If you're working in a mixed Windows NT/2000 environment, role-based security, while supported, is problematic. Consider the difference in security features offered by Windows 2000 and Windows NT for a moment and you'll understand why. If you've installed a Windows NT server on a Windows 2000 domain correctly, Windows 2000 will automatically provide a special user that allows access to your

COM+ applications. Figure 11-31 shows the Pre-Windows 2000 Compatible Access group. This is the group that will allow Windows 2000 and Windows NT to work together when dealing with COM+ applications. If users will be accessing COM+ applications through a Windows NT server connected to a Windows 2000 domain, you must add this group to one of the roles for your component and configure it correctly to ensure adequate access to the application. The error messages that you'll see for this particular problem usually have nothing to do with security and occasionally have nothing to do with object creation (depending on how you perform error trapping in the application). Again, this is a setting that you must verify when seeing odd problems with your COM+ application.

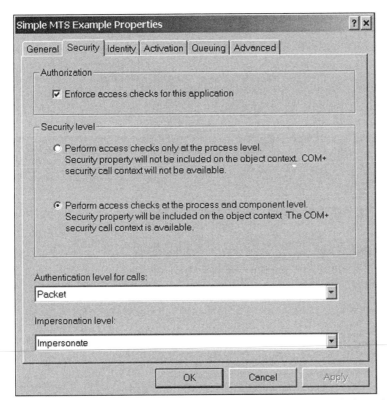

Figure 11-30: Make sure that you set the application to use role-based security if you plan to use role-based security interfaces and objects.

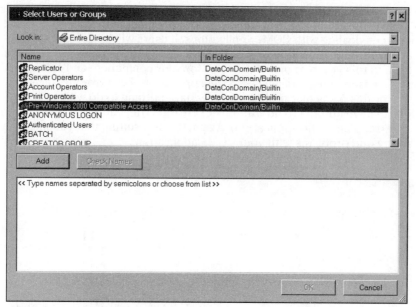

Figure 11-31: Windows 2000 provides a special group for pre-Windows 2000-compatible access.

A workaround for the SetAbort bug

There's at least one MTS-specific problem that affects only Visual Basic components under COM+. If a secondary object (one called by a server-side component, rather than the desktop application client) calls `SetAbort()` and raises an error that should propagate back to the root object, the custom error message that should accompany the error can get overwritten with a generic message. What the end user will see is a message that says, "Method '~' of object '~' failed" as shown in Figure 11-32. Because the tilde (~) symbol means nothing to most people, the user won't know what error occurred or where. In short, this particular bug can make it nearly impossible for you to troubleshoot an errant application.

Figure 11-32: This unfriendly error message tells the user nothing about the error that occurred.

The easiest way to fix this problem is to avoid using `SetAbort()` or `SetDeactivateOnReturn(True)` when working with a secondary object that raises an error (which means that you're going to have to do additional work to detect this condition). If you need to roll a transaction back, the best way is to call `SetMyTransactionVote(txAbort)` instead of using `SetAbort()`. You could also use `DisableCommit()` if you didn't want to include any new features within your component.

This bug exists in the lightweight proxy that COM+ builds for your Visual Basic component. That's why the bug doesn't show up for components built by using Visual C++ (although there are other bugs with that programming language). Fortunately, this bug only appears when working with COM+; the same component will work fine with MTS under Windows NT.

Of course, this bug raises several issues. For one thing, there's already a lot of code out there that calls `SetAbort()` when an error is detected. In most cases, this bug will force you to rewrite that code to ensure that it will work consistently under Windows 2000. If you're working on a team project, you'll also need to work with other developers on your team to break the habit of using `SetAbort()` automatically.

The second issue is that you now need to write components to either fill the root object or the secondary object. A root object should always call `SetComplete()` or `SetAbort()` in response to all of the events that occurred with secondary objects that it called. In short, you're now saddled with extra coding responsibilities that shouldn't be necessary.

A third issue is that you're also forced to choose between Windows NT and Windows 2000 development because of this bug. The best fix for the problem is to use `SetMyTransactionVote(txAbort)` when you need to abort a transaction. Unfortunately, this is one of the new methods introduced by COM+; it doesn't work with MTS under Windows NT. So, you may find yourself writing a version of a component for Windows NT use and another version for Windows 2000 use.

Microsoft is aware of the problems of using `SetAbort()` with Visual Basic components. They've provided two Knowledge Base articles to address developer concerns. You'll find the first at `http://support.microsoft.com/support/kb/articles/Q255/7/35.ASP`. The second Knowledge Base article appears at `http://support.microsoft.com/support/kb/articles/Q255/7/33.ASP`. Neither article tells when Microsoft will provide a permanent fix for this problem, but at least they provide detailed error information and potential methods for circumventing the error.

MTS component inaccessible on Windows NT

There's an odd problem that developers will see on Windows NT, but not on Windows 2000 and it has to do with the Registry changes that we talked about in the "Registry Entry Differences" section of the chapter. When you compile a component by using

Visual Basic, the IDE automatically registers the component for you. The only problem with doing this under Windows NT is that the Registry entries for a standard component are different from those for an MTS component or MTS package. Consequently, whenever you compile a component on Windows NT, the Registry entries for the MTS package are trashed and the component appears to malfunction.

Unfortunately, there isn't any way to turn off this behavior. The Visual Basic IDE will insist on registering the component for you every time that you need to make a coding change. Of course, one solution for this problem is to develop the component on your Windows 2000 machine and simply move it to the Windows NT machine as needed. This will allow you to check updates without trashing those all-important Registry entries.

MTS Explorer also provides a command that can fix the problem for you. Highlight the machine that you want to work with. Right-click the machine and you'll see a context menu similar to the one shown in Figure 11-33. Choose the Refresh All Components command and MTS Explorer will ensure that all of the Registry entries for your components are correct. You'll want to perform this task during off-peak hours because it appears to take some amount of time and the server won't be available during the refresh process.

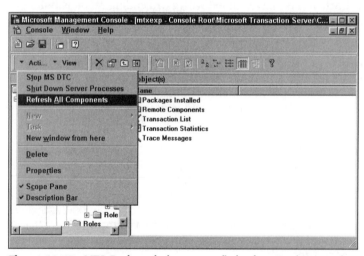

Figure 11-33: MTS Explorer helps you to fix broken Registry entries.

Quick Fixes for Event Problems

Events are one way to make applications more responsive and reduce application resource usage at the same time. Using an event allows you to place client applications on hold until a specific set of conditions is in place. The ability to fire an event within your component means that you can tell a client to wake up and do something. A common example of this behavior is a stock ticker that wakes up just long enough to show a new stock value, and then goes back to sleep until needed again.

Prior to COM+, all applications relied on the request/reply event model. The component and client were tightly coupled to each other through a callback system. These two elements have to know a lot about each other in order to make the event system work. A change in either element usually means making code changes to both. Although this system works well in a LAN environment with permanent connections, the system is not suitable for the COM+ distributed application environment in which the client and server may not even be available at the same time.

The publish/subscribe event model is the one that you'll use with COM+. It offers many advantages that developers could only dream about in the past, including the capability to fire events without worrying about any form of tight coupling. When using the publish/subscribe model the client and server need to know next to nothing about each other because an intermediary works with both.

Unfortunately, even in this updated application development environment, there are still times when the client and server will fail to communicate. In addition, the new stresses of this environment also incur new problems that you may not have dealt with in the past. The following sections discuss some of the more common problems that you'll run into while working with the COM+ publish/subscribe model. Some, but not all, of these problems are also common to the request/reply event model, but may take on a different appearance in that environment. In short, you should probably consider the following problem fixes specific to the publish/subscribe event model environment.

Finding subscription configuration errors

Subscriptions can fail for a number of reasons. A publish/subscribe model application relies heavily on getting all of the linkages between application elements right. In addition, configuration is a necessity, not an option. Failing to enable a subscription or start an application may mean that you get some very strange errors that will cost you hours in troubleshooting time. However, after you do get everything configured correctly, you'll find that publish/subscribe model applications are amazingly robust and bulletproof, so the initial effort is well worth the results.

A common error that developers make is to install the event object as a standard component. Make absolutely certain that you install the event object as an event component within Component Services or you'll never see the component as being available for use.

Another common problem is to reference the wrong component within a client application. This may seem like a very strange mistake to make, but given the number of components that could be floating around with precisely the same interface, the problem occurs more often than many developers will admit. If everything else looks like it's configured correctly, then check the object references in your application. Interestingly, because the other component could provide the same interface as the event object does, neither Visual Basic nor Windows will raise an error for this situation, making it difficult to find.

There are any number of ways to shoot yourself in the foot with configuration errors, but the most common way is to forget to enable the subscription. This is especially important to check when you create a subscription by using code rather than by relying on manual configuration methods. When you look at a dialog box you can see whether an option is checked; the same isn't true of your code. Make sure that the subscription is enabled before you try to use it. This is another kind of error that won't show up with an error message. Windows will continue to ignore your application as long as the subscription is disabled.

Publish/subscribe model applications are almost always used in a distributed environment, which means that you need to worry about machine references. The easiest way to get around machine reference problems is to use exported COM+ application proxies rather than to include hard coded references in your code or rely on Registry entries. An MSI file can be added to the user's login routine, making it quite easy to distributed changes to the network configuration by making a change to the original COM+ application and distributing proxies as required.

Understanding subscription failures

Checking every potential source of configuration error in your application isn't always sufficient to locate a subscription problem. In some cases, the source of a subscription failure is far more obvious, yet escapes detection because most developers aren't looking in the right place. For example, if you try to create a subscription with a name that already exists, the subscription will fail even if you already have the correct configuration in place. Unfortunately, Windows doesn't provide a straightforward response like, "That subscription already exists." Instead, it provides you with generic subscription failure message that tells you nothing about the problem.

One of the easiest and best ways to avoid the dual-subscription problem is to give the subscription a combination of the machine and user's name. There aren't any circumstances in which a given user on a machine will need more than one subscription to the same component. Using this technique also makes it easier to administer subscriptions because you can quickly identify who the subscription belongs to and on what machine.

However, this technique won't work with component subscriptions. In this case, you could use a combination of the originator and direct client names. It's unlikely that this combination would require more than one subscription to a single component and it also provides the means for you to track the subscriptions. The important consideration here is that components create permanent subscriptions and you want to reduce the number of duplicates to zero if possible.

Even though there aren't any unique error codes for this problem, you can still prevent it from happening. All you need to do is add code to your client's subscription routine that traverses the COM+ Catalog hierarchy in search of the subscription name before you request a new one. If you do find it, you can always provide detailed error information to the client and allow the client to override the default subscription name. Along with the override, you should also make an event log entry so the network administrator knows about the name change and can determine if there's a duplicate subscription on the server in question.

Dealing with resource drain

A publish/subscribe event-mode application relies on publishers to generate events and clients to subscribe to those events. Every time a client wants to receive events, it must subscribe to get them. Subscriptions can become a drain on system resources if clients start creating too many of them and not releasing them. That's why you should always use transient subscriptions for client applications. In some cases, especially when a server connects across a WAN, you'll also want to use a transient subscription for component subscriptions. Always consider the location of a subscriber as part of your strategy for determining a subscription type.

Does this mean that you should always use transient subscriptions? No, because creating a subscription requires processing time. If you have a local or LAN-based component subscription that you'll use on a regular basis, then it makes more sense to use a permanent subscription in order to reduce the amount of time that the server spends handling this type of request. Using transient subscriptions in place of permanent subscriptions means that the server will spend a lot more time answering requests and you'll have to perform a server upgrade that much faster.

Of course, the biggest resource drain comes from inappropriate use of the publish/subscribe model. Older event strategies still work fine with desktop applications, especially if those applications are working with noncritical data. In fact, many developers question the use of event technology in some cases. For example, if you're sending a broadcast message to thousands of users, event technology is the worst possible solution. You need an e-mail system, not an event handler.

There are other resource considerations when you do decide to create a particular kind of publish/subscribe application. For example, you need to choose between a client application and a server component. There are areas where either type of client will work, but you need to consider how many resources you're willing to part with for this application and environmental factors like the need for a user interface. Although a client application uses more resources, it spreads resource usage among at least two machines, making the client application more efficient from a single-machine perspective even though it uses more resources overall.

Summary

MTS is a good solution for many problems. In this chapter, we looked at various types of applications that you can create, examples of those applications, and how to fix those applications when they break. Here are some additional conclusions that you can draw from the contents of this chapter:

✦ Always consider using MTS for your application, but don't always use it because it's there. Determine in advance whether MTS will add anything to the application that it doesn't already have. In many cases, MTS will protect your data and ensure that it arrives at its destination without any loss of application functionality. In other cases, it's a deadly solution that could make your application act differently than you originally anticipated.

✦ Component Services adds many features that are not found in MTS Explorer. An important feature that it adds is the capability to export a client proxy version of a COM+ application that allows easy application configuration on the client machine.

✦ COM+ supports many MTS-related interfaces that are not found in MTS alone. Most of these interfaces expand on capabilities already found in earlier versions of MTS, and make component development both faster and easier.

✦ Remember that you can use `CreateObject()` with COM+, but that you don't need to use `SafeRef()`.

✦ COM+ makes it easy to avoid hard-coded reference problems. All you need to do is leave the reference out of your code and use the external configuration features that COM+ provides as an alternative.

✦ COM+ adds a number of new interfaces to the MTS environment. Using these new interfaces will make it easier to create applications fast.

✦ Always install your event object by using the event procedure (found in this chapter), rather than the standard component installation procedure (found in Chapter 2).

✦ Look for application and subscription failures in both obvious and nonobvious locations. Sometimes the source of an application failure is apparent if you look in the right location. For example, subscription failures aren't always the result of coding or configuration errors.

✦   ✦   ✦

Working with Disconnected Applications

We took a preliminary look at Microsoft Message Queue (MSMQ) in Chapter 1 and a theoretical look in Chapter 6. It's important to know that you'll normally use MSMQ in combination with Microsoft Transaction Server (MTS) for certain classes of applications, especially those that require high reliability like database management systems (DBMS). However, it's just as important to know that MSMQ is a standalone product that you can use for non-transaction-oriented applications that simply require the capability to work with messages.

This chapter will view MSMQ and it's wrapper Queued Components as a standalone technology that you can use to create asynchronously connected applications, better known as disconnected applications. MSMQ is essentially a freeform one-way messaging system that allows a server and client to exist at different times and still communicate with each other. You'll find that MSMQ incurs a small performance penalty, but that speed isn't necessarily as much of an issue with these types of applications.

The first section of the chapter discusses the ways that you can use MSMQ to build applications. We'll discuss the various categories of MSMQ application and some of the uses that you can put them to in any organization. All of the hottest applications today are likely to need MSMQ or a similar technology in the near future. For example, laptops, personal digital assistants (PDAs), and even cell phones will eventually rely on MSMQ to provide the delayed communication that a remote and portable communication device requires.

The second section of the chapter discusses the differences between MSMQ (the underlying technology used in both Windows NT and Windows 2000) and Queued Components (the wrapper technology introduced with Windows 2000). You'll find that Queued Components has capabilities that MSMQ doesn't, many of which help you to create applications faster and administer them with fewer problems.

The third, fourth, and fifth sections of the chapter show you how to create a simple MSMQ application. We'll begin with an MSMQ component that resides on a server on the local network. Next, we'll create an application that works equally well connected to the network or in disconnected mode on the road. Finally, we'll test the resultant application in both connected and disconnected modes.

In the sixth section, we'll look at a more advanced MSMQ application that also works with Active Directory. While you might not use this application directly as a real world application, it does give you a very good idea of what's possible. In addition, the sample code will provide you with valuable techniques that you can use in real-world applications. In this case, we'll create a disconnected application that sends time-check information to the office in the form of an Active Directory entry. The entry is attached to a particular user and will allow an administrator to better track user time on the road.

MSMQ and Queued Components have their own set of administrative tasks, just as MTS and Component Services do. The seventh section of the chapter explores the administrative tasks and provides information that you need to know to recover from errant applications during the debugging process. Unlike many other application types, MSMQ applications can leave bits and pieces that you'll want to clean up before making another test of your application.

The final section looks at some of the problems that you'll run into when working with MSMQ and Queued Components. We'll explore some of the fixes for these problems and how you can avoid them in the future. When a problem isn't avoidable, this section will provide aids on how to reduce the probability of seeing that problem occur, at least in certain circumstances. It's important to know what kinds of problems you'll run into when using an advanced technology like this because many of your standard debugging techniques won't work with an application running in disconnected mode. For example, a problem with an overfull queue is something that you'd never run into with a standard application.

Uses for MSMQ Applications

E-mail is a perfect example of a nontransaction-oriented application that you often need to work with in a disconnected state. Getting e-mail ready offline, then getting online just long enough to transmit the data to a server is are common tasks that we've all performed in the past. Obviously, there are enough e-mail packages on the market that you don't need MSMQ to create a custom e-mail package for your company. In most cases, text transfer between clients is better accomplished with one of these prepackaged applications.

However, there are types of e-mail-like applications that you might want to create using MSMQ. For example, a network administrator may want to track the status of all of the machines under the administrator's control. This is a relatively easy task to perform on the local network. All you need to do is load an agent on the client machine, then use some type of server-based product to query the agents for status information. Monitoring packages today can tell an administrator everything from what applications a user is currently working with to the speed of the cooling fan.

Laptops form a special class of machine because they're largely used on the road where the network administrator can't get in contact with them. How can a network administrator keep track of machines that are on the road? A message transmitted each time that the user makes contact with the home (main corporate or satellite office) network is one answer. Just like the agent on desktop machines, an agent on a laptop could make log entries that are transferred to a queue. Whenever the user is connected to the home network, these log entries automatically appear on the server immediately after they are made. On the other hand, when the user is on the road, the log entries will appear on the server whenever the user makes contact with the home network. As far as the user and the agent are concerned, everything is working in the same way no matter where the user is physically located. MSMQ provides the "magic" that allows a network administrator to track machine conditions even when that machine is on the road.

MSMQ applications are more commonly used for database updates. The user may require, for example, an updated sales list or a new list of client meeting times. All of this information is normally stored in a database for easy access. While it's common to use MTS for critical database information, these database uses hardly constitute something earth shaking, so using MSMQ alone is more than sufficient. While disconnected mode execution is essential in remote database updates, there are many times when using MTS would be overkill and could negatively affect network resource usage.

Another use of MSMQ for application development is the store-and-forward application type. In this case, the user creates some type of data that is stored on the local machine, which information is then forwarded to someone who needs it. Consider client-meeting notes. In the past, a company would need to wait until the user on the road got home and shared his or her notes with everyone. These notes will always remain on the user's machine, so if they're lost, it's more of an inconvenience than a catastrophe for the company. A store-and-forward approach is perfect in this situation because it allows the user to keep a local copy and also send one to interested parties at the home office.

MSMQ can also be used for asynchronous data transfers between user machines. A very simple example of this use is an application that transfers data from a user's home machine to the machine at work. The home machine would transfer data in the form of a message at night, after the user completes work for the day. The work machine would receive this message and update the user's data as required when the user logs in the next day. Machine-to-machine transfers of this sort are very useful for a variety of asynchronous data needs like collaborations. Users in different time zones can communicate without worrying about synchronizing their work hours.

There are also a few odd uses for MSMQ alone. Consider the application in which a user makes a request that isn't critical. For example, you may use some type of system for requesting office supplies through a central database. Requests like this aren't normally routed through MTS because they usually aren't considered critical enough to tie up system resources. So, why would you use MSMQ? It does, after all, consume system resources. The answer is that MSMQ would allow the server to process the requests for office supplies at night or other off-peak times. In short, using MSMQ, in this case, will actually extend system resources by making better use of those resources during noncritical times.

There are some applications that work best with MSMQ and MTS combined. For example, if you design an order-entry system for a user who works on the road as well as at home, you'll want to use both MSMQ and MTS. The reason is simple, MSMQ alone won't protect the user orders that the employee on the road generates. You have to protect that data, so using MTS is essential.

In some cases, MSMQ really isn't the right solution. For example, you wouldn't want to use MSMQ to set up an e-mail system for a large company. The e-mail system would require far too many resources with MSMQ — at least for general e-mail. MSMQ does provide a certain level of data protection, but the queue messages that it produces are larger than the original text. In addition, there are few e-mail messages that really need the internal transactional capability of MSMQ. MSMQ is the wrong solution when:

✦ **Time is a factor:** MSMQ isn't particularly slow, but you wouldn't want to use it for real-time data. Remember that the main advantage of using MSMQ is that you can generate data now for processing later.

✦ **Size is a factor:** MSMQ always bloats the size of the messages that it transfers. Even if you don't encrypt the message, there's a lot of other information that MSMQ adds to the message in order to make it easier to track.

✦ **Client drive space is critical:** MSMQ requires you to create queues to store data and load MSMQ support on the client machine. If your only goal is to transfer a few messages when the user connects to the network, then e-mail or some other text-only system might work better.

✦ **Security is essential:** Let's face it, you're storing application-generated data on the hard drive where the user can gain access to it relatively easily. Unless the encryption technology that you're using is perfect, storing the data locally presents a security risk. Just how big that security risk is depends on the encryption method used, the skill of the user, and the amount of time that the user has to decrypt the data.

Differences Between Queued Components and MSMQ

Two terms in this book may appear to refer to the same operating system feature: MSMQ and Message Queuing. There is, however, an important difference between the two. MSMQ is an underlying messaging middleware that originally appeared in Windows NT. Message Queuing, on the other hand, is a wrapper around MSMQ that only appears in Windows 2000.

Message Queuing makes using MSMQ easier for both the developer and the network administrator by enabling applications to asynchronously send and receive messages in a disconnected environment. It also provides the interface that you see when you work with MMC snap-ins like Component Services. So, when you see MSMQ in the book, you know that we're talking about the underlying messaging technology, and when you see Message Queuing, you know that we're talking about the new Windows 2000 interface technology.

There are differences, however, between the version of MSMQ for Windows NT and Windows 2000. Windows NT uses MSMQ 1.0 (MQOA10.TLB), whereas Windows 2000 uses MSMQ 2.0 (MQOA.DLL). If you plan to develop MSMQ applications for Windows 2000 alone, you'll use the Microsoft Message Queue 2.0 Object Library reference within your applications. Applications that need to run under Windows NT and Windows 2000 require the Microsoft Message Queue 1.0 Object Library reference instead. Fortunately, the Microsoft Message Queue 2.0 Object Library is a true superset of the Microsoft Message Queue 1.0 Object Library. Anything that you write with Windows NT in mind will work unaltered under Windows 2000. Table 12-1 tells you about the differences between the two libraries. This table doesn't provide a complete method and property listing; it only contains a list of new or modified properties and methods.

Note All of the applications in this chapter use the Microsoft Management Queue 2.0 Object Library. This means that you can't place the applications on the CD-ROM provided with this book on a Windows NT machine and expect them to work. While the simple MSQM component example could be modified to work under Windows NT, the Active Directory disconnection application example is a Windows 2000 only project.

Table 12-1
MSMQ 1.0 and MSMQ 2.0 Object Library Differences

Method or Property	Description
MSMQApplication Class	
IsDsEnabled	This property tells you whether MSMQ is using Active Directory.
MachineNameOfMachineId	A method that converts a machine name into a GUID path. You'd use this method to convert a machine name into a GUID so that you could retrieve messages from that machine by using the FormatName property of the MSMQQueueInfo class.
MSMQVersionBuild	A property that contains the version build of MSMQ in use.
MSMQVersionMajor	This property contains the major version number of the MSMQ in use.
MSMQVersionMinor	This property contains the minor version number of the MSMQ in use.
RegisterCertificate	A method that registers a user certificate in Active Directory.
MSMQMessage Class	
AuthenticationProviderName	A property that defines the name of the cryptographic provider used to generate a message's digital signature.
AuthenticationProviderType	A property that defines the type of the cryptographic provider used to generate a message's digital signature.
Class	This property is no longer supported by MSMQ 2.0. You can, however, use the MsgClass property to gain access to the same information. In both cases, the property shows the class of the message as enumerated by MQMSGCLASS.
ConnectorTypeGuid	A property that indicates that some of the message properties normally generated by MSMQ were generated by an external source. It contains the GUID of the external source as a string.
DestinationSymmetricKey	A property that contains the symmetric key used to encrypt the message. (Another key is normally used to encrypt the message properties.)

Method or Property	Description
Extension	A property that normally remains blank unless the application needs to send data in addition to the normal message properties.
IsFirstInTransaction	A property that indicates if this is the first message in a transaction.
IsLastInTransaction	A property that indicates if this is the last message in a transaction.
ReceivedAuthenticationLevel	An enumerated property that indicates the received authentication level of the message. These values are enumerated in MQMSGAUTHENTICATION.
SenderVersion	A property that indicates the MSMQ version number used to send the message.
Signature	This property contains the digital signature of the sender of the message.
TransactionId	This property contains the identification of the transaction that sent the message (if any).
TransactionStatusQueueInfo	This property contains information about the status queue on the source computer.
MSMQQueueInfo	
PathNameDNS	A property that contains the path of the queue. This is the physical location of the queue on the computer in DNS format.
MSMQTransaction	
InitNew	A method used to create a new MSMQ transaction object within an existing transaction.

As you can see from Table 12-1, many of the feature differences between the two versions of MSMQ are related to the induction of Active Directory, increased Windows 2000 security, or MSMQ integration with COM+. In one case, the Class property, the name was changed to avoid confusion. Unfortunately, the name change from Class to MsgClass may actually cause more problems than it solves.

There are a few new methods or properties that Microsoft added for developer convenience. For example, MSMQ 1.0 provides a method for changing a GUID into a machine name using the `MachineNameOfMachineId()` method. You could use this method to convert GUIDs stored in message headings into human readable form. MSMQ 2.0 provides a method that performs the opposite task, changing a machine name into a GUID by using the `MachineIdOfMachineName()` method. This method is used to create a format name entry that's used to retrieve the queue messages for a particular machine.

Besides the API differences discussed in this chapter, there are some functional differences between MSMQ 1.0 and MSMQ 2.0. In addition, Queued Components allows for easier administration of queues and the addition of the COM+ Catalog allows for better programmatic control of the application. We discussed many of these differences as part of the theoretical discussion in Chapter 6. However, it's important to mention them again here for the sake of completeness.

Creating a Simple MSMQ Listener/Player

MSMQ applications consist of three elements, as discussed in Chapter 6. The server side of the application consists of a listener and a player, while the client side of the application consists of a recorder. This section of the chapter shows you how to create a listener/player application. You could use these same techniques to create a listener/player component (as we'll do in the Active Directory example later in the chapter). I chose a listener/player application for the first example because it's easier to gain an instant appreciation for the mechanics of MSMQ by going this route.

 Note It's unusual to write a server-side listener/player application unless you want to provide some type of user interface with the application. For example, if you were using MSMQ to transfer data from one user machine to another, you'd need to write a listener/player application rather than a listener/player component.

This section of the chapter looks at the important issue of what you need in order to create a functional MSMQ listener/player. The first section of the chapter tells you about the requirements for the most common server-side element, the component. These same requirements apply to listener/player applications; however, an application also requires some form of user interface. (There isn't any reason to use the application form of the listener/player if there isn't any need for a user interface.)

Three of the sections that follow will help you to design a listener/player interface, add code to it, and then install the application on the server. You'll find that the application version actually requires less work than working with a component because the user interface reduces the number of items that you have to configure.

As part of the application creation process, we'll discuss some ways of reducing application development time, in addition to other tips for working with queued components. MSMQ technology has been around for a while now and you'll find that following a few simple rules when creating your component or application will definitely make development tasks easier to handle. We'll also talk about working with the queue itself. There are shortcuts that you can use that will make creating queues a lot faster and easier.

Requirements for MSMQ components

MSMQ components share many of the same requirements as the other components that we've covered in the book so far. For example, you still have to design an MSMQ component to use the fewest number of server resources possible and to free those resources when they're no longer required. In addition, an MSMQ component will lack an interface because there won't be anyone at the server to see any messages that it creates.

One option that we've already included for providing error feedback is returning an error code as part of the method call to the client application. This allows the client application to react to the error and potentially fix it. This won't work in an MSMQ component because data transfer is one way—there's no return path to the user application unless you specifically set up a recorder on the server side and a listener/player on the client side. Even if you do set up a return path, there's no guarantee that the user will be available to see the error code until sometime later when they reconnect to the server and pick up any waiting messages. Consequently, one of the special requirements for MSMQ components is that they always provide feedback in the form of event log messages so that the network administrator can react to them.

Every MSMQ component is also a single-call component. The client application has to provide all of the required information to complete the call the first time because there isn't any way to ask for more information. This means that the callback methodologies used by many other component types won't work with an MSMQ component. Even the use of collections may be limited because of the all-or-nothing approach that you have to take when creating an MSMQ component. For this reason, you should include special error handling for incomplete requests. When making an event log entry, make sure that the entry includes the reason that the call failed and the missing information so that the developer has a better idea of how to change the client application code.

You always have to provide some mechanism for starting an MSMQ component and keeping it running. The listener portion of the component has to be listening for new messages or the queue will remain full. I cover one of the easier ways of starting an MSMQ queue automatically in the "Starting a Queued Component Application By Using Code" section of this chapter. There are, however, other methods, including manually starting the queue. The only requirement is that the component be listening for messages to arrive in the queue that it's monitoring.

MSMQ components need to be extremely flexible. These components will run on more than a few machine types and under a variety of conditions. This means providing alternate paths of execution when necessary, checking the context in which the component is running and adapting, and providing enhanced error checking. A single component may run on everything from a laptop on the road to a super-server attached to the company network. In some cases, it may have a wealth of resources to use; in other cases, it may have to count every byte because resources are scarce. On some machines, security may be very strict; on other machines, the component may have complete access.

The last requirement for an MSMQ component is that it assumes nothing about either the client or the server. The same component might be used in both places, depending on the circumstances, so it can't even assume that it's working on the client or server side of the application equation. As previously mentioned, an MSMQ component should never assume that a client or server is available.

There's one optional requirement that you should consider when working with an MSMQ component. Even though the main error-reporting path is through the event log, you could set up a return path to the user to report the error as well. In this case, you should limit error reporting to things that the user can easily fix while on the road. For example, if an order is rejected because of incomplete or incorrect information, you should provide a detailed message on what the original request contained (the user may not have it anymore), the missing or incorrect information (so the user knows what to fix), and the reason the additional information is required. You may want to include individual field information in the message as well. For example, if there are specific choices for a field, then you should let the user know what they are and what each choice

Creating the Listener/Player shell

This listener/player application will sit on the server, listen for messages, and respond when it sees one in the queue. While this isn't a typical MSMQ application, it does demonstrate well the mechanics of how MSMQ works. Begin by creating a Visual Basic Standard EXE project. I've named the example project ListenerPlayer, but you can use any name that you'd like. Figure 12-1 shows what the initial form should look like once you configure it for use. Table 12-2 contains all of the form settings, including those of the form itself.

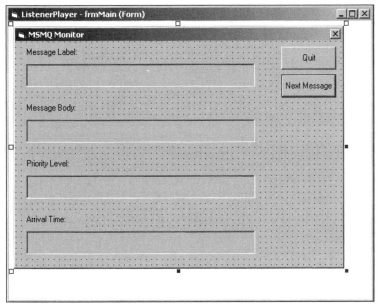

Figure 12-1: The example Listener/Player application form setup.

Object	Property	Value
Table 12-2		
Listener/Player Application Component Settings		
Object	**Property**	**Value**
Form	Name	frmMain
	BorderStyle	3 — Fixed Dialog
	Caption	MSMQ Monitor
	Height	5220
	ShowInTaskbar	True
	Width	7320
cmdQuit	Name	cmdQuit
	Cancel	True
	Caption	Quit
	ToolTipText	Exit the Application

Continued

Table 12-2 *(continued)*		
Object	**Property**	**Value**
cmdNext	Name	cmdNext
	Caption	Next Message
	Default	True
	ToolTipText	Get the Next Message from the Queue
lblMsgLabel	Name	lblMsgLabel
	BorderStyle	1 — Fixed Single
	Caption	""
	ToolTipText	Message Label or Title
	Width	5055
lblMsgBody	Name	lblMsgBody
	BorderStyle	1 — Fixed Single
	Caption	""
	ToolTipText	Message Label or Title
	Width	5055
lblPriorityLevel	Name	lblPriorityLevel
	BorderStyle	1 — Fixed Single
	Caption	""
	ToolTipText	Message Label or Title
	Width	5055
lblArrivalTime	Name	lblArrivalTime
	BorderStyle	1 — Fixed Single
	Caption	""
	ToolTipText	Message Label or Title
	Width	5055

Besides the required component configuration, you'll need to add a reference to the Microsoft Management Queue 2.0 Object Library to the example. This is the library that contains the API elements that we'll be working with in the code section. You may also want to ensure that the application is set to automatically update ActiveX controls by using the Upgrade ActiveX Controls option on the General tab of the ListenerPlayer Project Properties dialog box.

Shortcuts for working with Queued Components

Applications that require Queued Components and the services of the underlying MSMQ API always work with asynchronous communications. This means that you probably can't count on a server if you're the client or a client being present if you're the server. The asynchronous communication constraint means that you'll need to employ a few new coding techniques to create a successful application.

If you also add disconnected mode operation, the component and application development can become quite difficult. Most developers are used to working with applications where the client and the server exist at the same time and are hopefully in contact with each other. Even distributed applications based on COM+ or DCOM often rely on direct two-way client/server communication.

The following sections provide tips on how to create Queued Component applications that consider the needs of a disconnected application. In most cases, using these techniques will help reduce debugging time. Remember that it's possible to create a completely workable application that won't work in disconnected mode. The debugging tools and programming techniques that you've used in the past won't work in many cases.

Starting a Queued Component application by using code

It's essential to start a Queued Component application before you begin sending messages to it. The listener, in particular, needs to be active in order to "hear" the messages that you send across the wire. You could ask the network administrator to start the application for you, but it's actually easier to start the application from within the program by using the simple code shown here.

```
Dim oAdmin As Object
Set oAdmin = CreateObject("COMAdmin.COMAdminCatalog.1")
oAdmin.StartApplication ("MSMQ Application")
```

As you can see, all that you need is an object with access to the COM+ Catalog. Once you have that access, you can use the StartApplication() method to start any application within the COM+ Catalog. You'll only want to use this feature after you've performed any required application setups.

Write queue creation or access code first

Some developers will attempt to write an entire method before testing it. In many cases, this makes sense because you really can't test the functionality of a method until the entire method is in place. In addition, testing a method too often wastes time without much of an increase in productivity.

However, when working with MSMQ, you'll normally want to be sure that you can create the queue and access it before you write any other code. There are three reasons for doing this. First, queue-creation error messages tend to mask themselves as something else. A favorite Windows 2000 misdirection is to report the queue-creation error as an Active Directory access problem. Testing the queue-creation code first makes it possible to find the problem faster despite the misleading error message that Windows 2000 may provide.

Second, queue creation and access is a separate entity from the rest of the code in most cases. In other words, you'll normally open the queue for access as a first step in just about every piece of MSMQ code you write. The code that follows is the part that's component or application specific. Because the queue creation or access code is actually a separate module, you'll want to test this code first to ensure that it works before you write code that will use the contents of the queue.

Third, the queue-creation code is a must-have before you can manipulate the data in the queue. It always pays to makes sure that your queue code works so that any new error messages that you get when testing the code are likely to be within the queue manipulation code.

Use efficient queue-receive code

A lot of development time is spent optimizing and debugging code. You can reduce the amount of time required to optimize code by making good choices while writing the code. For example, many developers will retrieve data that they don't really need, which is fairly inefficient when working with a distributed application. This is especially true when working with messages.

The MSMQ Queue `Receive()` method allows you to specify five arguments. The first is whether you want to provide a transaction for the message. This is an internal MSMQ transaction, not an MTS transaction. Only use transactions when you need them because a transaction will always slow the transfer of data on your network in both directions. In most cases, if you don't need a transaction for the entire data path, you don't need it for the data transfer that uses MSMQ alone.

One item that you'll generally want to receive is the message body, no matter how large the message body is. However, this is an optional item, and there may be times when just reading the message label is sufficient. For example, you may want to download message labels first so that a user can determine whether he or she actually wants to download the contents of a long message. There are times when making two requests will reduce the overall amount of data transferred on the network and improve system performance.

MSMQ will allow you to detect the destination queue information. You need to tell the `Receive()` method that you want this information by specifying True for the WantDestinationQueue argument, then retrieve it by using the `Destination QueueInfo()` method of the MSMQMessage class. Asking for this information normally slows data transfer and you seldom need it for an application because you already know the destination queue information.

One of the new arguments for MSMQ 2.0 (so new that it doesn't appear in the documentation anywhere) is WantConnectorType. Specifying True for this argument tells MSMQ that you want to retrieve external connector type information. The only time that this information is generated is if message information that's normally generated by MSMQ is generated by another component. As with the destination queue information, specifying that you want this information will slow the message transfer down, so you need to use it with care. You can retrieve the connector type information by using the `ConnectorTypeGuid()` method of the MSMQMessage class.

An easy way to get LDAP paths

This isn't strictly an MSMQ tip, but given that we'll be using MSMQ with lightweight directory access protocol (LDAP) in this chapter, this tip is very helpful. Trying to figure out how to access a particular resource by using LDAP can get confusing at times. The string that you thought would work, often doesn't. Unfortunately, one of the faster ways to gain access to Active Directory resources is by using an LDAP string similar to the one shown here:

```
Private Sub Command1_Click()
    Dim oUser As IADsUser
    Set oUser = GetObject _
    ("LDAP://WinServer/CN=A. User,CN=Users,DC=DataConDomain")
    oUser.GetInfo
    MsgBox oUser.Get("streetAddress")
End Sub
```

This bit of code will retrieve information for a user named A. User. The oUser object will contain a wealth of information about this user, including a street address that is displayed by the MsgBox call. There isn't anything too surprising about this code except for the LDAP string.

You can use the ADSI Viewer to get the LDAP string right every time. Figure 12-2 shows a typical ADSI Viewer display. Notice the LDAP string at the top. You can highlight the string, press Ctrl+C to copy it to the clipboard, and then paste it in your code to get the display string correct the first time.

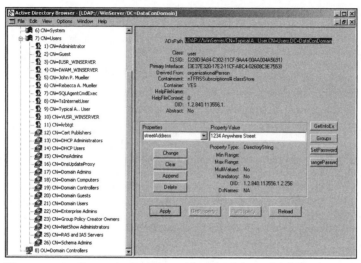

Figure 12-2: The ADSI Viewer provides a quick method for creating the right LDAP string every time.

Adding some code

Now that we've got a listener/player application shell ready, it's time to add some code to it. There are several pieces of code that we'll need to add to this application. The first is some code to ensure that the queue is in place before we begin waiting for the first message to arrive. The second is the initial message waiting code. Both of these sections appear in the Form_Load() method of the application as shown in Listing 12-1. This listing also contains three global variable declarations and some code to end the application when you're finished.

Listing 12-1: **Form_Load() Method for the Listener/Player Application**

```
'Create the required MSMQ variables.
Dim qInfo As MSMQQueueInfo
Dim qObject As MSMQQueue
Dim qMessage As MSMQMessage

Option Explicit

Private Sub cmdQuit_Click()
    'Exit the application.
    End
End Sub
```

```
Private Sub Form_Load()
    Dim CancelWait As VbMsgBoxResult

    'Create a queue info structure.
    Set qInfo = New MSMQQueueInfo

    'Fill out the queue structure
    qInfo.PathName = ".\TestQueue"
    qInfo.Label = "Test Queue"
    qInfo.BasePriority = MQ_MIN_PRIORITY

    'Try to create the queue.  Make sure you
    'mark the queue as non-transactional and
    'non-world readable. If the queue exists,
    'then recover from the error and proceed.
    On Error GoTo CheckQueue:

    qInfo.Create False, False
    GoTo QueueCreated:

CheckQueue:
    If Not Err.Number = MQ_ERROR_QUEUE_EXISTS Then
        MsgBox "Error: " + Hex$(Err.Number) + _
        vbCrLf + Err.Source + _
        vbCrLf + Err.Description, _
        vbCritical + vbOKOnly, _
        "MSMQ Error"
    End If

QueueCreated:
    'Once the queue is created, open it for reading.
    Set qObject = qInfo.Open(MQ_RECEIVE_ACCESS, MQ_DENY_NONE)

    'Display a waiting message and exit if necessary.
    CancelWait = MsgBox _
        ("Click OK to Wait for a Queued Message", _
        vbInformation + vbOKCancel, _
        "MSMQ ListenerPlayer Start")

    If CancelWait = vbCancel Then
        Goto NoWait
    End If

    'Wait an infinite amount of time for a message.
    'We don't want a transaction or the destination
    'queue, but do want the message body.
    Set qMessage = qObject.Receive _
        (MQ_NO_TRANSACTION, _
        False, _
        True)
```

Continued

Listing 12-1 *(continued)*

```
    'Fill the dialog with the message contents.
    lblMsgLabel.Caption = qMessage.Label
    lblMsgBody.Caption = qMessage.Body
    lblPriorityLevel.Caption = qMessage.Priority
    lblArrivalTime.Caption = qMessage.ArrivedTime

    'Now that we're done with the queue, close it.
NoWait:
    qObject.Close

    'Release the objects we created.
    Set qInfo = Nothing
    Set qObject = Nothing
    Set qMessage = Nothing
End Sub
```

As you can see, this application performs quite a few tasks when getting and displaying a message from MSMQ. The first thing that the code does is to create the CancelWait variable that will be used with a dialog box later. I wanted to provide the user with an option of exiting the application before it goes into the wait cycle.

Initializing the qInfo object comes next. You need this object to create or open the test queue. Once the qInfo object is instantiated, we need to define a path to the queue, the queue name, and the base priority for the queue. These three items represent the least that you can do to create a queue of any type. Notice that the path starts with a period. This represents the local machine. If you want to create a queue on another machine, then you replace the period with a machine name. This will be a public queue. Adding "\$Private" between the machine name and the queue path will create a private queue.

There are eight levels of queue priority supported by MSMQ. MQ_MIN_PRIORITY is the lowest priority at level 0, while MQ_MAX_PRIORITY is the highest priority at level 7. You'll find both of these constants in the MQPRIORITY enumeration. The base priority of a queue determines the normal message processing priority for that queue. You can also set the priority level of individual messages to ensure prompt servicing of high priority items.

Error trapping is important for two reasons when working with a queue in this case. The first reason is the normal trapping of coding, system, or user problems. The second reason is to allow you to check for the existence of the queue. Trying to create a queue that already exists will always generate an error. If you don't know for certain that the queue does exist, then you must always check for its existence prior to opening it. You can check for queues by using Active Directory on Windows 2000 machines, but private queues are registered locally.

The next bit of code uses the only technique available for checking queue availability in most cases. We'll try to create the queue so that it doesn't require a transaction and so that it isn't available for the whole world (the world being limited to your network) to read. If the queue already exists, it'll generate an error and we can check for that specific error number. The MQ_ERROR_QUEUE_EXISTS constant allows the code to bypass error handling if the queue already exists.

Execution continues when the queue is opened by using the qInfo.Open() method. In this case, we're opening the queue for receive access; that is, to remove messages from the queue and process them. The application doesn't need to add messages to the queue, so we don't open it for that purpose. Notice that the queue is also opened for nonexclusive use. You can open a queue for various types of exclusive use as well. The enumerations required for the Open() method appear in MQSHARE and MQACCESS.

Tip   You can also open a queue for peek access by using MQ_PEEK_ACCESS. This allows you to see which messages the queue contains without removing any of them. Peek access comes in handy for message preprocessing, and if you want to pass just the message labels to a user rather than the entire message. The user can select the messages that the user wants to look at and you can use receive access to remove the required messages from the queue.

At this point, the queue is ready for use, so we need to ask the user if he or she wants to wait for a message. If the user doesn't want to wait, the code skips right to closing the queue and getting rid of the objects. On the other hand, if the user wants to wait, the code uses the Receive() method to wait for a message to arrive in the queue. Notice that the call is set up in such a way that the message will be retrieved without a transaction. We do want the message body, but don't really care about the destination queue information. The default Receive() method setting is to wait for a message forever. If you don't want to wait that long, then you'll need to specify a wait value in milliseconds. After a message is received, the information is placed in the labels on the dialog box.

Now that you have a good idea of how to open a queue and perform some basic processing, let's look at some alternative ways to perform the task if you have several messages to process. The code shown in Listing 12-1 allows you to grab the first message from the queue. However, there might be more than one message and you'll want to view each message in turn. Listing 12-2 shows the code that you'll need for the Next button.

Listing 12-2: cmdNext_Click() Method Source Code

```
Private Sub cmdNext_Click()
    'Create a queue info structure.
    Set qInfo = New MSMQQueueInfo

    'Fill out the queue structure
    qInfo.PathName = ".\TestQueue"
    qInfo.Label = "Test Queue"

    'Try to open the queue.
    'On Error GoTo CheckQueue:
    Set qObject = qInfo.Open(MQ_RECEIVE_ACCESS, MQ_DENY_NONE)

    'Wait a short amount of time for a message.
    'We don't want a transaction or the destination
    'queue, but do want the message body.
    Set qMessage = qObject.Receive _
        (MQ_NO_TRANSACTION, _
        False, _
        True, _
        5)

    'See if there was a message waiting.
    If qMessage Is Nothing Then
        MsgBox "No Message Waiting", _
        vbInformation + vbOKOnly, _
        "Message Status"
        GoTo NoMessage:
    End If

    'Fill the dialog with the message contents.
    lblMsgLabel.Caption = qMessage.Label
    lblMsgBody.Caption = qMessage.Body
    lblPriorityLevel.Caption = qMessage.Priority
    lblArrivalTime.Caption = qMessage.ArrivedTime

NoMessage:
    'Now that we're done with the queue, close it.
    qObject.Close

    'Release the objects we created.
    Set qInfo = Nothing
    Set qObject = Nothing
    Set qMessage = Nothing
    Exit Sub

CheckQueue:
    MsgBox "Error: " + Hex$(Err.Number) + _
    vbCrLf + Err.Source + _
```

```
        vbCrLf + Err.Description, _
        vbCritical + vbOKOnly, _
        "MSMQ Error"
    End Sub
```

As you can see, this code is basically a repeat of Listing 12-1 with some notable exceptions. For one thing, because the queue is already created, we don't have to test it again. Depending on your application setup, this may or may not be a valid assumption because the user might remove the queue between queries. Because we don't have to test the queue, the error-handling code can appear at the end of the method, which is a more convenient place.

Notice that the Receive() method now contains a wait time as well. You'll want to set the wait time to reflect network conditions and the fact that the user might be willing to wait a few seconds rather than repeatedly push the Next pushbutton to get the next message. A value of five milliseconds is just fine for a test setup where you're already in control of when messages appear in the queue. The use of a wait time also makes the query message in the previous section of code unnecessary.

We do need to check whether there was a message in the queue because the call may not wait long enough for a message to arrive. Notice that the next section of code checks whether qMessage is equal to nothing. Even if you instantiate qMessage before you make the call to the Receive() method, it will still contain nothing on return if there was no message in the queue. If there wasn't a message, then we don't need to continue processing qMessage. The code closes the queue and sets all of the object variables to nothing. Otherwise, qMessage processing goes on as it did in Listing 12-1.

Shortcuts for queue setup

The focus of an MSMQ or Queued Component application is the queue. It's the place that data gets stored until the user on the road makes contact with the home office to transfer the data. As far as the user is concerned, the queue probably doesn't exist or is some fictional entity that they need not care about. Therefore, it's important to make sure that any queue setup is complete and as bulletproof as possible before the user goes on the road.

The following sections provide some ideas of how you can achieve this goal. We'll look at both physical setup methods and tasks that you can perform within an application to make queue setup faster and more likely to work the first time. While this isn't an exhaustive list of every potential technique, you'll find that these techniques will solve many of the problems that you face every day.

Programmatic versus manual queue setups

All MSMQ applications rely on a queue. If the queue isn't present, then the application is always going to fail because the calls to create any required components rely on the queue being in place. So, one of the main objectives of starting your application is to ensure that the queue is not only present but is also set up correctly for use.

There are a number of ways to get a queue set up correctly. You can perform this task as part of the application installation. Unfortunately, if the queue setup fails (and it can for a number of reasons), then the installation program is also likely to fail. While using the installation program as the means of adding a queue and configuring it is convenient, you'd probably want to save this method for situations when you know which machine the user will have and can control the installation environment.

Another technique is to provide instructions for the network administrator to follow. This technique has the greatest chance of success because the network administrator can make allowances for differences in network or machine setup. In addition, if the setup does fail, the network administrator will likely figure out the cause and fix it. Of course, this method assumes that the network administrator will actually perform the required setup and get the configuration correct. Choosing this method means knowing the market for your application well enough that you can judge how likely the network administrator is to perform the required setup.

The final method is to include a routine in the application itself. You can provide this routine as part of the application's Form_Load() method. Using this method is hardly bulletproof, but it's the most reliable of the available methods. The routine would need to check for the existence of the queue and add it if not found. In addition, the routine would also need to configure the queue once it was added. There are two problems with this technique. The first is that it adds complexity to the application development cycle for something that will essentially be used one time. The second is that it wastes system resources. The application will be slightly larger because of the extra code and the check will require additional processing cycles.

Although there are problems with the third method, I prefer the method. Checking for the queue each time that you start the application solves many problems. You can make certain assumptions throughout the application because you've checked the queue at the outset. For example, you know that the queue is present when you write to it because it was checked when you started the application, so you don't need to continuously check every write operation in the application. We'll be adding the queue-checking code to the Form_Load() method of every example in this chapter.

Check Active Directory

We've already talked about Active Directory collections in several places in this book. In fact, we've used them for the example in Chapter 11. Like everything else in Windows 2000, there are Active Directory collections that deal with MSMQ public queues. Notice that I didn't mention private queues. That's because private queues are registered locally, whereas public queues are registered on the server in Active Directory. If you're looking for a public queue and know for a fact that the queue should appear in Active Directory, it's often easier to search for a queue that you need there and then use the trial-and-error method shown in Listing 12-1. On the other hand, when working with private queues, you'll always need to check for the existence of the queue first, and then begin using it as shown in the listing.

Creating an MSMQ Client Application

Creating a listener/player application is only half of the job. We also need to create a recorder application; something to create messages that the first application can respond to. The following sections will show you how to create an application shell, and then add some code for sending the message to the listener/player application.

Creating the program shell and designing the dialog box

The recorder application sits on the client machine. It creates messages and places them in either a local or server queue. If the message is placed in a local queue, then MSMQ will transfer the message from the local queue to a server queue to await the listener application. The listener will get the message out of the queue, and the player will do something with it.

This section will show you how to create an application shell for a very simple recorder application. All that this application will do is transfer a message to the listener/player application that we created in the previous section. The example application uses a project name of Recorder, but you can use any name that you'd like. Figure 12-3 shows the form for this example. Table 12-3 tells you how to configure the various components.

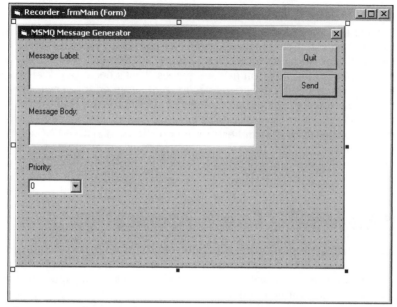

Figure 12-3: The example Listener/Player application form setup.

Table 12-3		
Recorder Application Component Settings		
Object	*Property*	*Value*
Form	Name	frmMain
	BorderStyle	3 – Fixed Dialog
	Caption	MSMQ Message Generator
	Height	5220
	ShowInTaskbar	True
	Width	7320
cmdQuit	Name	cmdQuit
	Cancel	True
	Caption	Quit
	ToolTipText	Exit the Application

Object	Property	Value
cmdSend	Name	cmdSend
	Caption	Send
	Default	True
	ToolTipText	Send a Message
txtMsgLabel	Name	txtMsgLabel
	TabIndex	0
	Text	""
	ToolTipText	Type a Message Label or Title
	Width	5055
txtMsgBody	Name	txtMsgBody
	TabIndex	1
	Text	""
	ToolTipText	Type a Message
	Width	5055
lstPriority	Name	lstPriority
	List	Entered one to a line: 0, 1, 2, 3, 4, 5, 6, 7 (press Ctrl+Enter between lines)
	TabIndex	2
	Text	0 (zero)
	ToolTipText	Select a Message Priority Level

In addition to the required component configuration, you'll need to add a reference to the Microsoft Management Queue 2.0 Object Library to the example. You may also want to ensure that the application is set to automatically update ActiveX controls by using the Upgrade ActiveX Controls option on the General tab of the ListenerPlayer Project Properties dialog box.

Adding some code

It's time to add some code to this part of the example. Listing 12-3 shows the code that you'll need to add for both the cmdQuit and cmdSend buttons.

Listing 12-3: **Simple Recorder Application**

```
Option Explicit

Private Sub cmdQuit_Click()
    'Exit the application.
    End
End Sub

Private Sub cmdSend_Click()
    'Create the required MSMQ variables.
    Dim qInfo As MSMQQueueInfo
    Dim qObject As MSMQQueue
    Dim qMessage As MSMQMessage

    'Create a queue info structure.
    Set qInfo = New MSMQQueueInfo

    'Fill out the queue structure
    qInfo.PathName = ".\TestQueue"
    qInfo.Label = "Test Queue"
    qInfo.BasePriority = MQ_MIN_PRIORITY

    'Try to create the queue.  Make sure you
    'mark the queue as non-transactional and
    'non-world readable. If the queue exists,
    'then recover from the error and proceed.
    On Error GoTo CheckQueue:

    qInfo.Create False, False
    GoTo QueueCreated:

CheckQueue:
    If Not Err.Number = MQ_ERROR_QUEUE_EXISTS Then
        MsgBox "Error: " + Hex$(Err.Number) + _
        vbCrLf + Err.Source + _
        vbCrLf + Err.Description, _
        vbCritical + vbOKOnly, _
        "MSMQ Error"
    End If

QueueCreated:
    'Once the queue is created, open it for reading.
    Set qObject = qInfo.Open(MQ_SEND_ACCESS, MQ_DENY_NONE)

    'Create a new queue message.
    Set qMessage = New MSMQMessage

    'Fill the message with the dialog contents.
    qMessage.Label = txtMsgLabel.Text
```

```
qMessage.Body = txtMsgBody.Text
qMessage.Priority = lstPriority.Text

'We also have to provide a sender ID type.
qMessage.SenderIdType = MQMSG_SENDERID_TYPE_SID

'Send the message without a transaction.
qMessage.Send qObject, MQ_NO_TRANSACTION

'Now that we're done with the queue, close it.
qObject.Close

'Release the objects we created.
Set qInfo = Nothing
Set qObject = Nothing
Set qMessage = Nothing
End Sub
```

The code in Listing 12-3 should look familiar by now. Before opening the queue, we begin by testing its presence. Because we're reading the queue, we'll open it for send access by using MQ_SEND_ACCESS instead of receive access as we did in the previous section.

Notice that, in this case, we need to set qMessage equal to a new message. You still need to instantiate the message object before you can fill it with information, so this step is necessary. Filling the message with data from the dialog box is similar to getting data out of the message and placing it on the dialog box. Notice that the code sets the SenderIdType when creating a message. You must set the SenderIdType to ensure that the message is created with the correct sender information. Otherwise, this information will appear blank in the queue.

When sending a message, you specify the name of the queue that you want to send it to and whether the message requires a transaction. You'll find the transaction constants in the MQTRANSACTION enumeration. The Send() method will allow you to specify a transaction for the entire message series, a transaction for a single message, a transaction coordinated by an external entity like MTS, or no transaction at all.

Testing the MSMQ Component

Testing this application is relatively easy if you have everything set up in advance. The problem is that the MSMQ environment isn't really all that simple to set up. What should be a fairly easy application type to test actually turns out relatively difficult to test for several reasons, the most important of which is the interaction of the various application elements over network cabling.

The first test step is to get a message in the test queue. There are actually two parts to this test. The first is the capability of the application to create the queue if it isn't already present. The message has to have somewhere to go, which means that the queue must be in place prior to sending the message. The second part of the first test is to ensure that the message actually gets in the queue. You have to verify that the message not only gets into the queue, but that it contains the information that you expect it to. For this reason, you'll probably want to conduct initial application tests without any encryption or other security measures in place. Sending the message in plain text will allow you to find out which part of the application is responsible for any corruption much faster than if you send the message in encrypted form and can't read it in the queue.

The second test step is to ensure that the receiving application works. I built a simple application, in this case, to test the capability of the listener/player to detect the message and read its contents. You'll probably want to perform the same step in any production development situation to keep the transmission sequence simple. Once the communication path and associated queues have been tested, you can begin to add complexity to the applications involved. This means converting any listener/player into a component or service.

Checking out the message

It's time to perform the first phase of the testing the process. Run the Recorder application, type some values in each of the three data fields, and then click Send. You won't see any action from the application, at this point, but something should happen. Open the Computer Management MMC snap-in and find the Public Queues folder. Highlight this folder and you should see a display similar to the one shown in Figure 12-4.

Notice that the Public Queues folder shows a testqueue entry, which is the name of the text queue for our application. Also notice that this queue has a single message in it, which is what you should have if you clicked Send only once. If you look at the code in Listings 12-1 and 12-3, you'll notice that the test queue should have a label of Test Queue. Part of checking communication with the queue is to see if the label appears as it should. Right click the testqueue entry, then choose Properties from the context menu. You'll see a testqueue Properties dialog box similar to the one shown in Figure 12-5.

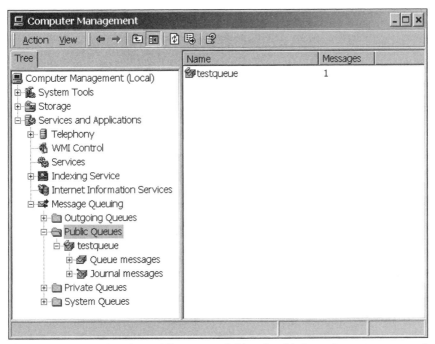

Figure 12-4: Opening the Public Queues folder should show the test queue and associated message count.

As you can see, the Label field of the testqueue Properties dialog box does indeed contain a value of Test Queue. Also notice that the Base priority field has a value of 0, as set by the MQ_MIN_PRIORITY setting in Listings 12-1 and 12-3. You can change any of the other fields in this dialog box by using various queue object properties, just as we set the Label field value for this example. The point is that when you create a queue from within the application, it should have all values set just as if you'd set them manually when creating the queue from Computer Management.

At this point, you should generate four or five additional messages at a variety of priorities so that you can see how the queue handles messages. Highlight the Queue messages folder that's beneath the testqueue folder. Figure 12-6 shows a typical example of the results that you should get from trying out various priorities. Notice that this list is in priority order — you could easily sort it by any of the other columns as well.

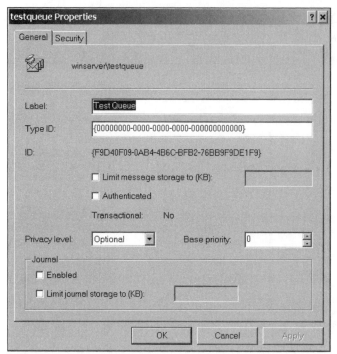

Figure 12-5: Always check the queue's Label field for the correct value when you evaluate application performance.

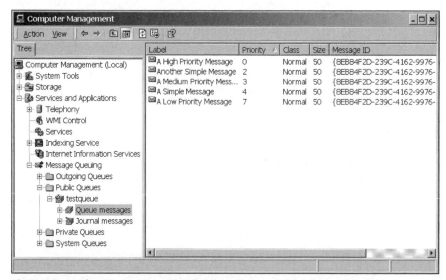

Figure 12-6: The Queue Messages folder will contain the messages that applications send to the queue.

There are a few additional points of interest that you should consider at this point. The first thing that you should see is that the Size column refers to the size of the text within the message, not the size of the entire message. This column will tell you the size of the body of the message and can help you to find messages that contain more data than an application could normally handle.

The Message ID column identifies the message in two ways. First, it tells you which machine sent the message. The GUID in the first part of the Message ID identifies a unique machine on the network. The second half of the Message ID contains the number of the message for that queue. The combination of the two identification parts gives each message a unique ID that you can sort on to determine which users are most often working with the queue.

As previously stated, all of the messages in the queue right now have a Class of Normal. That's because they were all generated by our test application. If this was a response queue, you might see other message classes, depending on the kind of message sent by either the server-side component or queue manager.

At this point, it might be interesting to look at one of the messages. Double-click one of the messages in the queue and you'll see a dialog box similar to the one shown in Figure 12-7.

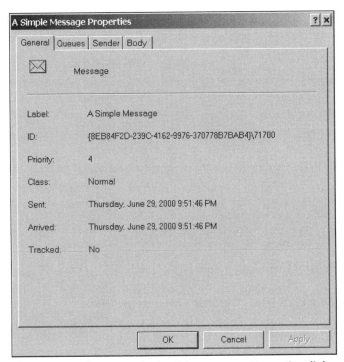

Figure 12-7: The General tab of the message Properties dialog box contains identification and time-oriented fields.

As you can see, the General tab starts out with essentially the same information as the entry in Computer Management. The Sent and Arrived fields tell you when the application sent the message and when it was received by the queue. A large difference in time here can indicate problems if the client isn't operating in disconnected mode. Although in some cases the entries in the Sent and Arrived fields won't be precisely the same, they should at least be close. If they aren't, you may have a latency problem with your network. The Tracked field simply tells you whether MSMQ is tracking the progress of the message as it traverses the network.

Every message will affect at least one queue—the one that you're sending it to. However, messages can affect more than just the queue that the application sent them to. Look at the Queues tab and you'll see a display similar to the one shown in Figure 12-8.

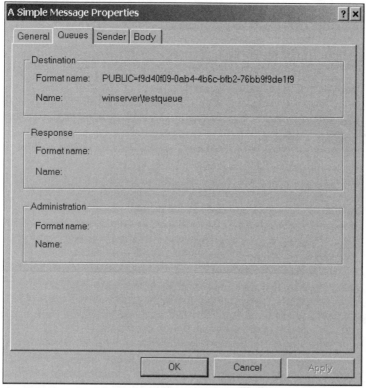

Figure 12-8: The Queues tab of the message Properties dialog box displays information about the three queues that a message will affect.

The message will report three queues. The first is the queue that the application specified as a final destination. If you decide to get a response from MSMQ about the message's final destination, then this tab will also have an entry for the Response queue. Finally, any kind of tracking requires an entry in the Administration queue. We didn't tell the application to create a journal entry for this message or to track it in any way, so there aren't any entries in these two additional queue fields. Every queue entry contains the GUID for the queue, along with the fully qualified path for the queue. This allows you to determine the precise locations of all copies of the message on the network.

Let's say that you do decide to add the administrative and response queues to a message. The code in Listing 12-4 will allow you to do just that. In this case, I decided to make both queues private. The error-trapping code was removed in order to better show the sequence of steps required to create the queues and add their content to the sample message. Figure 12-9 shows what the output from this code would look like.

Listing 12-4: **Adding an Administrative and Response Queue**

```
'Add these lines of code to provide an administration
'and response queue.

'Create the required MSMQ variables.
Dim qAdmin As MSMQQueueInfo
Dim qResponse As MSMQQueueInfo

'Create a queue info structure.
Set qAdmin = New MSMQQueueInfo
Set qResponse = New MSMQQueueInfo

'Fill out the administration queue structure
qAdmin.PathName = ".\Private$\MyAdmin"
qAdmin.Label = "MyAdmin Queue"
qAdmin.BasePriority = MQ_MIN_PRIORITY

'Fill out the response queue structure
qResponse.PathName = ".\Private$\MyResponse"
qResponse.Label = "MyResponse Queue"
qResponse.BasePriority = MQ_MIN_PRIORITY

'Create the queues.
qAdmin.Create
qResponse.Create

'Add the queues to the message after we create them.
Set qMessage.AdminQueueInfo = qAdmin
Set qMessage.ResponseQueueInfo = qResponse
```

All of the additional code shown in this section also appears in the Recorder example code in the Chapt12/Simple Recorder Example folder on the CD-ROM provided with this book. The extra code is commented out so that you can see the example in operation without the added coding in place. To test additional features mentioned in this section, uncomment the code to recompile the example.

Of course, simply adding an administration queue or a response queue entry to a message doesn't do very much for you. To activate the administration queue, you also need to specify what kind of acknowledgment you want from the receiving application by using the Ack property of the message. There are several levels of acknowledgment as we discussed in Chapter 6.

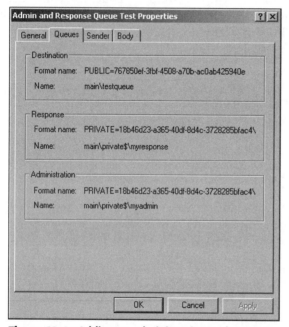

Figure 12-9: Adding an administrative and response queue to your message may take some work, but it's usually worth the effort.

Likewise, the response queue is only activated if the receiving application detects that you want some type of response and uses the ResponseQueueInfo property contained in the message to open the queue on the sending machine. Sending a message to the response queue works the same as with any other message. You create some content and specify the response queue instead of a local or server queue.

It's time to look at the message sender information. Click on the Sender tab and you'll see a display similar to the one shown in Figure 12-10.

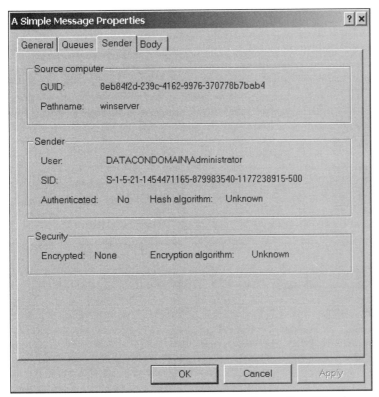

Figure 12-10: The Sender tab of the message Properties dialog box displays both user and computer information.

No matter how you send a message, the Source computer information will always get filled out. This information includes the GUID of the source computer, along with the source computer name. Note that the Pathname field contains the name of the computer only, it doesn't contain the fully qualified domain name for the source computer.

In Listing 12-3, we requested that MSMQ supply the security ID (SID) of the user that sent the message. It turns out that there's a little quirk with this particular entry that isn't really explained in the Microsoft documentation. You must request message authentication before this set of values will be filled in for the message. Windows 2000 requests this information because of the way that it controls security. Windows NT, on the other hand, won't request the authentication information automatically.

Because we didn't specify any form of authentication, MSMQ would place the message in the queue with an unknown user when working with Windows NT. Because this is a Windows 2000 server, the name of the user is known. However, notice that the Authenticated field is set to No and that the Hash algorithm field is set to Unknown. If you want to add encryption and authentication to a message, you'd need to add the three lines of code shown below to the application. Figure 12-11 shows a message that has both authentication and encryption enabled.

```
'Add these three lines of code to add authentication
'and encryption.
qMessage.AttachCurrentSecurityContext
qMessage.AuthLevel = MQMSG_AUTH_LEVEL_MSMQ20
qMessage.PrivLevel = MQMSG_PRIV_LEVEL_BODY_ENHANCED
```

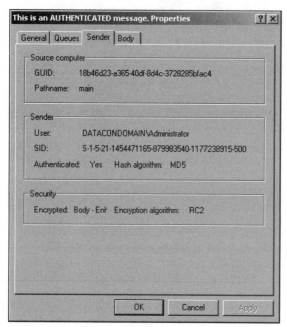

Figure 12-11: Authentication and encryption are easy to add to any message as shown here.

The final set of fields on the Sender tab deals with message security. Again, because we didn't include any security for this message, MSMQ hasn't filled this area out. The Security area tells you whether the message is encrypted or not and at what level. Fortunately, the entries in this section tend to be generic and don't compromise the integrity of the message in any way.

It's finally time to look at the body of the message. You'll definitely want to use plain text for the first phase of testing so that you can see any problems with the message body before it gets encrypted. After the message body is encrypted, it doesn't pay to look at the Body tab because all you'll see is gibberish. Figure 12-12 shows a typical example of a message body in plain text.

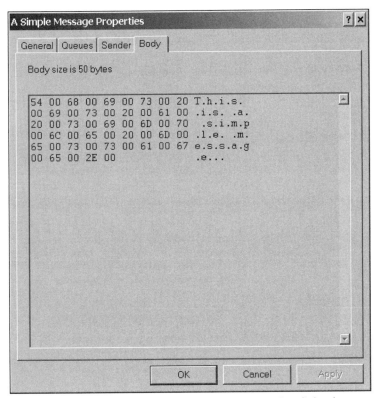

Figure 12-12: The Body tab of the message Properties dialog box displays the contents of the message.

Tip   There's an interesting problem with the Body tab of the message Properties dialog box. In some cases, you'll notice that the text gets cut off on the right side, yet there aren't any scroll bars to work with. You can reposition the text by clicking within the body text area and moving the arrow keys. At some point, the text will become visible so that you can see the contents of the message.

Viewing the message output

Getting the message into the queue and verifying that it's correct is actually the hard part of the testing process. What you'll want to do next is start the ListenerPlayer application that we created earlier. Figure 12-13 shows some typical output from the application.

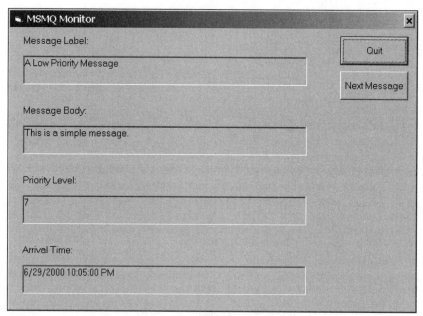

Figure 12-13: The MSMQ Monitor application will retrieve the messages placed in the queue.

There's an interesting anomaly that you should notice at this point. MSMQ gave us the lowest priority message in the queue to process first. Either the Microsoft documentation is wrong or there's something wrong with the queue setup in this example. Unfortunately, no one at Microsoft would comment about this apparent priority problem. The messages always appear to be retrieved in the opposite order, with 7 being the highest priority and 0 being the lowest priority. Needless to say, you'll want to test out potential problems like this as part of your application development process, which is one of the reasons why we ran this test application in the first place.

An Active Directory Disconnected Application

Active Directory represents one of the most anticipated features of Windows 2000 because it promises to reduce network administration problems while simultaneously making the Windows 2000 programming environment more flexible for the developer. It's one of the few times that an idea that's good for the user and the network administrator is also good for the developer. (It usually seems like a fancy new user-oriented feature only adds to the developer's programming burden and makes the development environment more complex than before.)

 Cross-Reference We talked about the procedures for creating COM+ application in Chapter 2. Chapter 2 also tells you about some of the implications of creating a COM+ application and how that process differs from what you may have done in the past. Be sure that you understand how to work with COM+ applications before you start the application in this chapter. We'll be creating MTS applications that you'll need to install by using the Component Services MMC snap-in to ensure proper operation.

Active Directory is above anything else a database. It has a schema, stores data, and everyone can retrieve the data that it contains within the bounds of their access rights. As a systemwide storage object, Active Directory is also the right place to store various kinds of long-term data for the system, users, administrators, applications, components, and developers. This new capability is long overdue and a very good replacement for the Registry in at least some situations.

This section provides an example of how this new capability can be used to track users on the road. We're going to create an application that allows a user to "punch the clock" while on the road. The application will create an MSMQ message that will get uploaded whenever the user makes contact with the company.

On the server, we'll create a component that runs all of the time and looks for messages from users on the road. When a user uploads his or her messages, the component will store the time values within Active Directory. In this way, a manager can always keep track of how much time employees on the road are spending performing certain tasks that require a login to the system. This type of application has many uses, I've chosen to implement a simpler example of something that could provide a lot of value to a company.

The following sections will help you to design, build, and test both a client-side application and a server-side component. I'm not going to go into as much detail as I did with the previous example because you already have a good idea of how a simple MSMQ application works.

After you've created the application, we'll look at some of the ways that you should and shouldn't use Active Directory, with an emphasis on shouldn't. One problem that will occur with Active Directory is that developers will see it as the latest and greatest toy. They'll want to create all kinds of applications for it, many of which simply don't fall into the realm of good Active Directory applications. This section isn't designed to inhibit your creativity, but it is designed to make you think twice about developing applications that won't work well with Active Directory. In some cases, these applications will require a separate database, in others they're actually better implemented by using the local Registry.

Creating the component

The first thing that we need to do to create this application is to design a component that will receive input from the client application on the user's machine. This component will interact with Active Directory by looking for the user's name. It will then place text in the user's "info" or Notes entry. The user's Notes entry appears on the Telephones tab of the User Properties dialog box as shown in Figure 12-14.

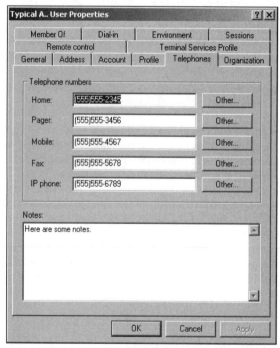

Figure 12-14: We'll use an easily accessible and freeform field to store user entries for this example.

In the following sections, we'll create a component shell, add two methods to it, and then some code to perform the required interactions. We'll need two different methods for this example. The first will add new login entries, and the second will clear all of the entries after the network administrator has viewed them or the user has come home.

Creating the component shell

Begin by creating an ActiveX DLL project. I've given the example project a name of QCOne, but you can use any name that you'd like. As with all of the other COM+ components that we've created in the book, you'll want to set at least three of the properties in the QCOne – Project Properties dialog box. Make sure that the Threading Mode property is set to Single Threaded, the Unattended Execution option is checked, and that you set the component up for Binary Compatibility after the first compile. In this way, you'll ensure that you know if you're breaking any COM rules when you create future builds of the component. The final project setup item is to add a reference to Active DS Type Library (ActiveDS.TLB) to your application.

The QCOne component has a class name of UserLog. You'll want to set the MTSTransactionMode property to "3 — Uses Transaction" so that the component can participate in client transactions, but doesn't require a transaction to function properly. This will allow more flexibility if you decide later to add transaction support to the client-side application in order to ensure that log entries are made while the user is on the road.

After you have these basic configuration needs completed, add two public Subs (methods) to the component. You may wonder why the component doesn't use functions in this case. The reason is simple: We're designing an MSMQ component where communication is one way. If the component runs into a problem, it has several options. It can make an event-log entry, send the user input in the form of an e-mail message or other communication, or make a response queue entry so that the user will receive feedback the next time the user makes contact with the company. An MSMQ component shouldn't assume any level of communication with the client at all. Call the first method `CreateLogEntry()` and the second method `ClearLogEntries()`. Both methods also require one input in the form of a string called strUserName.

Adding some code

It's time to add some code to the component. You'll find in a lot of cases that the MSMQ component that you create has a few limitations that standard components don't (like the inability to pass values out), but that the code itself is very much the same as any component that you created in the past. Listing 12-5 shows a typical example of component development in MSMQ. Notice that we're not talking about queues or doing anything queue related for the most part. The difference will be in the configuration, which we'll explore in the next section.

Listing 12-5: **Active Directory Log Component**

```
Option Explicit

Public Sub CreateLogEntry(ByVal strUserName As String)
    'Create the variables required for the log entry.
    Dim oUser As IADsUser
    Dim strLDAP As String
    Dim strLog As String

    'Build a connection string.
    strLDAP = "LDAP://WinServer/CN=" + _
            strUserName + _
            ",CN=Users,DC=DataConDomain"

    'Get the user object from Active Directory.
    Set oUser = GetObject(strLDAP)
    oUser.GetInfo

    'Create a new log entry string.
    strLog = oUser.Get("info") + _
        vbCrLf + "User Logged In: " + _
        Date$ + " " + Time$

    'Enter the string in the Notes field.
    oUser.Put "info", strLog
    oUser.SetInfo

    'Release the user object.
    Set oUser = Nothing
End Sub

Public Sub ClearLogEntries(ByVal strUserName As String)
    'Create the variables required for the log
    'deletion.
    Dim oUser As IADsUser
    Dim strLDAP As String

    'Build a connection string.
    strLDAP = "LDAP://WinServer/CN=" + _
            strUserName + _
            ",CN=Users,DC=DataConDomain"

    'Get the user object from Active Directory.
    Set oUser = GetObject(strLDAP)
    oUser.GetInfo

    'Delete the string from the Notes field.
```

```
        oUser.Put "info", " "
        oUser.SetInfo

        'Release the user object.
        Set oUser = Nothing
    End Sub
```

The Active Directory Services Interface (ADSI) allows you to work with Active Directory by using a standard set of interfaces. We're using one of those interfaces in this example. Both methods create an Active Directory user object that we'll use to access the Notes field of the Telephones tab of the User Properties dialog box. One of the more difficult tasks is building an LDAP string that we can use to access a particular resource, but using the ADSI Viewer makes that task a lot easier. See the "An Easy Way to Get LDAP Paths" section of this chapter for details.

You'll instantiate oUser by using the GetObject() method. The GetObject() method requires an object reference in the form of a string, which is where the LDAP string comes into play. However, instantiating oUser isn't enough to fill it with information that we can use. The code also calls on the GetInfo() method, which performs a function that's similar to the Populate method used for the COM+ Catalog searches that we discussed in Chapter 11.

Now that we have an object and some data to work with, it's time to do something with the "info" context, which is actually the Notes field in disguise. In one case, we'll add a new login entry to the existing contents of the Notes field; in the other case, we'll truncate the contents of the Notes field. Placing the new information in Active Directory is a two-step process. First, we use the Put() method to transfer the data to Active Directory. Second, we use the SetInfo() method to make the change permanent. Unless you follow both steps, the data change won't be reflected in Active Directory.

Installing the MSMQ component

Installation of an MSMQ component follows the same basic pattern as any other COM+ component, but there are a few twists that you need to know about. While the procedure in Chapter 2 will get the component installed, it won't make some of the configuration settings that you need for an MSMQ component. The following steps will help you to make the additional changes required for any COM+ application. Make sure that you check Chapter 2 for the standard installation procedures.

1. Begin by creating an empty COM+ application. Use the same procedures that you normally would as shown in Chapter 2. The example uses a name of Employee Logger, but any name will do. Make sure that you don't install the component right away, just create the empty application.

2. Right-click Employee Logger and choose Properties from the context menu. Select the Queuing tab and you'll see an Employee Logger Properties dialog box similar to the one shown in Figure 12-15.

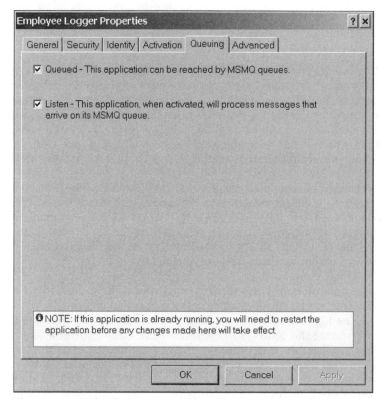

Figure 12-15: The first step in making this an MSMQ application is to change the application Queuing tab settings.

3. Check the Queued – This application can be reached by MSMQ queues option first, then check the Listen – This application, when activated, will process messages that arrive on its MSMQ queue option. These two options allow your application to receive and react to MSMQ messages. In effect, this is the listener part of your application, which is why the source code didn't contain specific listener code earlier. The older MSMQ 1.0 method is to create the listener as a separate item. The use of interceptors in COM+ allows MSMQ 2.0 components to be configured by using the method shown here.

4. Close the Employee Logger Properties dialog box.

5. Install the QCOne component just as you normally would by using the procedures in Chapter 2.

6. Right-click the _UserLog interface object and choose Properties from the context menu. Click the Queuing tab and you'll see an _UserLog Properties dialog box similar to the one shown in Figure 12-16.

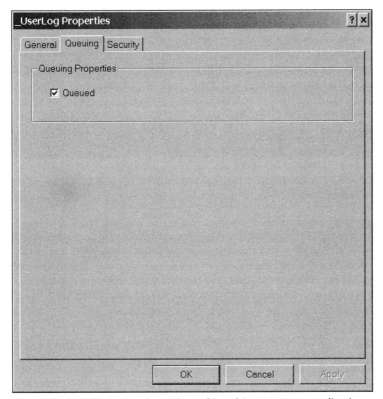

Figure 12-16: The second step in making this an MSMQ application is to change the interface Queuing tab settings.

7. Check the Queued option. This allows the interface to participate in message-driven applications. It's very important that you select queuing at both the application and component level. If you're having trouble checking this option, see the "Can't Set Interface as Queued" section of the chapter.

8. Close the _UserLog Properties dialog box.

9. Right-click the Employee Logger object, and then choose Start from the context menu. If you don't start the application, it won't be capable of listening for messages in the queue. You can also perform this task with the client application, but given the type of component that we're configuring in this case, manually starting the component is probably faster and more efficient than using program code.

After you've finished the server-side COM+ application configuration, you'll need to export the application as a proxy and install it on the client machine. We've already talked about the process for exporting a proxy and installing it in Chapter 2, so I won't discuss it again here. Make absolutely certain that the server-side application is fully configured before you export it and install it on the client machine or the proxy may not contain the required queue and server location information.

Creating the application

The test application will be relatively simple. All we really need is some way to trigger the creation or deletion of log entries, and a method of specifying the user name. The following sections will show you how to create the test application.

Creating the program shell and designing the dialog box

Begin the application by creating a new Standard EXE application. I named the example QCOneTest, but you can use any name that you'd like. Make sure that you add a reference to the QCOne – Active Directory Employee Log Entry Creator component in your application. Figure 12-17 shows what the form for this example will look like. Table 12-4 contains a complete list of component setting changes that you'll need to make.

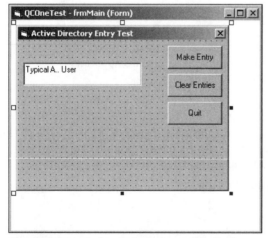

Figure 12-17: A simple form for testing both MSMQ and Active Directory.

Table 12-4
Listener/Player Application Component Settings

Object	Property	Value
Form	Name	frmMain
	BorderStyle	3 – Fixed Dialog
	Caption	Active Directory Entry Test
	Height	3750
	ShowInTaskbar	True
	Width	4770
cmdQuit	Name	cmdQuit
	Cancel	True
	Caption	Quit
	TabIndex	3
	ToolTipText	Exit the Application
cmdMakeEntry	Name	cmdMakeEntry
	Caption	Make Entry
	Default	True
	TabIndex	1
	ToolTipText	Create a New Log Entry
cmdClearEntries	Name	cmdClearEntries
	Caption	Clear Entries
	TabIndex	2
	ToolTipText	Delete an Existing Log Entry
txtUserName	Name	txtUserName
	TabIndex	0
	Text	The name of the test user.
	ToolTipText	Enter an Active Directory User Name
	Width	2655

The only entry in Table 12-4 that may require a little explanation is the txtUserName Text entry. This is just a convenience setting. Instead of typing the test user's name every time, you can simply enter it once and have it available whenever you need it.

Remember that the LDAP string requires a precise username that often varies from the login name that the user normally uses.

Adding some code

The client application is configured and ready for coding. Listing 12-6 provides the simple code that you'll need for this example.

Listing 12-6: **Active Directory Log Client Application**

```
Private Sub cmdClearEntries_Click()
    'Create an link to the MSMQ application on the server.
    Dim oEntry As QCOne.UserLog

    'Delete the log entries.
    Set oEntry = GetObject _
        ("queue:ComputerName=WinServer/new:QCOne.UserLog")
    oEntry.ClearLogEntries (txtUserName.Text)

    'Release the entry object.
    Set oEntry = Nothing
End Sub

Private Sub cmdMakeEntry_Click()
    'Create an link to the MSMQ application on the server.
    Dim oEntry As QCOne.UserLog
    Set oEntry = GetObject _
        ("queue:ComputerName=WinServer/new:QCOne.UserLog")

    'Create the log entry.
    oEntry.CreateLogEntry (txtUserName.Text)

    'Release the entry object.
    Set oEntry = Nothing
End Sub

Private Sub cmdQuit_Click()
    'Exit the application.
    End
End Sub
```

As you can see, there isn't anything out of the ordinary about this code except for one item. Notice that the GetObject() method uses an augmented string in this example. The queue keyword tells Windows that this is a queued application. You need to provide the name of the computer that has the queue for this component.

The string also contains the component name, as usual. After you have a reference to the queued component, you can call any methods that it provides, just like normal.

There's one thing to remember about MSMQ applications. Notice that I haven't included any error-handling code in the client application. The client won't receive any type of success value back from the component, so there isn't any way for the application to check the success of the call directly. A successful call, in this case, means that the message was stored in the local queue and nothing more.

Testing the application

It's time to test the Active Directory application that we've created. There's one additional setup task that you need to perform; you need to create a test user just in case something goes wrong with the application code. You don't want to wipe out a real user's record by accident. Changes made to Active Directory are permanent, so you need to test your Active Directory applications by using as many test objects as possible. If you're already familiar with adding a user, you can skip the first section that follows. If not, this section will provide a few tips that you can follow to make the creation process easier and better tuned to testing this application.

The next step of the process is to test the application in connected mode. You want to be sure that the application will perform well in connected mode first because it provides the fastest feedback on potential problems. In addition, every MSMQ application will eventually need to spend time in connected mode in order to accomplish any work; disconnected mode is an alternative operating mode akin to running a laptop on batteries rather than line power.

After you've completed connected mode testing, it's time to test the application in disconnected mode. There are a variety of tests that you should run in order to check for potential problems with connected mode operation. We'll look at all of these steps within the third section that follows.

Creating a test user

Creating a test user for this example isn't an option, it's a necessity. You don't have to provide good information, but every field in the user record should be filled out (within reason — you can't fill out mutually exclusive fields) so that you can verify which field you're working with at any time. Use a combination of long and short field values so that you can verify any data length problems in your application.

Adding a user is relatively easy. Open the Active Directory Users and Computers console (the entry appears under Start ➪ Programs ➪ Administrative Tools, or within the Administrative Tools folder of the Control Panel). Figure 12-18 shows what the Active Directory Users and Computers console looks like.

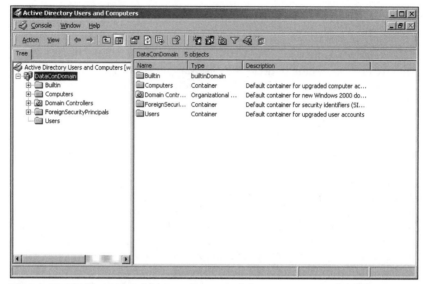

Figure 12-18: The Active Directory Users and Computers console allows you to add new users to Active Directory.

Right-click the Users node in the Scope (left) pane and choose New ⇨ User from the context menu. You'll see a New Object – User dialog box like the one shown in Figure 12-19. Simply follow the prompts to create a new user.

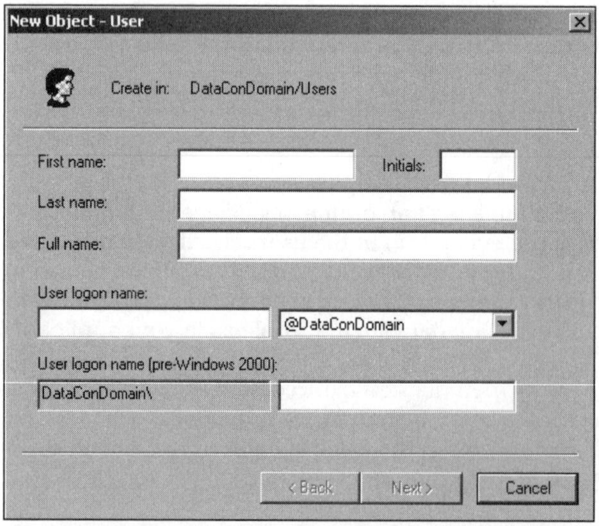

Figure 12-19: The New Object – User dialog box provides prompts for entering mandatory user information.

After you complete the initial data-entry process, right-click the new test user entry and choose Properties from the context menu. You'll see a user Properties dialog box. Fill out all of the information that you can for this text user so that you have data to work with during application development.

Connected mode

In most cases, you're going to want to test the application in connected mode first. However, because of the way that Queued Component applications work, you can actually perform the testing in two phases. First, send messages to the queue with the server-side application shut down. This will allow you to see how messages are added to the queue and can help you determine whether you need to add more parameters to your component and test application to create complete messages. More importantly, you can perform some analysis on various queue elements like the priority of messages that arrive from certain destinations. You may decide to handle local messages first, then those from remote locations if the queue will fill up during working hours.

Tip   You might initially think that the queue should remain relatively free of messages as the application runs. However, a backlog of messages isn't necessarily going to cause problems if you prioritize the messages as they arrive. Running the server 24 hours a day, even if there aren't any employees who access the server at night, allows the server to work more efficiently and reduces the amount of hardware that you need for message processing. Remote users are unlikely to notice whether their messages are processed at night after the daytime staff has left.

After you've checked out queue operation, it's time to purge the queue of existing messages (so that the component doesn't have to try to process them all when you start the application). Remember that all of the queues are found in the Message Queuing folder of the Computer Management snap-in. All you need to do to purge the queue is right click the Queue messages folder (under the Employee Logger folder) and choose Purge from the context menu.

Start the application by right-clicking Employee Logger in the COM+ Applications folder found in Component Services. Then choose Start from the context menu. Make sure that the little ball is rotating within the box. Now when you send a message by using Employee Logger, an entry will be made in the Notes field of the test user's Active Directory entry. Figure 12-20 shows a typical example of the results that you'll get with this application.

The point of this whole exercise is that the application really doesn't look any different than it did before and it'll be the same for the users of your application. Queued Components allow you to create applications with extended range without adding any additional functionality or really very much in the way of code.

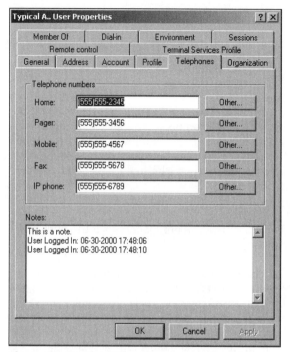

Figure 12-20: The Active Directory portion of our example will make entries in the test user's Notes field.

Disconnected mode

Testing a disconnected application with a server connection in place only ensures that the application will work at the most basic level. It doesn't really test the application in the way that it's designed to work on the road. The problem with testing the application in disconnected mode is getting your machine to a state in which it reflects what you'd expect the user to have on the road.

Note   At this point of the testing process, you must create a proxy application and install it on the client machine. While the test MSMQ application may have worked previously without this proxy, you must install one now for disconnected testing. Without a proxy, the application won't have access to a representative of the object on the server to work with in disconnected mode and the application will always fail.

There's one other small change that you'll need to make to the code for the client application. In Listing 12-6 we have several lines of code that look like this:

```
Set oEntry = GetObject _
   ("queue:ComputerName=WinServer/new:QCOne.UserLog")
```

You now need to change these lines of code to point to the queue on the client machine instead of the server. All this requires is to remove the ComputerName parameter so that the code looks like this:

```
Set oEntry = GetObject _
    ("queue:/new:QCOne.UserLog")
```

Recompile the application and ensure that it's ready to go by performing one more test with the client connected to the server. You should still see the log entry added to the test user's Notes field as you did before. The only thing that's changed is that the application is now ready for disconnected mode activity.

Before you begin this part of the test, you'll have to shut your machine down and disconnect any network connection. When you start the machine up again, it's going to be disconnected from the network and you'll probably see some error messages. The one message that you'll most definitely see is one that says that your machine can't be validated against the domain's list of users. This really isn't a big deal — the user on the road can't be validated either.

The first step in disconnected mode testing is to ensure that you still have access to the certificate for your machine. The way to check for this is to open the Message Queuing applet in the Control Panel. Click on the Security tab. Click Register and you should still see one or more certificates as shown in Figure 12-21. If you don't, then your machine isn't set up to work in disconnected mode and you'll have to reconnect it to the network. In short, you need to be able to support the security that MSMQ is expecting your machine to have before the test application will run. Click Cancel to close the Personal Certificates dialog box. You don't want to accidentally kill the certificate for the machine if it's installed and ready to go.

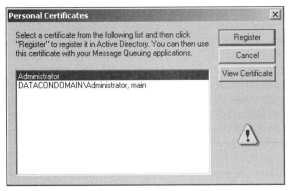

Figure 12-21: Make sure that you still have access to the required security for a disconnected test.

Start the QCOneTest application. Type a username and click Make Entry. It'll look like nothing has happened, but the application has stored a message locally that will be uploaded to the server when a connection is restored. Let's look at where that message was stored.

Open the Computer Management console and then open the Message Queuing folder. You won't find the message in the Public Queues folder this time. Look in the Outgoing Queues folder and you'll see a queue similar to the one in Figure 12-22 that's used to hold the messages for our application.

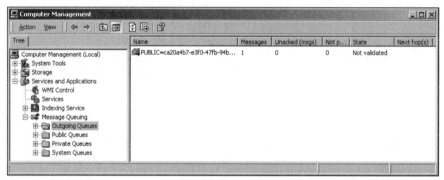

Figure 12-22: Messages that are waiting for a server connection are placed in the Outgoing Queues folder in a special folder for that application.

Note   You may see a snap-in failed to initialize message when you open the Computer Management console. This is natural because your machine has lost contact with the network. Click OK to clear the message and you'll see the Computer Management console as normal. Some features won't work because you're disconnected, but you'll still be able to check the status of your disconnected application.

You should notice several things about this dialog box. The first difference between this queue folder and the folders that we've used previously is that the queue name is actually a GUID. If you compare this GUID to the GUID of the Employee Logger queue on the server, you'll see that they're the same. The next thing that you'll notice is that this queue isn't validated. That makes sense considering that we don't have a connection to the server. Finally, there's a blank column called Next hop(s). We'll see where this comes into play in a few moments.

Shut down the client machine. Reconnect the network cable. Restart the client machine. A few moments after you log back into Windows 2000, the test user's Notes field will receive another entry. You'll be able to verify this by checking the test user's entry in the Active Directory Users and Computers console, yet you won't see anything physically happen on either machine. Neither machine will ask for any information from you that pertains to the test application. The application has automatically transferred the queued message to the server and the server-side component has already acted on it. This is precisely the way that a disconnected application will work in a production environment as well. The user won't see any difference in the way that the application operates and everything will happen automatically in the background.

There are a couple of final items that you should look at. The first is the Outgoing Queues folder. If you look right now, you'll see that the application queue shown in Figure 12-22 is gone. Now, run the QCOneTest application again. Send a message to the server and look at the Outgoing Queues folder again (you may need to right-click on the dialog box and choose Refresh from the context menu to refresh the display). You'll see a new queue similar to the one shown in Figure 12-23. We just created this queue with the QCOneTest application. However, in this case, the queue has a name in human-readable form and the Next hop(s) column will contain the IP address of the test server. Notice also that this queue is validated (connected) because we have a connection to the server.

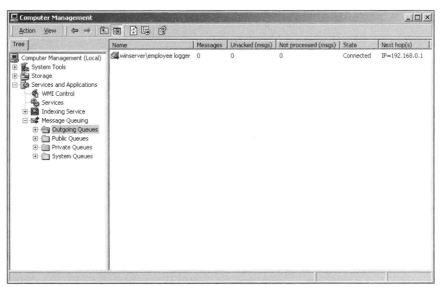

Figure 12-23: Queues created while connected to the server contain more human-readable information than those created while disconnected.

Situations in which Active Directory won't work

Active Directory isn't the correct solution for every application programming need. Even Microsoft acknowledges this because it provides quite a few compatibility solutions as part of its application strategy. So, it's very likely that you'll use Active

Directory for some tasks, the Registry for others, and a database or other storage methodology to fulfill still other needs.

Of course, this raises the question of when Active Directory is the appropriate choice to fulfill an application programming need. One of the ways that I decide whether to use Active Directory is by looking at where the application will be used. There are some situations when Active Directory can't work because it requires access to the network server. Any application settings that a user will need on the road are candidates for the Registry, not Active Directory. In fact, some settings, like the user's word processor preferences, should be stored in the Registry rather than in Active Directory anyway because you wouldn't want to raise network storage requirements and these settings are of limited use to anyone but the user.

There are types of data that you can store in Active Directory, even though you're on the road at the time. Consider the example application in this chapter. Data that everyone will use, but no one needs immediately, falls into this category. The user of the Active Directory example application is making an entry in Active Directory, but that entry won't appear in the log until the user makes contact with the company again. So, even though the user is ultimately working with Active Directory, in the interim, the user is interacting with MSMQ and nothing more.

Compatibility is another way to make a choice between the Registry and Active Directory. If an application already stores its information in the Registry and no one else needs access to that information, there's little reason to move the settings from the Registry to Active Directory. Besides making more work for company programmers, moving the data will more than likely break existing application installations. In short, sometimes it's better to leave settings where they are to ensure that applications continue to work as anticipated.

Custom databases are a stopgap solution to consider when user application settings will change while the user is on the road and those changes are generated at the home office, rather than by the user. For example, a company policy change could fall into this category. Working with the Registry from a remote location is difficult and error prone. Database updates can be accomplished with a background download from the home office while the user is doing other things like checking e-mail. A custom database is often the right solution when nothing else will work.

Performing MSMQ Administration

As a developer, you'll find that you need to perform certain kinds of administrative tasks, at least during the development process. We've already looked at a few of these issues throughout this chapter. For example, you need to know how to create and configure new queues as needed. It's also important to know how to read the messages that your application creates and determine whether there's any problem with them. The following sections will touch on a few additional issues that you need to be aware of. None of them are earth shattering, but it's handy to know about them so that you can fully test and maintain the applications that you create.

Basics of queue management

There are times, during the course of working with a complex application, when it would be nice to have some status information about the queues that you're dealing with. Unfortunately, the Computer Management MMC snap-in doesn't provide much in the way of quick documentation. However, you can create a quick overview of the queues on a certain machine by using the Export List command on the context menu for the various folders in Message Queuing. Selecting this option displays a Save As dialog box that you can use to export a list of entries at that level. Figure 12-24 shows a typical example of entries exported at the Private Queues level.

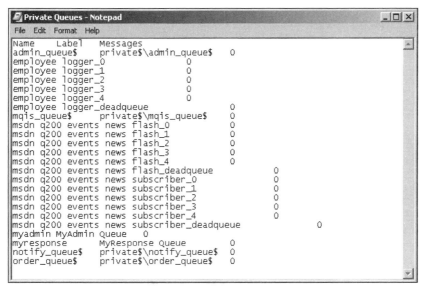

Figure 12-24: You can use the Export List command to create snapshots of your system setup for future analysis or recovery.

The exported list doesn't provide very much information, but it does provide the names of the queues that are currently in use and the number of messages that each queue contains. This is enough information, in most cases, to at least track the ebb and flow of message traffic on the network and determine if messages are moving along as anticipated. You can use this snapshot of the queue state to detect when certain events happened. For example, these snapshots could tell you when a component is being overloaded or even stops working completely.

Sometimes you'll need to clean out a test queue. It might be filled with messages that you'd rather not have in place. All you need to do to clear the messages is to right-click either the Queue messages or Journal messages folder and choose Purge from the context menu. Unfortunately, this is an all-or-nothing proposition — Computer Management doesn't provide any method for removing just one problematic message.

Some of you might be new to MMC and not know that Microsoft generally provides more display columns than you see by default. This is true of the various queues. By default you'll see the Label, Priority, Size, Class, and Message ID fields of the message. However, you can configure the display to show more than just these fields (or eliminate some of the fields if you don't want to see them). Right-click the Queue messages or Journal messages folder, and then choose View ➪ Choose Columns from the context menu. You'll see a Modify Columns dialog box like the one shown in Figure 12-25.

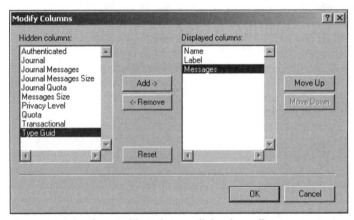

Figure 12-25: The Modify Columns dialog box allows you to choose how much or how little data you'll see within the console.

Obviously, the columns that you get to choose from depend on the kind of information presented at the level that you're looking at. The queue level is one area where you get many choices. A good selection of columns at this level can definitely help your troubleshooting efforts because you won't have to open messages individually to see certain types of information.

Dead letter messages queue

Checking the dead letter messages queue (or the dead letter queue associated with your application) might seem like an obvious thing to do, but because the dead letter queue is in a different place from the main queues for your application, you might not think to do it. After a while, the dead letter queue can fill with messages and slow system performance. There are a number of false indicators that you can get when this occurs, none of which will seem obvious at the time. For example, in one case, an application reported security errors when the dead letter messages queue overflowed with messages. In short, if you're having a weird application problem, check for some nonobvious problems with an overfilled dead letter messages queue.

Checking the event viewer

COM+ doesn't always display error messages that you can use to detect problems in your application. In fact, there are several situations in which your application will appear to work just fine (no errors returned from the calls), but where there will still be a problem. If you don't think to look in the Event Viewer, you might miss the information required to fix the problem. For example, there are situations when the Windows 2000 default recorder will report problems, yet you'll never see them at the application level. The COM+ Catalog also reports errors that will affect the operation of your MSMQ application. Figure 12-26 shows a typical example of such a problem.

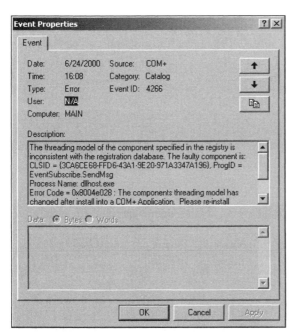

Figure 12-26: MSMQ, COM+, DCOM, and other sources of errors are reported in the event log, often without a corresponding error message.

At first, you may question why Microsoft would take this approach. Consider for a moment that like the components executing on your server, Microsoft can't assume that the application is still around to receive an error message. It's also in poor taste to display error messages on the server, because you can't be sure that the network administrator will find them anytime soon. Consequently, the only place that Microsoft could report some types of MSMQ application errors is within the Event Viewer. The point of this whole section is that the Event Viewer will normally contain some kind of useful information in those situations when it appears that the application is working, but you're not getting the desired results. It pays to check the Event Viewer when you're not sure whether an application is succeeding.

Quick Fixes for MSMQ and Queued Components

Very few technologies work perfectly, especially when they're new and virtually untested. MSMQ has been around for a while, so Microsoft has had a chance to work out a few of MSMQ's worst problems. Part of the problem resolution is the additional MSMQ 2.0 features that we've talked about in this chapter. Of course, MSMQ is partly new for Windows 2000 as well. MSMQ now includes advanced security support as well as better MTS support, and it enjoys a close relationship with COM. The new features are going to cause some problems — problems that you'll have to spend time fixing even though they have nothing to do with your code.

The following sections will help you to locate and fix some of the worst MSMQ and Queued Component problems that you'll find under Windows 2000. This isn't an exhaustive list, but it does provide you with some ideas on where to look for problems that you encounter when working with this technology. The important thing to remember is that Microsoft is working on a service pack for Windows 2000 as I write this, so some of the problems that you see here may be fixed by that service pack.

Leftover queues

In many cases, an application will leave what I call queue crumbs lying around after you uninstall it. There have been many times when I ran an application for a short time for test purposes, uninstalled it, and later found queues that had been left behind. These queues normally don't cause many problems. They do consume resources, but other than that, they just sit there, waiting for someone to notice them.

Eventually, these leftover queues begin to build up and they could become a problem, especially on those road warrior machines. Each queue consumes only a few resources. Stack several hundred of those queues, and you could begin to see the effects of the resource usage.

There's also a small chance that a leftover queue could interfere with a newly installed application. Although it's unlikely to happen, it's something to look for when you have a mysterious queue problem plaguing your current programming project.

Leftover queues don't serve a useful purpose. Like any housekeeping chore, many of us will just let them build up. It makes sense, though, to look through the queues on your machine from time-to-time to ensure that you keep the queue crumbs under control.

Application won't run or compile under Windows 2000

Remember that Windows NT uses MSMQ 1.0 and Windows 2000 uses MSMQ 2.0. In most cases, that won't cause a problem when you're moving up from one version to the other. There's only one case when MSMQ 2.0 doesn't directly support an MSMQ 1.0 feature and that's the Class property of the MSMQMessage class. This feature is supported, but under the name of MsgClass. If you run into problems when running your old applications under Windows 2000, this would be the first problem to look for.

Visual Basic should point out any problems with using the Class property when you compile your application under Windows 2000. However, it may just tell you that the property isn't supported under Windows 2000, rather than tell you that the property name has been changed. Again, you'll need to change any occurrences of the Class property in your code to MsgClass. The enumeration for both classes is the same, so the only thing that you'll need to change is the property name.

Application reports a full hard drive or other message error

Getting fixated on your own application code is easy to do when you've been working on an application for 10 or 12 hours straight. However, it's often the silly problems that take the longest time to fix. One problem that developers will face when working with MSMQ is that it doesn't follow one of the rules that other COM+ applications do: with MSMQ, you don't want the application to stop running immediately after the user is done in order to save resources. The second that an MSMQ component shuts down, it stops listening to the queue for new messages. If you're seeing a disk full or other strange message error, and your code isn't the cause of the problem, then you should probably check the component settings to ensure that the queue isn't getting full and staying that way.

This problem can also occur when there's a mismatch between the client and server. A client and server application must use the same queue name or the data won't be transferred from the client to the server. Make sure that you check the client-side queue when you see this problem. If the queue is full, start checking configuration items like the queue names.

It's also possible to shut off the Message Queuing service, and you can do it indirectly without too much trouble. Some people will shut down the Distributed Transaction Controller (DTC) when making a backup because this service keeps certain files open on the server hard drive (this isn't possible if your organization needs 7-day/24-hour service). The second that you shut down the DTC, you also shut down the Message Queuing service. Figure 12-27 shows the appropriate entry in the Services console. Notice that Message Queuing is started in the figure.

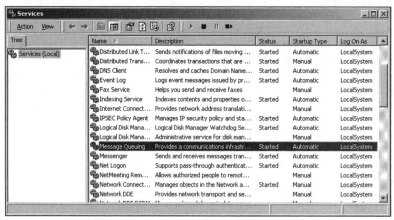

Figure 12-27: Always check the Message Queuing service if you suspect that someone may have shut it down accidentally.

Active Directory access problems

You'll find that there are times when you get an error message stating that you (or a user) don't have the access to Active Directory required to complete an action. In many cases, even though you do have the required access, the problem will persist no matter what you do to your code or how you configure security on the server. The problem may not even be with Active Directory or your code. Windows 2000 often generates Active Directory error messages when the problem is in some other service that's supposed to provide access to Active Directory.

A common source of this problem is when the local client doesn't have Message Queuing services installed. Running an application on such a machine often generates an Active Directory message. From a Windows 2000 point of view, the problem may actually appear to be that Active Directory is inaccessible. Always be sure to check that all of the required services are installed, configured properly, and running when you see an Active Directory error message. You'll be surprised when you discover how many Active Directory errors are actually some other problem in disguise.

Can't set interface as queued

It's absolutely essential that you set up both the application and the component interface for queued operation. Setting up the application for queued operation normally doesn't present much of a problem, but getting the component interface set up for queued operation can prove troublesome. If you open the Queuing tab of the interface Properties dialog box and find that the Queued option is grayed out, there are usually two sources for the problem.

The first problem can occur if you install the component before you set the application to act as a queued component. Always set up the application's queuing requirements first, and then add the component and set it up for queued operation.

The second problem is that Visual Basic always assumes that all method arguments are supposed to be set for input and output operation. Remember that MSMQ components are one-way only — the component can receive input from the client, but can't output to the client. Passing all arguments ByVal will usually fix the problem.

Summary

This chapter has shown you several ways that you can use MSMQ to build applications. We also looked at when MSMQ isn't the right tool. Finally, we spent time learning to work with MSMQ administration features. Here are some additional conclusions that you can draw from the contents of this chapter:

✦ The main reason to use MSMQ is to create data now, store it locally, and process it on the server later. MSMQ isn't a fast, efficient, or absolutely secure technology, but it does offer the capability to create reliable disconnected applications.

✦ Most of the differences that you'll see in the MSMQ API in Windows 2000 are due to the addition of Active Directory, changes in security, and integration of MSMQ with COM.

✦ Every message that you send can affect three different queues: destination, response, and administration. The destination queue is always affected. The administration queue is used for automatic acknowledgments of message receipt. The response queue contains responses from the receiving machine to the message sender.

✦ Always verify the precise operation of your MSMQ application. Some MSMQ behavior isn't very well documented, and you may end up with some surprises if you don't test your application thoroughly.

✦ Disconnected applications require small changes in the application code to ensure that the application relies on the local queue, rather than the one on the server.

✦ Always choose the right application configuration data storage methodology. In some cases, Active Directory is overkill; in other cases it would actually break the application rather than make it work more efficiently. In general, use Active Directory for data that's of interest to more than one person and isn't required in real-time by users on the road.

✦   ✦   ✦

Connecting to Remote Databases

The remote database application is one of the most complex applications that you can create today. There are so many different elements to consider that many developers give up or call in extra help to handle the load. Some problems are easy to see immediately. You need to consider data security because database applications tend to handle both sensitive and critical data. Making the situation more difficult is the inherent complexity of database applications. Relational databases force you to follow certain conventions and often those conventions make it difficult to create just the right query. Remote database applications need to handle both thick and thin clients; it's not impractical to think of someone entering small amounts of data by using something like a personal digital assistant (PDA) in the not too distant future. Finally, there are problems inherent with the network media. The Internet is hardly a reliable architecture to depend on for data transfers of this type, not to mention the problems that you'll encounter when trying to gain access to sufficient resources like network bandwidth. Suffice it to say, this type of application isn't for the faint of heart.

COM+ does help you to get around many of the problems mentioned in the previous paragraph. For example, MSMQ allows a user to keep entering data even if the connection to the remote server fails or isn't available when the user begins the session. MTS will allow you to store database updates in transactions, making it unlikely that data will get lost, even if it has to be transferred several times to ensure that a good copy goes into the database. Microsoft has also been promoting various thin-client technologies, most of which will work with either thick or thin clients.

There are also problems that COM+ won't help you to solve now or any time in the future. Database applications will always present the greatest developer challenge because they're always going to be large, require lots of interrelated tables, and handle massive quantities of sensitive data. As corporations get more of their business online and as mergers swell the size of previously small companies, the problem will become worse, not better. So, if you're looking for a magic bullet to kill the specter of database development problems of the past, COM+ probably won't help much.

Given what COM+ will and will not do for you, it's important to understand the applications that will benefit most from the capabilities that COM+ can provide. The first section of the chapter, "Uses for Remote Database Applications," tells you about these applications and just what COM+ can do to help. We'll also discuss the elements of application development that COM+ can't fix; even if COM+ is the perfect solution for a particular application, there's no reason to expect it to get rid of every potential problem that you'll run into.

The next section, "Creating the Server-Side MTS Component," helps you to build an MTS component that's optimized for database use. In this example, we'll concentrate on the elements of security and reliability, rather than speed or resource usage. In fact, we'll discuss the programming elements that are most important to database applications as part of the component-building discussion. This is also the section in which we'll look at ways of reducing the complexity of the MTS database component so that you're not dealing with both component and database schema complexities at the same time.

The third section of the chapter helps you to build a desktop client for the database component. The fourth section discusses what you'd need to do to adapt this example for thin client use. Many people are concentrating on thin clients today because they feel that PDAs and small handheld computers are the future. Whether they're the future or not remains to be seen. What's certain is that there's a vast stockpile of desktop machines that you'll need to work with for quite some time to come. Knowing how to develop both thick and thin clients is a real plus in an application that presents so many challenges at the outset. This section of the chapter also looks at shortcuts that you can use to make application development for either thick or thin clients faster.

As part of the thin-client discussion in the fourth section, we'll discuss the merits of static versus dynamic Web pages. Many developers think that live content is the only way to go in today's work environment. In many cases, they're right: Using dynamic content does have many advantages for the user, especially when constant information updates are required. There are, however, situations in which a static Web page is the only choice because the client is old or has an unreliable connection to the Internet. In some cases, you may want to develop both Web page types to ensure that users will always have maximum flexibility when working with your application.

The fifth section of the chapter, "Testing the Applications," begins by showing you how to install the component. It's important to make all of the right settings for a database application or you may suffer data loss, among other problems. After we've discussed component installation, it's time to look at the testing methodologies. Given the distinctly different natures of thick versus thin clients, we actually need to separate test procedures. As part of the testing discussion in this section of the chapter, we'll also look at the problems that you should watch for when working with a particular client type.

No matter how much work you put into an application, you're going to experience problems. If nothing else, the application will eventually break when enough of the equipment on the network changes. The final section of the chapter, "Quick Fixes for Remote Databases," will describe the kinds of problems that you're most likely to experience and will provide some solutions to those problems.

Uses for Remote Database Applications

Database applications, as a whole, perform a vast array of tasks within even the smallest company. These applications are used for everything from order entry to statistics gathering for a variety of purposes. People use the database for storing contact information and as a means to remember important commitments. In short, the database application is one of the most prevalent application types, and yet it's the one that's normally custom designed and built.

It's not too surprising that people started taking their database applications on the road with them when laptop computers became powerful enough to do so. The problem with copying a database to a local hard drive and making updates to it is that joining the old database to the new one is notoriously difficult and error prone. It's a lot better if an application can eliminate this separate step and update the remote database directly. That's where the functionality of COM+ comes into play. You can rely on COM+ to make those remote connections available, at least when it's actually possible to create a remote connection.

The following sections will take a brief look at some common remote application types that you may find yourself building tomorrow. We won't discuss every database application type, which is impossible given the flexibility of database management systems (DBMS) and the number of new ways that users consistently find for improving this application type. However, it's also important to know how you can use MTS with your favorite DBMS for your next application.

Order entry and status update

The order entry application is probably the oldest database application in existence. Of course, it's the fundamental need for these applications that make them so important; no company can survive long without accurate customer order recording and status update software. The order-entry system is also one of the easiest applications to convert to COM+ use and the most likely to provide large gains in both reliability and productivity for user and network administrator alike. In short, the order entry application represents one of the best application types to move from the desktop environment to the Internet.

Order entry programs have several advantages over other remote application types when it comes to getting them up fast by using COM+. Performing the main task of order entry doesn't require a connection to the company network. The user can enter orders, which MSMQ will store in a local cache. When the user does make a connection to the corporate network, the orders will be sent to the server automatically without any additional input from the user.

You can also make order entry programs more independent by using a preemptive download whenever possible. By looking at the user's itinerary, an application can anticipate potential data requirements and download the required information in the background. For example, when the user visits a customer's company, one of the first things that a customer will want to know is the status of a previous order. If you can't provide status information, the client tends to think that you came to the meeting ill-prepared to do any work. With a little work, a remote database application can anticipate this need, download the required data to the user's computer, and then allow the user to access that information offline while talking with the customer.

Another use of background downloads are information updates. You could combine this type of update with the use of a publish/subscribe event component. For example, the component could publish a price update that the user would get the next time that the user contacted the company. Status updates can go on while the user reads messages from other people in the organization, obtains required software or hardware updates, or simply takes a rest for lunch.

Contact information

A contact manager can be considered the right hand man of anyone on the road. It allows the road warrior to keep in contact with people at the home office and with customers who need new products, services, or other assistance from your company. In addition, a contact manager allows the road warrior to keep track of his or her appointments, avoid scheduling conflicts, and keep personal notes about trip expenses. A contact manager can also fulfill a variety of other needs, depending on the way that it's designed. In short, the road warrior would be lost without this application. It's important, therefore, to keep it as up-to-date and accurate as possible.

In the past, if a client changed an appointment, someone would have to search frantically for a way to contact the employee on the road. It wasn't an easy task and there were times that any contact was impossible. That's no longer the case. Schedule changes can be made locally, then distributed to the employee the next time that the employee checks in. If the employee checks in several times each day, then there won't be a problem with schedule changes.

In fact, this methodology can also solve other problems. For example, in the past, the employee on the road might have carried outdated client information. Today, however, a COM+ application can automatically update the employee's local database in the background and notify the employee of the change in the foreground. The problem is easily solved with little effort from the home office and no effort at all by the road warrior.

There are some potential problems with this system, but they'd be inherent in any system that you created. Some companies have literally hundreds of thousands of customers, and a database of that size won't fit on a laptop, let alone on a palm top, the kind of device used by many employees on the road today. Consequently, any download of data from the remote computer will have to be selective and consider the user's needs. Otherwise, the employee will run out of room for all of those orders that he or she is taking.

Another problem, albeit a small one, is the reliance of this system on the road warrior's ability to find a phone line to check in with. If the employee has a cell phone, the problem might be solved, but it's important to face the fact that there are times when communication will be less than optimal. Because everyone is counting on the system to handle these problems, they'll often go unnoticed until it's too late, making it more important to build time safeguards into the system whenever possible.

Equipment, network, or other status

Some companies encompass more than just one building. Some have buildings full of computer equipment that may physically reside in more than one country. In short, the network administrator can't be in every place at once, so it's difficult for the network administrator to know the status of the various pieces of equipment, the network itself, and various types of resources. Some type of remote connectivity is required so that the network administrator can stay up-to-date on potential and existing problems.

In days gone by, companies invested large sums on dedicated phone lines to keep all parts of the company in contact. Today, those same companies are moving toward using virtual private networks (VPNs) that are connected through the Internet. The network administrator's needs have to be taken care of using this same source of information and there isn't any reason that the Internet can't provide the required structure.

COM+ is an obvious choice for this type of communication because it allows fully secure transaction-oriented data transfers. In addition, the publish/subscribe event model allows components on remote servers to publish update information as needed. These events can be prioritized for the network administrator automatically, allowing for timely handling of critical situations.

There are a few potential problems with this strategy that you need to consider. The most important problem is that the Internet isn't known as a reliable medium. Although it's becoming more reliable, you still read about outages in the trade press and newspapers. Therefore, it's normally a good idea to have a backup plan in mind for critical network problems that need to be handled immediately, even if the network administrator can't look directly at the problem because of a downed phone line. The time-critical nature of this type of application makes careful planning necessary to avoid problems later.

Denial of Service (DOS) attacks are also a problem that you need to consider. In this scenario a cracker transmits messages that overwhelm the ability of the Web server to respond. As a result, normal traffic comes to a halt, which means that your application won't work correctly. Unlike a loss of connection problem, this problem affects your Web server, which means you have to have a local solution for the problem instead of relying on redundant ISP connections. In many cases bringing more servers online can counteract a DOS attack. Critical applications need to include some type of performance monitoring in order to detect impending problems like DOS attacks.

Configuration data

Business today changes rapidly. Even a few days can make a difference in how a business is run. A new technology might appear on the horizon, crackers might increase their attacks or become more subtle in their approach, clients may express an interest in getting additional services, even the needs of the employee on the road might change. In short, as a developer, you never have to worry about having enough work to do; the problem is one of too much work.

Because business changes rapidly, you need a way to communicate those changes to users on the road. The user needs to know not only the current prices, but also the current business strategy. Applications have to be configured to consider new requirements like increases in sales tax or a rise in gas prices. Configuration data controls how the computer feels to the user and the types of output that the computer can produce.

Obviously, there are alternatives to using a remote database update for configuration data. You might send updated Registry entries, or use some other form of configuration data update. The point is that even the Registry is a database of sorts.

Updates to the Registry will be similar to updates that you perform on a remote database.

A major consideration with configuration data updates is when to make the change. You need to consider the timing of a configuration update because it's essential not to make an update when the user is in the middle of a project that could be adversely affected by the change. In addition, it's normally a good idea to update all machines at once (which isn't always possible when you have employees on the road).

Business-to-business or business-to-customer sales

A remote database will be the central element in any online sales application that you want to set up. A remote database of this type would contain client lists and preferences, the results of sales made online, the sales catalog, and perhaps even some of the resources for the Web site itself. In short, the remote database is an integral part of any applications that you create for online use. Because many businesses are conducting business-to-business (B2B) sales over the Internet to reduce costs, time, risk, and other problems of getting sales in other ways, it's important to understand how COM+ can improve your ability to create the required database elements. In fact, B2B sales will eventually eclipse business-to-customer (B2C) sales if current predictions are correct.

COM+ is a perfect technology for B2C and B2B sales sites for several reasons. The most important reason for you as a developer is the disconnected application technology offered by MSMQ (as described in Chapter 12). Currently, if a major component of a Web site goes offline, the entire Web site is useless because of reduced access to resources and the inability of the application to access the databases that it requires to record any sales. As we saw in Chapter 12, MSMQ can help you to get around this problem by making every element of a Web site more independent. Sure, you may not be able to present a pretty picture of a new product to a client, but the system will be able to continue recording sales in a queue until the rest of the network comes back online.

There are other reasons that COM+ is an especially important technology for the developer when it comes to Web site sales. Security is a problem with any public site and everyone knows that crackers are always looking for new ways of gaining entrance where they're not wanted. Windows 2000 provides more in the way of security features than any previous version, which is good considering how many threats a computer network faces today compared to just a year or two ago.

The capability of MTS to guarantee a transaction is also central to the remote database scenario and this feature is especially important for online sites. The trade press has had a field day covering businesses that didn't quite make the grade during holiday sales or had a failure right after a major sales campaign. In many cases, the company was unaware that there was a problem until customers started complaining that their order wasn't recorded. Using transactions ensures that the order is entered and that you'll spend less time looking for error records in your system.

Creating the Server-Side MTS Component

Many of the components that we've created so far in the book have provided examples of how to access system resources or process small pieces of data. A database application, no matter what its purpose, is usually a major undertaking, so the component in this example will be more complex than any other components that we've looked at so far. Adding to the complexity of this example is the fact that we need to coordinate more of the features that COM+ provides in order to create a robust component that's capable of handling every task that a Web site is normally asked to perform.

 Cross-Reference We talked about the procedures for creating COM+ application in Chapter 2. Chapter 2 also tells you about some of the implications of creating a COM+ application and how that process differs from what you may have done in the past. Be sure that you understand how to work with COM+ applications before you start the application in this chapter. We'll be creating MTS applications that you'll need to install with the Component Services MMC snap-in to ensure proper operation.

Before we can do much, though, we need to define a database. That's what we'll do in the first section that follows. The SQL Server won't be too complex, but it will be complex enough so that you can see some of the problem areas of using COM+ for a remote database access scenario. The example will look at an extremely simple order-entry system and includes a few of the more common lookups like customer address information. We won't make this a full-featured application because even a small order-entry system could easily consume all of the space in a book this size.

The next section looks at some of the requirements for creating remote database access components. We'll talk about some of the problems that you can avoid by creating a robust component at the outset. This section will also discuss some of the elements that this type of component should always include. This section won't include any troubleshooting information; we'll discuss that in the "Quick Fixes for Remote Databases" section of the chapter.

Creating the component shell comes next. Obviously, getting the component configured correctly will avoid a lot of wasted time down the road. We'll look at some of the designers as your disposal for making database development easier. Visual Basic has a lot to offer in this area — database management is probably one of the tasks that Visual Basic best performs.

Database components tend to become very complex very quickly. The fourth section contains tips and hints on how you can reduce the complexity of the components that you create, simultaneously making them more reliable and efficient. We'll also talk about how complexity is often the cause of serious problems when it comes to database integrity and getting information to the database within a reasonable amount of time.

The final section shows you how to write the code required for this component. We'll look at both the client access issues and the database update problems that you'll face. It's important to understand that the features that we'll be placing in one component are usually found in several components of a large project. However, we won't discuss issues like coordination between multiple computers working with the same database in a cluster. While these problems do come up, the answers are usually too company specific (because each company has a custom configuration) to cover adequately within the small space of a single chapter.

Defining the SQL Server database

As with any application, the first thing that we'll need to do for this example is to define what we want the application to do. Normally, you'd do this as part of a complex specification document. We've all had to create design documents in the past, so I won't belabor the point of the importance of design documentation to creating a fully functional application in a minimum amount of time with the fewest number of bugs. This example will rely on Microsoft's DNA model to ensure that we get it put together in the least amount of time, with a minimum of problems, and with even fewer bugs.

 Chapter 8 contains a wealth of information about Microsoft's Distributed interNetwork Architecture (DNA) model and why the model is important for application development today. As you create more complex distributed applications, the benefit of understanding the DNA model becomes clearer. We won't talk much about the DNA model in this chapter, so you'll want to be sure to read Chapter 8 before spending much time with this example if your knowledge of DNA is limited.

Because you can't depend on seeing the application as a single entity anymore, it is imperative that you understand how the application works from a design perspective. Even using just two machines, as we'll do for this example, makes it much more difficult to see the application in action than in the days when everything resided on one desktop. As a result, monolithic applications don't work anymore. Modularity has taken on a new level of importance, which will become apparent as the chapter progresses.

The main reason that you'd use any component programming approach like COM+ is to ensure that you can move pieces of an application around without requiring any change to the application code. COM+ is all about application flexibility and the ability to write applications that don't depend on the ability to see the application as a whole. In fact, that's one of the main things that this example will demonstrate. The ability to place a component, which is part of a whole application, yet an independent part of that application, on a server and expect that an application will be able to access and use it is an important tenant of component programming.

Note   This example uses SQL Server 7.0. It isn't guaranteed to work with SQL Server 6.5, the version that ships with Visual Basic 6.0 Enterprise Edition. Chapter 1 tells you where to get the Visual Studio Option Pack, which includes a copy of SQL Server 7.0 Developer Edition. This version of SQL Server 7.0 will work fine for the example. Chapter 1 also tells you about the problems with installing and using SQL Server 6.5. In most cases, you'll find that upgrading to SQL Server 7.0 is one of the better ways to deal with those problems.

The following sections will help you to explore the definition for our example application. We'll look at two main application components: the tasks that the application will perform and the database used to store application data. The tasks define what the user will do with the data stored in the database, whereas the database design defines how the user will access the data. This section contains fairly complete database creation instructions that you can skip by looking at the field definitions provided in the tables. Make sure that you also define elements like the indexes used to keep the data in order and use the same field and table names as shown in the tables. The instructions are included to ensure that even developers with only a little database experience can work with the example.

An application task overview

As previously mentioned, the application that we'll create in this example is a very simple order-entry system. In this case, there are several sets of tasks that a user could perform, only a subset of which will actually appear in the example. The following list summarizes the types of tasks that a simple order-entry system normally performs from the user perspective. (Other tasks are occurring in the background.)

✦ Add new orders

✦ Edit an order

✦ Remove an order

✦ View the status of an order

✦ Print completed order forms

✦ Browse a list of orders

✦ Add new customers

✦ Edit customer information

✦ Remove a customer

✦ Perform various types of database maintenance

Defining what tasks you want the application to perform is only the first step. Now we have to divide each of those tasks into three elements as defined by the DNA description that I mentioned earlier. For example, the task of adding a new order could be divided into these three elements:

✦ **Client:** For this particular task, you'd need to display a form containing a series of fields for each field in the database. You'd need to check with the business logic tier to determine which fields the user is allowed to see. In addition, there might be special considerations, like list box entries, that the user isn't allowed to use and thus you wouldn't need to display. After the form is filled out, this client tier would check the results of the input before sending the data off to the business logic tier. This code would perform generic checks like the ranges of numbers or perhaps matching ZIP code to city and state. This is the only part of the application that will execute on the client machine for this example.

✦ **Business Logic:** There are a variety of things that you'd need to perform at this tier, depending on the size of your business. Our example will only use this tier to interface with the database management system (DBMS). However, a larger example might send a message to the company's inventory control system and check for product availability. As part of the order entry process, the business logic might assign a status or availability code to the order. The inventory control system would ask the shipping department to send the part if it's available or manufacturing to create the part if the warehouse is currently out of stock. In short, creating the order sets off a chain of events that your business logic would need to track to ensure that the order gets fulfilled.

✦ **Back-end processing:** Our example will use SQL Server for the DBMS, but the same idea will work with other products. The back-end processing element could even be a mainframe. The point is that the back-end processing element normally manages the data required to make your business work. Many people think of data as something that humans consume, but it's also needed by your applications. For example, the user may never see some of the status codes assigned to each order in the database, but those codes will be used by the various application components to make decisions automatically. It's important to understand that the back-end processing element refers to all data, no matter what form it takes or where it resides.

An overview of the database

In this case, our example application is relatively straightforward, but the database management part of the equation requires some additional explanation. The task list in the previous section makes it clear that a single table database won't do the job of storing the data that we need to manage. Minimally, we'll need a set of four tables for the example order entry application. Anyone working on database applications for any length of time knows that there are few, if any, database applications that can work with just one table and still provide efficient data access. Table 13-1 provides a name for each table in the database and defines its purpose.

	Table 13-1 **Tables in the Order Entry System**	
Name	***Description***	
Client	Contains a list of the clients and their contact information. Obviously, this is a simplistic view, but will work for a small order-entry system. Larger order-entry systems contain additional information like the client's current credit rating and pointers to past purchases. It might even include a hierarchy of contacts within the client company.	
Catalog	You need to know what you're selling before you can sell it. This example will use a small static table to list the items for sale. In a larger order-entry system, the catalog might be updated by the inventory control system to show only the items that meet a specific set of criteria like being in stock at the time of order.	
Orders	This table contains the one-time order information like a pointer to the client asking for the material and a method of payment. A more complex order-entry system might include status information for the order. In even larger systems, the order might be archived after fulfillment so that your company could track client buying habits.	
Items	A list of the items that the client has ordered from the catalog, along with the quantity of each item ordered. This is the lowest level table and it is similar in any order-entry system. The bottom line is that no matter how complex the rest of the order-entry system is, the whole process ends up listing items that you can supply to the customer and an indication of the client's need for those items.	

Note   I'm taking a couple of short cuts here that you wouldn't normally take with an order-entry system. For example, the Client table is normally divided into several related tables to ensure that you have enough flexibility for future needs. A client may have several addresses or you might need to accommodate several contacts for a single company. In this case, I'm using what amounts to a flat-file database for the client information. I've made every attempt to ensure that the shortcuts that I've taken with the database design won't affect the real-world perspective that I'm trying to maintain throughout the example.

An in-depth view of the individual tables

Now that you have a better idea of what the four tables will be used for, let's discuss the fields in each table. Remember that the purpose of this example is to create a simple order-entry system of the type that a small company would use, but one that could be expanded for a larger company's needs. In addition, we'll spend quite a bit of time looking at how various components can use MTS to ensure that the data gets from one end of the application to the other. The actual mechanics of the database are secondary in this example to the mechanics of the MTS-enabled components.

The client database is nothing more than a simple contact database with some order entry information thrown in for good measure. Table 13-2 provides a description of the Client table and the fields that it contains.

Note
The Nulls column of Table 13-2 contains two values. If you Check the Nulls column in the table definition, it means that Nulls are allowed in that field. You'd only allow Null values if the data in that field isn't absolutely essential to the operation of the database application. For example, not everyone has a middle name, so that information isn't crucial. On the other hand, the Not checked value indicates that the user has to enter a value for that field. This is especially important for key values, but is also important for field values that could affect the business logic of your application.

Table 13-2 Client Table Schema				
Column Name	*Datatype*	*Size*	*Nulls*	*Default*
CustomerID	Char	5	Not checked	
FirstName	Char	40	Not checked	
MiddleInitial	Char	1	Checked	
LastName	Char	40	Not checked	
Title	Char	40	Checked	'Owner'
Company	Char	40	Checked	
Address1	Char	50	Not checked	
Address2	Char	50	Checked	
City	Char	50	Not checked	
State	Char	2	Not checked	'WI'
ZIP	Char	10	Not checked	
Country	Char	40	Checked	'United States'
Telephone1	Char	13	Checked	
Telephone2	Char	13	Checked	
LastContact	DateTime	8	Not checked	

SQL Server 7.0 and above supports the ANSI NULL instead of the NULL value supported by previous versions. What this means to you as a developer is that you'll need to pay close attention to the upgrade information for SQL Server should you decide to move any SQL Server 6.5 project to SQL Sever 7.0. You may also need to modify your code, so be sure that you consider all potential changes.

Notice that I use a Char type for the CustomerID field. You'll find that all of the ID fields in this example use the Char type, even though many developers use an Int type in real-world databases. There are several reasons for this choice. The most important is flexibility. An Int field is limited to numbers alone. I could use a combination of numbers and letters for the ID fields should the need arise. The Char type is also less ambiguous than using Int. Depending on which version of Visual Basic you use, the value of an Int varies. Add to this mix the use of Visual C++ or other languages to access the component, and you have the potential for a real mess.

Of course, every design decision has a cost. There are some disadvantages to using the Char type as well. The most important problem is search time. It takes longer to search a Char type field than an Int type field. To gain the flexibility that a Char field provides, you have to give up some speed. The Char type also requires more space on disk than the Int type. Obviously, in today's world of huge hard drive arrays, the disk space concern is less important.

The Catalog table shown in Table 13-3 is another area where we're going to cheat a little for this example. In this case, it's not the format of the table that will differ from a standard database, but the content of that table. In this case, we'll use a very simple static table, to reduce the complexity of the application. Normally, you'd need some method for users to add or subtract catalog entries, and then track which catalog items are actually available for sale at any given time. Depending on the kind of database that you're setting up, the catalog may consist of items that are only sold during certain times of the year, like heavy coats near the end of summer, through fall, and during part of the winter. Our example application won't consider many of these complexities, but you'll need to consider them as part of a production application.

Table 13-3
Catalog Table Schema

Column Name	Datatype	Size	Nulls	Default
ProductID	Char	5	Not checked	
ProductName	Char	50	Not checked	
Price	Money	N/A	Not checked	
OnHand	Int	N/A	Checked	0

The Orders table shown in Table 13-4 merely tracks which order numbers belong to a particular client. Notice that it doesn't repeat the information found in the Client table because this information already appears in that table. However, the Client table only contains the information of the person placing the order, not the receiver of the order. In many cases, the shipping address will be different than the address of the Client contact, so we need to provide an additional set of fields for this purpose. You could automatically set both sets of fields to the same values to save data entry time when the addresses match. Fields missing from this table include normal business requirements like method of payment and the date agreed upon for delivery. These fields aren't all that important in the context of this example, but you'd need to include them with a production system.

	Table 13-4 Orders Table Schema			
Column Name	**Datatype**	**Size**	**Nulls**	**Default**
OrderID	Char	5	Not checked	
CustomerID	Char	5	Not checked	
FirstName	Char	40	Not checked	
MiddleInitial	Char	1	Checked	
LastName	Char	40	Not checked	
Title	Char	40	Checked	'Owner'
Company	Char	40	Checked	
Address1	Char	50	Not checked	
Address2	Char	50	Checked	
City	Char	50	Not checked	
State	Char	2	Not checked	'WI'
ZIP	Char	10	Not checked	
Telephone1	Char	13	Checked	
Telephone2	Char	13	Checked	

The final table for this database is the Item table shown in Table 13-5. This table contains a list of the items ordered by the client. Notice that the Price field is repeated from the Catalog table. The order entry database needs to reflect the price of a product at the time that the order was completed, not the current price of the product. Obviously, there will be times when you need to repeat information within a database for historical purposes, even though this practice is normally frowned upon.

Table 13-5 Item Table Schema				
Column Name	**Datatype**	**Size**	**Nulls**	**Default**
ItemID	Char	5	Not checked	
OrderID	Char	5	Not checked	
ProductID	Char	5	Not checked	
Quantity	Int	N/A	Not checked	1
Price	Money	N/A	Not checked	

Now that we have all of the tables defined, it's time to look at how they'll interact. Figure 13-1 shows how the primary keys and foreign keys of the various tables allow the order-entry system to work. We'll create indexes for each of these primary keys in the section that follows. For now, all you need to know is that the tables are designed to interact with each other. Although we won't use all of the interactions for the example program, a model like the one in Figure 13-1 is very important when working with any database project because it helps to keep the various data interactions in view. Large databases with lots of tables can quickly become so complex that you really can't see what the data is doing without a model of this type.

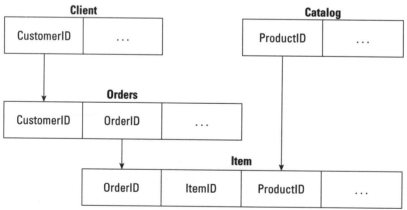

Figure 13-1: It's important to model the interactions between the various tables in a database application.

All of the relationships in Figure 13-1 are one to many. For example, one client can have many orders and each order can have many items within it. As you can see, this is a fairly standard database setup — there isn't anything too unusual to consider from a data-handling perspective if you've worked with database applications in the past.

Creating the database and associated tables

It's finally time to create the database and associated tables. In this section, we'll define the database itself, create a database structure, assign security, and, finally, create the required database indexes. We've already looked at the design of the database and associated tables in the previous sections, so I won't be covering that issue again. In fact, in some places, the procedures in this section have been shortened with the idea that creating these tables is a repetitive process in which only the schema changes.

After you've finished creating a database in SQL Server (step one of the process that we'll look at in this chapter), you need design the elements within it (the remaining three steps that I talked about in the previous paragraph). There are actually four steps in the design process (at least for this simple example). First, we'll need to create all of the tables used to store data. Next, we need to create the fields within those tables that the user will need to store the various kinds of order entry data. Third, we'll need to assign permissions to access the database. Without these permissions, no one will be able to access the database and enter data into it (except the system administrator, of course). Finally, we'll provide some indexes to order the data for display.

Now that you have some idea of what we're going to do, let's look at the process in more detail. The following sections of the chapter will help you to create the OrderEntry database, define the various tables that it contains, add security to those tables, and, finally, create indexes that will be used to interact with the tables.

Defining the OrderEntry database

As previously mentioned, the first thing that we need to do before any database design can take place is to create the database itself. The following procedure assumes that you have the Enterprise Edition of Visual Studio or Visual Basic, with SQL Server 7.0 Developer Edition installed. I also assume that you've set up any security required to access both the database server and the SQL Server installation.

Note   Your screen may or may not match the screen shots shown in this section of the chapter. I used a Windows 2000 Server and the version of SQL Server 6.5 Developer Edition that comes with the Visual Studio package for this example. If you're using a different version of Windows or a different configuration of SQL Server, your screen will most likely look different than mine. In addition, this chapter assumes that you've created a clean test installation of SQL Server on your server. Finally, the test application will always access the database over a network, which is what you'll need to do to check central file access.

1. Open SQL Server Enterprise Manager. You'll see a SQL Server Enterprise Manager window similar to the one shown in Figure 13-2. This is where you'll perform all management functions with SQL Server, including designing databases for use by clients. Notice that the figure shows the tree expanded, with the Databases folder selected. We'll use the Databases folder regularly as the example progresses. The first thing that we need to do is create a new database.

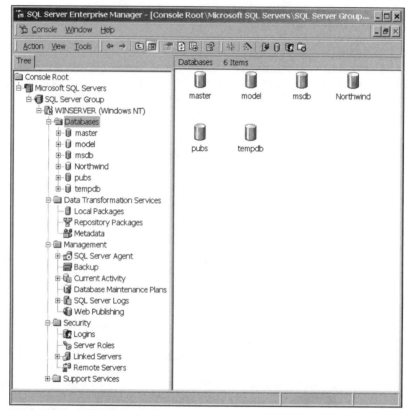

Figure 13-2: Microsoft SQL Server Enterprise Manager allows you to design and manage databases on your database server.

2. Right-click the Databases folder, and then select the New Database. . . option on the Context menu. You'll see the Database Properties dialog box shown in Figure 13-3. As you can see, creating the new database will require several steps, including defining the name of the file used to store the database and the location used to store the file on the hard drive. We'll also have to specify a number of other options like the initial size of the database file and whether we want the file to automatically grow in size.

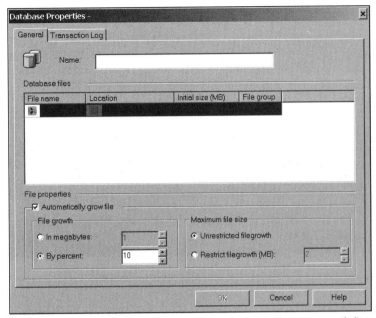

Figure 13-3: The Database Properties dialog box allows you to define the characteristics of a new database.

3. Type the name of your database in the Name field. I used OrderEntry for the sample application. Notice that SQL Server Enterprise Manager automatically provides a value for the File name and Location fields. It assigns an initial size of 1MB for the file and assigns it to the PRIMARY file group. We'll accept the entries in the File name, Location, and File group fields for this example.

4. Type the initial size of the database file in the Initial size (MB) field. I used 15 for this example because our test data won't be very large. Obviously, a production database will be much larger, and you'll need to provide additional space for growth while keeping the available space on your server in mind.

Tip

SQL Server Enterprise Manager automatically selects the Automatically grow file option for you. This is a good option to use if the database in question is the only one on the server and you have lots of space on the hard drive. However, this option can cause problems if you have several databases on the same server, lots of users accessing the databases, and a space limit on the hard drive. In this case, you'd want to ensure that the initial database size is large enough to hold the information that you need and either severely restrict the amount that the file can grow or uncheck the Automatically grow file option and resize the database manually as needed.

5. Click the Transaction Log tab and you'll see a Database Properties –OrderEntry dialog box similar to the one shown in Figure 13-4. Notice that SQL Server Enterprise Manager has provided a default set of values. The File name and Location field values will work fine for this example. However, if you normally save the transaction logs in a different location from the database (to use disk space more efficiently and, in some cases, to improve performance), you'll want to change the Location field as a minimum.

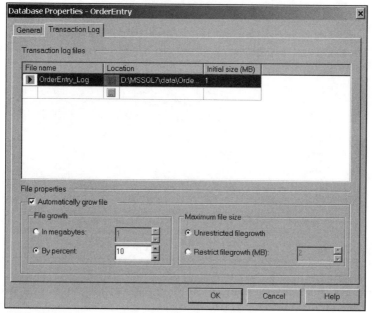

Figure 13-4: The Transaction Log tab allows you to set the size of the transaction log used to track database activity.

6. Change the Initial size (MB) field to 5 so that there's plenty of space to store transactions for the example database.

7. Click OK. You'll see the OrderEntry database added to the Databases folder.

Adding tables to the OrderEntry database

Now, we're ready to start designing the database. Let's begin by adding tables to our database as shown in the following procedure.

Note The system administrator account (sa) can access every part of SQL Server, including any new databases that you create.

1. Open the OrderEntry database hierarchy and you'll see a series of folders similar to those shown in Figure 13-5. Notice that the Tables folder is selected in the left pane and that the system files appear in the right pane. All of these system tables are used to maintain the database.

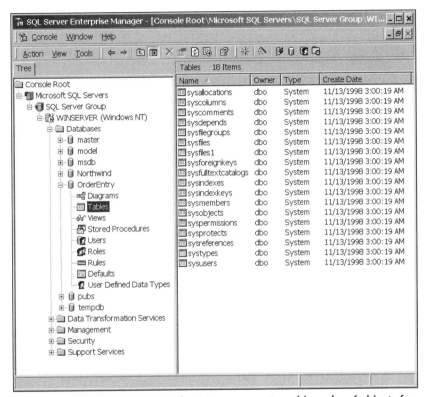

Figure 13-5: SQL Server Enterprise Manager creates a hierarchy of objects for each new database including system tables.

2. Right-click on the Tables folder and choose New Table. . . from the Context menu. A Choose Name dialog box will display.

3. Type a name for the table. If you're working on the first table for this example, you'd type Client. Click OK. You'll see a New Table dialog box (table design window) similar to the one shown in Figure 13-6.

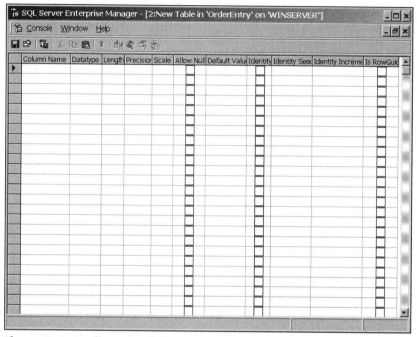

Figure 13-6: You'll need to define a set of characteristics for each field of the tables that you create using this dialog box.

Note

The New Table dialog box is where you'll type in the field names, decide on their data type and size, and assign them a default value (if required). The Allow Nulls column determines whether the field requires a value. A checked field allows null entries (no value). Tables 13-2 through 13-5 show the fields that we'll use for each table in this example. All you need to do is type the values for a particular table into the Manage Tables dialog box. A blank value in the Default column means that you don't need to type anything in the Default column of the Manage Tables dialog box.

4. Type the field entries for one of the tables listed in Tables 13-2 through 13-5. You won't need to worry about the Identity, Identity Seed, Identity Increment, or Is RowGuid fields for this example.

5. Right-click each primary key entry, and then choose Set Primary Key from the context menu. Figure 13-1 shows which fields are primary keys for each table. Setting the primary keys will help us link the tables together later in the database creation process.

6. Repeat Steps 2 through 5 for each of the tables.

Creating a diagram for the OrderEntry database

At this point, we've created the database and four tables. In addition, SQL Server Enterprise Manager has created some resources for us automatically. For example, when you select a primary key for a table, SQL Server Enterprise Manager automatically creates an index based on that primary key for you.

There are still several problems yet to tackle. A major problem is that there are no relationships set up between the four tables. While each table has a primary key that orders the table and allows for unique searches, the tables lack foreign keys that associate them with other tables.

SQL Server 7.0 provides a diagramming capability that SQL Server 6.5 lacks. We'll use the diagramming capability to set up the foreign keys for the OrderEntry database. You can also use this feature to create new tables, add columns to the tables, and perform other design tasks. In many cases, however, creating the tables first, and then using the diagram to add relations appears to work faster. The following steps show you how.

1. Close all table design windows that you may have open. Answer Yes when asked if you want to save the table information. Closing the table design windows ensures that any changes that you've made to the tables will be saved.

2. Right-click the OrderEntry\Diagrams folder in SQL Server Enterprise Manager and choose New Database Diagram from the context menu. You'll see a Welcome to the Create Database Diagram Wizard dialog box.

3. Click Next. You'll see a Select Tables to be Added dialog box like the one shown in Figure 13-7. Notice that this dialog box contains all four of the tables that we've designed so far.

4. Click Add four times to add all four tables to the Tables to add to diagram field. If we had created relationships between the tables during the initial creation process, you could have selected the Catalog and Client tables, and then checked the Add related tables automatically option. You would have needed to set the How many levels of related tables field to 2 because there are two levels of relations below the Client table.

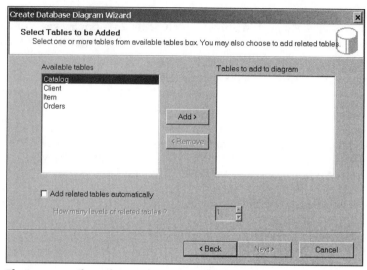

Figure 13-7: The Select Tables to be Added dialog box allows you to add tables to the new diagram.

5. Click Next. You'll see a Completing the Create Database Diagram Wizard dialog box similar to the one shown in Figure 13-8. You can use this dialog box to verify that you've added all of the required tables to the diagram. This dialog box also allows you to verify whether associated tables were added. If the number of tables on this dialog doesn't appear correct, you can click Back and change the settings on the Select Tables to be Added dialog box.

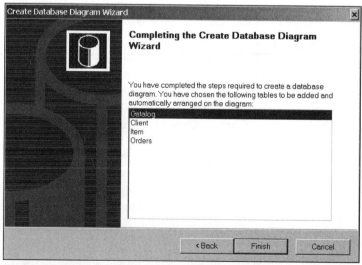

Figure 13-8: Always check the list of tables that will appear in the diagram before you create the diagram.

6. Click Finish. SQL Server Enterprise Manager will create the diagram, add the tables to it, and then display a message stating that the tables have been added to the diagram and arranged.

7. Click OK to clear the message and view the diagram. Figure 13-9 shows a typical example of what this diagram will look like. Notice that the tables are in alphabetical order. Clicking Arrange tables (last button on the toolbar) will always place them this way if there are no relationships established at the time.

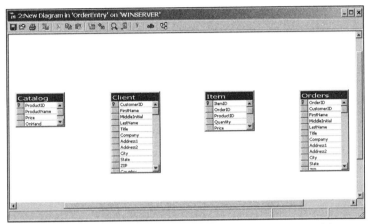

Figure 13-9: This is an example of the display that you should see after the tables from the OrderEntry database are added to a new diagram.

8. Click on the ProductID column in the Catalog table and drag it to the Item table. To make this work, the ProductID column in the Catalog table must be selected (shown in an alternative color). You must point to the ProductID column in the Item Table. You should see a Create Relationship dialog box similar to the one shown in Figure 13-10. Notice that this dialog box shows the two tables and the appropriate column in each table. The Catalog table should appear in the Primary key table field, while the Item table appears in the Foreign key table. After you've verified the information, click OK. You'll see a relationship line drawn on screen from the Catalog table to the Item table.

9. Repeat Step 8 for all of the relationships shown in Figure 13-1.

10. Save the diagram. The example uses a diagram name of OrderEntryDesign, but you can use any name that you like. You'll see a Save dialog box similar to the one shown in Figure 13-11. This dialog box gives you the option of saving the table changes directly to the database, removing the changes (by clicking No), or saving the changes to a text file for later incorporation into the database. In most cases, you'll select Yes to save the changes to the database.

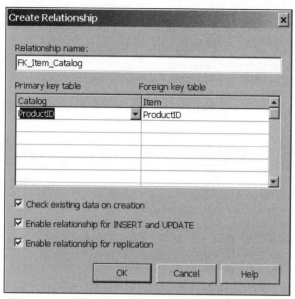

Figure 13-10: The Create Relationship dialog box allows you to set a relationship between two tables.

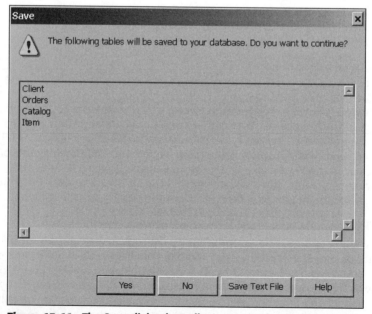

Figure 13-11: The Save dialog box allows you to choose how the relationships that you created are to be saved.

11. Click Arrange tables. The diagram shown in Figure 13-12 may not look precisely like Figure 13-1, but you can see that the relationships are the same. If you look at the relationship line closely, you'll see a gold key at the end of the line for the table containing the primary key. A silver key shows the table that has the foreign key.

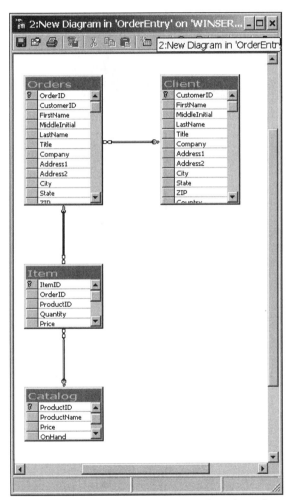

Figure 13-12: The relationship lines show how the tables in a database are connected.

At this point, all of the relationships in the OrderEntry database are defined. Using the visual aid provided by SQL Server 7.0 is much easier than the techniques required to create relationships in older versions of SQL Server. Keep the OrderEntryDesign diagram open so that we can use it to perform other database design tasks like creating indexes.

OrderEntry database security concerns

There are two tasks left to perform before we can start creating a connection to our database. The first task is to set the security for our database. To do that, we'll need to make changes to the Roles folder in the OrderEntry database (see Figure 13-5). For those of you who are used to working with SQL Server 6.5, two separate folders have replaced the Groups/Users folder. Users now appear in the Users folder, while groups appear in the Roles folder.

We need three roles for this database: Administrators, Users, and Public. The Public role is created by default, so we don't need to add it. Right-click Roles, then choose New Database Role from the context menu. You'll see a Database Role Properties – New Role dialog box similar to the one shown in Figure 13-13. Type Administrators in the Name field, and then click Add. You'll see Administrators added to the Roles hierarchy. Perform this same set of steps for both the Users role.

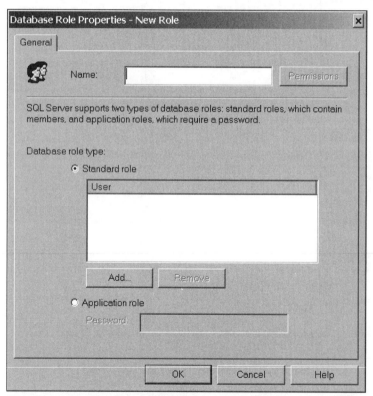

Figure 13-13: The Database Role Properties – New Role dialog box allows you to create a new role for your application.

Tip

It's important to remember that there are many levels of security used by a COM+ application to ensure that your data remains secure. Adding security to the database is just one part of a much larger overall picture. You'll also want to read about the security provided by Windows 2000 and COM+ in Chapter 7 as part of understanding the security measures in place for the example application. The easiest way to look at security under Windows 2000 is that every object, no matter what type of object it is, has some type of security attached to it. Even though different types of objects may employ a variety of security methodologies, all are protected to some extent. Of course, it's equally important to realize that no security scheme is perfect. Monitoring of your security measures is always essential because crackers are notorious for finding holes in supposedly perfect security measures.

After you create a role, you have to add permissions to it. A permission tells what the users in a specific role can do with the database. Right-click the Administrators role, and then choose Properties. You'll see a Database Role Properties – Administrators dialog box that looks similar to the dialog box in Figure 13-13. In this case, however, the Name field is grayed out (you can see the name of the role, but can't change it) and the Properties pushbutton is enabled. Click Properties and you'll see a Database Role Properties – Administrators dialog box similar to the one shown in Figure 13-14.

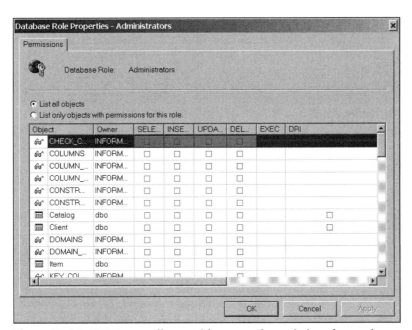

Figure 13-14: SQL Server offers a wide range of permissions for precise control of database access.

The public at large only needs to view the contents of the database. We really don't want them to change anything, so they only get the SELECT permission, which allows them to view the records. Part of the coding process will tie their CustomerID into the access that they get, so all that they can see are their records. This is useful for enabling the customer to see the current status of orders, without exposing the other data that the database contains. Users need to be able to view and modify the records. They also need to add new records and delete old ones, so users as a group get the SELECT, INSERT, UPDATE, and DELETE permissions. Because users can't change the schema of the tables nor back the data up, users can get work done with the database, but can't make any changes that could damage the entire database or compromise the security of the data. Finally, the Administrator group requires full access to the user tables (versus the user and system tables), so they get all of the available permissions. You'll need to be careful handing out this privilege because anyone in the Administrator group will have full access to everything that the table has to offer.

Note   The Roles folder contains a number of predefined roles such as the database owner (dbo), who is a member of the special db_owner group that has complete access to the database, including system tables.

You also need to assign permissions to use the various scripts in the database. For example, if an administrator lacks access to the dt_adduserobject script, then the administrator can't add new users to the database, making the Administrator role somewhat useless for anyone who needs it. On the other hand, even though the User role does require fairly complete access to the user tables, it doesn't require the capability to add users, so you wouldn't check the EXEC option for the dt_adduserobject script in this case. You'll also want to use extreme care when handing out access to any of the system tables. In many cases, you'll need to hand out the SELECT permission to allow a user to execute a script, but you won't want to provide any of the other permissions.

Caution   When working with SQL Server 6.5, it was possible to assign new roles to the dbo. The dbo in SQL Server 7.0 should only be assigned to the db_owner and public roles. If you want to create special administrator roles, create new users and assign them to a role containing just the permissions that you want them to have. Modifying the dbo security settings can have undesired effects on database access (like making the database inaccessible).

Creating a role is just the first step in setting a user up for database access. Once you have the roles in place, you need to create logins that the user can use to access the database. I usually create one login for each special role that I plan to support in an application, plus one for each standard role. This means that the OrderEntry database would require a minimum of three logins, one for each of the roles defined earlier in this section of the chapter.

Standard role access logins depend on the situation. For example, there might be a situation when a dbo might require access to only the database that the dbo is responsible for maintaining, and not any of the other databases that SQL Server supports. In this case, a special login is the only way to ensure that the database remains secure. The following steps show you how to create a new set of logins for the OrderAccess database.

1. Right-click the Security\Logins folder in SQL Server Enterprise Manager and choose New Login from the context menu. You'll see a SQL Server Login Properties – New Login dialog box similar to the one shown in Figure 13-15. This dialog box allows you to choose the type of login that the user will perform. Using the Windows NT authentication option is usually more secure.

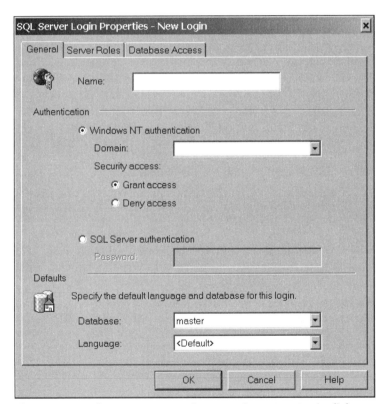

Figure 13-15: The SQL Server Login Properties – New Login dialog box allows you to create a special login for your database.

Note   If you choose to use the Windows NT authentication option, you'll also need to add an entry for the login to the Windows NT or Windows 2000 users list. SQL Server will attempt to access the entry from Windows NT or Windows 2000 security when you click OK in the SQL Server Login Properties – New Login dialog box. SQL Server Enterprise Manager will display an error message if it can't verify the name against the domain.

2. Type a name for the new login in the Name field. Using the name of the database provides an easy way to track logins. If you want separate logins for each of the major roles that a user could fulfill, you can add the name of the role to the database in order to create a unique login. The example will use OrderEntry Admin, OrderEntryUser, and OrderEntryPublic for the login names.

3. Select a domain from the Domain field if you're using Windows NT/2000 authentication, or select the SQL Server authentication option and type a password. The example uses SQL Server authentication for ease of demonstration purposes. You'll need to select a domain if you want to use Windows NT/2000 authentication rather than SQL Server authentication. Selecting a domain will automatically add the domain name to the Name field for you.

4. Select OrderEntry in the Database field. This allows the login to take the user right to the database in question, rather than to the master database, which is the default. A master database login allows you to work with all of the databases that you have permission to use; a specific database login is more secure and easier for the user. (You could also select a language, at this point, if your application supports more than one language.)

5. Click Database Access. You'll see a dialog similar to the one shown in Figure 13-16. This dialog allows you to grant access to the databases that the users can login to access. Because we're creating an application-specific login, the only database that you need to check is OrderEntry. If this were a general login, you'd need to decide which database to grant access to in addition to the master database. Notice that as soon as you check the OrderEntry option, the Database roles for 'OrderEntry' field becomes active.

6. Check the appropriate entries in the Database roles for 'OrderEntry' field. Every login requires Public access. The OrderEntryAdmin login will require access to the Administrators role and the OrderEntryUser login will require access to the Users role.

Tip   Selecting the Server Roles tab will allow you to add general SQL Server roles to a particular login. For example, you may also want to give the Administrators for an application-specific database access to the Setup Administrators role. In some cases, system-level access is required if you want the administrator to maintain certain database entities at a system level. Obviously, giving everyone the lowest level of access is one way to ensure that the database remains secure.

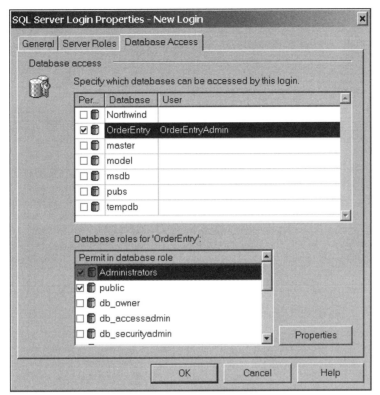

Figure 13-16: The Database Access tab determines which databases the user can access.

7. Click OK. SQL Server Enterprise Manager will create the new login for you.

8. Repeat Steps 1 through 7 for all three logins required for this example.

Creating the scripts

SQL Server will automatically generate scripts based on the selections that you've made so far. These scripts will allow you to access the database with relative ease in many situations, without a lot of additional programming. Even though you'll want to write custom code or use a designer to create the correct presentation within your Visual Basic application or component, it pays to generate the scripts for use during the initial design, code writing, and debugging process.

Creating the scripts is easy. Right-click the OrderEntry folder in SQL Server Enterprise Manager, and then choose All Tasks ⇨ Generate SQL Scripts from the context menu. You'll see the Generate SQL Scripts – <Server Name>\OrderEntry dialog box shown in Figure 13-17.

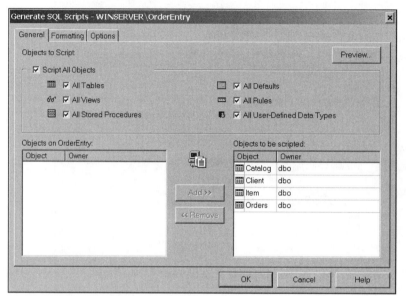

Figure 13-17: The Generate SQL Scripts dialog box will allow you to choose which objects to use when creating scripts.

As you can see, this dialog box provides options for generating scripts for quite a few different database objects. Because we haven't created all of these objects, we'll be able to save time by generating scripts for just the objects that we've created so far. In this case, all we need to generate scripts for is the All Tables and All Roles objects.

Now that you've selected some objects to script, you'll also want to select some formatting options. SQL Server Enterprise Manger always selects the common options for you, but there's at least one other formatting option that you should consider adding. Click Formatting and you'll see the dialog box shown in Figure 13-18. Notice the Include descriptive headers in the script files option. Clicking this option will increase the size of the script, but shouldn't affect script execution speed. This option also provides comments so that you can more easily figure out the automatically generated script code. Make sure that you check this option as shown in the figure.

Tip

If this is the first time that you've generated scripts for a new database, you may also want to select the Generate scripts for all dependent objects option to ensure that the scripts will work as anticipated. In some cases, SQL Server Enterprise Manager will fail to make a required change to a dependent script, causing the script to fail. This problem could lead you to believe that there's a problem in the database or your application code when there really isn't any problem to worry about.

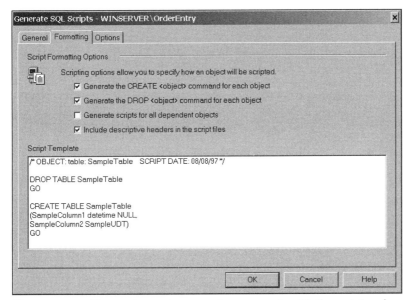

Figure 13-18: Always choose to generate comments with the script code.

SQL Server Enterprise Manager also provides some additional scripting options that you may want to consider, even though they're not required for this example. Click the Options tab and you'll see the dialog shown in Figure 13-19. Notice the options for scripting additional database objects. It's normally a good idea to script the database users and roles used for security purposes. You'll also want to script the indexes (including those automatically created for you by SQL server) and all of the keys for your database.

Click OK. SQL Server Enterprise Manager will ask where you want the scripts stored. The example uses the default directory and a filename of OrderEntry.SQL. Enter a filename and click Save. You'll see a Scripting in Progress dialog box while SQL Server Enterprise Manager creates the scripts for you. When the scripting process is complete, you should see a Scripting was completed successfully message box.

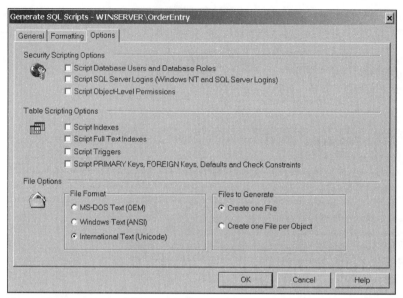

Figure 13-19: Some of the optional scripting tasks will make your setup more secure and easier to recover later.

OrderEntry database backup concerns

This chapter is showing you how to create a simple order entry database. If you lose the data, it's not going to be that big of a loss. However, losing the data in your production system is another matter. The data in a production system is worth more than the total cost of all of the systems that it runs on in most cases. Consider the time required to reenter the data if a system crash destroys the database, not to mention the business lost while the reentry process takes place. Of course, this assumes that you have a hard copy of the data to work with.

Regular data backups aren't an optional part of your application. You should plan to make daily backups as a minimum or even more often if the database or the amount of data entered each day is large. The reason is simple: It takes a lot less time to create a backup of your data than it does to recreate it later.

SQL Server provides a couple of different methods for backing up your data. The best method, at least from an administrator perspective, is to stop the three services associated with SQL Server and then backup the entire MSSQL directory (unless your data is stored somewhere else). This ensures that you'll get all of the data backed up and can restore the data later with minimum effort. Of course, this solution won't work in a lot of cases. For one thing, stopping the three SQL Server services makes the databases that it manages inaccessible. If your company runs 24 hours a day, then you won't be able to shut these services down.

There's another way to create a backup of your database — directly while the services are still running. Look in the Management folder shown in Figure 13-5. You'll see a Backup folder as shown in Figure 13-20. Within the Backup folder is a list of the backup devices and any database backups that you've created.

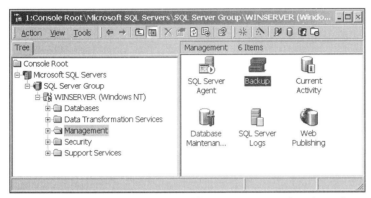

Figure 13-20: The Management folder contains a Backup icon that you can use to create backups of your system.

You need to create a backup device before you can perform the backup process. Don't confuse these backup devices with an actual piece of hardware like a tape drive. SQL Server will allow you to backup your data to a directory on the hard drive or to a physical piece of hardware. The default device provided with SQL Server will send the backup to \MSSQL7\BACKUP folder. Creating a new backup device is easy. Just right-click the Backup folder and then choose New Backup Device from the context menu. You'll see a Backup Device Properties – New Device dialog box similar to the one shown in Figure 13-21.

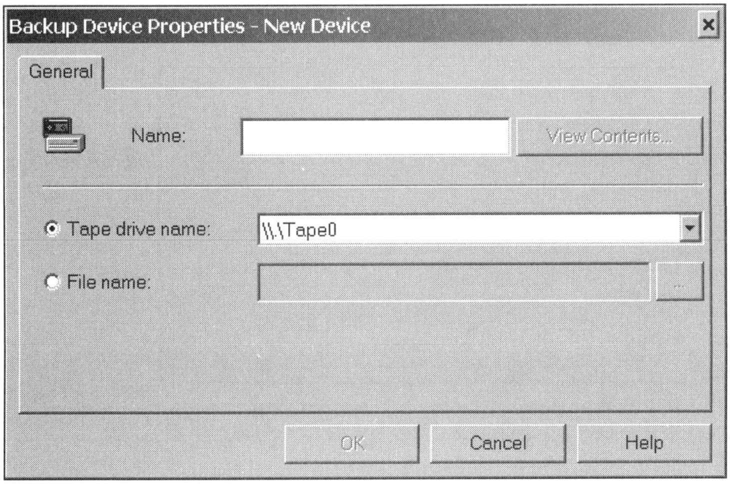

Figure 13-21: The first step in backing up your database is to create a backup device.

Notice that this dialog box allows you to choose between a disk backup device and a tape backup device. All you need to do is enter the name of a new backup device, and then supply a device location. Type the name of the backup device — I'll use MyBackup for this chapter, but you can use any name that you want. Placing the backup in the \MSSQL\BACKUP folder will work just fine. After you've chosen either tape or file and a backup location, click OK. SQL Server Enterprise Manager will create the backup device for you.

After you have a backup device, creating the backup is easy. Right-click the database that you want to backup, and then choose All Tasks ➪ Backup Database from the context menu. You'll see a SQL Server Backup – <Database Name> dialog box similar to the one shown in Figure 13-22.

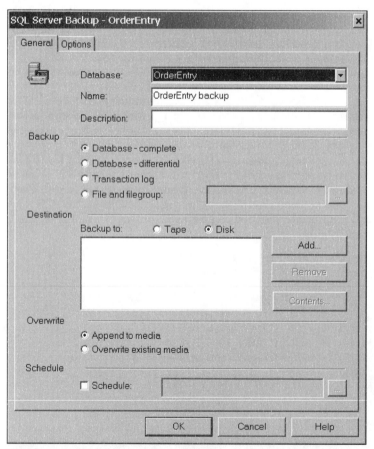

Figure 13-22: The SQL Server Backup dialog box lets you set the parameters for backing up your database.

Notice that there isn't any way to select all of the databases for backup; you'll have to back them up one at a time. Select the database that you want to back up from the Database drop-down list box, type a name for the backup in the Name field, and provide a description in the Description field. You'll need to choose the type of backup that you want to perform. In many cases, unless the database is very large, using the Database – complete option is the only way to ensure that you have a perfect backup of the database.

Providing a backup device comes next. Click Add in the Destination group and you'll see a Choose Backup Destination dialog box similar to the one shown in Figure 13-23. Choose a backup device or a location on the hard drive, and then click OK. The name of the backup device will appear in the Backing to field of the SQL Server Backup dialog box.

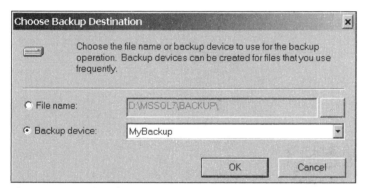

Figure 13-23: The Choose Backup Destination dialog box allows you to choose where the backup data will go.

There are two additional options on the General tab of the SQL Server Backup – <Database Name> dialog box. You can choose to append the backup to the current file, which means that the file will keep growing until you overwrite it, or you can overwrite the existing backup. Normally, it's a good idea to overwrite the existing backup and make a tape backup of the whole drive if you're working with a small-to medium-sized database and you're creating a complete backup. The option is to create a scheduled backup. If you want to use this method, select the Schedule option, and then click the ellipses button to set up a time and date.

Click the Options tab and you'll see a dialog box similar to the one shown in Figure 13-24. It's interesting that the Verify backup upon completion option isn't selected by default because you should always verify the backup. There are also options on this tab for ejecting a tape immediately after the backup is complete, removing inactive entries from the transaction log, setting a backup expiration date, and adding a name and description to the backup media. Most of these additional options are for tape backups and you should consider them if you plan to use a tape backup for your database.

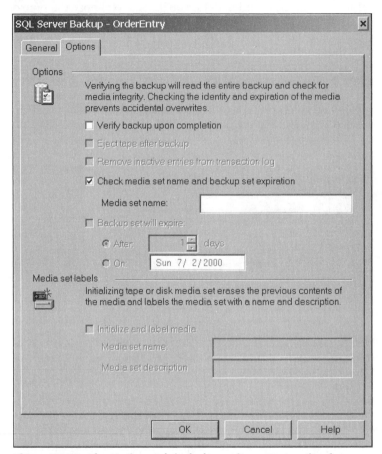

Figure 13-24: The Options tab includes an important option for verifying your data after you back it up.

Click OK and the backup will start. You'll see a backup message for some time, then the backup message will change to a success message. Click OK to clear the success message. All you need to do to complete the offline backup part of this process is to backup the data in the backup device file. The backup device file has a BAK extension and the same name as the backup device that you created. You'll find this device file in the directory that you chose for the backup.

Creating the OrderEntry database indexes

Our final task is to set up the required indexes for our table. An index allows the user to see the table in sorted order. All you need to do is right-click the Client table entry, and then choose All Tasks ➪ Manage Indexes. . . to open the Manage Indexes dialog box shown in Figure 13-25.

Figure 13-25: The Manage Indexes dialog box allows you to create indexes for your tables to keep them in sorted order.

We'll create two indexes for our Client table — the number that you actually need to set in a given circumstance depends on how many ways you need to see the data ordered. Click New and you'll see a Create New Index dialog box similar to the one shown in Figure 13-26. Notice that this dialog box contains a complete list of column names for the current table, options on how to build the database, like whether the index should only contain unique values, and the order in which the columns should appear.

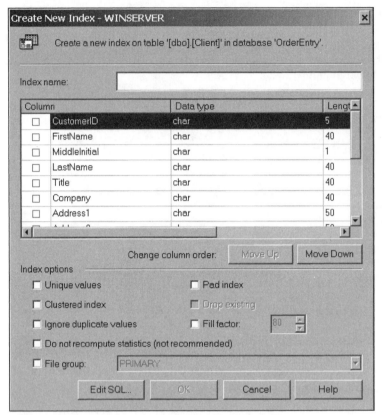

Figure 13-26: The Create New Index dialog box allows you to choose the columns and sort order for the index.

Type LastName in the Index Name field. Check the LastName, FirstName, and MiddleInitial fields. Highlight the LastName field, then click Move Up to ensure that it appears as the first field. Click OK.

Tip

As part of the process of creating primary keys for the tables, SQL Server will automatically generate one index for you. This index is for the primary key. For example, when you look at the Client table, there will already be a predefined index for the CustomerID field.

The second index is built by using the same technique. Type ZIPCode in the Index field. Choose the ZIP, LastName, FirstName, and MiddleInitial columns (use Move Up and Move Down to ensure that the columns are in the correct order). Click OK to close the Create New Index dialog box, and then Close to close the Manage Indexes dialog box.

The n-tier view of the project

To this point, we've taken a detailed look at the database and the various requirements for manipulating it. We really haven't looked at what's required to create the application for this example. By now you should realize that even the simplest COM+ application will be an order of magnitude more complex than other applications that you've created in the past. This means that you need to consider whether COM+ is really the solution that you need. If your goal is to create a simple application for working with data on a LAN, you'll probably be better off using one of these older approaches. In many cases, especially when using the new OLE-DB features in Visual Basic, the work required to create a simple LAN-based application is almost trivial.

The application in this chapter looks like a lot of work, and it is. However, it won't take long to realize that our sample application has many advantages over the simple applications of the past. Most notably, you'll see that accessing the data from any location is possible because of the arrangement of components servicing the application. The data is also more secure and access is more reliable. In short, all of the preparation time and coding will pay dividends that you can't easily equate to the work required to produce an old technology application. The COM+ application that we'll produce in this chapter really is a new kind of application that needs to be judged on its own merits.

We're going to take an n-tier approach to application development in this chapter that's very similar to what you saw in Chapter 8. In fact, the application overview shown in Figure 13-27 should look very familiar by now. No, you won't be required to run multiple servers to test this application — you could theoretically test it on a single machine. However, to get the full benefit out of the example and to really test the resulting code you need to test the application on two machines as shown in the diagram.

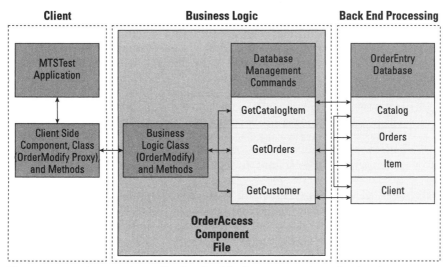

Figure 13-27: The sample application for this chapter uses the n-tier development approach.

Tip

There are some situations in which you may want to start out with one development machine, and then move to two machines as development progresses. A single-machine approach lets you test the application logic without any chance of outside interference from errant network connections and the like. In addition, a single-machine approach tends to hide some communication-related problems; allowing you to get the business logic in place for further testing. You must eventually test your application on a minimum of two machines because COM+ tends to hide some coding errors on a single-machine setup. For example, there was an error in the `CoCreateInstanceEx()` call in my original example that didn't show up with a single-machine setup. The problem only appeared when I moved to a two-machine (client and server) setup. In short, you can start developing your application on one machine to make things easy, but plan on using two machines for later development when working with COM+.

As you can see, the test application, MTSTest, and the client-side component will exist as separate files. MTSTest will use `CoCreateInstance()` to create a local copy of the client side component. The COrderRequest class methods will use `CoCreateInstanceEx()` to create a server-side copy of the server side component, OrderAccess. Within the OrderAccess file are the five classes that we'll use to implement business and database objects. COrderModify, which is the business object, will contain all of the methods required for the client to gain access to the data within the database. There's one database object class for each of the tables within the database. You'll see later in the chapter why we need this many classes. We would, in fact, need one class for every type of query required by the application and business logic. In other words, to execute a stored procedure, you need a separate class to perform that task.

Requirements for remote database components

Part of the problem with creating a remote database application is that most of us are used to thinking about applications in terms of the LAN. Even when there's a conscious decision to consider remote computing requirements, LAN thinking comes into play. For example, the idea that a connection won't be available for the user to work with often gets in the way of the design process because developers aren't used to considering this facet of design.

Unfortunately, not designing around some of the simple problems that you'll run across will cause just as many problems as missing a major design constraint like the lack of a connection. In many cases, small design problems produce subtle bugs that are difficult to trace because the developer often uses a desktop machine, rather than a laptop connected to the network through a dial-up Internet connection.

Unlike many of the other components that we've designed so far, a remote database component has to provide connectivity to the server for downloads. Attempting to fill a recordset with data using a ByVal variable just won't work. This means that while you can upload new records to the database by using individual records through MSMQ, you can't request a download from the server by using MSMQ. If a connection isn't available, the client-side component will need to use cached data or tell the user that the data isn't available. In short, you need to treat requests for data in a completely different way than you treat data uploads.

If you look back at the simple MSMQ example in Chapter 12, you'll notice that we marked the application and the interface for queuing. One way to handle the upload versus download problem is to include two separate interfaces within the component. The first would be marked as queued and would handle all of the data uploads like new records. The second wouldn't be marked as queued, meaning that it wouldn't work with MSMQ, and would handle client requests.

Even if you take this two-interface approach, there's a problem that we have yet to consider. Handling recordset downloads for the purpose of information is relatively easy because you can cache the recordset locally. New records aren't in the database yet, so caching them locally won't cause any problems either. However, how do you handle the situation when the user wants to edit an existing record? In this case, the data is already on the server and there's no locking mechanism that ensures that the user changes won't overwrite changes that someone else has made in the meantime. While there is a way to view data in disconnected mode and create new records, editing records should only occur with a live connection so that the usual record-locking mechanisms are in place.

Creating the component shell

Unlike many of the other components that we've created so far, this OrderAccess component will require quite a bit of setup. There's the usual amount of component setup, then we'll have to add a designer to access the OrderEntry database. A designer allows us to use graphical design techniques. Using the techniques in this section of the chapter will save you a substantial amount of coding later on.

Begin by creating an ActiveX DLL project. The example uses a project name of OrderAccess and a class name of OrderModify. As with all of the other COM+ components that we've created in the book, you'll want to set at least three of the properties in the QCOne – Project Properties dialog box. Make sure that the Threading Mode property is set to Single Threaded, that the Unattended Execution option is checked, and that you set the component up for Binary Compatibility after the first compile. In this way, you'll ensure that you know whether you're breaking any COM rules when you create future builds of the component.

Now we need to add a data environment to the component. The data environment shows the true magic of using Visual Basic for this type of component. Right-click OrderAccess in the Project window and then choose Add ➪ Data Environment from the context menu. Visual Basic will add a data environment to your component.

The example program uses a name of deOrderAccess for the data environment and connOrderAccess for the component. The following steps will help you to configure connOrderAccess.

Note
If you choose to use the code from the CD-ROM provided with this book, you must reconfigure the Data Link Properties dialog box for connOrderAccess to use the settings for your network. These configuration options are network specific and the component that I created for the example won't have the same server name as your network. After you reconfigure the Data Link Properties dialog box settings, you can recompile the component and install it on the server. The component should work without any additional code changes.

1. Right click connOrderAccess and choose Properties from the context menu. You'll see the Data Link Properties dialog box shown in Figure 13-28. This first dialog box allows you to select a database provider.

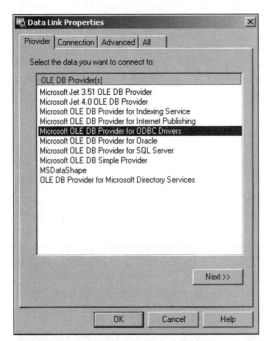

Figure 13-28: The first step in creating a connection is to choose a database provider.

2. Choose Microsoft OLE DB Provider for SQL Server, and then click Next. You'll see the Connection tab of the Data Link Properties dialog box as shown in Figure 13-29. This dialog box will allow you to configure options like the server name and database that you want to access. It also allows you to test the connection to ensure that it will work as anticipated.

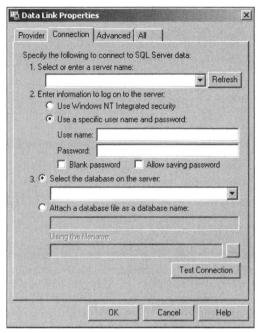

Figure 13-29: The second step in creating a connection is to set the server name and database name.

3. Choose the test server for your network in the Select or enter a server name field. Click Refresh if you don't see any servers in the list. Don't type the name of the server. If Visual Basic can't see the server now, it won't see the server when it's time to compile the component. You must correct any network problems before you proceed.

4. Type a username and password in the User name and Password fields. Use one of the usernames that we created earlier in the chapter or use the sa username and associated password.

5. Choose the OrderEntry database in the Select the database on the server field. If you don't see a list of databases, but you can access the server, it most likely means that you don't have proper access rights to SQL Server. Stop the procedure right now and correct any access problems before you proceed. If Visual Basic can't obtain a list of databases now, it won't be able to do so later.

6. Click Test Connection. You should see a Test connection succeeded message box. If you don't see this message box, then there's something wrong with your setup. Repeat Steps 3 through 5. Make sure that the username and password that you provided are correct.

7. Click OK to clear the Test connection succeeded message box, and then click OK again to save the connection settings.

At this point, we have a connection to the server, but no commands that tell the database to provide any information. The commands that you create will allow the component to grab data from the database in a specific way. The better you configure the commands, the easier it will be to write the component. In fact, there are at least a few situations when a correctly configured command can reduce the number of lines of code within the method to five. We'll see one of those instances in this example. The following steps will help you to create the first command for this example.

1. Right-click connOrderEntry and choose Add Command from the context menu. Visual Basic will add a new command to the database designer hierarchy. The example uses a command name of GetCatalogItem for this example, but you could use any name that you like.

2. Right-click GetCatalogItem and choose Properties from the context menu. You'll see the GetCatalogItem Properties dialog box shown in Figure 13-30. As you can see, this dialog box provides a number of ways to create a command. For example, you can use a stored procedure. The problem is that using a stored procedure will circumvent use of some COM+ features to protect the data — a better method of issuing a SQL statement and using the local component to manipulate the raw data.

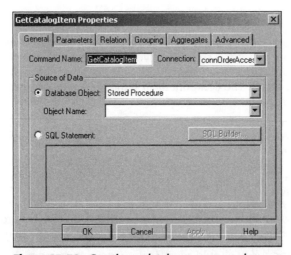

Figure 13-30: Creating a database command means creating a statement or accessing a predefined routine that will return data to the user.

3. Select the SQL Statement option, and then click SQL Builder. What you'll see are two dialog boxes similar to those shown in Figure 13-31. The Data View dialog box shows you what the database has to offer in the form of tables, views, and stored procedures. You can use any of these sources to create a command for your application. The Design dialog box shows the command that you're building. It allows you to add new tables, views, or stored procedures, and to then add attributes to those elements to ensure that they are displayed properly.

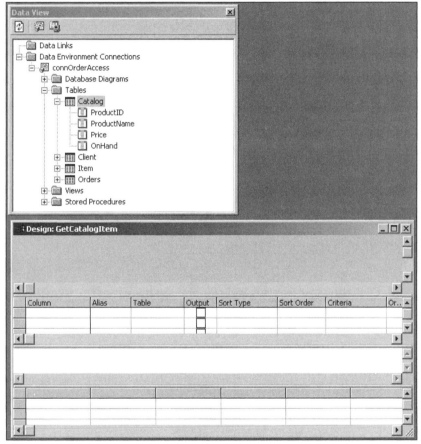

Figure 13-31: The Data View and Design dialogs allow you to create a command by using a graphical interface in place of code.

4. Drag the Catalog table from the Data View dialog box to the upper pane of the Design dialog box.

5. Click the * (All Columns) checkbox. The resulting command should look similar to the one shown in Figure 13-32. This command will allow you to retrieve all of the catalog items so that the user can view the products that the company has to sell and to make product updates as required.

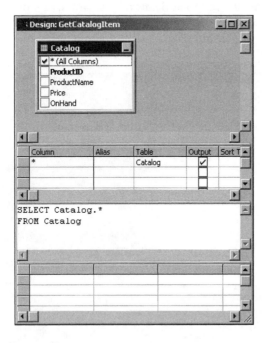

Figure 13-32: The graphical view of the GetCatalogItem command is simple.

6. Click the Close box. Visual Basic will ask if you want to save the command. Click Yes. At this point, your DataEnvironment window should look similar to the one shown in Figure 13-33.

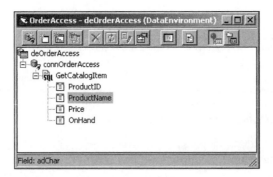

Figure 13-33: The database designer uses a hierarchy of objects to create a connection to the database.

As you can see, the graphical technique for creating a command is relatively painless and fast compared to writing all of the information code. You'll find that accessing a command requires a minimum of code and that the development process is much faster as a result. We'll need more commands to complete this example. Rather than take you through the construction of each command individually, I provide the required SQL statements in Table 13-6. The table also provides the name of the command and a description of its purpose.

If you get lost using the step-by-step instructions above and the information in Table 13-6, you can always look at the source code on the CD-ROM provided with this book. You'll find this example in the Chapt13\OrderAccess folder.

Table 13-6 OrderAccess Component Command Summary		
Command Name	**SQL Statement**	**Description**
GetCatalogItems	SELECT Catalog.* FROM Catalog	A command that gets data from the Catalog table.
GetCustomer	SELECT Client.* FROM Client	A command that gets data from the Customer table.
GetOrders	SELECT Catalog.*, Orders.*, Item.* FROM Client INNER JOIN Orders ON Client.CustomerID = Orders.CustomerID INNER JOIN Item ON Orders.OrderID = Item.OrderID INNER JOIN Catalog ON Item.ProductID = Catalog. ProductID	A command that combines the output of all of the tables.

Adding some code

It's time to add some code to the component that we've spent so long configuring. Listing 13-1 contains the source code for this example.

Listing 13-1: **OrderAccess Component Source Code**

```
Public Sub GetCatalogItem(rsCatalog As ADODB.Recordset)
    'Open the recordset
    deOrderAccess.rsGetCatalogItem.Open

    'Make it available to the client.
    Set rsCatalog = deOrderAccess.rsGetCatalogItem
```

Continued

Listing 13-1 *(continued)*

```
        'Close the recordset
        deOrderAccess.rsGetCatalogItem.Close
    End Sub

    Public Sub GetCustomers(rsCatalog As ADODB.Recordset)
        'Open the recordset
        deOrderAccess.rsGetCustomer.Open

        'Make it available to the client.
        Set rsCatalog = deOrderAccess.rsGetCustomer

        'Close the recordset
        deOrderAccess.rsGetCustomer.Close
    End Sub

    Public Sub GetOrders(rsCatalog As ADODB.Recordset)
        'Open the recordset
        deOrderAccess.rsGetOrders.Open

        'Make it available to the client.
        Set rsCatalog = deOrderAccess.rsGetOrders

        'Close the recordset
        deOrderAccess.rsGetOrders.Close
    End Sub
```

As you can see, all three methods use essentially the same code. The client application passes a recordset pointer to the method. The method opens the recordset that's created by one of the three commands that we configured. It places the recordset within the ADODB.Recordset object that the client passed, and then closes the recordset opened by the command. This should be a very fast process when working with smaller datasets. The point is that the client has a copy of the data to use and that there's little chance than any disruptions of the client's connection will cause problems on the server.

Creating a Desktop Client Application

Some people act as if the desktop client is dead or that they'll find some magic bullet solution that will allow them to create a one-size-fits-all solution to every client-side programming problem. The fact is that there will be desktop clients for the foreseeable future. Very few of us work from a home office and many of us spend the entire day at the office. The desktop application is still alive and well.

The following sections will help you to understand today's desktop client's programming needs in light of the current business climate, technology advances like

COM+, and the development of alternative computing platforms like the palmtop. The first section addresses the requirements for creating a thick client that provides robust access to a remote database. The next two sections discuss how you can create the application shell, including designing the complex forms that a database application normally requires. The fourth section provides some unique and helpful tips for creating your thick-client applications faster. Finally, we'll add some code to the application and get it ready for use.

Creating the application shell

This section will help you to create a thick-client application shell. There won't be too many twists and turns in this case, because most of the work is done in the OrderAccess component that we created earlier in the chapter. Begin by creating a Standard EXE project. I gave the example a name of ThickClient, but you can use any name that you'd like. Make sure that you add a reference to the OrderAccess – Database Order Entry Example component to your application. You'll also need to add two components: Microsoft ADO Data Control 6.0 (SP3) (OLEDB) and Microsoft DataGrid Control 6.0 (SP3) (OLEDB). Figure 13-34 shows what the form for this example will look like. Table 13-7 contains a complete list of component setting changes that you'll need to make.

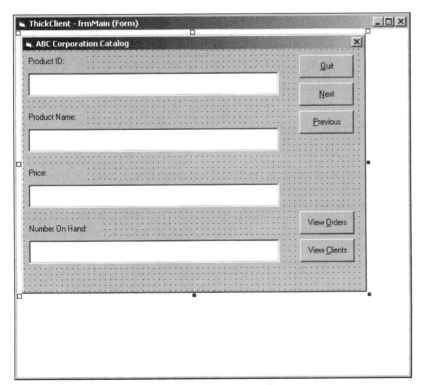

Figure 13-34: A simple form for the current catalog entries.

Table 13-7
View Catalog Component Settings

Object	Property	Value
Form	Name	frmMain
	BorderStyle	3 – Fixed Dialog
	Caption	ABC Corporation Catalog
	Height	5550
	ShowInTaskbar	True
	Width	7650
cmdQuit	Name	cmdQuit
	Cancel	True
	Caption	Quit
	TabIndex	4
	ToolTipText	Exit the Application
cmdNext	Name	cmdNext
	Caption	Next
	TabIndex	5
	ToolTipText	Go to the Next Record
cmdPrevious	Name	cmdPrevious
	Caption	Previous
	TabIndex	6
	ToolTipText	Go to the Previous Record
cmdViewOrders	Name	cmdViewOrders
	Caption	ViewOrders
	TabIndex	7
	ToolTipText	See the Current Orders

Object	Property	Value
cmdViewClients	Name	cmdViewClients
	Caption	View Clients
	TabIndex	8
	ToolTipText	See a List of Clients
txtProductID	Name	txtProductID
	TabIndex	0
	Text	""
	ToolTipText	Enter a unique Product ID
txtProductName	Name	txtProductName
	TabIndex	1
	Text	""
	ToolTipText	Enter a Product Name
txtPrice	Name	txtPrice
	TabIndex	2
	Text	""
	ToolTipText	Enter a Price
txtOnHand	Name	txtOnHand
	TabIndex	3
	Text	""
	ToolTipText	Enter the Quantity On Hand

This example will require two additional forms. The first will allow the user to view a customer list, while the second will allow the user to display the current orders. Figure 13-35 shows the customer list form, while Figure 13-36 shows the order entry form. You can use the figures and the contents of Table 13-7 as a basis for configuring these dialog boxes. The CD-ROM provided with this book also contains complete configuration information.

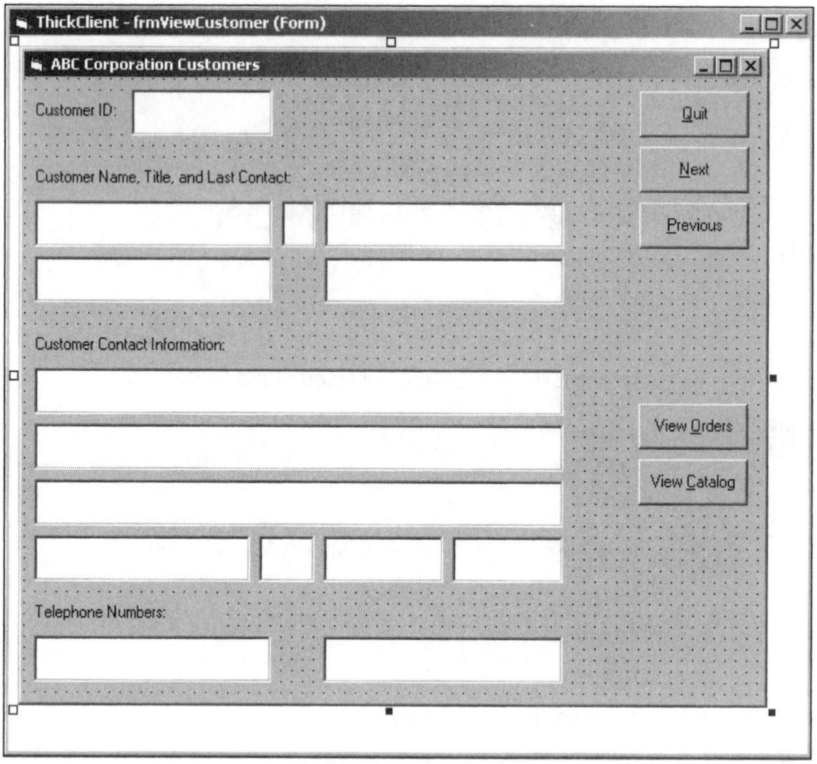

Figure 13-35: A simple form for the current customer entries.

Shortcuts for thick-client development

Desktop applications and thick-client applications are used synonymously by some people. In some respects, the usage is correct. A thick client usually refers to a desktop machine with a relatively large amount of processing power and other resources. These resources allow the thick client to perform a lot of local processing, reducing the load on the server and enhancing perceived application speed for the user. In short, a thick client is an independent node on the network that relies on the server more for data than for services.

There are still some problems with thick-client development that you need to avoid, especially if you want to use the same component for both thin and thick client deployments. We've already discussed issues like database record management with any client. You can't rely on a connection, so there are certain types of database activity that you should avoid like performing updates on a cached copy of the database.

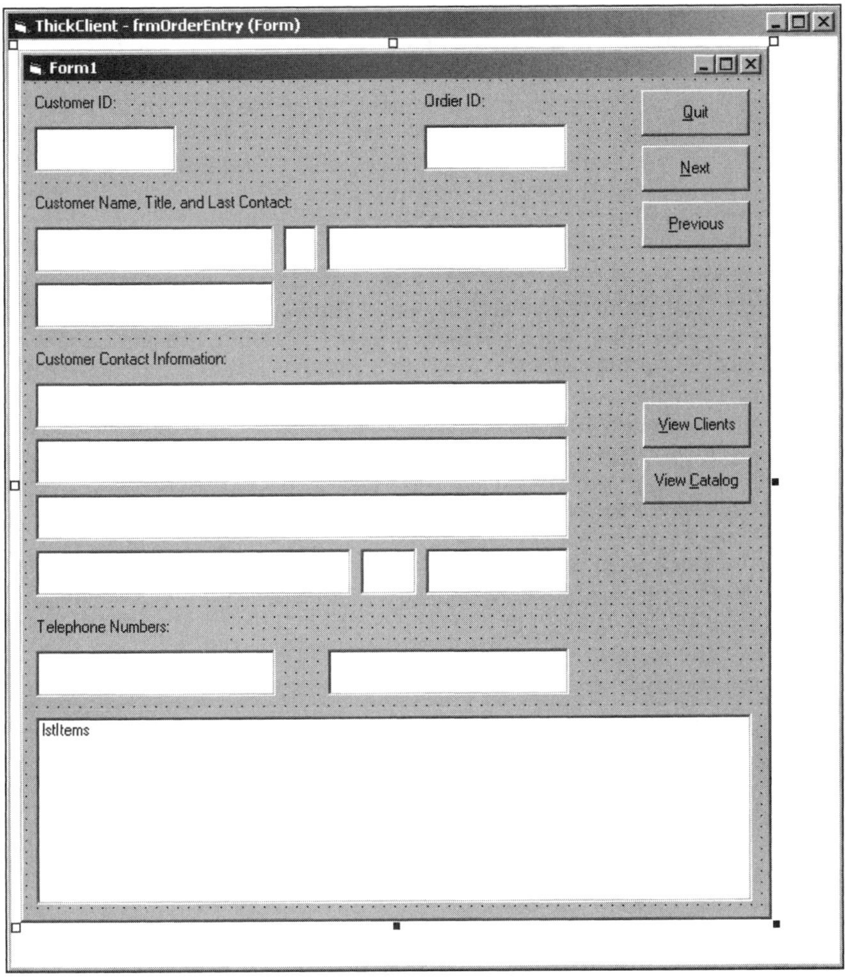

Figure 13-36: A simple form for the current orders.

One of the best shortcuts for thick-client development is to develop with thin clients in mind if your company is moving in that direction. Keeping one version of a component is definitely easier and less time-consuming than working with two versions. In some cases, you can optimize this arrangement by providing the thin client with a second server-side processing mechanism like scripts. A server-side script can access the database component, extract the required data, format it into a Web page, and send it off to the client. Inevitably, there are some tradeoffs to the single component setup, but the timesavings are well worth the effort.

Thick clients don't suffer from resource depravation like thin clients do. While using older libraries with modern thin clients is problematic to say the least, you can develop thick clients quite a bit faster by using them. Of course, you also need to watch out for potential problems when using someone else's code. Many of the older libraries on the market aren't thread safe. If you do decide to take advantage of one of the libraries on the market to reduce your coding time, it pays to spend some time looking at the threading model used and the features that the library provides.

Unlike thin clients, where you need to test the application using the worst-case scenario connection that the user will experience, thick-client testing can take place on the LAN for the most part. In many cases, it pays to develop the component on a thick client, and then fine-tune performance and other issues on a thin client. You can temporarily simulate a home user to office connection by disconnecting the client from the network and making the connection by using telephone lines.

Adding some code

It's time to add code to the three forms that we've created so far. The three forms are simple, so we'll discuss them as a group. Listing 13-2 contains the code for the catalog view form; Listing 13-3 contains the code for the customer view form; and Listing 13-4 contains the code for the order entry form.

Listing 13-2: **Catalog View Form Source Code**

```
'Create the required components
Dim oOrderModify As OrderAccess.OrderModify
Dim rsCatalog As ADODB.Recordset

Option Explicit

Private Sub PerformUpdate()
    'Make sure we can display the record.
    If Not (rsCatalog.EOF Or rsCatalog.BOF) Then

        'Display the four text fields.
        txtProductID.Text = rsCatalog.Fields(0).Value
        txtProductName.Text = rsCatalog.Fields(1).Value
        txtPrice.Text = rsCatalog.Fields(2).Value

        If IsNull(rsCatalog.Fields(3).Value) Then
            txtOnHand.Text = "0"
        Else
            txtOnHand.Text = rsCatalog.Fields(3).Value
        End If
    End If
End Sub
```

```
Private Sub cmdNext_Click()
    'Make sure there is a next record.
    If Not rsCatalog.EOF Then

        'Go to the next record.
        rsCatalog.MoveNext
        PerformUpdate
    End If
End Sub

Private Sub cmdPrevious_Click()
    'Make sure there is a previous record.
    If Not rsCatalog.BOF Then

        'Go to the previous record.
        rsCatalog.MovePrevious
        PerformUpdate
    End If
End Sub

Private Sub cmdQuit_Click()
    'End the application
    End
End Sub

Private Sub cmdViewClients_Click()
    'Display the client form.
    frmViewCustomer.Show
    frmMain.Hide
End Sub

Private Sub cmdViewOrders_Click()
    'Display the orders form.
    frmOrderEntry.Show
    frmMain.Hide
End Sub

Private Sub Form_Load()
    'Instantiate the server side component.
    Set oOrderModify = New OrderAccess.OrderModify

    'Gain access to the recordset.
    oOrderModify.GetCatalogItem rsCatalog

    'Make the data visible.
    rsCatalog.Open
    PerformUpdate
End Sub
```

Continued

Listing 13-2 *(continued)*

```
Private Sub Form_Unload(Cancel As Integer)
    'Close the recordset.
    rsCatalog.Close

    'Clean up the objects.
    Set oOrderModify = Nothing
    Set rsCatalog = Nothing
End Sub
```

Listing 13-3: Customer View Form Source Code

```
'Create the required components
Dim oOrderModify As OrderAccess.OrderModify
Dim rsCatalog As ADODB.Recordset

Option Explicit

Private Sub PerformUpdate()
    'Make sure we can display the record.
    If Not (rsCatalog.EOF Or rsCatalog.BOF) Then

        'Display the four text fields.
        txtCustomerID.Text = rsCatalog.Fields(0).Value
        txtFirstName.Text = rsCatalog.Fields(1).Value

        If Not IsNull(rsCatalog.Fields(2).Value) Then
            txtMiddleInitial.Text = rsCatalog.Fields(2).Value
        Else
            txtMiddleInitial.Text = " "
        End If

        txtLastName.Text = rsCatalog.Fields(3).Value

        If IsNull(rsCatalog.Fields(4).Value) Then
            txtTitle = "N/A"
        Else
            txtTitle = rsCatalog.Fields(4).Value
        End If

        If IsNull(rsCatalog.Fields(5).Value) Then
            txtCompany = "N/A"
        Else
            txtCompany = rsCatalog.Fields(5).Value
        End If

        txtAddress1 = rsCatalog.Fields(6).Value
```

```
                    If IsNull(rsCatalog.Fields(7).Value) Then
                        txtAddress2 = "N/A"
                    Else
                        txtAddress2 = rsCatalog.Fields(7).Value
                    End If

                    txtCity = rsCatalog.Fields(8).Value
                    txtState = rsCatalog.Fields(9).Value
                    txtZIP = rsCatalog.Fields(10).Value

                    If IsNull(rsCatalog.Fields(11).Value) Then
                        txtCountry = "N/A"
                    Else
                        txtCountry = rsCatalog.Fields(11).Value
                    End If

                    If Not IsNull(rsCatalog.Fields(12).Value) Then
                        txtTelephone1 = rsCatalog.Fields(12).Value
                    End If

                    If Not IsNull(rsCatalog.Fields(13).Value) Then
                        txtTelephone2 = rsCatalog.Fields(13).Value
                    End If

                    txtLastContact = rsCatalog.Fields(14).Value
            End If
    End Sub

    Private Sub cmdNext_Click()
        'Make sure there is a next record.
        If Not rsCatalog.EOF Then

            'Go to the next record.
            rsCatalog.MoveNext
            PerformUpdate
        End If
    End Sub

    Private Sub cmdPrevious_Click()
        'Make sure there is a previous record.
        If Not rsCatalog.BOF Then

            'Go to the previous record.
            rsCatalog.MovePrevious
            PerformUpdate
        End If
    End Sub

    Private Sub cmdQuit_Click()
        'End the application.
        End
    End Sub
```

Continued

Listing 13-3 *(continued)*

```
Private Sub cmdViewCatalog_Click()
    'Display the catalog.
    frmMain.Show
    frmViewCustomer.Hide
End Sub

Private Sub cmdViewOrders_Click()
    'Display the orders form.
    frmOrderEntry.Show
    frmMain.Hide
End Sub

Private Sub Form_Load()
    'Instantiate the server side component.
    Set oOrderModify = New OrderAccess.OrderModify

    'Gain access to the recordset.
    oOrderModify.GetCustomers rsCatalog

    'Make the data visible.
    rsCatalog.Open
    PerformUpdate
End Sub

Private Sub Form_Unload(Cancel As Integer)
    'Close the recordset.
    rsCatalog.Close

    'Clean up the objects.
    Set oOrderModify = Nothing
    Set rsCatalog = Nothing
End Sub
```

Listing 13-4: **Order Entry Form Source Code**

```
'Create the required components
Dim oOrderModify As OrderAccess.OrderModify
Dim rsCatalog As ADODB.Recordset

'OrderID field tracker.
Dim strOrderID As String

Option Explicit

Private Sub PerformUpdate()
```

```
'Make sure we can display the record.
If Not (rsCatalog.EOF Or rsCatalog.BOF) Then

    'Display the fields.
    txtCustomerID.Text = rsCatalog.Fields(5).Value
    txtFirstName.Text = rsCatalog.Fields(6).Value

    If Not IsNull(rsCatalog.Fields(7).Value) Then
        txtMiddleInitial.Text = rsCatalog.Fields(7).Value
    Else
        txtMiddleInitial.Text = " "
    End If

    txtLastName.Text = rsCatalog.Fields(8).Value

    If IsNull(rsCatalog.Fields(9).Value) Then
        txtTitle = "N/A"
    Else
        txtTitle = rsCatalog.Fields(9).Value
    End If

    If IsNull(rsCatalog.Fields(10).Value) Then
        txtCompany = "N/A"
    Else
        txtCompany = rsCatalog.Fields(10).Value
    End If

    txtAddress1 = rsCatalog.Fields(11).Value

    If IsNull(rsCatalog.Fields(12).Value) Then
        txtAddress2 = "N/A"
    Else
        txtAddress2 = rsCatalog.Fields(12).Value
    End If

    txtCity = rsCatalog.Fields(13).Value
    txtState = rsCatalog.Fields(14).Value
    txtZIP = rsCatalog.Fields(15).Value

    If Not IsNull(rsCatalog.Fields(16).Value) Then
        txtTelephone1 = rsCatalog.Fields(16).Value
    End If

    If Not IsNull(rsCatalog.Fields(17).Value) Then
        txtTelephone2 = rsCatalog.Fields(17).Value
    End If

    txtOrderID = rsCatalog.Fields(4).Value
```

Continued

Listing 13-4 *(continued)*

```
            'Prepare lstItems for use.
            lstItems.Clear
            lstItems.AddItem _
                "Order ID" + vbTab + _
                "Prod ID" + vbTab + _
                "Product Name" + vbTab + vbTab + vbTab + _
                "Each" + vbTab + _
                "Qty" + vbTab + _
                "Total"
            lstItems.AddItem ""
            strOrderID = rsCatalog.Fields(19).Value

            'Cycle through the times until we've gotten
            'through an entire order.
            While strOrderID = rsCatalog.Fields(19).Value

                lstItems.AddItem _
                    rsCatalog.Fields(18).Value + vbTab + _
                    rsCatalog.Fields(0).Value + vbTab + _
                    rsCatalog.Fields(1).Value + vbTab + _
                    CStr(rsCatalog.Fields(2).Value) + vbTab + _
                    CStr(rsCatalog.Fields(21).Value) + vbTab + _
                    CStr(rsCatalog.Fields(22).Value)
                rsCatalog.MoveNext

                If rsCatalog.EOF Then
                    Exit Sub
                End If

            Wend

            'Move back one record since so we're at the first
            'record of the next order.
            rsCatalog.MovePrevious

        End If
End Sub

Private Sub cmdNext_Click()
    'Make sure there is a next record.
    If Not rsCatalog.EOF Then
        'Go to the next record.
        rsCatalog.MoveNext
        PerformUpdate
    End If
End Sub

Private Sub cmdPrevious_Click()
    'Make sure there is a previous record.
```

```
        If Not rsCatalog.BOF Then

            'Go to the previous record.
            rsCatalog.MoveFirst
            strOrderID = CStr(CInt(strOrderID) - 1)
            strOrderID = Right("00000", 5 - Len(strOrderID)) _
                + strOrderID
            While rsCatalog.Fields(19).Value < strOrderID
                rsCatalog.MoveNext
            Wend
            PerformUpdate
        End If
End Sub

Private Sub cmdQuit_Click()
    'Exit the application.
    End
End Sub

Private Sub cmdViewCatalog_Click()
    'Show the catalog form.
    frmMain.Show
    frmOrderEntry.Hide
End Sub

Private Sub cmdViewClients_Click()
    'Show the customer form
    frmViewCustomer.Show
    frmOrderEntry.Hide
End Sub

Private Sub Form_Load()
    'Instantiate the server side component.
    Set oOrderModify = New OrderAccess.OrderModify

    'Gain access to the recordset.
    oOrderModify.GetOrders rsCatalog

    'Make the data visible.
    rsCatalog.Open
    PerformUpdate
End Sub

Private Sub Form_Unload(Cancel As Integer)
    'Close the recordset.
    rsCatalog.Close

    'Clean up the objects.
    Set oOrderModify = Nothing
    Set rsCatalog = Nothing
End Sub
```

As you can see from the listings, all three database access routines work about the same, with a few exceptions. For example, moving backward in the order entry view of the database is a little more difficult than simply using the `MovePrevious()` method of rsCatalog. In addition, a few of the fields require conversion before you can display them because in many cases, the application needs a string. The complexity of each table that the form displays also affects the associated code to some extent. However, after you put these differences aside, there's a general flow for these client applications that you can use when creating forms of your own.

The applications always begin with the `Form_Load()` method. The code begins by instantiating the OrderModify interface. Each of the forms has its own separate method within OrderModify that delivers the correct recordset, but the calling syntax is precisely the same each time. The rsCatalog recordset object returns with a complete copy of the database. Opening the recordset allows us to display the data that it contains. Finally, the `PerformUpdate()` sub displays the actual data according to the type of information that the recordset contains.

When the user is finished with a particular form, it's important to close the recordset first, and then release the objects that were created during application start. Otherwise, the database on the server could get left open, leaving the server to decide when to close the connection and release the resources used by it (or return the connection object to the object pool).

Moving forward and backward is straightforward. All you need to do is change the cursor position within the recordset and display the data again. It's also important to check for the beginning and end of file markers. Failure to do so can result in an application crash (or at least an incomprehensible message that the user will never figure out). Although the example code doesn't provide any error trapping, database code should always contain it.

Working with Thin Clients

The thin client is gaining in popularity for specific application types, especially those applications that are designed to run on smaller machines. Even as I write this, companies are trying to figure out better ways of making a cell phone into an all-in-one device for people on the road. Just think about how the thin client will affect everything from laptops to palmtop computers.

Some applications are better suited for thin-client development than are other applications. For example, every Web site on the Internet has the potential of becoming a thin-client application for you. When you shop online, you're actually using a thin-client application of some type.

This section of the chapter looks at the thin client. We'll discuss how you can use COM+ to make thin-client development easier. In addition, we'll look at how you can make a single component work for both your thick and thin clients. The second section provides a wealth of tips for making thin-client development faster and easier. I also include a few tips that involve both the thick and thin client because we discussed the thick client earlier. The last two sections discuss specific Web page types: static and dynamic. The static Web page requires few resources, but is also considered very dull and boring by most. Worst of all, you can't update it without asking the user to refresh the page. The dynamic Web page, on the other hand, is generally very resource intensive, but has the advantage of providing constantly updated content and a lot more pizzazz, which is designed to retain user interest.

Shortcuts for thin-client development

Thin clients are a relatively new phenomenon, so developing applications for them is on the same order as magic and psychic contact in some people's minds. Not only are thin clients disconnected from the network and mobile, but they also have a wealth of performance-inhibiting features that make application development almost impossible. Consider the small screen size of some of the thin clients on the market today. Getting all of the information that you need on one screen is impossible, so you use two or three screens to display the data, usually with a lot of complaints from the user. That the screens that you need to work with will become smaller doesn't help matters much.

Other resource problems include a small memory footprint, an even smaller hard drive, and processing speeds that are well below the range of desktop machines. In some cases, you may be dealing with a foreign operating system, so using any off-the-shelf aids, like canned libraries, is definitely out of the question, as are scripts.

After working with a thin client for a very short time, the resource problems become very obvious and most developers wonder how they'll get any kind of application delivered, much less a good one. An easy way to overcome at least a few of the resource problems of a thin client is to instantiate objects only when you need them, and then release them immediately. This allows the thin client to use its limited number of resources more efficiently. Of course, this tactic goes against what most people were saying as little as a year ago. When working with thin clients it's usually easier to trade some processing cycles for resources.

Avoid adding too many features to a thin client. Most users on the road need to add new records and review existing orders. If you can create a robust application that provides those two features, most users will be happy to wait for updates until they get back to the office. Whenever possible, try to keep functionality to reviewing records because that's the least resource and processor intensive task that the user can perform. Even the ability to review sales order status and get the latest catalog information can really help the user who is on the road.

Because you can't depend on the thin client to use the operating system that you're used to working with, it's usually a good idea to perform as much processing on the server as you can. The server application should check on the client's status occasionally, because the connection between a thin client and the server is often tenuous. Proactive monitoring of thin-client resource usage and the state of the connection can help you to recover some resources that are lost now to inefficient connection management.

Creating static Web pages

Even though Web sites have been using a variety of bells and whistles for a while now, most thin-client development still centers on the static Web page because of all the problems that we've talked about so far in the chapter. A static page is one in which the server creates the image and then sends it to the client. The image doesn't change until the client requests some sort of a refresh.

The static Web page will be with us for quite some time to come because the thin client can be very elusive when it comes to figuring out any form of client-side scripting that will work with it. Eventually the thin client's processing potential will catch up enough with the desktop so that developers won't have to worry about every byte used in making the display pretty versus displaying the information that the user is actually looking for from the application.

There are a few tricks that you can follow when working with static Web pages that won't cost much with regard to performance or resources. All static Web pages must be updated as an entire page; there isn't any way around this particular issue. So, when you upload the page to the user, some amount of the page will be updated instantly, while the rest languishes waiting for the dial up connection to catch up. If you place the information most likely to change near the top of the display and avoid using graphics (at least noninterlaced graphics), the user will see the update quickly.

The size of the Web page and client connection speed determines how fast the Web page will download. Because the thin client is only interested in information that it can display, and because you really don't need to provide search or other capabilities for a Web page that will be out of date in a few minutes, keep the Web page oriented toward data and avoid nonuseful elements like comments. You can also reduce nonfunctional elements like alternate text, which is a good addition for a public Web site, but generally not needed for an in-house application.

Creating dynamic Web pages

Using dynamic content on Web pages for thin clients isn't out of the question, but you do need to consider several factors before you include dynamic content. Dynamic content changes as conditions or user requirements change. Consequently, unlike the static Web page, you need a consistent connection to the server. A dynamic Web page is designed to download data almost constantly from the server.

Dynamic content may mean better updates without a refresh, but using dynamic content also means setting aside more resources on the client machine and allocating more network bandwidth. Always check the performance cost by creating the same content with a static Web page during testing. You may find that the benefits of using dynamic content are small compared to the performance costs.

There's also the issue of standardization to consider when using dynamic content. A client that obtains dynamic content is usually required to run scripts and perform some types of processing by using standard techniques. The lack of a standard operating system is also a problem because different operating system vendors implement standards, when they exist, in different ways.

Testing the Applications

It's finally time to test the applications that we've created. There are actually two separate applications in this example, even though both applications rely on the same component for data. The thick client is the perfect example of a desktop application that requires data from a remote source. You'd use this for a home office setup. The home machine uses a direct connection to the local company to gain access to data on the network. Because of the proliferation of small machines, the thin client is the direction in which many developers are heading. This version of the application could theoretically work on just about any machine that can create a Web connection.

Part of the testing process involves installing the database component and ensuring that it can access the database. It's important to test this connection out by using a local application, so we'll test the database with the thick client in local mode before we test it from a remote location. Next, we'll perform the two types of remote client testing: thick and thin.

Installing the database component

Install the database component by using the same techniques that we used in Chapter 2. The example application uses a COM+ application name of OrderModify. You'll need to export a proxy application for the client. After the component is installed on the client, you can begin to use it for development purposes. Because this is a database application, you may want to test it with MTS set on and off. You'll see for yourself that there's only a small performance penalty for using MTS on a COM+ application.

There's one problem that you should note with just about any database application. Trying to set up a database application for use with MSMQ is notoriously difficult for several reasons, most of which occur because of the amount of data that you're moving. Recordsets aren't MSMQ friendly and very often you'll find that the application fails to work because of the interactions with MSMQ. It's a good idea to avoid using MSMQ with the example in this chapter because of the way that the recordset is transferred from the server to the client.

Testing the thick client

Running the thick client on a desktop machine is relatively easy. You'll find that it can display records from the OrderEntry database, as well as move from record to record. It is fairly easy to add the capability to add new records to and delete existing ones from the database.

As previously mentioned, this application is large enough (just barely) to give you some idea of the performance hit of using MTS. Try configuring the application for an MTS setup the first time and test how long it takes to get the first record update. Make sure that you stop the application, and then reconfigure it for non-MTS operation. In most cases, using MTS will result in approximately a 5 to 10 percent loss in performance over a dial-up connection; less on a network.

To verify for yourself that the client is downloading a local copy of the recordset, start the application, look at a few records, and then remove the computer from the network. You'll find that the application continues to work as long as you don't try to update any of the records by typing new values in the fields. If this application also included local caching and MSMQ for new records, you'd find that you could perform quite a few tasks offline without doing anything special.

Testing a thin client

Thin-client testing is an error-prone process for several reasons. First, because you need to test the thin client by using it as it would be used normally, there are several layers of hardware and software that you wouldn't need to worry about normally. The addition of a dial-up or some other network connection can mean that problems get masked or that you'll chase what appears to be an application problem, only to learn later that it was a hardware failure.

It's important that you test a thin client by using the same type of connection that the user will have. In addition, you should try to duplicate the user's environment in order to check for usage or other problems with the client. For example, you may find that a screen that's perfectly readable on a desktop computer becomes totally unreadable on a thin-client screen.

Most of the testing that you perform using a thick client that requires the same component as a thin client is valid. However, because the thin client uses a different client-side processing methodology (Web pages for the most part), you'll find that you need to check all user interface elements again for interactions with the component.

Quick Fixes for Remote Databases

No one enjoys spending their Saturday or Sunday in the office fixing a remote database application, yet this happens more often than most developers care to think about. Any database application is similar to a complex piece of machinery. So many parts can break that they often do at the most inconvenient time imaginable.

The following sections discuss some of the more common problems that you'll encounter when working with remote database applications. We'll discuss problems that occur with both thick and thin clients, because it's very likely that you'll need to work with both types. Given the complexity of database applications, it's hard to predict just where one will break, so it's important to consider this a list of ideas, rather than an absolute guide to all that might happen to your application. In fact, it often surprises me when I find a new failure point in a database application that I thought I had completely figured out.

Internet connectivity issues

The Internet represents the weak link when it comes to connectivity for remote database applications. Any application that transfers data over the Internet will experience several problems that you wouldn't experience over a LAN. The following list outlines just a few of the major problem areas.

✦ **Data integrity:** It's hard to maintain data integrity over a network that's designed to connect disparate systems that wouldn't normally work with each other. Various packaging methods, such as the use of a VPN, are designed to help alleviate this problem. In addition, new technologies like Simple Object Access Protocol (SOAP) will eventually help with data integrity problems (although SOAP presents problems when it comes to security). In the short-term, however, it's better to add extra range and value-checking code to your applications to ensure that what you received is what the client sent.

✦ **Connections:** Unlike a LAN, MAN, or WAN, the connections for the Internet aren't under your control. The Internet has received more than a little press as an unreliable network medium that's prone to outages. It's possible to lose the connection to the client in the middle of a transaction. Normally, you'd use MTS to help prevent transaction problems on the Internet. Unfortunately, the Internet isn't COM friendly; firewalls and other Internet protection will usually reject COM packets before they can get to the server. Technologies like SOAP offer hope, in this case, because they use a pure text transfer that won't be rejected by the firewall. See the "Working with COM Internet Services Proxy" sidebar for alternatives that rely on DCOM, rather than SOAP.

✦ **Data security:** Retaining the integrity of the data as it traverses the Internet is one thing; keeping it safe from prying eyes is another. Windows 2000 provides a wealth of encryption techniques, as well as technologies such as VPN that create a secure data transmission path through the Internet. However, there are ways that you can keep your data less readable by coding components and applications to minimize data exposure.

Don't send entire recordsets unless absolutely necessary, use individual records or even single fields instead. Keep data in machine-readable form instead of converting it to human-readable form at the server. This means using strings as little as possible over the Internet.

✦ **Network security:** Crackers will often use open ports on a server as a means to get past security without alerting the network administrator to the problem. DCOM only makes the problem worse by requiring the network administrator to keep a large number of ports open (see the "Working with COM Internet Services Proxy" sidebar for details). Using SOAP or a firewall-friendly, DCOM-oriented technology like COM Internet Services (CIS) Proxy can help to reduce this problem.

✦ **Network bandwidth:** There are more articles appearing every day about the problems associated with network bandwidth limitations. This problem affects the capability of a client to reach a server with requests and for the server to respond with data. You can always ask your ISP for more bandwidth, but often you can't get it because the ISP doesn't have more to offer or the company doesn't have the money to spend. Keeping data transfers over the Internet small is one way to optimize network usage. Ensuring that you create applications in such a way that there's only one request and one response cycle will also help keep network bandwidth usage to a minimum (this means making requests and responses complete in the first pass, rather than including interrogation as part of the client/server exchange).

✦ **Data presentation:** Clients often vary in hardware capability, so it's hard for the server to know what form of data presentation to use. In most cases, you'll want to create the application in such a way that client requests also include the data presentation requirement. This way, the server can send the data in the format that the client requires.

As you can see, there are more than a few connectivity issues to deal with when working with the Internet. As the number of clients requesting data from your application becomes more diverse, the problem will get worse. It's time now to start figuring out strategies for dealing with connectivity issues like lost connections and thin versus thick client data presentation. In many cases, careful coding of the application and associated components will reduce the number of problems that you encounter (but is unlikely to get rid of them completely).

Working with COM Internet Services Proxy

Getting DCOM to work over the Internet is akin to teaching a pig to sing — it frustrates you and annoys the pig. The problem isn't a deficiency in DCOM as a technology, but a problem with the way that packets get transferred over the Internet. DCOM relies on packets that contain a great deal of binary information, in addition to the data that they transport.

Proxy servers often filter data (including binary data) before it leaves the confines of the local network and passes onto the Internet. ISP proxy servers will often filter the packets as well by removing anything that looks like it could cause problems for the ISP's servers or other equipment. Firewalls also filter incoming packets, getting rid of anything that looks suspicious (which normally means anything not pure text).

Another problem with DCOM and the Internet is that proxies and firewalls normally restrict the port addresses that a data transfer can use to a very narrow number of ports based on transport protocol. For example, HTTP is normally restricted to port 80. DCOM uses a wide range of network port addresses in the range from 1024 to 65,535. This means that at least some DCOM packets will be filtered simply because they're at the wrong port address. DCOM requires this wide range of port addresses to avoid conflicts that would occur when two clients use the same port number otherwise, but leaving such a large range of ports open on a firewall is an open invitation to a security breach, which makes DCOM firewall unfriendly. You can learn more about the problems of using DCOM with firewalls at `http://msdn.microsoft.com/library/backgrnd/html/msdn_dcomfirewall.htm`. All of these speed bumps have kept DCOM, and technologies like COM+ that rely on DCOM, from using the Internet as a transport medium.

Windows 2000 includes a Networking Services feature called COM Internet Services (CIS) Proxy. You can install this feature on any Windows 2000 server to allow DCOM to work as it should—at least in many cases. CIS Proxy isn't available for Windows NT at the time of this writing. The COM Internet Services Proxy appears in the Networking Services dialog box found in the Windows Components Wizard in the Add/Remove Programs applet. A full set of installation instructions appears at `http://msdn.microsoft.com/library/psdk/rpc/ov-http_4hgj.htm`.

The CIS proxy allows transfer of DCOM packets over Internet Information Sever (IIS) using port 80, the same one used by HTTP. It relies on tunneling transmission control protocol (TTCP) to accomplish its work. The purpose of CIS Proxy is to allow client and server to communicate over an Internet connection even if the network has a firewall attached or uses a proxy server that prevents certain types if data from getting through.

CIS Proxy also supports a new type of moniker (a name used to refer to an object) called OBJREF. You can use this new moniker within a Web page to refer to a running object on the server. The moniker also allows both ActiveX controls and client applets to bind the running object.

There are some additional sources of information for CIS Proxy on Microsoft's Web site. If you'd like a more in-depth overview of CIS Proxy, look at `http://msdn.microsoft.com/library/backgrnd/html/cis.htm`. You can learn how CIS Proxy fits into the overall planning strategy for a Windows 2000 Server at `http://www.microsoft.com/TechNet/win2000/win2ksrv/manuals/srvgs/sgsch03.asp`. The pertinent Windows 2000 Advanced Server information appears at `http://www.microsoft.com/TechNet/win2000/win2ksrv/manuals/asgs/agsch03.asp`. Because this is a new technology, there aren't any newsgroups for it at the time of this writing.

Security

Databases add security to the programming scenario, so you may find that a setup that normally works suddenly stops working when you add a database to the picture. For example, in our example, we chose to use the security that SQL Server provides instead of the Windows 2000 authentication. It's important to remember that this security is on top of the security that Windows 2000 normally provides. So, what you really have are additional layers of security where there's already an abundance of security. All of these additional security measures can cause conflicts that inevitably keep the user from accessing the application.

So, where do you begin looking for this problem? It's normally a good idea to look in the Windows 2000 event log. You won't want to look in the security log, however. The application log is more likely to contain the information that you need. In some cases, the message heading is so far off that you can't tell which message has the information that you need from looking at the headings alone, so a detailed look is required.

If you can't determine the source of problems by looking at the log files, try working through the various security layers. I normally set up a checklist of security points in the system, and then use it to systematically check for security problems. In many cases, you'll find one choke point in the security scheme that prevents a user from accessing the database application. Unfortunately, many problems are easy to overlook. For example, I once had a problem with one of my applications that turned out to be a capitalization problem. Remember that both Windows NT and Windows 2000 are case sensitive, so spelling and case are both important.

Make sure that any security settings in your code match those of the operating system. Given the extremely flexible nature of COM+ when it comes to configuring security outside of your component, it might be a good time to get rid of the internal security code. Doing so will get rid of a problem that will continue causing problems for you.

Server-side caching

Data caching can greatly increase system and application performance. Every read from the hard drive is years in terms of computer processing time. Because caching provides such a speed boost, you'll find it used in a lot of places that you may not have considered before you saw the application in action.

There are two major problems with using a cache, especially a cache that resides on the server because the local client doesn't have the required resources. The first problem is resource usage. A cache also uses RAM that could be used for running applications, rather than keeping them running faster. Trying to find a balance between caching and application needs is difficult, but you need to perform this task in order to gain the benefits of caching without crippling your applications.

The second problem can sneak up on you unexpectedly and the results are almost always unfortunate. Data caches require some sort of aging mechanism so that old data is removed from the hard drive. The caching problems on the Internet have become so severe, that some Web sites include code in their Web pages that always force an update. Some Webmasters have found that users get bad information or won't see a critical update because of problems in server-side or client-side caching. These same problems can affect your COM+ thin-client application with disastrous results.

Server-side caching also has an implication for the thin client in that the client is now tied to the server for all of its data needs. These very mobile thin clients are used to allow a user to travel and work without needing a connection to the local server. Tying the two together again with caching reduces the effectiveness of these devices to the point that the user is better off working at the home office.

Most of these caching problems can be overcome by using resources efficiently. If everything that your application needs can reside in memory without stressing system resources, then your application won't need to rely on server-side caching.

Summary

Remote database applications represent the bread and butter of many organizations, so it's an important application type to learn about. COM+ allows you to do many things with remote database applications that were impossible before COM+. Live updates from the field as users gain orders and the capability to update user information like price lists are important features in today's environment. Some additional conclusions that you can draw from the contents of this chapter are:

✦ Remote database applications represent a vast collection of application types that everyone uses on an almost daily basis. The order-entry system is obviously the application type that most developers are aware of and are used to working with, but there are many others that are just as important. The one piece of the puzzle that you need to consider when converting an application for remote use is just how well COM+ can handle the needs of that application. While delayed action or anticipated need applications work very well, applications that require immediate updates are almost never good choices for remote application conversion.

✦ Try developing as much of your combination thick- and thin-client application as you can on the local network before you begin testing by using the thin-client features alone.

✦ Always assume that a thin client will lack a good connection to the server at the home office. Doing so will force you to make design decisions that will create a better application.

✦ Reduce resource usage whenever possible and keep two-way communications to a minimum. New records can be cached on the local machine by using MSMQ. Record updates can't be cached, so they're harder to work with on a thin client.

✦ Take an n-tier view of your application whenever possible. You may find that distributed processing offers solutions for many of your database programming problems.

✦ Never use dynamic Web pages with a thin client unless you're absolutely certain that the client will provide a compatible operating system and browser. It's also important to consider the scripting capability of the thin client because this is a requirement for providing dynamic content in most cases. Finally, it's important to consider how dynamic content will affect system resources, especially network bandwidth.

✦   ✦   ✦

Working with Web-based Applications

Web sites are becoming more complex as remote users, business partners, and customers want Web sites to do more for them automatically. The remote user is especially affected by the complexity of the new Web pages that developers are creating to answer remote access requirements. An employee on the road requires full access to company resources, but transferring that data over a nonsecure medium to a client-side application that doesn't provide the greatest flexibility is a challenge.

We've already looked at several methods for enhancing the remote employee's ability to continue working. For example, the disconnected application in Chapter 12 offers one solution to the problem. But what if these other solutions won't work for whatever reason? What if the only real requirement is to provide the remote user with access to information, not exchange it with the company? There are a lot of situations where a Web-based application is the right answer to your application needs. Fortunately, you can augment the capabilities provided with Web-based solutions by using COM+.

This chapter will look at a typical example of a Web-based application that could enjoy the capabilities that COM+ will provide. We're going to create a help desk-type application that a user on the road can use to find solutions to problems like getting their orders entered correctly. Such an application could also help the user to find small, but significant problems on the user's laptop, and provide other forms of support as well.

The first thing that we'll need to complete this example is a help file. Instead of using a standard help file, we'll create the help file within a SQL Server database. This is the best method to use for a Web-based application because you won't need to transfer all of the information contained in the help file to the client, just the current topic of interest. We won't create a complex help file, but it will be representative of what you might need to create as part of your programming efforts.

Note   As with other database examples in the book, I'll be using SQL Server 7 for this example. You can obtain a copy of SQL Server 7 Developer Edition for free with the Visual Studio Option Pack as mentioned in Chapter 1. All screenshots and procedures in this chapter will reflect SQL Server 7 use, even though you could probably alter the examples to work with SQL Server 6.5, the version that comes with Visual Basic 6 Enterprise Edition.

Help desk applications often rely on a rule database and an application to perform analysis of a problem that the user may be having. This rule-based approach to problem solving is based on artificial intelligence (AI) research that has been around for quite some time. The principle is easy to understand. All that a company needs to do is keep track of support statistics and use those statistics as a basis for defining rules that reflect the probability of a certain problem happening and the probability of a particular answer fixing the problem. We'll look at the requirements for the rule database in the second section of the chapter and the analysis component in the third section of the chapter.

The fourth section of the chapter is where we'll create the Active Server Pages (ASP) script that the remote employee will use to interact with the help file and help desk. This example will look more at the practical requirements of such a script than at the aesthetic requirements of the Web page. (Obviously, we'll take user interface needs into account; the example will be usable, just not pretty.) The ASP script will need to call on the help desk component to perform analysis of a user's problem as required. The help desk component, on the other hand, will need the ASP script to ask the user questions based on the hierarchy of problem-solving requirements stored in the help desk database. The ASP script will also provide access to the static help files that the company will provide for problems of a general nature—those that don't require additional analysis to understand.

The fifth, and final, section of the chapter will put everything together. You'll see the application put to work in helping users on the road solve various problems without having to make a long distance phone call. We'll test the simple part of the application first, the help file. The second part of the test will look at how the help desk works to solve a user's problem and provide appropriate feedback that takes the user's particular situation into account.

Uses for Help Desk Applications

Many developers view the help desk application as a single-use item — to provide help to users. A help desk application normally allows a user to fix minor system problems or learn new application usage techniques without the intervention of company support staff, which reduces the total cost of ownership (TCO) for the application. In short, for many developers a help desk application is simply a help file with some refinements and nothing more. The format and content of the help file makes little or no difference in this perception. Because of this perception, many developers view the help desk application as something that they should avoid doing until the very last minute (the same treatment that help files have gotten for most of the history of DOS and Windows).

Help desk applications can be used for a lot more than simple or even complex help files, however. A help desk application can be used to provide any type of information to the user, not just help. For this reason, the help desk application is both more complex and more flexible than the help file. (Even a help file can be used for more than just help information; although this is the major use of a help file.) The following list provides some ideas on how you can use a help desk application to do more than just provide helpful information.

✦ **Company Policies:** The policies used to run your company are normally stored in printed format, making them difficult to access. Using a help desk application to make this information available online is one way to reduce the time required to search for a company policy, making it more likely that employees will follow such policies.

✦ **Bulletin Board:** Companies usually have bulletin boards containing announcements, employee regulations, and the like. In many cases, someone has to go from bulletin board to bulletin board making updates as required. A single help desk application can replace all of the company bulletin boards. Scanned images can replace paper counterparts. In addition, to saving time, using an electronic bulletin board allows more freedom in the presentation of information (use of animation is just one example) and closer monitoring of bulletin board content.

✦ **Forms:** Finding a required form can be a difficult and time-consuming process. In fact, it's a problem for many companies that results in the creation of duplicate forms because each person is absolutely certain that the form doesn't exist. Using a help desk application to allow employees to find forms can save time, money, and duplications.

✦ **Company Locator:** Give someone a company telephone book and they have to know something about the company before they can use it. A help desk application that provides the same functionality, on the other hand, is useful from the very first moment. Instead of knowing that James Smith is the personnel director, a user can simply ask for the personnel director and the help desk application will search for the required information.

As you can see, you can distribute just about any type of permanent or semipermanent information by using a help desk application. This type of application is more flexible than the help files of old. A help desk application can save any support person's time, even if support isn't normally part of that person's job description.

Don't confuse a help desk application with a Web site application like a search page. The differences are significant. A search page deals with individual documents, whereas a help desk application deals with a single document that contains related information. For example, a help desk application might be limited to a single application, while a search page would only be limited by the number of pages that it was designed to search for.

Creating the Help Desk Database

The first task that you need to perform when working with a help desk application is developing the database. The database will determine what type of information the help desk application will display. It also determines special component requirements. You need to know what you plan to provide for the user, how you plan to provide it, and the formatting requirements for that data before you can create an overall application plan.

You can use any database for a help desk application. For example, if the help desk application manages a large amount of data, you might want to use a full-fledged DBMS like SQL Server. On the other hand, small help desk applications can rely on something simpler, like a series of HTML pages accessed though the index services provided by Internet Information Server (IIS). Placing the help pages in a restricted area of the Web site ensures that only authorized personnel can view them and allows you to obtain usage statistics as users make requests.

We'll look at two different help desk database development topics in this section of the chapter. First, we'll build a simple database structure for our help desk applications. This structure is a very simplified form of what you may use on a large help desk application designed for enterprise use. Second, we'll look at some shortcuts that you can use to make building the help pages faster. Simply storing the content that you want to display isn't enough; you need to consider how the storage technique will affect the operation of the application.

Note   This chapter uses a somewhat compressed set of procedures for building the SQL Server database. We created another example database in Chapter 13, where I provided more detailed instructions. The instructions in this chapter provide all of the information that you require to build the database, associated tables, and indexes; however, I keep theoretical discussions to a minimum. I also won't talk much about security in this chapter's example, but you should always include it as part of your database design. See Chapter 13 for details on security as well.

Creating the database structure

We'll begin by creating a database for the help desk application. Figure 14-1 shows the details of the HelpMe database. As you can see, this database uses most of the default settings that SQL Server provides. In this case I decided to allow unrestricted growth and start with a small database size. The reason is simple, a help desk application will have strictly controlled entries and the network administrator should be able to keep a close watch on the size of the file. To better control how the file grows, you might want to use the In megabytes option in the File growth group. Using the In megabytes option allows you to specify specific growth intervals for the database.

You'll find an SQL script for creating this table in the Chapt14\Scripts and Data folder on the CD-ROM provided with this book. In addition, the data that I've used appears in this folder in a text file that you can import into the database once you've created it. Using the script and text files will save you the time of creating the database from scratch with the instructions found in this section of the chapter.

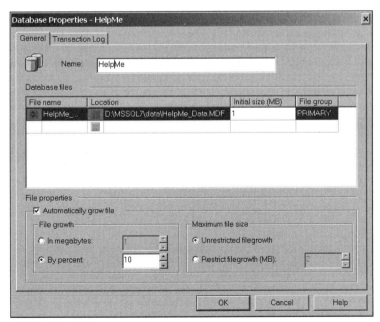

Figure 14-1: The HelpMe database will use most of the default settings provided by SQL Server.

There is just one table for this example. HelpInformation contains the actual data that will be displayed on screen. This includes a help title and associated content, as well as a help topic number used to coordinate various help topics. Figure 14-2 shows the structure of this table. Notice that the TopicNumber field is the primary key for this table.

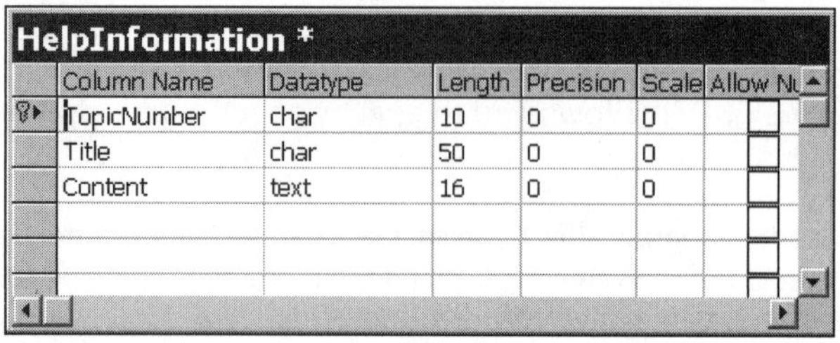

Column Name	Datatype	Length	Precision	Scale	Allow Nu
TopicNumber	char	10	0	0	
Title	char	50	0	0	
Content	text	16	0	0	

Figure 14-2: A simple table for storing help topics.

There are times when the user will want to search the help desk by topic, so we'll need to add an index to the database. You can add an index to the example for just this purpose. Right-click on the HelpInformation table entry and choose Manage Indexes from the context menu. You'll see a Manage Indexes dialog box similar to the one shown in Figure 14-3. Notice that this dialog box already contains an index for the primary key.

Click New in the Manage Indexes dialog box to display the Create New Index dialog box shown in Figure 14-4. All you need to do is select the Title entry as shown in the figure and give the index a name like TitleSearch. Click OK to create the index, then Close to close the Manage Indexes dialog box.

At this point, the design of our table is complete. As you can see, we're using a very simple database design for this application to ensure that there are no interactions or other problems to prevent the application from working the very first time. Remember to set security for the example table. All you really need to do is ensure that you can access the table from an external application.

Figure 14-3: Use the Manage Indexes dialog box to add new indexes to the HelpInformation table.

Creating data for this table does present a small challenge. Each help title's topic number has to be unique in order to ensure that every help topic can be accessed individually. Creating a title isn't much of a challenge, but there should be some logical scheme for naming the help topics. The content is the hard part. You need to consider how the client will use the data. For this reason, the text for each Content field entry has to include HTML tags so that the data will appear as the author intended within the target browser. Figure 14-5 shows a sample entry for this example.

Tip

Pressing Ctrl+M while in the Data in Table 'HelpInformation' window will allow you to add carriage returns to the end of each line of HTML code. This will make the text more readable when viewed as source code in the browser, as well as making the task of debugging the HTML content easier.

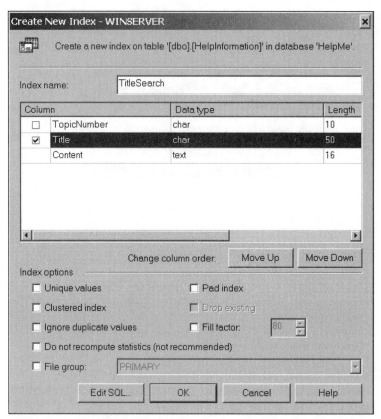

Figure 14-4: The example requires an index that will allow the user to search for information by title.

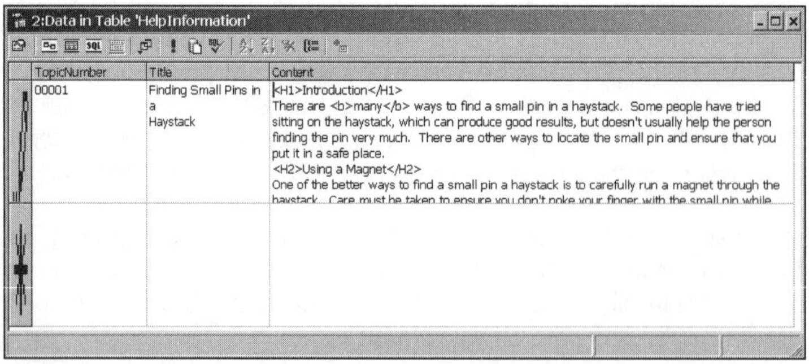

Figure 14-5: Creating the content for this example means including HTML tags.

Shortcuts for building help pages

A help desk database is a repository of information about a specific topic. In most cases, the type of data that you want to store determines the structure of the database. The amount of formatting that the data requires after it leaves the database is determined as much by the type of client as it is by the format used to store the data in the tables. There are, however, certain design elements that apply to any help desk implementation. The following sections provide you with shortcuts that will reduce the amount of work required when developing your help desk application and keep your help desk application running smoothly.

Data formatting

There are many ways that you could store the data for a help desk application. The method that you use determines how much formatting the client side of the application will need to perform once it receives the data from the server. For example, if you store the content of a help page with HTML tags in place, a Web-based application will need to perform little formatting. Of course, storing the data this way will mean that you can't easily use it with something other than a browser.

One of the easiest ways around this problem is to use the Microsoft Internet Controls (SHDOCVW.DLL) component, also known as WebBrowser, to display the data in clients that don't natively support HTML. You can use this component within a Visual Basic desktop application to support the embedded HTML tags. The `Navigate()` and `Navigate2()` methods within this component give you precise control over the contents displayed in the control window. There are also properties that you can monitor in order to ensure that the data is presented as originally anticipated. In fact, you can retrieve the document object and manipulate it directly when necessary. Using the WebBrowser does incur some application overhead, but its use also means that you can develop desktop and Web-based versions of the same application with little effort.

Another method is to use formatting hints within the application data. For example, you could store the data in rich text format (RTF). Because RTF is a common document formatting language, you can use it natively, or converted to a format that the client application is likely to understand. Using a formatting methodology like RTF orients the data toward desktop application use and means that any ASP script that you create will need to provide robust handling of the RTF tags.

You also need to consider data formatting to some extent when it comes to data input. Even though the help desk data will be used most often on a user's display, someone still has to input the original data. HTML tags are considered, even by the best professionals, as inadequate for most formatting tasks, even some of the simpler ones. Unless HTML provides enough formatting capability, you may need to use something similar to RTF to ensure that the data appears (at least on desktop machines) in the format that the originator had envisioned.

Statistics

A help desk application, unlike a standard help file, relies on input from a database. You can use the fact that the client must query the database for information to your advantage in many cases. Even though the query isn't client input per se, it does offer you the opportunity to set a triggering mechanism on the server side.

One such use for the query information is storing statistical information in the database. You can set up a separate table containing one entry for each help topic contained in the database. When a user makes a query, the ASP script or other client interface can automatically increment the appropriate help topic entry. This number will tell you how often the help topic is accessed by all users of the help desk. One refinement to this system is to add code to keep statistics on a per-session basis. In other words, once the user accesses the help topic in a given session, the number won't be incremented again. You could also keep statistics on a per-user basis. This would allow you to determine which users are accessing a specific help topic.

The uses for these statistics are almost unlimited, but two common uses come immediately to mind. First, you can use these statistics to determine which topics require additional explanation. A heavily accessed topic will indicate an area where the user needs the most help. Second, you can use the statistics to determine which topics you can safely remove from the help desk database or which topics you want to emphasize in training sessions. A topic that is seldom used may indicate an application feature that users don't understand or that users may not know about.

It's easy to create too many statistics for your help desk application. Obviously, you want to maintain the statistics in such a way that the application won't eat up too much valuable hard drive space, yet provide the input required to maintain the help desk. In many cases, all you really need to know is which topics are hot, and which are not.

Graphics

It's very unlikely that you'll create a help desk application that's devoid of graphics. The reason is simple. Showing a user a screenshot with callouts is much simpler than trying to describe the application setup with words. Even if users weren't able to understand graphics better than text, graphics offer solutions to problems that text alone can't provide. For example, it's easier for users to point to the area of the application that they don't understand than it is for you to provide them with a natural-language interface that they can use to describe the problem.

Obviously, you'll need a separate table to store graphics for a help desk application. As a minimum, you should consider adding fields for a unique identification code, the figure title, an alternative text description (if for no other reason than to help blind or PDA users who can't see the image, but who can hear a description of the image by using a reader), and the image itself. Along with these basic fields, you may want to include fields for the originator's name and other identifying information, the date that the image was created, and the location of any hand-drawn art used to create the computer image.

Adding all of this additional information may seem like a waste of time until you have to identify a graphic or find a graphic that you know is in the database, but that you can't locate by using simple identification. The ability to search for a given piece of art is important because many pieces of technical art are similar, but not precisely the same. You may have five different widgets that look almost the same and only vary by one specific characteristic. Documenting the graphics in your help desk application is very important if you want to keep the database small and easy to manage.

There is also the problem of graphics presentation. A desktop machine has a much larger display than a notebook computer does. As a result, you need more pixels to present a believable image on a desktop than you do on a notebook. There are several ways of dealing with this problem. For example, you can use scaling within the HTML to display the image at a size based on the client machine's display area. Of course, this means including a script with the HTML code to obtain the screen size from the operating system.

In many cases, Web-based applications also have the future complication of slow connection speeds. A dial-up connection won't provide enough bandwidth to download really complex graphics — at least it won't download them very fast. A user is likely to get impatient and stop the download long before the user can see the image. You can get around this problem by interlacing every image for the help desk application. Desktop application users won't see a difference in performance. In fact, anyone with a high-speed connection is unlikely to notice the interlaced image. A user with a dial-up connection, however, will see a fuzzy version of the graphic first. Once the graphic is clear enough to see, the user can stop the download and at least gain a marginal view of the graphic that you wanted to provide for the help desk application. Using something as simple as interlacing may seem obvious, but many Web sites still insist that you download the entire image before you can see it for the first time.

Tip   Once you've downloaded a graphic image to the user's machine, displaying it is very fast because the graphic already exists in the machine's cache. Using the same graphic image in several places can enhance the appearance of the Web page without the performance degradation of downloading a new graphic. For example, you could place the same company logo on every Web page. Using the logo on every Web page would provide company identification, dress up the display, and still provide a performance boost.

Links

One problem with creating a hypertext document is that the links within the document can get broken as the structure of the document database changes. This problem occurs all the time on Web sites and users find it very frustrating to click on a link that no longer works. Depending on the size of your help desk application, trying to keep all of the links updated can become a monumental task—one that you'll eventually fail to do completely.

One alternative to the link problem is to use indirect links within the document. You could provide an index in the document that points to an entry in another table. This table, in turn, would contain the link to the next document in line. Using this two-table system will result in some level of application performance degradation, but it also makes maintenance of large datasets possible. All an administrator needs to change during a help desk database restructuring is a single link reference, the one in the ancillary table.

If you choose to go this route, you'll need to ensure that every index value is unique. In addition, the index value should be assigned through code, rather than directly by the person entering the document data. In other words, what the user should think they're entering is the direct link to the next document. The modification of this link to an index to another table should occur in the background to avoid user confusion.

Human contact

Some developers are so concerned with the automation aspect of a help desk solution that they fail to add a human contact aspect as well. The human contact factor is required because no one can read minds. No matter how well you design your help desk application and no matter how much information it contains, someone will have a question that the help desk application isn't designed to answer. When this occurs, you need to provide some means of human contact. The human contact factor will keep users happy, and, more importantly, make them feel that using the help desk application isn't just a way of saving money at the expense of their ability to complete assigned tasks.

Unfortunately, the human contact information that is included in many help desk applications appears on the main page of the application. Some users bypass the help desk application to get what they think will be faster assistance with a human on the phone. The problem with this approach is that the support person has no idea of what the user has tried (if anything) to resolve a problem before calling. It's important, therefore, to place the human contact information at the end of a troubleshooting sequence, along with a contact code. The contact code will help the support person on the other end of the phone to understand what the user has tried and will result in lower support costs.

This design methodology will also save time for you, the developer. No longer do you need to create help desk data setups that use endless loops. Every troubleshooting scenario can have a logical conclusion where the user and the support staff know that everything that the user can do to fix a problem has been tried. In short, using a smart human contact methodology can make everyone happy and still dramatically reduce support costs for a company.

Creating the Server-Side Component

The server-side component provides a consistent method for accessing the database. This is an essential part of every COM+ application. Consistent access is important once you get to the server because without consistent access, testing becomes a nightmarish process of testing every potential combination of every access method. Using a single server-side component means that the middle tier and back-end processing will remain consistent even if the client side of the picture changes. In short, you should be able to use this same COM+ component whether the client is a browser (as in the case of this example) or a desktop application.

We talked about the procedures for creating COM+ application in Chapter 2. Chapter 2 also tells you about some of the implications of creating a COM+ application and how that process differs from what you may have done in the past. Be sure that you understand how to work with COM+ applications before you start the application in this chapter. We'll be creating MTS applications that you'll need to install by using the Component Services MMC snap-in to ensure proper operation.

Even though we don't cover the desktop application client in this chapter, you'll find one on the CD-ROM provided with this book in the Chapt14\Desktop Client folder. This client will allow you to test the server-side component in a second mode, as a desktop application. You'll find that the component works in the same way, whether using the ASP script or the desktop application — only the client changes, not the component or the business logic that it supports.

The following sections look at three aspects of server-side component building. First, we look at some special considerations for building Web-based applications. For example, you need to consider the use of MSMQ within your application, or whether you need the transactional support of MTS. Next, we create a component shell for the sample application. Finally, the third section will discuss the code for this server-side component.

Requirements for building Web-based applications

Web-based applications are more complex than desktop or LAN applications for many reasons. There are more transition layers to consider, the client is varied in both capability and needs, the user might not be the user that you originally envisioned for the application, and there are special reliability problems to address.

In addition, there are legal aspects that you may need to address within the application. For example, most countries now require you to keep user information confidential if your application will run in a public forum. Certainly, you wouldn't want your Web-based application to become the conduit for releasing company secrets or the means to giving away important user information like credit card numbers.

The following sections will help you to address some of the special requirements for Web-based applications. These requirements are in addition to many of the other requirements that we've already covered in other chapters. For example, if you decide to create a Web-based application that can run in disconnected mode, you'll want to look through the requirements for disconnected applications found in Chapter 12.

Using MSMQ

Building a help desk or any other Web-based application normally implies that the user has a direct connection to the server. After all, browsers aren't known for their capability to work offline unless the required Web pages are also stored offline. Of course, offline storage presents a problem for the Web-based application developer because you can't be sure that the data that the user is seeing is the data that actually exists on the server. As a result, you'll normally need to mark the downloaded pages for immediate destruction after the user sees them.

There is one way to use MSMQ in a Web-based application. A user may have a tickler or reminder file set up. The user simply notes that he or she needs to download data to better understand a company policy, procedure, or other information. For example, a client may ask about the particulars for a widget that your company sells and the salesperson on the road may need to look up this information. Rather than insist on an immediate connection to the server, a client-side application could rely on MSMQ to queue the requests for later download.

However, now we're getting out of the realm of the Web-based application because the user can no longer use a standard browser to do that job. In this case, you'd need to create a custom browser that acts like a browser from the user's perspective and like a disconnection application from the developer's perspective. In short, MSMQ is of limited use for a standard Web-based application.

Using MTS

Like MSMQ, MTS is less useful for a Web-based application than it is for other application types. Again, the problem is the browser interface on the client machine—it's not equipped to take MTS into account. MTS requires a direct client-to-component connection, something that you won't get with a standard Web-based application.

Aside from the browser limitations, you need to consider why you'd need MTS for a help desk application. Using a virtual private network (VPN) will keep secure the data that is transferred from the server to the client. The data request from the client is also protected using a VPN, so there is little chance of a security compromise. As you can see, there is little need to use MTS with a Web-based application because there aren't any special security or reliability requirements that can't be addressed by using other technologies.

The question, then, is why use COM+ at all? If MSMQ is of limited help and MTS isn't any help at all, what does COM+ have to offer the developer? In this case, the answer is in the efficiency of the COM+ architecture. A Web-based application will put a lot of stress on the server. Instead of hundreds of users that can make requests when a LAN connection is used, a Web-based application allows thousands of users to use a variety of connection methods to make requests (some of which will rely on dial-up connections).

A COM+ application allows the server to handle client requests efficiently. So, while we're relying on an older scripting technology to format the data for the client and to pass along the client request, COM+ is handling the bulk of the application processing. You'll find that using COM+ for the server portion of a Web-based application greatly enhances application throughput and makes the server more capable of handling large loads.

Server-side versus client-side locale support

The Internet isn't the vacuum that most corporate networks are. If your application will run on the Internet, then support for a variety of languages and ways of doing things is a requirement, not a luxury. Large companies, in fact, are finding that any assumptions that they may have made about single-language support for custom applications are wrong — today, even enterprise applications need to provide some level of support for more than one language. You'll need to provide some type of multiple-language support, even if that support is limited to providing captions in the user's native language.

Note   Every group of people has more than just a unique language. A nationality is often defined by the biases of its people and the ways that those people interact with the world around them. These differences create a lot of problems that you'll need to deal with when working with more than one language in an application. We'll talk about the problems that you'll face when incorporating various languages and nationality support into your application in the "Human language support" section of the chapter.

Part of designing a Web-based application is determining where you want to provide language and nationality support. Some items are taken care of for you. For example, the user configures Windows to use certain defaults. Figure 14-6 shows the Windows 2000 Regional Options dialog box (found in the Control Panel), which allows the user to adjust numeric, time, date, and currency formats. This same dialog box will also allow the user to change input locales, which, in most cases, has a smaller, but noticeable effect on your application.

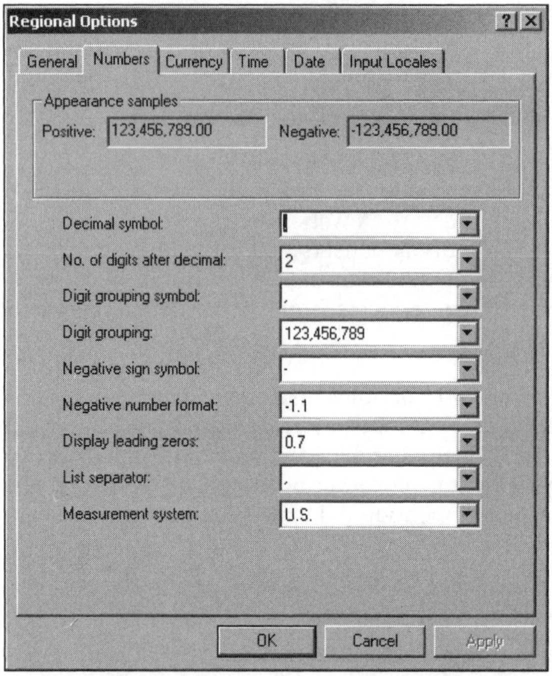

Figure 14-6: The Regional Options dialog box allows the user to configure preferred regional options that you can incorporate into your application.

Windows API calls like GetLocaleInfo() allow you to access this information and adjust the display appropriately. Visual Basic also provides native functions, like Format(), that are locale (regional setting) aware. The LocaleID ambient property allows you to check for user changes to the locale while your application is running. This allows you to change the display appropriately. You can conceivably perform this task as part of a script within the Web page, which means that the client will perform the required formatting work. Here's a very simple example showing how to use GetLocale() within a VBScript script in a Web page.

```
<HEAD>
<TITLE>
  Locale Demonstration
</TITLE>
<BODY>

The current local is: <INPUT TYPE="text" ID="Locale" SIZE="20">

<SCRIPT LANGUAGE="VBScript">

  Locale.Value = Hex(GetLocale)
```

```
</SCRIPT>
</BODY>
</HEAD>
```

The number that you'll see when you display this Web page depends on the current locale setting for your machine. For example, my machine displays a value of 409h because I live in the United States. Of course, you can change this value for testing purposes by changing the values in the Regional Options dialog shown in Figure 14-6. It's also possible to detect the locale and use it to select language specific DLLs. For example, you might have one version of a DLL that's named MyControl409.DLL for the United States and another version named MyControlCOC.DLL for French Canadian users. By creating a string using GetLocale(), you could select the right DLL for the user and download just that DLL from your Web site.

There are Locale ID (LCID) values for most language groups or countries in the world. It's important to know the LCID for each language that you plan to support with your application. You can find a list of currently supported LCIDs at http://msdn.microsoft.com/scripting/vbscript/doc/vsmsclcid.htm.

However, the problem with performing the required setup on the client side is that the client-side script can become quite complicated and browsers provide an interpreted environment. As a result, data display can become quite slow. In addition, if your application displays monetary values, you may need to provide some type of currency conversion routine, which is clearly outside the purview of most client-side scripts. In short, the client-side solution is limited to specific types of formatting if you want to present the user with a friendly display in the shortest possible time.

Windows 2000 provides the best level of international support of any version of Windows released at the time of this writing. You'll find that this product allows you to obtain and use more information about the user, making it possible to fully customize an application to meet a user's language requirements. You can find out more about the international support in Windows 2000 at http://msdn.microsoft.com/library/backgrnd/html/intl_sup_nt5.htm. This Web site also tells you how Windows 2000 international support differs from its predecessors.

Server-side processing of the same information can occur within a component. This means that the user will see the information faster and that you'll transfer far less data over the wire. After all, you'll send just the data, not the client-side scripts required to format the data once it arrives. The problem with server-side processing is that the server has no idea what the user preferences are and can't read the user's locale settings from a remote location.

Some Web sites have used a very simple solution for the problem of language support within Web-based applications. A main page allows the user to make the same selections found in the Regional Options dialog box. These options are then saved to a cookie on the user's machine. Of course, this solution is still less than elegant and in many cases requires a savvy user to make the required choices.

Another alternative is to allow two data transfers for each request from the client. The first would request the desired help topic, while the second would return regional information when requested. This solution is appealing because it requires no user intervention; everything is performed automatically. The downside to this approach is that the application now requires two trips to gain the required information; something you should avoid whenever possible for reliability and performance reasons.

In short, the decision whether to use client-side or server-side language and nationality support isn't easy to make. A good general rule of thumb is to look at the complexity of the application, the required performance factors, and the type of data being transferred from the server to the client. If the data includes data that may require translation like monetary, weight, or distance values, then server-side processing is probably the best choice. On the other hand, if the data is fairly plain and the user doesn't require immediate updates, using a client-side script will be the best choice because it offloads the burden from the server and allows a one-pass query.

Customization support

Other than the user's need to have an application that works as anticipated and one that supports national and language needs, a user also needs to have a certain level of customization within an application. For example, one user may like an uncluttered display containing only the data that the user requires to perform a task, while another user may want direct access to application commands through a toolbar or other direct access means. Some users may even want a combination of configurations depending on the task that they're performing at any given time. In short, although you can provide a specific set of features within an application, the user should control access to those features — at least to some extent.

Desktop applications are relatively easy to modify to provide customization support. Both Visual Basic and Visual C++ provide direct support for a variety of customization features like toolbars that you can detach from the rest of the application or get rid of entirely. Web-based applications, those that require a browser, are quite different. Now you're looking at the relatively difficult task of providing some type of customization support for something that is still a static media. Although Internet Explorer does provide support for all kinds of dynamic content, its interface is still relatively primitive.

One solution for this problem is to install ActiveX controls on the user's machine that allow the application to provide the same features found in desktop applications. This solution works very well for custom applications in an enterprise setting where you have direct control over the user's machine. It works relatively well in partner situations in which the person downloading data from your Web site has full confidence in your company's capability to provide Web content that is safe to use. This solution is probably not going to work well in an Internet setting where the public is downloading your Web-based application and there is no trust established between the user and your company.

The advantage of the ActiveX control solution is that all customization takes place on the client machine, which means that the server supplies the same page no matter who is requesting the data. Because ActiveX controls are persistable, the configuration information can be stored on the local machine in the Registry. This means that a user will see the same display no matter when the user looks at the Web page, even in disconnected mode. In fact, the user still has full configuration control in disconnected mode.

Another solution is to provide customization support through the use of onscreen configuration. The user's preferred Web page is generated on the server by using configuration settings supplied by the user during an initial query or uploaded from a cookie stored on the user's machine. Creating the customized version of the Web page allows greater flexibility because the client only needs to be capable of displaying the results; it does not need to be capable of performing any calculations. This is a good solution when you're unsure about the capability of the client, for example, when the same application has to work on both a desktop and a PDA. The downside to this approach is that it usually generates a little more network traffic because the server may have to communicate with the client more than once. In addition, the user will only see a static Web page. The user won't be able to change display settings while disconnected from the server.

Web-based application developers also need to consider how much customization is enough and what types of customization are required. For example, a PDA will barely have enough room on its display to show the data that the user has requested. There isn't any room for status bars, tool bars, or perhaps even menus. In some cases, the user might require an option to clear all extraneous text from the display so that a reader will be capable of providing the data to the user instead of the normal text display. These design requirements mean that an application designed for a broad range of application types will also need to provide full customization features.

Privacy and other legal concerns

We've talked about more than a little data gathering so far. You're probing the user's machine for regional settings, customization preferences, and other types of information. It might be necessary to download some personal information so that you can validate the user, and, in some cases, you might need the information to maintain localized stores of custom information.

There has been a lot of news in the trade press recently regarding user rights issues. The most important of these issues is user privacy. Crackers very often try to gain access to user information in an effort to perform misdeeds like steal the user's identity for the purpose of financial gain. The issue of user privacy is an important one no matter who the user is, and the Internet makes it difficult to protect that privacy.

A Web-based application needs to take more than the normal precautions when it comes to security. Not only do you have to protect the server, the client, the data, and the application, but now you have to protect the user as well. Encryption between client and server might not be enough to assure that the user's identity and associated information is protected.

This raises an interesting point: How do you secure the user's identity and still garner the identity information required to assure the safety of the server, client, data, and application? In some cases, the answer is that you really don't need to store identification information. If a user can provide proper credentials in the form of a digital certificate, you may have all the information that you need to ensure that the user is authorized to view data from your Web site or to use a customized Web-based application. The digital certificate can also be used in place of human-readable data within a database to associate stored configuration information with a particular user. After all, every digital certificate is guaranteed to be unique and you'll need to store the digital certificate locally for comparison purposes.

You'll want to spend some time talking with your company's legal department to ensure that any Web-based application that you create meets legal requirements for Internet access, not only in the country in which you live, but also in countries in which your application might be used. Many countries are attempting to establish legal protection and requirements at the time of this writing, so you may still find those requirements in a state of flux as you read this. The point is that the user has a right to privacy and the Internet, as a public network, requires special handling within a Web-based application that you may not be used to providing.

Note Checking with legal once about Web-based application requirements isn't enough. The Internet is a new territory for the legal profession, so new laws are created every day. With this in mind, you should check for new legal requirements and the enforceability of existing legal requirements on a regular basis. Make sure you update the legal requirements for your Web site every time you make a change to the content.

Bandwidth concerns

Transferring data on any network uses bandwidth. If you have a few clients, then the load on the network is usually negligible and you don't need to worry about it. A Web-based application is one application that will always require you to consider the amount of bandwidth that the application will use. The reason is simple. Unlike a desktop or LAN application, there is no way to predict how much the usage of a

Web-based application will grow, and therefore no way to tell how much bandwidth the application will eventually require.

In most cases, you can control this problem by enabling bandwidth throttling on the Web server. However, this treats the symptoms of the problem, not the cause. When you design a Web-based application, you need to consider how much data the application will transfer for every request and attempt to minimize the size of the data if possible.

One problem that developers run into is that they'll look at the actual size of the data, rather than its size on the network. It's not uncommon for some "optimized" applications to waste more network bandwidth than they save. A packet that contains only a small amount of data will get padded to a specific size. This means that the packet is wasting bandwidth because it's transferring padding, rather than real data.

In short, you need to consider the size of the data as well as the number of data transfers. A series of two small data transfers will always consume more bandwidth than a single data transfer that combines the data from both of the smaller data transfers. Remember that efficient data transfers minimize the number of packets as well as the size of those packets.

Creating the component shell

It's time to create the COM+ component that will enable the client to receive data from the database. We created a similar component in Chapter 13. However, the component in this chapter has a simpler task in that it only needs to work with one table. On the other hand, this chapter's component will need to search for a specific instance of the required data based on a field other than the help desk Title or TopicNumber field value. In addition, this component will need to retrieve a single record (to minimize network traffic) instead of an entire recordset. In other words, it's will be similar, but not the same because the task that this component is asked to perform is different. Because of the similarity between two components, however, I'll use abbreviated instructions in this chapter. The instructions are complete, but I haven't included some of the database theory details that appear in Chapter 13.

Begin by creating an ActiveX DLL project. The example uses a project name of SimpleHelpDesk and a class name of GetHelp. As with all of the other COM+ components that we've created in the book, you'll want to set at least three of the properties in the SimpleHelpDesk – Project Properties dialog box. Make sure that the Threading Mode property is set to Single Threaded, that the Unattended Execution option is checked, and that you set the component up for Binary Compatibility after the first compile. In this way, you'll ensure that you know whether you're breaking any COM rules when you create future builds of the component.

As with the other database example that we've worked with, we need to add a data environment to the component. Right-click SimpleHelpDesk in the Project window and then choose Add ⇨ Data Environment from the context menu. Visual Basic will add a data environment to your component. The example program uses a name of deSimpleHelpDesk for the data environment and connSimpleHelpDesk for the component. The following steps will help you to configure connSimpleHelpDesk.

Note   If you choose to use the code from the CD-ROM provided with this book, you must reconfigure the Data Link Properties dialog box for connSimpleHelpDesk to use the settings for your network. These configuration options are network specific and the component that I created for the example won't have the same server name as your network. After you reconfigure the Data Link Properties dialog box settings, you can recompile the component and install it on the server. The component should work without any additional code changes.

1. Right-click connSimpleHelpDesk and choose Properties from the context menu. You'll see the Data Link Properties dialog box shown in Figure 14-7.

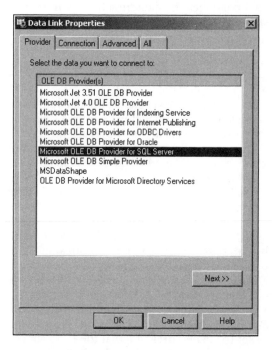

Figure 14-7: The first step in creating a connection is to choose a database provider.

2. Choose Microsoft OLE DB Provider for SQL Server, and then click Next. You'll see the Connection tab of the Data Link Properties dialog box as shown in Figure 14-8.

3. Choose the test server for your network in the Select or enter a server name field. Click Refresh if you don't see any servers in the list. Don't type the name of the server. If Visual Basic can't see the server now, it won't see the server when it's time to compile the component. You must correct any network problems before you proceed.

4. Type a username and password in the User name and Password fields.

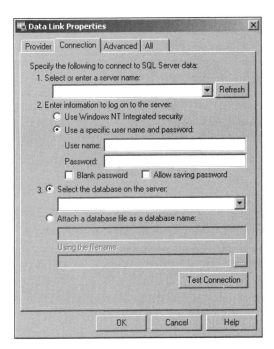

Figure 14-8: The second step in creating a connection is to set the server name and database name.

5. Choose the HelpMe database in the Select the database on the server field. If you don't see a list of databases, but you can access the server, it most likely means that you don't have proper access rights to SQL Server. Stop the procedure right now and correct any access problems before you proceed. If Visual Basic can't obtain a list of databases now, it won't be able to do so later.

6. Click Test Connection. You should see a Test connection succeeded message box. If you don't see this message box, then there's something wrong with your setup. Repeat Steps 3 through 5. Make sure that the username and password that you provide are correct.

7. Click OK to clear the Test connection succeeded message box, and then click OK again to save the connection settings. It's time to create the commands required to make the component work. We did the same thing for the component in Chapter 13 as a separate set of steps.

8. Right-click connSimpleHelpDesk and choose Add Command from the context menu. Visual Basic will add a new command to the database designer hierarchy. Use a name from the Command Name column of Table 14-1 below.

9. Right-click the new command and choose Properties from the context menu. You'll see the new command Properties dialog box shown in Figure 14-9.

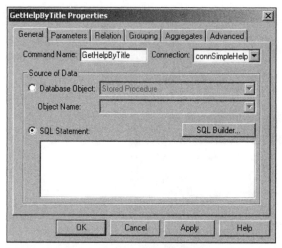

Figure 14-9: Creating a database command means creating a statement or accessing a predefined routine that will return data to the user.

10. Select the SQL Statement option, and then click SQL Builder. You'll see two dialog boxes. The Data View dialog box shows you what the database has to offer in the form of tables, views, and stored procedures. The Design dialog box shows the command that you're building.

11. Drag the HelpInformation table from the Data View dialog box to the upper pane of the Design dialog box.

12. Click each of the fields individually, rather than clicking the * (All Columns) option as we did in Chapter 13. Using this technique allows a little more flexibility than selecting all of the fields at once.

13. Select the proper sort order for the fields shown in the Sort Order column of Table 14-1 below. The resulting command should look similar to the one shown in Figure 14-10 for the GetHelpByTitle command.

14. Click the Close box. Visual Basic will ask if you want to save the command. Click Yes.

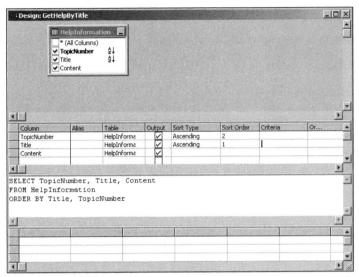

Figure 14-10: The graphical view of the GetHelpByTitle command is simple.

15. Perform steps 9 through 14 for each command in Table 14-1 below. When you've completed both commands in Table 14-1, the database designer window should look like the one shown in Figure 14-11.

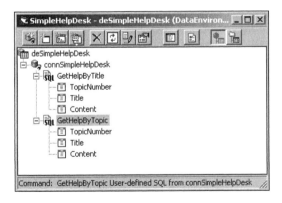

Figure 14-11: The database designer uses a hierarchy of objects to create a connection to the database.

On the CD-ROM

If you get lost using the step-by-step instructions above and the information in Table 14-1, you can always look at the source code on the CD-ROM provided with this book. You'll find this example in the Chapt14\Help Desk Component folder.

Table 14-1
SimpleHelpDesk Component Command Summary

Command Name	Sort Order	SQL Statement	Description
GetHelpByTitle	Title (Ascending) TopicNumber (Ascending)	SELECT TopicNumber, Title, Content FROM HelpInformation ORDER BY Title, TopicNumber	A command that retrieves data from the HelpMe database in Title order.
GetHelpByTopic	TopicNumber (Ascending)	SELECT TopicNumber, Title, Content FROM HelpInformation ORDER BY TopicNumber	A command the retrieves data from the HelpMe database in TopicNumber order.

Adding some code

There are a few things that we'll need to consider when putting the code together for this component. First, there have to be two method calls. The first will allow a user to look for a help topic by title. The ASP script will use the second method to look up topics by topic number. The ASP script will default to looking for the first topic in the help desk application. However, once the user begins to click on links within the help topics, the link numbers will be used for lookup purposes.

The second consideration is network bandwidth. This component will return a single record at a time to conserve network bandwidth. If the client application requires another help topic, then the component will look it up as a separate task.

Now that you have some idea of what will make the methods for this code special, let's look at some code. Listing 14-1 shows the code for the component.

Listing 14-1: SimpleHelpDesk Component Source Code

```
Public Sub GetTitle _
    (strTopicNumber As Variant, _
    strTitle As Variant, _
    strContents As Variant)

    'Create an array to hold the data values.
    Dim aFields

    'Create a string to hold the search value.
    Dim strSearch As String
    strSearch = "Title LIKE '*" + strTitle + "*'"
```

```
        'Open the recordset.
        deSimpleHelpDesk.rsGetHelpByTitle.Open

        'Look for the help topic by title.
        If Len(strTitle) > 0 Then
            deSimpleHelpDesk.rsGetHelpByTitle.Find strSearch
        End If

        'Determine if the search value was found.
        If deSimpleHelpDesk.rsGetHelpByTitle.EOF Then

            'If the search value wasn't found, report an
            'error to the user.
            strTopicNumber = "99999"
            strContents = "Couldn't find the search value: " _
                + strTitle
            strTitle = "Error Finding Value"

        Else

            'Get the current field values.
            aFields = deSimpleHelpDesk.rsGetHelpByTitle.GetRows(1)
            strTopicNumber = aFields(0, 0)
            strTitle = aFields(1, 0)
            strContents = aFields(2, 0)
        End If

        'Close the database.
        deSimpleHelpDesk.rsGetHelpByTitle.Close
    End Sub

    Public Sub GetTopic _
        (strTopicNumber As Variant, _
        strTitle As Variant, _
        strContents As Variant)

        'Create an array to hold the data values.
        Dim aFields

        'Create a string to hold the search value.
        Dim strSearch As String
        strSearch = "TopicNumber LIKE '" + strTopicNumber + "'"

        'Open the recordset.
        deSimpleHelpDesk.rsGetHelpByTopic.Open

        'Look for the help topic by title.
        If Len(strTopicNumber) = 5 Then
            deSimpleHelpDesk.rsGetHelpByTopic.Find strSearch
        End If
```

Continued

> **Listing 14-1** *(continued)*
>
> ```
>         'Get the current field values.
>         aFields = deSimpleHelpDesk.rsGetHelpByTopic.GetRows(1)
>         strTopicNumber = aFields(0, 0)
>         strTitle = aFields(1, 0)
>         strContents = aFields(2, 0)
>
>         'Close the database.
>         deSimpleHelpDesk.rsGetHelpByTopic.Close
>     End Sub
> ```

One of the very first things that you should notice about this code is that the arguments are passed as variants instead of strings. Quite a bit of experimentation showed that strings are error prone when working with ASP scripts, so you'll want to avoid them in components designed for use in this environment. Using a variant doesn't result in any performance problems and makes the component work more reliably with the script.

The code for both methods begins by creating two variables. The first, aFields, will hold the recordset query results, which is returned in a two-dimensional array. The second, strSearch, contains the modified search string. You need to specify the field that you want to search on and provide some comparison criteria. Using LIKE is the most flexible way to search for text values. SQL server also supports the standard comparison values that include > (greater than), < (less than), = (equal to), >= (greater than or equal to), and <= (less than or equal to). Asterisks (*) are used before and after the search value in GetTitle(). They serve as wildcard values that allow the application to search for topics based on one word queries. Because the TopicNumber field is always a precise value, we don't need to include the asterisks for GetTopic().

The code begins interacting with the recordset by opening it. Note that we use a different recordset value for each method because the ordering is different. If you want to allow the user to select from a list of topics instead of going to just one topic, the ordering would be important. In this case, it simply allows us to search more quickly.

Both methods check the value of their respective search inputs next. If the value isn't present, then the code ignores it and proceeds to display the first record depending on the ordering of the recordset. If the value is present, then both methods attempt to find it within the recordset. Because the user will never provide input for the GetTopic method, it's safe to assume that any value passed by the ASP script will be found. However, if the value isn't found, the user will see a distinctive error screen similar to the one shown in Figure 14-12.

The most important part of this display is the error message. It says, "Error Type: ADODB.Recordset (0x800A0BCD) Either BOF or EOF is True, or the current record has been deleted. Requested operation requires a current record." This is your cue that the parent page has a broken link. The reason that you don't want to override this behavior is that the user can click the Back button to get to the previous page; the application is still functional, but the link is broken. The distinctive message tells the user to notify the network administrator and provide the administrator with the message text. In most cases, you do want to handle errors with a friendly display; this is one of those situations in which the default message does a very good job and doesn't prevent the application from recovering.

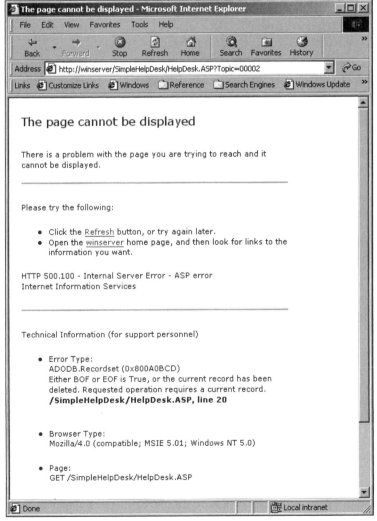

Figure 14-12: Broken links will display a distinctive error message to the user.

Unlike the GetTopic() method, the GetTitle() method does get input from the user and it's very likely that the user will occasionally search for items that don't exist in the recordset. As a result, the GetTitle() method checks for an EOF value immediately after the search is completed. If the user has entered a nonexistent title value, then they'll see the friendly error message display shown in Figure 14-13.

Figure 14-13: It's better to provide the user with a friendly error message screen than to use the default message if the user inputs an incorrect search value.

Notice how the values get returned from the recordset to the client. We place the rowset into the aFields array. The GetRows() method accepts the number of rows that you want to retrieve as the first argument. The default value of –1 retrieves all of the rows in the recordset. Each field is represented by the first array dimension. The second dimension contains the returned rows. As a result, the first TopicNumber row value appears in array element (0, 0) as shown in the code. If you wanted to get the second TopicNumber row value, you'd look at array element (0, 1). Likewise, because the Title is the second field, the first row value appears in array element (1, 0).

The final task performed by the code in both methods is to close the recordset. You always want to close the recordset or your component will leak resources. While Windows 2000 will eventually recover these resources, your server will run more efficiently if you close the recordset when you've finished using it.

Creating the Browser Application

One of the last pieces of the puzzle for a Web-based application is the browser support. A browser needs input in the way of HTML and script in order to provide the user with a display. In days past, it would have been possible to create individual Web pages by using HTML and links to allow the user to navigate from one portion of the Web site to another. A help desk application, however, provides too much information of a changeable nature to make individual Web pages a viable solution. That's why you need a combination of HTML, client-side scripting, and server-side scripting to make this type of solution work.

The first two sections that follow look at the important issues of how you can speed application development. Web applications have to be developed with ever-greater speed today, so getting the most out of your development time is very important. We'll begin by looking at methods for reducing script development time. The next section will help you to understand when scripting is a good solution and when you may need to look at some other methodology for getting the information to the user.

The third section will show you how to create the ASP script for this example. This ASP script relies on the component that we created earlier in the chapter. The component provides high speed access to the data, while the ASP script provides a flexible front end for formatting the data. The combination of speed and flexibility will allow the final application to create output quickly, yet allow the developer to make changes to the interface without recompiling the component.

Shortcuts for scripting

A lot of developers look at scripting as one of the faster ways to develop applications because scripts run in an interpreted environment where you can get instant feedback from the interpreter. The only problem with this scenario is that unlike most scripting environments, ASP scripts are notoriously difficult to troubleshoot because you don't get the instant feedback that you're expecting in many cases. The problem is twofold. First the script executes on a remote server, so many of the execution details are hidden from view. Second, until recently, Microsoft didn't provide any type of debugger for ASP scripts, making trial and error your best friend.

The debugger provided with Windows 2000 is pretty weak, but it's better than nothing at all. You'll have to install the Script Debugger separately by using the Add/Remove Programs applet. After you install the Script Debugger, you'll find a new View ⇨ Script Debugger entry in Internet Explorer that you can use to start the Script Debugger. You get Call Stack, Running Documents, and Command windows. The Call Stack window tells you the current call hierarchy within in the running document. The Running Document window allows you to choose other scripts to debug. The Command window is used to test variable values and code. Figure 14-14 shows a typical Script Debugger display.

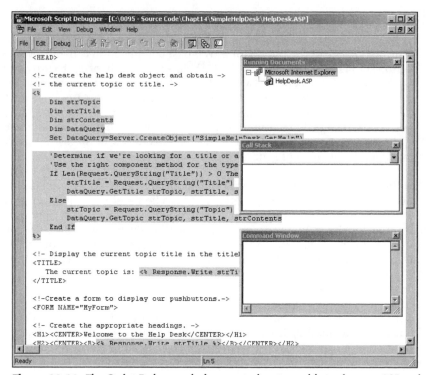

Figure 14-14: The Script Debugger helps you to locate problems in your ASP scripts.

Notice that the Script Debugger uses highlighting to help you to locate pieces of script to test. There are also debugging tools that allow you to single-step through the script, making it easier to find errant code. You can also set breakpoints or break at the next statement, which allows you to pass through the HTML portions of an ASP script with relative ease. Obviously, you'll want to use the Script Debugger whenever possible to speed your development along.

ASP is part script and part HTML. It's normally a good idea to write the HTML portion first so that you can get any HTML errors out of the way and check for element positioning on screen. In addition, by working on the HTML portion first, you can better see where you'll need to include specific script elements.

Fortunately, the perception that you can create a script in piecemeal fashion, testing each portion as you write it, is true. One of the better ways of avoiding problems with your script is to write functions individually and test them on a separate Web page. When the function is debugged, you can add it to the main script and test it again as part of the whole application. While this may seem to be time-consuming, using this technique will save you hours of debugging time and provide you with separate modules that you can use with other scripts as needed.

Determining what to script

Some developers look at the coding requirements for a Web-based application and immediately assume that there must be an easier way. To some, scripting looks easier because you can test the application in small segments, and making changes doesn't require recompiling the component and reinstalling it. There are, however, limits to what you can do with a script. For one thing, scripting languages aren't nearly as robust as full-fledged programming languages like Visual Basic. The following sections will help you to understand the role scripting plays with Web-based applications.

Advantages of scripting

Scripting has been termed as the novice's programming language by some people, but scripts are extremely useful tools when used correctly. It's important to understand that scripts have certain advantages when compared to the full-fledged applications that you normally create by using a standard language and compiler. The following list will help you to understand the advantages of using scripts for Web-based applications.

✦ **Development Speed:** Scripts are very fast to write; you can write them in sections; and mistakes are very easy to fix. You'll find that the loss of the compile portion of the debugging cycle does speed things up quite a bit.

✦ **Ease of Use:** Any text editor can be used to create a script. You don't need any fancy tools, just an interpreter. This means that any desktop machine can serve as a platform for building and testing scripts as long as it has the requisite interpreter installed.

✦ **Platform Independence:** To a certain extent, scripts are the most independent way to write code. Because they're written in text, there isn't any problem with transferring binary data to another machine. Any platform that has an interpreter capable of understanding the script can run it. Of course, therein lies the problem — finding an interpreter for every platform that needs it.

There are other advantages to using scripting languages that many developers overlook or are completely unaware of. For example, under Windows 2000, you can create very simple components by using scripting languages. These small components can perform simple tasks like converting monetary, distance, or weight values from one unit of measure to another. Here's a very simple example of a component written using a scripting language.

```
<SCRIPTLET>

<Registration
    Description="ConvertTemp"
    ProgID="ConvertTemp.Scriptlet"
    Version="1.00"></Registration>
```

```
<implements
 id=Automation
 type=Automation>

    <method name=Celsius>
        <PARAMETER name=F/>
    </method>

    <method name=Fahrenheit>
        <PARAMETER name=C/>
    </method>

</implements>

<SCRIPT LANGUAGE=VBScript>

  Function Celsius(F)
      Celsius = 5/9 * (F - 32)
  End Function

  Function Fahrenheit(C)
      Fahrenheit = (9/5 * C) + 32
  End Function</SCRIPT>

</SCRIPTLET>
```

As you can see, this very simple script converts degrees Celsius to degrees Fahrenheit and back. The two methods are very easy to understand, but it's the fact that you can write them within a script that's interesting. Right-click on the resulting script file and you'll see a context menu similar to the one shown in Figure 14-15. Notice that you can register and unregister this script as a component, just as you would any other component. Windows 2000 will even create a type library for the script so that you can use the component within environments like Visual Basic.

Figure 14-15: Scriptlets are treated like any other component, enabling you to create quick components for testing purposes.

Disadvantages of scripting

Scripts have a lot of disadvantages. Whenever you begin to approach the simplicity of the scripting environment, there are flexibility and extensibility concerns to weigh. The following list will help you to understand some of the disadvantages of using scripts.

✦ **Security:** Scripts are written in text. Anyone with a text editor and the proper rights can modify the script. Even someone who isn't looking to cause problems can inadvertently change a script and cause it to fail. Just imagine what crackers can to do the scripts on your server.

✦ **Debugging:** There isn't a formal IDE for writing scripts. As a result, you lose some basic support features that you'll find in a full-fledged programming language like debugging support. While the Script Debugger is a step in the right direction, it cannot replace the debugging capabilities found in a product like Visual Basic. In short, if you've got a bug in your script code, expect to spend some time researching the problem yourself.

✦ **Extensibility:** Script languages are usually limited versions of their full-fledged language cousins. When you look at the language features of Visual Basic and compare them to VBScript, you'll find that you're extremely limited in what you can do with VBScript, the scripting language version of Visual Basic. While you do have basic access to features like object creation, you'll find that other elements that you take for granted in Visual Basic, like access to the Windows API, are sorely lacking. Even Visual Basic for Applications (VBA) provides more capabilities than VBScript.

✦ **Flexibility:** Scripts are good for creating small applications. However, you'll find that the lack of some of the more common control structures and external file accessibility features will limit what you can create by using a script. Sure, you can go to extremes and write the next great chess game by using a scripting language, but you'll find that the effort of doing so far exceeds anything that you'd experience by using Visual Basic. So, while scripts are great for the small utility applications on your system, they're not really flexible enough for anything larger.

✦ **Execution Speed:** Because scripts are interpreted, you can't expect them to provide the same execution speed as a compiled version of an application. This lack of execution speed doesn't affect the small utility uses for which scripting languages are designed, but it will affect overall application speed if you try to use a script in places that it wasn't designed to go.

Methods of dividing application functionality

Trying to divide an application into compiled and scripted areas may prove difficult if you don't perform some application analysis first. It's important to create a full design specification for your application so that you know how complex each element will be, how often you'll need to change the code, where the code will be located, and what type of task the code will perform. The following list provides pointers on how you can divide an application into scripted and nonscripted areas after you get some of the basics figured out.

✦ **Size Matters:** One of the more important elements to consider is just how large a particular element will be. Interpreted code runs slowly compared to compiled code, so you'll want to reserve scripts for smaller utility functions.

✦ **Security:** Compiled code is inherently more secure than scripted code because it isn't in human-readable form. While it's very easy to change a script, changing compiled code is another matter. In addition, using compiled code will protect your company's research investment. Decompiling an application into human-readable form (so you can understand the code) takes more time than most crackers are willing to invest.

✦ **Changeability:** Scripts offer the advantage of quick changes. If your application is in a state of flux, you might consider using scripts to allow for quick changes. A script can even work for simple components that you eventually plan to convert to compiled code.

✦ **Client-Side Tasks:** In many cases, you don't know what capability the client will have when you write an application. Using a script that runs within the browser environment guarantees that no matter what capabilities the client has, it will be able to run your application.

Writing an ASP script

We've already created the component that we'll use for this application; now it's time to look at the script that will make the Web-based application complete. This script provides several features that may not be apparent at first. Because of the way that this script is designed, the user will always access the same URL. The only things that will change are the variables supplied to the script. If the user passes a Title variable, then the script will initiate a search of the recordset for a specific help desk title. On the other hand, if the user passes a Topic variable, then the script will initiate a search for that topic number within the recordset. This interface is designed to allow the user to save help pages that get used a lot in the user's Favorites folder, but the use of a consistent URL reduces the chance that broken links will render those Favorites folder entries invalid.

Caution   Most developers are aware of problems that occur when an operating system vendor fails to seal all of the security leaks, especially when those leaks occur on the Web server. However, few developers are aware of problems that their own code can cause, even when that code is syntactically correct and works as it's supposed to do. There is a new breed of security breach that virus writers and crackers are making use of that involves the interactions that take place between Web sites, especially if those Web sites dynamically generate the content for the Web pages that they provide. In fact, it's the dynamic generation part of the equation that makes this Caution so appropriate for this section of the chapter. The code for the individual Web site is correct, but when it interacts with the code from another Web site, the dynamic code causes security problems. The most severe form of this kind of programming problem is called Cross-Site Scripting. This coding error can allow a foreign executable to run within a user's Web session, causing a number of problems for the developer. Microsoft is currently working with the Computer Emergency Response Team (CERT) to derive solutions for this problem. You can find out more information about this problem at `http://www.microsoft.com/technet/security/crssite.asp`. This site tells you more about the potential for attack from crackers, and will also help you to understand what you can do to help prevent the problem on user machines until all of the code on your Web site can be examined for problems.

An important thing to remember about ASP, at least from a Visual Basic developer's perspective, is that an ASP script is equal parts VBScript and HTML. If you can write Visual Basic code and you know how to work with HTML, then ASP has absolutely nothing new to offer. All you need to do is combine the two technologies into a cohesive whole. This is one the reasons that many developers feel that ASP is the right technology for most of their Web programming needs.

Now that we've gotten some of the preliminaries out of the way, let's look at the ASP script for this example. Listing 14-2 contains the code that we'll use.

Listing 14-2: **Help Desk ASP Script**

```
<HEAD>

<!- Create the help desk object and obtain ->
<!- the current topic or title. ->
<%
    Dim strTopic
    Dim strTitle
    Dim strContents
    Dim DataQuery
    Set DataQuery=Server.CreateObject("SimpleHelpDesk.GetHelp")

    'Determine if we're looking for a title or a topic number.
    'Use the right component method for the type of call.
    If Len(Request.QueryString("Title")) > 0 Then
        strTitle = Request.QueryString("Title")
        DataQuery.GetTitle strTopic, strTitle, strContents
    Else
```

Continued

Listing 14-2 *(continued)*

```
            strTopic = Request.QueryString("Topic")
            DataQuery.GetTopic strTopic, strTitle, strContents
        End If
%>

<!- Display the current topic title in the titlebar. ->
<TITLE>
    The current topic is: <% Response.Write strTitle %>
</TITLE>

<!-Create a form to display our pushbuttons.->
<FORM NAME="MyForm">

<!- Create the appropriate headings. ->
<H1><CENTER>Welcome to the Help Desk</CENTER></H1>
<H2><CENTER><B><% Response.Write strTitle %></B></CENTER></H2>

<!- Display the content. ->
<%
    Response.Write strContents
%>

<!- Provide a place to search by topic. ->
<P><B>Search by Topic:</B><BR>
<INPUT TYPE=TEXTBOX NAME="SearchValue" SIZE=40><P>

<!- Allow the user to search for the topic. ->
<INPUT LANGUAGE="VBScript"
       TYPE="BUTTON"
       VALUE="Search"
       ONCLICK="window.location.href = 'HelpDesk.asp?Title=' _
                + MyForm.SearchValue.Value">

<!- Make it easy for the user to get back to the main page. ->
<%
    If Not RTrim(strTopic) = "00000" Then
        Response.Write "<P>Go Back to the "
        Response.Write "<A HREF=HelpDesk.ASP>Main Page</A>"
    End If
%>

</FORM>
</HEAD>
```

As you can see, the ASP script begins with the usual <HEAD> HTML tag and ends with the </HEAD> tag. Like all HTML pages, it has a body that's delimited by the <FORM> and </FORM> tag pairs in this case. So far, there isn't anything here that's different from a standard Web page.

The first scripting task that we have to perform is the creation of three variables to hold the contents of the database fields and make queries. We also need an object to hold the GetHelp interface pointer. The `CreateObject()` method instantiates the object and allows the user to make additional calls to the component, which will in turn, interact with the database that we created earlier in the chapter.

Once we have all of the required variables, it's time to check whether the user is at the main page or one of the other help topic pages, or has requested a search for a specific title within the database. Notice that I simply check for a Title variable. If there isn't a title, then there must be a Topic variable. Even if we're at the main Web page and there isn't any topic number to worry about, the component will ignore an empty Topic variable entry. The script uses the `GetTitle()` method for a title search and the `GetTopic()` method for everything else.

After the call to the component is completed, we can start displaying information. The title bar will contain the Title field of the table, along with some additional descriptive text. We use the `Response.Write()` method to send data to the browser. Because this data is within the <TITLE> tag, it will appear in the title bar.

Creating a form and appropriate headings comes next. Notice that we're using a combination of standard HTML and scripting code here as well.

Finally, we display the body of the page. This includes writing the information from the Content field of the database. Remember that this field contains tags that will format the data on screen. Two <INPUT> tags allow us to display a textbox and pushbutton for the user to make queries. If this isn't the main Web page, we also want to provide the user with some way of getting back to the main Web page. Notice that we can use a simple HREF to accomplish this task.

Testing the Web-based Help Desk Application

The Web-based application is a loosely coupled application. You can never tell when a client will request data, what the capabilities of that client will be, what type of client you're dealing with, or even what country that client is in. It's important, therefore, to test a Web-based application by using every conceivable client — at least those that your company has any notion of supporting at the time that the application is written. You also need to test the client's capability to adapt to unforeseen situations. The proliferation of new networking specifications like Bluenose will make wireless clients a reality soon and those clients will come in many different forms, some of which aren't even thought of today.

Of course, delaying the introduction of an application so that you can perform every conceivable test on it isn't really possible today. A delay of even a few days in Internet time can mean that a competitor will gain a significant advantage, something that most companies strive to avoid. So, it's important to categorize the testing criteria for your application by criticality. For example, it's absolutely essential that database access always works and that it works consistently, so this is an essential level of testing. On the other hand, you may find that you don't need to support French right away, so you may only test the English version of your application during its initial release, and then release other language modules as time progresses.

Our example is a fairly simple one. We're not incorporating many of the elements that you'd include in a production application like language support. The following two sections do perform essential testing of the application. We'll look at the database connection first and answer the question of whether it works consistently. The second section will test the application as a whole. We need to know that the application will work on several different clients (for this example I tested on desktop, laptop, and notebook computers).

Performing the help file test

One of the first things I did when working with this example was to create two Visual Basic applications. The first creates a direct connection to the HelpMe database, while the second relies on an indirect connection through the ASP script shown in Listing 14-2.

The main purpose of these two applications is to make it easier to check out the help desk data file. You want to ensure that any glitches that you see onscreen during browser testing have something to do with the browser, rather than with typing errors in the data file. It's very important to perform this initial level of testing before you begin browser testing so that you can reduce the potential sources of error and therefore the debugging time required to find them.

The use of two applications also allows you to isolate the ASP script. Remember that ASP scripts are notoriously difficult to troubleshoot. Isolating the ASP script by using two different testing methodologies allows you to find ASP-specific errors faster.

Performing the help desk test

After you know that everything else is correct, it's time to start browser testing. Figure 14-16 shows the browser output for one of the test pages in the database. Notice that this page is fully formatted. Even the content is properly formatted because of the tags included within the database table.

Make sure that you perform a reasonable amount of link testing when you first put the application together. For example, in this case, we'd want to check the ability of the application to get back to the main Web page with a single click, use links that are embedded within the database content, and perform title searches.

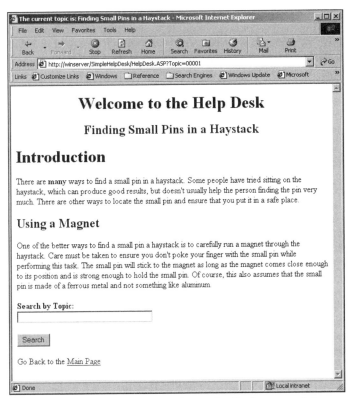

Figure 14-16: The browser test shows the final output of the Web-based application.

Quick Fixes for Web-based Applications

Web-based applications are one of the newest application types for any developer. The Internet has radically changed how developers create applications and how users interact with those applications. The Web-based application is no longer tied to a desktop machine, although it can certainly be used in that role. A developer needs to consider more than one client type now; everything from a desktop machine, to a laptop, to a notebook, and even to personal digital assistants (PDAs). It's little wonder then that there is actually more room for error in the new world of the Internet, not less.

Unlike the desktop or LAN application, the world of the Internet is largely unexplored at the moment. Every developer who creates an application for this environment is a pioneer and like all pioneers is subject to the vagaries of exploration.

You may find that the perfect application that you created works just fine on the company laptop machines, begins to falter on a notebook, and finally fails when it comes to PDA support. The use of multiple clients means that testing for a Web-based application is more extreme than anything created for the desktop.

Internet applications also have a worldwide appeal. You can no longer count on a particular set of biases when it comes to the user interface. Not only do you have language to consider, but every nationality has different ways of working with computer applications. In some cases, you may have to write the application for the lowest common denominator and allow a lot of user customization to account for differences in tastes.

All of these issues aside, the Web-based application is inherently different from anything that you may have created for the desktop in other ways. For example, there are more interfaces and data conversions to consider. The data that you store in SQL Server no longer undergoes a single transition from the DBMS to the client application; it undergoes several levels of change as it gets modified to fit within the HTML specification for browsers and browser-like applications.

The following sections can't help you to locate and kill every potential problem that you'll run into with Web-based applications. Rather, you should consider these sections as a starting point, a list of the most common problems that you'll run into as you work with the new Internet applications that your company will demand. We'll consider the most likely issues that every developer will run into.

Component interactions

Component interactions can take on a new meaning with Web-based applications. For example, in the application that we talked about in this chapter, there is an ASP script between the client and the server. The ASP script accepts data requests from the client, creates an instance of the required component, formats the data obtained by the component, and outputs it to the client. In short, the client and the server aren't even directly connected.

The loss of connection can create situations in which the client and server can't communicate well. Because of the way that HTML handles keep alives, the client could lose the context that it establishes with the server before the client completes whatever task needs to be accomplished. The point is that every ASP script query should be treated as a new call, even if the Web server keeps the original connection alive.

Scripting also presents other problems. Creating an instance of an object by using a script is seldom the same as creating an instance of the same object with a desktop application because of the scripting environment. As a result, you may find that components won't work at all with your script or may behave differently than you expect them to. You can get around this problem by testing a component thoroughly during development. Make sure that you include scripting tests as part of your test suite. It's also important to make sure that the component behaves in the same way no matter what type of desktop application or script is calling it.

A lot of components are designed with callbacks in mind. The client makes an initial query, and then the component uses a callback to obtain additional information from the client. Because Web-based applications are fairly unreliable when it comes to communication, it's important to design the component to rely on the client's initial query without any callbacks.

Scripting error handling

Scripts are a fact of life when working with Web-based applications. In fact, you'll probably need a combination of client-side and server-side scripts to make the application fully functional. Client-side scripts normally don't present much of a problem when it comes to error handling. Either the script works or it doesn't. While the error code that the user gets may seem somewhat cryptic, it's usually easy to locate the problem and fix it because client-side scripts are small and usually limited in scope.

Server-side scripts present other kinds of problems. Most scripting languages don't provide anything in the way of error handling. In addition, passing the error information along to the client may prove difficult without a lot of additional coding. Finally, unlike standard desktop applications or components, scripting languages provide little access to the event log, denying the developer of even this potential method of recording errors. In sum, the developer has to be exceptionally careful when creating the server-side script. Providing range and other nonerror-producing checks will help to reduce problems. If a range or other easily detectable problem is encountered, the script can always provide client feedback in the form of a special Web page.

Fortunately, Windows 2000 does provide rudimentary script debugging. You need to install this feature separately by using the Windows Components Wizard that is accessed by using the Add/Remove Programs applet in the Control Panel. Figure 14-17 shows the required entry. After you add this feature to your development platform, you'll always be able to debug scripts. You need to install this feature on both the client and the server; the Script Debugger doesn't provide remote debugging capability.

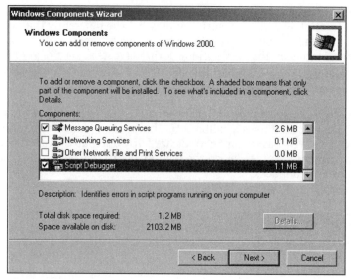

Figure 14-17: Windows 2000 provides a rudimentary script debugger that helps in locating potential problems in your Web-based application scripts.

Human language support

One of the biggest problems that you'll run into when working with a Web-based application is the issue of human language support. The Internet isn't a closed environment. If you plan on making a Web-based application open to the public through the Internet, you'll need to provide support for more than one language.

In many cases, the problem isn't one of translating the content of your Web site. There are many well-understood methods for translating text from one language to another. The main problem is one of application usage. For example, the captions on your application will need to change to support the other languages. You could place the required information in a database that the application could download as needed. The most recently used languages could be stored in a local database or even the Registry.

There are broader issues that you need to consider, however. For example, the layout of your application must be flexible enough to accommodate the way that people normally work or users will complain that the application is difficult to use. This means allowing users to configure the display. While this isn't a problem with most desktop applications, it is a little more difficult with a Web-based application because you don't have control over the position of the various components. In most cases, the best that you can do is to store the user preferences in a cookie, and then use the contents of the cookie to configure the display as data is down-loaded from the server.

ASP and component communication

A major problem with scripting is that you lose the direct connection between the client and the server. The COM+ application may generate an error, but unless the script that formats the Web page is designed to pass that error along, the user may never see it. Because a Web-based application normally has a direct connection (you wouldn't create a disconnected application in many cases), it's important to pass any component errors along to the client.

Unfortunately, simply passing the error along isn't enough in most cases. The problem is that the user won't know where the problem occurred unless you provide additional information. In most cases, the user will assume that an error has occurred locally, unless you make it clear that the problem occurred within the component.

Of course, complex applications may have several layers of component calls and it might be tempting to add code so the user sees the precise location of the problem. Rather than build overly complex components that do little for the user, it's better to simply report the error as a component error, then tell the user to contact the network administrator about the problem. An event log entry will allow the network administrator to determine the precise cause of the problem and take steps to fix it.

Component doesn't support locale error

More and more desktop applications are required to support multiple languages, but it's still possible to write a custom application and not worry about the locale. The same can't be said for a Web-based application. By its very nature a Web-based application requires multiple language support. Of course, this presents a problem for the developer because the developer may not know which locales an off-the-shelf component will support, or if it supports more than one language at all.

Visual Basic applications, including components, will generate a 477 error code when a component called by the application doesn't support the current local setting. When you detect this error in your Web-based application, you'll normally have three courses of action available to you. First, you can ask the user if some other language will work, in which case you'll have to try the call again with the new locale. Second, you can try to get around the problem by attempting to access the component with another dialect of the same language. For example, there are several locales that support French. The resulting text may not be perfect, but it should be readable. Third, you can register a failure with the user and present any data that you were able to get before the error occurred.

The 477 error code doesn't always occur when a component lacks support for a particular language. There have been several versions of the LCID table over the years and the one used by your component may be out of date. Getting a newer version of the component will usually help. If that isn't possible, you may need to find an alternative LCID that the component does support. Again, this isn't a perfect solution, but it may be the only choice in some cases.

Summary

This chapter showed you how to create one of the more useful applications from a user and support staff productivity standpoint, the help desk application. We've looked at a Web-based version of this application that relies on a COM+ component to provide the glue between the client and the server. Some additional conclusions that you can draw from the contents of this chapter are:

✦ One of the biggest mistakes that developers make is to underestimate the flexibility of the help desk application. This type of application can be used for more than simple user support. It can also be used to provide support for any type of semipermanent information like forms, company policies, and even the company bulletin board.

✦ Help desk applications in general require specialized databases that contain tables that may be indirectly linked. For example, there is an indirect link between the content displayed in a window and the graphics used to support it. Unlike many other types of relational database applications, the link in this case is buried in the content, rather than created directly.

✦ Unlike remote database applications, help desk applications require precise control over how information gets accessed and passed on to the client. A single-record lookup works best because it allows the Web-based application to format the data one record at a time and it keeps bandwidth requirements low.

✦ Always provide custom messages for user-oriented errors. However, the IIS default messages work fine for application-generated errors because those errors normally provide detailed information and allow the user to recover from an application-generated error with relative ease.

✦ Scripting is an essential tool for the modern developer. However, it's important to make sure that you use scripting only when appropriate. Scripting languages can't take the place of full-fledged programming languages.

✦ Always perform testing of Web-based applications in stages. At the very least, you should test the data file, the ASP script, and browser interface separately.

✦   ✦   ✦

Working with the Microsoft Windows Installer

This appendix is designed to help you learn about Microsoft's latest installation program technology, the Microsoft Windows Installer (MSI). Microsoft has changed the installation process for Windows 2000 for several reasons, most notably because the older setup file process is unreliable at best and often doesn't provide an easy method for uninstalling an application. Setup programs also require a lot of additional work on the part of the user and a poorly designed setup program can cause difficulties when situations that the developer didn't consider arise. In fact, the problems with using setup programs are so severe that Microsoft has also made MSI available on the other Windows platforms (Windows NT and Windows 9*x*).

There are good reasons for developers to switch to MSI as well. Creating a setup program normally ranks as one of the worst tasks for developers (right above creating help files) because writing a setup program is a difficult and thankless task. Nevertheless, the fact remains that the installation process can make or break an application. After all, the installation process is the user's first view of your application — the point at which the user begins to form a good or bad opinion of your product. In fact, the setup program is so important that I've never seen a product review that doesn't mention the ease of product installation. The new MSI file format promises easier installation and uninstallation for both users and developers.

Visual Studio doesn't come with MSI support built in; you have to add it as a separate SDK. You can obtain this SDK at `http://msdn.microsoft.com/downloads/sdks/platform/wininst.asp`. The first step if you're not running Windows 2000 is to install the MSI redistributable files. There are separate versions for Windows NT and Windows 9x, so make sure that you get the support that you need. These files will add MSI file support to your machine. After you complete this step, you need to download the Microsoft Windows Installer SDK installation program. This program will allow you to install the SDK. In addition to the Microsoft Windows Installer SDK, you'll need to download the Visual Studio Installer from `http://msdn.microsoft.com/vstudio/downloads/vsi/default.asp`. This product is based on MSI technology and makes the process of creating MSI files much easier. It's a better version of the Package and Deployment Wizard that ships with Visual Studio and should be a lot more flexible. The Microsoft Windows Installer SDK and Visual Studio Installer files may also be available on the Microsoft Developer Network (MSDN) CDs by the time that you read this (they weren't at the time of writing).

The first section of this appendix will provide you with a very quick overview of some packaging concerns that every developer needs to consider, no matter what type of setup program the developer is creating. We'll discuss the different types of packages that you can create based on the final destination of the particular package, how to determine which packaging model to use, and what to include in the package. Because all of this information is the same for any installation, you can also use it for creating setup programs.

The second section of the appendix introduces you to the MSI. Because this is a new Windows 2000 feature, some of you may not be as familiar with it as you are with the old setup program. We'll look at what this new feature will do for you as a developer and how it affects the user. This section will also provide an overview of the two tools that you need in order to create MSI files: the Microsoft Windows Installer SDK and the Visual Studio Installer.

The third section of the appendix will discuss why you should use MSI files instead of the older Setup technology. You may be surprised to find out that using this new technology really will save you time as a developer and make the task of creating installation packages just a little less repugnant.

The fourth, fifth, and sixth sections are the main event from many developer's perspectives. We'll create an installation program for one of the examples in the book, and then test the capability of the installation program to install and uninstall the application. One of the MSI features that you'll really like is the capability to perform both tasks in Windows Explorer.

This is a new technology, so in the seventh section of the appendix we'll discuss problems that you'll encounter when using it. It's important to understand that many of these limitations are temporary. Microsoft plans to provide updates to both MSI technology and the MSI file format. However, for right now, you'll still need ways to work around these problems.

A Quick Overview of Application Packaging

Many developers look at a setup program or an MSI installation file as just another application to create. However, that's not the best way to view any type of installation program. An installation program is actually a package for your application. It provides the window dressing that gives your application that shiny new look. Look at it this way: Designing an application without an installation package is akin to bringing a present to a birthday party without wrapping it first. Yes, the present is still appreciated, but all of the pizzazz is gone. The recipient doesn't get excited because the present is already open and exposed for everyone to see.

The following sections provide an overview of packaging concerns. For example, you need to answer the question of who will use your application when you create a package for it. Consider it this way, giving someone in their thirties a package with wrapping for a four-year-old may be cute, but hardly anticipated and, in some cases, definitely unwelcome (depending on the person's sense of humor). Likewise, you need to create the proper package for your application. An application designed for in-house use has different requirements than one designed for use outside of your company. As part of the packaging discussion, we'll also talk about what you need to include in the package. In some cases, you'll need to include more features because the user of the application won't have access on a regular basis to either the developer or a support team. In other cases, you want to reduce the feature set to make the application easy to transmit over a network or even the Internet.

An overview of the packaging models

Many different things need to be considered when creating a package in which to deliver your application. For most developers, the most important consideration is the environment that the application will be used in. An in-house developer won't have the same concerns as a software company that plans to deliver an application for use by an outside party. For one thing, the in-house developer probably won't have much time to get an installation program together — time is a factor in most in-house situations.

However, there are some common considerations, no matter what kind of application you want to create. For example, it really doesn't matter who will perform the installation or what kind of installation he or she plans to perform; in most cases you still need to write some type of installation program. The first section in this topic will address this and other common concerns. Make sure that you place these common concerns on your to do list, even if you're only a company of one.

The next four sections will look at the four most common types of installation environments: small-to-medium sized company, enterprise, shareware, and shrink-wrap. You'll likely fall into one of the four categories, but you may also want to look at the other categories because they'll contain a lot of helpful tips and hints. Some of you won't fall into a distinct category. For example, a consultant is part in-house (corporate) developer because most of the applications that the consultant creates are customized for a particular company. On the other hand, your client will want a little more from a consultant than something that works. As a minimum, the client will want something around the level of a shareware package (some clients will expect a shrink-wrap version of your product, but that's a little on the unreasonable side).

Figuring out what kind of packaging to provide can be a little tricky, but it's not impossible. All you really need to do is assess the needs of the people that you're writing the application for. If all that they're looking for is something that works well and doesn't include a lot of hype, then using the enterprise (corporate) packaging style will work just fine.

As more and more applications require the space offered by CD-ROMs and DVDs, it's becoming important to know how to create a bootable version of your disk. Creating a bootable CD-ROM isn't impossible. In fact, there's actually more than one way to do this (Microsoft actually uses two different methods for Windows 95/98 and Windows NT/Windows 2000). One of the ways to create a bootable CD can be found at the Adaptec site `http://users.knoware.nl/users/sanny/bootcd_ecdc.htm`. Of course, you need their Easy CD Creator product to make this solution work. Another version of this same process (using Easy CD Creator) can be found at `http://www.ias.berkeley.edu/i2net/Setup/bootcd.htm`. A more generic set of links for creating bootable CD-ROMs can be found at `http://idt-microsynergy.com/support/cdrfaq/part2/faq-doc-26.html`. In almost every case, these techniques rely on a feature found in many BIOS chips that allows for CD-ROM access prior to loading the operating system specific drivers. In addition, you'll likely find that some newer CD recording software also provides this feature without following special formatting procedures.

Common concerns

No matter what kind of application you've written or whom you've written it for, there are some common elements that everyone needs to think about. This section looks at the common concerns that all developers should have, no matter what kind of application package they put together.

Obviously, the first things that you need to put in the package are all of the required files. It may seem that this is obvious, but there have been a number of times when I tried to install an application only to discover that it didn't include everything. Consider, for a moment, the Visual Basic Virtual Machine or the files required for one version of Windows versus another. Some developers might not include them with their application, but the user might have an old version of the files that won't work with the developer's application. The result is a broken application and a disappointed user. One way to look at this particular need is the "batteries not included syndrome." Always include the batteries along with the new application.

Packaging also has a lot to do with an application's ease of use and the user's ability to install it quickly. Imagine for a moment a car that wasn't packaged correctly. Sure, it comes with directional signals, but there isn't any light on the dash to tell you which one of the directional signals is blinking. The engineer knows which way the directional lights work, so why bother to install indicator lights? You wouldn't buy a car like this and neither would anyone else. That's what an application without a good help file is like to a user who didn't design it. You may as well just tell them to guess about how to use the application because they'll never think to look at the README or other file that you placed on the disk with too few instructions.

Everyone should make his or her application look aesthetically pleasing, because appearance affects the user's attitude toward the application. Sure, you don't need to provide brilliant graphics worthy of an art gallery for an in-house application, but even a little color will dress up the display. I've found that attitude is about half the battle in getting a user up and running with a program. Anything that you can do to improve the user's attitude also benefits you by reducing service calls and complaints. In short, bells and whistles are nice, but a good interface is required. Even your installation program has to have a great interface; after all, it's the first part of your program that the user will see. First impressions are very long lasting—especially if you're a user who didn't particular want to use an application in the first place.

A complete application always includes an install program that you can use to test the setup as a whole. Here's another scenario to think about. One programmer that I know of decided to simply send out a batch file and a disk full of application files as a package. He never even bothered to test the application because it was only going to be used in-house. It didn't take too long before the programmer started getting a rash of calls from disgruntled users. It seems that he forgot to add a crucial file to the disk, and the users who were actually able to figure out the batch file couldn't get the program to work. No one ever liked that application—even after the programmer added a nice-looking interface and an install program, and fixed the bugs. The problem wasn't with the program; it was with the user's attitude toward the program. First impressions are crucial to a program's success.

Enterprise (corporate)

Enterprise-level programmers have the least to do with the beautification of their packaging and the most to do with customizing it. Let's face it, the enterprise programmer really doesn't have to impress anyone with fancy graphics or impressive sound effects. That the interface is both functional and user-friendly is enough. Frankly, your boss may not look very favorably on any time spent making an installation program look beautiful, especially if you have a stack of other programming projects awaiting your attention.

On the other hand, the enterprise programmer is most often engaged in creating custom applications that reflect a specific company's needs. It's not all that uncommon for custom applications, especially database applications, to require the use of specialized files to store both temporary data and global settings. You'll likely need custom Registry entries and a wealth of other custom settings as well. Creating a custom installation program that's guaranteed to work on all the workstations in an enterprise (corporate) environment, with little help from the programmer, is quite an undertaking. Plan on spending a lot of time hand-tuning the standard installation program that you can create with products like InstallShield.

Tip   If you've used a file located on the server or a central database to maintain application settings in the past, consider placing these settings in Active Directory instead. Using Active Directory will allow you to maintain the settings more easily, improve security, and reduce application overhead. In essence, Active Directory will replace global settings files much as the Registry has replace local INI files.

Media is another place where most enterprise (corporate) installation programs will differ from the other three categories. It's still not unusual (although it's becoming more so) for a shareware application to come on floppies. However, shareware vendors are about the only ones using floppies. Even shrink-wrap applications use CDs instead of floppies because of their superior storage potential and higher access speed (when compared to floppies). As an enterprise programmer, you need to find a fast and efficient solution for your installation media needs. You should not consider anything less than a CD for distributing your application.

Fortunately, there's probably a better choice of media at the enterprise developer's disposal. Unless the company that you're working for is living in the dark ages, you'll probably have a LAN on hand for distribution purposes. You can use this feature to your benefit when creating an application package. Unfortunately, some installation development programs don't support LAN installation. In this case, you can simply select the most efficient storage method possible — a CD. You'll find that you can create and test your installation program a lot faster if you rely on a CD version of the package and use a LAN to distribute it.

Tip   Even though this appendix is about the Microsoft Installer and the MSI file that you create is extensible enough to work over both LANs and remote connections like the Internet, you may have to consider other solutions because MSI is still in its infancy. InstallShield 6 Professional Edition comes with the capability to install an application over an intranet. Companies that occupy more than one building can simply extend the LAN distribution principle that we're talking about here to distribute the application as widely as needed. Make sure that you spend some time looking at the various distribution methods that InstallShield and other packaging applications provide before making the decision to commit your application to floppy or CD and distribute it manually. Using a LAN or intranet to distribute your application is almost always more efficient in the enterprise (corporate) setting than any other technique.

After you've packaged your application on the LAN, simply add an instruction to the main logon batch file for your server to install the program. The next time that the user logs on, your logon batch file will check whether the application is installed. If not, it'll call the installation program that you've placed on the LAN.

Tip

The enterprise (corporate) setting is one place where using UNC paths in place of standard drive identifiers comes in very handy. Using a UNC path for the source directory ensures that everyone will be able to access all the required source files for your application without too much effort.

There are some other packaging issue suggestions that you may want to consider for the enterprise (corporate) environment, although it's by no means certain that you'll actually be able to use all of them. The following list of ideas is meant simply to provide you with some things to think about when customizing your installation program. Whether they'll work in your particular situations depends on how your enterprise (corporate) structure is set up and on environmental factors like the availability of network connections for the user.

✦ **Centralized Common File Storage:** The standard procedure for distributing applications is to place all of the files on the user's machine. When you think about it, this is the only way to do things with shareware or shrink-wrap software. As an enterprise (corporate) programmer, though, you can choose to keep specific common files like DLLs on the file server instead of the user's machine. There are two benefits to this approach. First, you reduce the amount of space that the application requires on the user machine. Second, you reduce the time required to update custom DLLs should the user find an error in one of them. All you have to replace is one copy of the DLL on the server. There are also two downsides to this approach. First, the user has to have a network connection to make the technique work at all. Second, you could end up increasing network traffic substantially if the DLL is loaded and unloaded on a frequent basis.

✦ **Absolute Preferences:** A shareware or shrink-wrap application author can't assume anything about the application environment — not a source or a destination for the various application files. The machine is a total mystery as well. In fact, even the operating system is a mystery in some cases. You don't have that problem. All you really need to do is worry about the differences between the machines on your network. If you set up all the machines about the same way, you could assume a default destination. Using UNC paths means that you can always assume an absolute source because the server path name won't change from installation to installation. You may even be able to assume a certain amount about the workstation itself if your network is small and all the machines have similar capabilities. In sum, all this means is that you don't have to present the user with as many installation choices and can substantially reduce the complexity of the installation program. All it takes is a little preplanning on your part.

✦ **No Configuration Choices Needed:** Just about every available shrink-wrap program offers you a choice between three installation configurations: Custom, Typical, and Compact. The Custom choice allows you to choose specific program elements; the Typical configuration is designed for desktop users; and the Compact configuration is intended for people who own laptops. In most cases, you can limit your configuration options to two choices: Laptop and Desktop. In fact, you may want to use those terms to keep user confusion to a minimum.

Shareware

Shareware programmers probably have the most challenging job when it comes to packaging their application. Consider one of the main problems for a shareware programmer: installation size. Unlike the enterprise (corporate) developer who has a high-speed network connection to use, or a shrink-wrap developer who can distribute an application on CD, the shareware developer usually has to make do with a low-speed modem connection to a BBS, online service, or the Internet. If your application exceeds 1MB, the number of people downloading it will probably drop drastically.

> **Note**
>
> The file sizes in this section are meant as guidelines only. The amount of disk space or time that a potential user is willing to invest in your product depends on a good many factors like perceived value and the current level of exposure that you have. For example, one of my favorite shareware graphics packages takes up a whopping 7MB of hard disk space and is well over 1MB in size when compressed. People still download it and set aside the space that it requires because this program is well worth the investment. Because it's been around for a while, word-of-mouth also tends to give people a reason to download this file. What you need to consider is whether most people would be willing to pay the price to use your application — it's something that you'll have to learn by experience if you're serious about participating in the shareware market.

OK, so you're a little limited on space. How do you get around this problem? The key is in how you market your product. Most of the successful shareware products that I've seen use the same key graphics and sounds over and over again. In other words, instead of coming up with one really fancy graphic for the installation program and a totally different graphic for the application itself, the shareware programmer is content to use the same graphic for both the installation program and the application. In fact, using subtle programming techniques could allow you to get away with using the application's icon in several places.

Can a shareware developer emulate the enterprise (corporate) programmer and do without fancy graphics or sounds? Not likely. If you really want someone to pay for the application you've created, you'll need to add a little polish to it. No one will pay for something that looks drab even if it does provide much needed functionality. Obviously, trying to weight the space needed by a feature and the amount of pizzazz that it provides is difficult.

Another problem that a shareware developer will run into is one of resources. I know of many shareware developers who started out as one- or two-person shops. Many of these shops also deal with consulting jobs and other moneymaking ventures as they wait hopefully for a shareware product to take off. Time isn't on your side, and it's unlikely that you'll have a professional artist or sound person at your disposal to create the multimedia presentations provided by larger companies who create shrink-wrap applications. Most people are satisfied if they see a shareware product that's well designed, space conscious (consumes 5MB or less of hard disk space), and provides at least a modicum of polish.

We haven't yet discussed the biggest problem for shareware developers, and the installation program is the first place that you have to deal with it. Enterprise programmers have the most control over their environment by virtue of the fact that they have personal access to every machine that will use the program that they create. Enterprise developers can get by with a minimum of machine checks and configuration options. Small-to-medium-sized business and shrink-wrap developers come next. The small-to-medium-sized business developer has an intimate relationship with the customer that allows the developer to make some assumptions. The shrink-wrap developer can print a set of requirements on the box to ensure that no one will use the application without sufficient hardware. That the user is paying for the application tends to increase the user's awareness of the hardware requirements for installing it. The shareware developer has no such guarantees. A user of your program could have just about any kind of machine ever made—even an old 8088 PC.

What does this lack of control mean? First, it means that you have to build extra detection routines in your installation program to ensure that minimum hardware requirements are met. Users will rarely read the README file that you provide (the one stating the minimum requirements for using the application), and are even less likely to pay attention to the requirements if they do read the README file. When the installation fails, you can be sure that the user will blame you, not his or her own lack of attention to the minimum system requirements. Consequently, you have to build in some type of detection. You also need to build flexibility into your application with regard to configuration. For example, you may decide to allow the user with an older-technology machine to configure the application for text mode only and forgo those fancy graphics or sounds.

Tip   The installation program is a good place to sell your shareware product if you have the time and resources to design it properly. Make sure that users understand what they'll get in return for buying your product. In other words, because you have a captive audience during the installation process, you may as well use the time to sell your program.

Just like anyone else, the shareware developer does have a few tricks up his or her sleeve to make setting up the installation program easier. While the following list isn't inclusive of everything that you could try, it does provide some ideas on what could work. You'll need to try out a variety of packaging techniques with your application before you finally come up with something that works all of the time.

✦ **Granular Packaging:** One way for a shareware developer to get around the hard disk space and download time problems is to package the application in several pieces. For example, you could place the main program in one package, the graphics in another, and the sounds in a third package. The result is that users can choose what level of support they're willing to pay for with regard to download time and hard disk space. This concept doesn't come without a price, however. You have to write your application so that it can work without the graphics and sounds (or whatever elements you decide to place in a separate package). Your installation program has to provide similar flexibility. It has to know what do to if a user decides to download one packaging element but not another.

✦ **Amplified Help:** Creating two sets of help files for your users (for example, one for trial package users and another for registered users) is one way to cut down the trial package size. (This technique also tends to encourage the trial user to register his or her product.) One of the ways that you can do this is to make a main and an amplifying help file. The main help file contains explanations of basic commands, while the amplifying help file contains user tutorials, macro language descriptions, and detailed command descriptions. Again, the user could decide what level of help to pay for in the form of download time and disk space. You could also use this feature to your benefit. A shareware package is never guaranteed to sell. Making such a large investment in time without any guarantee of a payback is difficult, to say the least. Using this approach allows you to make a smaller initial investment until you could see whether a particular shareware product is worth fleshing out.

Tip

Many shareware companies have used modularized programs to enhance sales. For example, ButtonWare usually provides a simple help file and most of the features for a shareware application when you download it. Buying the application entitles you to download the full-featured program and complete program documentation. Many people are upset by what they call "crippleware" because it doesn't allow them to fully test the application before they buy it. Unfortunately, unless a shareware developer provides the user with a good reason to buy his or her product, most people won't. (You can test the veracity of this statement anytime by looking at the number of shareware companies that die due to a lack of sales even if downloads for their products are brisk.)

Small-to-medium-sized business

From a packaging perspective, a small-to-medium-sized business is a mix between the enterprise and the shareware model. These businesses don't have much in the way of complex equipment and don't normally have a programmer on staff. More likely than not, they don't have a large network; instead, they use workgroup computing to get the job done. In fact, many of these businesses rely on vertical market applications that a consultant customizes to meet their specific needs. In other words, the application isn't written from scratch. This environment both simplifies the packaging requirements (the consultant probably knows every machine on the premises) and at the same time makes it harder for the programmer to customize a package.

Like the enterprise developer, the small-to-medium-sized business developer can get by with very few graphics. However, because you're developing this application for multiple customers, you need to add a little more pizzazz than an enterprise programmer can get by with. In addition, unlike any other application packager, you might need to develop some unique graphics to go with your package like the individual company logos for each company that you deal with. It's important to realize, though, that your audience isn't expecting you to create an application that provides a lot of bells and whistles — they're usually happy if the application works as advertised.

The small-to-medium-sized business developer also shares one other problem with the shareware developer. The type of target platform is likely to vary a great deal because a small-to-medium-sized business typically can't afford to update its equipment as often as a large company can. So, while you probably won't have to worry about pre-80486 computers, you'll still have to deal with equipment that's a lot slower and older than most developers have to deal with.

Working in the small-to-medium-sized business environment has some advantages that you won't find in other markets. For example, you'll have a closer relationship with all of your clients, which means that you can better understand their needs. This close relationship also means that training is easier. A small-to-medium-sized business developer can create a training program that is likely to be more effective and consume less development time than any other developer category.

Obviously, the small-to-medium-sized business development environment is different from the other environments that we've discussed so far. Fortunately, there are a few ways that the small-to-medium-sized business developer can make his or her job easier. While the following list probably doesn't include everything that you've tried, it does provide a few ideas on how you can develop packages that reflect your client's needs.

✦ **Unique Code Included:** There are times when you won't want to give your customer all of the source code for a custom application. In fact, there might be times when it would be illegal to do so because you might need to include licensed source code to do so. However, in most cases, you'll want to provide the user with a package that contains the unique source code for his or her custom implementation of a generic application. Make sure that you provide this code in a separate directory so that it isn't loaded on the client machine.

✦ **Personalized Support Dialogs:** Unlike the enterprise programmer, you are more likely to service the needs of several clients. What this means is that you need to provide better support information in your application package. Make sure that you include support information as part of the installation program, the README file, and all of the help files, as well as within the application itself.

✦ **Customized License Agreement:** Enterprise programmers don't need to provide a license agreement for their software because it's written for a specific company and the licensing agreement (when there is one) is defined within the contract. A shrink-wrap or shareware developer will normally include a generic licensing agreement that applies to everyone equally. Only the small-to-medium-sized business developer is faced with a situation in which the licensing agreement for a generic application could differ from company to company. Make sure that you include this licensing as part of the package in both the installation program and within the application's About dialog.

Shrink-wrap

I'm not going to pretend to tell a company like Microsoft how to market or package its product; the effects of its sales force are already legendary and I doubt that I can do much to help it out. One thing that usually sets a shrink-wrap product apart from a shareware product is the size of the company producing the application. Larger software companies usually concentrate on one or more products and have a large professional group of people to help put the packaging together. However, the average programmer can learn can learn a few things by looking at these shrink-wrap packages.

During the past few months, I decided to start taking notes whenever I installed a shrink-wrap or shareware product. After installing about 30 products, I decided to review my notes. In some cases, the results were surprising. For example, the previous section mentions using the installation program as a means of selling your product if you're a shareware vendor, because you have a captive audience and fewer sales resources at your disposal. It may surprise you to find that shrink-wrap software commonly uses the installation program for this very purpose, but in a different way than a shareware vendor would use it. The user has already purchased the product that he or she is installing, but how about add-on products? Shrink-wrap vendors commonly use the installation program to sell some add-on product that relates to the application that the user is installing (one example is an extended dictionary or spelling checker for a word processor).

Another thing that I noticed is that shrink-wrap software commonly tells the user what's new about the program during the installation process. It doesn't surprise me too much, because the shrink-wrap companies must have figured out long ago that most users don't read the README file and the installation program is usually the last part of the product to be finished. Again, the shrink-wrap vendor has a captive audience and can use the installation program to give users an overview of what users would learn if they'd actually read the README file.

It should come as no surprise that the shrink-wrap installation programs are usually packed with all kinds of multimedia presentation materials. After all, the shrink-wrap vendor has the resources required to produce such a display. Even if you don't have the resources to duplicate the presentation provided by a shrink-wrap vendor, you can make notes as I have to figure out what works and what doesn't. Providing a smaller version of the same type of presentation in your installation program is a sure way to make it look more polished. Remember that you want to give users the best possible impression of your product from the outset to ensure that they enjoy working with it. Creating a nice-looking installation program won't do a single thing to make your application work better, but it'll affect the user's perception of your application, which is a very important part of getting the user up and running with a minimum of support.

There are also some negative lessons that you can learn from shrink-wrap vendors. One of the best things that I learned was that you can make your installation program too complex to test thoroughly. I recently tried installing one product and found that the help screens for the program were for the previous version. The vendor had forgotten to update the screens as needed for the new version of their product. The result? Because the product didn't come with any printed documentation, I didn't have a clue as to whether I should install certain product features. If the vendor had taken a few minutes to fully test the installation program, I would have had all the information needed to make an informed decision about which product features to install.

Another very strange problem occurred when the product failed to install at all. It seems that the installation program used special graphics that relied on a product feature that was incompatible with the machine that I was using. Moving the product to another machine where the installation program worked just fine showed that the product would work, even though the installation program wouldn't. Again, the vendor decided to add some really neat special effects to the detriment of the program as a whole.

As you can see from this section, looking at what other people are doing in the way of packaging a product can save you time and effort when it comes to packaging your own product. I find that taking notes and then reading them right before I write my installation program keeps me from making as many mistakes. (Very few people get an installation program right the first time around.)

Determining which packaging model to use

The previous section outlined four different packaging schemes based on common software usage environments. Unfortunately, while these four scenarios do cover a relatively large percentage of the development efforts out there, there may be times when the application that you've developed will be used in more than one of these environments.

Here's an example. What would happen if you wrote an accounting application that has vertical market add-ons? Many users will simply buy the shrink-wrapped version of the standard package because they don't require any additional functionality. These people would fit the shrink-wrap model. In other cases, your customer may be a developer who integrates the general package, one or more of the vertical market add-ons, and then adds some extra value in the form of custom modules. This person could fit into either the enterprise or the small-to-medium-sized business model. As you can see, there are times when the application that you develop might not fit into one packaging model, so it's important to provide some flexibility in the packaging system that you design.

There are other considerations when it comes to choosing a packaging model. Not every situation requires a large multistep installation program and associated help files. The following list provides some ideas on which factors you need to consider when creating your application package.

✦ **Application Size:** The size of your application determines just how much you need to add in the way of additional support. For example, if you're creating a package for a Notepad-style editor, you won't need an extensive help system as you would with a Word-style editor.

✦ **Application Complexity:** Don't confuse application complexity with application size. You can create a small application, like a network monitoring utility, that performs many complex tasks, but isn't very large. Complexity is a measure of how much knowledge a user requires to use the application, how many features the application provides, the depth of the menuing system, and the overall number of windows that the user will need to work with. The more complex the application, the larger the help file you need and the more options you need to add to the installation program.

✦ **Application Modularity:** Utility programs are normally the least modular applications that you can create. In most cases, they contain two modules: the application and an associated help file. On the other hand, major applications can contain literally hundreds of modules. The application package that you create should reflect the modularity of the application. More modules mean more options in the installation program. Make sure that you include options to tailor the help system to reflect the number of modules that the user chooses to install. If you choose to implement application advertising (discussed later in this appendix), make sure that you also advertise the modularity of your application so the users understand that they don't need to install everything to get the level of functionality that they require.

✦ **Audience:** A novice user requires more hand-holding than an experienced user. Extensive bullet help, higher levels of modularity, reduced complexity, and the use of wizards all help the novice user. On the other hand, some (if not most) experienced users will feel that you're talking down to them if you overwhelm them with help. This particular concern is so important that some applications actually consider the user level (as indicated by the user) when installing and configuring the application. A novice user might only gain access to a few very important features, while an experienced user will have access to everything that the application offers.

✦ **Target Platform:** The kind of hardware and operating system that your application will run on often determines the number of special effects that you add to the application package. Obviously, you don't want to provide multimedia presentations on an old 80486 machine. Likewise, you don't want to make your application package appear outdated by using text only displays on a modern machine with the latest operating system installed.

✦ **Network Functionality and Internet Capability:** Networks and the Internet present special challenges when putting an application package together. You might need to include special aids for helping the user get over potential network problems. In addition, your installation program may need to check for the presence of Internet support before installing specific Internet features.

✦ **Special Hardware or Hardware Specific:** Many applications rely on special hardware. For example, many graphics applications need a scanner attached to the target machine before they can grab images from print. Drivers are always a concern when it comes to special hardware. There have been more than a few situations when the application program that I've installed also installed the latest version of the vendor's drivers for me to ensure that the application will work as intended.

What to include in the package

Never get the idea that you can just slap an installation program together in a few seconds without doing any research. Any program that runs in the Windows environment is a lot more complicated than even the programmer may realize. For example, all of the examples in this book have relied on the Visual Basic and COM/COM+ runtime files. Yet, I've never mentioned adding these files to your application code, nor have you seen them referenced in any of the source code. (There have been references to individual DLLs, but this still doesn't give you the whole picture.)

The reason that I haven't mentioned the other files is because these files are automatically added to your SYSTEM folder when you install Visual Basic. You don't need to know about them while you design your application because their inclusion is automatic. The same can be said of the Visual Basic Virtual Machine files and those required for database applications. In most cases, Visual Basic takes care of these file additions for you without much, if any, thought on your part.

However, now you're trying to put everything needed to run your application into a package for the user. At this point in the product development cycle, you no longer have the luxury of ignoring those other files — they're part of your application and must be included with the package that you send to the user. The problem is figuring out which files to include with your program.

Figuring out which DLLs to ship with your application can be a time-consuming task, especially if you resort to trial and error to figure things out. However, there are three methods that you can use to remove some of the trial and error from the process.

1. You could use the Windows QuikView utility to view the Import Table entries for your application. Unfortunately, this utility isn't provided as part of Windows 2000, but you can still use it with other versions of Windows. The Import Table list tells you which DLLs your application relies on. Figure A-1 shows an example of a Quick View list for one of the applications on my machine. Notice that it not only shows which files your application uses, but also the function within those files.

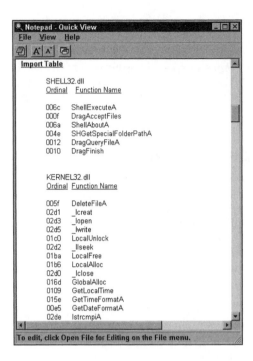

Figure A-1: The Windows Quick View utility provides one way to look for the files that your application depends on.

2. If you have the latest version of the Windows SDK, you'll find a superior version of the Depends utility, which you can use to get the DLL requirements for your program. Figure A-2 shows the Depends utility at work. Notice that the Depends utility provides a lot of information not provided by the other programs. For example, you can see the actual hierarchical relationship between the dependent files. The Depends utility also provides essential version information. In sum, although the Depends utility display looks a bit complex, it's also more informative than the QuikView utility.

Getting a list of files that your executable uses directly isn't the end of the process. You'll also need to check the DLLs that it uses for any dependencies that they may have. Obviously, you can ignore files like USER.EXE because the user will have them installed as part of Windows itself, but you'll need to watch for files that may not have been installed. In short, you'll need to manually check each file for it's dependencies, and then include those files with your application.

Once you have a complete list of the files that you need for your application, gather them into one place. Copy this set of files to a newly installed version of Windows (whichever version your application is targeting). Test your application to make sure that it works. You'll get messages if you're missing a file or if a file needs to go into the SYSTEM folder. Make sure that you keep track of the files that you place in the SYSTEM folder because you'll also have to place them there on the user's machine.

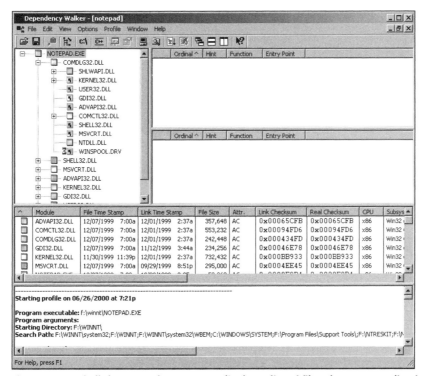

Figure A-2: Of all the ways that you can display a list of files that your application requires, the Depends utility is the most comprehensive.

Tip

Check a clean machine for a list of files that a specific version of Windows provides by default. You may want to maintain a list of these files for later reference if you plan on creating more than one installation program. In addition, make sure that you keep separate lists of the files that each version of Windows that you want to support contains. For example, the files in the OSR2 version of Windows 95 differ from those found in the OSR2.5 version, both of which differ from those in Windows 2000.

Note

Always try to keep all of the DLLs for your application in the application folder instead of automatically placing them in the SYSTEM folder. Keeping everything in one place will help to uninstall the program later should the user want to remove it from his or her machine. You'll also find that you have fewer problems with corruption from other programs that the user installs; for example, when a DLL that you need to run your application is overwritten by an older version of the same DLL used by another application.

About the Microsoft Windows Installer

MSI is a new technology that's supposed to provide a faster, easier, and cleaner way to install applications on any machine. That's the main reason that you'll want to begin using this technology right away. It represents the best method of making installation programs easier to build and easier to use, which means that you'll spend less time dealing with support calls and more time working on new code. The following sections introduce you to MSI, and then tell you about the two tools that you need to know about in order to use it.

Why is this technology important?

When a developer creates a standard installation program that relies on Setup.exe, everything that the installation program is capable of doing is hard coded into the setup application. A network administrator or other skilled person can't come back later and make changes to the installation package. When you create an MSI file, on the other hand, you end up with two files. The first contains the MSI package, while the second contains the configuration and installation files in an archive with a CAB (cabinet) extension. Figure A-3 shows the contents of the CAB file for the Simple Event Class application that we created in Chapter 11.

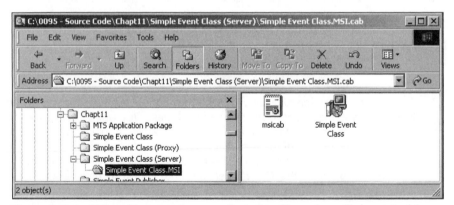

Figure A-3: An MSI archive contains a configuration file and any files required for installation.

Notice the msicab file in the archive. This is an editable text file that you can look into for installation information. Figure A-4 shows the msicab file for the Simple Event Class application. As you can see, this file doesn't differ much from any INF file that you may have worked with in the past. You could conceivably edit this file to add steps, change the destination directory, or perform any number of other tasks. The point is that while this installation program isn't fully configurable, it does provide more in the way of configuration options than the older setup route.

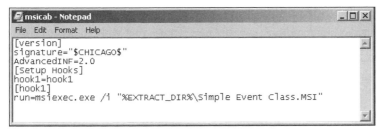

Figure A-4: The msicab file contains the same information that you'd find in any INF file.

If you do a lot of multiple-language development as I do, then you're also a bit tired of using one setup creation program for one language, and something entirely different for another language. In case you don't know what I'm talking about, Visual Basic relies on the Package and Deployment Wizard, while Visual C++ relies on an evaluation copy of InstallShield. You can conceivably use InstallShield for both Visual Basic and Visual C++, but the entire setup has the feel of something kludged together. Many serious developers end up buying a full-fledged third-party product for both languages, which means that every company ends up with its own custom installation program development solution.

Visual Studio Installer, a product created with the Microsoft Windows Installer SDK, is a free upgrade for Visual Studio users. It provides an easy-to-use and fully integrated solution for building installation programs. If you use more than one language product for development, the integration is more than welcome and it's something that Microsoft should have provided from the beginning. We'll look at the Visual Studio Installer later in this appendix so you can see for yourself how easy it is to use. The bottom line is that you get superior installation programs, at a reduced cost, and in less time.

Understanding the Microsoft Windows Installer SDK

The Microsoft Windows Installer SDK is designed to help developers write code that uses MSI technology. In other words, if you want to create an installation program the old fashioned way, you can do it with this product. However, the Microsoft Windows Installer SDK is useful for more than installation programs. You can use it to add install on-demand capability to your applications. The following sections answer three major questions about the Microsoft Windows Installer SDK for you. The first is why you'd want to add MSI capability to your applications. The second tells you what you get when you download the Microsoft Windows Installer SDK. The third is how you can use the Microsoft Windows Installer SDK even if you don't want to add MSI capability to your applications today.

Why MSI enable your applications?

Install on demand is an incredibly powerful new feature that you can add to applications. It allows an application to install new features that it needs, when they're needed. No longer will users complain about hard drive bloat because the hard drive only needs to contain the core features of an application. Using install on demand means that only the pieces of an application that are in use are installed on the hard drive.

Another problem that many developers have is that they create a very rich application, only to learn later that many users are completely unaware of all of the neat gizmos that the developer has provided. In some cases, users may ask for product updates for features that already exist in the application. Using the Microsoft Windows Installer SDK allows you to add feature advertising to your application. When an application detects that a user could benefit from a feature, it can ask the user if he or she would like to try the feature and install it for him or her. Using feature advertising means that users gain access to features that they may not realize exist with a lot less effort. It also means that users will be able to provide better feedback on what they'd really like to see in future versions of your product and which features just didn't make the grade.

The final reason that you'd want to MSI enable your applications is a feature known as self-repair. When an application is damaged for some reason, the user normally needs to uninstall and then reinstall it to get it working again. Unfortunately, this also means that the user loses time resetting the application configuration. Application repair allows a user to simply choose the repair option from a Support Info dialog box, similar to the one shown in Figure A-5, to repair an application, rather than having to reinstall the application. This dialog is automatically presented when the user selects the support information link in the Add/Remove Programs applet for that application.

Figure A-5: Using MSI allows you to build applications that can repair themselves.

An overview of the MSI Installer SDK contents

Now that I've piqued your curiosity a bit, let's look at what the Microsoft Windows Installer SDK has to offer. The package includes the usual documentation. You'll also find sample code and a sample application that you can use to learn more about this product. There are development tools, including a database validation tool that you can use to check the integrity of any installation database that you create. The development tools also include a database authoring tool and some VBScript tools. Finally, you'll find a directory that contains the redistributable files that you can use to make a user's machine MSI friendly.

An overview of a few tools

Let's look at some of the practical applications of this SDK, even if you don't want to create an MSI-enabled application today. I've often wondered how you could determine whether a problem with an MSI installation is the fault of the MSI file, the files contained in the CAB, or even something like a version change. Considering that MSI is new technology, the version question is especially important because you may find that your installation program works one day and not the next. The MSIInfo utility provided with the Microsoft Windows Installer SDK is the answer to this problem. It prints out information that you won't normally see about an MSI package, including the author of that package and the version number of MSI used to create it. Figure A-6 shows the MSIInfo utility in action. The file shown is the Simple Event Subscribe package for the example in Chapter 11.

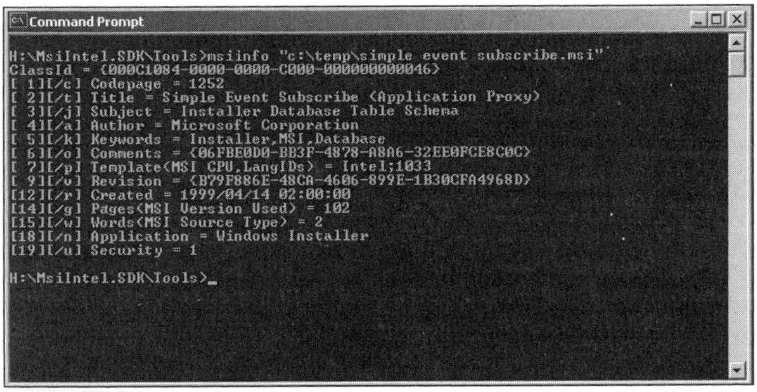

Figure A-6: The MSIInfo utility provides practical information about any MSI database on your machine.

Another interesting tool, MSIDB, allows you to export and import MSI database elements. Everything that MSI does while installing your application is part of a database element, so this is a very important utility to know about if you want to create a canned installation program and then replace only small pieces with custom elements. Figure A-7 shows what MSIDB looks like. Notice that I've opened the Simple Event Subscribe package again to show you a typical example of what an MSI database will contain.

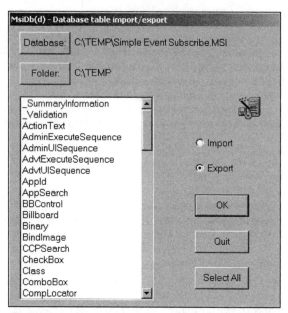

Figure A-7: MSIDB allows you to view the contents
of any MSI database.

On the
CD-ROM

You'll find copies of all the modified files shown in this section in the AppC\
Modified folder on the CD-ROM provided with this book. None of these modified
folders are designed for any use other than demonstration. Don't try to install any
of the files. You can, however, examine them for changes by using the utilities
described in this section of the chapter.

Notice that there's a _SummaryInformation in the MSI database. You'll find this entry
in every MSI database because it's the entry that the MSIInfo utility looks at. Highlight
this entry, select Export, and click OK. MSIDB will export the _SummaryInformation
entry to the location that you select on the hard drive. Now, use Notepad to open
the resulting _SummaryInformation.IDT file and you'll see something similar to the
entries in Figure A-8.

If you edited one of the text entries in this file, saved it, and then imported the file
back into the database, you'd find that the MSIInfo utility would report the changes
to the summary information. This is an example of how you can tweak a canned
installation to meet specific company needs with little effort on your part. The
installation program will run just as before with the subtle changes that you make
to it. Obviously, you'll want to be very careful making changes that could cause the
installation program to stop running. For example, changing GUIDs will almost certainly stop the MSI file from working.

```
 _SummaryInformation.idt - Notepad                          _|□|×|
File  Edit  Format  Help
PropertyId       Value
12       1255
_SummaryInformation       PropertyId
1       1252
2       Simple Event Subscribe (Application Proxy)
3       Installer Database Table Schema
4       Microsoft Corporation
5       Installer,MSI,Database
6       {06FBE0D0-BB3F-4878-A8A6-32EE0FCE8C0C}
7       Intel;1033
9       {B79F886E-48CA-4606-899E-1B30CFA4968D}
12      1999/04/14 02:00:00
14      102
15      2
18      Windows Installer
19      1
```

Figure A-8: MSIDB exports database entries to an IDT file in text format.

Note

MSIDB opens the database file for exclusive use, which makes sense when you consider the work that you're performing with it. Make sure that you close MSIDB before you attempt to access the database with any other utility. Nothing bad will happen if you don't follow this rule, but the new utility won't be able to access the database and will report an error instead of opening it for you. In other words, don't assume a change that you've made to the MSI database for an installation program has gone wrong until you check for the presence of MSIDB.

One problem that a developer faces when working on a new application is that the developer has to find an uncontaminated machine to test his or her application on. Normally, I have a machine set aside with just the operating system installed for testing purposes. If this machine gets "dirty," I reformat the hard drive and start with a fresh copy of the operating system. This is definitely not the way to test installation programs (unless you have plenty of time and an hourly wage instead of a salary). MSIZap, another utility that ships with the Microsoft Windows Installer SDK, will zap almost every trace of MSI data from your machine. You can completely clean off every application, or concentrate on just one or two applications with specific attributes.

Microsoft doesn't force you to hand edit the database with a text editor if you don't want to. Other utilities present the database in an easier to read format. For example, if you install the Orca utility (it doesn't install as part of the initial Microsoft Windows Installer SDK installation), you'll be able to use this editor to read and modify the contents of a database. Figure A-9 shows a typical example of what you'll see when you open a database by using this utility.

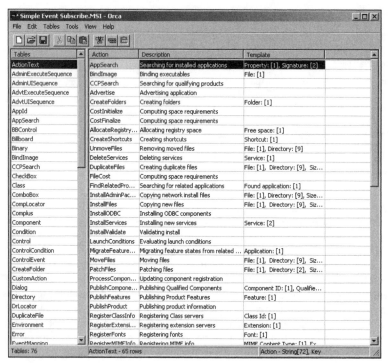

Figure A-9: The Orca utility allows you to modify the contents of an MSI database.

As you can see, the left pane displays all of the tables within the database. The right pane displays the rows and columns of the selected table. Right-click on any of these rows and you'll see options for adding or dropping a row. You can also edit the currently selected field by clicking it a second time. (The field will change to all bold characters when it's ready to edit.) The Microsoft Windows Installer SDK help file contains information about all of the standard tables within a database and how you can use them to create an installation application.

Tip   Text fields within a database are one of the items that a network administrator will want to modify. These fields allow a network administrator to provide company-specific information instead of the generic information provided by the developer. For example, you could include a text field that provides the name and telephone number of the person to contact in the event of an installation failure.

This is a brief overview of some of the Microsoft Windows Installer SDK tools. As you can see, this is a feature-rich product that's designed to change the way that you write installation programs. Instead of creating full-fledged inflexible applications, you can now create databases of installation steps that can be easily modified as needed to meet specific requirements. Add to that features like on demand installation, and you can see why this is a must have tool for any type of Windows 2000 development and a good add-on for development on other Windows platforms.

Understanding the Visual Studio Installer

The Visual Studio Installer represents the easy method for creating installation programs that use the MSI file format. This is a companion product to the Microsoft Windows Installer SDK. It allows you to add MSI features to applications and modify MSI databases. In addition, unlike the Microsoft Windows Installer SDK, this isn't a stand-alone product. It's designed to integrate with Visual Studio.

Before you install this product, you must have a copy of any of the Visual Studio products installed on your machine including Visual Basic and Visual C++. When you finish the installation, you'll see a new Visual Studio Installer entry in the Start ⇨ Programs ⇨ Microsoft Visual Studio 6.0 ⇨ Microsoft Visual Studio 6.0 Enterprise Tools menu. This product uses the same IDE as the Visual Studio Analyzer, so if you've used that product, you'll have a good idea of how to use this one.

Besides the application, you get a full-featured help file with the package. Microsoft didn't include any samples with this product. We'll discuss use of the Visual Studio Installer later in the appendix.

Why Should You Use the MSI File Format?

Some people may wonder why they should use the MSI file format at all. After all, the setup program has been working for quite some time now and you can even start it automatically with the right command line settings using a variety of methods. The fact remains that the setup program is a nonstandardized way of creating an installation program for any application. The lack of standardization has made the setup program less usable than it could be and many users still have a problem installing applications because every setup program seems to be different. The MSI file format promises to add standardization where chaos currently reigns.

Another good reason to use the MSI file format is that this is the file format used by Component Services for exporting COM+ applications. Using an MSI file for your installation program as well will give your application a uniform appearance and installation method. The user of your application won't have to figure out one installation method for the COM+ part of an application and another for the client application. Both applications will use the same installation procedure, which is quite simple.

All that a user needs to do to install any MSI file format application is right-click the Microsoft Windows Installer Package and select Install from the context menu (shown in Figure A-10). This same context menu allows the user to uninstall and repair the application, which means fewer trips to the Control Panel's Add/Remove Applications applet. If you have Orca installed, you can also use this menu to edit the database.

Figure A-10: Using the MSI file format means that you can install, repair, or uninstall an application within Windows Explorer

We've discussed the many network administrator and developer advantages to using MSI during the course of this appendix. However, it's important to realize that the ability to edit your installation routine after the fact is a big plus, one that you don't currently enjoy when using a setup application. If Microsoft provided a capability to edit the required database and support files, but it was hard to do, that would be one thing. MSI files, on the contrary, are very easy to edit and reconfigure. About the only problem that you might have using them is the speed of getting the application installed. It's possible that a custom setup program might do things faster.

Creating an MSI File for an Application

Creating an MSI file for a Visual Basic application is relatively easy and a lot more flexible when using the Visual Studio Installer. This section shows you how to create an installation package for a simple application. The Visual Studio Installer is designed to create very complex installation routines containing a number of merge packages as well as standard MSI packages. You'll also find that every aspect of the MSI file is configurable. This means that your installation package can look customized even though it uses the same MSI runtime as every other MSI file.

Note   A merge package has an MSM extension. It contains only the files required to install a single application element, but doesn't contain the installation instructions. You'll use a merge package to incorporate separate application elements. For example, when working with a COM+ application, the server-side component and the client-side application constitute two separate elements of the same application. After you build a merge package, you add it to an MSI file by using Visual Studio Installer to create a single package with two elements.

The first section that follows shows you how to set up the initial application. We'll discuss all of the customizations that you can perform for a simple application in the second section. The third section shows you how to create the package. Finally, we'll perform various types of testing on the package in the last two sections.

Creating the application

Creating the application is very simple. The following procedure shows you how to create a simple MSI package for a Visual Basic application. (I assume that you've already installed Visual Studio Installer.)

1. Start Visual Studio Installer, if you haven't done so already. You'll see a New Project dialog box similar to the one shown in Figure A-11.

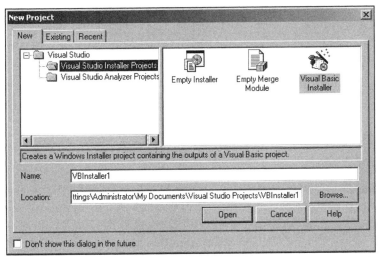

Figure A-11: The New Project dialog box is where you choose a Visual Studio Installer project type.

2. Open the Visual Studio folder and highlight the Visual Studio Installer Projects folder. Notice that there are three projects to choose from. You use the Empty Installer and Empty Merge Module projects with languages like Visual C++; Visual Basic includes it's own project type.

3. Highlight the Visual Basic Installer icon, type a name for your application (the example uses Event Receive Install), and choose a directory for the installation application.

4. Click Open. You'll see the Visual Studio Installer Setup Wizard – Visual Basic dialog box shown in Figure A-12. Notice that this dialog box allows you to create two different types of application. The merge module is used to create an addition for an existing application. We don't have an existing application to work with, so we'll create an installer project. This dialog box will also allow you to choose the application for which you want to create an installer.

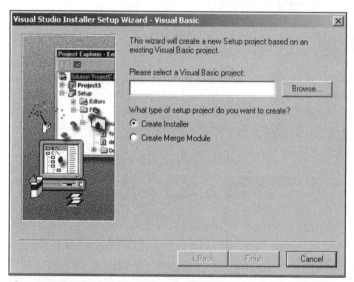

Figure A-12: The Visual Studio Installer Setup Wizard – Visual Basic dialog box allows you to choose the project type and source application.

5. Choose the Event Receive application from Chapter 11. You'll find it on the CD-ROM provided with this book in the Chapt11\Simple Event Receive folder. If you were creating an installer for another application, you'd use the Browse button to find that project on the hard drive.

6. Select the Create Installer option, and then click Finish. Visual Studio Installer will create a new project for you that contains all of the required application elements. You can see these elements in the Project Explorer window. Double-clicking on any of the Project Explorer window objects displays that object in the edit area, just as it would in Visual Basic. Figure A-13 shows a typical example of the Microsoft Development Environment display.

Note By the last step of the procedure, some people might be confused about where the Visual Studio Installer went. The Visual Studio Installer, like the Visual Studio Analyzer, depends on the Microsoft Development Environment as a container application. Most Microsoft language products are likely to use this container application as an IDE in the future.

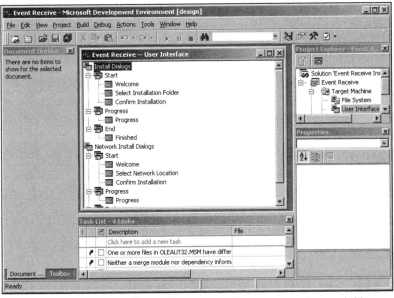

Figure A-13: The Microsoft Development Environment works much like Visual Studio, making installation program changes easy.

Customizing the installation features

Creating an installation program doesn't have to be hard if you follow some simple rules when creating one. The very first item that you should check is the list of files that will be installed with the application and the criteria for installing them. The Project Explorer window shown in Figure A-14 shows all of the files that are associated with the Event Receive application. You'd need to decide whether to install all of the files in this list, add to the list, or remove some items from the list.

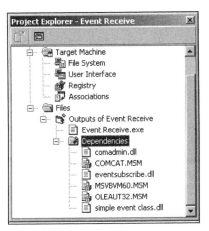

Figure A-14: Look in the Project Explorer window for the list of files that will be installed with your application.

There's something wrong with this list that a COM+ developer will always have to watch out for. Notice that the two COM+ application DLLs (eventsubscribe.dll and simple event class.dll) are included in this list, along with the files required for the application. These two DLLs are required on the server and you need to provide a separate installation for them. For this example, you'll need to remove the two files. Project Explorer won't remove them from the window, but they'll be removed from the project.

There are three files with an MSM extension. These are merge modules that were added to the installation program automatically because Event Receive relies on them for services. Because these files are already part of the operating system, the installation program can rely on the operating system's installation programs for them and not install them itself. This important new feature prevents some of the situations in which DLL hell existed in the past. These MSM files automatically check the version and language of the existing DLL before they overwrite the existing file with a new one. However, it always pays to check these files to ensure that you have all of the files that you need for the application and that the correct settings are made for each file.

The next task is to ensure that all of the files are going to the right place. Double-click on the File System entry in Project Explorer and you'll see an Event Receive — File System window similar to the one shown in Figure A-15. Notice that this window contains three default folders: the Application Folder, the User's Desktop, and the User's Start Menu. You can add more folders if you need them. For example, there is no Windows System32 folder and you may need to add files there.

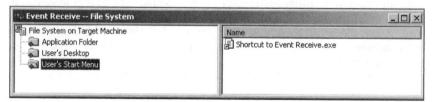

Figure A-15: The Event Receive — File System window tells you where all of the files will end up during installation.

Adding a new file is easy, just right-click on the File System on Target machine entry (or any other location in the file system hierarchy) and you'll see options for adding new folders. There's a Special Folders context menu entry similar to the one shown in Figure A-16 that allows you to add common Windows folders like the System32 folder to your installation program. We won't need any special folders for this application, but it's a good thing to keep in mind as you build other installation programs.

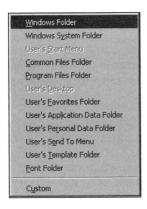

Figure A-16: This context menu allows you to create entries for standard Windows folders in the file system hierarchy.

The next part of the project to check is the User Interface. Double-click on this object in Project Explorer and you'll see an Event Receive — User Interface window similar to the one shown in Figure A-17. This window shows which dialogs the user will see and what order they'll see them in. Microsoft provides a standard set of dialogs for an MSI application in order to make every installation look the same to the user. You can, however, add customizations like a banner to each of these dialogs. The features that the user sees depends on the features that you add to the installation program. It's also possible to add custom dialog boxes to the installation program as needed. For example, you might require some special configuration settings for your application.

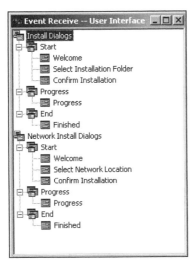

Figure A-17: The Event Receive — User Interface window shows how the installation will proceed from the user's perspective.

Note All banners for MSI files are either in BMP or JPG format. You'll want to test the installation application several times by using several different display resolutions to ensure that the banner appears as you want it to appear. It also helps to use different color settings and to test color depth. In some cases, poor color choices for a banner can make your installation program look strange with certain user machine settings.

Notice that this window actually contains two installations: standard and network. You can configure an MSI package to detect where it's being installed from and customize the installation for that installation scenario. This makes it easier to write installation programs that are flexible from the outset and will meet a broader range of client needs at the outset, rather than requiring modifications later.

Visual Studio Installer also allows you to check Registry entries, which should be the next step that you take. Double-click the Registry object in Project Explorer and you'll see an Event Receive — Registry window similar to the one shown in Figure A-18. Notice that this window looks like an abbreviated version of RegEdit and it works in the same way as RegEdit does. In most cases, the default Registry entries will work just fine, but make sure that you add any custom settings that your application requires.

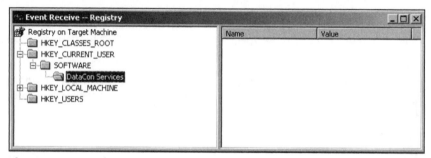

Figure A-18: Use the Event Receive — Registry window to customize any Registry settings for your application.

The final stop for most applications is to make any required file associations. For example, your application may open TXT files and you'll want to register it as an application that does so. Double-click the Associations object in Project Explorer and you'll see the Event Receive — Associations window shown in Figure A-19.

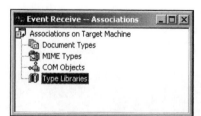

Figure A-19: The Event Receive — Associations window allows you to assign several types of file association to your application.

There are separate folders for documents, MIME types, COM objects, and type libraries. In short, you can create a variety of associations for both the desktop and the Internet.

Building the installation program

You should have noticed by now that we haven't written any code and you'll find that you don't need to. There are situations when the most that you'll need to do is perform a lot of configuration. After you finish with the setup process, you'll want to build the installation program.

Use the Build ⇨ Build command to build your installation program. The building process occurs in two phases. First, Visual Studio Installer gathers all of the required files, creates a database containing all of the required steps, and performs any customization that you requested. Second, Visual Studio Installer compresses the files so that they take the least amount of space possible. At this point, your installation program is ready to test.

Testing the install process

The first step for testing an installation program is to attempt to install the application in question. Move to a clean machine so that you can eliminate sources of outside interference and the contaminated environment of your development machine. It's important that you test the application in a clean environment to make it easier to verify the setup.

After you install the program, see if it runs. If it does, then you're at least halfway toward ensuring that the application will run as anticipated on a user's machine. You'll also want to check for potential problems like file associations.

After you've run the application for a while and checked all of the user elements, it's time to check under the hood. Look into the Registry and make sure that all of the Registry entries are as you expect them to be. Verify the locations of files and ensure that every file is in the appropriate place.

Testing the uninstall process

Applications written for Windows 2000 have to uninstall just as well as they install. Therefore, the next testing phase is to uninstall the application. In most cases, you won't see any problems with the application at this point; however, you'll sometimes find that appearances can be deceiving, so it pays to check further.

Make sure that the installation program removes the application directory and that all files associated with the application are gone. You'll also want to check that shared files are still available to other applications that may need them. Open RegEdit and verify that all of the application's Registry entries are gone. Look for little problems like Start menu entries that didn't get removed.

Problems with the Microsoft Windows Installer

The MSI is a new product, which means that there's a good chance that all of the bugs aren't worked out yet. Microsoft recognizes this fact and has included a list of bugs that it knows about in the Visual Studio Installer README file that accompanies the SDK. Make sure that you read this file before you begin the installation process because there are some significant limitations to this product. You may find, in rare cases at least, that one or more of these limitations will prevent you from using the MSI. However, the MSI file format is the wave of the future, and it's in your best interest to begin making the change sooner rather than later.

Non-Windows 2000 support

Just how much the problem of non-Windows 2000 support affects you as a developer depends on what type of installation package you need to create in most cases. Windows 2000 ships with MSI support. Microsoft has stated that MSI is the preferred installation method for this new platform. You can also get MSI support for Windows 9x and Windows NT machines because Microsoft would prefer that you also use this new technology for these older machines. However, because this support is unlikely to appear on older machines any time soon (it's a separate installation and not part of automated updates like Windows Update), you'll always have to include the MSI redistributable files with any shrink-wrap software package that you create.

This creates two problems. First, any installation program that you create will have to check for MSI support on the host machine and either fail gracefully if the support isn't present or offer to install the required support. Part of the reason to use MSI is to reduce installation program complexity; yet, the fact that MSI is new makes it possible that you'll actually increase application complexity in the short-term.

The second problem is one of support. Users already complain that installation programs are too difficult to understand and use. Microsoft is very aware of this problem. Microsoft has done everything possible to decrease installation program complexity during the last few years. Yet, there always seems to be a glitch in installation that keeps the user from getting the application installed on his or her computer. Using MSI means adding complexity to the setup if the user doesn't have MSI installed. You can be sure that some users will find this confusing and that support costs will increase as a result.

Database and INF corruption

MSI isn't an application per se; it's actually a database of instructions. You're not creating an application; it's more like a script that gets interpreted by the MSI Service. As we've seen throughout the appendix, the instructions used by MSI to install your product are very accessible and open. Anyone can look at them and it doesn't take very much knowledge at all to modify those instructions. In general, MSI is superior to any installation package that you may have used in the past for these very reasons.

Unfortunately, the very nature of MSI can also become a problem. Well-intentioned users or administrators could change vital information in MSI packages or archives, making the installation program perform in ways other than the way you intended. For example, changing a GUID will definitely lead to unanticipated results. Changing one of the lines of instruction in the INF file could make the installation program do a number of things that you didn't expect.

You can use policies and lock the CAB file to prevent these problems from happening. For example, the DisableBrowse machine policy will prevent users from locating the source of an application and modifying the files. In short, you need to be proactive about keeping corruption at bay. I hope that Microsoft will keep the flexibility and add a little more in the security department for the next release of MSI.

Summary

This appendix discussed two main topics. First, we looked at packaging applications in general. We discussed what you need to know in order to put together a good package that will address the needs of your users. Second, we looked in-depth at the MSI packaging methodology. Microsoft has provided this new method of packaging applications because the old method is flawed and difficult to use. Here are some additional conclusions that you can draw from the contents of this appendix.

✦ Always consider the application package that you create in light of the user who will install it. In many cases, you can design a package based on the user's environment and company size. You also need to consider the method used to distribute the application.

✦ Make sure that you create a complete package that includes all of the required files.

✦ The Microsoft Windows Installer SDK comes with a wealth of tools designed to make working with MSI databases easier. In addition, you can use this SDK to add new features to your applications like install on demand.

✦ The Visual Studio Installer is an application build with the Microsoft Windows Installer SDK. You'll find that it allows you to build installation programs quickly and easily.

✦ Always test both the install and uninstall features of your installation application before you release it to the public. In some cases, it also pays to simulate errors so that you can check the repair capability of your application.

✦ MSI is a new product, so you're going to run into problems. Microsoft has been very forthcoming with a list of problems for this product, so it pays to check the README first for problems that you can't work around. Besides the problems that Microsoft has listed, you'll also want to check for issues like non-Windows 2000 support.

✦   ✦   ✦

What's on the CD-ROM?

In This Appendix

Source Code Summary

Adobe Acrobat Reader

BootMagic and PartitionMagic

Microsoft Windows Platform SDK

Paint Shop Pro

PowerPoint Viewer

RoboHELP

VB Crash Shield and Photo Crunch

WinZIP

The CD-ROM that comes with this book contains many useful resources that will make your enjoyment of this book much greater. Obviously, one of the more important inclusions is the source code, which will reduce the amount of typing that you need to perform to see how things work. I've included some utilities like Jasc's Paint Shop Pro to make it easier for you to create the graphics required for this book. Other utilities, like Adobe Acrobat and the Microsoft PowerPoint Viewer, will make it easier for you to research information online. Finally, products like the Microsoft Windows Platform SDK are included because you need them in order to work with the code in this book. The following sections explain each of the major parts of the CD-ROM and provide details on why I chose the applications. We'll also talk about one of the most important inclusions — the source code for all of the examples in the book.

Source Code in the Book

Every one of the examples in this book is a fully functional program that you can compile and run at your leisure. By compiling and running the example applications, you can learn how COM+ applications work. An analysis of the code will show you what you'll need to do to make your own applications run.

Note Please be sure to check the README file for each example. This file tells you where to install the executable files on your machine. Obviously, you'll still need to install the software correctly to see it work properly. For COM+ applications, this means using two machines: a client and a server. One of the few applications that you can view in its entirety with a single machine is the MMC snap-in example shown in Chapter 9.

The source code in the book is complete enough for explanation purposes. In other words, when you read a chapter in the book, you're seeing just enough of the example code to understand a principle that I'm trying to demonstrate. However, the examples are much larger than what you'll see in the chapters—a lot of additional code is required to make a fully functional program. As a result, you'll want to look at the source code on the CD-ROM to get a better view of all of the code that's either created for you by the various wizards or added on later to make the code fully functional.

In some cases, there wasn't room in the book to fully demonstrate a principle. When this occurred, I created a second example on the CD-ROM that provides more functionality than the example in the book. These extra examples are always referenced in a Note so that you know that they exist. The CD-ROM contains these extra examples so that you can get the very best information on how an example works.

I've also included a compiled version of all of the examples. The reason is simple: Many of you will be using educational or other versions of Visual Basic, or may not have access to the Internet to download one of the ancillary programming aids that I talk about in the Preface to the book. I want to be sure that you can still run the examples and see how they work. Many times, running the code makes a principle a lot easier to understand.

Make sure that you take time to write to me about problems that you have with any of the source code in the book. I'm always on the lookout for a better way to do things or a way to improve my coding techniques. You can always contact me at JMueller@mwt.net. As people write in to me about this book, I'll upload their suggestions and code improvements to my Web site. Make sure that you also get the current URL updates for this book. You can find my Web site at http://www.mwt.net/~jmueller/.

Adobe Acrobat Reader

A lot of information is at your disposal on the Internet. The only problem is that some of this information is so bulky, that the presenter had to come up with a method to package it for easy download. In addition, the Internet isn't the easiest place to search through information or to present the complex graphics that are often required in our industry. Finally, reading the information online means that it won't be on your hard drive for very long and there are situations when you may not have a connection to the Internet. For these reasons and more, a lot of the information that you'll want to look at comes in a PDF file that you can download. Viewing a PDF file requires the Adobe Acrobat Reader.

Adobe is constantly upgrading their Acrobat Reader product and making it easier to use. Consequently, it's important to check their Web site at http://www.adobe.com/prodindex/ from time to time to ensure that you have the latest version of the product. This is a free download, so you can update it as often as you'd like.

PowerQuest BootMagic and PartitionMagic

I don't know of many programmers who don't have at least two different operating systems installed on their machine. For example, if you're developing for the corporate environment, you might have both Windows NT 4 and Windows 2000 installed on your machine right now. Often, programmers have to have far more than just two operating systems installed. Depending on whom you write applications for, just getting enough operating systems installed on your machine can become a nightmare. That's where these PowerQuest products come into play. They help you to maintain a variety of operating systems on one machine in a way that also allows you to keep your sanity.

The first part of the management picture is creating and maintaining partitions. What happens if you need to install a new operating system and there isn't any space left on your hard drive? In the past, you'd need to reformat the drive and create new partitions from scratch. If you're anything like me, reinstalling software isn't one of your favorite things. PartitionMagic allows you to modify your partitions as needed. You can resize partitions, delete and create partitions, and keep your system organized.

 It always pays to keep abreast of the latest product updates. You can find information about the most recent version of BootMagic at `http://www.powerquest.com/bootmagic/index.html` and download a demonstration version of PartitionMagic at `http://www.powerquest.com/partitionmagic/index.html`.

Obviously, creating the required partitions is only a first step. The next step is to install the required operating systems and provide some method for accessing them. In most cases, the best you can hope to achieve with operating system-specific solutions is a dual- or triple-boot system. BootMagic allows you to place more than one operating system on your machine and be assured that you'll be able to access it later. Not only that, you can also place operating systems that normally don't get along together on a single machine. For example, the current version of BootMagic (as of this writing) allows Windows NT 4 and Linux to get along on the same system—that's something that you wouldn't ordinarily be able to do with ease.

Microsoft Windows Platform SDK

Visual Basic users don't require a lot of the functionality that the Microsoft Windows Platform SDK (Platform SDK for short) provides. There are, however, two very good reasons to include this product on the CD-ROM. First, you can't build the MMC snap-in application in Chapter 9 without the Platform SDK. Visual Basic doesn't provide the required support natively, and none of the service packs provides the required wizard and developer. Second, the Platform SDK contains the latest set of tools that Microsoft provides to developers for creating applications and testing them. While you can always test a COM+ application with brute force methods, it's much easier to use the new tools that Microsoft provides in the Platform SDK. However, make sure to allocated 3GB for the full installation.

In addition to tools and product support, the Platform SDK also provides one indispensable resource, information. The help files that you got with Visual Basic are out of date now and you need the latest information in order to build COM+ applications. Unless you have a Microsoft Developer Network (MSDN) subscription, the only way that you can get the required information is to download the Platform SDK. So, even if you decide not to make use of anything else that the Platform SDK has to offer, you'll still want to get it installed for the information that it provides.

The Platform SDK version included with this book is the one that I used to develop the code that you're working with. The tools and documentation are more than sufficient to handle all of the applications in the book and just about any application that you'll build on your own. However, it's always helpful to have the most current version of any product. If you want to download the most current version of the Microsoft Windows Platform SDK, check out http://msdn.microsoft.com/downloads/sdks/platform/platform.asp. The Microsoft Windows Platform SDK is free for the price of download time, which can be substantial.

Jasc Paint Shop Pro

Most programmers are going to create a help file or two sometime in their career. In most cases, those help files are going to require some graphics — nothing fancy, just enough to get your point across. That's why you need a graphics program that's easy to use, easier to understand, and doesn't require a degree from an art college. Paint Shop Pro falls into this category. You can use it to draw simple pictures as well as capture screenshots of various types. Screenshots are the basis of many help files and are used for advertising purposes.

Graphics are the main type of application that Jasc works with, but it also produces an advanced form of Quick View called Quick View Plus that many people find quite handy. You can find out more about the products that Jasc makes at http://www.jasc.com/. The CD-ROM provided with this book contains a 30-day evaluation version of Paint Shop Pro. You can download the latest version of this and other Jasc products at http://www.jasc.com/download_4.asp.

Paint Shop Pro doesn't stop with graphics creation, though; it also allows you to read a wide variety of graphics formats and translate between them. You can take an interesting graphic that is in BMP format and convert it to the GIF file that you need for a Web site. Using the same image in several different formats allows you to develop a theme for your product in several different environments. Users build associations when they see the same background image in your application as they do on your Web site. These associations are important in building sales.

Microsoft PowerPoint Viewer

If you spend any time at all viewing data on Microsoft Web sites, looking at an MSDN subscription, or attending Microsoft seminars, you're going to need a PowerPoint viewer of some type. Every slide presentation that Microsoft produces is in PowerPoint format, which means that you'll need a viewer if you want to learn what happened at TechEd this year. However, instead of purchasing a full-fledged copy of Microsoft Office and consuming huge quantities of hard drive space to install the complete version of PowerPoint, it often makes sense to install just the viewer.

 Microsoft provides a wealth of viewers and converters that can make working with Microsoft Office a lot easier. Even people who don't own Office can look at the documentation that you create if it's converted to the right format or if they have a viewer that allows them to see the contents of the documentation without purchasing the product. All of these viewers are available for the price of a download. You can find out more about these converters and viewers at http://www. microsoft.com/Office/000/viewers.htm.

eHelp Corporation RoboHELP

If you're anything like me, building help files is your least favorite part of any project. It's still important to include help files or face the user's ire at not being able to figure anything out in your application. There are products that make this job a little easier and definitely more palatable. One of the most versatile and flexible help creation applications on the market is RoboHELP.

There are versions of RoboHELP on my machine for creating both standard Windows help files and more modern HTML help files. You'll also find versions of RoboHELP that integrate with Microsoft Office, as well as international versions that will help you to develop products for worldwide distribution. In short, RoboHELP can be the one product that answers all of your help file creation needs. Unfortunately, it still doesn't write content for you, but it will help you to organize your thoughts and get the content that you need put together faster.

 RoboHELP is one of the best ways to automate help creation that you'll ever find. It makes what's normally a white-knuckled adventure into the unknown world of product support a walk in the park for many developers. The 15-day evaluation copy of RoboHELP on the CD-ROM provided with this book is current as of the time of writing, but you may find this product so interesting that you've got to see the latest version available. You can find out the latest information and download the latest copy of RoboHELP at http://www.ehelp.com/RoboHELP/downloads.shtm.

Imron VB Crash Shield and Photo Crunch

Have you ever been working on a new project, made a programming error, and then watched several hours of work go down the drain because you forgot to save first? I know that many of you will say no to anyone who asks, but you'll also remember at least one time where it did happen. VB Crash Shield will help prevent little accidents like the forgotten save from happening. Even if you always remember to save your work, it's still annoying to have to reboot the machine every time an application crashes, so VB Crash Shield will at least save you some time in getting your system set back up for use.

So, how does this product work? No, it's not a magic barrier between your code and the machine it runs on. VB Crash Shield automatically inserts error-handling code into your application. When you compile the application, the error-handling code is already in place, making it a lot less likely that you or the user of your application will have to reboot when errors occur.

Have you ever wasted several minutes waiting for a graphic to download from a Web site and thought to yourself that there must be a faster way of getting the information that you needed? More than likely, if you didn't absolutely have to have the graphic image, you clicked Stop on your browser to end the whole painful process. Graphics are an essential download in many cases, though, so keeping the frustration level to a minimum is a real benefit to both you and the people who use your Web site. Sure, you can get by without a pretty map of the vendor's Web site or a logo that really doesn't thrill you, but many of the worst downloads are technical drawings or other critical information that you really can't do without.

Photo Crunch makes life a lot easier for everyone by compressing the image so that it downloads faster. The larger the image, the better Photo Crunch does in compressing it to a manageable size. This product is a perfect addition to Paint Shop Pro (described earlier) because it allows you to take the output from that application and make it Web-site friendly. Not only does compressing the image save download time, but it also saves space on your Web server.

Both VB Crash Shield and Photo Crunch are shareware products, which means that you get to try them before you buy. Both products provided on the CD-ROM for this book are current as of this writing, but you may want to check the vendor's Web site to ensure that you're getting the most current version of the product for testing purposes. You'll find VB Crash Shield at `http://www.imroncorp.com/vbcrash.htm`. Photo Crunch can be downloaded at `http://www.imrcorp.com/photo.htm`.

Nico Mak's WinZIP

The ZIP file format is one of the most popular ways to compress data in the world. Not only can compressing data save room on a hard drive, but it also allows you to reduce upload and download time for e-mail. A ZIP file is also a handy way of combining a multitude of files into a single file for ease of upload. In short, if you're going to work with files, you need to know about the ZIP file format. That's where WinZIP comes into play. Nico Mak has created one of the easiest ways to work with ZIP files. In fact, it's so easy that you don't have to know much more than how to right-click or drag and drop.

Web Resource

Like many other parts of the PC Industry, Nico Mak strives to make WinZIP faster and easier to use, while increasing the number of features. Of course, there are the usual bug fixes as well. You can always get the latest version of WinZIP plus patches and trial versions at http://www.winzip.com/.

✦   ✦   ✦

Glossary

This glossary has several important features that you need to be aware of. First, every relatively new or unfamiliar acronym in the entire book is listed here — even if there's a better-than-even chance that you already know what the acronym stands for. This way there is no doubt that you'll always find everything that you need to use the book properly. The second thing that you need to know is that these definitions are specific to the book. In other words, when you look through this glossary, you're seeing the words defined in the context in which they're used. This might or might not always coincide with current industry usage because the computer industry changes the meaning of words so often. Finally, the definitions here use a conversational tone in most cases. This means that they might sacrifice a bit of puritanical accuracy for the sake of better understanding.

Web Resource
What happens if you can't find the acronym that you need in the computer dictionary that you just bought? Fortunately, there are at least two sites on the Internet that you can go to for help. The first is the University of Texas site at `http://www-hep.uta.edu/~variable/e_comm/pages/r_dic-en.htm`. This site is updated fairly often and provides only acronyms (another page at the same site includes a glossary). The second site is Acronym Finder at `http://www.acronymfinder.com/`. Although this site isn't updated as often as the first one, it does have the advantage of providing an extremely large list of acronyms to choose from. At the time of this writing, the Acronym Finder sported 141,000 acronyms. If neither of these sites provides what you need, you might want to look at A Web of Online Dictionaries at `http://www.yourdictionary.com/`. An interesting feature of this Web site is that it provides access to more than one dictionary in more than one language.

There are always other online solutions, many of which are free. For example, Webopedia has become one of my favorite places to visit because it provides encyclopedic coverage of many computer terms and includes links to other Web sites. You can find Webopedia at `http://webopedia.internet.com`. In some cases, like Microsoft's Encarta (`http://encarta.msn.com`), you have to pay for the support provided, but it's still worth the effort to seek out these locations to ensure that you always understand the terms used by our jargon-filled trade.

Access Control List (ACL) Part of the Windows NT security API used to determine both access and monitoring properties for an object. Each ACL contains one or more ACEs (access control entries) that define the security properties for an individual or group. There are two major ACL groups: SACL (security access control list) and DACL (discretionary access control list). The SACL controls Windows NT auditing feature. The DACL controls access to the object.

Accessor functions Commonly known as get or set functions, these functions allow a client to manipulate object properties without directly manipulating the property. A property value is read using a get function, while a set function is used to change the property value. Certain programming languages like Visual Basic use accessor functions by default to reduce the potential for errant property value entries. Because the component can examine every request before it either grants access to the value or changes the property, the property value has a greater chance of remaining both secure and intact.

ACID An acronym commonly used to describe the four essential properties of any transaction. These properties include: atomicity, consistency, isolation, and durability.

ACL See Access Control List.

Active Directory A method of storing machine, server, and user configuration within Windows 2000 that supports full data replication so that every domain controller has a copy of the data. This is essentially a special-purpose database that contains information formatted according to a specific schema. Active Directory is designed to make Windows 2000 more reliable and secure, while reducing the work required by both the developer and network administrator for application support and distribution. The user also benefits because Active Directory fully supports roving users and maintains a full record of user information, which reduces the effects of local workstation down time.

Active Directory Services Interface (ADSI) A set of APIs used to access Active Directory, the central repository of information in Windows 2000. Active Directory is a hierarchical database used to store many types of information in a somewhat freeform format. ADSI allows access to both Active Directory data and the schema, which means that you can use it to create new database elements, as well as to remove elements that are no longer in use.

ActiveX Data Object (ADO) A local and remote database access technology that relies on OLE-DB to create the connection. ADO is a set of "wrapper" functions that make using OLE-DB and the underlying OLE-DB provider easier. ADO is designed as a replacement for DAO and as an adjunct to ODBC.

ADO See ActiveX Data Object.

ADSI See Active Directory Services Interface.

American Standard Code for Information Interchange (ASCII) A standard method of equating the numeric representations available in a computer to human-readable form. The number 32, for example, represents a space. The standard ASCII code contains 128 characters (7 bits). The extended ASCII code uses 8 bits for 256 characters. Display adapters from the same machine type usually use the same upper 128 characters. Printers, however, might reserve these upper 128 characters for nonstandard characters. Many Epson printers, for example, use the upper 128 characters for the italic representations of the lower 128 characters.

API See Application Programming Interface.

Application Programming Interface (API) A method for defining a standard set of function calls and other interface elements. It usually defines the interface between a high-level language and the lower-level elements used by a device driver or operating system. The ultimate goal is to provide some type of service to an application that requires access to the operating system or device feature set.

ASCII See American Standard Code for Information Interchange.

Atomicity The ability of a fault-tolerant system to identify a complete unit of work and either recover that unit of work or roll the work back to a previous stable state when a fault occurs. This term is normally associated with software systems like MTS.

Browser A special application normally used to display data downloaded from the Internet. The most common form of Internet data is the HTML (hypertext markup language) page. However, modern browsers can also display various types of graphics and even standard desktop application files such as Microsoft Word documents directly. The actual capabilities provided by a browser vary widely depending on the software vendor and platform.

Causality Identifier (CID) A form of globally unique identifier (GUID), it is used to link the method calls between two or more machines. For example, if machine A requests that machine B activate a component, and machine B has to request that machine C activate a component first, then the calls are causally related and DCOM will generate a CID for them. The CID will remain in effect until the original call that machine A created is satisfied by a return call from machine B.

CDS See Cell Directory Service.

Cell Directory Service (CDS) A part of the Open Software Foundation (OSF) distributed computing environment (DCE) remote procedure call (RPC) network protocol. This component provides name-service provider support.

CID See Causality Identifier.

Class ID (CLSID) A method of assigning a unique identifier to each object in the registry. Also refers to various high-level language constructs.

CLB See Component Load Balancing.

Client The recipient of data, services, or resources from a file or other server. This term can refer to a workstation or an application. The server can be another PC or an application.

CLSID See Class ID.

COM See Component Object Model.

Common Object Request Broker Architecture (CORBA) The purpose of this protocol is to describe data and application code in a way that a variety of computer types can use. Eventually, CORBA will allow you to go to a Web page and download a mini-application (applet) as part of that page. This is the Object Management Group's (OMG) alternative to Microsoft's ActiveX. IBM originally designed CORBA for inclusion with OS/2, but other companies, such as Sun Microsystems, now support this standard as well.

Compensating Resource Manager (CRM) This COM+ feature allows your application to work with the Distributed Transaction Coordinator (DTC) without requiring you to create a special resource dispenser. Normally, you'd be required to create a resource dispenser for your application. Depending on the complexity of your application, the resource dispenser might not have a lot of work to do. COM+ gets rid of the extra programming requirement by providing a default resource dispenser known as the CRM. All of the "magic" required to perform resource dispenser tasks is in the special interface that you add to your component. CRM accesses this interface and allows your component to vote on the outcome of a transaction based on the results of the individual transaction within the component. In short, you get all of the features of a full-resource dispenser implementation, without any of the work. The CRM also takes care of any recovery requirements for a failed transaction based on the log entries that it makes, which means that you get automatic error recovery without any additional work.

Component Load Balancing (CLB) A specialized form of load balancing that deals with the ability of COM+ applications to balance the processing load across multiple servers at the component level. CLB allows the application to perform load balancing at a finer level, which means that the processing load is better distributed across the processing elements. This also allows multiple servers to handle requests from a single client; potentially increasing data throughput by an order of magnitude.

Component Object Model (COM) A Microsoft specification for an object-oriented code and data encapsulation method and transference technique. It's the basis for technologies such as OLE (object linking and embedding) and ActiveX (the replacement name for OCXs, an object-oriented code library technology). COM is limited to local connections. DCOM (distributed component object model) is the technology used to allow data transfers and the use of OCXs within the Internet environment.

Connectivity A measure of the interactions between clients and servers. In many cases, connectivity begins with the local machine and the interactions between applications and components. LANs introduce another level of connectivity with machine to machine communications. Finally, WANs, MANs, intranets, and the Internet all introduce further levels of connectivity concerns.

Container Part of the object-oriented terminology that has become part of OLE. A container is a drive, file, or other resource used to hold objects. The container is normally referenced as an object itself.

CORBA See Common Object Request Broker Architecture.

Cracker A hacker (computer expert) who uses his or her skills for misdeeds on computer systems to which he or she has little or no authorized access. A cracker normally possesses specialty software that allows easier access to the target network. In most cases, crackers require extensive amounts of time to actually break the security for a system before they can enter it.

CRM See Compensating Resource Manager.

Cryptographic Service Provider (CSP) A specialty company that deals in certifying the identity of companies, developers, or individuals on the Internet. This identification check allows the company to issue an electronic certificate, which can then be used to conduct transactions securely. Several levels of certification are normally provided within a specific group. For example, there are three levels of individual certification. The lowest merely verifies the individual's identity through an Internet mail address; the highest requires the individual to provide written proof along with a notarized statement. When you access a certified site or try to download a certified document such as an ActiveX control, the browser will display the electronic certificate onscreen, allowing you to make a security determination based on fact.

CSP See Cryptographic Service Provider.

DACL See Discretionary Access Control List.

Data Encryption Standard (DES) A method of data encryption that relies on symmetric key encryption. This methodology was originally introduced in 1975 and standardized by ANSI in 1981.

DCOM See Distributed Component Object Model.

DDE See Dynamic Data Exchange.

DES See Data Encryption Standard.

Disconnected Applications An application that uses an intermediate storage mechanism, like Microsoft Message Queue (MSMQ), to process transactions like those used for databases. A disconnected application allows the user to create one-way messages while in a disconnected state. The application automatically uploads these queued messages to the server once a connection to the server is reestablished. In all cases, disconnected applications require clients that can operate in stand-alone mode without any support from the server.

Discretionary Access Control List (DACL) A Windows NT-specific security component. The DACL controls who can actually use the object. You can assign both groups and individual users to a specific object.

Distributed Component Object Model (DCOM) The advanced form of the component object model (COM) used by the Internet. This particular format enables data transfers across the Internet or other nonlocal sources. It adds the capability to perform asynchronous as well as synchronous data transfers, which prevents the client application from becoming blocked as it waits for the server to respond. See COM for more details.

Distributed interNetwork Architecture (DNA) A term used to describe Microsoft's vision of a three-tier development architecture. The three tiers include the user's desktop, business logic processing on a middle-tier server, and database processing on a back-end server. DNA is used to help emphasize various features of Microsoft products like Visual Studio and to help the developer modularize large-scale applications.

Distributed Password Authentication (DPA) A shared secret authentication method originally started by some of the larger online services like CompuServe and MSN. It allows a user to use the same membership password to access a number of Internet sites when those sites are linked together as a membership organization. In essence, this methodology replicates some of the same features that users can get when using the same password to access multiple servers on a local network. DPA relies on the Microsoft Membership Service for membership authentication and server-specific access information.

Distributed Transaction Coordinator (DTC) The Windows service responsible for managing transactions on the server. The DTC allows components to participate in transactions and handles transaction coordination between machines. The DTC also specifies a programming model and protocol for applications and components to use when engaging in a transaction.

DLL See Dynamic Link Library.

DNA See Distributed interNetwork Architecture.

Domain Controller One or more special servers that are used to store user, machine, server, and resource configurations. The domain controller maintains a database of information. It's also used to verify the identity of users or other entities that want to log onto the system and use resources under domain control. Windows installations normally have one Primary Domain Controller (PDC) that's in charge of the domain. Backup Domain Controllers (BDC) provide reliability in case the PDC becomes nonfunctional.

DPA See Distributed Password Authentication.

DS Directory Service.

DTC See Distributed Transaction Coordinator.

Dynamic Data Exchange (DDE) The capability to cut data from one application and paste it into another application. You can cut a graphics image created with a paint program, for example, and paste it into a word-processing document. After it's pasted, the data doesn't reflect any changes made to it by the originating application. DDE also provides a method for communicating with an application that supports it and a method for requesting data.

Dynamic Link Library (DLL) A specific form of application code loaded into memory by request. It's not executable by itself. A DLL does contain one or more discrete routines that an application may use to provide specific features. For example, a DLL could provide a common set of file dialogs used to access information on the hard drive. More than one application can use the functions provided by a DLL, reducing overall memory requirements when more than one application is running.

Dynamic Storage In reference to Active Directory, a method of storing changeable information in the Windows 2000 central database. Using Active Directory in this way allows an application or component to create a persistent data store of information that the user, client, or other operating system element may change from session to session. Dynamic storage is combined with data manipulation in components to preserve a snap shot picture of the operating system's state at any given moment and to allow that picture to change as conditions warrant.

Encapsulation A term normally associated with object-oriented programming (OOP), it defines the act of combining various elements that are designed to work together into a cohesive whole. For example, a recordset is essentially a type of encapsulation because it combines data elements to form a description of a higher-level data structure. Likewise, a procedure can be considered a form of encapsulation because it combines single-computer instructions to form a single instruction set. OOP combines both data and procedural elements to create a component that when instantiated becomes an object.

Event Log File (EVT) A file used to hold the event log entries for a particular aspect of system performance. For example, there are separate files for application, security, and system entries. Each log file can hold several different event types including informational, warning, and error events. An application never interacts with the EVT file itself because more than one application requires simultaneous access to the EVT file. A well-designed application will always use the Windows API to perform this task.

EVT See Event Log File.

Extensibility A measure of the flexibility of a data or programming element. It reflects the capability of the data or programming element to respond to situations outside the parameters of its original design.

FAT See File Allocation Table.

Fault Tolerance The capability an object to recover from an error. For example, the fault tolerance provided by MTS allows a network to recover from potential data loss that is induced by a system or use failure. Another example of fault tolerance is the capability of a RAID system to recover from a hard drive failure.

File Allocation Table (FAT) The method of formatting a hard disk drive used by DOS and other operating systems. This technique is one of the oldest formatting methods available. There have been several different versions of FAT based on the number of bits used to store disk locations. The original form was 12-bits, which was quickly followed by the 16-bit version used by many computers today. A 32-bit version of FAT, also called FAT32, was introduced with the OSR2 version of Windows 98. This new version of FAT stores data more efficiently on the large hard drives available on today's computers.

Firewall A system designed to prevent unauthorized access to or from a network. Firewalls are normally associated with Web sites connected to the Internet. Hardware or software can be used to create a firewall.

GDI See Graphics Device Interface.

GDS See Global Directory Service.

Global Directory Service (GDS) A part of the Open Software Foundation (OSF) distributed computing environment (DCE) remote procedure call (RPC) network protocol. This component provides repository services for data on an enterprise level. It keeps track of network objects like applications, files, printers, and people. GDS is normally use to name, describe, manage, locate, access, and secure these resources.

Globally Unique Identifier (GUID) A 128-bit number used to identify a component object model (COM) object within the Windows Registry. The GUID is used to find the object definition and allow applications to create instances of that object. GUIDs can include any kind of object, even nonvisual elements. In addition, some types of complex objects are actually aggregates of simple objects. For example, an object that implements a property page will normally have a minimum of two GUIDs: one for the property page and another for the object itself.

Graphical User Interface (GUI) 1. A method of displaying information that depends on both hardware capabilities and software instructions. A GUI uses the graphics capability of a display adapter to improve communication between the computer and its user. Using a GUI involves a large investment in both programming and hardware resources. 2. A system of icons and graphic images that replace the character-mode menu system used by many machines. The GUI can ride on top of another operating system (like DOS and UNIX) or be part of the operating system itself (like OS/2). Advantages of a GUI are ease of use and high-resolution graphics. Disadvantages consist of higher workstation hardware requirements and lower performance over a similar system using a character mode interface.

Graphics Device Interface (GDI) A main root component. It controls the way that artistic graphic elements are presented onscreen. Every application must use the API provided by this component to draw or perform other graphics-related tasks.

GUI See Graphical User Interface.

GUID See Globally Unique Identifier.

Hacker An individual who works with computers at a low level, especially in the area of security. A hacker normally possesses specialty software that allows easier access to the target application or network. In most cases, hackers require extensive amounts of time to actually break the security for a system before they can enter it. There are two kinds of hackers: those that break into systems for ethical purposes and those that do it to damage the system in some way. Members of the second group are known as crackers. Some people have started to call members of the first group "ethical hackers" to prevent confusion. Ethical hackers normally work for security firms that specialize in finding holes in a company's security. However, hackers work in a wide range of computer arenas. For example, a person who writes low-level code (like that found in a device driver) after reverse engineering an existing driver is technically a hacker.

HTML See Hypertext Markup Language.

HTTP See Hypertext Transfer Protocol.

Hypertext Markup Language (HTML) 1. A scripting language for the Internet that depends on the use of tags (keywords within angle brackets (<>)) to display formatted information onscreen in a nonplatform-specific manner. The nonplatform-specific nature of this scripting language makes it difficult to perform some basic tasks such as placement of a screen element at a specific location. However, the language does provide for the use of fonts, color, and various other onscreen enhancements. There are also tags for displaying graphic images. Scripting tags for using more complex scripting languages such as VBScript and JavaScript were recently added, although not all browsers support this addition. The latest tag addition allows the use of ActiveX controls. 2. A method of displaying text, graphics, and sound on the Internet. HTML provides an ASCII-formatted page of information read by a special application called a browser. Depending on the browser's capabilities, some key words are translated into graphics elements, sounds, or text with special characteristics, such as color, font, or other attributes. Most browsers discard any keywords that they don't understand, enabling browsers of various capabilities to explore the same page without problem. Obviously, there's a loss of capability if a browser doesn't support a specific keyword.

Hypertext Transfer Protocol (HTTP) A common data transfer protocol for the Internet. It specializes in the display of onscreen information such as data-entry forms or information displays. HTTP relies on HTML as a scripting language for describing special screen display elements, although you can also use HTTP to display nonformatted text.

IDE See Integrated Development Environment.

IMDB See In-Memory Database.

In-Memory Database (IMDB) A method of storing small amounts of data that are in constant use within the server's memory rather than on disk. Storing the database in memory increases system performance and reduces the amount of disk activity that the server encounters. A good example of an IMDB candidate is a database that stores all of the ZIP codes currently in use.

Integrated Development Environment (IDE) A programming language front-end that provides all the tools you need to write an application through a single editor. Older DOS programming language products provided several utilities — one for each of the main programming tasks. Most (if not all) Windows programming languages provide some kind of IDE support.

Interface The physical connection between two programs, a person, and the machine, or any other place where two entities touch.

Internet Packet Exchange (IPX) A Novell-specific peer-to-peer communication protocol based on the internet protocol (IP) portion of the TCP/IP pair. Think of this as the language used on the network. If everyone speaks the same language, then all the nodes can understand each other. Messages are exchanged in the form of packets on a network. Think of a packet as one sheet of a letter. There's a letterhead saying who sent the letter, an introduction saying who the letter is for, and a message that tells the receiving party what the sending party wants to say.

Internet Server Application Programming Interface (ISAPI) A set of function calls and interface elements designed to make using Microsoft's Internet Information Server (IIS) and associated products such as Peer Web Server easier. Essentially, this set of API calls provides the programmer with access to the server itself. Such access makes it easier to provide full server access to the Internet server through a series of ActiveX controls without the use of a scripting language. There are two forms of ISAPI: filters and extensions. An extension replaces current script-based technologies like CGI. Its main purpose is to provide dynamic content to the user. A filter can extend the server itself by monitoring various events like user requests for access in the background. You can use a filter to create various types of new services like extended logging or specialized security schemes.

Intranet A private network that relies on the connections provided by a LAN, MAN, or WAN to mimic the behavior of the Internet. An intranet always relies on a Web server to perform the same functions of this type of server on the Internet. It also relies on TCP/IP as the Internet does for a transport protocol. Users obtain access to company resources through browsers and other applications normally used to access resources on the Internet. The main criterion for an intranet is the private nature of this form of connectivity. Another, less important, factor is the local company nature of such connectivity.

IPX See Internet Packet Exchange.

ISAPI See Internet Server Application Programming Interface.

KDC Key Distribution Center.

LAN See Local Area Network.

Light Remote Procedure Calls (LRPC) A method for accessing data within another application. LRPC only work on the current workstation. Future versions of OLE promise to use Remote Procedure Call (RPC) technology, which means that OLE can search across a network for the programs that it needs.

Load Balancing Refers to the ability of an individual application, group of applications, individual server, or group of servers to maintain a consistent load across all processing elements. This, in turn, provides maximum processing throughput, greater processing efficiency, and reduced user waiting time. Load-balanced systems are inherently more reliable than assigned or single systems because the load-balanced system automatically compensates for downed or overloaded servers.

Local Area Network (LAN) Two or more devices connected together by using a combination of hardware and software. The devices, normally computers and peripheral equipment such as printers, are called nodes. An NIC (network interface card) provides the hardware communication between nodes through an appropriate medium (cable or microwave transmission.) There are two common types of LANs (also called networks). Peer-to-peer networks allow each node to connect to any other node on the network with shareable resources. This is a distributed method of files and peripheral devices. A client-server network uses one or more servers to share resources. This is a centralized method of sharing files and peripheral devices. A server provides resources to clients (usually workstations). The most common server is the file server, which provides file-sharing resources. Other server types include print servers and communication servers.

Local Procedure Call (LPC) A method of accessing a function that resides outside of the application's current process but within a process found on the same machine.

Locally Unique Identifier (LUID) Essentially a pointer to an object, the LUID identifies each process and resources for security purposes. In other words, even if a user has two copies of precisely the same resource option (like a document), both copies would have a unique LUID. This method of identification prevents some types of security access violation under Windows NT.

LPC See Local Procedure Call.

LRPC See Light Remote Procedure Calls.

LUID See Locally Unique Identifier.

MAN See Metro Area Network.

Message Queuing The act of storing a message for later processing by the client or server. Microsoft Message Queue (MSMQ) uses message queuing technology to allow a developer to create disconnected applications on independent clients. A disconnected application stores messages for the server on the local hard drive until the client establishes a connection to the server. The messages are then transferred in the background to the server's queue to await further processing by the server.

Message Transfer System (MTS) A method of transferring mail from one location to another. In most cases, this requires some form of encryption along with other transport-specific issues. Most NOSs provide some types of MTS as part of their base services. However, the Internet requires special transport mechanisms. Several standards are available on the Internet for providing MTS as part of a Web site. The two most notable specifications are the IETF RFC1421 from the IETF and X.400 from the ITU (formerly CCITT). (This term may also be known as a message transfer service in some operating systems.)

Metro Area Network (MAN) A partial extension and redefinition of the WAN, a MAN connects two or more LANs together using a variety of methods. A MAN usually encompasses more than one physical location within a limited geographical area, usually within the same city or state. (A WAN can cover a larger geographical area, and sometimes includes country-to-country communications.) Most MANs rely on microwave communications, fiber optic connections, or leased telephone lines to provide the internetwork connections required to keep all nodes in the network talking with each other.

Microsoft Management Console (MMC) A special application that acts as an object container for Windows management objects like Component Services and Computer Management. The management objects are actually special components that provide interfaces that allow them to be used within MMC to maintain and control the operation of Windows. A developer can create special versions of these objects for application management or other tasks. Using a single application like MMC helps maintain the same user interface across all management applications.

MMC See Microsoft Management Console.

Moniker A name associated with an object. For example, `http://www.microsoft.com` is a moniker associated with the IP address of Microsoft's Web site. Likewise, a moniker might provide a human-readable form of a component GUID.

MSMQ Microsoft Management Queue.

MTA See Multithreaded Apartment.

MTS See Message Transfer System.

Multithreaded Apartment (MTA) A term that refers to the method used to write the code for a COM component. The term apartment is a metaphor. Just as an apartment is a single room (or set of rooms) in an entire building, a COM apartment is a single part of an entire application. The best way to think of MTA is as a common area that anyone in the apartment building can access — like a laundry. A laundry contains multiple washers and dryers (objects of different types) that anyone can access. There's only one MTA per application and it contains all of the objects that any thread can access. This means that an MTA COM object has to be capable of keeping track of which thread is asking for what service.

Nested Objects Two or more objects that are coupled in some way. The objects normally appear within the confines of a container object. Object nesting allows multiple objects to define the properties of a higher-level object. It also allows the user to associate different types of objects with each other.

Network Interface Card (NIC) The device responsible for enabling a workstation to communicate with the file server and other workstations. It provides the physical means for creating the connection. The card plugs into an expansion slot in the computer. A cable that attaches to the back of the card completes the communication path.

NIC See Network Interface Card.

Object Conversion A method of changing the format and properties of an object created by one application to the format and properties used by another. Conversion moves the data from one application to another, usually without a loss in formatting, but always without a loss of content.

Object Linking and Embedding (OLE) The process of packaging a file name, application name, and any required parameters into an object, and then pasting this object into the file created by another application. For example, you could place a graphic object within a word-processing document or spreadsheet. When you look at the object it appears as if you simply pasted the data from the originating application into the current application (similar to DDE). The data provided by the object automatically changes as you change the data in the original object. Often, you can start the originating application and automatically load the required data by double clicking on the object.

Object-Oriented Programming (OOP) A method of programming that relies on objects. An object is one fully described section of code that includes properties and methods. Unlike procedural code, everything needed to describe a particular task is included in one object. OOP encourages code reuse and reduces interaction-type programming errors because each object is self-contained.

OCX See OLE Custom eXtension.

ODBC See Open Database Connectivity.

OLE See Object Linking and Embedding.

OLE Custom eXtension (OCX) A special form of VBX designed to make adding OLE capabilities to an application easier for the programmer. Essentially, an OCX is a DLL with an added programmer and OLE interface.

OOP See Object-Oriented Programming.

Open Database Connectivity (ODBC) A method for exchanging data between DBMSs. In most cases, this involves three steps: installing an appropriate driver, adding a source to the ODBC applet in the Control Panel, and using SQL statements to access the database.

Open Group A standards organization that's responsible for a number of popular standards efforts like DCE RPC. This organization includes what was originally the Open Software Foundation (OSF). The main goal of the Open Group is to bring buyers and sellers of information technologies together in order to reduce the time, money, and risk associated with integrating new technology into an organization. You can find the Open Group at `http://www.opengroup.org/`.

Packet Integrity A measure of a network's capability to protect data transferred on that network from damage due to various sources both natural and human-made. It may also include a measure of the network's capability to recover data after damage has occurred. Packet integrity is an essential element for any network transferring critical, real time, or sensitive data.

Packet Privacy A measure of a network's ability to protect data transferred on that network from observation or access by nonauthenticated parties. Packet privacy ensures that data remains secure.

PKI See Public Key Infrastructure.

Pointer 1. An arrow-shaped object used to show the currently selected menu item. 2. An arrow-shaped graphic used to show the viewer which object a label identifies.

POTS Plain Old Telephone Service.

Proxy When used in the COM sense of the word, a proxy is the data structure that takes the place of the application within the server's address space. Any server responses to application requests are passed to the proxy, marshaled by COM, and then passed to the application.

PSTN See Public Switched Telephone Network.

Public Key Infrastructure (PKI) A protocol that allows two sites to exchange data in an encrypted format without any prior arrangement. The default method for initiating the exchange is to create a secure sockets layer (SSL) connection. The main difference between this technology and other available technologies is that SSL relies on a public key system of certificates to ensure secure data transfer. The latest specification for SSL is SSL3, which the IETF is calling transport layer security (TLS) protocol. A newer addition to the mix is Private Communication Technology (PCT). PCT still uses public key encryption, but there are some distinct advantages to using it like extended cryptographic negotiation, improved message authentication keys, and simplified message and record structures. One benefit of using PKI is that there's no online authentication server required because the certificate is issued by a well-known certification authority (normally a company like Verisign when the technology is used publicly).

Public Switched Telephone Network (PSTN) The system of copper wiring normally used to carry analog voice communication. This network is associated with the telephone and modems. Data carried by this network is often referred to as the plain old telephone service (POTS).

QC See Queued Components.

Queue Commonly, a programming construct used to hold data while it awaits processing. A queue uses a FIFO (first in/first out) storage technique. The first data element in is also the first data element that is processed. Think of a queue as a line at the bank or grocery store and you'll have the right idea. There are also hardware queues that emulate the processing capability of their software counterparts.

Queued Components (QC) The COM+ version of Microsoft Message Queue (MSMQ). This integrated product offers enhanced support for transferring components from client to server by using messages. Because this version of MSMQ is also guaranteed full access to Microsoft Transaction Server (MTS), all message transfers may take place within a transaction.

RAS See Remote Access Server.

Recollimate A term applied to laser light. The act of making the individual light rays parallel to prevent dispersion as the light travels through a fiber optic cable. Recollimation reduces signal loss and allows the light to travel further without additional amplification.

Remote Access Server (RAS) An optional Windows service that allows users to call into the server from a remote location in order to access server resources. There are a variety of ways that this service can be used, including as a call back mechanism.

Remote Procedure Call (RPC) A method for accessing data within another application. RPC is designed to look for the application first on the local workstation, and then across the network at the applications stored on other workstations. This is an advanced capability that will eventually pave the way for decentralized applications.

Resource Pooling The act of maintaining a complex resource, like a COM object, in memory in a deactivated state until it's needed by another client. Normally, objects and other complex resources are completely destroyed and the individual simple resources made available for other purposes. Using resource pooling reduces the time required to create new objects by reallocating objects previously used by other clients.

ROT See Running Object Table.

RPC See Remote Procedure Call.

Running Object Table (ROT) A special Component Object Model (COM) table that is maintained by the operating system. Components that allow a client to create a connection to a running instance need to register themselves in the ROT. There are two levels of registration: strong and weak. The main difference between strong and weak ROT registrations is that a strong registration will prevent an object from shutting down until all of the connected clients have also shut down. A weak reference will be shut down automatically after all strong references to the object are cleared. In most cases, you'll want to use the default registration level of weak.

SACL See Security Access Control List.

Scalability A definition of an object's capability to sustain increases in load. For example, networking systems are often rated by their capability to scale from one to many users. Software scalability determines the capability of the software to run on more than one machine when needed without making it appear that more than one machine is in use.

SCM See Service Control Manager.

SDK See Software Development Kit.

Security Access Control List (SACL) A specialized access control lists (ACL) that is used to maintain object integrity. This list controls Windows' auditing feature. Every time a user or group accesses an object and the auditing feature for that object is turned on, Windows makes an entry in the audit log.

Sequential Packet Exchange (SPX) This is the part of the IPX/SPX protocol pair that guarantees delivery of a message sent from one node to another. Think of SPX as the postal clerk that delivers a certified letter from one place to another. In network terms, each page of the letter is called a packet. SPX delivers the letter one page at a time to the intended party.

Service Control Manager (SCM) The SCM is part of the load-balancing technology used by Windows servers. When a client makes a DCOM call to the load-balancing router, it's the SCM that actually receives the request. The SCM looks up the component in the load-balancing router table, and then makes a DCOM call to one of the servers in the application cluster to fulfill the request. The server in the application cluster creates an instance of the request object, then passes the proxy for it directly to the client. At this point, the server and the client are in direct communication; the router is no longer needed.

Simple Object Access Protocol (SOAP) A Microsoft-sponsored protocol that provides the means for exchanging data between COM and foreign component technologies like Common Object Request Broker Architecture (CORBA) by using XML as an intermediary.

Snap-ins Component technologies allow one application to serve as a container for multiple subapplications. A snap-in refers to a component that's designed to reside within another application. The snap-in performs one specific task, out of all of the tasks that the application as a whole can perform. The Microsoft Management Console (MMC) is an example of a host application. All Windows 2000 management tasks are performed through the use of snap-ins designed to work with MMC.

Sniffer A device or piece of software designed to examine raw network packets and to present those packets in human-readable format. A sniffer is commonly used to locate and repair network errors. It can also be used by crackers to break into networks by enabling them to view sensitive data like user passwords.

SOAP See Simple Object Access Protocol.

Software Development Kit (SDK) A special add-on to an operating system or an application that describes how to access its internal features. For example, an SDK for Windows would show how to create a File Open dialog box. Programmers use an SDK to learn to access special Windows components such as OLE.

SPX See Sequential Packet Exchange.

Stub When used in the COM sense of the word, the stub is the data structure that takes the place of the server within the application's address space. Any application calls to an object are received by the stub, passed to COM for marshaling, and then passed to the server for processing.

TCP/IP See Transmission Control Protocol/Internet Protocol.

Thread-Neutral Apartment (TNA) A new apartment type for Windows 2000 that's specifically designed to meet the needs of COM+ developers. Similar to the multi-threaded apartment (MTA), there's at most one TNA within a process. One thing that differentiates TNA from the single-threaded apartment (STA) and MTA apartment types is that it contains objects only; no threads are allowed within this apartment. Instead of executing within the TNA, when a thread requests access to a TNA object, it receives a lightweight proxy that switches to the object's context without the penalty of a thread switch. MTA threads can request this access directly, while STA threads will need to create a new thread-neutral object.

TNA See Thread-Neutral Apartment.

Transaction A single exchange of data or resources between a client and server. The transaction serves to document the data or resource transfer so that the process can be reviewed or reversed later.

Transaction List An organizational data structure used to track ongoing transactions for Microsoft Transaction Server (MTS).

Transmission Control Protocol/Internet Protocol (TCP/IP) A standard communication line protocol developed by the United States Department of Defense. The protocol defines how two devices talk to each other. Think of the protocol as a type of language used by the two devices.

UDP See User Datagram Protocol.

UNC See Universal Naming Convention.

Uniform Resource Locator (URL) A text representation of a specific location on the Internet. URLs normally include the protocol (http:// for example), the target location (World Wide Web or www), the domain or server name (mycompany), and a domain type (com for commercial). It can also include a hierarchical location within that Web site. The URL usually specifies a particular file on the Web server, although there are some situations when a default filename is assumed. For example, asking the browser to find `http://www.mycompany.com`, would probably display the default.htm file at that location.

Universal Naming Convention (UNC) A method for identifying network resources without using specific locations. In most cases, this convention is used with drives and printers, but it can also be used with other types of resources. A UNC normally uses a device name in place of an identifier. For example, a disk drive on a remote machine might be referred to as \\AUX\DRIVE-C. The advantage of using UNC is that the resource name won't change, even if the user's drive mappings do.

URL See Uniform Resource Locator.

User Datagram Protocol (UDP) Allows applications to exchange individual packets of information over a TCP/IP network. UDP uses a combination of protocol ports and IP addresses to get a message from one point of the network to another. More than one client can use the same protocol port as long as all clients using the port have a unique IP address. There are two types of protocol port: well-known and dynamically bound. The well-known port assignments use the ports numbered between 1 and 255.

VBA See Visual BASIC for Applications.

Virtual Private Network (VPN) A special setup that Windows 2000 and Windows 98 SE provide to allow someone on the road to use the server at work. This is where the virtual part comes in—the connection isn't permanent, you're using it for a short time. The reason that this connection has to be private is that you don't want anyone else to have access to your company's network. What you do is call into your ISP using Dial-Up Networking. Now that you have access to the Internet, you can use Dial-Up Networking to make a second connection to the server by using Point-to-Point Tunneling Protocol (PPTP). The setup is very secure because it actually uses two levels of data encryption: digital signing of packets and encrypted passwords.

Visual BASIC for Applications (VBA) A true subset of the Visual Basic language. This form of Visual Basic is normally used within applications in place of a standard macro language. Normally, you can't create stand-alone applications by using this language in its native environment; however, you could move a VBA program to Visual Basic and compile it there.

Visual Editing When used in the context of application development, the ability of a programmer to change an application's characteristics, procedural flow, or structure by using a designer or other graphical tool instead of direct coding. Using this methodology makes application development faster and less error prone by removing abstraction through the use of a visual interface.

VPN See Virtual Private Network.

WAN See Wide Area Network.

Wide Area Network (WAN) An extension of the LAN, a WAN connects two or more LANs together by using a variety of methods. A WAN usually encompasses more than one physical site, such as a building. Most WANs rely on microwave communications, fiber optic connections, or leased telephone lines to provide the internetwork connections required to keep all nodes in the network talking with each other.

Index

Continued

IDG Books Worldwide, Inc.
End-User License Agreement

READ THIS. You should carefully read these terms and conditions before opening the software packet(s) included with this book ("Book"). This is a license agreement ("Agreement") between you and IDG Books Worldwide, Inc. ("IDGB"). By opening the accompanying software packet(s), you acknowledge that you have read and accept the following terms and conditions. If you do not agree and do not want to be bound by such terms and conditions, promptly return the Book and the unopened software packet(s) to the place you obtained them for a full refund.

1. **License Grant.** IDGB grants to you (either an individual or entity) a nonexclusive license to use one copy of the enclosed software program(s) (collectively, the "Software") solely for your own personal or business purposes on a single computer (whether a standard computer or a workstation component of a multiuser network). The Software is in use on a computer when it is loaded into temporary memory (RAM) or installed into permanent memory (hard disk, CD-ROM, or other storage device). IDGB reserves all rights not expressly granted herein.

2. **Ownership.** IDGB is the owner of all right, title, and interest, including copyright, in and to the compilation of the Software recorded on the disk(s) or CD-ROM ("Software Media"). Copyright to the individual programs recorded on the Software Media is owned by the author or other authorized copyright owner of each program. Ownership of the Software and all proprietary rights relating thereto remain with IDGB and its licensers.

3. **Restrictions On Use and Transfer.**

   (a) You may only (i) make one copy of the Software for backup or archival purposes, or (ii) transfer the Software to a single hard disk, provided that you keep the original for backup or archival purposes. You may not (i) rent or lease the Software, (ii) copy or reproduce the Software through a LAN or other network system or through any computer subscriber system or bulletin-board system, or (iii) modify, adapt, or create derivative works based on the Software.

   (b) You may not reverse engineer, decompile, or disassemble the Software. You may transfer the Software and user documentation on a permanent basis, provided that the transferee agrees to accept the terms and conditions of this Agreement and you retain no copies. If the Software is an update or has been updated, any transfer must include the most recent update and all prior versions.

4. **Restrictions on Use of Individual Programs.** You must follow the individual requirements and restrictions detailed for each individual program in Appendix B of this Book. These limitations are also contained in the individual

license agreements recorded on the Software Media. These limitations may include a requirement that after using the program for a specified period of time, the user must pay a registration fee or discontinue use. By opening the Software packet(s), you will be agreeing to abide by the licenses and restrictions for these individual programs that are detailed in Appendix B and on the Software Media. None of the material on this Software Media or listed in this Book may ever be redistributed, in original or modified form, for commercial purposes.

5. Limited Warranty.

(a) IDGB warrants that the Software and Software Media are free from defects in materials and workmanship under normal use for a period of sixty (60) days from the date of purchase of this Book. If IDGB receives notification within the warranty period of defects in materials or workmanship, IDGB will replace the defective Software Media.

(b) **IDGB AND THE AUTHOR OF THE BOOK DISCLAIM ALL OTHER WARRANTIES, EXPRESS OR IMPLIED, INCLUDING WITHOUT LIMITATION IMPLIED WARRANTIES OF MERCHANTABILITY AND FITNESS FOR A PARTICULAR PURPOSE, WITH RESPECT TO THE SOFTWARE, THE PROGRAMS, THE SOURCE CODE CONTAINED THEREIN, AND/OR THE TECHNIQUES DESCRIBED IN THIS BOOK. IDGB DOES NOT WARRANT THAT THE FUNCTIONS CONTAINED IN THE SOFTWARE WILL MEET YOUR REQUIREMENTS OR THAT THE OPERATION OF THE SOFTWARE WILL BE ERROR FREE.**

(c) This limited warranty gives you specific legal rights, and you may have other rights that vary from jurisdiction to jurisdiction.

6. Remedies.

(a) IDGB's entire liability and your exclusive remedy for defects in materials and workmanship shall be limited to replacement of the Software Media, which may be returned to IDGB with a copy of your receipt at the following address: Software Media Fulfillment Department, Attn: *Visual Basic® 6 COM+ Programming Bible*, IDG Books Worldwide, Inc., 10475 Crosspoint Blvd., Indianapolis, IN 46256, or call 1-800-762-2974. Please allow three to four weeks for delivery. This Limited Warranty is void if failure of the Software Media has resulted from accident, abuse, or misapplication. Any replacement Software Media will be warranted for the remainder of the original warranty period or thirty (30) days, whichever is longer.

(b) In no event shall IDGB or the author be liable for any damages whatsoever (including without limitation damages for loss of business profits, business interruption, loss of business information, or any other pecuniary loss) arising from the use of or inability to use the Book or the Software, even if IDGB has been advised of the possibility of such damages.

(c) Because some jurisdictions do not allow the exclusion or limitation of liability for consequential or incidental damages, the above limitation or exclusion may not apply to you.

7. **U.S. Government Restricted Rights.** Use, duplication, or disclosure of the Software by the U.S. Government is subject to restrictions stated in paragraph (c)(1)(ii) of the Rights in Technical Data and Computer Software clause of DFARS 252.227-7013, and in subparagraphs (a) through (d) of the Commercial Computer — Restricted Rights clause at FAR 52.227-19, and in similar clauses in the NASA FAR supplement, when applicable.

8. **General.** This Agreement constitutes the entire understanding of the parties and revokes and supersedes all prior agreements, oral or written, between them and may not be modified or amended except in a writing signed by both parties hereto that specifically refers to this Agreement. This Agreement shall take precedence over any other documents that may be in conflict herewith. If any one or more provisions contained in this Agreement are held by any court or tribunal to be invalid, illegal, or otherwise unenforceable, each and every other provision shall remain in full force and effect.

my2cents.idgbooks.com

CD Installation Instructions

The source code on the CD-ROM provided with this book is arranged by chapter number and example name. I always provide the name of the example and associated files at the very beginning of each chapter's example sections so it'll be easy for you to find the file that you need on disk. To use the source code on the CD-ROM, perform the following steps.

1. Copy the associated file folder (the whole folder and any subfolders, not just the files listed in the example) from the CD-ROM to your hard drive by using Windows Explorer.

2. Use Edit ⇨ Select All to highlight all the files in the first folder.

3. Right-click the selected files and choose Properties from the context menu.

4. In the File Properties dialog box that appears, uncheck the Read-Only attribute.

5. Repeat Steps 2 through 4 for all folders associated with the example.

Some of the example files will install COM+ applications on your system. Always install the COM+ applications by using the Component Services MMC snap-in instead of the context menu option from Windows Explorer. You'll click the Install Pre-built Application button instead of creating an empty application. When asked for an installation directory, don't use the Default directory option — use the Specific directory option. Otherwise, when you attempt to run the application, Windows will look for the location on my machine, rather than your machine. Chapter 2 has additional instructions for working with COM+ applications if you need them.

The CD-ROM also contains trial versions of many third party products. For more information on these products, see Appendix B. Each of these products has an associated README file that you'll need to open and read before you attempt to install it. Some vendors may also include additional instructions and requirement files that are worth taking a look at.